Baseball Nicknames

Baseball Nicknames
A Dictionary of Origins and Meanings

JAMES K. SKIPPER, JR.

McFarland & Company, Inc., Publishers
Jefferson, North Carolina, and London

The present work is a reprint of the library bound edition of Baseball Nicknames: A Dictionary of Origins and Meanings, first published in 1992 by McFarland.

LIBRARY OF CONGRESS CATALOGUING-IN-PUBLICATION DATA

Skipper, James K., Jr.
    Baseball nicknames : a dictionary of origins and meanings / by James K. Skipper, Jr.
    p. cm.
    Includes bibliographical references and index.

    ISBN 978-0-7864-6717-4
softcover : 50# alkaline paper ∞

    1. Baseball players—Nicknames—Dictionaries. 2. Baseball players—Biography. I. Title.
GV867.3.S55 2012
796.357′03—dc20   91-43690

BRITISH LIBRARY CATALOGUING DATA ARE AVAILABLE

© 1992 James K. Skipper, Jr.. All rights reserved

No part of this book may be reproduced or transmitted in any form or by any means, electronic or mechanical, including photocopying or recording, or by any information storage and retrieval system, without permission in writing from the publisher.

On the cover: Washington, D.C., July 7, 1937. All-Star Game. Left to right: Lou Gehrig, Joe Cronin, Bill Dickey, Joe DiMaggio, Charley Gehringer (Harris & Ewing, photographer, Library of Congress)

Manufactured in the United States of America

McFarland & Company, Inc., Publishers
  Box 611, Jefferson, North Carolina 28640
  www.mcfarlandpub.com

*To six Skippers and one that used to be:
my sons, James K., III, and John Frederick
my brothers, Thomas Lewis and John Clyde
my late parents, James K., Sr., and Dorothy Ann
my former wife, Joan Lois*

and

*for my grandfather, Thomas "Haig" Lewis,
a semipro pitcher out of Jackson, Ohio,
before the turn of the century*

Table of Contents

Preface ix
Key to Abbreviations xiii
Introduction xv

I. Players, Umpires, Nonplayer Managers, Officials, Sportswriters, Broadcasters, Owners, Fans — 1

II. All American Girls Baseball League Players *(compiled by Brenda Wilson)* — 313

Appendix A: Negro League Players — 335

Appendix B: Umpires — 337

Appendix C: Influential Nonplaying Baseball Personalities — 339

Bibliography 341
Index 355

Preface

I am a sociologist and a rabid baseball fan. In July of 1979 I read an article by Stan Grosshandler, "Where Have Those Grand Old Nicknames Gone?" It appeared in the 1978 edition of the *Baseball Research Journal,* a publication of SABR, the Society for American Baseball Research. The gist of the article was that over time the number of major league players with nicknames had declined and the ones assigned in recent years lacked the color of those of the past. While Grosshandler provided some examples in support of his argument, the three page article was hardly a comprehensive study. I was aware that from time to time other writers had made the same point, but none had any hard evidence to back up their hypothesis. As a baseball fan I wanted to know if this hypothesis could be supported, and if so, as a sociologist I wanted to know why.

I was aware that the Macmillan *Baseball Encyclopedia,* edited by Joseph Reichler, listed nicknames among the information provided on every person who had played in the major leagues. This volume seemed to be a logical source to begin research. Using the fourth, 1979, edition I began to document by decade the number of players with nicknames. Analysis of the data verified the hypothesis: The number of players with nicknames did change over time and there were many fewer players with nicknames in the 1970s than in the peak periods of the 1920s and 1930s. Documentation of this and my explanation of why this might have occurred were published in an article, "The Sociological Significance of Nicknames: The Case of Baseball Players," which appeared in a 1984 issue of the *Journal of Sport Behavior* and which, in an edited form, is reprinted in this volume as the introduction even though it is now slightly out of date. It also contains a precise definition of what, for my research, I consider a nickname. This article serves as an introduction to the study of baseball player nicknames and places their use in the context of major changes which have occurred in the larger society. I urge the reader to look it over carefully.

During the course of working on this book I became interested in learning how the players received their nicknames, what they meant, and who gave the players their nicknames. Starting in 1980 I began to collect material related to those topics. I was able to discover only two works that attempted to compile the origin of more than just a few players' nicknames.

Preface

In 1946 Tom Shea published a pamphlet, *Baseball Nicknames—1870–1945*. It sold for 25 cents and contained the nickname origins of about 200 players. In 1980 Joseph McBride published *High and Inside: The Complete Guide to Baseball Slang*. One section provided material on the origins of about 600 player nicknames. I already was aware that the writings of baseball historian Lee Allen and sportswriter Fred Lieb often provided material on nicknames.

After that, it was a hit or miss proposition. Over the next ten years, I read every baseball publication I could get my hands on. I covered over 3,500 books, articles and newspaper accounts. I made three trips to the National Baseball Library at Cooperstown, New York, and drew information from 4,350 players files. In addition I sent a mail-back questionnaire to 467 living former players, inquiring about their nicknames; I achieved a 62 percent response rate. Seventy-seven other players were located and interviewed by telephone. As others in the baseball research community learned of my efforts, either from my publications and presentations or by word of mouth, I began to receive accounts that they knew of or had run across. These were helpful and those individuals are acknowledged below. Even after the years of researching, there are still many ballplayers whose entries in this volume read "Origin unknown." The nicknames most difficult to trace are those for "cup of coffee" players, those who played before the turn of the century, and those from Latin American countries. For another project not related to this one, my colleague, Brenda Wilson, secured data on the nicknames and their origins of the women who played professional (hardball) baseball in the All American Girls Baseball League, which existed from 1943 to 1954 and in one year drew over one million fans. This information is presented in Part II of this volume.

In perusing the literature in quest of information on the nicknames of major league players, I discovered the nicknames of a number of individuals closely associated with the game, but who had never played in the big leagues. At first I ignored them since I was only interested in major league players. Later, however, it dawned on me that no one had ever compiled even a short list of those individuals. I decided it would be interesting and valuable to bring them together for the first time. I created three categories: umpires, players from the Negro leagues who had never played major league ball, and a catch-all category to include baseball executives from commissioners to nonplayer managers, sportswriters, sportscasters, famous fans, and club house attendants. The nicknames of persons in these categories are interspersed through Part I but are also available through the use of one of the three appendices at the back. To the best of my knowledge, these lists are the first compilations of their type.

Many individuals were instrumental in providing me with information and encouragement for this project. I would like to acknowledge their contributions. *Members of the sociological community,* but especially Rebecca Adams, Clifton Bryant, Joann Clayton, Donna Darden, Daniel Dotter, Jon Epstein, William Knox, John Kramer, Mark Lefton, Jean Brittain Leslie, William Markham, Charles McCaghy, Dawn McCaghy, Jerry Michel, Dennis Peck, David Pratto, Donald Shoemaker, William Snizek, Donald South, Brenda Wilson, and Barbara Zaitzow. *Members of the American Name Society,* but especially Leonard Ashley, Edward Callary, Wayne Finke, Thomas Gasque, Kelsie Harder, Edwin Lawson, and W.F.H. Nicolaisen. The staff at the National Baseball Library at Cooperstown, New York, but especially Jon Blomquist, Bill Deane, and Tom Heitz. *Members of the Society for American Baseball Research, and the baseball community,* but especially Paul Adomites, Peter Bjorkman, Pat Boyer, Richard Clark, "Kit" Crissey, Jon Daniels, Marge Daniels, Paul Dickson, L. Robert Davids, Gene Elson, Jorge Figuerdo, Michael Frank, "Cappy" Gagnon, Bob Garfinkle, Larry Gerlach, Michael Gershman, Barbara Gregorich, Stanley Grosshandler, William Haber, John Holway, Jerry Jackson, W. Lloyd Johnson, Thomas Jorwik, Clifford Kachline, Jim Kaplan, Francis Kinlaw, Leonard Levin, Nathaniel Levinson, Ray Lowery, Philip Lowry, David Marks, Elmy Martinez, Ronald Mayer, "Skip" McAfee, Robert McConnell, Kenneth Nester, Joseph Overfield, John Pardon, Frank Phelps, Walter Robertson, Sharon Roepke, Fred Schuld, Thomas Shea, Johnny Shevalla, Dean Sullivan, Robert Tiemann, Richard Thompson, Stephen Thompson, John Thorn, Barbara Topp, Richard Topp, David Voight, Philip Von Bovries and Jay Westerfield.

Finally, a special acknowledgment is due my good friend and colleague, Paul Leslie. It was through his efforts that the logistics of putting this volume together was made possible. His contributions were invaluable. Thanks, Paul.

James K. Skipper, Jr.
Greensboro, North Carolina
Fall, 1991

Key to Abbreviations

C	catcher
DH	designated hitter
1B	first baseman
H	hitter
OF	outfield
PH	pinch hitter
PR	pinch runner
P	pitcher
RP	relief pitcher
2B	second baseman
SS	shortstop
3B	third baseman
Util	utility

Introduction

The Sociological Significance of Nicknames: The Case of Baseball Players*

A nickname is a name not derived from a person's given name but added to or substituted for it. "Red," "Bud," "Babe," and "Blondie" are examples of common American nicknames. Nicknames are an important part of American culture, yet remarkably little research on them has been reported in the literature. The leading onomastic journal *Names* has published only two articles on the subject (Lawson, 1973; Mook, 1967) in over a quarter century of its existence.

The word nickname is derived from the Old English *eke namé* based on the verb *ecan* meaning to add or augment. Thus, nicknames provide a richer or more explicit denotation (Harre, 1980). Nicknames tell us something more about a person. They often serve as illustrations of aspects of a person's personality, physical appearance, or mannerisms (Morgan, O'Neile, & Harre, 1980). A nickname may also serve as a capsule history of an individual by selecting and amplifying some incident which is particularly striking (Morgan et al., 1980). Smith (1970, p. 74) believes that giving people nicknames is the "most powerful way we can express our inherent sense of the significance of names."

What little research has been published indicates that nicknames are more often used with males than females and are more common during the early years than in later life (Smith, 1970; Van Buren, 1974). There is some evidence that nicknames may be associated with popularity and may affect self-concept and behavior in the sense that an individual may attempt to live up to a nickname such as "Silver Tongue" Sam, or live down one such as "Ever Eager" Eve (Dexter, 1949; Harre, 1980; Lawson, 1973). Several writers have suggested that people feel closer to individuals when they use nicknames for them even though they might not be acquainted with them personally (Allen, 1956; Harre, 1980; Lieb, 1943).

This is an edited and abbreviated version of an article published in 1984 in Journal of Sport Behavior *(vol. 7, no. 1), which was itself a revision of a paper presented in 1983 at the 13th Annual Alpha Kappa Delta Research Symposium, Richmond, Virginia.*

Introduction

The ultimate aim of the research to be reported here is to increase awareness of the sociological meaning, usage, and significance of nicknames in American society, by documenting their use with baseball players. Baseball players offer an unusually rich entry point for the study of nicknames for several reasons.

First, baseball has played an important role in our cultural heritage. It has been suggested that it is a reflection of the American way of life (Morrow, 1982; Skipper & Shoemaker, 1980). Baseball illustrates democratic values. Each player has the opportunity to demonstrate his value to the team in an objective competitive process. Both teams begin a game on equal terms.

Second, perhaps no other occupation or organization has kept as meticulous a record of its members, their everyday work performance, and sociodemographic characteristics as has major league baseball (Farrell, 1953). These data have been recorded on every person who played in a major league baseball game since 1871, even though the individual may have participated in no more than one inning of one game! The data include nicknames. This may be a unique data set for historical analysis. As Emrich (1972) has observed, a person's nickname will not usually be remembered much past his or her lifetime unless fame is achieved. Thus, in many other aspects of American life, data on nicknames have not been preserved.

Third, a number of writers familiar with professional sports have commented that many sports figures, but especially baseball players, attract nicknames. Blount (1977) states that sports are richer in nicknames than any other aspect of American culture. Smith (1970, p. 88) comments, "Men active in amateur and professional sports seem to have a tendency to acquire picturesque nicknames. As baseball is our leading sport in America, so baseball's stars are given nicknames by sports writers or others by which they are known to the public."

Emrich (1972) has suggested that the use of nicknames with baseball players increases the potential to become folk heroes and solicits greater fan identification. Schlossberg (1980) has observed that many baseball nicknames originate before individuals become professionals and are not usually related to the game at all. Finally, it is Grosshandler's (1978) opinion that there may be fewer baseball players with nicknames in the 1960s and 1970s than in decades before. He hints that this may have something to do with the meaning of baseball in American culture, the changing nature of society, and the way players are viewed by fans. It is with his hypotheses that this report will be most concerned.

It will be assumed, as has been suggested, that the use of nicknames implies a degree of intimacy identification which is lacking with given names. The argument will be made that the manner in which major league baseball players are perceived by the public has changed over time, since

1870. They have moved from folk heroes, implying closeness, and personal identification, to shrewd entrepreneurs, implying impersonality, distance, and a low degree of personal identification (Warshay, 1982). It is hypothesized that this pattern will be reflected in the use of nicknames with major league baseball players—that is, the use of nicknames has declined over time as measured by the number of individuals receiving nicknames.

Part of the American cultural tradition, especially before World War II, was a belief in the "American Dream" that anyone could be successful if he or she but tried hard enough. One kind of folk hero was the individual who came from lower class origins in a semiliterate and poverty-stricken area of the country whose rise to fame and fortune was due to such virtues as hard work, skill, determination, and honesty, and often included feats of strength and endurance. Folk heroes such as Daniel Boone, Davy Crockett and Abe Lincoln, or fictional ones such as Paul Bunyan and Horatio Alger exemplified democratic values.

By the 1940s, especially after World War II, belief in the folk hero complex began to decline. It became increasingly clear that the rags to riches story was more myth than reality. It was the exception rather than the rule. A reflection of this changing view was the growing social consciousness concerning the lower classes and minority groups. It was now assumed that members of disadvantaged groups would not increase their lot in life without special social support programs. This resulted, of course, in a host of social and welfare legislation. For all practical purposes the era of belief in the folk hero was dead by the mid-1960s. Roughly the same patterns prevailed in attitudes and beliefs toward baseball players as folk heroes. However, the reasons for the demise of the baseball player as folk hero are more specific and individualistic in nature.

Baseball grew up in the folk hero era. Before World War II most major league performers came from lower class origins in rural areas of large city ghettos. Many of them had ethnic backgrounds and were first or second generation immigrants. Their level of formal education was low or in some cases nonexistent. They were a colorful, rough and ready lot whose antics off the playing field, in terms of their capacity for eating, drinking, womanizing and general debauchery, often contributed more to their reputations than their skill at playing the game. Legends and myths abounded concerning their abilities and activities. Michael "King" Kelley, before the turn of the century, and later George "Babe" Ruth, personified the characteristics of the folk hero. For several generations after the Civil War, baseball players supplied Americans with a seemingly inexhaustible supply of folk heroes.

The appeal of the national pastime has always been foremost to the working classes. As former owner Bill Veeck (1963, p. 20) put it, "A baseball crowd is a beer-drinking crowd not a mixed drink crowd." Baseball players exemplified how "folk people" could receive recognition, financial success, and general social mobility. Spectators could achieve wish fulfillment through identification with the players. As Warshay (1982, p. 228) has remarked: "There appears to be as much interest in the fortunes and careers of individual players (heroes, "superstars," and lesser lights who are sympathetically perceived or even resented or disliked) as in the success of the teams themselves."

Americans' love affair with baseball may have peaked in the 1920s which is usually referred to as the "golden age" of sports (Warshay, 1982). Identification with the game itself is reflected by the number of slang expressions incorporated into the language from baseball jargon by the 1920s, such as homer, double header, southpaw, bullpen, hotdog, charlie horse, rain check, and so forth (McBride, 1980). Similarly, identification with baseball players was also, by that time, reflected in the use of nicknames, such as "King," "Georgia Peach," "Big Train," "Grey Eagle," "Three Finger," and so forth.

Before the end of World War II, few baseball fans would have doubted that baseball should be classified as a sport rather than a business. In fact, the distinction may not have even entered most people's minds. As Morrow (1982, p. 68) has pointed out, "The beauty of baseball is essentially an illusion. It demands a suspension of certain disbeliefs." One of the most important of these is the perpetuation of the mythical qualities of major league players which demands that they, as well as the basic institutions of the game, be kept both separate and distinct from the social organization of mainstream business and industry (Andreano, 1965). A second myth is that the major league baseball player plays for the love of the game rather than for financial gain. "As a folk hero he is expected to be innocent, fun-loving, and willing to sacrifice material and future plans for The Game" (Andreano, 1965, p. 143).

Less than a decade after World War II events began to occur which made it difficult to continue belief in these myths. "'Thou shalt not change the basic nature of the game' has always been baseball's first commandment" (Boswell, 1982). However, beginning in 1953 changes in the basic structure of baseball as an institution became the rule rather than the exception. In that year, the Boston Braves moved their franchise to Milwaukee. This was the first franchise move since 1902. In 1954, the St. Louis Browns moved to Baltimore, and in 1955, the Philadelphia Athletics moved to Kansas City. Shortly after, in 1958, two teams moved from coast to coast; the New York Giants moved to San Francisco, and the Brooklyn Dodgers moved to Los Angeles. The illusion of a team's loyalty to its fans and to its city was lost forever. The moves were made on strictly monetary grounds.

Money was also the reason that the American League added two new franchises in 1961, and the National League added two more in 1962. By 1969, each league expanded again by two teams, and in 1977, the American League added two more. In less than 25 years, the major leagues had grown from 16 teams, which had been maintained from 1900 to 1925, to 26, a 62 percent increase. It was obvious that expansion meant money, for it was during this period that the old sportsman type of owner was replaced by corporate ownership, thus marking the transition to big business. The enormous revenues garnered from television contracts were an integral part of this process.

During this same period the characteristics and attitudes of the players were changing. Their class origins began to rise as did their level of education. With the decline of minor league baseball, due in large part to the advent of televised major league games after World War II, colleges and universities became the early training ground for many future players. More and more major leaguers gained college experience, if not degrees. They became better educated, more independent, and materialistically oriented.

A series of events began in 1966 which were to make it crystal clear that the players were more interested in their own personal gain than love of the game or preserving its traditions, loyalty to fans, team, or metropolitan area. In that year, the Major League Players' Association was formed and would shortly become a union. In 1969, the players boycotted spring training over a dispute involving pension fund. In 1970, a player objected to being traded and filed suit in federal court against baseball's reserve clause, which binds a player to the team that holds his contract. While the United States Supreme Court eventually ruled against Curt Flood, his case paved the way for other changes which were to be quickly forthcoming. The first general strike in baseball history took place in 1972 and delayed the start of the season by ten days. Another strike was avoided in 1973, when the owners agreed to outside arbitration in salary negotiation and to the stipulation that players with ten years service—the last five with the same team—could not be traded without their consent. Also, through arbitration it was established that players who perform one season without a signed contract could become free agents, at liberty to sell their services to the highest bidder. In 1974, Jim Hunter did just that. Free of his contract with Oakland, he auctioned his services to the New York Yankees for $3.25 million.

The gates which Flood had helped crack were now wide open, and in 1977, with free agency a reality, 12 players were able to negotiate multi-million dollar contracts. The process has continued to accelerate to date with the help of a strike in 1981, which interrupted over one-third of the season. The age of innocence was over, with lawyers, agents, and union organizers becoming as important to the smooth functioning of a season as managers, umpires, and grounds-keepers. Perhaps the situation was best summarized in the following passage from the *Baseball Encyclopedia* (1979, p. 20): "The money mania gripped all the established players. Those who did not sever relations with their clubs were compensated with generous increases which caused the average player salary to leap to $97,500 in 1978, an enormous 62½% increase from the 1966 season."

By 1982 the average salary had risen to over $130,000. The players' higher education level, the unionization movement, the weakening of the reserve clause, and free agency all tended to make players more independent, hedonistic, and egotistical, with a view of baseball as work and as a means toward postcareer rewards.

The players with high incomes had an entirely different lifestyle than the millions of fans who followed their careers. The baseball player who is surrounded by agents, lawyers, accountants and investment brokers has moved outside of folk identification. He becomes more of an institution than an individual. This situation has led to a feeling of alienation between fans and players, and players and sportswriters or broadcasters, who, incidentally, are often responsible for coining and certainly popularizing nicknames. Noted sportswriter Kopplett (1982, p. 5) summarized the relationship in these words: "Regardless of justification in law or economics and entirely apart from the priceless charisma a Babe Ruth... [or] a Reggie Jackson can generate, there is absolutely no way for ordinary people to identify with $300,000 a year substitutes."

In 1969, Macmillan published the *Baseball Encyclopedia* to commemorate the 100th anniversary of professional baseball. It was the most complete compilation of information on baseball and baseball players ever printed. Among the information provided was player nicknames. The encyclopedia was kept up to date with revisions in 1974, 1976, 1979, and 1982. It was from these sources that the data for this report were derived. The nicknames listed in these volumes will be termed "official"; that is, the nicknames by which the players were known to the public. They are not necessarily the nicknames used for the players by friends, relatives, and acquaintances in everyday life, which in most cases have not been preserved. For example, George Ruth's official nicknames were: "Babe," "The Bambino," and the "Sultan of Swat." Yet, in everyday life, he was called "Jidge," a takeoff on George which never caught on with the public (Lieb, 1943). Such nicknames will be termed "Unofficial" and do not form a part of this analysis.

The *Baseball Encyclopedia* lists the names of 11,351 individuals who played in at least one major league baseball game from 1871 to 1979. Of these, 2,906 (over 25 percent) had nicknames which were not derivable from their given names. (These are unofficial statistics since they are based on the count made by the researcher and not by Macmillan publishers or by

Decade	Frequency of Nicknames	Number of Teams	Nickname Index
1870-1879*	75	71	1.06
1880-1889	186	159	1.17
1890-1899	214	136	1.57
1900-1909	363	160	2.27
1910-1919	502	160	3.14
1920-1929	452	160	2.83
1930-1939	379	160	2.37
1940-1949	374	160	2.34
1950-1959	164	160	1.03
1960-1969	147	198	.74
1970-1979	50	246	.20

* Correction factor used.

Frequency of Major League Player Nicknames by Decade 1870–1979

major league baseball authorities.) The table presented here shows the data by decades. Column one lists the 11 decades of recorded major league baseball. Column two lists the number of players with nicknames who began their careers in a particular decade. Column three lists the total number of teams participating in a decade. For example, two 8-team leagues (the norm from 1900 to 1959) would have 160 teams competing in a decade. Column four represents a frequency-of-name index. It is derived by dividing the number of nicknames by the number of teams. An average correction factor is used for the 1870–1879 decade since data are not recorded for the year 1870.

From the table it can be seen that 75 players with nicknames began their careers during the 1870–1879 decade. With 71 teams competing, the index is 1.06. During the next four decades both the number of players with nicknames and the index value continue to increase, reaching a high point of 502 players and an index of 3.14 in the 1910–1919 decade. In the next three decades, 1920–1949, there is a gradual decline in the number of players with nicknames and in the index value. Then, during the 1950–1959 decade there is 50 percent decline, with the number of players with nicknames dipping to 164 and the index value to 1.03. The downward trend continues in the 1960–1969 decade, but not as steeply. The index value for the sixties drops below 1.0 for the first time. The 1970–1979 decade brings an even greater decline than the one in 1950–1959. The number of players receiving nicknames falls to 50 and the index value drops to .20. (It must be understood that the 1970– data may be incomplete. Some players, especially those who began their careers late in the decade, may not as yet have been accorded nicknames. Thus, the number of players with nicknames and the index may rise slightly in the future. However, analysis indicates that this would be an exception rather than the rule. Most players with nicknames bring them with them to the major leagues.)

Thus, the use of nicknames with baseball players as measured by the number of players accorded nicknames increases by decade from 1870–79 through 1910–1919. This is during the period of time when one would expect the folk hero complex to have great influence. However, nicknames peak in the decade before the 1920s and the so-called "Golden Age" of sports and then start declining roughly after World War I in a continuing pattern through the 1970–1979 decade. The steepest declines take place during the 1950–1959 decade when the first franchise changes were made and the 1970–1979 decade when the first players' strike occurred, arbitration and free agency were established, and multimillion dollar contracts became common.

The data offer support for the hypothesis that the use of nicknames has declined over time since 1920, but especially after 1950. The evidence indicates that this decline parallels a similar decline in Americans' belief in folk heroes. It also parallels a steep decline in fans' ability to identify with baseball players as ordinary folks dedicated to the traditions of the game. This supports the argument that nicknames reflect the degree of identification and intimacy that fans feel toward baseball players.

The decline in the use of nicknames may be part of the more general process of the transition of American society from a folk-rural orientation to a mass-urban.

There are certain conclusions about baseball and the use of nicknames that are suggested. First, one would predict that the use of "official" nicknames for baseball players in the 1980s will be slight, about the same as the 1970s. It is doubtful that nicknames will ever regain the popularity they had over a half century ago. Second, the lack of identity with players does not appear to be associated with interest in the game, if interest can be measured by attendance figures. Attendance for major league baseball reached an all time high in 1982, with one team, the Los Angeles Dodgers, drawing over 3,600,000 fans. Such a total would have been considered impossible in the heyday of the use of nicknames. Third, given the demise of the belief in the folk hero complex and the almost simultaneous reduction in the use of nicknames with baseball players, and assuming that baseball is a reflection of American culture, then it would follow that the use of nicknames with other types of public figures would emulate the same pattern. Thus one could hypothesize that after World War II one would find a decline in the use of nicknames, not only for other sports figures but also for politicians, high ranking military personnel, entertainers, and perhaps even members of organized crime and other underworld figures.

In conclusion, this report does not even begin to tap the potential for research on the significance and meaning of nicknames in baseball. This is true not only from the sociological point of view, but also the psychological, ethnological, historical, linguistic, onomastic, and so forth. The origin of nicknames, how they affect one's self-concept, the meaning they have in a particular interaction, the difference between those used as terms of address, such as "Babe," and those used as terms of reference, such as the "Sultan of Swat," are just a few of the fertile areas for research which readily come to mind. (For an example of this type of research see Skipper, 1982.)

References

Allan, L. "Red, Lefty and a Few Animals." In C. Einstein (ed.), *The Fireside Book of Baseball.* New York: Simon & Schuster, 1956, pp. 6–10.
Andreano, R. *No Joy in Mudville: The Dilemma of Major League Baseball.* Cambridge: Schenkman, 1965.
Baseball Encyclopedia. New York: Macmillan, 1969.
Blount, R. "Games." *Esquire,* 87 (March 1977), pp. 46–47.
Boswell, T. "Off the Base, on the Mark, a Season for the Record." *Washington Post,* July 25, 1982, PMl-2.
Dexter, E. (1949). "Three Items Related to Personality: Popularity, Nicknames, and Homesickness." *The Journal of Social Psychology,* 30 (1949), pp. 155–158.
Emrich, D. *Folklore on the American Land.* Boston: Little, Brown, 1972.
Farrell, J. "Baseball Statistics." In Franklin Watts (ed.), *Pocket Book Magazine,* no. 2. New York: Pocket Books, 1955, pp. 159–175.
Grosshandler, S. "Where Have Those Grand Old Nicknames Gone?" *Baseball Research Journal,* 7 (1978), pp. 61–63.
Harre, R. "What Is in a Nickname?" *Psychology Today,* 31 (Jan. 1980), pp. 78–79, 81–84.
Koppett, L. "Why a Decline in Fun and Laughter?" *The Sporting News,* March 13, 1982, p. 5.
Lawson, E. "Men's First Names, Nicknames, and Short Names: A Semantic Differential Analysis." *Names,* 21 (1973), pp. 22–27.
Lieb, F. "Dizzy, Lippy, Babe or Cy Give an Image to the Eye." *The Sporting News,* Nov. 18, 1943, p. 10.
McBride, J. *High and Inside: The Complete Guide to Baseball Slang.* New York: Warner Books, 1980.
Maestri, B. *Little Eva, Baby Doll, and Blondy Ryan.* Smithtown, N.Y.: Exposition Press, 1981.
Mook, M. "Nicknames Among the Amish." *Names,* 15 1967), pp. 111–118.
Morgan, J., O'Neile, C., & Harre, R. *Nicknames and Their Social Consequences.* London: Routledge & Kegan Paul, 1980.

Morrow, L. "The Lessons of Steinbrennerism." *Time*, August 23, 1982, p. 68.
Reichler, J. (ed.). *The Baseball Encyclopedia*. (4th ed.), New York: Macmillan, 1979.
Schlossberg, D. *The Baseball Catalog*. Middle Villege, N.Y.: Jonathan David Publishers, 1980.
Skipper, J. "Feminine Nicknames 'Oh You Kid' from Minnie to Tilly to Sis." *Baseball Research Journal*, 11 (1982), pp. 92–96.
Skipper, J., & Shoemaker, D. "Tradition and Rationality in Baseball: The Case of Pitching." *Sociological Symposium*, 30 (Spring 1980), pp. 109– 125.
Smith, E. *The Story of Our Names*. Detroit: Gale, 1970.
Van Buren, H. "The American Way with Names." In R. Breslin (ed.), *Culture Learning: Concepts, Applications and Research*. Honolulu: University of Hawaii Press, 1974.
Veeck, B. *Veeck as in Wreck*. New York: Bantam, 1963.
Warshay, L. "Baseball in Its Social Context." In R. Pankin (ed.), *Sociological Approaches to Sport*. East Brunswick, N.J.: Associated University Presses, 1982, pp. 225–282.

I. Players, Umpires, Nonplayer Managers, Officials, Sportswriters, Broadcasters, Owners, Fans

1. Aaron, Henry Louis (1954–76 OF) "Hammerin' Henry." The nickname was assigned by the media early in Aaron's career and refers to his hitting ability. In addition to being the all time home run hitter with 755, Aaron ranks first in RBIs, 2,297; second in runs scored, 2,174, and times at bat, 12,367; third in games played, 3,298, and hits, 3,271; and eighth in doubles 624.

2. Abbott, Ody Cleon (1910 C) "Toby." "Toby" is a take off on the first name of Ody.

3. Abernathy, Theodore Wade (1953–72 P) "Angleworm." Tristram Coffin states; "Although now and then an inglorious Milton unmutes his poetic urge in these names, labeling Ted Abernathy 'Angleworm' because he pitches underhand and his stuff seems to rise out of the ground..."

4. Ables, Harry Terrell (1905–11 P) "Hans." "Hans" denotes Ables' German background. It was said that Ables had the largest hands in baseball. Since Hans Wagner also had large hands, it is possible the "Hans" nickname is in reference to Wagner.

5. Abner, Albert Julius (1950–57 P) "Lefty." Abner pitched left handed and batted left handed.

6. Abreu, Joseph Lawrence (1942 3B) "The Magician." Abreu was a professional magician and a member of the Society of American Magicians.

7. Abstein, William Henry (1906–10 1B) "Big Bill." Abstein was 6'0" and weighed 190 pounds.

8. Acker, Thomas James (1956–59 P) "Shoulders." Acker at 6'4" and 215 pounds was said to have a physique equal to that of Charles Atlas, with huge shoulders.

9. Acosta, Balmadero Pedro (1913–18 OF) "Mento." Origin unknown.

10. Adair, James Aubrey (1931 SS) "Choppy." Origin unknown.

11. Adair, Marion Danne (1970 Manager 1970) "Bill." Adair managed the Chicago Cubs for ten games in 1970. He wrote me: "When I first signed a contract, a veteran player, George 'Mickey' O'Neill, said Marion was not a good baseball name and since there were no other 'Bill's' on the team at the time, he gave me that name."

12. Adams, Charles Benjamin (1906–26 P) "Babe." Adams was the first player with an illustrious career with the nickname of "Babe." As a 26-year-old rookie pitcher for pennant winning Pittsburgh in 1909, he won 12 games and lost three, but was the fourth starter on the club. During the World Series, the first three starters did not win a game, but Adams wrote his name in the record book by winning three. He shut out Detroit in the seventh game to make Pittsburgh World

---

The most widely known nickname appears after the parenthetical years-and-position indicator. Others may be found in quotation marks within the text of the entry.

Champions. In his 19-year career, he posted a 194-140 won-lost record with an ERA of 2.76. Adams received his nickname while playing for Louisville in the American Association in 1908. Women fans used to yell, "Oh you Babe" when he was on the mound. It referred to his good looks and according to Tom Shea, it was the 1908 equivalent of the 1940s "Hubba Hubba."

13. **Adams, Daniel Leslie** (1914–15 P) "Rube." Even though he was from St. Louis, Adams was considered backward in his ways and was nicknamed after "Rube" Waddell.

14. **Adams, Earl John** (1922–34 2B) "Sparky." Adams original nickname was "Rabbit" which referred to his speed. In 1925, James "Rabbit" Maranville became manager of the Chicago Cubs and decided he did not want two "Rabbits" on the same team. Since Adams was the spark plug of the ball club, he decided to give him the nickname of "Sparky."

15. **Adams, Elvin Clark** (1939–48 OF). "Buster." Adams was a right handed slugger. "Buster" referred to his power.

16. **Adams, George** (1879 OF) "Partridge." Origin unknown.

17. **Adams, Joseph Edward** (1902 P) "Wagon Tongue." "Wagon Tongue" refers to the big bat Adams used.

18. **Adams, Karl Tutwiler** (1914–15 P) "Rebel." "Rebel" denotes Tutwiler's southern heritage. He was born in Columbus, Georgia.

19. **Addy, Robert Edward** (1876–77 OF) "The Magnet." The nickname refers to Addy's fielding ability. The ball seemed to come to him as if he were a magnet.

20. **Adkins, Grady Emmett** (1928–29 P) "Butcher Boy." Origin unknown.

21. **Adkins, Merle Theron** (1902–03 P) "Doc." Many players with the nickname of "Doc" had close associations with either the medical or dental professions. In the case of Adkins, however, the origin of "Doc" is unknown. Adkins was also called "Babe," the origin of which is also unknown.

22. **Agganis, Harry** (1954–55 1B) "The Golden Greek." Agganis, a former college football star, was of Greek background, but had blond hair.

23. **Aitchinson, Raleigh Leonidas** (1911–15 P) "Redskin." Aitchinson was born in Tyndall, South Dakota, and was of American Indian background.

24. **Aker, Jack Delane** (1964–74 P) "Chief." Aker had an American Indian background. "Chief" was reinforced by his great relief pitching. He was the "Chief" on the mound. In 1966, he won eight and lost four in relief, and led the American League in saves with 32.

25. **Akers, Thomas Ernest** (1929–32 SS) "Bill." Origin unknown.

26. **Alberts, Francis Burt** (1979 DH) "Butch." Alberts wrote me that "Butch" was a childhood family nickname, which had no special meaning.

27. **Alberts, Frederick Joseph** (1910 P) "Cy." Alberts probably was nicknamed after Denton "Cy" Young, but this is undocumented.

28. **Albosta, Edward John** (1941–46 P) "Rube." Albosta was thought to be rather slow and backward in his style of life. He was nicknamed after "Rube" Waddell. In two seasons his won-lost record was 0-8.

29. Alcock, John Forbes (1914 3B) "Scotty." Alcock was of Scottish background.

30. Aldridge, Victor Eddington (1917–28 P) "Hoosier Schoolmaster." Aldridge was a school teacher in Indiana before his baseball career. He later became a lawyer and served in the Indiana state legislature.

31. Alexander, David Dale (1929–33 1B) "Moose." Alexander was 6'3" and weighed 210 pounds.

32. Alexander, Grover Cleveland (1911–30 P) "Pete." Alexander was one of the greatest pitchers the game has ever known. His 373 wins ranks him third on the all time list behind only Denton "Dy" Young and Walter "Big Train" Johnson. He is best remembered for coming out of the bull pen in the seventh inning of the seventh game of the 1926 World Series and striking out the Yankee slugger Tony Lazzeri with the bases loaded and then shutting out the Yankees in the eighth and ninth innings to preserve the St. Louis Cardinals 3–2 lead which made them World Champions. Since Alexander was a heavy and frequent drinker, and had pitched the sixth game of the series the day before and did not figure to pitch in the seventh game, it was commonly thought he was hung over when he pitched to Lazzeri. In 1950, at the All-Star game in Chicago, Alexander told reporters that: "There were plenty of other nights before and since that I have not been sober, although I have been cold, but the night before I struck out Lazzeri, I was as sober as a judge should be." Alexander's nickname in the minor leagues was "Dode." When he joined the Philadelphia Phils in 1911, there was already a "Dode" on the team, outfielder George Paskert. Because of confusion, the nickname was dropped. There are two versions of how "Pete" or "Old Pete" came about. The first is that he was called that after he slipped off a buckboard on a Texas hunting trip and landed on his kisser in a large pool of alkali and mud—peat moss. The second account has to do with his drinking. During Prohibition the slang term for liquor was "Sneaky-Pete." Alexander spent much of his off-the-diamond time tracking down the illegal beverage. In either event, "Pete" was an affectionate nickname applied to Alexander during the latter years of his career.

33. Alexander, William Henry (1884 C) "Nin." At 5'2", Alexander was one of the shortest players in major league history, especially for a catcher. "Nin" may refer to size, but the exact origin is unknown.

34. Allen, Artemus Ward (1914–20 C) "Nick." Origin unknown.

35. Allen, Cyrus Alban (1879 3B) "Jack." Origin unknown.

36. Allen, Fletcher Manson (1910 C) "Sled." Origin unknown.

37. Allen, Horace Tanner (1919 OF) "Pug." Allen had a snub nose.

38. Allen, Mel (1940– Announcer) "The Voice." Allen started broadcasting New York Yankee games in 1940 and did so until 1964. He has continued to broadcast a wide variety of sporting events through 1990.

39. Allen, Newton Henry (1922–44 2B, Negro League) "Colt." "Colt" refers to Allen's 5'8", 155 pound build. Over 21 seasons Allen compiled a .296 batting average.

40. Allenson, Gary Martin (1979–78 C) "Hardrock." Allenson had the reputation as an aggressive hard-nosed player. He was also called "Muggsy" after John McGraw who was the ultimate hardrock player.

41. Allison, Milo Henry (1913–17 OF) "Pete." Origin unknown.

42. Alomar, Conde Santos (1964–78 2B) "Iron Pony." Lou Gehrig earned the nickname of "Iron Horse" by playing in 2,130 consecutive games. Sandy, as Alomar was addressed, was called "Iron Pony" when he played in 648 straight games.

43. Alomo, Luis (1950–53 P) "Witto." Alomo reported he had no idea where the nickname "Witto" came from, or what it might mean.

44. Alou, Jesus Rojas (1963–79 OF) "Jay." Jesus Alou was the youngest of the three Alou brothers who played in the major leagues at the same time. "Jay" was used as an alternative to Jesus, primarily because most Americans did not pronounce the "J." in Jesus with the Spanish "H."

45. Alperman, Charles Augustus (1906–09 2B) "Whitey." The nickname refers to Alperman's light grey hair. He was a 27-year-old rookie in 1906.

46. Alston, Walter Emmons (1936 1B) "Smokey." Walter Alston's playing days in the major leagues were limited to a "cup of coffee." He played in but one game for the St. Louis Cardinals in 1936. He fanned in his only appearance at the plate and was charged with one error at first base. As a relative unknown, he began managing the Brooklyn Dodgers in 1954 and continued to manage the Dodgers through the 1976 season even after they had moved to Los Angeles in 1958. In that 23-year span, his teams had a winning percentage of .558 and copped seven National League flags as well as five World Championships. Despite this success, Alston's 1967 Dodger team finished in last place. Alston was raised in the small Ohio community of Darrtown. During his tenure as manager of the Dodgers he acquired the nickname of "Squire of Darrtown." But most baseball people called him "Smokey." This nickname was a product of Alston's youth although it related to baseball. As a pitcher on a grade school baseball team, he threw a live fast ball. The kids said he put plenty of "smoke" on the ball.

47. Altizer, David Tildon (1906–11 SS) "Filipino." Altizer was not a Filipino, but he did serve with the Army in the Philippines during and after the Spanish-American war and in China during the Boxer Rebellion.

48. Alton, Ernest Matthias (1920 P) "Lefty." Alton pitched left handed, but batted right handed.

49. Alton, George Wilson (1912 OF) "Bill." Origin unknown.

50. Alusik, George Joseph (1958–64 OF) "Turk." Alusik was one of the few ball players of Turkish background. He was also called "Glider."

51. Alvarado, Luis Cesar (1968–77 SS) "Pimba." Alvarado explained to me: "When I was a small boy, my mother called me "Pimba" because I called all the Ovachados pimbas. In baseball they first called me 'Ovachado Pimba' and then just 'Pimba.'

52. Alvarez, Rogelio Hernandez (1960–62 1B) "Barrego." Origin unknown.

53. Alvord, William C. (1885–93 3B) "Uncle Bill." Origin unknown.

54. Ames, Leon Kessling (1903–19 P) "Red." The nickname refers to hair color. Kessling posted a 183-167 career won-lost record with an ERA of 2.63 for 17 seasons.

55. Amole, Morris George (1897–98 P) "Doc." Many of the players with the nickname of "Doc" had close associations with either the medical or dental professions. In the case of Amole however, the origin of "Doc" is unknown.

56. Amoros, Edmundo Isasi (1952–60 OF) "Sandy." Manager Bert Hass gave him the nickname of "Sandy" in 1952 when Amoros was tearing up the International League for St. Paul. He was built like the featherweight boxing champion, Sandy Sadler. Amoros is remembered most as a defensive change for the Brooklyn Dodgers in the sixth inning of the seventh game of the 1955 World Series. He made an impossible catch of a drive off the bat of Yogi Berra down the left field line at Yankee Stadium which he turned into a double play. The Dodgers went on to win 2–0, and took the series four games to three.

57. Anderson, Arnold Revola (1937–41 P) "Red." The nickname refers to hair color.

58. Anderson, Edward John (1907 OF) "Goat." Origin unknown.

59. Anderson, George Edward (1950 2B) "Sparky." While playing in the Texas League in 1959, the future manager was called "Sparky" by his Ft. Worth teammates because like "Sparky Adams" and others with that nickname, he was the spark plug of the team. When he managed Cincinnati, he was called "Captain Hook" because of his tendency to yank (hook) pitchers when they showed the least signs of tiring. The "Captain Hook" reference is to the villainous pirate character in J.M. Barrie's *Peter Pan*.

60. Anderson, John Fred (1909–18 P) "Spitball." Anderson's best pitch was a spitball.

61. Anderson, John Joseph (1894–1908 OF) "Honest John." An umpire once told him he was hit by a pitched ball and to take his base. Anderson convinced the umpire that the ball did not hit him and he did not deserve to take a base. He then struck out. But, it was written that not a fan in the stands did not admire his honesty. In 1904, Anderson immortalized himself by stealing second base with the bases loaded!

62. Anderson, Karl Adam (1982–83 P) "Bud." "Bud" was a childhood nickname.

63. Anderson, Robert Carl (1957–63 P) "Hammond Hummer." This is a place nickname. Anderson was a fastball pitcher from the East Chicago–Hammond, Indiana area.

64. Anderson, Walter Karl (1917–19 P) "Lefty." Anderson pitched left handed and batted left handed.

65. Anderson, William Edward (1925 P) "Lefty." Anderson pitched left handed, but batted right handed.

66. Andre, John Edward (1955 P) "Long John." Andre was 6'4" and weighed 200 pounds.

67. Andres, Ernest Henry (1946 3B) "Junie." Origin unknown.

68. Andrews, Hubert Carl (1947–48 P) "Hub." "Hub" is just the first three letters of the first name Hubert, but it has a different pronunciation.

69. Andrews, Ivy Paul (1931–38 P) "Poison." "Poison" is a response to the first name of Ivy.

70. Andrews, Stanley Joseph (1939–45 C) "Polo." Origin unknown.

71. Ankenman, Fred Norman (1936–44 SS) "Pat." Ankenman told me his uncle started calling him "Pat" in childhood, but he could not recall any particular reason for it.

72. Anker, Walter (1913 P) "Gee." Origin unknown.

73. Anson, Adrian Constatine (1876–97 1B) "Cap." Anson was one of the foremost figures in baseball before the turn of the century. He compiled a batting average of .334 in 22 years with the Chicago White Stockings. For 20 of those years, he was a player-manager. Anson was prejudiced against blacks and refused to let his team take the field against a team with a black player. In 1885, he led a team of all-star performers on a world tour to promote the game of baseball. When he first entered baseball, he was called "Baby" and "The Marshalltown Infant." He was from Marshalltown, Iowa. After he became manager of the White Stockings in 1879, he was called "Cap" which was short for Captain. In the latter stages of his career, he was called "Pop" and referred to as "Old Anse."

74. Aparico, Luis Ernesto (1956–73 SS) "Little Louie." Aparico was one of the premier shortstops of the 1950s and 1960s noted for his fielding ability. He was also a talented base stealer with speed. He led the American League in stolen bases for the first nine years of his career. His career total was 506. The "Little Louie" nickname was one of affection and referred to Aparico's size, 5'9" and 160 pounds.

75. Applegate, Frederick Romaine (1904 P) "Snitz." Origin unknown.

76. Appleton, Edward Sam (1915–16 P) "Whitey." The nickname refers to hair color.

77. Appling, Lucius Benjamin (1930–50 SS) "Old Aches and Pains."

Appling played 20 years in the major leagues, all for the Chicago White Sox, and compiled a .310 batting average. He was noted for fouling off pitches he did not like. One of the results was that he walked 1,302 times in his career compared to just 528 strikeouts. Appling was a notorious hypochondriac always complaining about the various maladies he suffered. Thus the nickname "Old Aches and Pains." In later years, his timely hitting earned him the nickname of "Luscious Luke!"

78. Aragon, Angel Valdez, Jr. (1941) "Little Bing." Aragon appeared in only one major league game and did not have an official time at bat nor did he play in the field. He inherited the "Bing" nickname from his father. His widow told me he was also called "Angel Jack."

79. Aragon, Angel Valdez, Sr. (1914–17 3B) "Bing." Origin unknown.

80. Archdeacon, Maurice John (1923–25 OF) "Flash." Archdeacon had great speed. He was also called "Comet." Tom Shea reports he was "a small streak on the straightaway."

81. Archer, Frederick Marvin (1936–37 P) "Lefty." Archer pitched left handed and batted left handed.

82. Arcia, Jose Raimundo (1968–70 SS) "Flaco." "Flaco" means skinny and refers to Arcia's 6'3", 170-pound build.

83. Ardizoia, Renaldo Joseph (1947 P) "Rugger." Origin unknown.

84. Ardner, Joseph A. (1884–90 2B) "Old Hoss." Origin unknown.

85. Arft, Henry Irwin (1948–52 1B) "Bow Wow." "Bow Wow" is a response to the last name of Arft.

86. Arlett, Russell Louis (1931 OF) "Buzz." Arlett played but one year in the major leagues batting .313 with 13 home runs, but he had an outstanding minor league career. "Buzz" was short for "The Human Buzz Saw." In 1921, for Oakland in the Pacific Coast League, he led the league as a pitcher with 29 wins. In 1929, he hit .374 with 70 doubles, 39 home runs and 189 RBIs. In 1932, for Baltimore in the International League, he hit 54 home runs and drove in 144 runs.

87. Armbruster, Herman (1906 OF) "Buster." "Buster" is a takeoff on the bruster portion of the last name.

88. Armstrong, George Noble (1946 C) "Dodo." Armstrong told me his older sisters gave him the nickname as a child. He said: "Dodo means a dumb bird."

89. Arnovich, Morrie (1936–46 OF) "Snooker." "Snooker" referred to Arnovich's large nose.

90. Arntzen, Orie Edgar (1943 P) "Old Folkes." Arntzen was a 34-year-old rookie.

91. Arroyo, Louis Enrique (1955–63 P) "Yo Yo." When he played for Greensboro, North Carolina, in 1948, fans had difficulty pronouncing his name and shortened it to "Yo Yo." In his native Puerto Rico, Arroyo was known as "El Zurdo de Tallaboa," the Southpaw of Tallaboa. Tallaboa is the name of the barrio where Arroyo was born in his home town of Penuelas.

92. Arundel, John Thomas (1882–88 C) "Tug." Origin unknown.

93. Ashburn, Don Richard (1948–62 OF) "Put Put." Richie, as Ashburn was addressed, was a speedster in the outfield and on the base paths. Ted Williams once reparked, "That Put Put has twin motors on his pants." He was also called "The Cornhusker Express" denoting his speed and home, Tilden, Nebraska. "Whitey" was a third nickname, describing Ashburn's hair color.

94. Ashford, Emmett L. (1966–70 AL Umpire) "Pata Ditas." Ashford was the first black umpire. "Pata Ditas" or "Little Kicks," was the nickname he had when he umpired in the Dominican Republic. He had no public nickname as an American League umpire.

95. Ashford, Thomas Steven (1976–78 2B) "Tucker." Ashford wrote me: "My nickname came from the nursery rhyme, 'Little Tommy Tucker.' At age 2, my brothers and sisters knew all the nursery rhymes and I liked that one best. At first, I was called Tommy Tucker and by grade school, kids just Tucker. Most people thought that was my real name."

96. Atherton, Charles Morgan Herbert (1899 3B) "Prexy." Origin unknown.

97. Atkins, James Curtis (1950–52 P) "Buddy." "Buddy" was a childhood nickname.

98. Atkinson, Hubert Burley (1927 PR) "Lefty." Atkinson batted left handed, and threw left handed, but he never got a chance to do either in the major leagues.

99. Atwell, Maurice Dailey (1952–56 C) "Toby." Atwell's uncle nicknamed him "Toby" because he did not like the name of Maurice.

100. Atwood, William Franklin (1936–40 C) "Dad Gum." "Dad Gum" was the strongest expletive the mild mannered Atwood ever used.

101. Auker, Eldon LeRoy (1933–42 P) "Big Six." Auker was a 6'2" right hander who reminded people of Christy "Big Six" Mathewson.

102. Aulds, Leycester Doyle (1947 C) "Tex." Aulds played in the Texas league before joining the Boston Red Sox for a cup of coffee in 1947.

103. Austin, James Philip (1909–29 3B) "Pepper." "Pepper" denoted Austin's enthusiasm. It was said he could shout louder and longer than any other player in the game. Austin was also known for his hustle.

104. Autry, Gene (1961 Owner) "Singing Cowboy." Autry, a life long lover of baseball, was awarded the California Angels franchise in 1961. The wealthy, but long time retired entertainer, made 95 movies and more than 125 records. He hosted a national radio show and toured the country many times in concerts and rodeos. As a singing cowboy, he was a movie hero in an age of heroes. Autry is most associated with the tune "I'm Back in the Saddle Again."

105. Autry, Martin Gordon (1924–30 C) "Chick." Autry was nicknamed after William "Chick" Autry.

106. Autry, William Askew (1907–09 1B) "Chick." "Chick" refers to Autry's relatively small size for a first baseman, 5'11" and 165 pounds.

107. Averill, Howard Earl (1929–41 OF) "Rock." Averill liked the nickname of "Rock." He was called "The Rock of Snohomish," a place nickname. He was born in Snohomish, Washington. He was also called "Orange-Outang" which called attention to his simian build.

108. Avila, Roberto Gonzaltz (1949–59 2B) "Beto." "Beto" is Bobby in Spanish.

109. Ayers, Yancy Wyatt (1913–21 P) "Doc." Ayers studied medicine, but there is no evidence he practiced the profession.

110. Azue, Jose Joaquin (1960–72 C) "The Immortal Azue." Azue got his nickname during a hot streak with the bat at Cleveland in 1963. On July 30, 1968, Azue had the misfortune of hitting into an unassisted triple play which reinforced his immortal status.

B

111. Babbit, Mack Neal II (1981 2B) "Shooty." Origin unknown.

112. Babe, Loren Rolland (1952-53 3B) "Bee Bee." "Bee Bee" is a take off on Babe-Babe.

113. Baczewski, Frederic John (1953-55 P) "Lefty." Baczewski pitched left handed, and batted left handed.

114. Bader, Lore Verne (1912-18 P) "King." "King" referred to Bader's royal pitching.

115. Badgro, Morris Hiram (1979-80 OF) "Red." The nickname refers to hair color.

116. Bagby, James Charles Jacob, Sr. (1912-23 P) "Sarge." Several of Bagby's Cleveland Indian teammates saw a Broadway play in which one of the main characters was named Sergeant Jimmy Bagby. They began calling Bagby "Sarge."

117. Bagwell, William Mallory (1923-25 OF) "Big Bill." Bagwell was 6'1" and weighed 175 pounds.

118. Bailey, Abraham Lincoln (1919-21 P) "Sweetbreads." Lee Allen indicated that Bailey was in fact fond of sweetbreads.

119. Bailey, Frederick Middleton (1916-18 OF) "Penny." Origin unknown.

120. Bailey, Lemual (1895 P) "King." Origin unknown.

121. Bailey, Robert Sherwood (1962-78 3B) "Beetle." Bailey was nicknamed after the comic strip character, Beetle Bailey.

122. Bakely, Edward Enoch (1883-91 P) "Jersey." This is a place nickname. Bakely was from Blackwood, New Jersey.

123. Baker, Charles (1901 P) "Bock." Origin unknown.

124. Baker, John Franklin (1908-22 OF) "Home Run." Baker collected 1,838 hits for a career average of .307 for 13 seasons. Only 96 were home runs. Although he led the American League in home runs four consecutive years, 1911-14, his highest total was 12. Rodger Creamer explains that in the dead ball area, a home run, was not considered a particularly significant event in and of itself, any more than a triple would be today. It was just considered a long hit. Weekly statistics in the Sunday newspapers listed sacrifices, stolen bases and batting averages, but not home runs. Baker's nickname "Home Run" came from the special circumstances of two home runs he hit in the 1911 World Series for the Philadelphia A's against the New York Giants John McGraw. The first was a two run shot in the second game of the series with the A's down one game to the Giants, off Rube Marquard. This broke a 1-1 tie and gave the A's the game. The second came in third game off Christy Mathewson in the ninth inning and cost the Giant ace a 1-0 shutout and eventually the game. It was the circumstances of the home runs and the fame of the pitchers which created the nickname. Or did it? Joseph McBride maintains that "Home Run" for Baker started during his minor league career, and the events of the 1911 World Series merely reinforced, rather than created the nickname. Regardless, for a time, home runs were often called "Bakers" much as they are called "Taters" today.

125. Baker, Johnnie (1968–86 OF) "Dusty." Baker told me he received the nickname of "Dusty" as a child because he and his dog whose name was Dusty always used to play in the dirt rather than on the grass lawn. Both the dog and boy would come home when someone called for Dusty. Both his mother and aunt take credit for the nickname. Baker says he has always been called "Dusty" and few people know his real name.

126. Baker, Norman Leslie (1883–90 P) "Bones." Baker was tall and thin, but his exact height and weight are not recorded.

127. Baker, Thomas Calvin (1935–38 P) "Rattle Snake." Baker was always telling tall tales of his experiences with rattlesnakes in Texas. For example: "But as I was sayin', here was this big rattler on the road fixin' fer a fight. I slowed down somewhat and bore over, tryin' to get around him. Would he let me? No suh. He just whirred that ol' tail of his, opened his big mouth, and struck at my front tire. And do you know what happened? Well sir, when them fangs of his punctured the tire why the air just natcherilly poured right out and down that rattler's throat. In less'n no time he looked like one of these balloons they sell at this County Fair. And then when his hide couldn't stretch no more, why he just busted right in my face."

128. Balboni, Stephen Charles (1981– 1B) "Bye Bye." The nickname refers to the home runs he hit while playing for Kansas City. They went bye-bye. Balboni does not like the nickname because when he strikes out during road games, the opposing fans chant "Bye-Bye Balboni."

129. Baldwin, Charles Busted (1884–90 P) "Lady." Baldwin did not smoke, drink, use profanity, or engage in rowdy behavior on or off the diamond.

130. Baldwin, Clarence Geoghan (1884–90 C) "Kid." "Kid" referred to Baldwin's small size, especially for a catcher, 5'6" and 147 pounds.

131. Baldwin, Henry Clay (1927 SS) "Ted." Origin unknown.

132. Baldwin, Marcus Elmore (1887–93 P) "Fido." In his rookie year, Baldwin did not get along with Chicago manager, "Cap" Anson. He was always in the doghouse. "Fido" was a popular name at the time for a dog. In 1889, Baldwin led American Association pitchers in losses with 34. The following year, he led Players League pitchers in wins with 32.

133. Bales, Wesley Owen (1966–67 2B) "Lee." Bales told me: "My brother, Terry, could not pronounce my name and called me 'Lee.' The rest of the family picked it up and I have been called that by everybody all my life."

134. Ballanfant, E. Lee (1936–57 NL Umpire) "Joe Doaks." Umpire expert, Larry Gerlach, quotes Bellanfant: "I got that nickname playing semipro ball. C.K. Martin, the manager of the Royse City Club, called me that [Doaks] one day and it stuck. A few months later we were in a theater watching a song-and-dance act set in a graveyard scene; there was a big tombstone that read, 'Joe Doaks 15 a.c.' The guys let out a holler and from then on it was 'Joe Doaks.' That's all they knew me by in the army; I don't think my commander knew my real name."

135. Ballow, Noble Winfield (1923–29 P) "Old Pard." The nickname is short for "Old Pardner" meaning partner or buddy, or chum. The term was often used to refer to a faithful horse. It appears to have been used in reference to Ballow throughout his career.

136. Bamberger, Harold Earl (1948 3B) "Dutch." Bamberger was of German background.

137. Bancroft, David James (1915–30 SS) "Beauty." Bancroft was a superb fielding shortstop. He was at his best at fielding bad hop balls and as a cut-off man. In addition, he collected 2,004 hits and had a career average of .279 over 16 seasons. Lowell Reidenbaugh suggests "Beauty" denotes Bancroft's superlative play. Robert Smith states it was because Bancroft would mutter "Beauty" when he let a good pitch go by for a strike. Hy Turkin and S.C. Thompson report it was because Bancroft would yell "Beauty, Beauty" when ever a teammate would make a good play. It could be, that all three accounts contributed to the nickname. Perhaps in keeping with the nickname, Bancroft, managed the South Bend Blue Sox from 1949–50, and in 1951, the Battle Creek Belles of the All American Girls Baseball League.

138. Banks, Ernest (1953–71 1B) "Mr. Cub." Banks was a star short stop–first baseman for 19 pennantless years for the Chicago Cubs, collecting 2,583 hits of which 512 were home runs. In 1955, he hit five grand slam home runs. Surprisingly, Banks had no public nickname until his tenth season when Chicago sportswriter, Jim Enright, dubbed him "Mr. Cub." Banks was famous for his: "It's a beautiful day, let's play two."

139. Bannon, James Henry (1893–96 OF) "Foxy Grandpa." Origin unknown.

140. Bannon, Thomas Edward (1895–96 OF) "Uncle Tom." Origin unknown.

141. Barbare, Walter Lawrence (1914–22 3B) "Dinty." Origin unknown.

142. Barbary, Donald Odell (1943 PH) "Red." The nickname refers to hair color.

143. Barbeau, William Joseph (1905–10 3B) "Jap." Tom Shea states the "Jap" referred to Barbeau's small build, 5'5" and 140 pounds, and swarthy complexion.

144. Barber, Walter Lanier (1934–78 Announcer) "The Ol' Redhead." Curt Smith writes of Barber "the most resplendently talented announcer in baseball's tide of times." The redheaded Barber began broadcasting Cincinnati Reds games in 1934, moved to Brooklyn in 1939, and was the New York Yankees announcer from 1954–67. He was elected to the Hall of Fame in 1978. The professional's professional, Barber syndicated radio spots were still being aired as late as 1990.

145. Barclay, George Oliver (1902–05 OF) "Deerfoot." "Deerfoot" referred to Barclay's speed, especially on the base paths.

146. Barger, Eros Bolivar (1906–15 P) "Cy." "Cy" referred to Barger's rustic origins in rural Kentucky. He was also called "The Old Home Remedy" by Brooklyn sportswriter, Tommy Rice, because he was strong medicine to opposing teams, or as Tom

Shea put it, he was "like sulphur and molasses"—hard to take.

147. Barker, Raymond Herrell (1960–67 1B) "Buddy." Barker wrote me that he was nicknamed by an aunt. "When she first held me she said, 'Oh, what a Buddy he is going to be.'"

148. Barkley, John Duncan (1937–43 2B) "Red." The nickname refers to hair color.

149. Barlick, Albert J. (1940–43, 1946–55, 1958–71 NL Umpire) "Prodigy." "Prodigy" referred to Barlick's age. He became a major league umpire before he was 30 years old.

150. Barma, Herbert Paul (1927–43 OF) "Babe." Barma was about the size of Babe Ruth, 6'2", weighed 210 pounds and batted left handed. In the minor leagues, he was a powerful hitter. He hit 49 home runs for Nashville in the Southern Association in 1949.

151. Barmes, Bruce Raymond (1953 OF) "Squeaky." Barmes reported to me: "A scout for the Washington Senators tagged me 'Squeaky' because I was always hollerin' at batters from my left field position. After a while, my voice would become hoarse."

152. Barnes, Emile Derring (1927–30 OF) "Red." The nickname refers to hair color.

153. Barnes, Everett Duane (1923–24 1B) "Eppie." "Eppie" is a take off on Everett.

154. Barnes, Frank Samuel (1929–30 P) "Lefty." Barnes pitched left handed, and batted left handed.

155. Barnes, John Francis (1926 C) "Honey." Origin unknown.

156. Barnes, June Shoaf (1934 P) "Lefty." Barnes pitched left handed, and batted left handed.

157. Barnes, Robert Avery (1924 P) "Lefty." Barnes pitched left handed, and batted left handed. He pitched but 4.2 innings in the major leagues giving up 14 hits and 9 runs.

158. Barnes, Virgin Jennings (1919–28 P) "Zeke." Origin unknown.

159. Barnes, William Henry (1983–87 3B) "Skeeter." Barnes told me, "My mother gave me the nickname when I was newborn. I have been called that all my life. When I was drafted by the Reds, it was announced by the media as William Barnes. My friends didn't know if that was me or not."

160. Barnhart, Clyde Lee (1920–28 OF) "Pooch." Origin unknown.

161. Barnhill, David (1938–48 P, Negro League) "Impo." At 5'7" and 155 pounds, Barnhill had an impish appearance. Barnhill compiled a winning percentage of .666 for his career.

162. Barnie, William Harrison (1883–86 C) "Bald Billy." Barnie, was in fact, bald, when he batted .180 for his 19-game major league career.

163. Barr, Hydor Edward (1908–09 OF) "Scotty." Barr was of Scottish background.

164. Barragan, Facundo Anthony (1961–63 2B) "Cuno." Barragan was nicknamed "Cuno" by his mother as a child. It was really short for Facundo.

165. Barrett, Charles Henry (1937–49 P) "Red." The nickname refers to hair color. On August 10, 1944, Barrett used a record-setting total of only 58 pitches in pitching the Boston Braves to a 2-0 win over the Cincinnati Reds.

166. **Barrett, Francis Joseph** (1939–50 P) "Red." The nickname refers to hair color.

167. **Barrett, Robert Schley** (1923–29 3B) "Jumbo." Barrett was 5'11" and weighed 175 pounds. It would not seem he was large enough to qualify for "Jumbo" nor small enough for the nickname to be an opposite. Origin unknown.

168. **Barrett, Tracey Souther** (1933–45 P) "Kewpie." Barrett had a baby face and looked like a big kewpie doll at 5'9" and 175 pounds.

169. **Barrett, William Joseph** (1921–30 OF) "Whispering Bill." Joseph McBride reports that this is a nickname opposite. Barrett had a loud voice and was prone to use it.

170. **Barron, David Irenus** (1929 OF) "Red." Barron was given the nickname "Red" by fans. It was a response to his last name, not to the color of his hair. The reference is to the German fighter pilot in World War I.

171. **Barrow, Edward G.** (1894–1930 Executive Manager) "Cousin Ed." Barrow is best known as the longtime general manager of the New York Yankees but he had been in baseball since 1894. He managed the Boston Red Sox to a world championship in 1918 and was the person most responsible for converting Babe Ruth from pitcher to outfielder. Boston owner Harry Frazee dubbed Barrow "Simon" as in Simon Legree because of his ability to make people who worked for him feel inferior and replaceable. Barrow had a cold personality and was a tough person both mentally and physically who often turned to fisticuffs to settle disputes. Sportswriter W.O. McGeehan nicknamed him "Cousin Egbert" and Barrow was often referred to in print as "Cousin Egbert" or "Cousin Ed." In later years he was called the "Man Behind the Yankees" but interestingly, Ruth always addressed him as "Eddie," and "Ruppert Barrows" adding an "s" where none existed. According to Barrow, these were the only individuals to use such terms.

172. **Barrow, Roland** (1909–12 OF) "Cuke." Origin unknown.

173. **Barry, Edward** (1905–07 P) "Jumbo." Barry was a big man, but exact statistics on his height and weight are not available.

174. **Barry, Hardin** (1912 P) "Finn." Richard Topp, SABR researcher, reports that "Finn" is short for "Mickey Finn." The reference is to knock out drops. When Barry pitched, he gave the opposing team a "Mickey Finn."

175. **Barry, John C.** (1899–1908 OF) "Shad." Origin unknown.

176. **Bartell, Richard** (1927–46 SS) "Rowdy Dick." The peppery, hard playing Bartell collected 2,165 hits over 18 seasons with a career batting average of .284. The talkative Bartell was also called "Pepper Pot." Warren Brown recounts the following incident. During the 1939 season, Bartell insulted a newspaper reporter, and Cubs' traveling secretary, Bob Lewis, about their weight. The reporter retaliated by announcing over the public address system at Wrigley Field every time Bartell made an error, which was often that year, in a loud voice, "ERROR BARTELL." Fans picked it up and would chant "Error Bartell, Error Bartell." Teammates often called Bartell "Shortwave."

177. **Barthold, John Francis** (1904 P) "Hans." "Hans" denotes Barthold's German background.

178. **Basgall, Romanus** (1948–51 2B) "Monty." Origin unknown.

179. Basinski, Edwin Frank (1944–47 SS) "Fiddler." Basinski played classical music on the fiddle. When he was with the Pittsburgh Pirates, he played off-season violin with the Buffalo Symphony Orchestra.

180. Baskett, James Blain (1911–13 P) "Big Jim." Baskett was 6'0" and weighed 185 pounds.

181. Bass, William Capers (1918 PH) "Doc." Many of the players with the nickname of "Doc" had close associations with either the medical or dental professions. For Bass, however, who failed to get a hit in his one time at bat in the major leagues as a pinch hitter, the origin of "Doc" is unknown.

182. Bassett, Lloyd (1934–50 C, Negro League) "Rocking Chair Catcher." Bassett, who was called "Pepper" because of his spirit and chatter, received the "Rocking Chair Catcher" tag when he caught for the touring Indianapolis clowns in the 1940s. As a crowd pleaser, he would catch a few innings in a rocking chair.

183. Batch, Emil Henry (1904–07 3B) "Heinie." "Heinie" denotes Batch's German background.

184. Batchholder, Joseph Edmund (1923–25 P) "Win." "Win" refers to Batchholder's winning ways in his pre-major league days.

185. Bates, George (1889 P) "Bush." "Bush" may have been short for Bush League. The term would describe Bates single appearance in the major leagues. He pitched eight innings in one game allowing ten runs on 15 hits and five walks.

186. Bates, Hubert Edgar (1939 OF) "Bud." "Bud" was a family nickname, dating from Bates' youth.

187. Bauer, Lou (1918 P) "Kid." "Kid" refers to Bauer's age. He was still in his teens as a rookie in the majors.

188. Baumann, Charles John (1911–17 2B) "Paddy." Origin unknown.

189. Baumann, Frank Matt (1955–65 P) "The Beau." Baumann told me: "When I joined the Red Sox in 1955, owner Tom Yawkey called me 'The Beau' because of my size and name."

190. Baxes, Dimitrios Speros (1959 2B) "Jim." Baxes told me: "Dimitrios is a Greek name. When I came to bat, and it was announced over the loud speaker, it made people laugh, so I just decided to use Jim instead."

191. Bay, Harry Elbert (1901–08 OF) "Dearfoot." Bay won the American League stolen base title with 45 thefts in 1903. His career total of 169 still ranks high among Cleveland's all-time leaders.

192. Baylor, Don Edward (1970–87 DH) "Groove." The nickname "Groove" referred to Baylor's hitting. He was always in the "Groove." Baylor was best known for getting hit by pitched balls. As the all-time leader he was hit over 240 times.

193. Bayne, William Lear (1919–30 P) "Beverly." I can find no mention of Beverly in the literature. Bayne is referred to as "Lefty." He pitched left handed and batted left handed.

194. Beatty, Aloysisus Desmond (1914 SS) "Desperate." "Desperate" is a take off on Desmond. Beatty was addressed as "Des." Anything would be better than Aloysisus for a ball player.

195. Beaumont, Clarence Howeth (1899–1910 OF) "Ginger." Beaumont had a career batting average of .311 for

12 years and led the National League at .357 in 1902. He possessed good speed and on July 22, 1899, he made six infield hits in six times at bat and scored six runs. In 1903, Beaumont was the first player to bat in a World Series. "Ginger" which he much preferred over Clarence, denoted Beaumont's shock of red hair.

196. Becannon, James Melvin (1884–87 P) "Buck." "Buck" is a generic nickname of which the circumstances of origin are almost never documented. It refers to a virile, well developed, aggressive, high spirited young man. It is usually bestowed on the individual during his teenage years.

197. Beck, Clyde Eugene (1926–31 3B) "Jersey." Origin unknown.

198. Beck, Erwin Thomas (1899–1902 2B) "Dutch." "Dutch" refers to Beck's German background.

199. Beck, Walter William (1924–45 P) "Boom Boom." Beck won 38 games and lost 69 with a 12-year career ERA of 4.30. He was nicknamed "Boom Boom" by Brooklyn sportswriter, Edward T. Murphy because of the sound of the balls hit off his pitches as they banged off the tin walls of the old Philadelphia Baker Bowl. At the start of his career, Beck was called "Elmer the Great" because he reminded people of the Ring Lardner egotistical baseball character of that name. The reference comes from the short story.

200. Beckendorf, Henry Ward (1909–10 C) "Heinie." "Heinie" denotes Beckendorf's German background.

201. Becker, Charles S. (1911–12 P) "Buck." "Buck" is a generic nickname of which the circumstances of origin are almost never documented. It refers to a virile, well developed, aggressive, high spirited young man. It is usually bestowed on the individual during his teenage years.

202. Becker, Heinz Reinhard (1943–47 1B) "Bunions." Becker suffered from bunions throughout his major league career.

203. Beckley, Jacob Peter (1888–1907 1B) "Eagle Eye." Beckley was one of the games premier performers around the turn of the century. He collected 2,931 hits, of which 244 were triples, which ranks fourth of all time. His career average was .308 for 20 seasons. "Eagle Eye" recognizes his ability to distinguish balls from strikes. Beckley struck out but 270 times, or less than 14 times per season. He was credited with developing a novel hidden ball trick in which he concealed the baseball under one corner of first base.

204. Bedrosian, Stephen Wayne (1981– P) "Bedrock." "Bedrock" is a takeoff on the last name of Bedrosian.

205. Beecher, Edward (1897–98 OF) "Scrap Iron." Beecher was known for his hard aggressive no-holds-barred type of play.

206. Beecher, Leroy (1907–08 P) "Colonel." Origin unknown.

207. Beeler, Joseph Sam (1944 3B) "Jodie." "Jodie" is a take off on Joseph.

208. Beggs, Joseph Stanley (1938–48 P) "Fireman." Beggs was an excellent relief pitcher for his time. In nine seasons, he won 29 games in relief and saved 29 others.

209. Begley, James Lawrence (1924 2B) "Imp." Begley was 5'5" and weighed but 140 pounds. He was impish looking.

210. Behan, Charles Frederick (1921–23 P) "Pete." In a 1921 article from an unidentified Philadelphia newspaper it states: "They call him Pete because his name is Charles." During spring training of 1921 Behan swallowed a toothpick and needed an operation to remove it from his stomach.

211. Bejma, Aloysius Frank (1934–39 2B) "Ollie." "Ollie" was a take off on the first name of Aloysius.

212. Belardi, Carroll Wayne (1950–56 1B) "Footsie." Belardi wrote me, "I have always been clumsy, since childhood, stepping on people with my big feet. After my first home run in 1953, I stepped on Ralph Branca's foot in the dugout and he started the nickname of 'Footsie.' When I hit my first major league triple, I tripped over second base, fell at shortstop, then lost my hat and went back to grab it, and tripped over third base. It should have been an inside the park home run."

213. Belinsky, Robert (1962–70 P) "Bo." Early in his rookie year on May 5, 1962, Belinsky threw a no-hit game against Baltimore. Although he was only 10-11 that year, and 28-51 for his entire eight-year career the handsome Belinsky became a celebrity in Hollywood's finest tradition. He built a reputation as a playboy and dated Hollywood starlets, which far surpassed his baseball exploits. Maury Allen quotes Belinsky's mother on the origin of the "Bo" nickname. "When he was small, we called him Robert or Bobby. My mother called him Bubbaleh, you know that's Jewish for little boy or little Bobby or something like that. I'll tell you the truth, I don't even know where the Bo came from. We called him Bobby. I think his boy friends at school called him Bo. I think it had something to do with some fighter, Bobo Olson, who was always getting knocked down, just like 'Bo' in school."

214. Bell, David Gus (1972–88 3B) "Buddy." Bell was the son of David "Gus" Bell (1950–64). In childhood, he was called Gus' "Little Buddy." Bell collected over 2,400 hits over 16 seasons with a .292 career average.

215. Bell, David Russell (1950–64 OF) "Gus." Bell's parents were fans of catcher Gus Mancusco. Bell was a catcher in his youth and his parents nicknamed him "Gus."

216. Bell, Fern Lee (1939–40 OF) "Danny." Origin unknown.

217. Bell, George Glenn (1907–11 P) "Farmer." Tom Shea points out that "Farmer" was in the same genre as "Rube." Bell came from the small town of Academy Corners in Tioga County, Pennsylvania.

218. Bell, Herman S. (1924–34 P) "Hi." "Hi" was simply short for, and more acceptable for baseball than the first name of Herman.

219. Bell, James Thomas (1922–46 OF, Negro League) "Cool Papa." Many people who saw him play contend that Bell was the fastest runner who ever played the game of baseball. He was a terror on the base paths. Even when he grounded to the pitcher on one hop, it was a wise hurler who threw quickly to first base. Surprisingly, the "Cool Papa" tag does not stem from the latter years of Bell's career, or his speed. While there are several different stories as to how "Cool Papa" originated, Bell himself says it came from the early 1920s. In his words, "We left and went to Detroit. We would charter a Pullman then, and I was back there asleep, and those guys came in there with a newspaper about this new pitcher, this young pitcher going to open this game in Detroit. They said, 'Wake up, Wake up. Lookie here, you're on this train sleeping and this headline says you're going to pitch in Detroit.' I didn't pay it much attention. I guess that had something to do with my name "Cool." They said, 'He's so cool, he don't get excited.' They started calling me Cool Bell, but Gatewood [Manager, Bill] said, 'We've got to add something to it. We'll call him "Cool Papa."'" Lowell Reidaubany offers a different story. "When he started playing with the St. Louis Stars at age 19, Manager Frank Duncan was afraid Bell would be hampered by nervousness. But Bell told him that he had already played before crowds as large as 1,000. A teammate said, 'He's a cool one, isn't he?' 'Yeah,' replied Duncan, "Cool Papa."'" When Bell played in Cuba, fans called him "Guineo" which means Guinea hen. It referred to his great speed.

220. Bell, Roy Chester (1935–41 OF) "Beau." "Beau" referred to Bell's dapper dress and association with Bohemian girls. Players called him "Bo-Beau."

221. Bell, William Samuel (1952–55 P) "Ding Dong." Ed Walton reports that "Ding Dong" was just a response to the last name of Bell.

222. Bella, John (1957–58 OF) "Zeke." Origin unknown.

223. Bender, Charles Albert (1903–25 P) "Chief." Bender won 210 games in the major leagues in 16 seasons, and won six World Series games in five series. He was a half Ojebwa (Chippewa) parentage, but his swarthy appearance resembled that of a full blooded Indian. When he joined the Philadelphia A's in 1903, he was immediately nicknamed "Chief." Stephen Thompson comments on the usage of "Chief" as a nickname. "Indeed, the nickname 'Chief,' which applied to virtually every Indian baseball player from the 1890s to the 1950s is itself a subtle indication of racism. Although James Skipper's 1981 *Baseball Research Journal* article on nicknames placed 'Chief' in the miscellaneous rather than ethnic category, a glance through the Macmillan *Baseball Encyclopedia* reveals that almost every bearer of that coynomen in baseball history has been Indian—'Chief' Meyers, 'Chief' Bender, 'Chief' Yellow Horse, Allie 'Big Chief' Reynolds and so on. Many modern Americans, who do not have much opportunity to interact with Indians, should be advised that calling an Indian 'Chief' may tend to generate much the same reaction as calling a black man 'Boy'!"

224. Benes, Andrew Charles (1989– P) "Rainman." Benes' San Diego teammates nicknamed him "Rainman" in 1990 because he was the starting pitcher in a number of games in which there was a rain delay.

225. Benge, Raymond Adelphia (1925–38 P) "Silent Cal." Benge was a man of few words and received the nickname of "Silent Cal" even before he made the major leagues. When asked how he acquired his nickname, he replied, "Don't talk much." The reference is to President Calvin Coolidge, who had the nickname "Silent Cal" because he too was a man of few words, especially for a politician.

226. Benners, Isaac B. (1884 OF) "Windy." Benners had the reputation of a long talker. He just as easily could have been called "Noisy."

227. Bennett, Francis Allen (1927–28 P) "Chip." "Chip" was a childhood family nickname, but had no particular meaning.

228. Bennett, James Fred (1928–31 OF) "Red." The nickname refers to hair color.

229. Bennett, Joseph Harley (1918–21 P) "Bugs." Tom Shea attributes the nickname "Bugs" to Bennett's eccentric humor.

230. Bennett, Justin Titus (1906–07 2B) "Pug." Tom Shea reports that Bennett looked pugnacious, but I cannot document that he actually was.

231. Benson, Allen Wilbert (1934 P) "Bullet Ben." Benson was primarily a fastball pitcher.

232. Benton, Alfred Lee (1978–85 C) "Butch." Origin unknown.

233. Benton, John Celbon (1910–25 P) "Rube." Steve Boren points out that Benton was nicknamed after "Rube" Waddell. He was a free wheeling left hander who acquired the reputation of a heavy drinker and carouser. Benton was at the center of two major baseball controversies. The first involved pitching for the wrong team. The second involved his being declared ineligible to play, and yet allowed to continue to pitch in the major leagues.

234. Benton, Stanley W. (1922 2B) "Rabbit." Benton was small, 5'7½", weighed 159 pounds, and was very fast.

235. Benz, Joseph Louis (1911–19 P) "Blitzen." Joseph McBride reports that Benz, a fastball pitcher, was nicknamed after the fastest car of the day, Mercedez Benz. According to Tom Shea, Benz as a kid, threw a rock through a windshield of a Blitze Benz car. That accounts for the "Blitzen" nickname. In addition, Benz was not a fastball pitcher, but relied on a variety of pitches leading to the nickname of "Stuff." Finally, Richard Lindburg maintains that Benz's real nickname was "Butcher Boy" since he was an apprentice butcher in Batesville, Indiana.

236. Berger, Charles (1907–10 P) "Heinie." "Heinie" refers to Berger's German background.

237. Berger, John Henry (1890–92 SS) "Tun." "Tun" refers to Berger's weight which was well over 200 pounds during his career. Information on his height, however, is not available.

238. Berger, Joseph August (1913–14 2B) "Fats." Berger was 5'10½" and weighed 170 pounds.

239. Berger, Louis William (1932–39 2B) "Boze." Berger wrote me, "In 1910, when my maternal grandmother saw my mother holding me and my twin sister she said, 'Look at the two little Boseys.' It had no particular meaning. She said it was the first thing that came into her head. My sister has always been called Louise or Lou. There have been several spellings of my nickname: Boz, Boze, Bo, Bos and Bosey."

240. Bergman, Alfred Henry (1916 2B) "Dutch." "Dutch" denotes Bergman's German background.

241. Bernard, William Henry (1899–1907 P) "Strawberry Bill." The nickname referred to the color of Bernard's hair.

242. Bernhardt, Walter Jacob (1918 P) "Sarah." Bernhardt was nicknamed after the famous French actress Sarah Bernhardt, who was popular during the 1875–1903 era. Oscar Wilde nicknamed her, "The Divine Sarah."

243. Berra, Lawrence Peter (1946–65 C) "Yogi." Berra was one of the best of post-war catchers. He collected 2,150 hits of which 358 were home runs over 19 seasons, with a career average of .285. Berra played in 14 World

Series. He ranks first in series games played, 75; times at bat, 259; hits, 71; and doubles 10. "Yogi" was a childhood nickname. While watching a movie travelog about India as a kid in St. Louis, one of the actors was a Hindu Fakis who was called a Yogi. Jack Maguire, who later played shortstop for the New York Giants thought he looked like Berra and said. "I'm gonna call you 'Yogi'." The nickname stuck. However, when Berra joined the Yankees in 1946, he was also called "Little Kong," after Charlie "King Kong" Keller.

244. Berry, Claude Elzy (1904–15 C) "Admiral." Origin unknown.

245. Berry, Jonas Arthur (1942–46 P) "Jittery Joe." Berry went through a number of nervous moves between pitches while he was on the mound. Joe was a replacement for Jonas.

246. Berry, Joseph Howard, Jr. (1921–22 2B) "Nig." Berry had a dark complexion.

247. Berry, Joseph Howard, Sr. (1902 C) "Hodge." "Hodge" was a take off on Howard.

248. Bertrand, Roman Mathias (1936 P) "Lefty." Bertrand pitched left handed, but batted right handed.

249. Besse, Herman A. (1940–46 P) "Long Herm." Besse was a tall 6'2" and weighed 190 pounds.

250. Bessent, Fred Donald (1955–58 P) "The Weasel." Origin unknown.

251. Bethea, William Lamar (1964 2B) "Spot." Bethea told me, "During my college days at the University of Texas, I was called 'Spot' by Coach Bibb Falk. 'Spot' relates to the heavy covering of freckles that was amassed across my face and arms during the sunny baseball season."

252. Betts, Walter Martin (1920–35 P) "Huck." Betts wrote me, "In 1920, coming north with the Philadelphia Phils on the train, I was quite tan and reading a western magazine. Shortstop, Dave Bancroft, walked by and said, 'We have a Huckleberry Finn with us.' The name was picked up after that and even carried into my private life."

253. Betzel, Christian Frederick Albert John Henry David (1914–18 2B) "Bruno." Even with his host of names, Betzel was called "Bruno" after the name of his childhood pal dog. Betzel liked the nickname and asked other players to call him that.

254. Bevacqua, Kurt Anthony (1971–85 3B) "Dirty." "Dirty" did not refer to Bevacqua's play, but his uniform, which never seemed to be clean for very long.

255. Beville, Clarence Benjamin (1901 P) "Candy Ben." Origin unknown.

256. Biancalana, Roland Americo (1982–88 SS) "Buddy." Biancalana wrote me that his parents started calling him "Buddy" a few days after he was born.

257. Bicknell, Charles Stephen (1948–49 P) "Bud." Bicknell wrote me, "I was called 'Bud' by my aunt Nadie Bicknell after actor Charles 'Buddy' Rodgers. All my family uses 'Bud'."

258. Bigbee, Carson Lee (1916–26 OF) "Skeeter." "Skeeter" refers to Bigbee's slight build, 5'9" and weight of 157 pounds.

259. Bigbee, Lyle Randolph (1920–21 P) "Al." Origin unknown.

260. Bigelow, Elliott Alladice (1929 OF) "Gilly." "Gilly" appears to be a childhood family nickname but the exact origin is unknown. Bigelow was also called "Babe" and "The Babe Ruth of the Citrus Circuit" because of his lusty hitting for teams in Florida.

261. **Bildilli, Emil** (1937–41 P) "Hillbilly." Richard Wurman reports that Bildilli was from the backwoods county of Diamond, Indiana. But the nickname was also a response to the last name.

262. **Bilko, Stephen Thomas** (1949–62 1B) "Humphrey." Bilko was nicknamed "Humphrey" by St. Louis Cardinal teammates in 1953. The reference is to the character Humphrey Pennyworth, a big strong blacksmith type, created by Ham Fisher as Joe Palooka's manager in the comic strip of that name, which first appeared in 1923.

263. **Billings, John Augustus** (1913–23 C) "Josh." "Josh" is a take off on the first name of John.

264. **Binks, George Alvin** (1944–48 OF) "Bingo." "Bingo" is in response to the last name. When he played for Milwaukee in the American Association, manager Casey Stengle gave him the nickname of "Magnificent Unpredictable." "You never exactly knew what he would do in a game. Would he make a good play, get a key hit, miss signs, forget to take sunglasses to the outfield?"

265. **Bird, Frank Zephenin** (1892 C) "Dodo." "Dodo" is a response to the last name of Bird. The reference is to the extinct Dodo bird.

266. **Bird, James Edward** (1921 P) "Red." The nickname refers to hair color.

267. **Birkofer, Ralph Joseph** (1933–37 P) "Lefty." Birkofer pitched left handed and batted left handed.

268. **Birmingham, Joseph Leo** (1906–14 OF) "Dode." Origin unknown.

269. **Birrer, Werner Joseph** (1955–58 P) "Babe." Birrer earned the nickname of "Babe" on July 19, 1955. He pitched four innings of relief for Detroit and hit a pair of two run homers in his first two trips to the plate.

270. **Biscan, Frank Stephen** (1942–48 P) "Porky." Biscan was 5'11" and weighed 190 pounds.

271. **Bischoff, John George** (1925–26 C) "Smiley." Bischoff was well known for his pleasant disposition.

272. **Bishop, Max Frederick** (1924–35 2B) "Tilly." "Tilly" referred to Bishop's high girlish sounding voice. He was also called "Camera Eye" because of his ability to attract walks. In 1929, he led the American League in walks with 128 free passes.

273. **Bishop, William Henry** (1921 P) "Lefty." Bishop pitched left handed and batted left handed.

274. **Bittmann, Henry** (1839 2B) "Red." The nickname refers to hair color.

275. **Black, Harry Ralston** (1981– P) "Bud." Black wrote me, "My sister gave me the nickname of 'Bud' as an infant. She was 8 years old and she called me her little Buddy. My father's name was also Harry, so it helped to avoid confusion."

276. **Black, John William** (1924 2B) "Jigger." Origin unknown.

277. **Black, Joseph** (1952–57 P) "Gentleman Joe." Black had an outstanding rookie year for Brooklyn going 15–4, but in the next five years, he was able to win only 15 more games while

dropping eight. When he won games, he always gave the credit to others, especially catcher Roy Campanella. When he failed to win, he always took the blame. Thus, the "Gentleman Joe" tag.

278. Black, William Carrol (1952–56 P) "Bud." Black told me his father's name was also William, but he was not a Junior. "Bud" was used by the family to distinguish father and son.

279. Blackburn, Foster Edwin (1915–16 P) "Babe." Origin unknown.

280. Blackburne, Russell Aubry (1910–29 SS) "Lena." Blackburne had the nicknames of "Slats" and "Lean" referring to his build. While in the minor leagues, a fan in Worcester, Massachusetts converted "Lean" into the girl's name "Lena," after Blackburne made an outstanding play in the field.

281. Blackwell, Ewell (1942–55 P) "The Whip." Blackwell received his nickname "The Whip" in 1947, when he won 22 and lost 8 for Cincinnati. At 6'6" and weighing 195 pounds, he had a unique pitching style which reminded people of a buggy whip.

282. Blaemire, Bertrum (1941 C) "Rae." "Rae" is a take off on the "Bla" in Blaemire.

283. Blair, Clarence Vic (1929–31 2B) "Footsie." A quote from an unauthored article in the *Chicago Tribune*, 1930, reads, "Blair is a speedy fellow despite enormous contact with the ground, which accounts for his nickname."

284. Blair, Louis Nathan (1942 3B) "Buddy." Blair told me, "It started when I was playing semi-pro ball. Friends started calling me Buddy. Maybe they thought I was family."

285. Blair, Paul L.D. (1964–80 OF) "Motormouth." Blair had the reputation of a fast talker, who was always talking. Although he batted only .250 over 17 seasons, he had a .288 average in six World Series.

286. Blair, Walter Allen (1907–15 C) "Heavy." Blair was 6'0" and weighed 185 pounds.

287. Blake, Harry Cooper (1894–99 C) "Dude." Origin unknown.

288. Blake, John Frederick (1920–37 P) "Sheriff." Lee Allen recounts the surprising manner in which Blake received his nickname. "One day in 1924, a young pitcher with the Cubs, John Fred Blake, was sitting around a Chicago hotel room talking with his cronies . . . the talk turned to Prohibition, bootleggers and revenue officers . . . one of the men began to refer to Blake as Sheriff, though for no observable reason." A nickname was born.

289. Blank, Frank Ignatz (1909 C) "Coonie." Origin unknown.

290. Blanks, Larvell (1972–80 SS) "Sugar Bear." Blanks wrote me, "In the months of August and September, while I was in the Arizona Instructional League, there was a hit single being played on the radio called 'Sugar, Sugar.' Ralph Garm Darrell Evans and others started calling me 'Sugar Bear' because of my aggressiveness at the plate." The song "Sugar, Sugar" was recorded by the Archies and reached number 40 on the charts in 1970. Wilson Pickett also cut a version of the tune in 1970, but it did not reach chart ranking.

291. Blanton, Darrell Elijah (1934–42 P) "Cy." Blanton came from the small town of Waurika, Oklahoma. He was a country boy nicknamed after Denton "Cy" Young.

292. Blasengame, Don Lee (1955–66 2B) "The Blazer." Blasengame told me, "Blazer is a combination of my name and the fact I was pretty fast. The nickname started in my third year in pro-ball, when I was playing for Omaha."

293. Blatnic, John Lewis (1948–50 OF) "Chief." "Chief" denotes Blatnic's American Indian background.

294. Blattner, Robert Garnett (1942–49 2B) "Buddy." Blattner wrote me, "I was a junior, and since my father's name was Bob, he started calling me 'Bud' at about age 3."

295. Blemker, Raymond (1960 P) "Buddy." "Buddy" was a childhood family nickname.

296. Blethen, Clarence Waldo (1923–29 P) "Climax." Origin unknown.

297. Block, John James (1907–14 C) "Bruno." Origin unknown.

298. Block, Seymour (1942–46 3B) "Cy." Block wrote me that he nicknamed himself because he didn't think Seymour sounded like a major league name. Even though he only played 17 games in the major leagues, in 1965, he wrote a self-help book titled, *So You Want to Be a Major Leaguer.* For what it's worth, he said when he played in Puerto Rico, his nickname was, "Don Jose Blocke el Dirigente de Aquadilla Teborines."

299. Bloomfield, Clyde Stalcup (1963–64 2B) "Bud." Bloomfield told me "Bud" was short for "Buddy," which was his family nickname given to him by his father.

300. Blue, Bird Wayne (1908 C) "Bert." "Bert" was a take off on the unusual first name of Bird.

301. Bluege, Otto Adam (1932–33 SS) "Squeaky." A long time Cincinnati fan told me that Bluege's nickname referred to his voice. However, I have been unable to document this as the origin.

302. Bluhm, Harry Fred (1918 PH) "Red." The nickname refers to hair color.

303. Bodie, Frank Stephen (1911–21 OF) "Ping." Bodie's case is both interesting and unusual. Although a number of ball players have seen fit to change their last names, as well as first, Bodie is the only one to change his last name to a place name. Bodie was born Franceto Sanguenitta Pezzola in San Francisco, California. His family adopted Bodie from the name of the now almost forgotten mining town in Western California between Yosemite National Park and the Nevada border, where Frank's father worked. Franceto was changed to Frank at age two. Frank was nicknamed by his parents after a friend of the family, "Ping." The "Ping" nickname was reinforced during his baseball career. It was said that when his bat connected with a pitch, it gave forth a distinctive ping sound. Thus Franceto Pezzola at birth, went through life being called "Ping" Bodie.

304. Boeckel, Norman Doxie (1917–23 3B) "Elmer." Origin unknown.

305. Bogart, John Ronzie (1920 P) "Big John." Bogart was 6'2" and weighed 195 pounds.

306. Boggess, Tyton R. (1944–48, 1950–62 NL Umpire) "Dusty." "Dusty" is a childhood nickname. Boggess, as a young boy, used to play in the dust of a sawmill in Waco, Texas. He was always dusty when he came home.

307. Boggs, Raymond Joseph (1928 P) "Lefty." Boggs pitched left handed and batted left handed.

308. **Bogiovanni, Anthony Thomas** (1938-39 OF) "Nino." Origin unknown.

309. **Bohen, Leo Ignatius** "Pat." "Pat" denotes Bohen's Irish background.

310. **Bold, Charles Dickens** (1914 1B) "Dutch." It is unclear if "Dutch" in Bold's case indicates a German background. He was born in Karlstroma, Sweden, and the names Charles and Dickens would suggest an English background.

311. **Bolden, William Horace** (1919 P) "Big Bill." Bolden was 6'4" and weighed 200 pounds.

312. **Boley, John Peter** (1927-32 SS) "Joe." "Joe" was used as an alternative to John, without any special meaning attached.

313. **Bolger, James Cyril** (1950-59 OF) "Dutch." Bolger was of German background.

314. **Bolton, Cecil Glanford** (1928 1B) "Lefty." Bolton batted left handed and threw left handed.

315. **Bonds, Barry Lamar** (1986- OF) "Sledge Hammer." The nickname refers to the tremendous swing Bonds takes with the bat.

316. **Bonham, Ernest Edward** (1940-49 P) "Tiny." "Tiny" is a nickname opposite, Bonham was 6'2" and weighed 215 pounds.

317. **Bonner, Frank J.** (1894-1903 2B) "The Human Flea." The nickname referred to Bonner's build. He was 5'7½" and weighed 165 pounds.

318. **Bonura, Henry John** (1934-40 1B) "Zeke." Bonura at 6'0" and 210 pounds was an all-around athlete. At Notre Dame, he became AAU javelin champion in 1925. A sportswriter kept saying, "Oh! what a physique." Bonura shortened it to "Zeke" for a nickname. Over seven seasons in the majors, he hit .307 with 119 home runs. He was, however, a poor fielding first baseman often smiling and waving at balls that went past him. A colorful player, he was notorious for missing signs. He once stole home thinking he had gotten a sign to do so.

319. **Booker, Richard Lee** (1966-68 C) "Buddy." "Buddy" was given to Booker as a small child by his parents.

320. **Booles, Seabron Jessie** (1909 P) "Red." The nickname refers to hair color.

321. **Boone, Raymond Otis** (1943-60 3B) "Ike." Boone wrote me: "From age 12 on, I was called 'Ike' after former outfielder Ike Boone. Dee Ballinger, a former minor league catcher started it."

322. **Booth, Amos** (1876-82 C) "The Darling." Origin unknown.

323. **Borbon, Pecho** (1969-80 P) "Dracula." In 1974, Borbon was guilty of biting an opposing player during a fight.

324. **Bordagaray, Stanley George** (1934-45 OF) "Frenchey." Bordagaray wore a mustache and goatee which, in addition to his French background, gave him the look of a French headwaiter. In 1938, while with the St. Louis Cardinals, Bordagaray batted .465, 20 for 42 as a pinch hitter. It is the third highest average completed for pinch hitters appearing at the plate at least 35 times in a season.

325. **Borden, Joseph** (1880s Groundskeeper) "Josephus the Phenomenal."

According to Harold Keese, in 1876 the Boston Nationals signed a pitcher who had pitched a no-hit game in the National Association. (Borden is not recorded as playing in the National Association in Macmillan's 1969 *Encyclopedia of Baseball*.) He was given a three-year contract at $2,000 a year. It was a fabulous income and the baseball writers gave him his distinctive nickname. It turned out that he was unable to pitch for the Nationals and later became their grounds keeper, but retained his nickname.

326. Borkowski, Robert (1950–55 OF) "Bush." Borkowski told me, "As a kid, I had long blond hair and since the kids could not pronounce Borkowski, they called me Bush."

327. Borland, Thomas Bruce (1960–61 P) "Spike." Origin unknown.

328. Borom, Edward Jones (1944–45 2B) "Red." The nickname refers to hair color.

329. Borton, William Baker (1912–16 1B) "Babe." Origin unknown.

330. Boss, Elmer Harley (1928–33 1B) "Lefty." Boss batted left handed, and threw left handed.

331. Bostock, Lyman Wesley (1975–78 OF) "Abdul Jibber-Jabber." Joseph McBride reports that Bostock's teammates believed he had the same "aggressive, loquacious qualities as boxer Muhammad Ali and basketball star Kareem Abdul Jabbar. Jibber-Jabber refers to excessive chatter.

332. Bottomley, James LeRoy (1922–37 1B) "Sunny Jim." Bottomley was one of the finest first basemen of the 1920s and 1930s. He batted .310 over a span of 16 years and collected 2,313 hits of which 219 were home runs. In 1927, he led the National League in home runs, 31; triples, 20; and RBIs, 136. Bottomley was a handsome, affable fun-loving player. Women found him charming and attractive. His happy-go-lucky attitude and the jaunty angle at which he cocked his hat lead to the "Sunny Jim" nickname.

333. Botz, Robert Allen (1962 P) "Butterball." Botz told me the nickname was given to him by sportswriter Dick Young, who thought he had a "robust" stomach.

334. Boucher, Medric Charles Francis (1914 C) "Bush." "Bush" is short for the way Boucher is pronounced.

335. Boudreau, Louis (1938–52 SS) "The Boy Manager." Boudreau was one of the premier shortstops of the 1940s. He had a career batting average of .295 for 15 seasons and led the American League in hitting in 1942 with a mark of .327. Boudreau became player-manager of the Cleveland Indians in 1942 at the age of 24, and earned the nickname of "Boy Manager." In 1948, he led the Indians to the American League flag with a batting average of .355. In 1960, he was broadcasting Chicago Cub games, when 13 games into the season, he replaced Charlie Grimm as manager, and Grimm took his place as announcer.

336. Bouton, James Alan (1962–78 P) "Bull Dog." Bouton, who is probably best known, not as a pitcher who once won 21 games for the New York Yankees in 1962, but for his exposé book on baseball, *Ball Four*. He wrote me, "Elston Howard, the Yankee catcher gave me the nickname during the 1963 season. After a tough game when I hung in there in spite of not having my good stuff, Ellie told some sportswriters that I was a 'Bull Dog' out there. The next day, there it was in the newspapers."

337. **Bowen, Emmons Joseph** (1919 OF) "Chick." "Chick" refers to Bowen's height, 5'7".

338. **Bowen, Sutherland McCoy** (1896 P) "Cy." A small town boy from Kingston, Indiana, he was nicknamed after Denton "Cy" Young.

339. **Bowerman, Frank Eugene** (1895-1909 C) "Mike." "Mike" is short for "Iron Mike." It refers to his tenacity behind the plate. The following is from *The Sporting News*, "Necrology" of December 8, 1948. "Frank Bowerman is the gamest guy whoever put on a uniform," remarked George Gibson, former catcher and manager of Pittsburgh. Bowerman once was hit on the temple and knocked out and taken to the hospital. Everyone thought he was dead. Somehow, he turned up the next day, ready to play. Before another game, machinery fell on his chest with a crushing effect. Yet after a few moments, Bowerman recovered enough to get to the ball park and catch another game.

340. **Bowers, Stewart Cole** (1935-36 P) "Doc." Many of the players with the nickname of "Doc" had close associations with either the medical or dental profession. With Bowers, however, the origin of "Doc" is unknown.

341. **Bowles, Emmett Jerome** (1943-45 P) "Chief." Bowles was of American Indian background.

342. **Bowlin, Louis Weldon** (1967 3B) "Hoss." Bowlin had six older brothers. When he was born, his mother wanted a girl so badly, she named him Lois! In school, he was called Louis to avoid the stigma of a girl's name. He was so fast afoot, that the kids called him "Little Hoss." It finally was shortened to just "Hoss."

343. **Bowman, Alvah Edison** (1914-15 P) "Abe." "Abe" was an acceptable alternative as a baseball name for Alvah.

344. **Bowman, Elmer William** (1920 PH) "Big Bo." Bowman was 6'1½" and weighed 195 pounds.

345. **Bowman, Ernest Ferrell** (1961-63 SS) "Squeaky." Bowman told me: "Willy Mays and Harvey Kuenn gave me the nickname of Squeaky during my rookie year, 1961, because of my high pitched voice."

346. **Bowser, James H.** (1910 OF) "Red." The nickname refers to hair color.

347. **Boyd, Dennis Ray** (1982 P) "Oil Can." Boyd picked up the nickname while pitching for Jackson State University. Beer was called oil at Jackson State, and Boyd drank a lot of beer after games. Boyd often refers to himself as "Oil." That is the account of Joe Giuliotti. Bruce Schlain presents a slightly different version. He relates that the nickname "Oil," meaning beer, came from Boyd's home town of Meridian, Mississippi. Boyd had the reputation before he turned pro of being able to down one six-pack after another like it was nothing at all for his 6'2", 145-pound frame. He was known to drink beer prodigiously before games.

348. **Boyd, Robert Richard** (1951-61 1B) "The Rope." When he played for Baltimore, it was said he hit line drives like a frozen rope. Boyd was the only player of the hundreds I contacted who refused to give information about his nickname without receiving a fee. He asked, but did not get, $100.

349. **Boyer, Cletis Leroy** (1955-71 3B) "Spike." "Spike" was in response to the first name of Cletis. The ref-

erence is to cleats, which on baseball shoes, are often called spikes.

350. Boyer, Cloyd Victor (1949–55 P) "Junior." Boyer was in fact a Junior.

351. Boyle, Henry J. (1884–89 P) "Handsome Henry." Boyle was considered to be one of the most handsome players of his time.

352. Boyle, John Anthony (1886–98 C) "Honest Jack." Throughout his career, Boyle was considered a person of integrity and a perfect gentleman. Besides catching 544 games, he was at first base in 453, second base in 7, shortstop in 44, third base in 52 and also played 15 games in the outfield over a 15-year career.

353. Boyle, Ralph Francis (1929–33 OF) "Buzz." Origin unknown.

354. Boyles, Harry (1938–39 P) "Stretch." Boyles at 6'5" and 185 pounds, had a long stretch.

355. Bradford, Charles William (1966–76 OF) "Buddy." Bradford told me his mother started to call him "Buddy" when he was five years old.

356. Bradley, George H. (1976 P) "Foghorn." Bradley had an unusually loud voice, which he used frequently on the diamond.

357. Bradley, George Washington (1876–88 P) "Grin." When Bradley was pitching, it appeared he always had a grin on his face.

358. Bradley, Hugh Frederick (1911–15 1B) "Corns." Bradley's play was hampered by corns on his feet.

359. Bradshaw, Dallas Carl (1917 2B) "Rabbit." The 5'7", 145 pound Bradshaw was known for his speed. He was also called "Windy" for the same reason.

360. Brady, James Joseph (1956 P) "Diamond Jim." Brady's classmates at St. Peters Prep school in Jersey City, New Jersey, gave him the nickname of "Diamond Jim," when he signed a bonus contract with Detroit. Brady turned out to be one of the bonus babies of the 1950s who did not make it in the major leagues. He pitched a total of 6.1 innings for Detroit in six games in 1956, allowing 15 hits, 11 walks and an ERA of 28.42.

361. Branca, Ralf Theodore Joseph (1944–56 P) "Hawk." Branca won 88 major league games while dropping 68. In 1947, he won 21 games for Brooklyn and a game in the World Series. It was Branca who threw the home run ball to the New York Giants Bobby Thompson in the 9th inning of the last game of the 1951 season which won the flag for the Giants over the Brooklyn Dodgers. To make matters worse, the home run has gone down in the baseball history as, "The Shot Heard 'Round the World." Branca received the nickname "Hawk" while playing basketball at New York University. He was like a hawk around the basket.

362. Branch, Norman Downs (1941–42 P) "Red." The nickname refers to hair color.

363. Brandom, Chester Milton (1908–15 P) "Chick." "Chick" refers to Brandom's slight build 5'3", 155 pounds.

364. Brandon, Darrell G. (1966–73 P) "Bucky." Brandon wrote me, "I purchased a glove from my first roommate in pro-ball, Bucky Poodry. It had Bucky written across it. The following year my teammates, Cliff Davis and John Harms of the 1962 Houston Colts made fun of it. These guys used to turn the glove inside out and kick it like a football. It was old and the insides were all eaten up. My nickname came from that glove."

365. Brandt, John George (1956–67 OF) "Flakey." Sportswriters called Brandt "Jackie," but players and friends called him "Flakey" because of his crazy antics on and off the field. For example, he once drove teammates several miles to a fancy ice cream parlor advertising 50 flavors and then ordered vanilla. Brandt liked his nickname, and wanted people to use it.

366. Bransfield, William Edward (1898–1911 1B; NL Umpire 1917) "Kitty." "Kitty" referred to Bransfield's hair style. He had a large shock of hair which dangled over his eyes in much the same way some girls wore their hair at the time.

367. Brasher, Norman C. (1902 1B) "Kitty." Brasher was nicknamed after William "Kitty" Bransfield whom he was thought to resemble.

368. Bratcher, Joseph Warwick (1924 P) "Goobers." Origin unknown.

369. Bratchi, Frederick Oscar (1921–27 OF) "Fritz." "Fritz" denotes Bratchi's German background.

370. Bray, Clarence Wilbur (1941 OF) "Buster." "Buster" referred to hitting ability.

371. Brazle, Alpha Eugene (1943–54 P) "Cotton." "Cotton" referred to the light blond color of Brazle's hair.

372. Breadon, Sam (1917–47 Owner) "Lucky Sam." Breadon began buying stock in the St. Louis Cardinals in 1917 and he held control of the club until he sold it to Fred Saigh and Postmaster General Robert Hannegan in 1947. Breadon's tenure with the Cardinals saw the development of baseball's first and most successful farm system, the emergence of one of baseball's best known teams, the famed "Gas House Gang" and National League championships in 1926, 30, 31, 34, 42, 43, 44 and 46. He earned the nickname "Lucky" for his rapid success in the developing automobile business. He was also called "Singing Sam" for his gift of gab and oratory.

373. Brecheen, Harry David (1940–53 P) "The Cat." Brecheen was a good fielding pitcher. Roy J. Stockton of the *St. Louis Post Dispatch* gave him the nickname of "The Cat" because of his cat like moves in fielding the ball off the mound. In Brecheen's biography in the 1945 *Baseball Register* his nickname is listed as "Weasel," but no explanation is given. Brecheen is known best for his three victories for the St. Louis Cardinals in the 1946 World Series.

374. Bremer, Herbert Frederick (1937–39 C) "Butch." "Butch" was a childhood nickname.

375. Brenegan, Olaf Selmer (1914 C) "Sam." Origin unknown.

376. Brennan, James Augustus (1884–90 C) "Old Sport." Origin unknown.

377. Brennan, Thomas Martin (1981–85 P) "The Gray Flamingo." Brennan wrote me, "I got my nickname from the bird that stands on one leg. In my wind-up, I would come to a complete stop making it appear that I was standing like a flamingo. In 1978, playing in the Venezuelan Winter League, the Cleveland newspapers coined the phrase 'Flamingo' and then added the 'Gray' because of my premature gray hair."

378. Brenner, Delbert Henry (1912 P) "Dutch." "Dutch" denotes Brenner's German background.

379. Brenton, Lynn David (1913–21 P) "Buck." "Buck" is a generic nickname. The circumstances of origin are almost never documented. It refers to a virile, well developed, aggressive, high spirited young man. It is usually bestowed during teenage years.

380. Bresnahan, Rodger Philip (1897–1918 C) "The Duke of Tralee." Bresnahan was one of the best catchers just after the turn of the century. He batted .279 in 17 seasons and also played games at each infield position as well as the outfield and even pitched in nine games. He was born in Toledo, Ohio, but always maintained he was born in Tralee, Ireland. Sportswriters of the time called him "The Duke of Tralee."

381. Bressler, Raymond Bloom (1914–32 OF) "Rube." Bressler was a real country boy in the best sense of that phrase. He was born in Coder, Pennsylvania, which no longer exists. It was a lumber town. When the trees were cut down, the company moved out and that was it for the town. His family moved to a town called Ashtola, but the same thing happened. The nickname "Rube" is after George "Rube" Waddell.

382. Brett, Herbert James (1924–25 P) "Duke." "Duke" refers to Brett's fancy dress off the field.

383. Brewer, Jack Herndon (1944–46 P) "Buddy." Brewer wrote me, "When I reported to the New York Giants in 1944, I was an unknown and the writers did not know whether my correct first name was Jack or John so they decided 'Buddy' sounded good with Brewer. Dick Young was responsible for this. My given name is Jack, not John."

384. Brewer, Marvin Howard (1939–43 P) "Baby Face." Joseph McBride reports that Brewer was handsome, but with a baby face. He was also called "Adonis."

385. Brickhouse, Jack (1940–81 Announcer) "Hey Hey." Brickhouse broadcast 5,060 major league games, the majority of which were contests involving the Chicago Cubs. His nickname stems from his shouting "Hey Hey" when a Cub or White Sox hit a home run.

386. Bridges, Everett Lamar (1951–61 SS) "Rocky." Bridges related, "One day in 1948, I was playing ball with the Dodgers farm club in Greenville, South Carolina, and the public address announcer said, 'Playing shortstop, Lamar Bridges.' Well, that ball park just about stopped dead. I thought they were upset that I was playing. I couldn't blame them, I'd seen me play before. 'What's a Lamar?' one of my teammates asked. A lot of people offered answers to that question, and none of which can be repeated here, and it was finally decided that Lamar was no name for a baseball player. I could've told them that. 'Let's call him Rocky,' someone else suggested. They weren't too creative in Greenville. I didn't mind though. I thought they were talking about my physique. Turned out, they were talking about my face."

387. Bridges, Marshall (1959–65 P) "Sheriff." "Sheriff" is a response to the first name of Marshall. The reference is to law enforcement officers.

388. Brief, Anthony Vincent (1912–17 1B) "Bunny." "Bunny" refers to Brief's speed. But as Tom Shea put it, at 6'0" and 185 pounds, Brief was a very big bunny. Brief was a home run hitter in the minor leagues. In 1916, he led the Pacific Coast League with 33, and is the American Association career leader with .256. Yet he hit but five home runs in the major leagues.

389. Briggs, Herbert Theodore (1896–1905 P) "Buttons." Briggs was nicknamed "Buttons" by his teammates. When he first joined the Chicago team in 1896, he wore a long gray robe in the locker room that had huge white pearl buttons down the front. About all his teammates could see, was the huge white buttons when they looked his way. From then on, Briggs was known as "Buttons."

390. Briggs, Walter Owen (1920–50 Owner) "Spike." Briggs bought into the Detroit Tigers in 1920 and remained in control until 1950 when his son succeeded him. The nickname "Spike" may have come from Briggs' teenage years when he was a car checker for the Michigan Central Railroad. The exact origin, however, is unknown.

391. Briggs, Walter Owen, II (1950–56 Owner) "Spike." Briggs II was president of the Detroit Tigers succeeding his father from whom he inherited the nickname of "Spike."

392. Briley, Gregory (1988– OF) "Pee Wee." Briley is 5'8" and 165 pounds.

393. Brinker, William Hutchinson (1912 OF) "Dode." Origin unknown.

394. Briody, Charles F. (1880–88 C) "Fatty." Briody was 5'8½" and weighed 190 pounds. He was also called "Alderman," because he was a public official in Troy, New York, during the off season.

395. Brissie, Leland Victor (1947–53 P) "Lou." "Lou" was the product of sportswriter "Scoop" Latimer of the Greenville, South Carolina, *News*. He thought "Lou" was more appropriate than Leland.

396. Bristol, James David (1966–80 Manager) "0010." Bristol never played in the major leagues. Tommy Helms gave him the nickname because he wore the number 10 on his uniform and was a big fan of James Bond movies.

397. Brodie, Walter Scott (1890–1902 OF) "Steve." Brodie batted .303 over a 12-year career, but was best known for his zany behavior. Today, he would be labeled as a flake who seemed always to be in a different state of consciousness from the rest of the world. Consequently, he was nicknamed "Steve" after the eccentric who some years earlier had become a national celebrity by allegedly jumping off the Brooklyn Bridge.

398. Brokett, Lewis Albert (1907–11 P) "King." "King" refers to Brokett's royal pitching.

399. Bronkie, Herman Charles (1910–22 3B) "Dutch." "Dutch" refers to Bronkie's German background.

400. Brookens, Edward Dwain (1975 P) "Ike." Brookens wrote me that his mother gave him the nickname as a child, but he has no idea why.

401. Brooks, Jonathan Joseph (1925–26 OF) "Mandy." Origin unknown.

402. Brosnan, James Patrick (1954–63 P) "Professor." Brosnan read books, wore glasses, wore a beret, smoked a pipe and wrote two books about baseball. In his *Long Season*, 1960, and *Pennant Race*, 1964, Brosnan provided a look at the way ball players really perceive the game they play.

403. Brouthers, Dennis Joseph (1879–1904 1B) "Big Dan." Brouthers was 6'2" and weighed 210 pounds. In his day, he set standards for long distance hitting. Over 19 seasons he batted .343, collecting 2,304 hits. He hit 106 home runs through 1896, and was the Babe Ruth of his era.

404. Brovia, Joseph John (1955 PH) "Ox." Brovia was 6'3" and weighed 200 pounds.

405. Brower, Francis Willard (1920–24 OF) "Turkeyfoot." Brower's daughter wrote me her father's real nickname was "Tuckey" which he got as a child. Sportswriters thought he said Turkey because of his southern accent. Later it was changed to "Turkeyfoot" because he was so fast. She said her father did not like the nickname, no one ever used it, and she would like me to change it in the baseball documents.

406. Brown, Alton Leo (1951 P) "Deacon." Origin unknown.

407. Brown, Carroll William (1911–15 P) "Boardwalk." "Boardwalk" is a place nickname. Brown was raised close to the Boardwalk in Atlantic City, New Jersey.

408. Brown, Charles E. (1897 P) "Yank." Origin unknown.

409. Brown, Charles Edward (1905–13 P) "Buster." Brown was nicknamed after the mischievous, but ingenious comic strip character "Buster Brown" appearing in the strip by that name created by R.F. Outcault in 1902. Brown pitched for nine years in the major leagues and managed to win just 51 games while dropping 105. His .327 is the lowest career winning percentage since 1901 for pitchers with a minimum of 150 decisions.

410. Brown, Charles Roy (1911–15 P) "Lefty." Brown pitched left handed, and batted left handed. He was also called "Curley" referring to his hair.

411. Brown, Edward William (1920–28 OF) "Glass Arm Eddie." Brown was rated as having the worst (weakest) throwing arm from the outfield of his time. He made up for the deficiency by batting .303 over seven seasons.

412. Brown, Elmer Young (1911–15 P) "Shook." Origin unknown.

413. Brown, Hector Harold (1951–64 P) "Skinny." Brown was 6'2" and weighed 185 pounds. But the nickname of "Skinny" was really a nickname opposite. Brown was chubby as a child and his parents called him "skinny." During the 1961 season, Brown pitched 36 scoreless innings for Baltimore.

414. Brown, James Donaldson (1915–16 OF) "Moose." Brown was 6'0" and weighed 178 pounds.

415. Brown, John Christopher (1984 3B) "Tin Man." Brown was given this nickname by his teammates at San Francisco because they felt he lacked a competitive spirit. "He has no heart." The reference is to the Tin Man character in the movie *The Wizard of Oz*.

416. Brown, John Lindsay (1937 SS) "Red." The nickname refers to hair color.

417. Brown, Lewis J. (1876–84 C) "Blower." "Blower" refers to Brown's profinity for boasting. He thought so much of his ability to box, that he challenged Joe Goss, the bare knuckle heavyweight champion of the world to a bout. Goss dismissed the challenge with such contempt, that Brown was the laughing stock of the baseball world. In 1875, Brown was the catcher when Joe Borden was credited with pitching the first no-hit game.

418. Brown, Lloyd Andrew (1925–40 P) "Gimpy." Brown ran with the hint of a limp. While attending high school, he broke his left leg playing football in Beeville, Texas. After the cast was removed, his leg was 1½ inches shorter than the right. Over time, the injury seemed to correct itself, so that Brown actually became fleet of foot. When Brown played around Tampico, Mexico, his nickname was "El Grande Burro"—the big burro.

419. Brown, Mordecai Peter Centennial (1903–16 P) "Three Finger Brown." Brown worked as a coal miner and one of his nicknames was "Miner." As a young boy, he lost his index finger on his right hand below the second joint, not in a coal mine accident, but from a cornshredder. Compensating for the missing finger led Brown to an unorthodox delivery, which produced one of the most baffling curveballs of the time. Brown used it to win 239 major league games with a 2.06 ERA, third best on record. In addition, Brown won five world series games.

420. Brown, Ollie Lee (1965–77 OF) "Downtown." Brown acquired the nickname when he hit 40 home runs for Fresno in the Pacific Coast League in 1964. Many of them were hit towards downtown Fresno.

421. Brown, Richard P. (1893–97 P) "Stub." "Stub" short for "Stubby" is a nickname opposite. Brown was 6'2" and weighed 220 pounds.

422. Brown, Robert William (1946–54 3B) "Golden Boy." Sportswriters called him "Golden Boy," when he received a $50,000 bonus from the New York Yankees for signing. Brown studied medicine while playing for the Yankees and subsequently practiced medicine. There is no mention of Brown ever being called "Doc." Even in 1990, as president of the American League, he is referred to as Dr. Bobby Brown, never "Doc."

423. Brown, Thomas Michael (1944–53 SS) "Buckshot." Brown had an unpredictable throw to first. No one knew exactly where it was likely to go when he let loose of the ball. His throwing arm was strong, however. Playing for the Brooklyn Dodgers against Boston at old Braves Field, he once threw a ball to first that was so wild, it ended up in the twentieth row of the grandstand.

424. Brown, Walter George (1925–41 P) "Jumbo." Brown may have been the largest pitcher of all time at 6'4" weighing 295 pounds. When Hy Goldberg of the *Newark Evening News* was asked what stuff Brown threw, he replied, "He throws a fastball, curve and the biggest shadow in baseball." Jumbo was the name of a gigantic elephant exhibited by P.T. Barnum.

425. Brown, Willard (1887–94 1B) "Big Bill." Brown was 6'2" and weighed 190 pounds. He was also called "California Bill." He came from San Francisco at a time when there were few other players in the major leagues who came from the west coast.

426. Brown, Willard (1935–49 OF, Negro League) "Home Run." Brown was a slugger who led the league in home runs five times and had a .355 batting average over 13 seasons.

427. Brown, William James (1963–75 OF) "Gates." Brown was recruited out of prison by the Detroit Tigers. It is sometimes thought that the "Gates" nickname refers to prison gates. However, Brown wrote me, "When I was five years old, I used to hang out at the gate of the family farm. My mother started calling me Gates." Over 13 seasons, Brown became a proficient pinch hitter, collecting 107 for his career.

428. Browne, Earl James (1935–38 OF) "Snitz." Tom Shea reports that "Snitz" referred to Brown's small flat nose.

429. Browne, Prentice Almont (1962 P) "Pidge." Origin unknown.

430. Browning, Louis Rogers (1882–94 OF) "The Gladiator." None other than famed pitcher, Charles Radbourne remarked that Browning, "Is the most wicked batter in the business." For 13 seasons, Browning maintained a batting average of .343. He was also rated as a "superb" center fielder making many difficult catches, although on occasion not making routine plays. Browning could not read or write, suffered from mastoiditis, and was a chronic alcoholic. He once remarked "I can't hit the ball, until I hit the bottle." His lusty hitting and constant battles with the press led to the nickname of "The Gladiator." Browning himself, used this nickname and also called himself "Old Pete" while playing for Louisville in the American Association, he asked a local lumber businessman, John Hillench to make a bat to his specifications. It was known as the Louisville Slugger. Brownings success with the made-to-order bat created a demand from other players for custom made bats and led to the firm of Hilbrich and Bradsby and the famed Louisville Slugger bats.

431. Brunansky, Thomas Andrew (1981– OF) "Bruno." "Bruno" is a take off on the last name of Brunansky.

432. Bruner, Jack Raymond (1949–50 P) "Pappy." Bruner told me, "In high school, I was awkward and uncoordinated playing basketball, especially my feet. My coach, Bill Walter, said I looked like a Grandpappy. It was shortened to Pappy."

433. Brunet, George Stuart (1956–71 P) "Lofty." Brunet pitched left handed, but batted right handed. After leaving the major leagues, Brunet continued to pitch in the minor leagues. Through 1985, at age 50, he pitched for 33 seasons, the all-time record.

434. Brush, John T. (1880s Owner) "Tooth." Brush owned the Indianapolis American Association team during the 1880s. He was responsible in 1889 for a classification rule which graded players and capped their salaries. The nickname "Tooth" fit his last name.

435. Bryant, Ronald Raymond (1967–75 P) "Bear." Bryant was nicknamed after the famous football coach, Paul "Bear" Bryant.

436. Brynan, Charles Ruby (1888–91 P) "Tod." Origin unknown.

437. Buckeye, Garland Maiers (1918–28 P) "Gob." Buckeye stood 6'0" tall and weighed between 250–270 pounds during his playing days. "Gob" referred to his stint in the U.S. Navy. According to SABR researcher, Fred Schuld, alternative nicknames for Buckeye were: "Great Lakes Dread-Naught," "Indians Bologna," "Indians' Bambino," "Ponderosa," and two which described his pitching, "Hooks" and "Lefty." In addition, Schuld provides another 25 phrases, if not nicknames, that were used for Buckeye including: "Pitching Pachyderm," "Dining Car Addict," and "The Mastodon Moundsman." Buckeye also played professional football in its infant days 1920–26 with the Chicago Tigers, Chicago Cardinals, and Chicago Bulls.

438. Buckles, Jess Robert (1916 P) "Jim." "Jim" was an alternative to Jess.

439. Buelow, Frederick William (1899–1907 C) 'Fritz." "Fritz" refers to Bullow's German background.

440. Buker, Henry L. (1884 SS) "Happy." Buker was known for his easy going ways and pleasant personality.

441. Bullard, George Donald (1954 SS) "Curly." Origin unknown.

442. Bullas, Simeon Edward (1884 C) "Derby." Origin unknown.

443. Bullheart, James Benson (1922–31 P) "Buck." "Buck" is a generic nickname. The circumstances of origin are almost never documented.

It refers to a virile, well developed, aggressive, high spirited young man. It is usually bestowed during teenage years.

444. Bullock, Malton Joseph (1936 P) "Red." The nickname refers to hair color.

445. Burdock, John Joseph (1876–91 2B) "Black Jack." Burdock had dark brown hair and dark complexion.

446. Burgess, Forrest Harrill (1949–67 C) "Smoky." Burgess inherited the nickname of "Smoky." It may have been a response to the first name of Forrest. Burgess was a fine hitter with a career average of .295. He is best remembered, however, as an effective pinch hitter. He appeared 507 times in that capacity, the most of any player, and banged out 145 hits, third on the all-time pinch hitter list.

447. Burgess, Thomas Roland (1954–62 1B) "Tim." Burgess was nicknamed "Tim" by his high school teammates.

448. Burgmeir, Thomas Henry (1969–84 P) "Bugs." Burgmeir inherited his nickname from his father.

449. Burk, Leslie Kingston (1923–26 2B) "Buck." "Buck" in Burk's case is just a take off on the last name of Burk.

450. Burk, Robert James (1927–37 P) "Lefty." Burk pitched left handed, and batted left handed.

451. Burke, James Timothy (1898–1905 3B) "Sunset Jimmy." Joseph McBride maintains that "Sunset" referred to Burke's "deep-red" complexion. Lee Allen, on the other hand, says Burke had a superstition that made it impossible for him to eat dinner until the sun went down.

452. Burkett, Jessie Cail (1890–1905 OF) "The Crab." Burkett earned the nickname of "The Crab" because of an overall cranky disposition. He always played with a scowl on his face, was irascible and caustic to teammates, traded insults with spectators and fought with umpires. Burkett, was however, a great hitter, collecting 2,873 hits and a .343 average in 16 seasons. Three times he hit over .400, .423 in 1895, .410 in 1896, and .402 in 1896.

453. Burkhart, Elmer Robert (1936–39 P) "Swede." "Swede" referred to Burkhart's build 6'2" and weight of 190 pounds, and his light colored hair.

454. Burleson, Richard Paul (1974–78 SS) "Red Rooster." Johnny Pesky, Boston Red Sox coach, called Burleson "Red Rooster" not because of his hair color, but because of his cocky and competitive spirit.

455. Burnham, George W. (1883, 1886–87, 89, 93, 95, NL Umpire) "Watch." During his rookie year as an umpire, Burnham received a watch from his fans in Cleveland inscribed: "Presented to George Burnham by his Cleveland friends, July 25, 1883." Burnham was often criticized for his poor officiating. A Chicago newspaper reporter once wrote of him: "More unjust decisions in Chicago in three days than all the errors made in Chicago by all the umpires all season."

456. Burns, Charles Birmingham (1902 PH) "CB." C.B. were Burns initials.

457. Burns, George Henry (1914–29 1B) "Tioga George." This was a place nickname. Burns lived in North Philadelphia on Tioga Street when he played for the Philadelphia A's. The nickname was used to distinguish him from the contemporary out fielder,

George Joseph Burns, 1911–25. Outside of "Broadway," and "Boardwalk," Tioga is the only other example of a player being nicknamed for a street. Burns batted .307 over 16 years, collecting 2,018 hits.

458. Burns, James (1901 P) "Farmer." "Farmer," in Burns case, has the same meaning as "Rube." He was backward in his ways.

459. Burns, John Irving (1930–36 1B) "Slug." "Slug" is short for "Slugger." It was given to Burns by teammates when he was playing semi-pro ball in New England.

460. Burns, Thomas P. (1884–95 OF) "Oyster." Lee Allen reports that Burns was fond of eating oysters. However, it appears that most of the time, he was simply called Tommy.

461. Burns, William Thomas (1908–12 P) "Sleepy Bill." Burns earned the reputation as baseball's all-time gold bricker. On days he did not pitch, he slept through the game on the bench. On days he did pitch, he slept only between innings. Burns was the alleged go-between during the 1919 Black Sox scandal to fix the World Series.

462. Burrell, Frank Andrew (1891–97 C) "Buster." There is some indication that "Buster" may have referred to hitting ability, but it is not really documented.

463. Burright, Larry Allen (1962–64 2B) "Possum." Burright wrote me, "During spring training, my rookie year in 1962, Tim Harkness and Duke Snider gave me the nickname because I was always smiling, but had little to say."

464. Burrus, Maurice Lennon (1919–28 1B) "Dick." Origin unknown.

465. Burtschy, Edward Frank (1950–56 P) "Moe." Burtschy wrote me, "Moe is short for molasses foot. In high school, I did not like to do wind sprints during football practice, and always finished last. My high school coach, John 'Socko' Wothe started the Mo business. Few people even know my real name."

466. Busby, Paul Miller (1941–43 OF) "Red." The nickname refers to hair color.

467. Busch, August Adolphus, Jr. (1953–89 Owner) "Big Eagle." Busch inherited the Anheuser-Busch beer industry. In 1953 he purchased the St. Louis Cardinals. The ultra conservative Busch opposed what he considered inflationary player salaries in the late 1960s and was adamant in his resistance to the 1972 and 1981 player strikes. "Big Eagle" referred to the bird in the Anheuser-Busch trademark.

468. Bush, Guy Terrell (1923–45 P) "The Mississippi Mudcat." This is a place nickname. Bush was raised on a Mississippi plantation where the muddy streams contain catfish. Although Bush won 176 major league games, he is probably best remembered for serving up balls for Babe Ruth's 713th and 714th home runs.

469. Bush, Leslie Ambrose (1912–28 P) "Bullet Joe." Bush used a bullet-like fastball to win 194 major league games in 17 seasons. However, in five World Series, he won just two games while dropping five. Fred Lieb remarks that everyone called Bush "Joe," but I have been unable to establish the reason for this.

470. Bush, Owen Joseph (1908–23 SS) "Donie." Harold Johnson writes, "In 1908, when Bush first went to the Detroit Club, he was struck out by the left-handed offerings of Jess Tannehill, then in the twilight of his career. The kid came back to the bench completely puzzled. 'What was that old buzzard throwing me?' Bush asked. Whereupon the late Ed Killian said, 'He was foolin' you with his donieball.' For no more pertinent reason than this, Bush for twenty-five years has been known as Donie."

471. Bushong, Albert John (1876–90 C) "Doc." Bushong received his DDS degree in 1882, from the University of Pennsylvania and became a practicing dentist while still catching in the major leagues.

472. Butka, Arthur Edward (1943–44 1B) "Babe." Butka told me, "I was a long ball hitter. After winning a game with a long home run in the minor leagues, teammates started calling me Babe."

473. Butler, Cecil Dean (1962–64 P) "Slewfoot." Butler at 6'4" was a big man who moved very slowly on the bases and fielding balls off the mound.

474. Butler, Charles Thomas (1933 P) "Lefty." Butler pitched left handed, but batted right handed.

475. Butler, Frank Dean (1895 OF) "Stuffy." Origin unknown.

476. Butler, Frank E. (1884 OF) "Kid." "Kid" referred to Butler's small stature.

477. Butler, John Stephen (1926–29 SS) "Trolly Line." Butler received his nickname while playing for Brooklyn who were once known as the Trolley Dodgers.

478. Butler, Willis Everett (1907 2B) "Kid." Butler was a teenager when he played 20 games in the major leagues in his only season.

479. Butts, Thomas (1938–50 SS, Negro League) "Pee Wee." Butts was 5'9" and weighed 145 pounds.

480. Buxon, Ralph Stanley (1933–49 P) "Buck." "Buck" was a play on the last name of Buxon.

481. Byers, James Williams (1904 C) "Big Bill." It appears that Byers, as a catcher, was a big man. However, statistics on his height and weight are not available.

482. Byrd, Samuel Dewey (1929–36 OF) "Babe Ruth's Legs." From 1929–34, Byrd's primary role with the New York Yankees was a pinch runner for Babe Ruth or a late inning replacement for him in the outfield. Byrd was also called "Babe Ruth's Caddy." The reference was to Byrd's golfing ability. He was the best pro golfer who played major league baseball.

483. Byrnes, Milton John (1943–45 OF) "Skippy." Byrnes was nicknamed after the "Skippy" comic strip character.

484. Byron, William J. (1913–19 NL Umpire) "The Singing Umpire." Byron, who as might be expected, was often referred to as "Lord" made up rhymes and sung them to protesting players. For example, to a player squawking on a called third strike:

"Let me tell you something, son
Before you get much older,
You cannot hit the ball my friend
With your bat upon your shoulder."

To a player who had just waved at a pitch:

"It cut the middle of the plate
You missed because you swung too late."

Once Byron bounced John McGraw out of a game singing the following to the tune of a familiar nursery song:

"To the clubhouse you must go
You must go
To the clubhouse you must go
My fair manager."

485. Caballero, Ralph Joseph (1944–52 2B) "Putsy." As a young child, his father thought he liked to "putt" around.

486. Cady, Forrest LeRoy (1912–19 C) "Hick." Cady came from the small town of Bishop Hill, Illinois. "Hick" like "Rube" and "Cy" was used by players to indicate unsophisticated roots.

487. Caffie, Joseph Clifford (1956–57 OF) "Rabbit." "Rabbit" indicated Caffie's speed and recognized his base stealing ability in the minor leagues.

488. Cahill, John Patrick Francis (1884–87 OF) "Patsy." "Patsy" is derived from Patrick. It has no feminine connotations.

489. Cain, Merritt Patrick (1932–38 P) "Sugar." "Sugar" is in response to the last name of Cain. Cain was the pitcher for the Detroit Tigers when Bill Veeck sent the midget, Eddie Gaedel, to the plate for the St. Louis Browns in 1951. Cain walked him on four pitches.

490. Cain, Robert Max (1949–54 P) "Sugar." "Sugar" is in response to the last name of Cain. In Cain's case, the nickname came from kids in high school.

491. Caldwell, Earl Welton (1928–48 P) "Teach." Before signing a baseball contract, Caldwell taught history in his hometown of Rogers, Texas. Although Caldwell's major league career spans three decades, he only spent eight years in the major leagues. He pitched five games for the Philadelphia Phils in 1928, and then was out of the majors until 1935 when he went with the St. Louis Browns. The Browns dropped him after the 1937 season and he did not reappear until 1948 with the Chicago White Sox.

492. Caldwell, Ralph Grant (1904–05 P) "Lefty." Caldwell pitched left handed and batted left handed.

493. Caldwell, Raymond Benjamin (1910–21 P) "Slim." Caldwell was 6'2" and weighed 190 pounds. In 12 seasons he won 133 games and batted .248 with eight home runs. He was given the nickname of "Slim" by pitcher Russ Ford when both were with the Yankees in 1910.

494. Calhoun, John Charles (1902 3B) "Red." The nickname refers to hair color.

495. Calhoun, William Dovitte (1913 1B) "Mary." Origin unknown.

496. Callahan, James Joseph (1894–1913 OF) "Nixey." Origin unknown.

497. Callahan, James Timothy (1884 3B) "Red." The nickname refers to hair color.

498. Callahan, Ray James (1915 P) "Pat." "Pat" recognized Callahan's Irish background.

499. Cameron, John Wesley (1906 P) "Happy Jack." "Happy Jack" referred to Cameron's easy going personality during his minor league career. He pitched only six innings in the major leagues and did not allow an earned run.

500. Camnitz, Samuel Howard (1904–15 P) "Red." The nickname refers to hair color. Tom Shea states that Camnitz was known as "The Kentucky Rosebud," a place nickname. He had red hair and was from Covington, Kentucky.

501. Camp, Howard Lee (1917 OF) "Red." The nickname refers to hair color.

502. Camp, Winfield Scott (1892–94 P) "Kid." Camp was the kid brother of Llewellan Camp who also played in the majors at the same time, 1892–94.

503. Campau, Charles Columbus (1888–94 OF) "Count." Campau inherited the "Count" nickname from his father who had been a captain in the Union Army during the Civil War, most remembered for his retreat at the Battle of Bull Run. After the war, he traveled to France and became a trusted counselor to Napoleon III who gave him the honorary title of "Count."

504. Campbell, Archibald Stewart (1928–30 P) "Iron Man." "Iron Man" comes from Campbell's minor league career where he appeared in many games each year.

505. Campbell, Clarence (1940–41 OF) "Soup." The nickname is in response to the last name of Campbell. The reference is to the soup company.

506. Campbell, Marc Thaddeus (1907 SS) "Hutch." Origin unknown.

507. Campfield, William Holton (1896 P) "Sal." Origin unknown.

508. Candelaria, John Robert (1975–89 P) "The Candy Man." The nickname is derived from the last name. It has nothing to do with candy.

509. Cannady, Walter (1922–39 SS, Negro League) "Rev." Origin unknown.

510. Cannell, Virgin Wirt (1904–05 OF) "Rip." Cannell was a good minor league hitter and earned the nickname of "Rip" a much more acceptable baseball tag than the first name, Virgin.

511. Cantillon, Joseph D. (1907–09 Manager) "Pongo Joe." Cantillon never played in the major leagues but managed the Washington Senators to eighth, seventh, and eighth place finishes in three years. San Francisco sportswriter, Charley Dryden, was responsible for the nickname. In answer to a fan's question about Joe's nationality (Irish), Charley wrote that his real name was Pelipe Pongo Cantilono, an Italian nobleman, who fled the country to escape an idle life of social ease. San Francisco bay area Italians took Dryden's spoof seriously and claimed him as one of theirs, cheering "Pongo Pongo" when he came to bat for the Seals. Cantillon despised the nickname, but he carried it with him when he managed in the major leagues.

512. Cantrell, Dewey Guy (1925–30 P) "Gunner." Tom Shea reports that "Gunner" referred to Cantrell's fastball pitching.

513. Capra, Lee William (1971–77 P) "Buzz." A Chicago neighbor saw Capra playing ball with his father and said that the youngster had a buzz saw swing.

514. Caray, Harry, Jr. (1976– Announcer) "Skip." Caray is the son of Hall of Fame announcer Harry Caray, Sr. He started working Atlanta Braves games in 1976. The popular Caray, Jr., was not at all like his father on the air, as described by Curt Smith: "He consolidated interest with *Anschauung* and a sassy twist...." "Skip" appears in this case to be the equivalent of Junior.

515. Cardenas, Leonardo Lazaro Alfonso (1960–75 SS) "Chico." "Chico" means kid in Spanish. He was also called "Mr. Automatic" because of his fancy fielding.

516. Cardini, Armand Joseph (1943–45 P) "Big Ben." Cardini was 6'3" and weighed 195 pounds.

517. Carey, George C. (1895–1903 1B) "Scoops." Carey was a fancy fielding first baseman known for his ability to scoop throws out of the dirt.

518. Carey, Max (1910–29 OF) "Scoops." Carey, as one story has it, was nicknamed after George "Scoops" Carey a fancy fielding first baseman 1895–1903. Carey, however, may have earned the nickname in his own right because of the way he scooped in line drives in the outfield. In six of his best seasons he handled 400 or more putouts with a high of 450 in 1923. Carey batted .285 for his career collecting 2,665 hits. He was an outstanding base stealer leading the National League ten times with a career total of 738. Before his baseball career when attending Concordia College in Fort Wayne, Indiana, and thinking of preparing for the Lutheran ministry, he was called "Carmarius." The "Scoops" tag was first used in 1909 when Carey played for South Bend. In 1944 he managed the Milwaukee Chicks of the All American Girls Professional Baseball League. From 1945–49 he served as president of the league, and in 1950–51 he managed the Fort Wayne Daisies.

519. Carey, Thomas Francis Aloysius (1935–46 2B) "Scoops." Carey was nicknamed after Max "Scoops" Carey.

520. Cargo, Robert J. (1892 SS) "Chick." Although exact statistics are not available, in Cargo's case, "Chick" refers to small size.

521. Carleton, James Otto (1932–40 P) "Tex." "Tex" is a place nickname. Carleton was from Comanche, Texas. Baseball historian, Ernest Lanigan, gave Carleton the nickname in 1926.

522. Carlisle, Walter (1908 OF) "Rosy." "Rosy" referred to Carlisle's complexion.

523. Carlson, Leon Alton (1920 P) "Swede." Carlson was of Swedish background.

524. Carlstrom, Albin Oscar (1911 SS) "Swede." Carlstrom was of Swedish background.

525. Carlton, Stephen Norman (1965–88 P) "Lefty." Carlton pitched left handed and batted left handed. He was one of the greatest left hand pitchers of all time winning 329 major league games and striking out 4,136 batters. Perhaps his greatest feat was a 27-10 record with 30 complete games for the 1972 last place Philadelphia Phils.

526. Carmell, Leon James (1959–65 OF) "Duke." Carmell told me: "Growing up in the era of Willie, Mickey and the Duke and being a Dodger fan at the time, I thought Snider was the best. So I started calling me Duke at about age 14."

527. Carnett, Edwin Elliot (1941–45 OF) "Lefty." Carnett batted left handed and threw left handed.

528. Carney, John Joseph (1889–91 1B) "Handsome Jack." Carney was considered one of the most handsome players of his time.

529. Carney, Patrick Joseph (1902–04 OF) "Doc." Carney studied medicine while a player and later became a practicing physician.

530. Carpenter, Warren William (1879-92 3B) "Hick." The real origin of "Hick" seems to have been lost over time. Carpenter was called "Old Hick" for so long that no one remembers why. He was one of three men, according to Lee Allen, who played third base left handed, the other two being Wee Willie Keeler (44 games) and Charles Marr (129 games). Carpenter played 1,059 games at third left handed, but he was a right handed batter. It must be noted that Don Mattingly appeared in three games in 1986 as a left handed third baseman for the New York Yankees.

531. Carr, George (1920-34 1B, Negro League) "Tank." "Tank" referred to Carr's size, 6'2", 230 pounds. Carr was not slow, however. In 1925 he led the league in stolen bases with 24.

532. Carrasquel, Alejando Aparicio Elroy (1939-49 P) "Chico." "Chico" means kid or little boy in Spanish. His nephew, Alfonso "Chico" Carrasquel told me his uncle was also called "Carrasquelito."

533. Carrasquel, Alfonso Colon (1950-59 SS) "Chico." Carrasquel wrote me: "Chico means little boy, little one, or kid in Spanish. I was named by my teammates at Fort Worth when I was in the Texas League. I had an uncle, Alex Carrasquel, who pitched for Washington 1939-49. He was called 'Kid' Carrasquel or 'Carrasquelito'."

534. Carrick, William Martin (1898-1902 P) "Doughnut Bill." Carrick liked to eat doughnuts. He was also called "Poker Bill" because of ineptness in playing cards.

535. Carrigan, William Francis (1906-16 C) "Rough." Carrigan was well mannered off the field. On it was a different story. He was hard, tough and aggressive. In other words he played rough, giving no quarter and asking none. He enjoyed holding his ground at home plate against the flying spikes of would-be scorers, including Ty Cobb.

536. Carroll, Clay Palmer (1964-78 P) "Hawk." Carroll had a long sharp nose.

537. Carroll, Dorsey Lee (1919 P) "Dixie." "Dixie" is a place nickname referring to the Southern section of the country. Carroll was from Paducah, Kentucky.

538. Carroll, Edward (1884 OF) "Chick." "Chick" refers to small size.

539. Carroll, John E. (1884-87 OF) "Scrappy." Carroll was but 5'7" but he built a reputation as a fighter who was not afraid to mix it up with much larger men.

540. Carroll, Ralph Arthur (1916 C) "Red." The nickname refers to hair color. Carroll was also called "Doc" but it is unknown whether he had an association with either the medical or dental professions.

541. Carroll, Richard Thomas (1909 P) "Shadow." Carroll was so thin that he looked like a shadow on the mound.

542. Carsey, Wilfred (1891-1901 P) "Kid." Joseph McBride reports that "Kid" referred to Carsey's 5'7" height. Carsey won 116 games in ten seasons, but lost 138. In 1895 he posted a 24-16 won-lost record, but his ERA was the highest for any 20-game winner in history, 4.92.

543. Carson, Albert James (1910 P) "Soldier." Origin unknown.

544. Carson, Walter Lloyd (1934-35 OF) "Kit." The nickname of "Kit" is in response to the last name of Carson. The reference is to the famous American frontiersman and guide of the 1840s.

545. Carswell, Frank Willis (1953 OF) "Tex." "Tex" is a place nickname. Carswell was from Palestine, Texas. He was also called "Wheels" because of his speed.

546. Carter, Arnold Lee (1944–45 P) "Lefty." Carter pitched left handed and batted left handed.

547. Carter, Conrad Powell (1908 P) "Nick." Carter told people that "Nick" came from his "cutting up" on the field of play.

548. Carter, Gary Edwards (1974– C) "The Kid." In Carter's case, "Kid" refers to boyish looks.

549. Carter, Otis Leonard (1925–26 C) "Blackie." The nickname refers to hair color.

550. Carter, Solomon Mobley (1931 P) "Buck." "Buck" is a generic nickname of which the circumstances of origin are almost never documented. It refers to a virile, well-developed, aggressive, high spirited young man. It is usually bestowed on the individual during his teenage years.

551. Cartwright, Edward Charles (1890–97 1B) "Jumbo." Cartwright was 5'10" and weighed in excess of 225 pounds, unusual for a first baseman.

552. Caruthers, Robert Lee (1884–93 OF) "Parisian Bob." One version has it that Caruthers was a fancy dresser, which reminded people that Paris was the center of fashion. Robert Tiemann, SABR 19th century expert, however, suggests the nickname may have come from the fact that after the 1885 season Caruthers went to Paris the "Doc" Bushong and at first refused to sign a contract for the 1886 season.

553. Cary, Scott Russell (1947 P) "Red." The nickname refers to hair color.

554. Cascarella, Joseph Thomas (1934–38 P) "Crooning Joe." Cascarella was a talented and accomplished tenor singer.

555. Casey, James Peter (1898–1907 3B) "Doc." Casey was a practicing dentist. Nap Lajoie credited Casey for bringing him in to pro baseball.

556. Cassini, Jack Dempsy (1949 PR) "Scat." "Scat" refers to Cassini's speed. He was very fast. Cassini's major league career consisted of eight games as a pinch runner.

557. Caster, George Jasper (1934–46 P) "Ug." "Ug" is a response to the last name of Caster. The reference is to Castor oil, infamous for its bad taste.

558. Castleman, Cydell (1934–39 P) "Slick." Joseph McBride reports "Slick" referred to Castleman's fancy dress, not his fancy pitching.

559. Castner, Paul Henry (1923 P) "Lefty." Caster pitched left handed and batted left handed.

560. Castro, Louis M. (1902 2B) "Jud." Origin unknown.

561. Cathey, Hardin (1942 P) "Abner." Origin unknown.

562. Caton, James Howard (1917–20 SS) "Buster." "Buster" refers to his hitting ability. Caton received the nickname in 1915. While playing for Portsmith in the Ohio State League he once belted 11 straight hits and went 13 for 15.

563. Caulfield, John Joseph (1946 SS) "Jake." "Jake" was used as an alternative to Joseph.

564. Causey, Cencil Algeron (1918–22 P) "Red." The nickname refers to hair color.

565. Cavarretta, Philip Joseph (1934–55 1B) "Philabuck." In Charlie Grimm's words: "When I first saw Cavarretta back there in the mid-thirties, I started calling him 'Philabuck.' It just came to me and was inspired, if you can call it that, by my reaction that here was a hard-nosed athlete. Phil liked it." Chicago Cub broadcaster, Bert Wilson, helped popularize the nickname.

566. Cavet, Tiller H. (1911–14 P) "Pug." Cavet had a pug nose.

567. Cavney, James Christopher (1922–25 SS) "Ike." Origin unknown.

568. Ceccarelli, Arthur Edward (1955–60 P) "Chick." "Chick" is a contraction of the last name of Ceccarelli.

569. Center, Marvin Earl (1942–46 P) "Pete." Origin unknown.

570. Cepeda, Orlando Manuel Penne (1958–74 1B) "The Baby Bull." Cepeda batted .297 in a 17-year career with 2,351 hits, 379 home runs and 1,365 RBIs. Cepeda's father, Pedro, was known as the "Babe Ruth of Puerto Rico" because of his reputation as a slugger and home run hitter. He was nicknamed "The Bull" and "Perucho." When Orlando became a star, he was called "The Baby Bull" and "Peruchin." Orlando was also called "Cha Cha" for his movements around first base. This nickname was popularized by broadcaster Harry Caray when Capeda played for the St. Louis Cardinals.

571. Cey, Ronald Charles (1971–87 3B) "Penguin." Los Angeles manager, Tom Lasorda, was responsible for making the nickname "Penguin" stick. It was because of Cey's short legs which gave him a waddling walk and run just like a penguin. It first had been used when Cey was in college.

572. Chadbourne, Chester James (1906–18 OF) "Pop." Chadbourne received the nickname "Pop" after he returned to the major leagues in 1914 after a seven-year lapse.

573. Chadwick, Henry (1858–1908 Chronicles) "Father of Baseball." Chadwick was not only the chronicler of early baseball, but also a promotor, shaper and its conscious. As Frederick Ivor-Campbell writes: "Chadwick wrote voluminously about baseball in newspapers, pamphlets and books. He reported its games, chronicled its development, taught its skills, recommended changes in its rules, and battled the drinking and gambling that threatened its integrity." He was responsible for the box score and the system for scoring games.

574. Chagnon, Leon Wilbur (1929–35 P) "Shag." "Shag" merely replaces "S" for "C" in the last name. Shag is a baseball term meaning to chase fly balls.

575. Chakales, Robert Edward (1951–57 P) "Chick." Teammates in high school had difficulty pronouncing Chakales and used "Chick" instead. He was also called "The Golden Greek."

576. Chalmers, George W. (1910–16 P) "Dut." Origin unknown.

577. Chamberlain, Elton P. (1886–96 P) "Icebox." Lee Allen wrote: "Chamberlain's nickname was devised from his austere calm in the face of all hostility on the part of the enemy. Sportswriters of that era seem to have bestowed on the athletes a happier nomenclature than is used today."

578. Chambers, Clifford Day (1948–53 P) "Lefty." Chambers pitched left handed and batted left handed.

579. Chance, Frank Leroy (1898–1914 1B) "Husk." Chance was the first baseman in the Chicago Cubs' famous double-play combination, Tinkers to Evers to Chance. In addition to a 17-year playing career in which he compiled a batting average of .297, Chance managed for 11 years including leading the Cubs to four National League pennants and two World Championships. He once got into a barroom fight with heavyweight champion, James J. Corbett. After the battle, players began calling Chance "Husk," short for "Husky." He joined the Chicago Cubs in 1898 from Fresno of the Pacific Coast League where he had been a catcher. He had the reputation of being slow on the bases. His nickname at that time was "Slouth Foot." As a manager of the Chicago Cubs and winning championships in the 1906–08 era, sportswriter Charlie Dryden of the *Chicago Examiner* dubbed him "The Peerless Leader."

580. Chandler, Albert Benjamin (1945–51 Commissioner) "Happy." According to Lee Allen: "He worked his way through Transylvania College and first demonstrated his talent for politics as a joiner in almost every campus activity imaginable." It was at this stage of life that his perpetual grin secured for him the nickname of "Happy." He was a former governor of the state of Kentucky.

581. Chandler, Spurgeon Ferdinand (1937–47 P) "Spud." Chandler was a college football star. His nickname "Spud" was a corruption of his first name Spurgeon. In a game in 1940 while pitching for the New York Yankees against Chicago, he hit two home runs, one a grand slam, and drove in six runs.

582. Channell, Lester Clark (1910–14 OF) "Dude." Origin unknown.

583. Chaplin, James Baily (1928–36 P) "Tiny." "Tiny" is a nickname opposite. Chaplin was 6'1" and weighed 195 pounds.

584. Chapman, Glenn Justice (1934 OF) "Pete." Origin unknown.

585. Chapman, John Curtic (1874–76 OF) "Death to Flying Things." Joseph McBride reports of Chapman: "The left fielder for the Philadelphia Athletics of the 1860s, Chapman played barehanded, as was then the custom and thrilled fans with his spectacular one-handed catches. Sportswriters gave him the quaint name of 'Death to Flying Things'."

586. Chapman, William Benjamin (1930–46 OF) "Blazer." Chapman had great speed on the base paths. He led the American League in stolen bases four times. His career batting average was .302 with 1,958 hits in 15 seasons. Chapman was a hard-nosed player who was easily angered. As a member of the New York Yankees he even had altercations with teammate "Babe" Ruth.

587. Chappelle, William Hogan (1908–14 P) "Big Bill." Chappelle was 6'2" and weighed 210 pounds.

588. Charboneau, Joseph (1980–82 OF) "Super Joe." Charboneau had a fine rookie year for Cleveland in 1980 batting .289 with 23 home runs, but injuries kept him from playing much after that year. He was nicknamed "Super Joe" by Cleveland fans because of his bizarre off-the-field antics. They included: bench pressing 401 pounds, opening beer bottles with his arm muscles and eye socket bones, drinking beer through his nose, eating lighted cigarettes, swallowing uncracked eggs and pulling his own teeth.

589. Charles, Edwin Douglas (1962–69 3B) "The Poet." "The Poet" refers to Charles' skill in handling rhyme and verse. When he first began his pro career he was called "Ez" after heavyweight boxing champion Ezzard Charles. Charles was also called "The Glider" for the way he got around the bases so easily.

590. Charles, Raymond (1908–10 2B) "Chappie." Origin unknown.

591. Charleston, Oscar McKinley (1915–50 OF, Negro League) "The Black Ruth." Robert Peterson writes of Charleston, "Built like Babe Ruth with a barrel chest and spindly legs, Charleston combined speed, power at the plate, a strong arm, and an unerring sense of where a ball was hit in the outfield." Charleston had natural fast ball hitting ability with power to all fields, plus the knack of the swinging bunt.

592. Chartak, Michael George (1940–44 OF) "Shotgun." "Shotgun" referred to Chartak's strong throwing arm. He was also called "The Volga Batman" in 1942 because of his lusty hitting for the St. Louis Browns. Chartak was of Russian background.

593. Charton, Frank Lane (1964 P) "Pete." Charton's grandmother called him Peter Rabbit because of his prominent front teeth. It led to the nickname of "Pete."

594. Chase, Harold Homer (1905–19 1B) "Prince Hal." Chase is generally regarded as one, if not the best, fielding first baseman of all time. His range on bunts and balls hit to his right was truly amazing. He was nicknamed "Prince Hal" by fans because of his fielding ability. Chase was also an excellent hitter compiling a career .291 batting average for 15 years. Chase's career was marred by wrong doing and alleged wrong doing. The worst charges involved the throwing of games, bribing opposing players and having prior knowledge of the Black Sox scandal, the throwing the 1919 World Series.

595. Chase, Kendall Fay (1936–43 P) "Lefty." Chase pitched left handed, but batted right handed.

596. Chatham, Charles L. (1930–31 3B) "Buster." "Buster" referred to Chatham's batting ability, stemming from his minor league career.

597. Cheeves, Virgil Earl (1920–27 P) "Chief." Cheeves was of American Indian background. He was also called "The Giant Killer" when he beat the New York Giants six straight times in 1921–22.

598. Chesbro, John David (1899–1909 P) "Happy Jack." Chesbro won 198 games in 11 years including a 28-6 season in 1902 and 41-12 in 1904. Chesbro always seemed to have a smile on his face. He was also called "Algy" which was a slang term of the time meaning sissy, which in Chesbro's case was a nickname opposite. He was anything but a sissy. The "Happy Jack" tag dates from 1894 when Chesbro was working in a mental institution in Middleton, New York.

599. Chester, Hilda (1940s and 50s Fan) "Howling Hilda." Hilda was a famous Brooklyn Dodger fan. She sat in the bleachers at Ebbets Field and shouted to players and rang cowbells. Players would wave to her. She earned the price of admission to games by hawking song sheets. Hilda preferred to be called "Queen of the Bleachers."

600. Childs, Clarence Algernon (1888–1901 2B) "Cupid." There is some controversy over the meaning of "Cupid." Joseph McBride states it referred to Childes' loveable but fierce temper. Stan Grosshandler believes it is a nickname opposite. Childes was far from angelic. There is also evidence that it might have denoted his build 5'8" and 185 pounds and his cupid-like facial features.

601. Childes, Pearce Nuget (1899–1900 OF) "What's the Use." Jack Connerlly suggests that Childes was the leading baseball pessimist of his time. I have not, however, been able to verify the opinion. Bill O'Neal lists the nickname as "No Use" stating, "His peculiar nickname derived from his favorite insult as a dedicated bench jockey."

602. Childress, Rodney Osborne (1985– P) "Rocky." Childress wrote me: "Rocky comes from my initials R.O.C. My step-great-grandfather started calling me Little Roc, since my father's name was also Rodney and he went by Rod. My mother particularly wanted me to have a nickname. So when Little Roc was being started, my parents decided to call me Rocky. I was around two years old when I became familiar with my nickname. I have always liked it and appreciated being the only boy among my friends and classmates with the name of Rocky."

603. Chiozza, Dino Joseph (1935 SS) "Dynamo." "Dynamo" was a takeoff on the first name of Dino. Chiozza was hardly a dynamo in the major leagues appearing in but two games without a time at bat.

604. Chipman, Robert Howard (1941–52 P) "Mr. Chips." The nickname is in response to the last name. The reference is to the popular novel *Goodbye Mr. Chips*.

605. Chouneau, William (1910 P) "Chief." Chouneau was of American Indian background.

606. Christenburg, Lloyd Reid (1919–22 OF) "Low." "Low" referred to Christenburg's height of 5'7".

607. Christenson, Walter Neils (1926–27 OF) "Cuckoo." Christenson was a clowning off-season gardener who delighted fans turning flip-flops in the outfield after he had made a good catch. He also kept up a constant conversation with umpires and opposing players. He was known to read a newspaper in the outfield. He would poke holes in it so he could see through. At times he would catch pop-ups in his hip pocket. Fans said he was cuckoo. Christenson was also called "Seacap."

608. Christopher, Lloyd Eugene (1945–47 OF) "Feather." Christopher was slim at 6'2" and 170 pounds.

609. Christopher, Russell Ormand (1942–48 P) "Daddy." "Daddy" is short for "Daddy Long Legs." Christopher at 6'3½" had exceptionally long legs.

610. Chunn, Clarence Nottingham (1957–59 P) "Chuck." "Chuck" was just used as a more acceptable alternative to Clarence.

611. Church, Emory Nicholas (1950–55 P) "Bubba." Church's younger sister could not pronounce brother. It came out Bubba and became a nickname.

612. Ciaffone, Lawrence Thomas (1951 OF) "Symphony." The nickname "Symphony" is a response to the last name of Ciaffone. The reference is to the last name sounding like a musical instrument.

613. Cicero, Joseph Francis (1929–45 OF) "Dode." Cicero played pro ball while still in high school and protected his eligibility by using the name of Doughty. "Dode" was short for

Doughty. Cicero played for the Red Sox in 1929–30. He did not appear again in the major leagues until the war year of 1945 with the Philadelphia Athletics.

614. Cicotte, Alva Warren (1957–62 P) "Bozo." In Cicotte's neighborhood in Melvinville, Michigan, near Detroit, ice cream cones were available call Bozos. As a kid, he liked Bozos so well that an uncle began calling him "Bozo."

615. Cicotte, Edward Victor (1905–20 P) "Knuckles." Cicotte won 208 major league games in 14 seasons before he was banned from baseball for life by Judge Landis for his involvement in the Chicago Black Sox scandal in throwing the 1919 World Series. Joseph McBride claims "Knuckles" stems from Cicotte throwing a shineball which acted like a knuckleball. Kevin Nelson agrees that Cicotte did not throw a knuckleball, but attributes the nickname to the fact that Cicotte had very large knuckles.

616. Cihocki, Edward Joseph (1932–33 OF) "Cy." "Cy" is a popular nickname. For Cihocki the "y" replaced the "i" in his last name.

617. Clabaugh, John William (1926 OF) "Moose." Clabaugh was big and slow of foot. In 1926 for Tyler in the East Texas League he hit 62 home runs. As a power hitter in the minor leagues, he accounted for 340 home runs.

618. Clack, Robert S. (1876 OF) "Gentlemanly Bobbie." In an era of rough and ready play, Clack was known for his proper decorum. He did not smoke or drink.

619. Clancy, John William (1924–34 1B) "Bud." Clancy received the nickname as a child from his parents.

620. Clanton, Eucal (1922 1B) "Uke." "Uke" was a play on the first name of Eucal. Clanton was also called "Cat" because of his quick fielding moves at first base.

621. Clark, Harry (1903 3B) "Pep." Clark was a pepper pot at third base in the minor leagues.

622. Clark, Harvey Daniel (1902 P) "Ginger." "Ginger" referred to hair color.

623. Clark, John Carroll (1938 C) "Cap." He was nicknamed after Fred "Cap" Clarke (1894–1915).

624. Clark, Owen E. (1889–90 OF) "Spider." Clark was 5'10" and weighed but 150 pounds. He looked all arms and legs. He was a versatile performer whose career consisted of 43 games in the outfield, 28 as catcher, 15 at second base, 14 at shortstop, 6 at first base, and one as pitcher.

625. Clark, Roy Elliot (1902 OF) "Pepper." Clark was noted for his hustle and spirited play in the minor leagues.

626. Clark, William Nuschler (1986– 1B) "Will the Thrill." Clark hit a home run his first time at bat in the minor leagues for Fresno in the California League. He also gave fans a thrill by hitting a home run off Nolan Ryan in his first time at bat in the major leagues. Clark likes the nickname and has it painted on his batting helmet. In college at Mississippi State, he was called "Thunder" because of his lusty hitting.

627. Clark, William Otis (1895–99 1B) "Wee Willie." While there is no data available on Clark's size, there is mention of it in the literature that he was short for a first baseman.

628. Clark, William Watson (1924–37 P) "Needle." Wattie, as Clark was addressed was a relief pitcher for the Brooklyn Dodgers. When he was needed, he was needed in a hurry. The "Needle" comes from a Sherlock Holmes remark: "Quick Watson, the needle."

629. Clarke, Alan Thomas (1921 P) "Lefty." Clarke pitched left handed and batted left handed.

630. Clarke, Fred Clifford (1894–1915 OF) "Cap." In 21 seasons Clarke collected 2,708 hits, stole 506 bases and had a career average of .315. He was a player-manager from 1897–1915. "Cap" meant he was the captain or manager of the team.

631. Clarke, Jay Justin (1905–20 C) "Nig." On June 15, 1902, Clarke, a Wandotte Indian, while playing for Corsicana against Texakana in the Texas League hit 8 home runs in 8 times at bat, driving in 16 runs scoring 8 runs, making 24 extra bases and a total of 32 bases. The nickname of "Nig" stems from his dark complexion.

632. Clarke, Joshua Baldwin (1898–1911 OF) "Pepper." Clarke was known for his spirited and inspirational play. It was said he had a lot of pepper.

633. Clarke, Richard Grey (1944 3B) "Noisy." Clarke wrote me that "Noisy" was a nickname opposite. "It was given to me by Art Evers, a left handed pitcher for Macon, Georgia, in the South Atlantic League because I was so quiet."

634. Clarke, Vibert Ernesto (1955 P) "Webbo." "Webbo" is a corruption of the names of Vibert and Ernesto.

635. Clarke, William H. (1888–98 P) "Dad." Tom Shea suggests that Clarke received the nickname at the tail end of his career because of his age. If so, he was only 33 when he ended his major league career.

636. Clarke, William Jones (1893–1905 C) "Boileryard." Origin unknown.

637. Cleary, Joseph Christopher (1945 P) "Fire." Cleary told me: "I was short tempered and would fight at the drop of a hat. I also had red hair. The combination led a boyhood friend to give me the nickname when I was 16 after a sandlot game."

638. Clemens, William Roger (1984– P) "Rocket." Clemens is a fastball strikeout pitcher for the Boston Red Sox. On April 29, 1986, he struck out 20 Seattle batters. He is also called "Big Tex" because he pitched for the University of Texas in college.

639. Clemente, Roberto Walker (1955–72 OF) "Arriba." During the 1960s, Clemente became baseball's best all-around right fielder. He possessed an awe-inspiring throwing arm. He won National League batting titles in 1961, 1964, 1965, and 1967. He collected a career 3,000 hits with a batting average of .317. His career was cut short when he died in an airplane crash in 1972, attempting to carry relief supplies to victims of a Nicaraguan earthquake. "Arriba" or "Let's go" is what Latin-American fans would shout to Clemente. As a child, he was called "Monte Irvin." He was called several derogatory terms by teammates and other players such as: "Goldbrick," "Crybaby," and "No Votes" because of his refusal to play from allegedly minor aches and pains. Teammate Vernon Law called him "Herschel."

640. Clemons, Verne James (1918–24 C) "Fats." Clemons was 5'9½" and weighed 195 pounds.

641. Clevenger, Truman Eugene (1954–62 P) "Tex." I cannot document any association with the state of Texas. Origin unknown.

642. Clift, Harlong Benton (1934–45 3B) "Darkie." Clift wrote me: "I got my nickname from St. Louis Browns teammate, Alan Strange in West Palm Beach, Florida, in 1934. He thought my name was Harlem. Because of that I was called 'Darkie,' 'Nig,' and 'Nigger Dark'." The reference is to Harlem, a section of New York City inhabited by blacks.

643. Clifton, Herman Earl (1934–37 3B) "Flea." Fred Lieb commented, "A strong wind could blow Flea Clifton from one corner of the diamond to the other." But Clifton wrote me: "Flea was hung on me by Del Baker, a former manager of the Detroit Tigers in Beaumont, Texas, in 1933. I was a good-sized flea at 5'11", and 165 pounds. If you have ever been bitten by a Sand Flea, you know why I got my name."

644. Cline, John P. (1882–91 OF) "Monk." Cline did not smoke or drink. At 5'3" and 140 pounds, he was one of the smallest of all baseball outfielders.

645. Clines, Eugene Anthony (1970–79 OF) "Road Runner." With his great speed on the bases and the outfield, Clines was nicknamed after the lightening quick bird character in the "Road Runner" cartoon series created by Chuck Jones.

646. Clinton, James Lawrence (1876–86 OF) "Big Jim." A 5'8½" and 175-pounder, Clinton was big-around.

647. Clinton, Lucien Louis (1960–67 OF) "Ponca City Lou." This is a place nickname. Clinton was from Ponca City, Oklahoma.

648. Clouth, Edgar George (1924–26 OF) "Specs." Clouth wore eyeglasses.

649. Clymer, William Johnstone (1891 SS) "Derby Day." Joe Overfield provides several versions of "Derby Day." Before the days of sunglasses Clyman played the outfield wearing a long-billed cap, more like a jockey would wear to shield his eyes from the sun. Another story has it that at a rained-out game in the 1890s players from Buffalo took off for the race track where the Providence Derby was being run. Clymer bet on a horse he thought was a sure thing. When the horse lost, the other players began to kid him and call him "Derby Day." Overfield suggests yet a third possibility. A quote from the *Buffalo Express* in 1924 read: "Billy Clymer will be able to revive his famous 'Derby Day' cry when he is in the coaching box for Cincinnati this year. He'll also be close to the race track." Joe Overfield wrote me: "Can't you just picture Clymer on the coaching lines, trying to get a rally started? 'Come on guys, let's go, it's Derby Day'!"

650. Cobb, Tyrus Raymond (1905–28 OF) "The Georgia Peach." Cobb must be considered one of the greatest players of all time. He led the American League 12 times in batting average finishing with a career mark of .367, the highest of all time. Eight times, he led the American League in slugging average, seven times in hits, six times in stolen bases, five times in runs scored, four times in triples, and three times in doubles. Cobb's best season was 1911 in which he batted .420 with 248 hits, 147 runs scored, 144 RBIs, and 83 stole bases. Larry Gerlach catches the essence of Cobb's personality, behavior and performance in the following passage: "Cobb's brilliance was due more to a careful mastery of skills combined with a maniacal will to succeed then to native talent. His unrelenting quest to be the best featured and aggressive style of play simultaneously admired and abhorred by teammates, opponents and fans alike. Cobb exhibited in extreme form all the aggressive, extroverted human characteristics—bravery, egotism, unyieldingness, hypersensitivity. He also proved to have a dyspeptic personality, being obstinate, paranoid, vituperative and racist." His nickname "The Georgia Peach" was a place nickname. He was from Royston, Georgia, and Georgia is known as the peach state. He received the nickname from sportswriter, Joe H. Jackson, of the Detroit Free Press during spring training in 1906. It was strictly a newspaper nickname since no one called him "Georgia," "Peach," or "Georgia Peach."

651. Cochran, Alvah Jackson (1915 P) "Goat." Origin unknown.

652. Cochrane, Gordon Stanley (1925–37 C) "Mickey." Cochrane was one of the finest catchers of the 1920s. In 13 seasons, he collected 1,652 hits and a career batting average of .320. "Mickey" reflected his Scotch-Irish background. It was given to him by the manager of Dover in the Eastern Shore League, before he reached the major leagues. He was also called "Black Mike" in reference to his black hair and dark complexion. In his early days as a football player at Boston University, he was called "Kid." Cochrane did not like the nickname of "Mickey." He preferred to be called Gordon.

653. Coffman, George David (1937–40 P) "Slick." Coffman tole me: "My nickname originated when I played for the St. Louis Browns in 1940. I was known as a flashy dresser."

654. Coggins, Franklin (1967–72 2B) "Swish." In Coggins' major league career, he struck out 50 times in 247 official appearances at the plate, a little better than 1 in 5. He collected but 12 walks.

655. Coimbre, Francisco (1940–44 OF) "Pancho." "Pancho" refers to Coimbre's Latin background. He was born and raised in Puerto Rico. In 1943 he hit for a .436 batting average.

656. Cole, Leonard Leslie (1909–15 P) "King." The "King" nickname is in response to the last name of Cole. William Patten and J. Walker McSpadden explained the meaning in the following 1911 passage: "It did not take long for the 'fans' to find a suitable nickname for him 'King Cole' perhaps on account of our nursery-rime [sic] hero, and as 'King Cole' he will be recorded in baseball epics."

657. Coleman, Clarence (1961–65 C) "Choo Choo." "Choo Choo" may be due to Coleman's speed as a catcher. He told me, however, that he did not know where he got it or what it meant. Coleman called all his teammates and many others "Bub."

658. Coleman, Walter Gary (1955–60 P) "Rip." In high school, Coleman played first base and tried to imitate former St. Louis star Jim "Rip" Collins.

659. Colgan, William H. (1884 C) "Ed." Origin unknown.

660. Collard, Earl Clinton (1927–30 P) "Hap." "Hap" was short for "Happy" and was in reference to Collard's pleasant personality.

661. Collins, Edward Trowbridge (1906–30 2B) "Cocky." Collins was the second baseman on the Philadelphia A's $100,000 infield. In 25 seasons, he batted .333 with 17 seasons over .300. "Cocky" referred to his personality. He had a big ego and carried a chip on his shoulder.

662. Collins, Harry Warren (1920–31 P) "Rip." Joseph McBride suggests that "Rip" refers to the speed of Collins' pitches. The reference being to the British slang term ripping. Collins was also called "Two Gun" because he was an officer in the Texas Rangers.

663. Collins, James Anthony (1931–41 1B) "Rip." Collins acquired the nickname of "Ripper" during his days in semi-pro ball. The cover of a ball he tagged was ripped off after it struck a nail on the outfield fence.

664. Collins, John Edgar (1914–21 OF) "Zip." "Zip" referred to the strength of Collins' throw from the outfield.

665. Collins, John Francis (1910–25 OF) "Shamo." "Shamo" was a result of the comparison between his English first name of John and its Gaelic equivalent—Sean.

666. Collins, Kevin Michael (1965–71 3B) "Casey." "Casey" spells out Collins' initials K.C.

667. Collins, Orth Stein (1904–09 OF) "Buck." "Buck" is a generic nickname of which the circumstances of origin are almost never documented. It refers to a virile, well developed, aggressive, high spirited young man. It is usually bestowed on the individual during his teenage years.

668. Collins, Philip Eugene (1923–35 P) "Fidgety Phil." Collins was very nervous on the mound, always moving his body, neck, arms and legs.

669. Collins, Robert Joseph (1940–43 OF) "Chub." "Chub" is short for Chubby, which Collins was.

670. Collins, Tharon Leslie (1919–29 C) "Pat." "Pat" denoted Collins' strong Irish background. Collins batted .500 in three World Series for the New York Yankees, 1927–29.

671. Combs, Earle Bryan (1924–35 OF) "The Kentucky Colonel." Combs compiled a .325 career batting average in 12 seasons with the New York Yankees and .350 in four World Series. "Kentucky Colonel" is a place nickname. Combs came from Pebworth, Kentucky. He was also referred to as "The Southern Gentleman" because he did not smoke, drink or use profanity. Combs was also a church goer and had a warm personality. He had great speed and in the minor leagues, he was called the "Mail Carrier." In his years with the Yanks, he was a lead-off man and dubbed "Waiter." He got on base and waited for "Murders' Row" to knock him in.

672. Comellas, Jorge (1945 P) "Pancho." "Pancho" denotes Comellas Cuban background. "Pancho" is a common nickname in Cuba.

673. Comiskey, Charles Albert (1882–94 1B) "The Old Roman." Charles Comiskey began his playing career in 1882. In 13 years, primarily as a first baseman, he batted .264. He began managing in 1883 and led St. Louis of the American Association to four straight first place finishes 1885–1888. In 11 years as a manager, he achieved a winning percentage of .607, the third best of all time. However, in 1894, his Cincinnati team could do no better than tenth out of 12 contenders. During this period of time, he was called "Charlie" and "Commy." The former is a diminutive of his first name and the latter a derivative of his last name. Comiskey was instrumental in the formation of the American League. In 1901, as owner of the newly formed Chicago White Sox he induced star pitcher, Clark Griffith of the crosstown Chicago National League team, then called "Colts," to jump to the

White Sox. Griffith won 24 games for the Sox in 1901 helping them to their first pennant. At about this time, Hugh Keough, a Chicago journalist, began to refer to Comiskey as "The Old Roman," and the nickname followed him for the rest of his life. Tom Shea suggests that the nickname was a composite of Comiskey characteristics—breeding, a patrician bearing and manner, shrewdness, and a noble mane of flowing white hair which crowned a classical profile.

674. Compton, Anna Sebastian (1911–18 OF) "Pete." Compton told me: "I was never called Anna, which was my mother's maiden name. I was known as Pete from the very first day I played ball. Some called me 'Bash' because of my hitting."

675. Conception, Davis Ismael Benitez (1970–88 SS) "Elmer." Conception is known to ball players and intimates as "Elmer." Art Rosenbaum explains: "The handle was put on Conception by Larry Bowa of the Phils. Seems the Reds shortstop was having a little trouble with his glove one week, and Bowa stopped him to ask, 'Say Conception, is your first name Elmer?' Before he could get an answer, Bowa produced a couple of newspaper box scores with an underline E Conception. 'I figured',' Bowa said, "'that the E stands for Elmer.' Elmer, he remains."

676. Congalton, William Millar (1902–07 OF) "Bunk." Origin unknown.

677. Conigliaro, Anthony Richard (1964–75 OF) "Tony C." "Tony C" was an affectionate nickname given to Conigliaro by teammates. It also helped to distinguish him from his brother Billy, who was a teammate with the Boston Red Sox. "Tony C" hit 24 home runs in 1964 at age 19. He led the American League the next year with 32, hit 28 in 1966 and had 20 in 90 games in 1967, when on August 18, a wild fastball by California Angels Jack Hamilton fractured his left cheekbone and left his vision permanently impaired, although he continued to play in the major and minor leagues through 1975. In 1982, Conigliaro suffered a heart seizure, was in a coma for three weeks, and was left with irreversible brain damage. He required constant care until his death in 1990.

678. Conkwright, Allen Howard (1920 P) "Red." The nickname refers to hair color.

679. Conlan, John Bertrand (1934–35 OF) "Jocko"; (NL Umpire 1941–64) "Jocks." Conlan writes in his book *Jocko:* "When I was playing ball in Rochester there was a sportswriter on the *Democrat and Chronicle* named Corri. We called him 'Geechy.' I don't remember why.... He was the fellow who hung the name 'Jocko' on me. I've heard several people say that I got the name because I was a bench jockey. I never liked that, because I wasn't a bench jockey. I fought like a devil to win, but I didn't rack people. I had a few words with somebody now and then, but I wasn't one of those pop-offs. Just about the time I was with Rochester there was a fellow named Conlon who played second base for a while with the Braves. He spelled it with two O's.... This fellow Conlon on the Braves was called 'Jocko' and Corri started calling me Jocko too. It stuck. It seemed to fit. I wouldn't know what to do now if I didn't have Jocko as part of my name." Conlan became a major league umpire in the National League, 1941–64.

680. Conley, James Patrick (1914–18 P) "Snipe." Origin unknown.

681. Conlon, Arthur Joseph (1923 2B) "Jocko." Conlon was best known as a bench jockey.

682. Connally, George Walter (1921–34 P) "Sarg." During World War I, Connally served in the Marine Corps with the rank of sergeant. He was awarded the Congressional Medal of Honor.

683. Connally, Mervin Thomas (1925 SS) "Mike." "Mike" was used as a more acceptable baseball tag than Mervin. Connally, however, was usually addressed as "Bud," a childhood nickname.

684. Connaster, Broadus Milburn (1931–32 1B) "Bruce." "Bruce" simply replaced the odd first name of Broadus.

685. Conner, Roger (1880–97 1B) "Dear Old Rodger." Conner played for 18 years and was the all-time home run kings with 136 until the Ruth Era. Once one of his home runs went over the right field wall in the old Polo Grounds out onto 112th Street. Several members of the New York Stock Change saw it and were so astonished, they took up a collection for "Dear Old Rodger."

686. Connerlly, William Wirt (1945–53 P) "Wild Bill." Connerlly had difficulty at times getting his pitches close to the plate.

687. Connolly, John M. (1886 3B) "Red." The nickname refers to hair color.

688. Connolly, Joseph George (1921–24 OF) "Coaster Joe." "Coaster" is a place nickname referring to the West Coast. Connolly was from San Francisco. It was given to him when he was playing in the Texas League before his major league days.

689. Connolly, Thomas Francis (1915 3B) "Blackie." Connolly had dark brown, almost black hair.

690. Connolly, Thomas H. (NL 1898–1900, AL 1901–21 Umpire) "Mr." Players called Connolly "Mr." out of respect. Although he never played organized baseball, Connolly worked the first American League game in 1901. He was a neat and conservative dresser with a high hard collar on his shirts and a tie held in place by a jeweled stick pin. Connolly believed that the best umpires were those that attracted the least attention.

691. Conroy, William Edward (1901–11 3B) "Wid." "Wid" is short for "Widow." As a kid, Conroy displayed motherly interest in taking care of youngsters smaller and younger than himself, who were members of his group. Sometimes, he missed out with boys his own size and age.

692. Conroy, William Frederick (1923 3B) "Pep." Conroy displayed a good deal of vim and verve in his play. "Pep" is short for "Pepper."

693. Constable, Jimmy Lee (1956–63 P) "Sheriff." "Sheriff" is a response to the last name of Constable which suggests a law enforcement officer.

694. Consuegra, Sandalio Castellon (1950–57 P) "Sandy." "Sandy" does not refer to hair color, but is a contraction of the first name of Sandalio.

695. Contreras, Arnaldo Juan (1980 P) "Nardi." Contreras told me he was called "Nardi" from birth. "Most Spanish speaking families use Nardi as short for Arnaldo," he said.

696. Conway, Richard Daniel (1918 2B) "Rip." In Conway's case, "Rip" probably meant he was a nice person (English) rather than denoting power or speed.

697. Conwell, Edward James (1911 3B) "Irish." Conwell was of Irish background.

698. Cook, Luther Almus (1913–16 OF) "Doc." Many of the players with the nickname of "Doc" had close associations with either the medical or dental professions. With Cook, however, the origin of "Doc" is unknown.

699. Cooke, Allen Lindsey (1930–38 OF) "Dusty." Tom Shea states that Cooke was very fast and made the dirt fly as he rounded the bases.

700. Cooley, Duff Gordon (1893–1902 OF) "Sir Richard." Origin unknown.

701. Coombs, John Wesley (1906–20 P) "Colby Jack." This is a place nickname. Coombs attended Colby College in Maine and was a star on the baseball team. In 1911, Coombs led the American League in wins with 28. In three World Series he won five games and lost none, including three wins in the 1910 Series for the Philadelphia A's.

702. Cooney, James Edward (1917–28 SS) "Scoops." Cooney was a good fielding shortstop who could scoop grounders out of the dirt.

703. Cooper, Andy (1920–30 P, Negro League) "Lefty." Cooper pitched left handed, but I have no data showing from which side of the plate he batted. In 11 years Cooper won 118 games and lost all except for a winning percentage of .674.

704. Cooper, Guy Evans (1914–15 P) "Rebel." "Rebel" refers to the southern section of the country. Cooper was from Rome, Georgia.

705. Corcoran, Arthur Andrew (1915 3B) "Bunny." Corcoran was small of stature, although exact statistics are not available on him.

706. Corhan, Roy George (1911–16 SS) "Irish." Corhan was of Irish background.

707. Corkhill, John Stewart (1883–92 OF) "Pop." Origin unknown.

708. Cornelius, Willie (1929–46 P, Negro League) "Sug." Cornelius was nicknamed "Sugar." "Sug" was short for "Sugar." In his own words, "I got my nickname from around home. All I know is, when I was big enough to know anything, my mother told me I used to eat all the sugar I could find. And they just started calling me 'Sugar,' and when I went to school it was not 'Sugar' anymore, it was 'Sug'."

709. Corrales, Patrick (1964–73 C) "Ike." Origin unknown.

710. Corriden, John Michael, Sr. (1910–15 SS) "Red." The nickname refers to hair color.

711. Corridon, Frank J. (1904–10 P) "Fiddler." Corridon was a concert violinist, during his baseball career.

712. Cortazzo, John Francis (1923 PH) "Shine." Origin unknown.

713. Corwin, Elmer Nathan (1951–55 P) "Al." Corwin inherited the nickname of "Al" from his father. It was a more acceptable name than Elmer.

714. Cosell, Howard (1962– Announcer) "Howard the Humble." A lawyer of training, the egotistical Cosell began his formal broadcasting career doing a New York Metropolitan pregame show with Ralph Branca and Bobby Thomson in 1962. He then started interviewing players for ABC and did color on "Game of the Week" and other special events. The self-centered, all-knowing Cosell began to knock baseball on the air by the 1970s and Commissioner Bowie Kuhn even tried to get him removed from the air. The nickname "Howard the Humble" is, of course, a nickname opposite. Cosell was also referred to as "The Mouth."

715. Costello, Daniel Francis (1913–16 OF) "Dashing Dan." Costello was considered handsome. He received the nickname "Dashing Dan" while playing for Mt. St. Marys seminary team in Maryland.

716. Cotton, Harvey Louis (1922–24 1B) "Hooks." Origin unknown.

717. Coughlin, William E. (1890–91 P) "Roscoe." Origin unknown.

718. Coughlin, William Paul (1899–1908 3B) "Roudy Bill." Coughlin was known as a fighter and a tough one. After his playing days, he became a minor league umpire.

719. Coumbe, Frederick Nicholas (1914–21 P) "Fritz." Coumbe was of German background.

720. Courtney, Clinton Dawson (1951–61 C) "Scrap Iron." Courtney was dubbed "Scrap Iron" by teammate Duane Pillette and broadcaster Buddy Blattner. Courtney hurt himself running a race at a train station with those two men, but suited up and played the next game. He was also called "Red Neck" because he came from the south and had a temper that was quick to flare. "Toy Bull Dog" was yet another nickname for Courtney indicating his propensity for battle. In July of 1952, he got the worst of a fist fight with Billy Martin. Later that year he spiked Yankee shortstop Phil Rizzuto with a high slide at second base. Both the Yankee and St. Louis Browns benches erupted with both teams swinging. Courtney was mauled by the bigger and more powerful Yankee players.

721. Cousineau, Edward Thomas (1923–25 C) "Dee." Origin unknown.

722. Coveleski, Harry Frank (1907–18 P) "The Giant Killer." In the closing week of the 1908 season, Coveleski won three games for the Philadelphia Phils against the New York Giants. His record for the entire season was only 4-1. The losses to Coveleski left the Giants in a dead heat with the Chicago Cubs, who beat them in a playoff for the pennant.

723. Covington, Chester Rogers (1944 P) "Chesty." Covington was a big man 6'2", 225 pounds with an extremely well developed chest.

724. Covington, Clarence Otto (1913–18 1B) "Sam." Origin unknown.

725. Covington, William Wilkes (1911–12 P) "Tex." "Tex" is a place nickname. Covington was raised in the state of Texas.

726. Cox, Elmer Joseph (1925–26 OF) "Dick." Origin unknown.

727. Cox, Ernest Thompson (1922 P) "Elmer." Origin unknown.

728. Cox, Frank Bernhart (1884 SS) "Runt." Cox was 5'8", but his weight is unknown. He batted only .127 in his only major league season in 27 games.

729. Cox, Glen Melvin (1955–58 P) "Jingles." Origin unknown.

730. Cox, Plateau Rex (1920 P) "Red." The nickname refers to hair color.

731. Craft, Maurice Montague (1916–19 P) "Molly." "Molly" is a take off on Maurice, but the meaning is not documented.

732. Craghead, Howard Oliver (1931–33 P) "Judge." Origin unknown.

733. Craig, George McCarthy (1907 P) "Lefty." Craig pitched left handed, but there is no record of how he batted.

734. Cramer, Rodger Maxwell (1929–48 OF) "Doc." Cramer attracted the nickname of "Doc" from a boyhood job driving a local physician around town in a horse and buggy. When Cramer was a rookie for the Philadelphia A's in 1929, he was supposed to be the fastest man in baseball. Teammates called him "Flit." He extinguished fly balls in the outfield just like a flit.

735. Crandall, James Otis (1908–18 P) "Doc." Crandall was a right handed spitball pitcher, who became one of the first to specialize in relief in 1909 for John McGraws' New York Giants. Writer Damon Runyon called him "The Doctor of Ball Games."

736. Crane, Edward Nicholas (1884–93 P) "Cannonball." Crane threw one of the fastest pitches of his era. He also held the record for long-distance throwing. In Cincinnati on October 12, 1884, he threw a ball 406'1½". Crane had a reputation as a prodigious eater. His favorite snack, according to Lee Allen, consisted of an order of one dozen soft-boiled eggs served in a soup bowl, topped off with two dozen clams.

737. Crane, Samuel Byren (1914–22 SS) "Red." The nickname refers to hair color.

738. Cravath, Clifford Carlton (1908–20 OF) "Cactus." It is all but forgotten, that for his day, Cravath was the premier home run hitter leading the National League six times. Yet his career total for 11 years was only 119. He was called "The Flower of the Desert Cactus" even though he came from Escondido, California. Cravath was often addressed as "Cavvy."

739. Crawford, Clifford Rankin (1929–34 2B) "Pat." "Pat" denotes Crawford's Irish background.

740. Crawford, Glenn Martin (1945–46 OF) "Shorty." Crawford was 5'9" and weighed 165 pounds.

741. Crawford, Henry C. (1956–75 NL Umpire) "Shag." In Crawford's own words: "Everybody seems to think my nickname came from shagging fly balls, but it didn't. My old man didn't make too much money, so we didn't have very much. We had enough to eat, but our clothes were a little on the shabby side—holes in the pants, holes in the shoes, and so on. The kids used to call me 'shaggy' because of my appearance. My mother objected to it, but the name stuck, and as I grew older, it was shortened to 'Shag'."

742. Crawford, Rufus (1952 OF) "Jake." Crawford wrote me: "I acquired the nickname 'Jake' in high school. My brother was called 'Jake' and after he graduated, they all started calling me 'Jake'."

743. Crawford, Samuel Earl (1899–1917 OF) "Wahoo Sam." In 19 seasons Crawford collected 2,964 hits and had a career average of .309. The best years of his career for Detroit were played in the shadows of Ty Cobb. For example, his career high of .378 in 1911 fell far short of Cobb's .420 that year. "Wahoo Sam" is a place nickname. Crawford was from Wahoo, Nebraska. Crawford liked his nickname and insisted it be put on his plaque at the Baseball Hall of Fame in Cooperstown, New York.

744. Cree, William Franklin (1908–15 OF) "Birdie." Cree was once a musician, playing under the name of Burdee.

745. Creeden, Patrick Francis (1931 2B) "Whoops." "Whoops" refers to Creeden's ineptness in the field. In his brief major league career he fielded .846.

746. Creel, Jack Dalton (1945 P) "Tex." "Tex" is a place nickname. Creel was born in Kyle, Texas.

747. Cregan, Peter James (1899–1903 OF) "Peekskill Pete." This is a place nickname. Cregan was from Peekskill, New York.

748. Creighton, James (1860–62 P) "Unbeatable Jimmy." "Unbeatable Jimmy" is the earliest recorded player nickname I have been able to document. Connie Mack writes: "The first big star in the game was a nineteen-year-old boy wonder, James Creighton, who toured with the Brooklyn Excelsiors in 1860. Jimmy was like the first shot at Fort Sumter, for his achievements were heard around the world. He hurled the ball with a wrist throw that created speed. The sensation of his times, he became known as 'Unbeatable Jimmy.' Young pitcher Creighton was the first baseball casualty. While standing at the plate in a game of the Brooklyn Excelsiors versus the Unions on October 15, 1862, he was felled by a heart attack. Carried from the field, he passed away three days later, when only twenty-one years of age. This was baseball's first tragedy."

749. Cremins, Robert Anthony (1927 P) "Lefty." Cremins pitched left handed and batted left handed.

750. Crespi, Frank Angelo Joseph (1935–42 2B) "Creepi." Crespi wrote me: "I received the name playing for an amateur team as a teenager. It was because I could run almost full speed crouched for ground balls, looking as if I were creeping up on the ball."

751. Cress, Walker James (1948–49 P) "Foots." Cress had very large feet.

752. Criskall, William Arthur (1901 P) "Lefty." Cristall pitched left handed and batted left handed.

753. Crist, Chester Arthur (1906 C) "Squack." Crist had the habit of arguing with the umpire on ball and strike calls, while catching.

754. Cromp, Herbert Bryan (1937–45 C) "Workhorse." "Workhorse" refers to Cromp's tireless work behind the plate while in the minor leagues.

755. Crompton, Edward (1909–10 OF) "Ned." Ned was simply a take off on the first name of Edward.

756. Cronin, William Patrick (1928–31 C) "Crungy." "Crungy" refers to Cronin's less than pleasant personality.

757. Crosby, Harry Tillis (1947–Owner) "Bing." The famous entertainer became part owner of the Pittsburgh Pirates in 1947. Crooning Crosby was given the nickname "Bing" at the age of seven because of his fondness for a Sunday comic strip called "Bingville Bugle."

758. Crosetti, Frank Peter Joseph (1932–48 SS) "The Crow." Crosetti was the long time shortstop of the New York Yankees and then coach. He played in seven World Series. His constant chatter from his shortstop position and later the coaches box sounded like a crow, from the dugouts and stands.

759. Cross, Clarence (1884–87 SS) "Cleary Daddy." Origin unknown.

760. Cross, Frank Atwell (1901 OF) "Mickey." Origin unknown.

761. Cross, George Lewis (1893–94 P) "Lem." "Lem" was a take off on Lewis.

762. Crouch, Jack Albert (1930–33 C) "Roxy." In 1931, as a pinch hitter for the St. Louis Browns, the public address announcer in Shibe Park, Philadelphia, shouted through the megaphone "Roxy Batting for St. Louis" and that sired a nickname.

763. Crouch, William Elmer (1910 P) "Skip." Origin unknown.

764. Croucher, Frank Donald (1938–42 SS) "Dingle." Origin unknown.

765. Crouse, Clyde Ellsworth (1923–30 C) "Buck." "Buck" is a generic nickname of which the consequences of origin are almost never documented. It refers to a virile, well developed, aggressive, high spirited young man. It is usually bestowed on the individual during his teenage years.

766. Crowder, Alvin Floyd (1926–36 P) "General." Crowder won 167 American League games in an 11-year career. In 1932 and 33, he led Washington with 26-11, 24-15 records. He was nicknamed for General Enoch Crowder who originated the conscription lottery for the United States military in World War I. In the spring of 1918, he pronounced a work or fight order. It meant that baseball players were not immune from the draft. Some did opt to take jobs that were designated to help the war effort. The name General Crowder was well known to all baseball players. Alvin Crowder served in the Army with the rank of sergeant.

767. Crowell, Minot Joy (1915–18 P) "Cap." Neither Minot or Joy are much for baseball names, but the origin of "Cap" is unknown.

768. Crump, Arthur Elliott (1924 OF) "Buddy." "Buddy" was a childhood family nickname.

769. Crutchfield, John Wilbain (1930–45 OF, Negro League) "The Black Lloyd Waner." Crutchfield compiled a career average of .325 and always played with hustle and enthusiasm. He earned "The Black Lloyd Waner" sobriquet because of his ability to execute the hit and run play.

770. Cuccinelli, Anthony Francis (1930–45 2B) "Chick." Tom Shea reports that "Chick" referred to Cuccinello's small build, 5'7" and 160 pounds. In 1945, Cuccinello batted .308 and came within one point of the American League batting title, yet was unable to make the Chicago White Sox post-war 1946 roster. He never played in another major league game.

771. Cuccurillo, Arthur Joseph (1942–45 P) "Cookie." Origin unknown.

772. Cuellar, Miguel Angel (1959–77 P) "Crazy Horse." According to David Petreman: "Mike Cuellar was called 'Crazy Horse' because he believed in the spirit of a special baseball hat that he had to wear or he would not pitch. Once when he forgot it in Baltimore, he demanded that they fly it up to him before he would pitch a game in Baltimore."

773. Cullop, Henry Nicholas (1920–31 OF) "Tomato Face." Cullop's face had a ruddy complexion at times, appearing almost red. This was especially true when he became excited.

774. Culloton, Bernard Aloysius (1925–26 P) "Bud." "Bud" was short for the childhood nickname of "Buddy."

775. Culp, Benjamin Baldy (1942–44 C) "Nitro." Culp received the nickname "Nitro" when he banged out three hits in his first major league game.

776. Cummings, William Arthur (1872–77 P) "Candy." Cummings was 5'9" and just 126 pounds. He is credited with developing the curve ball around 1864. He began using it seriously in games around 1866–67. In 1876, as a member of the Hartford Dark Blues of the newly formed National League, manager Bob Ferguson had him pitch a double header against the Cincinnati Redlegs. He won both ends of the double header. The Hartford Historical Society declared that this was the first time a pitcher performed such a feat. After the games, manager Bob Ferguson remarked: "God never gave him any size, but he's the Candy." However, it is quite likely that Cummings had been called "Candy" long before that. "Candy" meant that his pitching was a sweet thing to watch.

777. Cuppy, George Joseph (1892–1901 P) "Nig." Cuppy won 162 games in his ten-year career, winning 24 games or more three times. "Nig" denotes his dark complexion. Cuppy was one of the first pitchers to wear a glove. An article in the *Cleveland Press* 11/17/1906, recalls Cuppy's style on the mound. "It was his delight to have the Baltimore bleacherites 'count' time on him and to tire them out by delaying the delivery of the ball to the utmost possible limit. By this time, the batter would be in a nervous frenzy and generally an easy victim."

778. Curley, Walter James (1899 2B) "Doc." Many players with the nickname of "Doc" had a close association with either the medical or dental professions. In the case of Curley, however, the origin of "Doc" is unknown.

779. Curran, Simon Francis (1902 P) "Sam." "Sam" was a more acceptable baseball name than Simon.

780. Curtis, Vernon (1943–46 P) "Turk." Origin unknown.

781. Curvy, George James (1911 P) "Soldier Boy." Origin unknown.

782. Cutshaw, George William (1912–23 OF) "Clancy." "Cutty," as Cutshaw was often addressed, was nicknamed "Clancy" by infielder Walter Barbare for his ability to drive in runs. Barbare said he was just like Clancy lowering the boom. The reference is to an Irish folk song.

783. Cuyler, Hazen Shirely (1921–38 OF) "Kiki." Bill James reports that Cuyler stuttered as a youth and when he tried to pronounce his own name, it came out "KiKi." This, however, is not the way Cuyler himself explains the origin. "When I was a kid, the boys called me 'Cuy' the first half of my name. This clung to me and, after I joined Nashville, it was 'Cuy' this and 'Cuy' that. The newspapers spelled it 'Ki.' It got so when I went after a ball the shortstop would yell 'Ki' indicating that it was my catch to make and the second baseman would pipe up immediately with another 'Ki.' This caught the fans and it was no time before they were calling me 'KiKi'."

D

784. Daglia, Peter George (1932 P) "Rig Pete." Origin unknown.

785. Dagres, Angelo George (1955 OF) "Junior." His grandmother started calling him "Junior" when he was still in grammar school. It followed him into his baseball career and then later life, even though he grew to 6' and weighed more than 200 pounds.

786. Dahlen, William Frederick (1889-1911 SS) "Bad Bill." Dahlen earned his name for arguing with umpires and being ejected from many more games than the norm. He was also known for intensity and clutch hitting.

787. Dahlgren, Ellsworth Tenny (1935-46 1B) "Babe." His stepfather began calling him "Babe" because of his small size, and teachers began using it as well. Although he grew to be 6', the name stuck throughout his baseball career.

788. Dahlke, Jerome Alex (1955 P) "Joe." In this case, "Joe" is a corruption of Jerry which is what Dahlke was usually called.

789. Daily, Hugh Ignatius (1882-87 P) "One Arm Daily." The nickname is an exaggeration. In 1882, his left hand (not his left arm) was amputated as the result of a gunshot wound. Daily was regarded as a mean character with a quarrelsome personality. When he was scheduled to pitch, he would not talk to anybody, not even the waiter who served him breakfast, until after he had taken batting practice.

790. Daley, Leavitt Leo (1955-64 P) "Buddy." "Buddy" is a childhood nickname.

791. Daley, Thomas Francis (1908-15 P) "Pete." Origin unknown.

792. Dallesandro, Nicholas Dominic (1937-47 OF) "Dim Dom." Usually addressed as Dom, Dallesandro was also "Dim Dom" because of his (5'6", 170) diminutive stature. Cub manager Charlie Grimm is credited with first using "Dim," and radio announcer Bert Wilson popularized it. Dallesandro had extremely short legs, and it sometimes appeared as if he were standing in a hole in the outfield grass at Wrigley Field. One day, as a prank, Grimm called, "Time out" and started to look quizzically towards left field. When umpire Harry "Beans" Reardon asked what was going on, Grimm replied, "I can't find Dim Dom." Dallesandro was also called "Fire Hydrant," a reference to his Hack Wilson build.

793. Dalton, Talbot Percy (1910-16 OF) "Jack." Origin unknown.

794. Daly, George Joseph (1909 P) "Pecks." Origin unknown.

795. Daly, James J. (1892 OF) "Sun." Daly received his nickname while playing minor league ball in Buffalo. He would never use sunglasses or a sun shade while playing the outfield.

796. Daly, Thomas Peter (1887-1903 2B) "Tido." Daly played for 16 years in the major leagues and collected 1,582 hits, yet little is known about his nickname. It may be a take off on Thomas, but the origin is unknown.

797. Dam, Elbridge Rust (1909 OF) "Arbie." This nickname was derived from a play on the expression, "I'll be damned." "Arbie" batted .500 in the majors, one hit in two times at bat!

798. Damman, William Henry (1897–99 P) "Wee Willie." The nickname refers to Damman's diminutive stature—5'7", 150 pounds.

799. Dandridge, Raymond (1933–49 3B, Negro League) "Hooks." "Hooks" referred to Dandridge's bowlegs which some said you could drive a truck through, but not hit a baseball. At 5'7" Dandridge was also called "Squat." He was such an excellent fielding third baseman that he was dubbed "Brooks Robinson of the Negro Leagues." He was particularly good on the swinging bunt, coming in fast to make the play. When he played in Latin America, he was called "El Sambo Maravelloso," Sambo because he was bow-legged and Maravelloso because he was marvelous. Dandridge was signed by the New York Giants in 1949 and sent to Minneapolis where he hit .362 and roomed with Willie Mays. In 1950 he was named the American Association's most valuable player.

800. Daney, Arthur Lee (1928 P) "Chief Whitehorn." Daney also pitched under the name of Arthur Lee Whitehorn. He was a full-blooded Choctaw Indian. William "Kid" Gleason was responsible for the nickname. The "Chief" pitched in only one major league game, that being for Philadelphia against the Yankees in 1928. His performance was memorable for the towering pop-up hit by Babe Ruth, hit so high that infielders lost sight of it and it dropped for a hit.

801. Danforth, David Charles (1911–25 P) "Dauntless Dave." He was known for working himself out of jams. He is alleged by some to have been the first to make use of what now is called a slider pitch. Although he was a practicing dentist, he did not carry the nickname of "Doc."

802. Daniels, Frederick Clinton (1945 2B) "Tony." Origin unknown. Daniels refused to discuss with me any details of his nickname.

803. Daniels, Harold Jack (1952 OF) "Sour Mash." Daniels was addressed as Jack. The nickname is a play on his names referring to a popular brand of sour mash whiskey, Jack Daniels.

804. Danner, Henry Frederick (1915 SS) "Buck." "Buck" is a generic nickname of which the circumstances of origin are almost never documented. It refers to a virile, well developed, aggressive, high spirited young man. It is usually bestowed on the individual during his teenage years.

805. Danning, Harry (1933–42 C) "Harry the Horse." Danning had a long face. It reminded people of one of writer Damon Runyon's famous characters, "Harry the Horse" who was later brought to life in the musical and movie *Guys and Dolls*. The nickname was given to him by radio announcer Ted Husing an avid reader of Runyon.

806. Dantonio, John James (1944–45 C) "Fats." A reference to his stature (5'8", 170 pounds). Since Dantonio was from New Orleans, he may also have received the name as a tribute to budding New Orleans rhythm and blues star, Antoine "Fats" Domino.

807. Darby, George William (1893 P) "Deek." This nickname refers to Darby's ability to fake batters out, confuse them. He had little chance to do this in the major leagues, appearing in only four games. He did, however, manage to get three hits in ten times at bat.

808. Dark, Alvin Ralph (1946-60 SS) "Blackie." The name stems, not from his last name or hair color, but from the black bats he preferred as a player. As manager of the Giants, he was called "The Swamp Fox" for his southern Louisiana background and also for his tactic of ordering groundskeepers to water the dirt around first base to slow down opposing base stealers, particularly Maury Wills.

809. Darraugh, James S. (1891 1B) "Jack." During this era, "Jack" was sometimes used as an alternative to James. Darraugh appeared in only one major league game, but singled in one of his two times at bat.

810. Dasher, Lee Claire (1913 P) "Lefty." Dasher pitched left handed, but batted right handed. A cup of coffee player, he pitched only 1.2 innings in the majors and never did get to bat.

811. Datz, Elmer L. (1890 P) "Babe." Origin unknown.

812. Daubert, Jacob Elsworth (1910-24 1B) "Gentleman Jake." The nickname refers to his meticulous dress and dapper appearance off the playing field. Daubert compiled a lifetime average of .303 with over 2,300 hits. Playing for Brooklyn, he led the National League in hitting in 1913 and 1914 with averages of .350 and .329.

813. Daugherty, Harold Ray (1951 PH) "Doc." Many of the players with the nickname of "Doc" had close associations with either the medical or dental professions. However, in the case of Daugherty, the origin of "Doc" is unknown.

814. Daughters, Robert Francis (1937 PH) "Red." "Red" refers to hair color. "Red" struck out in his only official time at bat in the majors.

815. Dauss, George August (1912-26 P) "Hooks." The nickname refers to Dauss' tantalizing curve ball, which helped him win 221 games for Detroit.

816. Davalillo, Pompeyo Antonio (1953 SS) "Yo-Yo." At 5'3", 140 pounds, Davalillo was one of the shortest players ever to perform in the major leagues. His small size led a Washington Senator's play-by-play broadcaster to nickname him "Yo-Yo."

817. Davenport, David W. (1914-19 P) "Big Dave." Davenport was an extremely large player for his time—6'6" and 220 pounds. He was one of the best pitchers in the Federal League. In 1915, he won 22 games and led the league in complete games, 30, and strikeouts, 229.

818. Davidson, David L. (1969-84 NL Umpire) "Satch." Davidson told me he was given the name of "Satch" as a youth because he idolized Hunter Hall who played "Satch" in the movies as one of the Dead End or East Side Kids. Davidson turned his cap backwards as Hunter did in the movies. After Davidson became an umpire, he met Hall, who was an avid fan, and they became good friends.

819. Davidson, Homer Hurd (1908 C) "Divvy." "Divvy" is really a mispronunciation of "Davey" stemming from his last name. He played in nine major league games, but failed to record a hit.

820. Davies, Lloyd Garrison (1914-26 P) "Chick." In this case "Chick" refers to Davies' size 5'8", 143 pounds. At least his career batting average of .193 was 50 points higher than his weight!

821. Davis, Alfonzo DeFord (1901–07 OF) "Lefty." Davis batted left handed and threw left handed.

822. Davis, Arthur Willard (1965–69 1B) "The Jolly Green Giant." Davis was given the nickname by Portland fans while he was playing in the Pacific Coast League. He was 6'7", and reminded people of the character in the TV commercial advertising green vegetables.

823. Davis, Brysher Barnett (1963–72 OF) "Brock." This nickname was given to Davis by his little league teammates who could not pronounce his first name.

824. Davis, Charles Theodore (1981– OF) "Chili." As a youngster, Davis was known as "Chili Bowl" because of a particularly poor hair cut. Friends said his hair must have been cut around a chili bowl. As an adult, the bowl was dropped in favor of just "Chili."

825. Davis, Curtis Benton (1934–46 P) "Old Coonskin." Davis was a crack shot with a rifle and enjoyed hunting. This along with his homespun philosophy reminded people of Daniel Boone and his coonskin cap.

826. Davis, Frank Talmadge (1912–26 P) "Dixie." The nickname refers to Southern heritage. Davis was born in Wilson Mills, North Carolina.

827. Davis, George Allen (1912–15 P) "Iron." George received his nickname while attending Williams College. He broke all existing strength records. He did the same thing while obtaining his law degree at Harvard. At first, he was called "Iron Man." In 1914, he pitched a no-hitter for the Boston Braves but had a 3-3 record for the year. In fact, his life time won-lost record was 7-10 with an ERA of 4.48. He practiced law until 1961. Five months after retirement, he committed suicide.

828. Davis, George Earl (1982– P) "Storm." Shortly before his birth, his mother read the novel, *Doctor on Trial*. The main character was Dr. Storm Linders. Mrs. Davis admired this fictional hero and decided to nickname her son after him.

829. Davis, George Willis (1926–38 OF) "Kiddo." According to Roy J. Stockton: "They called him 'Kiddo' because when he was obtained from St. Paul in 1932, he made a crack about being so happy to play for the fans in Philly."

830. Davis, Harry Albert (1932–37 P) "Stinky." Davis was nicknamed by his Rochester teammates in 1928, after the comic strip character by that name, whom they thought he resembled.

831. Davis, Harry H. (1895–1912 OF) "Jasper." "Jasper" was not a nickname that was used by sportswriters, and its origin is unknown. The more common moniker was "Home Run Harry." Davis led the American League in home runs in four consecutive years, 1904–07.

832. Davis, J. Ira (1899 SS) "Slats." There is little data available on this player, not even his height and weight. Best guess is that "Slats" refers to a lean and thin body build.

833. Davis, James J. (1884–91 3B) "Jumbo." The nickname refers to body size. Davis was 5'11" and usually played at well over 200 pounds.

834. Davis, John (1941–49 OF, Negro League) "Cherokee." Davis was of part Cherokee Indian background.

835. Davis, John A. (1884–85 P) "Daisy." Origin unknown.

836. Davis, John Humphrey (1941 3B) "Red." The nickname refers to hair color.

837. Davis, John Wilbur (1915 P) "Country." Davis came from the small rural town of Merry Point in Virginia. He was usually addressed as "Bud," a childhood nickname.

838. Davis, Lawrence Columbus (1940–42 2B) "Crash." "Crash" wrote me: "When I was about 14, a character 'Crash Davis' appeared in the comic strip 'Freckles.' He had the same characteristics as I, aggressive with lots of chatter. Later, sportswriters began to call me that, and I have been 'Crash' ever since. 'Crash' to me is more real than Lawrence. It is easy to remember and once introduced, always remembered. There is a disadvantage though, when I am away from home, I always have to explain to people how I got the nickname. Sometimes, they are disappointed to learn it was not because of some type of car crash." As a public figure, Davis was in obscurity after his playing days until 1988. His nickname was used for one of the main characters in the popular movie "Bull Durham." It led to the rediscovery of the real "Crash" Davis.

839. Davis, Lorenzo (1943–50 1B, Negro League) "Piper." "Piper" was a place nickname. Davis came from the coal mining town of Piper, Alabama.

840. Davis, Otis Allen (1946– PR) "Scat." In 1943, a sportswriter in Jamestown, New York, gave him the nickname because of his speed of foot. Davis never got used to his speed in the major leagues appearing in only one game and without an official time at bat.

841. Davis, Ray Thomas (1936–39 P) "Peaches." In his own words "Peaches" wrote me: "As a kid, I loved peaches. One day I slipped out of the house and went to a nearby orchard and picked a ripe peach. I sat down to eat it, but my behind landed on a red ant hill. The ants began to bite me and I started yellin.' My brothers and mother came running to get me. My brother said 'you like peaches so much, from now on that's what we are going to call you'."

842. Davis, Thomas Oscar (1949–51 SS) "Tod." Davis told me his nickname is derived from his initials.

843. Davis, Virgil Lawrence (1928–45 C) "Spud." Davis was given the nickname of "Spud" by his boyhood chums because he ate potatoes at all three meals every day. Davis thought it would make him a better hitter. In fact, he was one of the better hitting catchers of the time, compiling a .308 average in 16 years. It was cause for amusement in 1928, when "Spud" was traded from Philadelphia to St. Louis for a player named Peel!

844. Davis, Wallace McArthur (1983–84 OF) "Butch." "Butch" is a childhood nickname.

845. Davis, Woodrow Wilson (1938 P) "Babe." Davis was from the small town of Nicholas, Georgia. He was known as a "Babe in the Woods" because of his lack of sophistication.

846. Dawson, Andre Fernando (1976 OF) "Hawk." The nickname stems from Dawson's extraordinary ability to chase down balls hit to the outfield. He is a gold glove outfielder, but is best known for his hitting. In 1987, he won MVP honors in the National League even though his team, the Cubs, finished in last place.

847. Dawson, Ralph Fenton (1924–29 P) "Joe." Dawson always remembered being called "Joe," but never knew the reason why. It came from childhood.

848. Day, Charles Frederick (1969–74 OF) "Boots." As a young child, Day had extraordinary big feet which always got in the way. They allowed him to kick off his booties. An older sister started calling him "Boots" and it stuck as a nickname.

849. Day, Clyde Henry (1924–31 P) "Pea Ridge Day." Day carried the nickname of his hometown, Pea Ridge, Arkansas. Day committed suicide in 1934 a short three years after he left the major leagues.

850. Deal, Ellis Ferguson (1947–54 P) "Cot." As a child, Deal was a "Tow" head and people called him "Cotton Top." It was shortened later to just "Cotton."

851. Deal, John Wesley (1906 1B) "Snake." According to Joseph McBride, Deal earned the nickname of "Snake" because of his deft moves on the basketball court. If so, Deal must have been one of the first major league baseball players to be skilled at basketball. Basketball was invented in 1891, when Deal was 12 years old.

852. Dean, Alfred Lovill (1936–43 P) "Chubby." Al was nicknamed by his older brother Dayton Dean, who thought he looked chubby at birth. Al was a cousin of Dizzy and Paul Dean, whose pitching careers overlapped with his and gained much more notoriety.

853. Dean, Charles Wilson (1876 P) "Dory." "Dory" was a childhood nickname.

854. Dean, Jay Hanna (1930–47 P) "Dizzy." White Sox manager Lena Blackburne is credited as the first person to tag Dean as "Dizzy." Pitching for a U.S. Army team in 1928, Dean was mowing down one White Sox batter after another in an exhibition game. Blackburne yelled at his batters: "Don't let that dizzy rookie fool ya." The nickname was reinforced in 1930 when Dean joined the St. Louis Cardinals, because of his zany behavior and colloquial speech. During spring training he told three different St. Louis sportswriters three different birth places in three different states. He could not be bothered getting up early enough to make a morning practice. Lieb quotes him saying, "Let the other clucks work out for places on the staff; nobody can beat me out." He talked so much about fogging in his fastball, that at first "Foggy" became an alternative nickname. In spite of the "Dizzy" moniker friends usually addressed him as "Country."

855. Dean, Paul Dee (1934–43 P) "Daffy." Sportswriters started calling him "Daffy" when he came up with the St. Louis Cardinals in 1934. It seemed a natural in tandem with his brother's nickname "Dizzy." Paul, however, was neither dizzy or daffy and the nickname did not fit. It was strictly a newspaper nickname. In fact, Paul was so serious and non-talkative in contrast to "Dizzy," he was sometimes referred to as "Harpo," the non-talking Marx brother.

856. Dear, Paul Stanford (1927 2B) "Buddy." "Buddy" was a childhood nickname. "Buddy" Dear failed to get a hit in his only trip to the plate in the majors.

857. DeArmond, Charles Hommer (1903 3B) "Hummer." The nickname is derived from the middle name. There is no indication that DeArmond liked to hum.

858. Deasely, Thomas H. (1881–88 C) "Pat." Deasely was of Irish descent. It was common during the early days of baseball for players of Irish origin to receive the nickname of "Pat." In addition to catching, "Pat" appeared in games at all outfield and infield positions.

859. Dedaux, Raoul Martial (1935 SS) "Rod." "Rod" is simply a shortened and easier-to-say version of Raoul. A cup of coffee player, "Rod" had a single and RBI in four times at bat in the major leagues.

860. Dee, Maurice Leo (1915 SS) "Shorty." "Shorty" refers to Dee's small stature, 5'6". Dee failed to get a hit in his three chances at bat in the major leagues.

861. Deegan, William John (1901 P) "Dummy." Deegan was one of the several ballplayers in the early days of baseball who were deaf and dumb. "Dummy" pitched in only two major league games and lost them both.

862. DeFate, Clyde Herbert (1917 3B) "Tony." Origin unknown.

863. DeGroff, Edward Arthur (1905–06 OF) "Rube." DeGraff was nicknamed after the great black ballplayer "Rube" Foster who he played against in an exhibition game in 1902. Exactly why is unknown.

864. Deinninger, Otto Charles (1902 P) "Pep." "Pep" referred to Deinninger's enthusiasm while playing the game, which he must have needed during the 12 innings he pitched in the major leagues. He gave up 19 hits and 9 walks.

865. Deisel, Edward (1902–03 C) "Pat." Origin unknown.

866. Delahanty, Edward James (1888–1903 OF) "Big Ed." Ed at 6'1" was the tallest and oldest of the five Delahanty brothers to play major league baseball. He was also the most famous. He compiled a .345 lifetime batting average for 16 seasons. Delahanty may just have been the best badball hitter of all time. Smith reports that he had such a quick eye, he could pick balls out of the dirt with the end of his bat and send them out of the park. Despite his exploits on the diamond, "Big Ed" is probably best remembered today for the events surrounding his tragic death. While with Washington in 1903, he was suspended for drinking. Traveling on the Michigan Central Express train bound for Buffalo, he caused a row in the dining car and was put off the train at the time it was about to cross the International Bridge at Fort Erie, Ontario. Fumbling in the darkness in a highly inebriated state, he tried to run up the tracks and reboard the train. The draw was open at the bridge and he fell and was carried over Niagara Falls. His body was found a week later. A leg and arm were mangled. It was presumed that his body had been hit by the propeller of the *Maid of the Mist*, the small tourist boat which makes excursions in those waters.

867. Delahanty, Frank George (1905–15 OF) "Pudgie." Frank was the youngest of five baseball playing Delahanty brothers. As a youngster, he was pudgy. In his playing days, however, his build 5'9", 160 pounds, was about the same as his brothers Jim, Joe and Tom, although he was four inches shorter than big brother Ed.

868. Delaney, Arthur Dewey (1924–29 P) "Swede." Origin unknown. There is no evidence that Delaney was of Swedish origin. His blond hair may account for the nickname.

869. Delhi, Lee William (1912 P) "Flame." The nickname refers to the speed of Lee's fastball. Unfortunately he did not get to throw it much in the major leagues. He pitched in three innings allowing seven hits and three runs.

870. Dell, William George (1912–17 P) "Wheezer." Dell was nicknamed after the small town of Weiser, Idaho, where he grew up. An alternative explanation is that a broken nose led to heavy breathing.

871. Delock, Ivan Martin (1952–62 P) "Ike." Delock was nicknamed by Barney Hearn, the manager for the Auburn team in the Border League in 1948. He did not think that Ivan was a good baseball name.

872. Demaestri, Joseph Franklin (1951–61 SS) "Oats." He was nicknamed by a childhood friend in reference to the color of his hair.

873. DeMars, William Lester (1948–51 SS) "Kid." "Kid" is short for "Billy the Kid," after the legendary outlaw of the Old West. When DeMars broke into the majors he was known as a tough, scrapping bantam shortstop.

874. DeMerit, John Stephan (1957–62 OF) "Thumper." "Thumper" stems from his college playing days when he hit some long home runs. He does not recall the nickname being used during his major league career.

875. De Mose, Elwood (1905–43 2B, Negro League) "Bingo." De Mose was an adapt gloveman at second base with impeccable defensive skills and a wide range. He was a spray hitter who almost always made contact with the ball and rarely struck out. This ability earned him the nickname of "Bingo."

876. Denning, Otto George (1942–43 C) "Dutch." "Dutch" refers to Denning's German background.

877. Dent, Russell Earl (1973–84 SS) "Bucky." Dent's grandmother gave him this nickname as a child because she thought he looked like a little Indian boy, that is, an Indian buck. Dent, however, never played for the Cleveland Indians, spending most of his career with the New York Yankees and Chicago White Sox.

878. Dente, Samuel Joseph (1947–55 SS) "Blackie." When Dente was a rookie with the Boston Red Sox he reminded people of the radio (and later the television) detective character "Boston Blackie."

879. Derrick, Claud Lester (1910–14 SS) "Deek." "Deek" is a play on the name of Derrick. "Deek" Derrick sounded better than Claud Derrick.

880. Derringer, Samuel Paul (1931–45 P) "Duke." The nickname of "Duke" was given to him by teammates because of his fancy and expensive wardrobe. He was also called "Dude" for the same reason. Sportswriters sometimes referred to him as "Oom Paul" because of his resemblance to South African leader "Oom" Paul Krueger.

881. Derrington, Charles James (1956–57 P) "Blackie." Derrington's father was "Black Irish," that is, an Irishman with black hair who came to Ireland from Spain. His nickname was "Blackie." As a child Derrington was called "Blackie, Jr." As an adult the Jr. was dropped.

882. Denzer, Roger (1897–1901 P) "Peaceful Valley." Roger was born in Le Sueur, Minnesota, which is in a region called "Peaceful Valley." Today we recognize "Peaceful Valley" as the land of the Jolly Green Giant from the television vegetable commercials.

883. Desautels, Eugene Abraham (1930–46 C) "Red." The nickname refers to hair color.

884. **DesJardien, Paul Raymond** (1916 P) "Shorty." In this case "Shorty" is a nickname opposite. DesJardien, who only pitched one inning in the major leagues, was 6'4½" and weighed well over 200 pounds.

885. **Dessau, Frank Roland** (1907–10 P) "Rube." "Rube" was a nickname given to players from rural areas and or were slow in learning big-city ways. They generally lacked social graces and were not "streetwise." Dessau hailed from New Galilee, Pennsylvania.

886. **Detwieler, Robert Sterling** (1942–46 3B) "Ducky." While in high school, Detwieler hit a line drive down the third base line so hard that the third baseman ducked rather than trying to catch the ball. From then on Bob was called "Ducky." Although "Ducky" only got to play in 12 major league games, he hit .311.

887. **Devine, William Patrick** (1918–25 C) "Mickey." "Mickey," similar to "Pat," was a nickname given to players with an Irish background.

888. **Diaz, Baudlio Jose** (1977– C) "Bo." "Bo" is derived from the first name Baudlio. "Bo" is easier to pronounce.

889. **Diaz, Michael Anthony** (1983–88 OF) "Rambo." The 6'2", 210-pound Diaz was nicknamed after the macho movie character of the same name in a series of movies in the 1970s and 1980s.

890. **Dickerson, Louis Pessano** (1878–85 OF) "Buttercup." Dickerson loved flowers.

891. **Dickey, George Willard** (1935–47 C) "Skeets." George was the younger brother of Hall of Fame catcher Bill Dickey. When he was young he was very tall and very thin and his nickname was "Skeeter." It was later shortened to "Skeets."

892. **Dicksen, Walter R.** (1910–15 P) "Hickory." "Hickory" was a nickname given to players who were tall, lean, but well built, and tough. Walt was 6'1" and weighed 180 pounds, and was tough.

893. **Dietrich, William John** (1933–45 P) "Bullfrog." Before World War II it was fairly unusual for players to wear glasses, especially pitchers. Doing so resulted in a nickname. For Dietrich it was "Bullfrog." The glasses gave him a popeyed look.

894. **Dietz, Lloyd Arthur** (1940–43 P) "Dutch." "Dutch" refers to Dietz's German background.

895. **Dietz, Richard Allen** (1966–73 C) "Mule." Dietz played like a stubborn mule even when injured. In mid-1971 he played the stretch drive with his head heavily bandaged.

896. **Dihigo, Martin** (1923–45 2B, Negro League) "El Maestro." It is difficult to place Dihigo at any one position, since, with the exception of catcher, he played them all, and sensationally. The Mexicans called him "El Maestro" and in his native Cuba he was referred to as "El Immortal." John Holway writes, "Virtually everyone who saw Martin Dihigo agrees that he was the greatest all-around ball player who ever lived, black or white." He batted a career .304 with power, and as a pitcher won 256 games while dropping but 133. Dihigo was a superb fielder at any position and had an arm like a rocket. He performed with class and grace.

897. **Dillhoefer, William Martin** (1917–21 C) "Pickles." "Pickles" is a take off on the Dill in Bill's last name.

898. **Dillinger, Harley Hugh** (1914 P) "Hoke." The origin of "Hoke" is unknown. Dillinger, however, was also called "Lefty" because he pitched left handed.

899. Dillon, Frank Edward (1899–1904 OF) "Pop." "Pop" is a nickname usually associated with older players. In Dillon's case it refers to his relatively advanced age for a rookie, at the turn of the century. He was 26.

900. DiMaggio, Dominic Paul (1940–53 OF) "The Little Professor." Dom was the shortest and youngest of the three DiMaggio brothers to play outfield in the major leagues. Although he was a fine fielder and a good hitter, his career average was .298, he was always in the shadow of his older brother Joe. His studious looks and wire-rimmed glasses reminded people of the stereotypical college professor.

901. DiMaggio, Joseph Paul (1936–51 OF) "Joltin' Joe." As a rookie Joe was called "Big Dago" by his teammates. Sportswriters began to refer to him as "Joltin' Joe" during the 1939 season when he led the league with a .381 average. In 1941 Joe hit safely in 56 consecutive games. His feat was immortalized in the song "Joltin' Joe DiMaggio" recorded that year by the Les Brown Band with Betty Bonney doing the vocal. Joe was also called the "Yankee Clipper" in reference to the swift and graceful sailing ship. That is the way he looked patrolling center field. He made hard plays appear routine. After his retirement, and especially after 1970, sportswriters and broadcasters began to call him just "Joe D.," indicating that his fame was so widespread that the initial alone was enough to indicate which Joe. During the 1980s Joe made television commercials for a manufacturer of coffee makers. So popular were these commercials that some people know him simply as "Mr. Coffee."

902. Dinneen, William Henry (1898–1909 P) "Big Bill." Dinneen was 6'1", 190 pounds, large for the era in which he played.

903. Dismukes, William (1913–50 P, Negro League) "Dizzy." Dismukes, was a journeyman pitcher for 13 years for nine different clubs including the Brooklyn Royal Giants and American Giants of Chicago. He later became a field manager and business manager for a host of teams. As far as I can ascertain, "Dizzy" is a play on the name Dismukes and does not describe behavior.

904. Distel, George Adam (1918 2B) "Dutch." "Dutch" refers to Distel's German background.

905. Dixon, Herbert Albert (1922–37 OF, Negro League) "Rap." Dixon threw right handed, but batted left handed. He compiled a career batting average of .340, and in 1929 playing for the Baltimore Black Sox, was credited with 15 straight hits against the Homestead Grays. The nickname "Rap" is short for Virginia's Rappahannock River denoting Dixon's southern origin. As such, it qualifies as a place nickname.

906. Dixon, John Craig (1953–56 P) "Sonny." Dixon writes: "My mother and father felt that I was the ray of their life. I was called "Sonny" from the day I was born. I was teased when I grew to be 6'3½" and 215 pounds, but it never bothered me and few people knew my real name.

907. Dixwell, Arthur (1880s Fan) "Hi Hi Dixwell." Boston "fanatic," independently wealthy, Dixwell became famous for giving Boston players rewards for outstanding plays. In addition he created the Dixwell trophy given to the outstanding minor league team in New England. When he got excited he screamed "Hi Hi" which became his nickname.

908. Doak, William Leopold (1912–29 P) "Spittin' Bill." Doak was one of the last great spitball pitchers. He had 170 career wins, and twice won 20 games in a season.

909. Dobb, John Kenneth (1924 P) "Lefty." Dobb pitched left handed, but batted right handed. His entire major league career was wrapped up in two innings pitched.

910. Dobens, Raymond Joseph (1929 P) "Lefty." He pitched left handed and batted left handed. Dobbens pitched 28 innings in the majors without receiving a decision. However, he had three hits in eight at bats for an average of .375.

911. Dobernic, Andrew Joseph (1939-49 P) "Jess." Dobernic was given this nickname by playmates as a young child and it all but replaced his first name.

912. Dobson, Joseph Gordon (1939-54 P) "Burrhead." The nickname refers to Dobson's tight curly hair. In the 1946 World Series, Joe did not allow the St. Louis Cardinals an earned run in 12⅔ innings pitched.

913. Dobson, Patrick Edward (1967-77 P) "Snake." According to Thurman Munson, "Snake" referred to Dobson's intelligent way of pitching, rather than simply a curveball.

914. Dockins, George Woodrow (1945-47 P) "Lefty." Dockins pitched and batted left handed.

915. Dodd, Oran A. (1912 3B) "Ona." "Ona" is a take off on Dodd's first name and middle initial. In nine times at bat in the majors, he failed to get a hit.

916. Doe, Alfred George (1890 P) "Count." It is reported in the *Brockton Massachusetts Times*, October 29, 1907, that Doe carried the nickname "Mary Ann" during his minor league career. A fellow player, Tom Cotter, received two new bats which he called "Mary Ann" and "Mary Ellen." In one of the next games he used "Mary Ann" to hit a triple. When Doe stepped to the plate Cotter yelled out "Mary Ann, Mary Ann!" meaning use that bat. The fans were confused, thinking that was Doe's nickname and started chanting "come on Mary Ann." Doe got a hit and drove Cotter in. After that, he was called "Mary Ann." I found no mention of "Count" being used as a nickname.

917. Dolan, Albert J. (1909-22 OF) "Cozy." Al was nicknamed after Pat "Cozy" Dolan an outfielder who he resembled and who preceded him by just a few years.

918. Dolan, E.L. (1914 1B) "Biddy." "Biddy" might be an Irish equivalent of "Buddy," but the exact origin is unknown.

919. Dolan, Patrick Henry (1895-1906 OF) "Cozy." Pat was the original "Cozy" Dolan. He was given the name as a youth, but the exact reason is unknown.

920. Donahue, Charles Michael (1904 SS) "She." During the time Donahue was playing, the nickname of "She" had several different meanings: a person with feminine characteristics; a person with a different sexual orientation; or a person who didn't smoke, drink or swear.

921. Donahue, Francis Rostell (1893-1906 P) "Red." The nickname refers to hair color. "Red" was an excellent pitcher who won 20 games or more in a season three times. In 1896, however, his won-lost record was 7-24, followed in 1897 by 11-33. Going 18-57 for the two years, it is small wonder that the St. Louis Cardinals traded him to the Philadelphia Phils before the start of the 1898 season.

922. Donahue, John Augustus (1900-09 1B) "Jiggs." At first base John was constantly moving his feet as if he was doing a jig. One writer said it looked as if he was doing a clog dance.

923. Donahue, John Frederick (1923 OF) "Jiggs." Nicknamed after first baseman John Augustus "Jiggs" Donahue.

924. Donahue, John Michael (1943–44 P) "Deacon." The nickname "Deacon" was often applied to players active in the church or who did not drink, smoke, or swear. A war time player, John appeared in only eight major league games. He was credited with 0 wins and 2 losses.

925. Donald, Richard Atley (1938–45 P) "Swampy." Atley, as he was usually addressed, was born in Morton, Mississippi, but grew up in the swampy bayou country of Louisiana.

926. Donalds, Edward Alexander (1912 P) "Skipper." Origin unknown.

927. Donders, Leonard Peter (1909 3B) "Mike." Origin unknown.

928. Donlin, Michael Joseph (1899–1914 OF) "Turkey Mike." Kavanaugh suggests that Donlin's nickname came from his long sunburned neck which protruded from the back of his uniform. Lieb, however, provides quite a different explanation. He reports it was because of Mike's walk which reminded one of a Turkey strut. Donlin left baseball during the 1909 and 1910 seasons to star in a Vaudeville act with his wife. When he returned in 1911 Harry Cross of the *New York Times* wrote: "'Turkey' Mike has been dancing the boards with his wife for two seasons, but he still does the turkey strut when he walks on the diamond." Dolan, who despised the nickname, told the writer in no uncertain terms to never use the name "Turkey" for him in the newspaper again.

929. Donnelly, Sylvester Urban (1944–51 P) "Blix." "Blix" was Donnelly's father's name and it was his father who gave him the nickname.

930. Donovan, William Edward (1898–1918 P) "Wild Bill." Bill was an excellent pitcher with a career record of 186-139. However, he had a propensity for being wild, hitting batters, and giving up walks. In 1902 he won 25 games and struck out 225 batters, but he also walked 156. For a pitcher Donovan was also a bit wild on the base paths. In 1906 he stole second, third and home in one inning! His career total of 36 swipes is the best mark ever for pitchers. In addition, he stole a base for Detroit against the Chicago Cubs in the 1908 World Series.

931. Dooin, Charles Sebastian (1902–16 C) "Red." The nickname refers to hair color.

932. Dorish, Harry (1947–56 P) "Fritz." Harry inherited the nickname from his father. It indicated a German background.

933. Dorman, Dwight Dexter (1923–28 OF) "Red." "Red" refers to the color of Dorman's hair which was, in addition to being red, also very thick. For this reason he was often addressed as "Curly."

934. Dorsett, Calvin Leavelle (1940–47 P) "Preacher." The nickname comes from Dorsett's first name reminiscent of the famous clergyman, John Calvin.

935. Dotterer, Henry John (1957–61 3B) "Dutch." Dotterer writes: "When I was a teenager my friends began calling me 'Little Dutch' since I played baseball like my dad and 'Dutch' was his nickname. He was German in background. When I was

936. Dotz, Elmer L. (1890 P) "Babe." Origin unknown.

937. Dougherty, Charles (1909–15 P, Negro League) "Pat." Dougherty was one of the better pitchers in the early days of the Negro leagues. A left hander, he earned the sobriquet of the "Black Marquard." The origin of "Pat" is unknown, but we are sure it does not indicate an Irish background.

938. Dougherty, Thomas James (1904 P) "Sugar Boy." Origin unknown.

939. Doughit, Taylor Lee (1923–33 OF) "Ball Hawk." The nickname of "Ball Hawk" celebrated Doughit's defensive ability in the outfield.

940. Douglas, Charles William (1957 P) "Whammy." Douglas had an artificial right eye. It gave the appearance that he had an evil eye which put the "whammy" on batters.

941. Douglas, Phillip Brooks (1912–22 P) "Shufflin' Phil." Phil was 6'5" and weighed between 220 and 250 pounds during his playing days. His heavy, stooped shoulders, thin legs, big feet, and alcoholic haze all contributed to movement which was more a shuffle or a stagger rather than a walk. Probably because of his drinking problem his personality and behavior were erratic. It was never certain if he would show up to play and he took frequent "vacations" which were really drinking bouts. In 1922, under the influence of alcohol, he wrote a letter to outfielder Les Mann of the St. Louis Cardinals indicating that he did not want his team, the New York Giants, to win the flag. For "goods" he would be willing to leave his team for the rest of the season. This letter was eventually used by Judge Landis as a basis to ban Douglas from organized baseball for life.

942. Douglas, William Bigham (1896–1904 1B) "Klondike." Origin unknown. It may refer to his size, 6', 200 pounds, or the large territory in Canada.

943. Dowd, James Joseph (1910 P) "Skip." Origin unknown.

944. Dowd, Raymond Bernard (1919–26 2B) "Snooks." Origin unknown.

945. Dowd, Thomas Jefferson (1891–1901 OF) "Buttermilk Tommy." Origin unknown.

946. Downey, Alexander Cummings (1909 OF) "Red." The nickname refers to hair color.

947. Downing, Brian Jay (1973– OF) "The Incredible Hulk." For the 1978 season Downing was disappointed with his .255 average and 46 RBIs. He embarked on a large scale body-building program. In 1979 his average was .326 with 75 RBIs. The turnabout was so great that California Angels teammate Nolan Ryan nicknamed him after the main character in the TV series "The Incredible Hulk." When angry, the character is quickly transformed from a normal sized man into a giant.

948. Downs, James Willis (1907–12 2B) "Red." The nickname refers to hair color.

949. Doyle, John Joseph (1889–1905 1B; NL umpire 1911) "Dirty Jack." Doyle used every tactic in the book to win games. Many of them did not conform to the rules of the game.

950. Doyle, Judd Bruce (1906–10 P) "Slow Joe." The nickname referred not the speed of his pitches but the time it took to deliver them. When a game started at 3:00 P.M. and Judd was on the mound, fans knew they would be late for supper.

951. Doyle, Lawrence Joseph (1907–20 2B) "Laughing Larry." Doyle had a pleasant, optimistic personality and disposition. Baseball was fun and a laugh for him. He once remarked: "Gee it's great to be young and a Giant" (New York Variety that is).

952. Dozier, William Joseph (1947–49 P) "Buzz." Dozier's fastball was clocked at 98 MPH, but his nickname did not come from the speed of his pitches. When he was just a year old his grandfather started calling him "Buzzard." Later it was shortened to "Buzz."

953. Drabowski, Myron Walter (1956–72 P) "The Snake Man." "Moe," as he was addressed, liked to play pranks and scare his teammates by using snakes. He had five little snakes that he used to place in the more squeamish player's lockers. Once while with Baltimore, he put a boa constrictor in Paul Blair's locker. Brooks Robinson was the victim in 1984 when Moe came back to a sports banquet in Baltimore. He put a 4' Florida king snake in the basket of dinner rolls. When Brooks reached into the basket for a roll he found himself face to face with a beady eyed little black reptile. He jumped a foot from his chair.

954. Drake, William (1916–27 P, Negro League) "Plunk." Drake had a reputation as a beanball specialist. However, John Howlay quotes Drake as not knowing how he received the nickname of "Plunk." "Here's me, 'Plunk' Drake! That's what I was known as. I don't know where I got that name. Like this boy named Sue, I guess, I don't know why they called me that."

955. Dreisarerd, Clement John (1944–48 P) "Steamboat." Clem was born in the small Missouri town of Old Monroe, close to the Ohio river, where he worked on steamboats.

956. Dreschler, William Clayton (1944–46 C) "Dutch." Dreschler was of German background. He was also called "Moose" because of his size, 6'2" and around 200 pounds.

957. Driscoll, John F. (1880–85 P) "Denny." Origin unknown.

958. Driscoll, John Leo (1917 2B) "Paddy." "Paddy" refers to Driscoll's Irish background. Driscoll was a great football player for Northwestern University, the Chicago Cardinals, and later coached the Chicago Bears. He was elected to the Pro Football Hall of Fame.

959. Dropo, Walter (1949–61 1B) "Moose." Dropo was 6'5" and weighed 225 pounds. This would qualify him for a nickname of "Moose" and certainly reinforced its use. However, the nickname stems from the fact that he came from the town of Moosup, Connecticut.

960. Drott, Richard Fred (1957–63 P) "Hummer." The nickname refers to the speed of his fastball. It was said that it hummed. Drott is probably best remembered for leading the cheers of Chicago Cubs' "Bleacher Bums" at Wrigley Field while stationed in the bull pen down the left field line.

961. Drysdale, Donald Scott (1956–69 P) "Big D." Don stood a shade over 6'5" and weighed better than 200 pounds. He was one of the premier pitchers of his day so everyone knew to whom the initial belonged. He was known as a mean pitcher and fierce competitor who thought nothing of throwing his 95-mile-an-hour fastball or wide sweeping curveball close to batters, or at them. His "close shaving" batters triggered more than one bench-clearing brawl. His streak of 58 straight scoreless innings in 1968 was finally broken by Orel Hershiser in 1988.

962. Dubiel, Walter John (1944–52 P) "Monk." Walter's facial features and mannerisms reminded people of a monk.

963. Dubuc, Jean Joseph Octave (1908–19 P) "Chauncy." Origin unknown.

964. Duffee, Charles Edward (1889–93 OF) "Home Run." Charlie was a long ball hitter in the American Association when home runs were relatively rare. In 1889, his rookie year, he hit 15 "dingers" to finish third in the league.

965. Dugan, Joseph Anthony (1917–31 3B) "Jumpin' Joe." The nickname does not refer to his ability to, or propensity to rise off the ground, but to the number of times he went AWOL from his team. The nickname was attached to him by sportswriter "Tiny" Maxwell of the *Philadelphia Ledger* after one of Joe's frequent jumps. A teammate said he was gone 36 times while with the Athletics 1917–21. He was a sensitive person and when the fans hooted at him he took it personally and left for his home or the beach. He also left over contract disputes.

966. Duggleby, William James (1898–1907 P) "Frosty Bill." Duggleby was known for a mean disposition which some feel enhanced his pitching. Despite that, his career won-loss record was but 92-104. On April 21, 1898, Bill became the first, and to this date, only player to hit a grand slam home run in his first time at bat.

967. Duliba, Robert John (1959–67 P) "Ach." Bob's name bears a resemblance to the German song "Ach Der Lieber Augustine." Manager "Whitey" Kurowski began calling him "Ach Duliba" while he was playing for Peoria in 1954.

968. Dumont, George Henry (1915–19 P) "Pea Soup." Origin unknown.

969. Dundon, Edward Joseph (1883–84 P) "Dummy." Dundon was deaf and dumb.

970. Dunham, Henry Houston (1902 P) "Wiley." Origin unknown.

971. Dunlap, Frederick C. (1880–91 2B) "Sure Shot." Dunlap was known for his fielding ability even though he never wore a glove. Mike "King" Kelly gave him the nickname of "Sure Shot" because of the accuracy of his throws. His low sizzling throws from second base were usually flung underhand with almost the same motion he used to gather in the ball. They barely skimmed the turf in flight, yet they never seemed to lose altitude and were almost always on target.

972. Dunlap, Grant Lester (1958 OF) "Snap." Grant received his nickname while playing college basketball. One of his teammates thought he played the game so easily, as if it were "a snap." Writers and fans preferred "Snap" to Grant. Even the PA announcers at the games called him "Snap" or "Slim."

973. Dunnbaugh, Robert Eugene (1957 SS) "Scroggy." Origin unknown.

974. Dunne, Michael Dennis (1987– P) "Iceman." Dunne was nicknamed during his rookie year by his Pittsburgh teammates for his cool, calm, and quiet performance on the mound.

975. Durbin, Blaine Alphonsus (1907–09 OF) "Kid." The nickname referred to his size, 5'8", 150 pounds, and his boyish looks.

976. Duren, Rinold George (1954–65 P) "The Flame." Ryne, as he was called, had a sizzling fastball which accounts for the nickname. He wore extra thick glasses which gave the appearance of not being able to see very well. He also had an alcohol problem. The rumor was that on some of his relief appearances he was slightly intoxicated. Duren would intimidate batters by demonstrating his wildness by throwing warm-up pitches over the catcher's head all the way to the backstop.

977. Durham, Donald Cary (1972–73 P) "Bull." Don is one of several players with the last name of Durham who have been nicknamed "Bull." The reference is to the Bull Durham tobacco advertisements placed on outfield walls during the early years of the game.

978. Durham, Edward Fant (1929–33 P) "Bull." Ed was another pitcher who was nicknamed after the Bull Durham tobacco advertisements placed on the outfield wall during the early years of the game.

979. Durham, Joseph Vann (1954–59 OF) "Pop." Joe was given the nickname "Pop" at age four before he even started playing baseball. That may account for why he was never called "Bull." Once his grandfather gave him five cents to buy a treat and he bought a 16-ounce can of soda pop and drank it so quickly that his grandfather began calling him "Pop" short for "Soda Pop."

980. Durham, Leon (1980– OF) "Bull." Leon is the most recent of the players named Durham to be tagged "Bull" after the Bull Durham tobacco advertisements on the outfield wall during the game's infant days.

981. Durham, Louis Staub (1904–09 P) "Bull." This Durham was the first to reach the major leagues and be nicknamed "Bull" but in a sense it was manufactured. According to Haber, Durham was born Louis Staub. Around 1902 he had his name changed to Louis Staub Durham. Relatives believe that he used the pseudonym of "Bull" Durham because of his deep appreciation for the tobacco product. Whether that accounts for the name change, is a matter of conjecture. But it does appear that Louis nicknamed himself.

982. Durocher, Leo Ernest (1925–45 SS) "The Lip." Durocher had several nicknames of which "The Lip" was the most famous, but not the first. Durocher related in his book, *The Dodgers and Me: The Inside Story*, that his nickname as a kid was "Frog" which evolved into "Bullfrog" and then "Swamp." By the time he began playing organized baseball it had become "Swamper." In 1925 he played two games for the Yankees and was called "Fifth Avenue" because he strutted around in fancy clothes. "Broadway" was another term used for his sharp dress. In fact even "Sharpie" was used for his immaculate appearance even in baseball uniform. He reportedly remarked that anyone who did not change his shirt three times a day was a slob. In 1928, Leo's first full year in the major leagues, his fresh disrespectable and cocky talk led members of the Yanks' "Murderers Row" to call him "Lippy." Both sportswriters Will

Wedge and Ford Frick began calling the voluble and loquacious rookie Leo "The Lip." Babe Ruth disliked Durocher because Leo did not pay him any deference. In 1929 when Durocher's average fell into the .240s, Ruth coined the nickname "All American Out." In 1930 when he was traded to Cincinnati Leo brought with him a string of debts so great that money was deducted from his paycheck. According to Lee Allen, his nickname during the Cincinnati years was not so much "Lip" as "C Note." He was always in need of money. Talking out of the side of his mouth in gangster fashion he would barge into the club's office demanding to borrow a "C note." Allen remarks he usually had to settle for a double sawbuck. Finally, Tom Gorman reports that: "A lot of umpires called him 'Hook' because of that big schnozz of his." This was the nickname which Durocher disliked the most.

983. Durrett, Elmer Charles (1944–45 OF) "Red." The nickname refers to hair color.

984. Duryea, James Whitney (1889–93 P) "Cyclone Jim." Early in his career it was said his pitches came in like a cyclone. In 1889, the year before Denton "Cy" Young pitched in the majors, Duryea won 32 games for Cincinnati in the American Association. It may be that the fans in Ohio thought Young resembled Duryea when they began to call him "Cy" short for "Cyclone."

985. Dusak, Ervin Frank (1941–52 OF) "Four Sack." The nickname rhymes with his last name. In addition, Erv was supposed to be a great home run hitting prospect when he came to the Cardinals in 1941. He never lived up to his nickname, hitting only 24 home runs in bits and pieces of nine seasons.

986. Dwyer, John F. (1904 AL Umpire) "Blinky." As a player, Dwyer was called Frank. "Blinky" was the nickname used by Nap Lajoie who once threw a wad of tobacco in Dwyer's face when he thought he had made a poor call. It is unclear how widespread the use of the nickname was.

987. Dwyer, Joseph Michael (1937 PH) "Double Joe." Joe relates that as a teenager he played semi-pro ball in Orange, New Jersey, in a park which had a short right field fence. Over that fence was a ground rule double. He hit so many balls over the fence that when he came back from a game, neighborhood kids would ask "How many doubles, Joe?" The nickname was reinforced in 1936 when he hit 65 doubles for Nashville, a Southern League record which still stands.

988. Dyer, Don Robert (1968–81 C) "Duffy." Dyer was born on August 15, 1945—VJ day. Don's mother was listening to her favorite radio program, "Duffy's Tavern," when a special news broadcast interrupted to announce that the war with Japan was over. In the excitement of the news, Mrs. Dyer went into labor and was taken to the hospital. After giving birth and attempting to wake up from the anesthesia, she seemed to have one thought on her mind which was: how did her favorite radio show turn out? She looked at the nurse and asked: "How's Duffy?" The nurse assumed she was asking about the baby and replied: "'Duffy's' just fine. He is a beautiful healthy baby, and what a cute name—Duffy Dyer."

989. Dygert, James Henry (1905–10 P) "Sunny Jim." Origin unknown.

990. Dykes, James Joseph (1918–39 2B) "Roundman." Dykes did not have a nickname as a player. He received the "Roundman" tag during his days managing the Chicago White Sox 1934–46. During those years he began to carry 220–230 pounds on his 5'9" frame. The nickname was most popular with the press.

991. Dykstra, Lenny Kyle (1985– OF) "Nails." Len was nicknamed for his style of play reminiscent of McGraw's Giants, aggressive, serious, hard-nosed, win at any cost.

992. Eagan, Charles Eugene (1901 2B) "Truck." Eagan was 5'11" and weighed 190 pounds. He moved like a truck at second base.

993. Eagan, James (1882 OF) "Troy Terrier." This is a place nickname. Egan played for the Troy, New York, team and was small of stature.

994. Eagan, William (1891–98 2B) "Bad Bill." Eagan was illiterate. He could not read or write. But he knew the rules of the game backwards and forwards and could quote them. He was an umpire baiter and used his knowledge of rules to take advantage of umpires. Eagan was ill tempered and used hoodlum tactics to pick fights during games. He was not liked by players, umpires or fans.

995. Earl, Howard J. (1890–91 OF) "Slim Jim." Earl was 6'1" and skinny.

996. Earle, William Moffat (1889–94 C) "The Little Globe Trotter." At 5'10½" and weighing 170 pounds, Earle could not be considered little. He played for five different teams in five major league seasons. In 1988–89 Earle barnstormed around the world with A.G. Spaulding's All-Stars.

997. Earley, Thomas Francis Aloysius (1938–45 P) "Chick." Origin unknown.

998. Earnshaw, George Livingston (1928–36 P) "Moose." "Moose" describes Earnshaw's size 6'4", 210 pounds. He won four and lost three World Series games for the Philadelphia A's (1929–31) with an E.R.A. of 1.58.

999. Easler, Michael Anthony (1973–78 OF) "Hit Man." "Hit Man" refers to Easler's batting skills. In his words: "My philosophy of hitting has always been a simple one: You throw it, I hit it. That's why Willie Stargell and my brother Ted, hung my nickname, 'Hit Man' on me."

1000. Eason, Malcolm (1900–06 P) "Kid." There is no exact data on Eason's height and weight, but there is evidence he was of small stature.

1001. Easterwood, Roy Charles (1944 C) "Shag." Easterwood was excellent at catching foul pop-ups.

1002. Easton, John David (1955–59 PH) "Goose." Easton told me he was nicknamed by sportswriter, Dick Emery of the *Newark News* during his sophomore year at Princeton University. He has no idea what the nickname may mean.

1003. Eaton, Zebulon Vance (1944–45 P) "Red." The nickname refers to hair color.

1004. Eaves, Vallie Ennis (1935–42 P) "Chief." Eaves was of American Indian background.

1005. Ebright, Hiram C. (1889 C) "Buck." "Buck" is a generic nickname of which the circumstances of origin are almost never documented. It refers to a well developed, aggressive, virile, high spirited young man and is usually bestowed on the individual during his teenage years.

1006. Eccles, Harry Josiah (1915 P) "Buggs." Origin unknown.

1007. Eckert, Albert George (1930–35 P) "Obbie." Origin unknown.

1008. Eckert, Charles William (1919–22 P) "Buzz." "Buzz" referred to the sound of Eckert's fastball. Eckert also had a place name, a section of Philadelphia. "It is customary to refer to Eck as 'The East Falls Boy' because he votes here."

1009. Eckert, William D. (1966–68 Commissioner) "The Unknown Soldier." Eckert was also known as "The Faceless Functionary." He was a retired Air Force Lieutenant General with a distinguished record in World War II, called "Spike" by his friends. He was recommended for commissioner to baseball owners by General Curtis Le May, head of the Strategic Air Command. Eckert had no knowledge of baseball and his ineptitude was obvious from the beginning to one and all. He was fired in December, 1968.

1010. Eckhardt, Oscar George (1932–36 OF) "Ox." Lee Allen states, "His bulk made him as durable as his nickname would imply." As a rookie in 1932 with the Boston Braves, he requested a double room at spring training—not for his wife, but for his St. Bernard dog!

1011. Edelen, Edward Joseph (1952 P) "Doc." Many of the players with the nickname of "Doc" had close associations with either the medical or dental professions. For Edelen however, the origin of "Doc" is unknown.

1012. Edge, Claude Lee, Jr. (1979 P) "Butch." "Butch" was a childhood nickname.

1013. Edington, Jacob Frank (1912 OF) "Stump." Edington was 5'6½" and weighed 180 pounds.

1014. Edmonson, Earl Edward (1913 OF) "Axel." Edmonson was known for his strength.

1015. Edmonson, George Henderson (1922–24 P) "Big Ed." Edmonson was 6'1" and weighed 180 pounds.

1016. Edwards, Charles Bruce (1946–56 C) "Bull." Edwards was 5'8" and weighed 180 pounds plus. "Bull" referred to his build. He received the nickname during a tour of duty in the Army.

1017. Edwards, Howard Rodney (1962–70 C) "Doc." Edwards explained to me: "I was a Navy medic with the 5th Marines. All the Marines called medics 'Doc.' After discharge, I went to Miracosta College in Oceanside, California, but I had no intention of pursuing a medical career. When I would see friends from the Marines, they would call me 'Doc' and the college kids picked it up."

1018. Egan, Aloysius Jerome (1902–06 P) "Wish." "Wish" is simply a shortened form of the first name of Aloysius.

1019. Ehmke, Howard Jonathan (1915–30 P) "Bob." "Bob" is listed in the Macmillan *Baseball Encyclopedia* as Ehmke's nickname. However, I failed to document its use in print, or even its origin.

1020. Ehret, Philip Sydney (1888–98 P) "Red." The nickname refers to hair color.

1021. Ehrhart, Welton Claude (1924–29 P) "Rube." Ehrhardt reminded people in size, looks and mannerism of "Rube" Waddell.

1022. Elberfeld, Norman Arthur (1898–1914 SS) "The Tabasco Kid." Elberfeld received his nickname because of his size 5'5½" and 134 pounds and his violent temper. It was said he was "hard as nails and tough as an Apache." He may have given more base runners the shoulder as they rounded second base than any player before or since. Elberfeld felt he had to be rough and tough so others would not push him around because of his size. New York sportswriter, Sam Crane is given credit for "The Tabasco Kid" nickname. Elberfeld was also called "Brownie" referring to his size.

1023. Elco, Peter (1943–44 3B) "Piccolo Pete." Elco wrote me, "Three sportswriters and I were drinking at a bar in Chicago. The sportswriters had a couple of beers and I had one bottle of beer and about 20 strong whiskeys. I didn't come to for the next couple of days. Then they started to call me 'Piccolo Pete' in the sports pages."

1024. Elder, Henry Knox (1913 P) "Heinie." "Heinie" calls attention to Elder's German background.

1025. Ellam, Roy (1909–18 SS) "Whitey." The nickname refers to hair color. Ellam was also called "Slippery" because his last name honored slippery elm, a substance used by spitball pitchers.

1026. Eller, Horace Owen (1917–21 P) "Hod." "Hod" is a short take off on Horace and a more acceptable baseball nickname than Horace.

1027. Ellerbe, Francis Rogers (1919–24 3B) "Governor." Ellerbe was from Marion, South Carolina, and nicknamed "Governor" after William Ellerbe, who was governor of South Carolina, 1897–99. Francis was his son.

1028. Ellingsen, Harold Bruce (1974 P) "Little Pod." Origin unknown.

1029. Elliott, Allen Clifford (1923–24 1B) "Ace." Origin unknown.

1030. Elliott, Claude Judson (1904–05 P) "Chancer." Origin unknown.

1031. Elliott, Harold B. (1910–20 C) "Rowdy." Elliott had a reputation for hard and tough play and questioning umpire decisions.

1032. Elliott, Harold William (1929–32 P) "Ace." "Ace" referred to pitching skill.

1033. Elliott, Herbert Glenn (1947–49 P) "Lefty." Elliott pitched left handed, but was a switch hitter.

1034. Elliott, James Thomas (1923–34 P) "Jumbo." Elliott was 6'3" and weighed in excess of 230 pounds.

1035. Ellis, George William (1909–12 OF) "Rube." Ellis was from the small town of Dowley, California, and not familiar with the big city ways. He was nicknamed after "Rube" Waddell. Walter Nagel describes Ellis' joining the Los Angeles team in the Pacific Coast League: "He arrived in his own uniform—an awesome combination of blue stockings, red pants, yellow shirt and a little red cap about three sizes too small perched precariously on top of his head. His face was a mess of adolescent pimples. With the usual bashfulness of a busher, he asked for Cap Dillon. 'Over there Rube' one of the players pointed. From that moment on, for the rest of his life, that name 'Rube' never left him." Mac Davis mentions that Ellis once refused to sign his contract with St. Louis until he got what he was holding out for, $2.50 to buy a new fielder's glove.

1036. Ellison, Herbert Spencer (1916–20 1B) "Babe." Origin unknown.

1037. Elsh, Eugene Roy (1923–25 OF) "Dory." Origin unknown.

1038. Elson, Bob (1929–68 Announcer) "The Old Commander." Elson broadcast Chicago Cub and White Sox games for 38 years. He was known for his laid back style, few words, and monotone delivery. Glancing at the scoreboard at Comiskey Park, he once said excitedly *over the radio:* "Look what the Red Sox hit the Yankees with in the 6th." It was an inning later before he reported the Red Sox had scored six runs in the 6th inning. Elson became a public relations director in the Navy in 1942. After that he dubbed himself "The Old Commander."

1039. Ely, Frederick William (1884–94 SS) "Bones." Ely was 6'1", but weighed just 155 pounds. Lee Allen comments, "When he batted, he presented such a delicate picture that fans were afraid a pitched ball might splinter him."

1040. Embree, Charles Willard (1941–49 P) "Red." The nickname refers to hair color.

1041. Embry, Charles Akin (1923 P) "Slim." Embry was 6'4½" and weighed 195 pounds. He pitched 2.2 innings in the big leagues and walked two, allowed seven hits and three runs.

1042. Emerson, Chester Arthur (1911–12 OF) "Chuck." "Chuck" was used as an alternative to Chester.

1043. Emery, Herrick Smith (1924 OF) "Spoke." Emery was nicknamed after outfielder Tris "Spoke" Speaker.

1044. Emmerick, William Peter (1945–46 P) "Slim." Emmerick was 6'1" and weighed 170 pounds. He told me: "I have always been Bill to my friends and relatives. It was only the New York City writers who called me Slim."

1045. Emslie, Robert D. (1891–1924 NL Umpire) "Blind Bob." The nickname was bestowed by John McGraw during the 1908 National League season.

1046. Engle, Arthur Clyde (1909–16 OF) "Hack." Engle's strength and build reminded people of the great wrestler, George Hackenschmidt.

1047. Engle, Charlie (1925–30 SS) "Cholly." "Cholly" is simply a take off on Charlie.

1048. English, Elwood George (1927–38 SS) "Woody." "Woody" is a take off on the first name of Elwood. When he first came up to the Chicago Cubs at age 20, he was called "Kid" because of his age, and "Flash" for his fielding ability.

1049. Ennis, Russell Elwood (1926 C) "Hack." Origin unknown.

1050. Enzmann, John (1914–22 P) "Gentleman John." Origin unknown.

1051. Epperly, Albert Paul (1938–50 P) "Pard." Epperly wrote me: "Win Ballou, a former major league pitcher started calling me that when I played for San Francisco in the Pacific Coast League in 1940. He could not remember my name. After that, all the players started calling me that."

1052. Epps, Aubrey Lee (1935 C) "Yo-Yo." Origin unknown.

1053. Epstein, Michael Peter (1966–74 1B) "Super Jew." Epstein was of the Jewish faith. He was nicknamed by Rocky Bridges for his exploits at Stockton, California, in 1965. He led the league with 30 home runs and a .338 batting average.

1054. Erauti, Joseph Michael (1930–51 C) "Stubby." Erauti was 5'9" and weighed 175 pounds.

1055. Erickson, Henry Wels (1935 C) "Popeye." According to Joseph McBride, Erickson entertained his Cincinnati teammates imitating the facial contortions of the comic strip character Popeye. The reference is to the comic strip character created by E.C. Seagar which first began to appear in newspapers in January of 1929.

1056. Erickson, Paul Walford (1941-48 P) "Li'l Abner." Erickson was nicknamed by his Chicago Cub teammates after the comic strip character because he was strong red blooded American boy. This was in spite of the fact that he had blond hair, and Li'l Abner's was black. The reference is to the "Li'l Abner" comic strip created by Al Capp, which first appeared in newspapers in 1935.

1057. Erickson, Richard Merriwell (1938-42 P) "Lief." Teammates nicknamed Erickson after the Norse explorer, Lief Erickson, who discovered America in 1002.

1058. Erickson, Rodger Farrell (1973-83 P) "Pudge." Joseph McBride quotes Erickson: "When I was three-years-old, I had a teddy bear that had a pug nose and my brother started calling me Pudge."

1059. Erskine, Carl Daniel (1948-59 P) "Oisk." Erskine was a popular pitcher for the Brooklyn Dodgers during their glory years in the mid-1950s. Erskine was one of the star pitchers and pitched in five World Series. "Oisk" is what Erskine sounded like when spoken with a Brooklyn accent.

1060. Erwin, Ross Emil (1907-14 C) "Tex." This is a place nickname. Erwin was born in Forney, Texas.

1061. Escarrega, Ernesto Acousta (1982 P) "Chico." "Chico" means kid in Spanish.

1062. Esper, Charles H. (1890-98 RP) "Duke." "Duke" referred to Esper's fashionable dress.

1063. Espinosa, Anulfo Acevedo (1974-81 P) "Nino." "Nino" in Spanish means little boy or my boy.

1064. Essick, William Earl (1906-07 P) "Vinegar Bill." In 1906, when he was a rookie with Cincinnati, Rhinelander fans mispronounced his name as it were spelled Essig. That is the German word for Vinegar. Although he had only a brief career in the major leagues, Essick became a famous scout for the New York Yankees. He sent such players to the Yanks as: Joe DiMaggio, Bob Meusel, "Lefty" Gomez, Frank Crosetti, Joe Gordon, Gerry Priddy, and Ralph Houk.

1065. Esterbrook, Thomas John (1880-91 3B) "Dude." Tom Shea reports that "Dude," in the 1880s, meant one who wore fancy clothes.

1066. Estrada, Charles Leonard (1960-67 P) "Droopy." When Estrada was a baby, his father was listening to a radio program in which a character was introduced by the name of "Droopy." He took a fancy to the name and used it as a nickname for his son.

1067. Etchison, Clarence Hampton (1943-44 1B) "Buck." "Buck" is a generic nickname of which the circumstances of origin are almost never documented. It refers to a well developed, virile, aggressive, high spirited young man and is usually bestowed upon the individual during his teenage years.

1068. Etheridge, Bobby Lamar (1967-69 3B) "Luke." Origin unknown.

1069. Eubank, John Franklin (1905-07 P) "Honest John." Origin unknown.

1070. Eubanks, Vel Melvin (1922 P) "Poss." "Poss" is short for "Possum," but the origin is unknown.

1071. Evans, Dwight Michael (1972 OF) "Dewey." "Dewey" is a short name for Dwight.

1072. Evans, Jacob (1879–85 OF) "Bloody Jake." Origin unknown.

1073. Evans, Joseph Patton (1915–25 OF) "Doc." Evans was a practicing physician.

1074. Evans, Russell Edison (1936–39 P) "Red." The nickname refers to hair color.

1075. Evers, John Joseph (1902–39 2B) "The Crab." Evers played for 18 years in the major leagues and was one of the best second basemen of his time. He was the middle man in the famous double-play combination immortalized in the poem "Tinkers to Evers to Chance." Charley Dryden first called him "The Crab" because of the crablike way he gripped the ball when throwing it. The nickname took on a new dimension when National League President John Tener announced that Evers was the number one problem player in the league. Evers was also called "Trojan" because he came from Troy, New York, and "Toy Trojan" referred to his size, 5'9" and 125 pounds.

1076. Evers, Walter Arthur (1941–56 OF) "Hoot." Joseph McBride reports that Evers used to pretend to be the cowboy movie star, Edward "Hoot" Gibson and was nicknamed by his uncle. Evers wrote me that his uncle nicknamed him "Hoot" because he hooted as a baby.

1077. Ewing, George Lemuel (1902–12 P) "Long Bob." Ewing was 6'1½" tall and weighed 170 pounds. The origin of Bob is unknown.

1078. Ewing, William (1880–97 C) "Buck." Ewing was one of the premier catchers and players of the 1880s and 1890s. Most researchers believe "Buck" was a boyhood nickname bestowed by friends. Some sportswriters have given him the middle name of Buckingham and claimed "Buck" is short for that name. There does not appear to be any evidence to support such a claim. Ewing had no middle name. In fact, his looks and actions are a prototype of the generic nickname of "Buck."

1079. Ewoldt, Arthur Lee (1919 3B) "Sheriff." Origin unknown.

F

1080. Faber, Urban Clarence (1914–33 P) "Red." The nickname refers to hair color. Faber won 254 games over 20 seasons. He had four decisions in the 1917 World Series, winning three and dropping one for the Chicago White Sox.

1081. Fabrique, Albert LaVerne (1916–17 SS) "Bunny." "Bunny" referred to Fabrique's size. He was 5'8½" and weighed 150 pounds.

1082. Fagan, William A. (1887–88 P) "Clinkers." "Clinkers" is a derogatory nickname which refers to a player prone to making boners and errors.

1083. Fahey, Howard Simpson (1912 OF) "Kid." "Kid" refers to Fahey's size and age when he was a 20-year-old, 5'7½", 145-pound rookie with the Philadelphia A's. Fahey was also addressed as "Cap."

1084. Fahr, Gerald Warren (1951 P) "Red." The nickname refers to hair color.

1085. Fain, Ferris Roy (1947–55 1B) "Burrhead." Fain was a fancy fielding first baseman and two-time American League batting champion. He was nicknamed "Burrhead" by roommate Win Ballow when they played for San Francisco of the Pacific Coast League in the 1940s. Fain was also called "Cocky," not because of his demeanor, although it fit, but as short for "Cockeyed." A team trainer didn't think his eyes were matched. In 1985, and again in 1988, Fain was arrested and convicted of growing marijuana plants in El Dorado County, California.

1086. Fairbank, James Lee (1903–04 P) "Smoky." "Smoky" refers to the speed of Fairbank's fastball.

1087. Faircloth, James Lamar (1919 P) "Rags." is a response to the last name of Faircloth.

1088. Falk, Bib August (1920–31 OF) "Jockey." Falk was a noted bench jockey throughout his career. The nickname was reinforced by the fact that Falk was a constant follower of the sport of horse racing.

1089. Falk, Chester Emanual (1925–27 P) "Spot." Origin unknown.

1090. Falkenberg, Frederick Peter (1903–17 P) "Cy." Falkenberg was a fastballing strikeout pitcher who reminded people of Denton "Cy" Young.

1091. Fallenstin, Edward Joseph (1931–33 P) "Jack." "Jack" was used as an alternative to Joe early in life.

1092. Fallon, George Decatur (1937–45 2B) "Flash." Fallon was nicknamed after Yankee star second baseman Joe "Flash" Gordon who some felt he resembled in the field.

1093. Fannin, Clifford Bryson (1945–52 P) "Mule." Fannin had the reputation of a hard worker and was always ready to pitch.

1094. Fanok, Harry Michael (1953–54 P) "The Flame Thrower." Fanok was a fastball pitcher. He struck out 35 batters in the 33.1 innings he pitched in the major leagues.

1095. Fanovich, Frank Joseph (1949–53 P) "Lefty." Fanovich pitched left handed, and batted left handed.

1096. Farmer, Floyd Haskell (1916–18 OF) "Jack." Origin unknown.

1097. Farrell, Charles Andrew (1888–1905 C) "Duke." As far as I can ascertain, "Duke" does not refer to Farrell's dress, but is really part of a place nickname. In 1891, Farrell was playing for the Beantown Reds. Before an exhibition game on the road, a concessionaire introduced him: "Now batting 'The Duke of Malborough'." Farrell was from Marlborough, Massachusetts.

1098. Farrell, Edward Stephen (1925–35 SS) "Doc." Farrell was a practicing dentist. He received his DDS degree from the University of Pennsylvania.

1099. Farrell, John (1879 OF) "Hartford Jack." This is a place nickname. Farrell was from Hartford, Connecticut.

1100. Farrell, John A. (1879–89 2B) "Moose." At 5'9" and 165 pounds, Farrell did not have a Moose build. The nickname referred to how he moved and acted off the field.

1101. Farrell, Richard Joseph (1956–69 P) "Turk." "Turk" was a family nickname. Farrell is one of just a few pitchers to win over 100 games, (106) but lose more than he won (111).

1102. Fasyholz, John Edward (1953 P) "Preacher." Fasyholz explained to me: "During the years I was playing pro ball, I was attending Concordia Theological Seminary in St. Louis. In the early 1950s, players on the Rochester Red Wings started calling me 'Preacher.' Since I always had pretty good success pitching on Sundays, Manager Harry Walker would say, 'You can't beat the Preacher on Sundays'."

1103. Faulkner, James LeRoy (1927–30 P) "Lefty." Faulkner pitched left handed, but was a switch hitter.

1104. Fausett, Robert Shaw (1944 3B) "Leaky." The nickname is a response to the last name. Fausett was often addressed as "Buck."

1105. Faust, Charles Victor (1911 P) "Victory." At first "Victory" appears to be no more than derivation of the middle name of Victor, but there is much more to the story. In 1911, Faust was told by a fortune teller that he was to become the world's greatest baseball pitcher, despite the fact that he had never pitched a game in organized baseball. Shortly after, he asked and received a tryout with John McGraw's New York Giants. As it turned out, he was so poor that the Giants decided to keep him around for a few days as a non-player, just for laughs. They even outfitted him in an ill-fitted uniform. His main function was to entertain fans before games. While he was with the team, however, the Giants put together a string of victories. Some of the more superstitious players thought Faust was good luck, a jinx killer, and wanted him to remain on the bench. He was allowed to do so, and when he was present the Giants made some amazing comebacks for more victories. In fact, as the Giants wrapped up the flag, Faust actually did more than warm-up in the bull pen. He was allowed to pitch in two games for a total of two innings. He spent part of the 1912 season on the Giant bench, sans uniform, until it became clear that his presence did not insure victories and the team tired of him. Faust died in 1915 in a hospital for the insane.

1106. Fauver, Clayton King (1899 P) "Pop." Fauver was a 27-year-old rookie when he pitched and won the only major league game in which he played.

1107. Favrell, Luther (1926–34 P, Negro League) "Red." On October 8, 1927, pitching for the Atlantic City Bacharach Giants against the Chicago American Giants in the Negro World Series, Favrell pitched a seven inning no-hitter, winning 3–2. Favrell won two games and lost two games in that series. The nickname "Red" referred to his light skin.

1108. Federoff, Alfred (1951–52 2B) "Whitey." The nickname refers to hair color.

1109. Fehring, William Paul (1934 C) "Dutch." Fehring played in only one major league game and struck out in his only trip to the plate. He told me that while playing football for Columbus, Indiana, high school, he once blocked a punt and carried it back 70 yards for a touchdown. The next day, the local newspaper called him "The Flying Dutchman." "After that," he said, "people started calling me 'Dutch' because of my German descent."

1110. Feinburg, Edward (1938–39 SS) "Itzy." "Itzy" is short for "Itzy Bitzy" referring to Feinburg's size of 5'9" and 165 pounds.

1111. Feller, Robert William Andrew (1936–56 P) "Rapid Robert." Feller's blazing fastball gave rise to his "Rapid Robert" nickname while pitching for Cleveland in 1936, even before he graduated from high school. At that time he was also called "The Van Meter School Boy." His home was Van Meter, Iowa. Feller led the American League in strikeouts seven times and set the record of 348 in 1946, which was the standard for many years. Even with 3½ of his potentially most productive years lost to military service, Feller still managed to win 266 major league games.

1112. Felsch, Oscar Emil (1915–20 OF) "Happy." Felsch had an easy going disposition and was well liked. His father said he was born laughing. It may have been his easy going ways which paved the way for his part in the 1919 "Black Sox" scandal. Felsch along with seven other Black Sox players were banned for life by Judge Landis for throwing the World Series to the Cincinnati Reds.

1113. Fenwich, Robert Richard (1972–73 2B) "Bloop." Origin unknown.

1114. Ferguson, Robert V. (1871–84 2B; NA Umpire 1871–75) "Death to Flying Things." Ferguson was a sure handed infielder. It is assumed that he was adept at catching balls on the fly. However, there is no documentation of this. Lacking such, it has been suggested to me that one might equally assume that the nickname refers to Ferguson's adeptness with a fly swatter in a hotel lobby!

1115. Fermin, Felix Jose (1987 SS) "Gato." "Gato" is Spanish for cat and refers to his fielding ability. He received the tag in the minor leagues.

1116. Fernandez, Humberton Perez (1956–62 SS) "Chico." "Chico" is Spanish for kid or little boy.

1117. Fernandez, Lorenzo Marto (1968 SS) "Chico." "Chico" is Spanish for kid or little boy.

1118. Ferns, Stanley (1942–46 P) "Lefty." Ferns pitched left handed, but was a switch hitter.

1119. Ferrara, Alfred John (1963–71 OF) "The Bull." Ferrara was 6'1" and weighed a shade over 200 pounds.

It was said he played as tenaciously as a bull.

1120. Ferrarese, Donald Hugh (1955–62 P) "Midget." Ferrarese stood 5'9" and weighed 170 pounds.

1121. Ferris, Albert Soyles (1901–09 2B) "Hobie." Origin unknown.

1122. Ferris, David Meadow (1945–50 P) "Boo." Ferris won 21 games as a rookie for the Boston Red Sox and 25 games the next year, but he was only able to capture 19 more wins in his career. He told me: "As I was just beginning to talk in early childhood, I tried to call my older brother, 'big brother,' but the word 'Boo' came out. My family began to call me 'Little Boo' and then just 'Boo'."

1123. Ferry, Alfred Joseph (1904–05 P) "Cy." Ferry was one of many pitchers who at the start of their careers reminded people of Denton "Cy" Young.

1124. Ferson, Alexander (1889–92 P) "Colonel." Origin unknown.

1125. Fidrych, Mark Stephen (1976–80 P) "The Bird." The first time he set foot on the field at Bristol, Tennessee, in the Appalachian League, he startled teammates with a high pitched squawk—GAAWK! GAAWK! which was to become his trademark. Coach Jeff Logan took one look and said: "A bird, a Bird, you are a bird." Fidrych's frizzy hair, long legs and lopping stride reinforced the bird image. He reminded teammates of "Big Bird," the character from the children's TV show "Sesame Street" which was played by Frank Oz and Carroll Spinney and premiered in 1969. Fidrych was one of the strangest characters the game has ever known. Bruce Shalain in his book *Odd Balls* catches the essence of Fidrych in the following passage: "He sprinted on and off the field between innings and after each out he strutted around like a mad stork on the balls of his feet, long curls bouncing as his head bobbed like an excited turkey, calling for the ball back. He had his own style and was into his own moves, which were definitely ornithological. When he got in a grove, he would flap his arms and shriek like a bird, a gawky display resembling a punch-drunk pelican trying to take wing. And, Fidrych talked to the ball especially before he pitched it and asked for a new ball after giving up a hit." Finally, Bruce Shalain reports that in 1976, when Fidrych learned he was going to make the Detroit Tiger team, he got so excited he brought a girl to the stadium and made love to her on the side of the mound to show her where he worked.

1126. Fieber, Clarence Thomas (1932 P) "Lefty." Fieber pitched left handed, and batted left handed.

1127. Fielder, Cecil Grant (1985 DH) "Big Daddy." The nickname is a combination of Fielder's build, 6'3", 235 pounds and his ability to hit the long ball. In 1990 Fielder hit 51 home runs for the Detroit Tigers.

1128. Fields, John Joseph (1887–92 OF) "Jocko." In Fields' case, "Jocko" was a take off on the first name of John.

1129. Fiene, Louis Henry (1906–09 P) "Big Finn." "Big Finn" does not refer to Finnish ancestry, but is a play on the way Fiene is pronounced.

1130. Finley, Charles O. (1960–81 Owner) "Charlie O." Finley was an eccentric and controversial owner of the Kansas City A's which he moved to Oakland in 1968. His shenanigans led opponents to rumor that the initial "O" stood for "outrageous." Thus the nickname "Charlie O." Probably more was written about Finley than his players, even when they won the World Series. His years as an owner brought a continuous battle with players, managers, fans, owners, and the commissioner's office.

1131. Finn, Cornelius Francis Neal (1930–33 2B) "Mickey." "Mickey" is a response to the last name of Finn.

1132. Fiore, Michael Garry Joseph (1968–72 1B) "Lefty." Fiore pitched left handed, and batted left handed.

1133. Fischer, Chauncy Burr (1893–1901 P) "Peach." Origin unknown.

1134. Fischer, Henry William (1962–67 P) "Bull Dog." Fischer explained to me, "I was compact and would challenge any hitter in the league. I had the personality of a bull dog. I got the nickname during my rookie year in 1962 with Milwaukee. My manager, Birdie Tebbets used signs instead of the telephone to motion to the bull pen from the dugout. His sign for Don McMahan was to stand up and raise both arms up with his fists clenched. When he would motion for me, he would use the same signal but he would do it from a squatting position. I guess it indicated 'Bull Dog.' Well, it was quite a sight for a fan if you didn't understand what he was doing."

1135. Fisher, Frederick Brown (1964 P) "Fritz." "Fritz" denotes Fisher's German background.

1136. Fisher, George Aloys (1923–32 OF) "Show Boat." In the minor leagues Fisher built the reputation of being a show-off or showboat hitter. Once he got ten straight hits. On another occasion he was credited with 23 hits in 31 trips to the plate.

1137. Fisher, John Gus (1910 OF) "Red." The nickname refers to hair color.

1138. Fisher, John Howard (1959–69 P) "Fat Jack." Fisher's record for 11 years was 86 wins and 139 losses, a .382 percentage with a career ERA of 4.06. He was 6'2" and weighed 220 pounds.

1139. Fisher, Thomas Chalmers (1904 P) "Red." The nickname refers to hair color.

1140. Fisher, Wilbur McCullough (1916 PH) "Levy." Fisher failed to get a hit as a pinch hitter in his only appearance in the major leagues. The origins of "Levy" and his other nickname "Hod" is unknown.

1141. Fisher, William Charles (1876–78 P) "Cherokee." Fisher was of Cherokee Indian background.

1142. Fisk, Carlton Ernest (1969 C) "Pudge." Fisk was on the heavy side as a child. He was 5'4" and weighed 155 pounds in the eighth grade. He says the nickname was given to him either by an aunt or grandmother. He can't remember which. As a player at 6'3" and 200 pounds, Fisk did not fit the nickname as an adult.

1143. Fiske, Maximillian Patrick (1914 P) "Mox." "Mox" is a short take off on the first name of Maximillan.

1144. Fitzberger, Charles Casper (1928 PH) "Hon." "Hon" denotes Fitzberger's German background. It is a corruption of "Hun."

1145. Fitzgerald, Howard Chumney (1922–25 OF) "Lefty." Fitzgerald pitched left handed and batted left handed.

1146. Fitzke, Paul Frederick Herman (1924 P) "Bob." Origin unknown.

1147. Fitzsimmons, Frederick Landis (1925–43 P) "Fat Freddie." Fitzsimmons won 217 games during his

19-year career. He stood 5'11" and in the latter stages of his career weighed up to 250 pounds.

1148. Flagstead, Ira James (1917–30 OF) "Pete." Origin unknown.

1149. Flaherty, John F. (1953–73 AL Umpire) "Red." The nickname refers to hair color.

1150. Flair, Albert Dell (1941 1B) "Broadway." In Flair's case, "Broadway" referred to the love of night life and having a good time.

1151. Flanagan, Edward J. (1887–89 OF) "Steamer." Origin unknown.

1152. Flaskamper, Ray Harold (1927 SS) "Flash." "Flash" is a take off on the last name of Flaskamper.

1153. Fleming, Leslie Fletchard (1940–46 P) "Bill." Fleming wrote me: "Leslie is a family name. My father gave me the name Bill as a child, because he did not think Leslie was appropriate for a boy. I could always tell when my father was angry with me. He would use Leslie. I knew everything was all right when he used Bill."

1154. Fleming, Leslie Harvey (1939–49 1B) "Moe." Origin unknown.

1155. Fleming, Thomas Vincent (1899–1904 OF) "Sleth." Origin unknown.

1156. Flick, Elmer Harrison (1898–1910 OF) "Bedford Sheriff." This is a place nickname given to Flick by his teammates. He was from Bedford, Ohio. I cannot, however, find any documentation that he was ever a sheriff.

1157. Flint, Frank Sylvester (1878–89 C) "Silver." According to SABR researcher Mark Rucker, "Silver" had pale blond hair. When he caught Ed "The Only Nolan" in 1878, he was called "The Only Flint." Adrian "Cap" Anson in his book *Ball Player's Career* describes Flint: "He was generally reliable, and that in spite of the fact that he was a hard drinker, the love of liquor being his besetting weakness. A plucker man never stood behind a bat, there never coming a ball his way that was too hard for him to handle, or at least to attempt to. In 'Old Silver's' day, the catcher's glove had not come into use, and all his work was done with hands that were unprotected. Those hands of his were a sight to behold, and if there is a worse pair today in the United States, or a pair that are as bad, I should certainly like to have a look at them. His fingers were bent and twisted out of all shape and looked more like knotted and gnarled branches of a scrub oak than anything else that I can think of."

1158. Flohr, Moritz Herman (1934 P) "Dutch." "Dutch" refers to Flohr's German background.

1159. Florence, Paul Robert (1926 C) "Pep." When he was attending Georgetown University, Florence showed great energy or pep, by participating in many different activities including, among other things, drama and four sports.

1160. Flowers, D'Arcy Raymond (1923–34 2B) "Jake." The name D'Arcy, was thought to be "too highfalutin" for a ball player, and when Flowers was in high school, classmates substituted "Jake."

1161. Floyd, Leslie Roe (1944 SS) "Bubba." Origin unknown.

1162. Flynn, Cornelius Francis Xavier (1894–96 P) "Carney." "Carney" is a take off on the first name of Cornelius.

1163. Flynn, George A. (1896 OF) "Dibby." Origin unknown.

1164. Flynn, John A. (1886–87 P) "Jocko." In Flynn's case, "Jocko" is a take off on the first name of John.

1165. Fodge, Eugene Arlan (1958 P) "Suds." Fodge wrote of his nickname "Suds": "It refers to one game in the Pacific Coast League in 1956 at Los Angeles. I gave up 7 runs without retiring a batter. So I got an early shower and a full bar of soap. My roommate, Johnny Briggs, jokingly approached me and said 'Hey Suds' as I exited the shower and it has stayed with me ever since."

1166. Foley, Charles Joseph (1879–83 P) "Curry." Origin unknown.

1167. Force, David W. (1876–88 SS) "Tom Thumb." Force was 5'4" and weighed 130 pounds. He was nicknamed after the dwarf, Charles Stratton who was 3'4" and weighed 70 pounds. Stratton was exhibited by P.T. Barnum under the name of General Tom Thumb in the 1840s.

1168. Ford, Darnell Glenn (1975–85 OF) "Disco Danny." Ford wrote me that he did not dance at discos. But in 1977, in Minneapolis some of his fans began to sell T-shirts with his name and or likeness on them at discos. This is where the nickname came from.

1169. Ford, Edward Charles (1950–67 P) "Whitey." Ford originally had strawberry blond hair color, which turned to white. In 16 years, Ford posted a 236-106, won-lost record for a winning percentage of .690, third highest in major league history. He pitched in 11 World Series winning ten games and dropping eight. Both figures are the highest of all time. Casey Stengel christened him "Slick" and he was called that by teammates. "Slick" may have referred to the ways in which he "doctored" the ball and got away with it and for the way he drank liquor. "Chairman of the Board" was a nickname of respect bestowed on Ford, by his catchers, "Yogi" Berra and Elston Howard.

1170. Ford, Horace Hills (1919–33 SS) "Hod." "Hod" is a take off on the first name of Horace.

1171. Ford, Percival Edmund (1973 P) "Wentz." Origin unknown.

1172. Foreman, August (1924–26 P) "Happy." The nickname refers to Foreman's pleasant disposition.

1173. Foreman, Francis Isaiah (1884–1902 P) "Monkey." Fred Lieb attributes the "Monkey" tag to the way Foreman screwed up his face when he pitched. He looked like a monkey.

1174. Foreman, John Davis (1895–96 P) "Brownie." Origin unknown.

1175. Foss, George Dueward (1921 3B) "Deeby." Foss' middle name was selected from the novel *Lena Rivers* which his mother was reading at the time of his birth. The nickname of "Deeby" is a corruption of his middle name.

1176. Foster, Andrew (1902–26 P, Negro League) "Rube." As a 22-year-old pitcher, Foster defeated George "Rube" Waddell in an exhibition game in 1902. His teammates paid him deference by nicknaming "Rube." Thus the nickname had a positive meaning when applied to Foster, rather than its more common use in baseball to refer to a country bumpkin. Honus Wagner thought Foster was the smartest pitcher he had seen in all his years of baseball. Foster's pitching ability is usually forgotten since his main accomplishments were as a manager and league operator.

It was largely through Foster's efforts that black baseball became respectable.

1177. Foster, Clarence Francis (1898–1901 OF) "Pop." In Foster's case, "Pop" is a nickname opposite. He began his major league career at age 19, and it ended at age 24.

1178. Foster, Eddy Lee (1908 P) "Slim." Foster was 6'1", but there is no information available on his weight. It is assumed that he was thin.

1179. Foster, Edward Cunningham (1910–23 3B) "Kid." "Kid" refers to Foster's size. He was 5'6" and weighed 145 pounds.

1180. Foster, George (1913–17 P) "Rube." Foster came from the small Oklahoma town of Leigh. He was not familiar with big city ways. He was nicknamed after "Rube" Waddell.

1181. Foster, Oscar E. (1896 PH) "Reddy." The nickname refers to hair color.

1182. Fothergill, Robert Roy (1922–33 OF) "Fatty." Fothergill was 5'10" and began his career at a rather heavy 230 pounds. It was estimated that in the last two years of his stay in the major leagues, he had reached 300 pounds.

1183. Fournier, John Frank (1912–27 1B) "Jacques." "Jacques" is John in French. The nickname denotes Fournier's French background.

1184. Fournier, Julius Henry (1894 P) "Frenchy." Fournier was of French background.

1185. Foutz, David Luther (1884–94 P) "Scissors." Foutz at 6'2" and 170 pounds had very long legs. Tom Shea reports he looked like a pair of scissors when he was at the plate.

1186. Fowler, John W. (1872–99 2B, Negro League) "Bud." According to SABR founder, Bob Davids, Fowler, whose real name was John W. Jackson, was born in Cooperstown, New York. He may have been the first black professional player. The nickname "Bud" resulted from his inclination to call most others by that name.

1187. Fox, Charles Frances (1942 C) "Irish." Fox was of Irish background.

1188. Fox, Erwin (1933–45 OF) "Pete." The nickname "Pete" stems from Fox's days in the Texas League where fans were impressed with his speed and called him "Peter Rabbit."

1189. Fox, George B. (1891–99 1B) "Paddy." "Paddy" was an affectionate nickname denoting Fox's Irish background.

1190. Fox, Jacob Nelson (1947–65 2B) "Little Nel." Nellie as he was addressed, was one of the most popular performers ever to play for the Chicago White Sox. In 19 seasons, he collected 2,663 hits and a career average of .288. Fox could not be considered small at 5'10" and 160 pounds, but he looked smaller than that. Teammate "Minnie" Minoso called him "Little Bit." "Little Nel" was an affectionate nickname used by players, fans and media. Probably radio announcer, Bob Elson, did as much as anyone else to publicize the nickname.

1191. Foxx, James Emory (1925–45 1B) "Double X." Somewhat unusually, Foxx's name was spelled with two x's. When he first came up to the majors, his name was erroneously listed on the score cards with the normal one "x." To emphasize the variation, he was called "Double X." Fox had great strength and was one of the finest power hitters of all time, blasting 534 career home runs, 58 of them in 1932. For such power and strength, he was called "The Beast." In 1952, Fox managed the South Bend Daisies of the All American Girls Baseball League, the women's professional league which existed from 1943–54.

1192. Francona, John Patsy (1956–70 OF) "Tito." Francona told me: "Tito means little in Italian. My father began calling me that as a little boy."

1193. Franklin, Murray Asher (1941–42 SS) "Moe." "Moe" is a take off on the first name of Murray.

1194. Frantz, Arthur F. (1969–77 AL Umpire) "Bud." "Bud" was a childhood nickname.

1195. Frazier, Joseph Filmore (1947–56 OF) "Cobra Joe." Frazier's batting style was like the uncoiling of a snake. "The Snake" was the nickname given to Frazier by Houston sportswriters when he played there in the Texas League in 1953. In 1954, St. Louis Cardinal Manager, Eddie Stanky, changed the nickname to "Cobra Joe" because of his good batting eye, rather than his propensity to uncoil.

1196. Freeman, Alexander Vernon (1921–22 P) "Buck." Alexander Freeman was nicknamed "Buck" after John Frank "Buck" Freeman.

1197. Freeman, Frank Ellsworth (1908–09 1B) "Buck." Frank Freeman, who was addressed as Jerry, was nicknamed after John Frank "Buck" Freeman.

1198. Freeman, Harvey Boyard (1921 P) "Buck." Harvey Freeman was nicknamed "Buck" after John Frank "Buck" Freeman.

1199. Freeman, Hershell Baskin (1952–58 P) "Buster." Origin unknown.

1200. Freeman, John Edward (1927 OF) "Buck." John Edward Freeman was nicknamed "Buck" after John Frank "Buck" Freeman.

1201. Freeman, John Frank (1891–1907 OF) "Buck." Freeman was a popular player and so was his nickname of "Buck." Several other players after his time with the name of Freeman were assigned the nickname of "Buck." John Frank Freeman was the original "Buck Freeman." In his case, "Buck" referred to his robust nature.

1202. Freese, Eugene Lewis (1955–66 3B) "Augie." In his rookie year when Pittsburgh was playing at Brooklyn, public address announcer Tex Rikards didn't know Freese's first name. He asked some Brooklyn players, who as a joke told him "Augie," since Umpire August Donatelli was scheduled to be behind the plate that day. The joke created a nickname.

1203. Freeze, Carl Alexander (1925 P) "Jake." Origin unknown.

1204. Freeze, George Walter (1953–61 3B) "Bud." Freeze received the nickname of "Bud" from his parents at an early age.

1205. Friegan, Howard Earl (1922–28 3B) "Ty." Origin unknown.

1206. French, Frank Alexander (1917 OF) "Pat." Origin unknown.

1207. French, Walter Edward (1923–29 OF) "Fitz." Origin unknown.

1208. French, Walter Edward Raymond (1920–24 SS) "Ray." Origin unknown.

1209. Frey, Linus Reinhard (1933–48 2B) "Junior." When Frey first came up to the majors, he looked much younger than he was, and teammates called him "Junior."

1210. Frias, Jesus Maria (1973–81 SS) "Pepe." Origin unknown.

1211. Friday, Grier William (1923 P) "Skipper." Origin unknown.

1212. Fridley, James Riley (1952–58 OF) "Big Jim." Fridley was 6'2" and weighed 205 pounds.

1213. Fried, Arthur Edwin (1920 P) "Cy." Similar to so many other players with the nickname of "Cy," Fried was probably nicknamed after Denton "Cy" Young. I have not, however, been able to document this origin.

1214. Friend, Owen Lacey (1949–56 2B) "Red." The nickname refers to hair color.

1215. Friend, Robert Bartness (1951–66 P) "Warrior." Friend was well educated and serious about his work on the mound and all other aspects of his life. He was a heavy duty pitcher who led the National League in games started for three straight years, 1956–58. Perhaps the nickname "Warrior" refers to this. However, I was unable to find the term "Warrior" used in print in reference to Friend, or its origin. Friend was called "Nervous" by his teammates. Myron Cope explains why: "When he drew a starting assignment, he would warm up for his warmup. He would pace back and forth in the clubhouse bending his pitching arm up and down at the joint while massaging it nervously with his left hand."

1216. Frierson, Robert Lawrence (1941 OF) "Buck." "Buck" is a generic nickname of which the circumstances of origin are almost never documented. It refers to a well developed, aggressive, virile, high spirited individual and is usually bestowed on the person during his teenage years.

1217. Frisbee, Charles Augustus (1899–1900 OF) "Bunt." Frisbee was known as a frequent and adept bunter. With Frisbee as a last name, I suspect his nickname would be much different if he played today.

1218. Frisch, Frank Francis (1919–37 2B) "The Fordham Flash." Frisch was one of the great second basemen of all time, collecting 2,880 hits in 19 seasons with a career batting average of .316. As a player manager, he led the famous 1934 St. Louis Cardinals "Gas House Gang" to the world championship. "The Fordham Flash" is a place nickname. Frisch came directly from Fordham University to the New York Giants where he was an instant star (flash) and a hit with the fans. Players sometimes called him "Dutchman" denoting his German background. When he managed the St. Louis Cardinals, 1933–38, he was sometimes referred to as "Onkel Frantz."

1219. Frisella, Daniel Vincent (1967–76 P) "Bear." Frisella was called "Bear" by teammates because he did not shave before games.

1220. Fritz, Harry Koch (1913–15 3B) "Dutchman." "Dutchman" refers to Fritz's German background.

1221. Froelich, William Palmer (1909 C) "Ben." Origin unknown.

1222. Fry, Johnson (1923 P) "Jay." The initial "J" was used for Johnson. In print it came out "Jay."

1223. Fuentes, Rigoberto Peat (1965–78 2B) "Tito." "Tito" means small in Italian, but Fuentes was

Cuban and spoke Spanish. Teammates called him "Parakeet" because he talked to everyone when he was on base. Fuentes had a son born on September 29, 1971, the day his team, the San Francisco Giants, won the National League Western Division championship. To celebrate, he named his son Clinch.

1224. Fuhrman, Alfred George (1922 C) "Ollie." Fuhrman was from Jordan, Minnesota, and of Swedish background.

1225. Fulghum, James Lavoisier (1921 SS) "Dot." Fulghum was nicknamed after John "Dots" Miller who was finishing his career with the Philadelphia Phils in 1921, while Fulghum was playing for the Philadelphia A's.

1226. Fuller, Charles R. (1902 C) "Nig." "Nig" refers to Fuller's dark complexion.

1227. Fuller, Frank Edward (1915–23 2B) "Rabbit." "Rabbit" refers to Fuller's speed.

1228. Fuller, William Benjamin (1888–96 SS) "Shorty." There is no information available on Fuller's height or weight. It is assumed he was short.

1229. Funk, Elias Calvin (1929–33 OF) "Liz." "Liz" is a take off on the first name of Elias. It has no feminine connotations.

1230. Furillo, Carl Anthony (1946–60 OF) "Skoonj." Furillo was an excellent hitter with a career average of .299 for 15 seasons, but he had little speed, especially on the bases. "Skoonj" is short for the Italian word scungelli which means snail. It referred to his lack of speed. Furillo was noted for his strong throwing arm. While playing for Reading, Pennsylvania, in the Eastern League, he was credited with throwing out six runners at first base while playing right field. This feat earned him the place nickname of "The Reading Rifle." Some players called him "Rock," short for "Rock-Headed," because of his lack of education.

1231. Fussel, Frederick Morris (1922–29 P) "Moonlight Ace." In 1933, Fussel pitched the first twilight no hitter in International League history.

G

1232. Gabler, Frank Harold (1935-38 P) "The Great Gabbo." Tom Shea reports: "Name taken from the stage success of F. Scott Fitzgerald's novel to indicate player's complete lack of mike freight, with or without benefit of the instrument."

1233. Gaddy, John Wilson (1938 P) "Sheriff." Origin unknown.

1234. Gaff, Brent Allen (1982-84 P) "Willy." Origin unknown.

1235. Gaffney, John H. (1884-89, 91-95 NL Umpire) "King of the Umpires." The nickname was a phrase of deference. Gaffney had the reputation of making good calls. He helped fans distinguish between strike two and strike three by shouting "Strike two-o-o-o-o-o."

1236. Gagnon, Harold Dennis (1922-24 SS) "Chick." "Chick" refers to Gagnon's small stature, 5'7½", 158 pounds.

1237. Gaines, Willard Roland (1921 P) "Nemo." Gaines was nicknamed after the comic strip character "Nemo" in "Little Nemo in Slumberland" created by Windsor McKay, which first appeared in 1905 in the *New York Herald* newspaper.

1238. Gainor, Dallos Clinton (1909-22 1B) "Sheriff." Origin unknown.

1239. Galan, August John (1934-49 OF) "Goo Goo." Galan was called "Goo Goo" by his teammates referring to his prominent eyes. Charles Grimm may have been the first to use the tag when Galan joined the Chicago Cubs in 1934.

1240. Galarraga, Andres (1985- 1B) "Big Cat." In size, hitting ability and quick moves at first base, Galarraga reminds many of John "Big Cat" Mize.

1241. Gallagher, Alan Mitchell Edward George Patrick Henry (1970-73 3B) "Dirty Al." Gallagher was an only child born to his parents after they had waited eight years to have a child. They assigned to him many of the names they had been considering during that time, six to be exact. "Dirty Al" as a nickname refers to the state of his uniform which some said was always so dirty that it made the "Gashouse Gang" look like men from Glad. Gallagher was also called "Pig Pen," "The Dirty Man," and "Filthy McNasty." Mike Mandel lets Gallagher himself explain the origin of the "Dirty Al" nickname: "My ol' buddy Sam McDowell once said, he was with about ten reporters one day and they were asking him all sorts of questions. He said, 'I'll tell one the way you want to hear it.' So I think this goes back to the 'Dirty Al' story. People just called me 'Dirty Al' for a long time because of the way I played, I always got dirty. I wasn't interested in girls, I was interested in sports. That was kind of dirty to begin with. Guy's got to be goofy, he loves baseball instead of a broad.... How could somebody be so idiotic? But I did. When I was in college, they had a greased pig contest. And I wasn't even in it. I had my regular clothes on, but I decided to catch the greased pig. Caught the greased pig, threw it up in the air and went to the microphone. I had a couple drinks. And I made an announcement that the world's greatest greased pig catcher was Al Gallagher in my typical manner. Then I went to the dance with this pig still all over me smelling up high heaven. And I'd be asking all these debutante girls we had at Santa Clara. We had some pretty high class girls, because it's a pretty high class school. And I'd be asking them to dance and we'd start dancing and then all of a sudden they'd smell that pig. Oh! They got excited! That was a big joke and I'd do it five or six times before it got around all over the place. Then I couldn't get no more dancing so I had to go home. I had a hitting streak at Santa Clara and it went twenty-two games in a row and I didn't change my uniform. Which doesn't sound too bad in professional baseball, except here we played about three games a week, so we're talking about eight weeks I never changed anything, my jock strap, my sanitaries, my sweatshirt, nothing. And I wouldn't let 'em wash 'em either. So I had a couple of open stalls next to my locker. But I was kind of superstitious and I didn't want to wash out those hits. So pick out whichever 'Dirty Al' story you like best."

1242. Gallagher, Edward Michael (1932 P) "Lefty." Gallagher pitched left handed, but was a switch hitter.

1243. Gallagher, Joseph Emmett (1939–40 OF) "Muscles." Gallagher was strong and well built with large biceps, at 6'2" and 210 pounds.

1244. Gallagher, Lawrence Kirby (1922 SS) "Gil." "Gil" is a short take off on the last name of Gallagher.

1245. Gallia, Melvin Allys (1912–20 P) "Bert." Origin unknown.

1246. Galloway, Clarence Edward (1919–28 SS) "Chick." As a child, playmates began to call Galloway "Chick" in place of Clarence.

1247. Galloway, James Cato (1912 2B) "Bad News." While he was playing semi-pro baseball, Galloway was a telegrapher. In order to break away for games, he would have a friend in another office fake a message to him that a relative was ill and needed to see him. He received so many of these bad news messages during the course of the season, that other employees began calling him "Bad News."

1248. Galvin, James Frances (1875–94 P) "Gentle Jeems." Galvin was one of the great 19th century pitchers, winning 361 games in just 14 years. In 1884, he won 46 games for Buffalo while dropping 22 with an ERA of 1.99. Galvin had a pleasant personality which accounts for why he was called "Gentle." "Jeems" is an affected way of saying James. Tom Shea reports this was a common literary expression of the times. Galvin was often addressed as "Pud," which is short for "Pudding." He made pudding out of opposing batters. "The Little Steam Engine" was another nickname used for Galvin. Joseph McBride reports that it referred to his tireless work. Bill James suggests it referred to his fastball and he may have been the first hurler to have his pitches likened to a train. Galvin was 5'8" and weighed about 190 pounds at the start of his career. Bill Borst reports that in the latter stages of his career, Galvin approached 300 pounds.

1249. Gammons, John Ashley (1901 OF) "Daff." "Daff" is short for "Daffy" and refers to Gammons' eccentric behavior off the field of play.

1250. Gandy, Robert Brinkley (1916 P) "String." "String" refers to Gandy's build. He was 6'3" and weighed 180 pounds.

1251. Gannon, James Edward (1895 P) "Gussie." "Gussie" was a pet name given to Gannon by friends with no apparent meaning.

1252. Gantenbein, Joseph Steven (1939–40 2B) "Sep." Origin unknown.

1253. Ganter, James Elmer (1976– 2B) "Gumby." The nickname was given to Ganter by his Milwaukee Brewer teammates. Ganter was a master of "gumming" things up with a mixed metaphor, a non-sequitur, or the nonsensical. Once, when he failed to show up for a radio appearance his explanation was: "I must have ambrosia."

1254. Ganzel, Foster Pirie (1927–28 OF) "Babe." Ganzel was a home run hitting outfielder in the minor leagues. He was so respected that in 1927, he drew 114 walks with Birmingham of the Southern Association, before joining Washington at the end of the season. His father, Charles Ganzel, was a major league catcher, 1884–97. Foster, as he was addressed, was the baby Ganzel. He also had an uncle, John Henry Ganzel who appeared as a pitcher in one game for Pittsburgh in 1898.

1255. Garcia, Alfonso Rafael (1976–85 SS) "Kiko." Garcia wrote me: "'Kiko' is the nickname for Frank or Francisco in Spanish. But my grandmother used to call me Chicquito which means small boy in Spanish. Eventually, it became 'Kiko'."

1256. Garcia, Edward Miguel (1948–61 P) "The Big Bear." Garcia was 6'1" and weighed 195 pounds. He was nicknamed by his Cleveland Indian teammates because of his size, and broad, rounded, sloped shoulders, in addition to long arms.

1257. Garcia, Vinicio Uzcanga (1954 2B) "Chico." "Chico" is a common Latin American nickname meaning kid or small.

1258. Gardella, Daniel Lewis (1944–50 OF) "Dauntless Dan." Fred Stein describes Gardella: "He was an amusing colorful native New Yorker with a blithe, free-spirited approach to life in general and baseball in particular."

1259. Gardner, Franklin W. (1879–88 OF) "Gid." "Gid" was a take off on the last name of Gardner.

1260. Gardner, Richard Frank (1965–73 P) "Rob." Origin unknown.

1261. Gardner, William Frederick (1954–63 2B) "Shotgun." The nickname, "Shotgun" refers to Gardner's strong throwing arm. He was also dubbed "Goofball" by teammates because of his idiosyncracies off the field.

1262. Garner, Philip Mason (1973–88 2B) "Scrap Iron." Garner told me: "In 1977, my first year with Pittsburgh, Willie Stirgell said you could bend me, twist me, beat on me, but you could not break me like a piece of scrap iron."

1263. Garr, Ralph Allen (1968–80 OF) "Road Runner." Garr possessed great speed. He was nicknamed after the lightning quick bird character in the "Road Runner" cartoon series created by Chuck Jones.

1264. Garrett, Clarence Raymond (1915 P) "Laz." "Laz" is short for "Lazy" for which Garnett had a reputation.

1265. Garriott, Virgil Cecil (1946 PH) "Rabbit." Garriott was 5'8" tall and very swift. However, he had little chance to show his speed in the major leagues appearing in but six games and failing to get a hit in five times at bat.

...Officials, Writers, Broadcasters   Gehrig   99

1266. Garrison, Robert Ford (1943–46 OF) "Snapper." Garrison told me: "At about 8 years of age, my dad nicknamed me after a famous jockey after the turn of the century. He always hoped I would be a jockey." Garrison grew to 5'10½" tall and weighed 180 pounds, hardly jockey size.

1267. Garrity, Francis Joseph (1931 C) "Hank." Origin unknown.

1268. Gassaway, Charles Cason (1944–46 P) "Sheriff." In the off season Gassaway was a member of the Tennessee State Police force.

1269. Gaston, Clarence Edwin (1967–78 OF) "Cito." While in high school in San Antonio, Texas, Gaston was nicknamed by a friend after a famous Mexican wrestler named "Cito."

1270. Gau, George Joseph (1920 P) "Chippy." Origin unknown.

1271. Gautreau, Walter Paul (1925–28 2B) "Doc." Gautreau had no medical or dental training. The "Doc" nickname began about the time he started performing in the major leagues, but the reason why is unclear.

1272. Gautreaux, Sidney Allen (1936–37 C) "Pudge." At 5'8" and weighing 195 pounds, Gautreaux was on the heavy side.

1273. Gearin, Dennis John (1922–24 P) "Dinty." "Dinty" is a take off on the first name of Dennis.

1274. Geary, Eugene Francis Joseph (1942–43 SS) "Huck." Geary reminded people of the character "Huckleberry Finn" in the novels of Samuel Clemens, *Tom Sawyer*, and *The Adventures of Huckleberry Finn*.

1275. Geary, Robert Norton (1918–21 P) "Speed." "Speed" recognizes Geary's fastball pitching.

1276. Gebrian, Peter (1947 P) "Gabe." "Gabe" is the way the first part of the name of Gebrian is pronounced.

1277. Gee, John Alexander (1939–46 P) "Whiz." "Whiz" is a response to the last name of Gee. He was one of the tallest players in major league history at 6'9". Because of his height, he was declared 4F in the military draft during World War II.

1278. Gehrig, Henry Louis (1923–39 1B) "Iron Horse." If George Herman "Babe" Ruth was the heart of the great New York Yankee teams of the 1920s and early 1930s, then Lou Gehrig was the soul. The less boisterous, less gregarious, less colorful Gehrig probably contributed as much to the Yankee's success as Ruth. Perhaps his most amazing feat is that which led to the "Iron Horse" nickname. From June 1, 1925, until May 2, 1939, Gehrig played in 2,130 consecutive games. The reference was to the old wood-burning locomotives that traversed the plains in the 1880s. Gehrig removed himself from the lineup, because of what was later diagnosed as a rare muscle disease called amyotrophic lateral sclerosis. It would claim his life in just over two years. Ironically, today, what might be called this malady's nickname is "Lou Gehrig's Disease." Gehrig's consecutive game streak overshadows some of his other accomplishments which led to the affectionate sobriquet, "Pride of the Yankees." For example: Gehrig hit 535 doubles, 493 home runs, scored 1,188 runs and drove in 1,990 runs, collected 1,503 walks and posted a career average of .340. He was the first American League player to hit four home runs in a game and had 23 career grand slam home runs. In 1931, he became baseball's all-time run producer by scoring 163 runs and driving in 175. Gehrig led the American League in RBIs three times, runs scored and total bases four times, and slugging percentage twice. He won the triple crown (home runs, RBIs and batting average) twice and in 1936, he won the American League's most valuable player award. Finally, today an almost forgotten statistic seems incredible for a slugger: Gehrig stole home 15 times during his career. When he was still in high school, Gehrig played for New York's Commerce High School in a game against Chicago's Lane Technical High School in Wrigley Field. He hit a grand slam home run out of the park. The next day, New York newspapers referred to him as "The Babe Ruth of the High Schools." In 1924, he was called "Babe Ruth of the Rookies." During the early years of his career, he was given the place nickname of "Columbia Lou" because he had attended Columbia University. A strictly media hype nickname was "Larrupin Lou." He was also called "Biscuit Pants" because of his running back's low center of gravity. Six inches off the ground. Teammates often addressed Gehrig as "Buster" a nickname borrowed by Ruth who had difficulty remembering names. Finally, for what it's worth, Yankee teammates sometimes called Gehrig "Little Joe" because he wore the number 4 on his uniform. A four on the roll of the dice was known as a "Little Joe" in the game of Parcheesi, which was popular at the time.

1279. Gehringer, Charles Leonard (1924–42 2B) "Mechanical Man." In 19 seasons, Gehringer collected 2,839 hits with a career average of .320. He attracted 1,185 walks compared to just 372 strike outs. Detroit Tiger teammates said of Gehringer: "All you have to do is wind him up on opening day and he runs on and on—doing everything right." "Mickey" Cochrane, Detroit manager, once remarked about Gehringer's Sphinx-like demeanor: "He says hello on opening day, and goodbye on closing day, and in between he hits .350."

1280. Gehrman, Paul Arthur (1937 P) "Dutch." "Dutch" referred to Gehrman's German background.

1281. Geier, Philip Louis (1896–1904 OF) "Little Phil." Geier was 5'7" and weighed 140 pounds.

1282. Genins, C. Frank (1892–1901 OF) "Frenchy." Genins was of French background.

1283. Gentile, James Edward (1957–66 1B) "Diamond Jim." Gentile had the reputation of being a big, hot-headed, free spirit.

1284. George, Charles Peter (1935–45 C) "Greek George." George was of Greek background. He wrote me that he received his nickname "Greek George" in 1932, while attending Oglethorp College. Classmates stole an advertisement about a movie featuring Greeks and attached it to the door of his dorm room. Larry Gerlach quotes umpire Joe Rue describing George's behavior in 1945. "He was a habitual bellyacher, a real crybaby," a busher of the worst sort. The umpires in every league he had been in always had trouble with this fellow. Well, he was catching that day, jerking the ball, trying to fool me, and complaining. So I told him if he didn't shape up I would run him. At the end of the tenth inning I was brushing off the plate when he hit me over the left eye. (He said I called him a Greek son of a bitch, but I never cursed a ball player in my life.) I staggered back but then went after him with my mask. I chased him all around the back of the plate.... I'm yelling and cursing and now I probably am calling him a Greek son of a bitch."

1285. George, Thomas Edward (1911–18 P) "Lefty." George pitched left handed, and batted left handed.

1286. Gerber, Walter (1914–29 SS) "Spooks." "Spooks" referred to his quick hands at shortstop. They were spooky. He led American League shortstops in double plays four times.

1287. Gerhard, David Frederick (1962 P) "Jug." Gerhard's best pitch was a curveball.

1288. Gerhardt, Allen Russell (1974 P) "Rusty." "Rusty" is a take off on the middle name of Russell.

1289. Gerhardt, John Joseph (1876–91 2B) "Move Up Joe." Joseph McBride reports that Gerhardt used to shout from the coaching box for runners to "move-up." However, an article by John Halderman in the *Louisville Courier Journal* of June 6, 1877, suggests that "Move Up Joe" referred to Gerhardt's ability to take an extra base. David Nemec interprets "move up" to mean moving runners on, which, he points out, Gerhardt did very little of once he had to face over-hand pitching.

1290. Gerheauser, Albert (1943–48 P) "Lefty." Gerheauser pitched left handed, and batted right handed.

1291. Gerken, George Herbert (1927–28 OF) "Pickles." "Pickles" is a response to the last name of Gerken.

1292. Gerkin, Stephen Paul (1945 P) "Splinter." "Splinter" refers to Gerkin's 6'1", 160-pound build. Playing only in the war time year of 1945, Gerkin compiled a 0-12 won-lost record for the Philadelphia Phils, while batting .039. Gerkin holds the National League record for most losses in a season without a win.

1293. Gerner, Edwin Frederick (1919 P) "Lefty." Gerner pitched left handed, and batted left handed.

1294. Gervais, Lucien Edward (1919 P) "Lefty." Gervais pitched left handed, and batted left handed.

1295. Gessler, Harvey Homer (1903–11 OF) "Doc." Gessler was known for his feats of strength. He was one of three "Docs" in the 1906 World Series (with White and Owen). Gessler became a practicing physician after graduating from Johns Hopkins Medical School.

1296. Getz, Gustave (1909–18 3B) "Gee Gee." Getz was known by his initials G.G., but in print it turned out to be "Gee Gee."

1297. Gettman, Jacob John (1897–99 OF) "Quick." Gettman had great speed and led the Texas League in stolen bases in 1897 before coming up to the Washington Senators for the last 37 games of the season and stealing another eight bases.

1298. Getzien, Charles H. (1884–92 P) "Pretzels." According to Fred Lieb, Getzien came from a German background. In the 1890s, Germans were closely associated with beer and pretzels. So, "Pretzels" referred to German background and not to any physical characteristic or pitching mannerisms.

1299. Geyer, Jacob Bowman (1910–13 P) "Rube." Geyer came from a rural background and was not comfortable with big city ways. The "Rube" reference is to George Waddell.

1300. Geygan, James Edward (1924–26 SS) "Chappie." Origin unknown.

1301. Giard, Joseph Oscar (1925–27 P) "Peco." Origin unknown.

1302. Gibbs, Jerry Dean (1962–71 C) "Jake." Gibbs, an All American football player in college, was given the nickname of "Jake" by his mother at an early age. For all practical purposes, it replaced his first name of Jerry.

1303. Gibson, George C. (1905–18 C) "Moon." "Moon" described the roundness of Gibson's face. Gibson was born in London, Ontario, Canada. In 1925, he became interim manager for the Chicago Cubs and posted a 12-14 won-lost record. Gibson was the first, and to this date, the only Canadian born major league manager.

1304. Gibson, Joshua (1930–46 C, Negro League) "Boxer." In the Negro leagues his Homestead Gray teammates called him "Boxer." They said he caught foul balls as though he was wearing boxing gloves. Batting in the third slot for the Homestead Grays in front of "Buck Leonard" ("The Black Lou Gehrig"), Gibson's power and long home runs earned him the title of "The Black Babe Ruth." He was one, if not the greatest of Negro League home run hitters. It is alleged that he once hit a ball out of Yankee Stadium and that he had 72 home runs in a year. When he played in Latin America, his Spanish nickname was "Chimpance," meaning chimpanzee.

1305. Gibson, Leighton Henry (1888 C) "Whitey." The nickname refers to hair color.

1306. Gibson, Robert (1959–75 P) "Hoot." Gibson was a fierce competitor and perhaps the most intimidating pitcher of the 1960s. He worked rapidly with little time spent between pitches and would not hesitate to throw a brush back pitch to his closest friend. In 1968, Gibson started 34 games and completed 28, allowing just 198 hits and 62 walks and compiled an incredible ERA of 1.12 in 305 innings. He pitched 13 shutouts of which five were in succession, and allowed just one run in 11 other appearances. In the first game of the 1968 World Series, he struck out 17 Detroit Tigers. Gibson won 251 games in his 17-year career and was credited with 3,117 strikeouts. He was nicknamed "Hoot" after the cowboy movie star, Edmund "Hoot" Gibson.

1307. Gilbert, Drew Edward (1959 OF) "Buddy." Gilbert told me: "My parents did not particularly like Drew or my middle name Edward. Very early they decided to call me 'Buddy'."

1308. Gilbert, Harold Joseph (1950–53 1B) "Tookie." At age two, Gilbert mispronounced cookie. It came out "Tookie," and his older brother began calling him that and soon the whole family did.

1309. Gilbert, John Robert (1898–1904 OF) "Jackrabbit." "Jackrabbit" refers to Gilbert's speed on the base paths and in the outfield.

1310. Gile, Donald Loren (1959–62 C) "Bear." Gile was 6'6" and weighed 220 pounds. Teammate San Jose gave him the nickname of "Bear" when they were playing in the Pacific Coast League in 1955.

1311. Gilhooley, Frank Patrick (1911–19 OF) "Flash." "Flash" referred to Gilhooley's speed in the outfield.

1312. Gill, Harold Edward (1923 P) "Haddie." "Haddie" is a take off on the first name of Harold.

1313. Gill, John Westley (1927–36 OF) "Patcheye." There is a suggestion in the literature that Gil may have played a game with a patch over an injured eye. However, I have not been able to document that this happened.

1314. Gill, Warren Darst (1908 1B) "Doc." Many of the players with the nickname of "Doc" had a close association with either the medical or dental professions. With Gil, however, the origin of "Doc" is unknown.

1315. Gillespie, John Patrick (1922 P) "Silent John." Gillespie was one of those players who had little to say to anyone on or off the field.

1316. Gillespie, Robert William (1944–50 P) "Bunch." Gillespie stood 6'4". It was said he was a "Bunch," meaning big.

1317. Gilliam, James William (1953–66 2B) "Junior." Gilliam was one of the unheralded players of the great Dodger teams of the 1950s and 60s both in Brooklyn and Los Angeles. He performed more than adequately at second base, third base and in the outfield collecting 1,889 hits in 14 seasons and playing in seven World Series. He was 17 years old when he joined the Baltimore Elite Giants in the Negro Leagues. Teammates immediately christened him "Junior." Gilliam hated the nickname, but it stuck with him throughout his career.

1318. Gilliford, Paul Gant (1967 P) "Gorilla." Gilliford, who pitched in only 2 major league games, told me he received the nickname of "Gorilla" while playing for the Miami Marlins of the Florida State League. A fight started on the field during a game in which he was coaching first base, not pitching. He said, "I arrived on the scene and grabbed a player and put a gorilla hold on him and that ended the fight. After that, manager Billy Demars called me 'Gorilla'."

1319. Gilmore, Leonard Preston (1944 P) "Meow." Gilmore wrote me: "When I played in California, there was a brand of gasoline called Gilmore. It had a Lion as a trademark. A San Francisco sportswriter wrote in an account of a game that I roared like a lion, but purred like a kitten. The next day, players on the bench started to call me 'Meow,' but it was short lived." Gilmore started and lost the only game he pitched in the major leagues, giving up 8 runs and 13 hits in 8 innings.

1320. Gilson, Harold (1968 P) "Lefty." Gilson pitched left handed, but batted right handed.

1321. Ginsberg, Myron Nathan (1948–62 C) "Joe." Ginsberg did not like the name of Myron and decided to use his father's name Joe, instead. In other words, he chose his own nickname.

1322. Gionfriddo, Albert Francis (1944–47 OF) "The Little Italian." Gronfriddo was 5'6" and of Italian background. He is best known for his sparkling catch of Joe DiMaggio's 415-foot blast in game six of the 1947 Dodger-Yankee World Series.

1323. Giordano, Thomas Arthur (1953 2B) "T-Bone." Origin unknown.

1324. Gladman, John H. (1883–86 3B) "Buck." "Buck" is a generic nickname of which the circumstances of origin are almost never documented. It refers to a well developed, virile, aggressive young man. It is usually bestowed on the individual during his teenage years.

1325. Glaiser, John Burke (1920 P) "Bert." "Bert" was an alternative to the middle name of Burke, but was not used much. Glaiser was usually addressed as John.

1326. Glasscock, John Wesley (1879–95 SS) "Pebbly Jack." Glasscock was the best fielding shortstop of the 1880s and '90s. The infields of the day contained many pebbles, which often caused the ball to change directions. Glasscock earned his nickname by the tireless way he would pick up small stones from the diamond and toss them away. Glasscock was also a good hitter, collecting 2,040 hits in 17 seasons with a career average of .290.

1327. Glaviano, Thomas Giatano (1949–52 3B) "Rabbit." Glaviano told me he got the nickname in 1946 when he stole 64 bases for Fresno in the Pacific Coast League. Paul Bowa, the father of future major league shortstop Larry Bowa, thought he was fast as a rabbit.

1328. Glazner, Charles Franklin (1920–24 P) "Whitey." The nickname refers to hair color.

1329. Gleason, William J. (1888–1912 2B) "Kid." Gleason played for 22 years in the major leagues. From 1888–94, he was primarily a pitcher; in fact, in 1890, he won 38 games while dropping 17. For the remainder of his career he played second base collecting a career 1,944 hits. The "Kid" nickname came early in his career because he wore his cap on the back of his head like a little boy.

1330. Gleeson, James Joseph (1936–42 OF) "Gee Gee." Gleeson told me: "It started in high school as my initials J.G. and then turned into G.G. While I was in college a sportswriter from a Kansas City newspaper wrote it out in print Gee Gee."

1331. Gleich, Frank Elmer (1919–23 OF) "Inch." Origin unknown.

1332. Glenn, Burdette (1920 P) "Bob." Origin unknown.

1333. Glenn, Joseph Charles (1932–40 C) "Gabber." Glen was very talkative, especially to batters when he was catching.

1334. Goan, Joshua Mercer (1896–98 P) "Jot." "Jot" was a take off on the first name of Joshua.

1335. Goldstein, Leslie Elmer (1943–46 1B) "Lonnie." "Lonnie" was used as an alternative to the first name of Leslie.

1336. Goletz, Stanley (1941 PH) "Stash." "Stash" denoted Goletz's Polish background.

1337. Gomez, Jose Luis Rodriguez (1935–42 2B) "Chile." "Chile" brought attention to Gomez's Mexican background. He was from Villoumion, Mexico.

1338. Gomez, Ruben Colon (1953–67 P) "El Divino Loco." Gomez built a reputation for doing "crazy" things on and off the field. The nickname translates "The Divine Crazy." It was given to him by players.

1339. Gomez, Vernon Louis (1930–43 P) "Lefty." Gomez pitched left handed and batted left handed. In 14 seasons, Gomez posted a .649 winning percentage in 189 wins, 102 losses. In 1934, he won 26 and lost only 5 for a winning percentage of .839. Gomez was also called "The Gay Castillian" referring to his fun-loving personality and Spanish heritage. In addition, Gomez earned the tag "Goofy" early in his career after he told a sportswriter he had invented a revolving gold fish bowl so that the fish would be able to see everything without having to swim! Jimmy Powers reports the following incident: "His reputation as 'El Goofy' was established solidly when asked about his greatest ambition. He thought a moment and then said solemnly, 'It's a critical game before a packed crowd at the stadium. In the ninth inning, the bases are loaded, our pitcher is beginning to fade and McCarthy orders me to the mound.'

'And then I come roaring out of the bull pen riding a motorcycle and wearing a full suit of armor'."

1340. Good, Wilbur David (1905–18 OF) "Lefty." Good threw left handed, and batted left handed.

1341. Goodell, John Henry (1928 P) "Lefty." Goodell pitched left handed, but batted right handed.

1342. Gooden, Dwight Eugene (1984 P) "Dr. K." E.M. Swift quotes Gooden's father on the nickname. "You know how he got that name, Dr. K? A friend of mine used to yell to him in little league, 'come on doctor operate on him!'" Kevin Nelson reports it differently. He says that as a young boy Gooden admired Julius Erving, the great basketball player, whose nickname was "Dr. J." Ralph Kiner, New York Mets announcer, adds a third version. "During his rookie year a group of young fans showed up at the ball park with 'K' signs which they posted in the upper left field stands after each Gooden strikeout. In a short time, it became a craze and Gooden was dubbed as 'Dr. K.' It was a play on Julius Erving's 'Dr. J.' tag."

1343. Goodwin, Claire Vernon (1914–15 SS) "Pep." Goodwin played with great enthusiasm and energy.

1344. Goolsby, Raymond Daniel (1946 OF) "Ox." At 6'1" and weighing 185 pounds, writers thought he was big, strong and strapping—tough as an ox.

1345. Gorden, Joseph Lowell (1938–50 2B) "Flash." According to Tom Shea, and Joseph McBride, Gorden was considered flashy at both bat and with the glove at second base when he first came up with the Yankees. The nickname came from the futuristic character, Flash Gordon, in the comic strip and movie-serial of the same name created by Alex Raymond which first appeared in Sunday newspapers in 1934.

1346. Gore, George F. (1879–92 OF) "Piano Legs." Gore had extremely stocky legs. But despite that, he once stole seven bases in a game, and in another recorded five extra base hits. Gore was known for his love of night life, wine and women, which his manager on the Chicago White Stockings, "Cap" Anson said were his downfall.

1347. Gorman, Howard Paul (1937–38 OF) "Lefty." Gorman threw left handed, and batted left handed.

1348. Gorman, John F. (1883–84 1B) "Stooping Jack." Origin unknown.

1349. Gorman, Thomas David (1939 P) "Big Tom"; (NL Umpire 1951–76) "Easy." Gorman was 6'2" and weighed 200 pounds. He was called "Big Tom" during his playing days. As an umpire, Richie Allen thought Gorman did his job very easily and gave him the nickname of "Easy."

1350. Gornicki, Frank Ted (1941–46 P) "Hank." "Hank" is a substitute for Frank, but the exact origin is unknown.

1351. Goslin, Leon Allen (1921–38 OF) "Goose." Goslin was one of the premiere hitters of the 1920s and '30s. In 18 years he batted .316 with 2,735 hits including 258 home runs. During his rookie year with Washington in 1921, he had difficulty catching fly balls. Sportswriter Denmar Thompson gave him the nickname "Goose" because of his goose-like nose which many felt might be pulverized if Goslin misjudged a fly ball.

1352. Gossage, Richard Michael (1972–89 P) "Goose." Gossage at 6'3" and 180 pounds, with a mean look and an over powering fastball became one of the most intimidating relief pitchers of the 1970s and '80s. He recorded 104 relief wins, second on the all-time list, and 307 saves forth on the all list. Joseph McBride reports the nickname stems from 1977 when he was with Pittsburgh and kept a pet goose in the bull pen.

1353. Gossett, John Star (1913–14 C) "Dick." Origin unknown.

1354. Goulait, Theodore Frank (1912 P) "Snooze." Origin unknown.

1355. Gowdy, Curt (1948– Announcer) "The Cowboy." Gowdy was born, raised and went to school in the cowboy country of Wyoming. He earned six letters in varsity baseball and basketball at the University of Wyoming. Gowdy started broadcasting Yankee games in 1948 and was with the Boston Red Sox from 1953–65 before leaving for NBC. Curt Smith's comments on Gowdy: "He was, at heart, a small-town boy and his style was a basic, earthy one. It was streaked with numbers, anecdotes, and a penchant for fact; and if less poetic than Scully, or exciting as Prince, or dependent on punch lines than Garagiola, revealed a natural, honest delivery that made one intersperse the terms *meticulous, professional,* and *fair.*"

1356. Grabowski, John Patrick (1924–31 C) "Nig." Grabowski was called "Nig" because of his dark complexion. It is sometimes forgotten that Grabowski caught in 68 games for the 1927 Yankees, one if not the best teams of all time.

1357. Grabowski, Reginald (1932–34 P) "Hook." Grabowski was a curveball pitcher.

1358. Graff, Louis George (1890 C) "Chappie." Origin unknown.

1359. Graham, Arthur William, Jr. (1934–35 OF) "Skinny." "Skinny" is a nickname opposite. Graham stood but 5'7" and weighed 181 pounds.

1360. Graham, Dawson Francis (1914 1B) "Tiny." "Tiny" is a nickname opposite. Graham was 6'2" and weighed 185 pounds.

1361. Graham, George Frederick (1905 OF) "Moonlight." Furman Bisher suggests that Graham liked to "Whoop" it up at night, but there is no evidence to substantiate that allegation. Bisher is not the most reliable source on nicknames. Graham appears as a character in W.P. Kinsella's novel, *Shoeless Joe* and the subsequent movie, *Field of Dreams.* Graham appeared in one game in the outfield for the New York Giants in 1905, but never got to bat. According to Kinsella, in the novel, one night as a minor league player he could not sleep. He got up and dressed in his uniform and was seen roaming the nearby ballpark in the moonlight by his teammates. Graham, in the novel, later becomes a physician in Minnesota.

1362. Graham, George Frederick (1902–12 C) "Peaches." Tom Shea reports that fans called Graham a "peach" of a catcher.

1363. Graham, Kyle (1924–29 P) "Skinny." Graham was 6'2" and weighed 172 pounds.

1364. Grant, Charles (1896–1910 2B, Negro League) "Chief Tokahoma." Manager John McGraw of the American League Baltimore Orioles tried to use Grant in 1901 masquerading him as an Indian by the name of "Chief Tokahoma." Grant was unmasked as a Negro not Indian in Chicago, and the color banner was preserved. Although not strictly a nickname, it seems worth including in this list.

1365. Grant, Edward Leslie (1905–15 3B) "Harvard Eddie." This is a place nickname, Grant attended Harvard University. After the 1915 season he joined the Army and was killed in the battle of the Argon Forest, October 15, 1918, in World War I. A monument was erected in his honor in far center field of the Polo Grounds. The New York Giants had been the last team for which he played.

1366. Grant, Frank (1886–1903 2B, Negro League) "The Black Dunlap." Grant was compared with a contemporary second baseman, Fred "Sure Shot Dunlap" who played in the major leagues 1880–91. Robert Peterson writes of Grant: "The first Negro in organized baseball in 1886 was a cherubic twenty-year-old named Frank Grant, who was probably the best of the black players who appeared in white leagues during the early years. He was a strong hitter, and his play at second base earned him the sobriquet 'The Black Dunlap': a single compliment, because Fred Dunlap, the St. Louis second baseman and the first player to reach the $10,000 a year salary level, was regarded as the best at the position."

1367. Grant, James Timothy (1958–71 P) "Mudcat." When Grant was playing for Fargo-Moorehead in the Northern League in 1954, teammate Bartow Irby thought he was from Mississippi. He nicknamed him "Mudcat" because Mississippi is called the "Mudcat" state. The nickname stuck even though Irby was wrong. Grant was from Lacoochee, Florida.

1368. Grantham, George Farley (1922–34 2B) "Boots." In 1922 while playing for Omaha, he made 57 errors. In 1923 as a rookie for the Chicago Cubs he made 99 errors at second base in 150 games. He was dubbed "Boots" by Chicago sportswriters.

1369. Grasso, Newton Michael (1946–55 C) "Mickey." Grasso was nicknamed after catcher Gordon "Mickey" Cochrane who he was thought to resemble.

1370. Grate, Donald (1945–46 P) "Buckeye." This is a place nickname. Grate was from Greenfield, Ohio. Ohio is called the "Buckeye" state.

1371. Gray, George Edward (1899 P) "Chummy." Origin unknown.

1372. Gray, James D. (1890–92 P) "Reddy." The nickname refers to hair color.

1373. Gray, Samuel David (1924–33 P) "Sad Sam." Gray was nicknamed after Samuel Pond "Sad Sam" Jones who he resembled in size, pitching style, ability, and whose career he overlapped.

1374. Gray, Stanley Oscar (1912 1B) "Dolly." Gray was nicknamed after William Denton "Dolly" Gray whose career ended in 1911.

1375. Gray, William Denton (1909–11 P) "Dolly." Gray was nicknamed from the lyric in the song "Oh My Darling" which uses Nellie Gray. Teammates garbled "Darling" and it came out "Dolly."

1376. Greason, William Henry (1954 P) "Booster." Origin unknown.

1377. Green, Edward (1898–1905 OF) "Danny." Origin unknown.

1378. Green, Elijah Jerry (1959–63 2B) "Pumpsie." Green's mother is responsible for the nickname of "Pumpsie." It is merely a take off on "Pumpkin." Green told me that everyone in his hometown calls him by his nickname. "Few would know my real name."

1379. Green, Harvey George (1935 P) "Buck." "Buck" is a generic nickname of which the circumstances are almost never documented. It refers to a well developed, virile, aggressive, high spirited young man. It is usually bestowed on the individual during his teenage years.

1380. Green, Joseph Henry (1924 PH) "Tilly." Origin unknown.

1381. Greenburg, Henry Benjamin (1933–47 1B) "Hammerin' Hank." Greenburg was a 6'4" and 210-pound power hitting first baseman for the Detroit Tigers. He led the American League in home runs four times, including 1938 when he hit 58. Only Ruth with 59 and 60 and Maris with 61 have surpassed that total. Greenburg also led the American League in RBIs four times. In his banner year of 1937 he drove in 183 runs. Only Hack Wilson with 190 and Lou Gehrig's 184 rank higher than Greenburg. For these feats he earned the nickname of "Hammerin' Hank."

1382. Greene, Nelson George (1924–25 P) "Lefty." Greene pitched left handed, and batted left handed.

1383. Greenlee, William Augustus (1931–38 Owner) "Big Red." During the 1930s nearly everyone in Pittsburgh's black community knew Greenlee. They patronized his nightclubs (especially the Crawford Grill, a mecca for jazz aficionados), drank his bootleg liquor, spent money on his numbers operations, cheered his stable of boxers (especially John Henry Lewis, the first American black light-heavyweight champion) and attended numerous other sporting events he sponsored. For blacks he was Pittsburgh's "Mr. Big." In 1931 he became the owner of one of the area's top sandlot teams, the Crawfords. Between 1931–38 Greenlee built the club into one of the finest in the Negro leagues, and constructed one of the nation's finest black controlled stadiums. Such future Hall of Famers as Oscar Charleston, "Judy" Johnson, "Cool" Papa Bell, "Satchel" Paige, and Josh Gibson toiled for the Crawfords. Greenlee resurrected the Negro National League and as president, managed to achieve financial stability for the organization. At 6'3", 200 pounds and light skinned, Greenlee fit his "Big Red" nickname.

1384. Gregg, David Charles (1913 P) "High Pockets." Gregg stood 6'1" and had very long legs.

1385. Gregory, Paul Edwin (1913 P) "Pop." Origin unknown.

1386. Gremminger, Lorenzo Edward (1895–1904 3B) "Battleship." Gremminger was 6'1" and weighed 200 pounds. In 1893–94 he played for a topflight independent team called the Canton Marines.

1387. Gremp, Louis Edward (1940–42 1B) "Buddy." "Buddy" is a childhood nickname of family origin.

1388. Grey, Romer Carl (1903 OF) "Reddy." The nickname refers to hair color. Romer was the brother of the famous author Zane Grey. He was probably one of the characters in Zane Grey's famous short story "The Red Headed Outfield."

1389. Grier, Claude (1925–28 P, Negro League) "Red." On October 3, 1926, pitching for the Atlantic City Bacharach Giants against the Chicago American Giants in the Negro World Series, Grier pitched a no-hitter. The nickname "Red" referred to his light skin.

1390. Griesenbeck, Carlos Phillipe (1920 C) "Tim." Origin unknown.

1391. Griffin, Francis Arthur (1917–20 1B) "Pug." Origin unknown.

1392. Griffin, James Linton (1911–12 P) "Hank." Origin unknown. Also known as "Pepper."

1393. Griffith, Clark Calvin (1891–1914 P) "The Old Fox." Clark Griffith pitched in the major leagues for 21 years, and won 240 games while losing only 141. Seven times he won 20 games or more in a season. He managed for 20 years, 1905–19 with a winning percentage of .522. Ironically, his only first place finish was during his first year as player-manager of the Chicago White Sox in 1901. His worst finish was seventh with the Washington Senators in 1916. By this time he was part owner of the team. While Griffith was known as a wily manager and executive, his nickname "The Old Fox" derives from his playing days as a pitcher. He was guilty of much chicanery on the mound. Allen explains through the words of umpire Bill Bryan: "For a little fellow he was pretty good. He used to stand out there on the rubber and spend minutes knocking the ball against his spikes, pretending there was dirt on them, and meanwhile scuffing up the cover of the ball." It is not known who first used "The Old Fox" nickname, but likely it was one of his opponents. It is sometimes forgotten that when Griffith first arrived in the major leagues in 1893, he was called "Dago" by his Chicago teammates because of his dark hair and complexion. This term is usually used to refer to individuals of Italian decent of which Griffith was not.

1394. Grimes, Burleigh Arland (1916–34 P) "Old Stubblebeard." Grimes won 270 games in his 19-year career and collected 380 hits for a .248 average. He was the last of the spitball pitchers. The spitball was not allowed after 1920 except for 17 pitchers. Grimes outlasted all the others. He claimed he did not throw it more than six times a game, but often faked it. Grimes did not shave on the days he pitched because the slippery elm he chewed and used to moisten the ball irritated his skin. This accounts for his nickname of "Old Stubblebread." Grimes made good use of the brush back pitch. He once decked a player who was swinging in the on-deck circle. His explanation was the potential hitter looked too eager to get up to the plate to face him. His idea of an intentional walk was four brush back pitches. The following incident was reported in Grimes obituary in *The Sporting News:* "Long after he retired, Bill Terry . . . had the occasion to ask Grimes why the pitcher always seemed to throw at Terry's feet rather than his body or head. 'Because you always hit with your feet together' Grimes replied, 'And you couldn't move them as fast as you could your head'."

1395. Grimm, Charles John (1916–36 1B) "Jolly Cholly." Grimm had the reputation as a "happy go lucky" sort who never took the game of baseball too seriously. In fact Grimm enjoyed life to the fullest and baseball was just part of it, albeit a large part. The attitude earned him the nickname of "Jolly Cholly" which over the years carried a great deal of affection. Eddie Gold and Art Ahrens quote Grimm: "I had fun playing baseball. I tried to make it fun for my players after I became manager. I was 'Jolly Cholly' and I always thought a pat on the back, an encouraging word, or a wise crack paid off a lot more than a brilliantly executed piece of strategy." As manager of the Chicago Cubs, he called himself "Der Kapitan." Grimm had a particular penchant for giving players odd and colorful nicknames. He may have been baseball's leading nicknamer. Grimm was also a prankster extraordinary on and off the field. One of his most on-the-field stunts was recalled in *The Sporting News'* Grimm obituary. In 1920 Grimm and "...second baseman Cotton Tierney another fun loving type, once pulled off a variation of the 'absolutely positively' routine popularized by Vaudeville's Gallagher and Shean. Grimm fielded a sharply hit grounder at first, but instead of going to the bag for a routine out, he threw the ball to Tierney, asking loudly: 'Have we got him Mr. Tierney?' Cotton threw back to first in plenty of time, shouting, 'Absolutely Mr. Grimm'." From 1916 to 1981 Grimm's career is a chronicle of 65 years of baseball history. As a player, Grimm was a fine fielding first baseman who collected 2,299 hits and a career average of .290 in 20 seasons, plus 12 hits and a .364 average in nine World Series games. In 19 seasons as a major league manager Grimm's winning percentage was .546 including three National League flags. He also managed Milwaukee of the American Association to two Little World Series championships. In addition Grimm's baseball career included service as coach, executive and special consultant. He was a baseball author and the most entertaining banquet circuit speaker of his time. Finally, he was also a play-by-play broadcaster. In fact Grimm was involved in one of the oddest switches in baseball history. Eighteen games into the 1960 season for the Chicago Cubs, Grimm was replaced as manager by broadcaster Lou Boudreau, and Grimm took Boudreau's place in the broadcasting booth. It could only happen at Wrigley Field! If baseball should ever decide to admit individuals to the Hall of Fame based on total career accomplishments and contributions, all phases of the game considered, "Jolly Cholly" should be the first person elected.

1396. Grimshaw, Myron Frederick (1935–37 1B) "Moose." Grimshaw was 6'1" and weighed 175 pounds.

Although not as big as a moose, it was said Grimshaw played as tough as one.

1397. Grimsley, Ross Albert, II (1971–82 P) "Scuzzy." Grimsley was somewhat of a flake. Don Baylor writes: "In 1974, we got a crazy pitcher from the Reds named Ross Grimsley, known as 'Scuzzy' because of his long, stringy hair and weird, some say sick, sense of humor. Grimsley always carried very strange paraphernalia to put on display in his locker including a two-foot-long dildo. He's lucky he did not have to work in the present-day world, with all the women reporters around, because Scuzzy did not have a PG-rated bone in his body."

1398. Griner, Donald Dexter (1912–18 P) "Rusty." The nickname refers to hair color.

1399. Grissom, Lee Theo (1934–41 P) "Lefty." Grissom pitched left handed, but was a switch hitter.

1400. Groth, Henry Knight (1912–27 3B) "Heinie." "Heinie" denotes Groth's German background. Groth was one of the better third basemen of the dead ball era. He batted .292 and collected 1,774 hits in 16 seasons, playing in five World Series with three different National League Clubs, Cincinnati, 1919, New York, 1922–24, and Pittsburgh, 1927. Groth was noted for using a thick bat called the "bottle bat" and an old batting stance which was described as a soldier standing at present arms. He would face the pitcher head-on, with his feet together and the bat held straight up in front of him.

1401. Groth, Lewis Carl (1919 3B) "Silver." Groth was 35 years old with grey silvery hair before he got his opportunity to play in two major league games. Unfortunately, he went hitless in four times at bat.

1402. Gross, Ewell (1925 SS) "Turkey." "Turkey" refers to Gross' lack of speed.

1403. Grove, Robert Moses (1925–41 P) "Lefty." Grove pitched left handed, and batted left handed. His career won-lost record of 300-141 figures to a winning percentage of .680 the fourth best on record. Grove led the American League in strikeouts seven times, games won four times and ERA eight times. He was also called "Old Mose" because of his grey, silvery hair. From 1920–24 Grove played with the Baltimore Orioles, considered by many the best minor league team of all time. Although he was a consistent winner, he had difficulty with his control, and at that time his nickname was "The Wild Oriole."

1404. Grover, Charles Byrd (1913 P) "Bugs." Grover once told his teammates about a fictitious play which supposedly happened in a game. Nobody believed him, and players began to call him "Buggy."

1405. Grubbs, Thomas Dillard (1920 P) "Judge." Origin unknown.

1406. Grube, Franklin Thomas (1931–41 C) "Hans." "Hans" refers to Grube's German background.

1407. Grunwald, Alfred Henry (1955–59 P) "Stretch." Grunwald was 6'4" with long legs. When pitching, it was said his stretch was half way to the plate.

1408. Guese, Theodore (1901 P) "Whitey." As a 29-year-old rookie, Guese had grey, silvery hair.

1409. Guidry, Ronald Ames (1975–87 P) "Louisiana Lightning." This is a place nickname. Guidry came from Lafayette, Louisiana. Lightning refers to the speed of Guidry's fastball. In 1978 Guidry posted a 25-3 won-lost record for the New York Yankees with an ERA of 1.74, and also led the American League in strikeouts with 248, and shutouts, 9.

1410. Guinn, Drannon Eugene (1968–71 P) "Skip." "Skip" is a childhood nickname. John Wilson wrote: "His full name is Drannon Eugene Guinn which is explanation enough of why he prefers Skip."

1411. Guise, Witt Orison (1940 P) "Lefty." Guise pitched left handed, and batted left handed.

1412. Gumbert, Harry Edward (1935–50 P) "Gunboat." Gumbert wrote me: "In the 1930s a sportswriter said I came on to the mound like a gunboat. Nobody ever used it though, even the players. I didn't either."

1413. Gunkel, Woodward William (1916 P) "Red." The nickname refers to hair color.

1414. Gust, Ernest Herman Frank (1911 1B) "Red." The nickname refers to hair color.

1415. Guth, Charles Henry (1972 SS) "Bucky." Guth wrote me: "My mother didn't want me called Chuck, so she called me Bucky so no one would call me Chuck."

1416. Guthrie, William J. (1913–15, 1922, 28–32 NL Umpire) "Bull-Necked Bill." The nickname describes Guthrie's build. He was a rough and tough umpire who handled no player with kid gloves. They were all the same to him. Guthrie in his speech was a "dees-does" guy. He would not tell batters that a pitch was at the knees or it just missed the corner. He'd say, "It's eider dis or dat wid me. Dere ain't no inbetween."

1417. Gutierrez, Cesar Dario (1967–71 SS) "Coca." Teammates called Gutierrez "Coca" to indicate his Latin background. He was also called "Bandito" for his base stealing ability. In 1970, he got seven hits in seven times at bat in one game—a major league record.

1418. Gutierrez, Joaquin Fernando Hernandez (1983– SS) "Whistler." When he plays in the field Gutierrez is constantly whistling to himself.

1419. Gwosdz, Douglas Wayne (1981–84 C) "Eyechart." When he joined San Diego in 1981 none of the players knew how to pronounce his name. So they nicknamed him "Eyechart."

1420. Haas, Bryan Edmund (1976-87 P) "Moose." Haas was hardly a moose at 6', 180 pounds. The nickname was given to him by his father on the day he was born. His father thought he would grow up to be a moose.

1421. Habenicht, Robert Julius (1951-53 P) "Hobby." "Hobby" is derived from the way the last name of Habenicht is pronounced.

1422. Hach, Irvin William (1897 2B) "Major." Origin unknown.

1423. Hack, Stanley Camfield (1932-47 3B) "Smiling Stan." Hack had a very easy going disposition and usually had a smile on his face. Manager of the Chicago Cubs, Charlie Grimm, called Hack "Stanislous," and the nickname was popularized by Cub broadcaster Bert Wilson.

1424. Hackett, James Joseph (1902-03 P) "Sunny Jim." The nickname refers to Hackett's pleasant disposition.

1425. Haddix, Harvey (1952-65 P) "The Kitten." Haddix was nicknamed "The Kitten" by St. Louis Cardinal fans and players after former Cardinal pitcher Harry "The Cat" Brecheen. He had the same cat-like moves on the mound that made Brecheen a good fielding pitcher. On May 26, 1959, Haddix pitched 12 perfect innings against Milwaukee at County Stadium only to lose the game in the 13th inning 1-0.

1426. Hadley, Irving Darius (1926-41 P) "Bump." Hadley received his nickname when he played football at Mercersburg Academy. He was a rough fullback who liked to bump people. The nickname stuck with him when he played football at Brown University, although he quit as a sophomore opting for professional baseball.

1427. Haefner, Milton Arnold (1943-50 P) "Mickey." According to Tom Shea, "Mickey" is short for "Mickey Mouse." It refers to Haefner's slight build, 5'8" and 160 pounds.

1428. Hafey, Charles James (1924-37 OF) "Chick." "Chick" is a fairly common nickname for the name of Charles. Hafey did not know where "Chick" came from saying he had been called that as long as he could remember.

1429. Hafey, Daniel Albert (1939 P) "Bud." "Bud" was a childhood family nickname.

1430. Hafey, Thomas Francis (1939-44 3B) "The Arm." Hafey had an unusually strong throw from third base to first.

1431. Hageman, Kurt Moritz (1911-14 P) "Casey." Origin unknown.

1432. Hagerman, Zeriah Zequiel (1909-16 P) "Rip." Hagerman was a fastball pitcher. He "ripped" the ball toward the plate.

1433. Hahn, Frank George (1899-1906 P) "Noodles." Lee Allen explains the origin of the nickname in the following manner: "A friend recalls the origin. 'When Hahn was a boy in Nashville,' the man explained, 'he always had to carry his father's lunch to him. His father worked in a piano factory and the lunch was always noodle soup. You never saw the boy without the noodle soup. So the nickname was a natural'." Hahn was one of the best left handed control pitchers of all time. He allowed only 379 walks in 2,012 career innings pitched, for an average of just 1.70 per nine innings. Besides Steve Carlton, Hahn is the only other left handed pitcher to win 20 or more games for a last place team. He won 22 and lost 19 for last place Cincinnati in 1901.

1434. Haines, Henry Lurther (1923 OF) "Hinkey." In 1919 Haines played under the name of Hinkey in the Virginia League to protect his eligibility to play college football.

1435. Haines, Jessie Joseph (1918–37 P) "Pop." "Pop" refers to Haines grey, silvery hair which he developed late in his career. Although well past his prime, Haines did pitch in 37 games for the 1934 St. Louis Cardinal "Gas House Gang" winning four and losing four games.

1436. Hale, Arvel Odell (1931–41 2B) "Bad News." The nickname meant he was bad news to opposing pitchers. In the minor leagues he had the propensity for breaking up ball games in the late innings. In 1929 playing for Alexandria in the Cotton States League, he hit seven home runs in six days.

1437. Hale, George Wagner (1914–18 C) "Ducky." Origin unknown.

1438. Hale, Ray Luthur (1902 P) "Dad." Origin unknown.

1439. Haley, Richard Timothy (1915–17 C) "Ray." Origin unknown.

1440. Hall, Charles Louis (1906–18 P) "Sea Lion." According to Boston Red Sox teammate Harry Hooper, Hall could imitate the bark or call of a sea lion. He had a voice that could be heard anywhere on the field and in the stands. Some said his sea lion roars awakened babies in the next county. Usually, he did not roar when pitching, but from the coach's box. It was common at the time that an idle pitcher would assume the duties of a base coach.

1441. Hall, Charles Walter (1887 OF) "Doc." Many of the players with the nickname of "Doc" had a close association with either the medical or dental professions. For Hall, however, the origin of Doc is unknown.

1442. Hall, Herbert Silas (1918 P) "Iron Duke." Hall was 6'4", weighed 220 pounds and came from Steelville, Illinois.

1443. Hall, Thomas Edward (1968–77 P) "The Blade." Hall was 6'0" but weighed just 150 pounds. Some said he looked more like a hunger strike victim than a pitcher.

1444. Hall, William Bernard (1913 P) "Beanie." Origin unknown.

1445. Hallahan, William Anthony (1925–38 P) "Wild Bill." Hallahan lacked control and led the National League three times in bases on balls. He had a tendency now and then to throw the ball all the way to the back stop. The "Wild Bill" tag was reinforced when Hallahan once posed on a horse. His teammates called him "Moon" because of the shape of his face.

1446. Haller, William E. (1961, 63–82, AL Umpire) "Fox." Origin unknown.

1447. Halligan, William E. (1890–92 OF) "Jocko." Origin unknown.

1448. Hallstrom, Charles E. (1885 P) "Swedish Wonder." Hallstrom was born in Jonkeping, Sweden.

1449. Hamann, Elmer Joseph (1922 P) "Doc." Many of the players with the nickname of "Doc" had a close association with either the medical or dental professions. For Hamann, however, the origin of "Doc" is unknown.

1450. Hamby, James Sanford (1926–27 C) "Cracker." "Cracker" refers to people of Southern origin. Hamby was from Wilkesboro, North Carolina.

1451. Hamilton, Jack Edwin (1962–69 P) "Hairbreadth Harry." Hamilton had the tendency as a pitcher to bring himself close to danger and then escape. For instance, in one game he walked three straight batters to bring Hank Aaron up to the plate. He then managed to get Aaron to pop out.

1452. Hamilton, William Robert (1888–1901 OF) "Sliding Billy." Hamilton was one of the great base stealers of all time copping 937 in 14 seasons. In 1889 he stole a career high of 117 and earned the tag of "The Human Rocket." It was said that he was "fast as a deer" on the base paths, but "slippery as an eel" when sliding into a base. In 1894 Hamilton compiled a batting average of .399, but finished behind Hugh Duffy, .428; Sam Thompson, .404; and Ed Delahanty, .400.

1453. Hamlin, Luke Daniel (1933–44 P) "Hot Potato." A New York sportswriter called him "Hot Potato" when he played for Brooklyn. He handled the ball like a hot potato between pitches.

1454. Hammond, Walter Charles (1915–22 2B) "Wobby." Hammond was addressed as Wallie. "Wobby" is a take off on Wallie.

1455. Hamner, Ralph Conant (1946–49 P) "Bruz." Hamner's brother had difficulty in pronouncing "brother" and called Hamner "Bruz."

1456. Hancken, Morris Medlock (1940 C) "Buddy." "Buddy" was a childhood family nickname. Hancken's older brother called him his little buddy when he was two years old.

1457. Handiboe, Aloysius James (1911 OF) "Coalyard Mike." Origin unknown.

1458. Handiboe, James Edward (1886 P) "Nick." Origin unknown.

1459. Handley, Lee Elmer (1936–47 3B) "Jeep." According to Joseph McBride, Handley's nickname refers to his bouncing around the infield like an army jeep.

1460. Haney, Fred Girard (1922–29 3B) "Pudge." "Pudge" referred to Haney's build, 5'6" and 175 pounds.

1461. Hanlon, Edward Hugh (1880–92 OF) "Foxy Ned." According to Fred Lieb, Hanlon, who was usually addressed as Ned, was one of the most intelligent players of his day. As a manager from 1889–1907 he was known for the crafty trades he engineered.

1462. Hanlon, William Henry (1903 1B) "Big." Hanlon was 5'9½" and weighed 170 pounds. It would not seem Hanlon's build was large enough to warrant the "Big" tag or small enough to warrant the nickname to be an opposite. Origin unknown.

1463. Hannah, James Harrison (1918–20 C) "Truck." In the minor leagues Hannah was a work horse behind the plate, catching over 2,400 games. In 1917 he caught 185 games for Salt Lake City in the Pacific Coast League.

1464. Hansen, Andrew Viggo (1944–53 P) "Swede." "Swede" referred to Hansen's blond hair. Hansen was of Danish rather than Swedish background.

1465. Hansen, Roy Emil Frederick (1930–35 P) "Snipe." In 1927 at age 17 Hansen was on a training trip with the Chicago Cubs on Catalina Island. The players organized a snipe hunt with Hansen as the butt of the joke. The nickname stems from that incident.

1466. Hanson, Earl Sylvester (1921 P) "Ollie." Hanson was of Swedish background.

1467. Harder, Melvin LeRoy (1928–47 P) "Chief." Harder carried the nickname of "Chief" because he was the Cleveland Indians leading pitcher in the 1930s. He had not one drop of Indian blood, and was about the only player to be nicknamed "Chief" who did not have an American Indian background. Harder was also called "Wimpy," not because he was fond of hamburgers, but because of an unusually short hair cut he showed up with at the ball park one day. It reminded teammates of the "Popeye" strip character, J. Wellington Wimpy.

1468. Hardgrove, William Henry (1918 PH) "Pat." Origin unknown.

1469. Hardin, William Edgar (1952 SS) "Bud." "Bud" was a childhood family nickname.

1470. Harding, Charles Harold (1913 P) "Slim." Harding was 6'2½" and weighed 170 pounds.

1471. Harding, Louis Edward (1886 C) "Jumbo." Harding packed 215 pounds on a 5'9" frame.

1472. Hardy, Francis Joseph (1951 P) "Red." The nickname refers to hair color.

1473. Hargrave, Dudley Michael (1974–85 1B) "The Human Rain Delay." Hargrave was fidgety at the plate and took a long time getting ready to hit, adjusting his batting glove, helmet, shirt, pants, shoes, belt and so forth. Some said he made the most of his television time.

1474. Hargrave, Eugene Franklin (1913–30 C) "Bubbles." Hargrave, according to Joseph McBride, stuttered. He had great difficulty pronouncing the letter "B" which resulted in the unkind nickname of "Bubbles." Hargrave detested the nickname and would start a fight if it was mentioned in his presence.

1475. Hargrave, William McKinley (1923–33 C) "Pinky." "Pinky" Hargrave was the younger brother of Eugene "Bubbles" Hargrave. "Pinky" did not refer to skin complexion as it did with several other players, but to his red hair.

1476. Harkins, John Joseph (1884–88 P) "Pa." Harkins was 25 years old as a rookie, old for the 1880s.

1477. Harkness, Frederick Harvey (1910–11 P) "Specs." "Specs" refers to the freckles on Harkness' face.

1478. Harley, Henry Risk (1905 P) "Dick." Origin unknown.

1479. Harmond, Robert Green (1909–18 P) "Hickory Bob." Harmond had a lean, straight and hard appearance.

1480. Harper, Charles William (1899–1906 P) "Jack." Origin unknown.

1481. Harper, William Homer (1911 P) "Blue Sleeve." Origin unknown.

1482. Harrah, Colbert Dale (1969–86 3B) "Toby." Harrah wrote me that his grandmother gave him the nickname of Toby at an early age because she did not like the name Colbert and he was tow-headed as a little boy.

1483. Harrell, Oscar Martin (1912 P) "Slim." Harrell was 6'3" and weighed 180 pounds.

1484. Harrell, Raymond Jones (1935–45 P) "Cowboy." "Cowboy" refers to Harrell's origin in Petrolia, Texas.

1485. Harrelson, Derrel McKinley (1965–80 SS) "Bud." Harrelson wrote me: "My two-year older brother called me Bubba and then it became Bud. In grade school I was called 'Buddo.' In high school some kids called me 'Butthole' which I hated." He went on to say that New York Met teammate Tom Seaver always called him "Buddy."

1486. Harrelson, Kenneth Smith (1963–71 1B) "Hawk." This outspoken player was not called "Hawk" because of his fielding ability, but because of his large pointed nose.

1487. Harrelson, William Charles (1968 P) "Chief." Harrelson was one-half Cherokee Indian.

1488. Harris, Alonzo (1967 PH) "Candy." Origin unknown.

1489. Harris, Charles (1948–51 P) "Bubba." Harris told me the nickname stems from his childhood when he had difficulty pronouncing "brother."

1490. Harris, David Stanley (1925–34 OF) "Sheriff." In the off season Harris was a deputy sheriff in his native North Carolina.

1491. Harris, Frank Walter (1884 1B) "Buddy." "Buddy" was a childhood family nickname.

1492. Harris, Joseph (1914–28 1B) "Moon." Origin unknown.

1493. Harris, Stanley Raymond (1919–31 2B) "Bucky." Harris played second base for 12 years, 1919–29, 1931, in the American League for Washington and Detroit with a lifetime batting average of .274. In 1924 he became the player-manager of the Washington Senators and directed them to straight flags in 1924 and 1925 and the World Championship in 1924. For this achievement he received the nickname "Boy Wonder." Harris managed 29 years in the major leagues with a winning percentage of .493. His second World Championship came 23 years after his first with the New York Yankees in 1947. His worst finish was seventh place in 1931. The "Bucky" nickname stems from Harris' youth, playing basketball and not baseball. As Harris himself relates, "Gary Schmeelk made it stick on me when I was playing basketball. I had a couple of players on my back in a rough game. When I shook them off and shot a basket he said I bucked like a tough little bronco."

1494. Harris, Walter Francis, Jr. (1970–71 P) "Higbe." Harris wrote me he was nicknamed in the minor leagues after Brooklyn pitcher Kirby Higbe. His name is often listed in baseball documents as "Buddy." He says that is incorrect.

1495. Harrison, Charles William (1963–71 1B) "Pound Cake." According to Rich Marazzi and Len Fiorito, "Pound Cake" referred to Harrison's 5'10" and 190-pound build.

1496. Harriss, William Jennings Bryan (1920–28 P) "Slim." Harriss was 6'6" and weighed 180 pounds. He was also called "The Texas Ranger" referring to his build and the fact he was from Brownsville, Texas.

1497. Harrist, Earl (1945–53 P) "Irish." Harrist was of Irish background.

1498. Hart, James Henry (1905–07 C) "Hub." Tom Shea indicates this is a place nickname. Hart was from the Boston area, and Boston is known as the "Hub" city.

1499. Hart, Robert L. (1890 P) "Billy." Robert Hart was nicknamed "Billy" after Bill Hart, a contemporary pitcher who he resembled.

1500. Hart, William Woodrow (1943–45 3B) "True Gun." "True Gun," according to Tom Shea, refers to Hart's swift and sure throw from third base to first base. It also refers to cowboy movie start William S. Hart and his "True Gun."

1501. Hartenstein, Charles Oscar (1965–77 P) "Twiggy." Hartenstein was nicknamed by Chicago Cub teammate, Dick Radatt, after the thin English model who was popular during the mid–1960s.

1502. Harter, Franklin Pierce (1912–14 P) "Chief." Harter was of American Indian background.

1503. Hartley, Grover Allen (1911–34 C) "Slick." Hartley was a good defensive catcher with a good head for the game in calling pitches.

1504. Hartley, Walter Scott (1902 OF) "Chick." Origin unknown.

1505. Hartman, Frederick Owen (1894–1902 3B) "Dutch." Hartman was of German background.

1506. Hartnett, Charles Leo (1922–41 C) "Gabby." Hartnett was one of the best catchers of the 1920s and 1930s with a career average of .297 over 20 years. He is best remembered for the home run he hit in semi-dark Wrigley Field on September 28, 1938, with two outs in the ninth inning to break a 5–5 tie with Pittsburgh and put the Chicago Cubs in first place. They went on to win the flag. The home run has gone down in baseball history as "The Homer in the Glowin." As a boy in New England, Hartnett built a reputation as a champion marble player. He won over 55,000 marbles and kept them in 25-pound sugar sacks. At age 21 he signed a contract with the Chicago Cubs. Before he went for spring training, his mother told him to keep his mouth shut until he got the "lay of the land." On the train to California and Catalina Island, Hartnett sat quietly beside Dean Sullivan, sports editor of the *Chicago Herald Examiner*. Sullivan, finally remarked "You're certainly a gabby guy." The nickname of "Gabby" was picked up by older players and was originally a nickname opposite. Hartnett, however really had a gregarious personality, and a year later he fit the nickname by chirping so constantly that sportswriters were asking, "Who is that gabby kid?" Hartnett, who hit .420 in four World Series was also called "Old Tomato Face" because when he laughed hard, which was often, his face turned scarlet.

1507. Hartnett, Patrick J. (1890 1B) "Happy." Hartnett enjoyed having a good time. Playing baseball was fun for him.

1508. Hartsel, Tully Frederick (1898–1911 OF) "Topsy." Fred Lieb reports that "Topsy" referred to the fact that Hartsel was tow-headed, almost to the point of being an albino. Charles Dryden wrote that as a hobby, Hartsel collected sugar bowls. He had a trunk made, fitted and padded to keep safe the sugar bowls he bought while on the road.

1509. Hartung, Clinton Clarence (1947–52 P) "Floppy." Teammates called Hartung "Floppy" because of his large angular ears. Sportswriters, however, liked to call him "The Hondo Hurricane." He was 6'5" and his hometown was Hondo, Texas. Thus this was a place nickname.

1510. Harvel, Luther Raymond (1928 OF) "Red." The nickname refers to hair color.

1511. Harvey, Douglas H. (1962-77, 79-88, NL Umpire) "God." According to Tony Kubeck, "God" was used out of respect for Harvey. He was also called "Silver" when he first started umpiring in the National League because of his premature grey hair.

1512. Harvey, Erwin King (1900-02 OF) "Zaza." Tom Shea reports that Harvey had red hair. "Zaza" was a popular theater play of the time in which Mrs. Leslie Carter was the heroine and she had red hair.

1513. Hasbrook, Robert Lydon (1916-17 1B) "Ziggy." Origin unknown.

1514. Hass, Bruno Philip (1915 P) "Boon." "Boon" is derived from the first name of Bruno.

1515. Hass, Bryan Edmund (1976- P) "Moose." Joseph McBride claims Hass' 5'10" and 185 pounds build accounts for the nickname of "Moose."

1516. Hass, George William (1925-38 OF) "Mule." Hass is the German word for rabbit, but this Hass ran more like a donkey. "Mule" referred to his slowness of foot. He was also called "Donk" for the same reason.

1517. Hassamaer, William Louis (1894-96 OF) "Roaring Bill." Hassamaer had an extremely loud voice which could be easily heard all over the playing field and stands.

1518. Hassett, John Aloysius (1936-42 1B) "Buddy." Hassett wrote me, "'Buddy' means friend to me. My mother gave me the nickname because a very good friend she admired in her youth was called Buddy. That way she didn't have to worry about calling John which was also my father's name."

1519. Hassey, Ronald William (1978- C) "Babe." Origin unknown.

1520. Hatfield, Fred James (1950-58 3B) "Scrap Iron." Hatfield was nicknamed "Scrap Iron" because he was a hard nosed player who would do anything for the team to win.

1521. Hatter, Clyde Menlo (1935-37 P) "Mad." Hatter's behavior was sometimes considered strange. He was nicknamed after the Mad Hatter character in the book *Alice in Wonderland* by Lewis Carroll, published in 1865.

1522. Haughey, Christopher Francis (1943 P) "Bud." "Bud" was a childhood family nickname.

1523. Hauser, Arnold George (1910-15 SS) "Pee Wee." Hauser was 5'7" and weighed 135 pounds, yet he had a career batting average of .300.

1524. Hauser, Joseph John (1922-29 1B) "Unser Choe." Hauser was of German background from Milwaukee which had a high concentration of German Americans. "Unser Choe" is German for "Our Joe." Although Hauser hit .284 in the major leagues with 79 home runs in six seasons, he was at his best in triple-A ball. He hit 63 home runs and drove in 175 runs for Baltimore in 1930, and 69 home runs and 182 runs batted in for Minneapolis in 1933.

1525. Hawke, William Victor (1892-94 P) "Dick." Origin unknown.

1526. Hawkes, Nelson Louis (1921-25 1B) "Chicken." The nickname is in direct response to the last name.

1527. Hawley, Emerson P. (1892–1901 P) "Pink." Hawley had a twin brother. To distinguish between them, parents pinned a pink ribbon on Emerson, and a blue ribbon on his brother.

1528. Haworth, Homer Howard (1915 C) "Cully." Origin unknown.

1529. Hayden, Eugene Franklin (1958 P) "Lefty." Hayden pitched left handed, and batted left handed.

1530. Hayes, Franklin Witman (1933–47 C) "Blimp." Tom Shea suggests "Blimp" refers to Hayes' weight, even though his listed playing weight was 190 pounds on a 6'1" frame. He really played at 30–40 pounds more than that.

1531. Hazelton, Willard Carpenter (1902 1B) "Doc." Many of the players with the nickname of "Doc" had close associations with either the medical or dental professions. However, with Hazelton the origin of "Doc" is unknown.

1532. Hazle, Robert Sidney (1955–58 OF) "Hurricane." Hazel was the name of a particularly devastating storm of the 1950s. Robert Hazle joined the Milwaukee Braves in June of 1957 and batted .403 in 41 games. In a game in which he hit several balls hard in Philadelphia, someone in the press box said "That guy is a real hurricane." Bob Wolf of the *Milwaukee Journal* was the first person to use the nickname in print.

1533. Healy, John J. (1885–92 P) "Egyptian." Healy was from Cario, Illinois, a sister city to Cario, Egypt.

1534. Hearn, Elmer LaFayette (1926–29 P) "Bunny." Hearn was nicknamed after pitcher Bunn "Bunny" Hearn who pitched from 1918–28.

1535. Heath, Minor Wilson (1931–32 1B) "Mickey." "Mickey" in this case was an acceptable baseball replacement for the first name of Minor.

1536. Heathcote, Clifton Earl (1918–32 OF) "Rubberhead." St. Louis fans began to call Heathcote "Rubberhead," when as a rookie with the Cardinals, he lost a fly ball in the outfield in the sun and it bounced off his head. The fans never let him forget the mishap, taunting him with the nickname whenever he took the field.

1537. Hebert, Wallace Andrew (1931–43 P) "Preacher." People in his hometown of St. Charles, Louisiana, called Hebert "Preacher" because he was always talking. However, it was also used as a nickname opposite. Hebert was a man of few words. He seldom spoke to anyone without being spoken to. In 1932 he won only one game while dropping 12, but he had the distinction of striking out Ruth twice and Gehrig once in the same game.

1538. Hecker, Guy Jackson (1882–90 P) "Blond Guy." Hecker had striking blond hair. In 1884 he won 52 games for Louisville and lost 20 with an ERA of 1.80. In 1886 he became the only pitcher to win a batting title. He led the American Association with an average of .342.

1539. Hedlund, Michael David (1965–72 P) "Red." The nickname refers to hair color.

1540. Heffner, Donald Henry (1934–44 2B) "Jeep." Heffner was given the nickname "Jeep" by St. Louis Browns teammate, Ralph "Red" Kress. It was because he bounced around like an Army jeep.

1541. Heffner, Robert Frederick (1963–68 P) "Butch." Heffner's brother gave him the nickname when he was a small child.

1542. Heidrick, R. Emmet (1898–1908 OF) "Snags." Heidrick was an excellent fielding center fielder. It was said he snagged everything that came his way.

1543. Heilemann, John George (1901 3B) "Chink." Heilemann's facial features resembled those of a Chinaman.

1544. Heilmann, Harry Edwin (1916–32 OF) "Slug." Heilmann was one of the great hitters in the late deadball era. His career average for 17 seasons was .342. He led the American League in 1921, .394; 1923, .404; and 1925, .393. Heilmann had to earn his hits, since he was slow of foot. "Slug" and "Harry the Horse" referred to his lack of speed.

1545. Heimach, Frederick Amos (1920–33 P) "Lefty." Heimach pitched left handed and batted left handed.

1546. Heine, William Henry (1921 2B) "Bud." "Bud" was a childhood nickname given to Heine by his family.

1547. Heise, Clarence Edward (1934 P) "Lefty." Heise pitched left handed and batted left handed.

1548. Heitmann, Harry Anton (1918 P) "Boy Wonder." In 1918 Heitmann was the "Boy Wonder" of spring training for Brooklyn. A great future was predicted for him. As the season started he made his debut against the St. Louis Cardinals. The first batter singled, the next tripled, the third doubled and the fourth hit a home run. Heitmann tossed his glove in the air, marched off the mound and went straight to the clubhouse. He dressed, left the park and enlisted in the Navy, never to return to the major leagues.

1549. Heitmuller, William Frederick (1909–10 OF) "Heinie." Heitmuller was of German background.

1550. Held, Melvin Nicholas (1956 P) "Country." Held came from the small country town of Edon, Ohio.

1550a. Helfer, Al (1950–70 Announcer) "The Ghost of Hartsdale." In 1950 Helfer began broadcasting the "Game of the Day" for the Mutual network. Working six days a week, he would board a plane once or twice a week for 25 weeks each year. He was seldom seen in his hometown of Hartsdale, New York, hence the nickname.

1551. Helfrick, Emory Wilbur (1913 2B) "Ty." Origin unknown.

1552. Heltzel, William Wade (1943–44 3B) "Heinie." Heltzel was of German background.

1553. Hemming, George Earl (1890–97 P) "Old Wax Figger." Hemming possessed one of the finest physiques in professional baseball. His carriage was that of the proverbial Indian, straight as an arrow. His physical appearance with his poise and coolness under fire won for him the nickname of "Old Wax Figger."

1554. Hemp, William H. (1887–90 OF) "Ducky." "Ducky" referred to Hemp's build. He was 5'9" and 160 pounds.

1555. Hemphill, Charles Judson (1899–1911 OF) "Eagle Eye." Hemphill was an excellent judge of pitches. He did not swing at bad pitches. In 11 years he walked 435 times and fanned only 207 times.

1556. Hemsley, Ralston Burdett (1928–47 C) "Rollicking Rollie." At the start of his career Hemsley was a heavy drinker and was continuously partying. This led to the "Rollicking Rollie" nickname. He became an alcoholic and drank himself off the Pirates, Cubs, Reds, and Browns. In 1938 while with Cleveland on a train road trip, he threw lighted matches into the berth of traveling secretary Lewis Mumaw. He was taken to an Alcoholic Anonymous meeting in Akron, Ohio. This 12-step support group program had its origin in Akron in 1935, but was still in its infancy. It was of great help to Hemsley. Franklin Lewis quotes Hemsley in 1940, "It's been just a year now since the most wonderful thing in the world happened to me, so I feel safe in telling you boys about it. You know I didn't have a drink at all last season. Well, Alcoholic Anonymous did that for me. I'd like to give credit to this great organization and you'll do me a favor by writing a story about Alcoholic Anonymous." Bob Feller was a strong supporter of Hemsley who continued catching in the major leagues until 1947. Feller devotes a whole chapter to the Hemsley story in his 1990 book, *Now Pitching: Bob Feller, A Baseball Memoir.*

1557. Henderson, Arthur (1922–31 P, Negro League) "Rats." In 1927 Henderson led the Negro League East pitchers with a 19-7 won-lost record. He also led the league in 1923 with a surprising 7-9 mark. The origin of "Rats" is unknown.

1558. Henderson, Bernard (1921 P) "Barnyard." Origin unknown.

1559. Hendrick, George Andrew (1971–87 OF) "Silent George." Hendrick was a man of few words on and off the field. He tried to ignore the press whenever possible.

1560. Hendrick, Harvey (1923–34 1B) "Gink." As a rookie with Memphis of the Southern Association in 1920, Hendrick got into an argument with his manager, Spencer Abbott. In the heat of the moment Abbott called him a "Gink."

1561. Hendricks, Edward (1910 P) "Big Ed." Hendricks was 6'3" and weighed 200 pounds.

1562. Hendrikson, Olaf (1911–17 OF) "Swede." Hendrikson was of Swedish background.

1563. Hengle, Emery J. (1884–85 2B) "Moxie." In Hengle's case, according to Bob Considine, "Moxie" meant guts, a combination of strength and courage. Moxie was a popular soft drink sold at ball parks on the East coast in the 1880s. A familiar call at the ball parks was "Ice Cold Moxie." It began to be associated with "ice cold nerves."

1564. Henke, Thomas Anthony (1982 P) "The Terminator." As a relief pitcher, Henke gained the reputation of ending the game by retiring the opposition in the late innings. In 1987 with Toronto, Henke led the American League in saves with 34.

1565. Henline, Walter John (1921–31 C) "Butch." "Butch" referred to his rugged, independent nature as a child.

1566. Hennessey, George (1937–45 P) "Three Star." The nickname is a response to the last name of Hennessey. "Three Star" refers to a trade name of Brandy under the label of Hennesey.

1567. Henniney, Ernest Herman (1914–15 P) "Pete." Origin unknown.

1568. Henrich, Frank Wilde (1924 OF) "Fritz." Henrich was of German background.

1569. Henrich, Thomas David (1937–50 OF) "Old Reliable." New York Yankee broadcaster Mel Allen gave Henrich the nickname "Old Reliable" because of his ability to come through in the clutch.

1570. Henrichs, William Louis (1910 P) "Dutch." Henrichs was of German background.

1571. Henry, Earl Clifford (1944–45 P) "Hook." Henry's best pitch was a curveball. However, in 17 major league games he posted only a 1-4 won-lost record.

1572. Henry, Eugene (1977–88 AL Umpire) "Ted." Umpire expert Larry Gerlach wrote me that Ted was used as an alternative to Eugene, but for unknown reasons.

1573. Henry, Frank John (1921–32 P) "Dutch." Henry was of German background.

1574. Henry, Frederick Marshall (1922–23 1B) "Snake." "Snake" referred to Henry's long stretch at first base. Henry was best known as a minor league player. He belted 3,384 minor league hits.

1575. Henry, John Park (1910–18 C) "Bull." At 5'10" and 190 pounds Henry was a hard-nosed catcher who protected the plate like a bull.

1576. Henshaw, Roy Knickelbine (1933–43 P) "Kid." Henshaw came off the campus of the University of Chicago to pitch for the Chicago Cubs. He was only 5'8" and weighed 155 pounds.

1577. Hensiek, Philip Frank (1935 P) "Sid." Origin unknown.

1578. Herbert, Ernie Albert (1913–15 P) "Tex." Herbert was born in Missouri, but he was raised in the state of Texas.

1579. Herman, Floyd Caves (1926–45 OF) "Babe." Floyd Herman was a contemporary of "Babe Ruth" and played for Brooklyn the first six years of his career. Thus greater New York area fans had two "Babes" to root for. In fact in 1936, Herman hit for a .393 average compared to Ruth's .359. Herman played through the 1937 season and then came back in 1945 as a pinch hitter for the wartime Dodgers. In 13 seasons he averaged .324 with 181 home runs. Originally Herman was called "Lefty." The "Babe" tag dates from his days in the minor leagues. One version has it that while he was playing first base for Edmonton in the Western Canada League, a coach, Dan Howley, knew a fighter in Canada named "Babe" Herman and insisted on calling Floyd "Babe." Sportswriters picked it up immediately. Joseph McBride in *High and Inside* reports that when he was a rookie in 1926, Ty Cobb told Herman the 45-ounce bats he was using were even heavier than those Ruth swung. Herman replied that if he used heavier bats he would hit the ball even farther than Ruth did. From this time on players picked up the nickname of "Babe." Lawrence Ritter in his *Glory of Their Times* presents a slightly different account of the origin of "Babe" from Herman himself, "I got the nickname 'Babe' way back when I was playing with Edmonton in the Western Canada League, my very first year in organized baseball. There was a popular champion flyweight prize fighter at the time called Babe Herman, and a fog-horn lady fan at Edmonton started calling me 'Babe' after Babe Herman the fighter, not after Babe Ruth. She'd yell 'Go get 'em Babe,' or 'Get a hit Babe' so loud you could hear her all over the park and somehow the name stuck." Larry Gerlach in his *The Men in Blue: Conversations with Umpires*, quotes umpire Ben Reardon: "Turkey Neck— that's what I always called Herman."

1580. Hernandez, Guillermo Villanueva (1977– P) "Willie." "Willie" is a derivation of Villanueva. In 1988 Hernandez wanted to be called Guillermo and not Willie which he said he never liked.

1581. Hernandez, Keith (1974– 1B) "Mex." Hernandez wrote: "Despite my surname Hernandez and my nickname 'Mex' I am not one of the 'official' Hispanic players. My father's parents came from Spain early in the century; my mother's family is Scottish living in South Texas."

1582. Hernandez, Salvadore Jose Ramos (1942–43 C) "Chico." "Chico" is a common Latin American nickname meaning kid.

1583. Herndon, Larry Darnell (1974–88 OF) "Hondo." When he was playing high school basketball in Memphis, fans and teammates thought he played like John "Hondo" Havlicek of the Boston Celtics.

1584. Herrera, Jose Conception Ontiverous (1967–70 OF) "Loco." In Spanish "loco" means crazy or insane. The nickname refers to Herrera's eccentric behavior.

1585. Herrera, Juan Francisco Willavencio (1958–61 1B) "Pancho." Herrera was from Havana, Cuba, where "Pancho" is a common nickname. It means big. Herrera was 6'3", 220 pounds.

1586. Herrera, Procopto Rodriguez (1951 P) "Tito." Origin unknown.

1587. Herrin, Thomas Edward (1984 P) "Dutch." Herrin was of German background.

1588. Herring, Arthur L. (1929–47 P) "Sandy." Teammate, Bob Fothergill of the Detroit Tigers called Herring "Sandy" because of his light blond hair.

1589. Herring, Silas Clarke (1899 P) "Lefty." Herring pitched left handed and batted left handed.

1590. Herring, William Francis (1915 P) "Smoke." Herring had a high speed fastball.

1591. Herrmann, Martin John (1918 P) "Lefty." Herrmann pitched left handed and batted left handed.

1592. Hershiser, Orel Leonard Quinton (1983– P) "Bull Dog." The devoutly religious Hershiser was nicknamed "Bull Dog" by Dodger manager Tom Lasorda because of his competitiveness. In 1988 incuding the LCS opener against the Mets, Hershiser went 67 innings without giving up a run.

1593. Herzog, Charles Lincoln (1908–20 2B) "Buck." Herzog was an extra aggressive player. He once picked a fight with Ty Cobb. Because of his hard play he was called "Choke 'em Charlie." He urged his teammates: "When you get 'em down, choke 'em."

1594. Herzog, Dorrel Norman Elvert (1956–63 OF) "Whitey." Herzog says: "At McAlester a sportscaster named Bill Speith called me 'Whitey' because of the color of my hair. At Denver with the Yankee chain in 1955, coach Johnny Pesky called me 'White Rat' because he thought I looked like a left handed pitcher, Bob Kuzava, whom the Yankees had for a while. Kuzava's nickname was the 'White Rat'."

1595. Hesketh, Joseph Thomas (1984– P) "Fungo." Hesketh's 6'2", 165-pound build reminded teammates of a long thin bat.

1596. Heusser, Edward Burlton (1935–48 P) "The Wild Elk of the Wasatch." Heusser was from Murray,

Utah, near the Wasatch Mountains. He joined the St. Louis Cardinals in 1935 when John "Pepper" Martin was one of the heroes of the 1934 World Series. Martin was called "The Wild Horse of the Osage." Heusser's nickname was a takeoff on Martin's, concocted by sportswriters.

1597. Hickery, James Robert (1942–44 P) "Sid." Hickery wrote me: "Sid was the name of a bull in the rodeo show at the Boston Arena in 1944. I was kidding around and told some of the guys I could ride the bull. I never did, but after that the players started calling me 'Sid'."

1598. Hickman, Charles Taylor (1887–1907 1B) "Piano Legs." Hickman was 5'8" and weighed 185 pounds. He had thick legs like those of a piano.

1599. Hicks, Clarence Walter (1956 SS) "Buddy." Hicks wrote me, "My youngest sister could not pronounce my name when I was born and started calling me Buddy."

1600. Higbe, Walter Kirby (1937–50 P) "Old Hig." "Old Hig" is how Higbe use to refer to himself. In other words he was one of the few players who nicknamed himself.

1601. Higgins, Michael Franklin (1930–46 3B) "Pinky." Tom Shea reports that "Pinky" is a childhood nickname referring to Higgins' complexion.

1602. Higgins, Thomas Edward (1909–10 P) "Irish." Higgins was of Irish background.

1603. High, Andrew Aird (1922–34 3B) "Handy Andy." High was a versatile infielder equally at home at second base, shortstop, or third base. At 5'6" he was also called "Knee High."

1604. High, Edward Thomas (1901 P) "Lefty." High pitched left handed, but was a switch hitter.

1605. High, Hugh Jenken (1913–18 OF) "Lefty." High batted left handed and threw left handed. His speed also earned him the tag of "Bunny."

1606. Hilcher, Walter Frank (1931–36 P) "Whitey." Hilcher had light blond hair.

1607. Hildebrand, George Albert (1902 OF) "Dumplings." "Dumplings" referred to Hildebrand's 5'8" and 170-pound build. For the same reason he was also called "Squatty."

1608. Hildebrand, Palmer Marion (1913 C) "Pete." "Pete" was a more acceptable baseball name than Palmer and was used as an alternative.

1609. Hill, Carmen Proctor (1915–30 P) "Specs." Hill was one of the first pitchers to wear eyeglasses.

1610. Hill, Clifford Joseph (1917 P) "Red." The nickname refers to hair color.

1611. Hill, J. Preston (1904–25 OF, Negro League) "Pete." As a player and manager Hill ranked as one of the finest hitters in the early years of Negro baseball. With the Chicago American Giants he was known as Rube Foster's "money hitter." Hill, a part Indian, captained the incredible Chicago Leland Giant team of 1910 which compiled a 123-6 won-lost record. The nickname "Pete" is a takeoff on the name of Preston, and of course, was a popular baseball nickname.

1612. Hill, Marc Kevin (1973–86 C) "Booter." Hill writes that Willie McCovey, his San Francisco Giant teammate was responsible for his nickname. "One day Willie said that everybody had heard of Bunker Hill and everybody had heard of Boot Hill, but nobody had ever heard of Marc Hill. So on that day I became Booter. It could have been worse, I suppose I could have been Bunkie!"

1613. Hill, William Cicero (1896–99 P) "Still Bill." Origin unknown.

1614. Hiller, Charles Joseph (1961–68 2B) "Iron Hands." As a second baseman, Hiller was slow and clumsy in getting the ball away, especially on double play attempts.

1615. Hiller, Frank Walter (1946–53 P) "Dutch." Hiller was of German background.

1616. Hiller, Harvey Mox (1920–21 3B) "Hob." Origin unknown.

1617. Hilley, Edward Garfield (1903 3B) "Whitey." Hilley had light blond hair.

1618. Hillis, Malcolm David (1924–28 2B) "Mack." "Mack" was a takeoff on Malcolm.

1619. Hillman, Darius Dutton (1955–62 P) "Dave." "Dave" was a takeoff on Darius.

1620. Hines, Henry Fred (1895 OF) "Hunkey." "Hunkey" refers to Hines stocky 5'7" and 170-pound build.

1621. Hinrichs, Paul Edwin (1951 P) "Herky." Hinrichs told me: "In a class in Greek during my second year at preparatory school at Concordia College, unexpectedly the professor asked me to translate a passage of Hercules. I was saved by the bell. I was so relieved I told the other students, 'That's right just call me Herky for short.' They did and it stuck. My mother never accepted it and always called me Paul even though others did not."

1622. Hinton, John Robert (1901 3B) "Red." The nickname refers to hair color.

1623. Hitt, Roy Wesley (1907 P) "Rhino." "Rhino" referred to Hitt's 5'10" and 200-pound build and the way he carried it on the playing field.

1624. Hittle, Lloyd Eldon (1949–50 P) "Red." The nickname refers to hair color.

1625. Hoak, Donald Albert (1954–64 3B) "Tiger." Hoak was a professional fighter before his baseball career. He was called "Tiger" by Brooklyn Dodgers teammate Clem Lebine because he liked to pick fights. Hoak once hosted a television show in Pittsburgh called "Tiger by the Tail." On May 2, 1956, while playing for the Chicago Cubs he struck out seven times in a 17-inning game at the Polo Grounds in New York.

1626. Hobson, Clell Lavern, Jr. (1975–82 3B) "Butch." Hobson told me, "My parents thought Butch suited me more than Clell. I have been called Butch since childhood."

1627. Hockette, George Edward (1934–35 P) "Lefty." Hockette pitched left handed and batted left handed.

1628. Hodge, Clarence Clement (1920–22 P) "Shovel." Tom Shea indicates that "Shovel" refers to Hodge's feet, big as shovels.

1629. Hodge, Harold Morris (1971 3B) "Gomer." Hodge wrote me: "I come from North Carolina. In 1964 in the minor leagues my teammates from the North thought I talked like Gomer Pyle on the television show."

1630. Hodkey, Aloysius Joseph (1946 P) "Eli." Origin unknown.

1631. Hoerst, Francis Joseph (1940–47 P) "Lefty." Hoerst pitched left handed and batted left handed.

1632. Hoff, Chester Cornelius (1911–15 P) "Red." The nickname refers to hair color.

1633. Hoffer, William Leopold (1895–1901 P) "Wizard." Joe Overfield indicated "Wizard" referred to Hoffer's pitching. In his first three seasons he was 30-7, 25-7, and 22-11.

1634. Hoffman, Clarence Casper (1929 OF) "Dutch." Hoffman was of German background.

1635. Hoffman, Edward Adolph (1915 3B) "Tex." "Tex" is a place nickname. Hoffman was from San Antonio, Texas.

1636. Hoffman, Frank J. (1988 P) "The Texas Wonder." This is a place nickname. Hoffman was from Houston, Texas.

1637. Hoffman, Harry C. (1904–07 OF) "Izzy." Origin unknown.

1638. Hoffman, John Edward (1964–65 C) "Pork Chop." "Pork Chop" referred to Hoffman's compact build as a catcher.

1639. Hoffman, Otto Charles (1879 C) "Hickey." Origin unknown.

1640. Hofman, Arthur Frederick (1903–16 OF) "Circus Solly." Hofman was known for his circus catches in the outfield. He was named after a comic strip character popular in the early 1900s.

1641. Hofmann, Fred (1919–28 C) "Bootnose." According to Jack Connelly, the nickname described Hofmann's nose.

1642. Hogan, James Francis (1925–37 C) "Shanty." Hogan was of Irish background and from the Boston area. "Shanty" refers to the shacks which many of the poor Irish were forced to live when they first arrived in this country. Hence the phrase "Shanty Irish."

1643. Hogan, William Henry (1911–12 OF) "Happy." Hogan was nicknamed after William L. Bray who managed Vernon in the Pacific Coast League and had the tag of "Happy Hogan."

1644. Holbrook, James Marbury (1935 C) "Sammy." Origin unknown.

1645. Holden, Joseph Francis (1934–36 C) "Socks." Origin unknown.

1646. Holdsworth, James (1876–84 OF) "Long Jim." The nickname refers to Holdsworth's height, although exact figures are not available.

1647. Hogg, William (1905–08 P) "Buffalo Bill." Origin unknown.

1648. Hogsett, Elon Chester (1929–44 P) "Chief." Hogsett wrote me, "I was a bellhop in my sister's hotel while I was in school. One time I took a salesman to his room. He said, 'What the hell are you, an Indian?' I said, 'Yep' and he started calling me Chief. Later I roomed with a full-blooded Indian. He was called 'Chief' and I guess it rubbed off on me."

1649. Holke, Walter Henry (1914–25 1B) "Union Man." Holke was always prompt and on time.

1650. Hollahan, William James (1920 3B) "Happy." Hollahan was easy going and usually had a smile on his face.

1651. Holland, Howard Arthur (1926–29 P) "Mul." "Mul" was short for "Mule." Holland was a hard worker.

1652. Holland, Robert Clyde (1932–34 OF) "Dutch." "Dutch" was a response to the last name of Holland.

1653. Holliday, James Wear (1889–98 OF) "Bug." At 5'7" Holliday looked like a bug in the outfield. Yet he compiled a career batting average of .316 over ten seasons.

1654. Hollingsworth, Albert W. (1935–46 P) "Boots." Before he became a pitcher, Hollingsworth played first base. He booted so many ground balls, players called him "Boots" even after he started pitching.

1655. Hollingsworth, John Burnett (1922–28 P) "Bonnie." Hollingsworth told me there were three Johns in his family, therefore, he was called Burnett. A neighbor boy had a speech impediment and could not pronounce Burnett. It came out "Bonnie." The nickname stuck from childhood.

1656. Hollison, John Henry (1892 P) "Swede." Hollison was of Swedish background.

1657. Hollmig, Stanley Ernest (1949–51 C) "Hondo." Origin unknown.

1658. Holloman, Alva Lee (1953 P) "Bobo." On May 6, 1953, in his first major league start, Holloman pitched a no-hit game for the St. Louis Browns against Philadelphia. It was to be one of only three games he won in the major leagues. He finished the 1953 season with a 3-7 won-lost mark and an ERA of 5.23. It was his only major league season. Holloman told me, "In 1948 with the Nashville Vols', owner Larry Gilbert said, 'You remind me of Bobo Newsom. You are big like him and you pitch like him. I am going to nickname you Bobo Holloman'."

1659. Holloway, Crush (1921–34 OF, Negro League) "Crush." "Crush" *is not* a nickname but Holloway's first name. But it is so unusual, that many people thought it was a nickname and used it as such. John Holway lets Holloway explain how he came by the name of Crush. "Crush, that's my real name, that ain't no nickname, and I'll tell you how I got it. The day I was born, September 16, 1896, down in Hillsboro, Texas, my father was fixing to go see a 'crash,' a collision. They'd take two old locomotive engines and crash them together for excitement, sort of a fair, and my father was going to see it. Before he got on the train, somebody pulled him off and said, 'Your wife is about to have a child.' And when I turned out to be a boy, he named me 'Crush.' That's how I got my name."

1660. Holm, Roscoe Albert (1924–32 OF) "Wattie." Origin unknown.

1661. Holmes, Elwood Marter (1918 P) "Chick." "Chick" referred to Holmes' small stature. Exact statistics, however, are not available.

1662. Holmes, Howard E. (1923–24, AL Umpire) "Ducky." "Ducky" may have referred to small size, but I cannot document this.

1663. Holmes, James William (1895–1905 OF) "Ducky." "Ducky" refers to Holmes' build and walk. He was 5'6" and weighed 170 pounds.

1664. Holmes, Thomas Francis (1942–52 OF) "Kelly." Holmes had a career batting average of .302 in ten seasons. In 1952 he hit .352 for the Boston Braves, but lost the batting title to Dixie Walker's .357. "Kelly" was the name he used to play professional baseball while preserving his amateur status while he was still in high school.

1665. Holt, James Emmett Madison (1925 1B) "Red." The nickname refers to hair color.

1666. Holtgrave, Lavern George (1965 P) "Woody." Origin unknown.

1667. Homes, Howard Elbert (1906 C) "Ducky." Howard Homes was nicknamed after James "Ducky" Homes.

1668. Honeycutt, Frederick Wayne (1977–84 P) "Rick." Honeycutt told me, "My parents always called me Rick because it sounded better than Frederick. Players called me 'Honey'."

1669. Hook, James Wesley (1957–64 P) "Jay." "Jay" is a takeoff on James.

1670. Hooker, William Edward (1902–03 P) "Cy." Hooker was nicknamed after Denton "Cy" Young.

1671. Hooton, Burt Carlton (1971–84 P) "Happy." This is a nickname opposite. Los Angeles manager, Tom Lasorda, called him "Happy" because he seldom was. He was more likely to be morose.

1672. Hoover, Robert Joe (1943–45 SS) "The Carpet Sweeper." The nickname is a response to the last name. Hoover, however, was a smooth fielding shortstop for Detroit during the war years.

1673. Hoover, William J. (1884–92 OF) "Buster." "Buster" referred to Hoover's prowess with the bat. He "busted" the ball.

1674. Hopkins, John Winton (1907 OF) "Sis." The origin of "Sis" is unknown. Since Hopkins was also called "Buck," "Sis" may have been a nickname opposite.

1675. Hopkins, Lolly (1940s–50s) "Megaphone Lolly." Hopkins used a megaphone in Boston ballparks to cheer not only Red Sox and Brave players but also opposing players when they pleased her.

1676. Hopp, John Leonard (1939–52 OF) "Hippity." Hopp was called "Cotney" by his godparents as a child because of his light blond hair. "Hippity" is a response to both cotton as in tail (bunny) and to the last name of Hopp.

1677. Hopper, Clarence F. (1898 P) "Lefty." Hopper pitched left handed. There is no information on how he batted.

1678. Hopper, William Booth (1913–15 P) "Bird Dog." Origin unknown.

1679. Horan, Joseph Patrick (1924 OF) "Shags." Horan was good in the outfield shagging down fly balls.

1680. Horne, Berlyn Dale (1929 P) "Sonny." "Sonny" was a childhood nickname. Horne was also called "Trader" because he played for so many minor league teams.

1681. Horner, James Robert (1978–88 3B) "Red Devil." Horner had no public nickname when he played in the major leagues. When he was not signed as a free agent in 1987, he decided to play in Japan for the Yakult Swallows. As a gaizin (foreigner) he was called the the "Red Devil" because of his reddish hair and the stern look on his face while on the playing field. He was also dubbed "Mr. Ho-Mah" after he delivered 11 home runs in his first 29 games.

1682. Hornsby, Rogers (1915–37 2B) "Rajah." "Rajah" was a nickname of admiration indicating royalty. Hornsby was an outspoken, aggressive driving player with a fierce competitive spirit in the mold of Ty Cobb. He is ranked by many experts as the greatest right hand hitter of all time. In addition he was one of the finest fielding second basemen of his time. Among his many achievements are seven National League batting titles and an average of .424 in 1924, the highest batting average since 1900.

1683. Hornung, Michael Joseph (1879–90 OF) "Ubbo Ubbo." Sam Crane reporting in *The New York Journal* stated that Hornung was called "Ubbo Ubbo" because that is what he yelled whenever he got a hit or made a good play in the field. It started out at first as a sort of self-satisfied grunt and later became a loud habit with him. Both players and fans gave him the nickname.

1684. Horton, Elmer E. (1896–98 P) "Herky Jerky." Lee Allen reports that the nickname refers to the way Horton delivered his pitches.

1685. Host, Eugene Earl (1956–57 P) "Twinkles." Host's wife told me Gene, as he was addressed, received the nickname "Twinkles" when he first started playing organized baseball. He does not know what it means, but it might have referred to his pitching style.

1686. Hotaling, Peter James (1879–88 OF) "Monkey." According to Bob Tremann and Mark Ricker, "His primary position was centerfield, but he also was an infielder and a catcher. The latter position was probably responsible for his nickname, "Monkey."

1687. Houch, Byron Simon (1912–18 P) "Duke." "Duke" noted Houck's propensity for fancy clothes.

1688. Houck, Sargent Perry (1879–87 SS) "Sadie." Origin unknown.

1689. Houk, Ralph George (1947–54 C) "Major." Houk held the rank of major in the Marine Corps. He was a reserve catcher for the New York Yankees for eight years, six of which the Yanks won the World Championship. Yet Houk played in only 91 games during that time obtaining 43 hits in 158 times at bat for a .272 average and drove in 20 runs. In other words, he averaged 5.4 hits per year and drove in 2.5 runs per year. Not bad for getting all those World Series checks!

1690. Houtz, Fred Fritz (1899 OF) "Lefty." Houtz batted left handed, and threw left handed.

1691. Howard, David Austin (1912–15 2B) "Del." Howard was nicknamed after George Elmer "Del" Howard who played from 1903–09.

1692. Howard, Frank Oliver (1958–73 1B) "Hondo." When he played basketball and baseball for Ohio State, Howard was called "Chico." According to Joseph McBride, John Wayne starred in the movie *Hondo* based on a Louis L'Amour western novel in 1953. Hondo means big in Spanish. John Havlicek, who also attended Ohio State before playing basketball for the Boston Celtics, was given the nickname of "Hondo." At 6'7" and 255 pounds, Howard also got the nickname when he started to play professional baseball. When he played for Washington, the media called him "The Capital Punisher" because of his many long home runs.

1693. Howard, George Elmer (1905–09 OF) "Del." "Dell" is a take-off on Elmer.

1694. Howard, Paul Joseph (1909 OF) "Del." Paul Howard was nicknamed "Del" after George "Del" Howard who played in the major leagues 1905–09.

1695. Howe, John (1890–93 2B) "Shorty." Howe was a diminutive second baseman, but his exact height and weight is unknown.

1696. Howe, Lester Curtis (1923–24 P) "Lucky." Origin unknown.

1697. Howell, Henry Harry (1898–1910 P) "Handsome Harry"; (FL Umpire 1915) "Handsome." Howell was considered good looking, especially by women.

1698. Howell, Homer Elliott (1947–56 C) "Dixie." "Dixie" is a place nickname indicating the southern section. Howell was from Louisville, Kentucky. The nickname was given to him while he was still in high school.

1699. Howell, Millard (1940–58 P) "Dixie." "Dixie" is a place nickname indicating southern section of the country. Howell was from Bowman, Kentucky.

1700. Howell, Murray Donald (1941 PH) "Red." The nickname refers to hair color. Howell was also called "Porky." He was 6'0" and weighed over 200 pounds.

1701. Howell, Roland Boatner (1912 P) "Billiken." Origin unknown.

1702. Howerton, William Roy (1949–52 OF) "Hopalong." Howerton wrote me, "When I was 9 years old I sprained my ankle and developed osteomyelitis. It left the ankle practically stiff. So, when I ran it gave me a hopalong appearance. Pitcher Howard Pollet gave me the nickname when I joined the St. Louis Cardinals in 1949."

1703. Howley, Daniel Philip (1913 C) "Dapper Dan." Howley was soft spoken off the field, a classy dresser and a gentlemen with polish. However, he was also called "Howling Dan" because of his strong voice on the field which he used often.

1704. Hoy, William Ellsworth (1888–1902 OF) "Dummy." Hoy was a 5'4", 148-pound deaf mute, but he played 14 years in the major leagues and lived to be 99. He made 2,054 major league hits and had a career average of .288. Meningitis caused his malady at age three. Since he could not hear, he had to be signaled about balls and strikes by hand. This may have started the tradition of umpires using hand signals. Fans, realizing that Hoy could not hear would wave handkerchiefs at him when they appreciated his play. On June 19, 1889, while playing for Washington against Indianapolis, Hoy was credited with three assists from the outfield to home plate. In the minor leagues while playing for Oskosh against St. Paul he jumped on a horse to catch a fly ball. Today, a nickname like "Dummy" would seem cruel and out of order. It was not, however, viewed in that light in Hoy's time. In fact, Hoy liked the nickname and insisted that people refer to him by it.

1705. Hoyle, Roland Edison (1952 P) "Tex." Hoyle was not from Texas but Carbondale, Pennsylvania. He wrote me, "In 1940 I was playing with Butler in the Penn State League. Al Rizzuto, the brother of Phil, and Sal Recca called me 'Tex' because I was so tall." Hoyle was 6'4" and weighed 210 pounds.

1706. Hoyte, Waite Charles (1918–38 P) "Schoolboy." Hoyt won 221 games in the major leagues and appeared in seven World Series. Hoyte pitched batting practice at Ebbets Field in Brooklyn before graduating from Brooklyn's Erasmus High School and signed a contract at age 16. From then on he was known as "Schoolboy."

1707. Hrabosky, Alan Thomas (1970–82 P) "The Mad Hungarian." Hrabosky was of Hungarian background. He could be a devastating relief pitcher at times. In 1975 he led the National League in saves with 22. Hrabosky wore a Fu Manchu mustache and carried a menacing look on his face to go along with his live fastball. He appeared to have Rasputin-like powers on the mound. He would become so angry while pitching that he often lost his concentration. He would then step off the mound between pitches, turn his back to the hitter, hunch his shoulders, lower his head and squeeze the ball savagely. Then throw it in his mitt and charge back to the pitching rubber ready to face the batter. His manner was entertaining to fans and disconcerting to batters.

1708. Hubbard, Jessie (1919–34 P, Negro League) "Mountain." Donn Rogosin remarked that Hubbard was a hulk of a country boy. He also played outfield when he was not pitching.

1709. Hubbard, R. Cal (1936–51, 54–62 AL Umpire) "Big Cal." Hubbard was 6'2½" and weighed 265 pounds. Before he became an umpire, Hubbard played professional football as a lineman.

1710. Hubbell, Carl Owen (1928–43 P) "King Carl." Hubbell won 253 major league games in 16 seasons, winning 20 or more three times. He also won four World Series games. He received the "King Carl" tag after pitching two complete game victories over Washington in the 1933 World Series. The nickname was reinforced the next year in the All Star game when he struck out Ruth, Gehrig, Foxx, Simmons and Cronin consecutively. From 1933 on Hubbell was also called "The Meal Ticket" because of his ability to win crucial games and prevent losing streaks. He also carried the tag of "Long Pants" because of his habit of fastening his knee pants just above his ankles.

1711. Huber, Clarence Bill (1920–28 2B) "Gilly." "Gilly" was a takeoff on "Billy."

1712. Hudlin, George Willis (1926–44 P) "Ace." Hudlin was called "Ace" by his Cleveland teammates in 1927. As a rookie he won 18 games for the sixth place club.

1713. Hudson, Hal Campbell (1952–53 P) "Lefty." Hudson pitched left handed and batted left handed.

1714. Hudspeth, Robert (1920–32 1B, Negro League) "High Pockets." The nickname refers to Hudspeth's long legs. In 1926 he led the league with a .365 batting average.

1715. Huggins, Miller (1904–16 2B) "The Mighty Mite." Miller Huggins stood 5'6½" and weighed 140 pounds. He played second base in the National League for 13 years, 1904–16. He began his career in organized baseball however, in 1899, with the Mansfield, Ohio, team in the Inter-State League, using the name of "Proctor," since he was attending college at the time. While playing for the St. Louis Cardinals, his size and ability to get on base, steal bases, and score runs earned him the nickname of "Rabbit." Most often, however, he was addressed as "Hug." "Hug" managed in the major leagues for 17 years, 1913–29. His worst finish was seventh place in 1925. Between 1921–28 he won six pennants and three World Series with the New York Yankees. It was during his years with the Yankees when he had to control the strong-willed Yankee players such as Babe Ruth, Joe Bush, and Joe Dugan, that "the Mighty Mite" sobriquet was most appropriate.

1716. Hughes, James Michael (1974–77 P) "Bluegill." According to

Joseph McBride when Hughes was on a hot streak in 1975, St. Paul sportswriter, Pat Reusee, started calling him "Bluegill" reasoning that if the Yanks could have their "Catfish" (Hunter), the Twins could have their "Bluegill." Bluegills are another name for the sunfish which are common in the waters of Minnesota.

1717. Hughes, Roy John (1935–46 2B) "Jeep." "Jeep" referred to Hughes' speed. He was also called "Sage" referring to his knowledge and "Whispering" because he talked softly and close to the listener's ear.

1718. Hughes, Thomas L. (1906–18 P) "Long Tom." Hughes was 6'2" and weighed 175 pounds.

1719. Hughes, Vernon Alexander (1914 P) "Lefty." Hughes pitched left handed and batted left handed.

1720. Hughey, James Ulysses (1891–1900 P) "Coldwater Jim." This is a place nickname. Hughey was from Coldwater, Michigan.

1721. Hughson, Cecil Carlton (1941–49 P) "Tex." "Tex" is a place nickname. Hughson was from Kyle, Texas.

1722. Huhn, Emil (1915–17 1B) "Hap." "Hap" is short for "Happy" referring to Huhn's disposition.

1723. Hummell, John Edwin (1905–18 2B) "Silent John." Hummell was uncommunitive. He talked little on or off the field, even to close friends.

1724. Hundley, Cecil Randolph (1964–77 C) "Rebel." Hundley was from Martinsville, Virginia. He had a very deep southern drawl which left no doubt what section of the country he called home. Hundley was one of the first catchers to place his right hand behind his back when catching a pitch.

1725. Hundling, Bernard Herman (1922–30 C) "Bud." "Bud" in Hundling's case was a boyhood family nickname.

1726. Hunnefield, William Fenton (1926–31 SS) "Wild Bill." Origin unknown.

1727. Hunt, Benjamin Franklin (1910–13 P) "Highpockets." Hunt had unusually long legs on his 6'1" frame.

1728. Hunter, Frederick Creighton (1911 1B) "Newt." Origin unknown.

1729. Hunter, Harold James, III (1971–75 2B) "Buddy." Hunter told me his grandmother gave him the nickname of "Buddy" because she thought there were too many Harolds in the family.

1730. Hunter, James Augustus (1965–79 P) "Catfish." Hunter was one of the premier American League pitchers of the late 1960s and 1970s. He won 224 games in 15 seasons. Oakland owner Charles Finley signed Hunter upon his graduation from high school in 1964 for a $50,000 bonus. At the press conference signing, for publicity purposes, Finley decided Hunter needed a nickname. Assuming his being from Hartford, North Carolina, he had done a lot of fishing, Finley introduced him as "Catfish" Hunter. As it turned out Hunter had no association with "catfish" before or after the conference. But that was to be his nickname throughout his career. In 1974 Hunter sued Finley for breech of contract for not paying $50,000 of his $100,000 salary on a deferred basis, and won the case. He was declared a free agent. After an unprecedented bidding war, Hunter signed a five-year contract with the New York Yankees for an estimated $3.75 million. This was the real start of free agency for baseball players and multi-year, multimillion dollar contracts.

1731. Huntzinger, Walter Henry (1923–26 P) "Shakes." Kit Crissey reports that "Shakes" refers to Huntzinger's poker playing. Whenever he had a hot hand, his hands began to shake.

1732. Hurd, Thomas Carr (1954–56 P) "Whitey." Hurd had very light blond hair.

1733. Hurley, Edwin H. (1947–65 AL Umpire) "Butch." "Butch" was a childhood nickname.

1734. Hurley, Jerry J. (1901–07 C) "Pat." Origin unknown.

1735. Husta, Carl Lawrence (1925 SS) "Sox." Origin unknown.

1736. Husting, Berthold Jeneau (1900–02 P) "Pete." Origin unknown.

1737. Hutcheson, Joseph Johnson (1938 OF) "Poodles." Hutcheson had large feet. When he ran, it reminded people of the way a poodle dog runs.

1738. Hutchinson, William Forrest (1889–97 P) "Wild Bill." Hutchinson gave up an unusually high number of walks. From 1889–96 he averaged 160 walks. At the same time, however, he averaged better than 25 wins per season and 175 strikeouts. In 1891 he won 43 games and dropped only 19. Hutchinson was a graduate of Yale University.

I

1739. Iburg, Herman Edward (1902 P) "Ham." The nickname of "Ham" is a play on Herman's last name.

1740. Imlay, Harry Miller (1913 P) "Doc." Imlay was a practicing dentist, having received his D.D.S. degree from the University of Pennsylvania.

1741. Ingerton, William John (1911 3B) "Scotty." The nickname refers to Ingerton's Scottish background.

1742. Iott, Clarence Eugene (1941-47 P) "Hooks." This left handed pitcher was known for his curveball.

1743. Iott, Fred John (1903 OF) "Dimples." Iott was addressed as "Happy." His dimples gave him the appearance of always having a smile on his face.

1744. Irelan, Harold (1914 2B) "Grump." Hal, as he was addressed, always had a serious look on his face, and in fact, was a very serious person.

1745. Irwin, Arthur Albert (1884-89 P) "Cut Rate." As a player Irwin did not have a distinctive nickname. As a manager, he was called "Cut Rate" because he would work for less money than other managers would. This made him in demand, and on the move for a ten-year period—1889 Washington (NL), 1891 Boston (AA), 1892 Washington (NL), 1894 Philadelphia (NL), 1896 New York (NL), 1898-99 Washington (NL).

1746. Irwin, Walter Kingsley (1921 PH) "Lightning." "Lightning" refers to Walt's speed which he was never able to demonstrate in the major leagues, appearing in only four games, and striking out in his only trip to the plate.

1747. Isabel, William Frank (1898-1909 1B) "Bald Eagle." Frank was completely bald, and selfconscious about it. He always kept his cap tightly on his head. Although first base was Isabel's primary position, he saw action at all other positions including pitcher and catcher. In the 1906 World Series for example, he played exclusively at second base for the Chicago White Sox.

1748. Izquierdo, Enrique Roberto (1967 C) "Hank." Origin unknown.

J

1749. Jackson, Charles Herbert (1915–17 OF) "Lefty." Jackson pitched left handed, and batted left handed.

1750. Jackson, George Christopher (1911–13 OF) "Hickory." Jackson was nicknamed after President Andrew Jackson whose nickname was "Old Hickory." At 6'1½" and 180 pounds, Jackson somewhat resembled the seventh president of the United States.

1751. Jackson, Grant Dwight (1965–82 P) "Buck." For Jackson, "Buck" has a specific connotation. Jackson wrote me, "My father gave me the nickname when I was 12 years old. I was plowing a field and my dad called. I stopped the tractor and ran across the field. He said I looked like a young buck running. I liked it, and it stuck."

1752. Jackson, Joseph Jefferson (1908–20 OF) "Shoeless Joe." In his biography, *Say It Ain't So, Joe!* Donald Gropman gives Scoop Latimer, a writer for the Greenville, South Carolina, newspaper, credit for first using the nickname of "Shoeless Joe" in print in 1908. Jackson, playing for Greenville against Anderson in a Carolina Association game, did so without wearing shoes. A fan shouted, "Look at 'Shoeless Joe'." The day before, Jackson's feet blistered when he tried to break in a new pair of shoes. The next day, he went back to the old pair, but his feet still hurt, even in them. Therefore, rather than not play, he went without shoes. Jackson's play was of Hall of Fame quality. One of the games greatest pure hitters, his average for 13 seasons was .356. However, Jackson was involved in the Chicago White Sox scandal to throw the 1919 World Series and was banned from baseball for life by baseball commissioner Judge Landes. As yet, he has not been admitted to the Hall of Fame. Jackson became the main character and hero of W.P. Kinsella's 1982 novel, *Shoeless Joe* and the subsequent 1989 movie *Field of Dreams*. Both helped revive the memory of Jackson to new generations of baseball fans.

1753. Jackson, Ransom Joseph (1950–59 3B) "Handsome Ransom." Jackson's looks were particularly appealing to women. His little boy smile, soft brown eyes and chiseled chin, led women to either want to mother him, or date him depending on their age.

1754. Jackson, Reginald Martinez (1967–87 OF) "Mr. October." The outspoken and controversial Jackson slugged 563 career home runs in 21 seasons, the sixth, best total of all time. None of them, however, brought him the recognition that the 16 he hit in post season play during the month of October did, six in League Championship Series, and ten in the World Series. Yankee teammate Thurman Munson called Jackson "Mr. October" for his key hitting during the 1977 League Championship Series. The media picked it up when he hit five home runs in the World Series. Jackson liked the nickname. "That's what I call home runs. Dingers. I've hit a bunch of them when it mattered, in Oakland and Baltimore and New York and now in California. I guess that's why the late Thurman Munson started calling me 'Mr. October.' That was a nickname I liked."

Players usually addressed Jackson as "Buck."

1755. Jackson, Roland Thomas (1963–74 SS) "Sonny." "Sonny" was a boyhood nickname that fit Jackson's diminutive size. With Joe Morgan at Houston in 1963 Jackson was part of a youthful and phenomenal double-play combination.

1756. Jackson, Travis Calvin (1922–30 SS) "Stonewall." Jackson was nicknamed after the Civil War general, Thomas "Stonewall" Jackson. Jackson was a "stonewall" at shortstop. Sometimes he was referred to as "Jax" in the press.

1757. Jackson, Vincent Edward (1986– OF) "Bo." Ira Berkow quotes Jackson, a Heisman Trophy winner in football. "When I was a boy coming up, I was a real bad kid, the bully of the neighborhood. My older brothers said I was mean as a boar hog. Bo is short for boar hog. My real name is Vincent, but nobody calls me that anymore. Even my mother calls me Bo."

1758. Jacobs, Forrest Vandergrift (1954–56 2B) "Spook." The nickname refers to the type of hits Jacobs got. Many were not well hit, but somehow eluded fielder's grasp. They were spooky. Jacobs is one of only seven players to collect four hits in his first major league game.

1759. Jacobs, Newton Smith (1937–40 P) "Bucky." "Bucky" was a childhood nickname.

1760. Jacobson, Albert L. (1904–07 P) "Beany." Jacobson had a tendency to pitch batters inside, and consequently hit a number of them.

1761. Jacobson, William Chester (1915–27 OF) "Baby Doll." Jacobson, a 6'2½" and 210-pound slugger, earned his nickname "Baby Doll" while playing for Mobile in the Southern Association in 1912. In the home opener on April 15th, he hit a prodigious home run and the band immediately broke out with one of the popular tunes of the day, "Oh You Beautiful Doll." An enterprising sports reporter picked it up and the next day the *Mobile Register* carried a picture of Jacobson with the overhead caption, "That Baby Doll."

1762. Jaeger, Charles Thomas (1904 P) "Zip." "Zip" referred to the sound of Jaeger's fastball as it approached the plate.

1763. Jakucki, Sigmund (1936–45 P) "Jack." "Jack" is a takeoff on the last name of Jakucki.

1764. Jamerson, Charles Dewey (1924 P) "Lefty." Jamerson pitched left handed and batted left handed.

1765. James, Berton Huldon (1909 OF) "Jessie." The last name recalls the post–Civil War bank and train robber Jessie James.

1766. James, Jeffery Lynn (1968–69 P) "Jessie." James was nicknamed after the post–Civil War train and bank robber Jessie James.

1767. James, Philip Robert (1977–78 1B) "Skip." Origin unknown.

1768. James, Robert Eugene (1929–33 2B) "Bernie." Origin unknown.

1769. James, William A. (1912–14 P) "Lefty." James pitched left handed, but batted right handed.

1770. James, William Henry (1911–19 P) "Big Bill." James was 6'4" and weighed 195 pounds. When he played for Portland in the Pacific Coast League he was known as "Portland Bill." This was to distinguish him from

William Laurance James a 6'3" and 196-pound pitcher for Seattle.

1771. James, William Lawrence (1913–19 P) "Seattle Bill." When he pitched for Seattle in the Pacific Coast League, James was nicknamed "Seattle Bill" to distinguish him from William Henry James, who was pitching for Portland at the same time.

1772. Jantzen, Walter C. (1912 OF) "Heinie." "Heinie" denotes Jantzen's German background.

1773. Janvrin, Harold Chandler (1911–22 SS) "Childe Harold." Tom Shea reports that Janvrin was a Boston schoolboy who went directly to the Red Sox. He was nicknamed after the Knight who gives the title to the poem by George Byron, *Childe Harold*.

1774. Jasper, Henry W. (1914–18 P) "Hi." "Hi" was a short alternative for Henry coming from boyhood days.

1775. Javery, Alva William (1940–46 P) "Bear Tracks." According to Tom Shea, Javery's big feet displaced large chunks of turf when he stomped around the diamond.

1776. Javier, Manual Julian Liranzo (1960–72 2B) "The Phantom." "Hoolie" (from his middle name) as Javier was usually addressed, earned "The Phantom" nickname from his ability to make the pivot on the double play and avoid the runner sliding in. Shortstop Del Maxvill said he looks, "like a ghost dancing in the air."

1777. Jeanes, Ernest Lee (1921–27 OF) "Tex." This is a place nickname. Jeanes was from Maypearl, Texas.

1778. Jelincich, Frank Anthony (1941 OF) "Jelly." "Jelly" is a takeoff on the last name of Jelincich.

1779. Jenkins, Clarence (1920–40 OF, Negro League) "Fats." According to Robert Peterson, Jenkins was not even chubby let alone fat. For some unknown reason, he inherited the nickname from his brother who was fat.

1780. Jenkins, Warren Washington (1962–69 P) "Hog." Jenkins told me his Washington teammate Bob Chance called him a "Hog" because he tried to steal the spotlight after hitting a home run.

1781. Jennings, Alfred (1878 C) "Alamazoo." This is a place nickname. According to an unidentified newspaper article dated November 29, 1890, "Alamazoo" is short for Kalamazoo, Michigan, where Jennings once played.

1782. Jennings, Hugh Ambrose (1891–1918 SS) "Ee-Yah." Jennings was a cocky, tough and talented member of the Baltimore Orioles who terrorized the National League in the 1890s. In compiling a .312 average over 17 seasons, the shortstop fractured his skull three times. His greatest fame and his nickname, however, come from his managerial career when he led Detroit to three straight flags, 1907–09. "Ee-Yah, Ee-Yah" was his famous and popular cheer from the coaching box. Fred Lieb describes, "He pulled up fistfuls of grass from around the coach's box, raised his left foot and with clenched fists gave vent to his famous cry."

1783. Jensen, Forrest Docenus (1931–39 OF) "Woody." Jensen claims he received the nickname of "Woody" because he played ball in the Timber League, an independent organization in the state of Washington. However, a response to the first name of Forrest likely reinforced the nickname.

1784. Jethroe, Samuel (1950–54 OF) "Jet." Jethroe had great speed. As a 28-year-old rookie, he led the National League in stolen bases with 35 for the Boston Braves and then duplicated the feat the following year.

1785. Jimenez, Alfonso Gonzalez (1983–87 SS) "Houston." In this case Houston is not a place nickname. It refers to a Mexican cowboy TV character of whom Jimenez identified.

1786. Jimenez, Manuel Emilio (1962–69 OF) "Houston." Origin unknown.

1787. Johns, Augustus Francis (1926–27 P) "Lefty." Johns pitched left handed, and batted left handed.

1788. Johns, William R. (1915–18 3B) "Pete." Johns' father did not like the name of William and always called him "Pete."

1789. Johnson, Adam Rankin, Sr. (1914–18 P) "Tex." This is a place nickname. Johnson was born in Burnet, Texas.

1790. Johnson, Charles Cleveland (1908 OF) "Home Run." Johnson was at bat only 16 times in the major leagues and did not hit a home run. He was, however, a slugger in the minor leagues. In 1912 he hit .403 for Trenton in the Tri-State League.

1791. Johnson, Clifford (1953–58 P) "Connie." Johnson wrote me, "I got the tag while playing in the minor leagues because I liked the music of the Boswell sisters. I started calling everybody Connie [the most famous of the Boswell sisters] after the lead singer. I don't know why. After that everybody started calling me Connie."

1792. Johnson, Clifford, Jr. (1972–86 DH) "Heathcliff." Johnson was nicknamed "Heathcliff" after the central character in Charlotte Brontë's novel *Wuthering Heights* because of his mountainous size. He was also called "Boomer" for his power and "Top Cat."

1793. Johnson, Donald Spore (1943–48 2B) "Pop." Johnson became a rookie at age 32.

1794. Johnson, Earl Douglas (1940–51 P) "Lefty." Johnson pitched left handed, and batted left handed.

1795. Johnson, Elmer Ellsworth (1914 C) "Hickory." "Hickory," in Johnson's case refers to hard and tough play behind the plate.

1796. Johnson, Frederick Edward (1922–39 P) "Cactus." Johnson came from the Texas cactus country. He was born in Hanley, Texas. Johnson pitched for the New York Giants in 1922–23, and then did not pitch again in the major leagues until 1938 with the St. Louis Browns.

1797. Johnson, George (1899–1921 C, Negro League) "Chappie." Johnson was noted as a smooth catcher, one of the best at the turn of the century. "Chappie" refers to Johnson's propensity to dress in cane and spots.

1798. Johnson, Grant (1895–1921 2B, Negro League) "Home Run." A powerful right hand swinger, Johnson earned the nickname during the deadball era. His most notable achievement came in 1910 when he out-hit Ty Cobb and Sam Crawford of the Detroit Tigers in a 12-game series in Cuba playing for the Havana Reds.

1799. Johnson, Harry S. (1915 NL Umpire) "Steamboat." Johnson was from Memphis, Tennessee, and owned a restaurant called Steamboat Johnson's Eat Shoppe, a favorite gathering place for men in the cotton trade. The "Steamboat" nickname was reinforced because Johnson bellowed like a fog horn on a Mississippi River steamboat. He spent almost his entire career in the Southern League where he became a tradition. Johnson had his eyes checked regularly to verify he possessed 20/20 vision. He carried a certificate to verify his excellent sight. If a batter called him blind, he would quickly produce his certificate.

1800. Johnson, Howard Michael (1982– 3B) "Ho Jo." "Ho Jo" used the first two letters of his first and last names. The hotel and restaurant chain that bears the same name houses Ho Jo's ice cream parlors.

1801. Johnson, John Clifford (1944–45 P) "Swede." Johnson was of Swedish background.

1802. Johnson, John Louis (1894 P) "Youngy." Origin unknown.

1803. Johnson, John Ralph (1889–91 OF) "Spud." Origin unknown.

1804. Johnson, Kenneth Wandersee (1947–52 P) "Hooks." Johnson had a terrific curveball, but sometimes had difficulty getting it over the plate.

1805. Johnson, Lloyd William (1934 P) "Eppa." Origin unknown.

1806. Johnson, Louis Brown (1960–69 OF) "Sweet Lou." The nickname refers to how Johnson swung the bat, loved the game and his disposition. He had a style and dash about him that was contagious. He was also called "Slick."

1807. Johnson, Oscar (1922–30 OF, Negro League) "Heavy." Johnson weighed in excess of 250 pounds. With the Kansas City Monarchs in 1922, he led the league in batting with an average of .389.

1808. Johnson, Randall David (1988– P) "Unit." Johnson was nicknamed by his Seattle teammates. "Unit" refers to his height of 6'10", the tallest pitcher in major league history.

1809. Johnson, Richard Allan (1958 PH) "Footer." Johnson failed to get a hit in five times at bat in the major leagues. He wrote me, "I have 13B feet, large for someone 5'11". My teammate on the basketball and baseball teams at Duke, Dick Groat, give me the nickname." For the same reason Johnson was also called "Treads."

1810. Johnson, Robert Lee (1933–45 OF) "Indian Bob." Johnson was a Cherokee Indian. In 13 years he batted .296 with 2,081 hits.

1811. Johnson, Roy Cleveland (1929–38 OF) "Hard Rock." Johnson really did not have a public nickname as a player. "Hard Rock" refers to his minor league managerial days when he became a stickler for hard play from his players.

1812. Johnson, Russell Conwell (1916–28 P) "Jing." Origin unknown.

1813. Johnson, Walter Perry (1909–27 P) "The Big Train." Johnson was one of the two or three greatest pitchers of all time. In 21 years he won 416 games with a career ERA of 2.17. For years his career strikeout mark of 3,509 was a mark which seemed untouchable. His 110 shutouts still tops the all-time list. Johnson's best pitch was a fastball which players claimed whizzed by batters like a fast express train by a flag stop. Sportswriter Grantland Rice either created or popularized "The Big Train" nickname when in 1911 he wrote of the 6'1" and 200-pound fire balling right hander, "'The Big Train' comes to town today." In 1911 big trains were among the fastest modes of movement humans could conceive. However, many players and fans addressed Johnson as "Barney." The reference was to Barney Oldfield a race car driver who was setting speed records. Other nicknames used for Johnson were "The Kansas Cyclone"—he was from Humbolt, Kansas—and "Sir Walter."

1814. Johnson, William J. (1921–38 3B, Negro League) "Judy." Johnson was called Billy as a child. When he started playing organized baseball, he was nicknamed "Judy" after Robert "Jude" Gans, outfielder, pitcher, manager in the Negro leagues from 1910–38. When he played in Cuba, his Spanish nickname was "Platanito," meaning banana. Johnson was 5'11½" but weighed only 145 pounds, yet his batting average was always around .300. At third base, he had sure hands and a strong throw. He was always regarded as one of the smartest players in the game.

1815. Johnson, William Russell (1943–53 3B) "Bull." Johnson earned the nickname of "Bull" during his rookie season in 1943 for his hard work at bat, in the field and on the base paths.

1816. Johnson, William T. (1884–92 OF) "Sleepy Bill." Origin unknown.

1817. Johnston, Wheeler Rodger (1909–22 1B) "Doc." Many of the players with the nickname of "Doc" had an association with either the medical or dental professions. For Johnston, however, the origin of "Doc" is unknown.

1817a. Johnston, Wilfred Ivy (1924 3B) "Red Top." The nickname refers to hair color.

1818. Johnstone, John William (1966–85 OF) "Moon Man." Johnstone played in the major leagues for 20 years and terrorized eight different teams with his wild antics and numerous pranks. The *Los Angeles Times* described Johnstone as "The Man Who Fell to Earth." When he played outfield for the White Sox in the early 1970s, a joke going around the league was, "Question: Where did the Sox get Johnstone? Answer: Neil Armstrong brought him back from the moon!" Among his stunts was to spray "GH" on players shoes and bats (Green Hornet). One hot day when he was playing for Los Angeles he put a melted brownie in Steve Garvey's glove and wiped the excess on pitcher Jerry Reuss' pants. Then he watched Garvey go after Reuss for messing around with his glove. Bruce Shlain recounts the following incident, "In spring training at Vero Beach, with the help of catcher Steve Yeager, he tied a sailor's knot around a palm tree and tied the other end to the door of manager Tommy Lasorda's room, making it impossible for him to get out. They disconnected his phone before that, and so he was trapped. He screamed until a hotel employee let him out, but by then—tragically for Lasorda—it was too late for breakfast if he wanted to catch the team bus." These, and many other incidents are described in Johnstone's two books, *Temporary Insanity* and *Over the Edge*.

1819. Joiner, Roy Merrill (1934–40 P) "Pop." Joiner was a 28-year-old rookie with grey, silvery hair.

1820. Jok, Stanley Edward (1954–55 3B) "Tucker." Origin unknown.

1821. Jolley, Smead Powell (1930–33 OF) "Smudge." Jolley was a notoriously poor outfielder which led to the nickname of "Smudge." He was also called "Guinea" after he once ordered a $6 guinea hen special for dinner. Jolley had a reputation as a playboy and womanizer which led to the tag of "Big Stud."

1822. Jolly, David (1953–57 P) "Gabby." Jolly was known for his gift of gab.

1823. Jones, Albert Edward (1898–1901 P) "Cowboy." Jones was from the cowboy country of Colorado and was involved with horses in the off season. He was also called "Bronco."

1824. Jones, Carroll Elmer (1916–18 P) "Deacon." Jones inherited the nickname from his father.

1825. Jones, Charles C. (1901–08 OF) "Casey." Jones was nicknamed after John Luther "Casey" Jones, the legendary Illinois Central railroad engineer who gave his life to save the lives of his passengers and crew on April 29, 1900. At Vaughan, Mississippi, engine 382 struck the rear of a two freight trains protruding from a siding. "Casey" was found dead with one hand on throttle and one on the air brakes. If he had not stuck with the engine, the crash would have been much worse. The train was called "Cannonball," and was a speedster between Chicago and New Orleans.

1826. Jones, Charles Leander (1892–93 P) "Bumper." Jones was from the small town of Cedarville, Ohio, and thought to be something of a "Country Bumpkin" or "Rube."

1827. Jones, Charles Lesley (1876–88 OF) "Long Charlie." Origin unknown.

1828. Jones, Dale Eldon (1941 P) "Nubs." Origin unknown.

1829. Jones, Daniel Albion (1883 P) "Jumping Jack." Jones had an odd pitching motion which made it appear he was jumping when he threw a pitch.

1830. Jones, David Jefferson (1901–15 OF) "Kangaroo." Tom Shea attributes the "Kangaroo" tag to the fact that Jones leaped from Milwaukee to Chicago to St. Louis and back to Chicago during the first years of National League–American League conflict (1901–03).

1831. Jones, Douglas Reid (1982– P) "Special Delivery." According to Tony Kubeck, Jones is a relief pitcher who delivers the mail.

1832. Jones, Earl Leslie (1945 P) "Lefty." Jones pitched left handed, and batted left handed.

1833. Jones, Elijah Albert (1907–08 P) "Bumpus." Jones was from the small town of Oxford, Michigan, and was thought to be a "Country Bumpkin" or "Rube."

1834. Jones, Grover William (1962–66 1B) "Deacon." Jones told me, "I received my nickname in childhood by school chums. It was because of my father who was a bonafide deacon at the Union Baptist Church in Greensburgh, New York."

1835. Jones, Henry M. (1884–90 2B) "Baldy." Jones was almost completely bald.

1836. Jones, Howard (1921 OF) "Cotton." Jones had light blond hair.

1837. Jones, James Murrell (1941–48 1B) "Jake." "Jake" was used as an alternative to James. Jones was a Navy fighter pilot in World War II and won the Silver Star, three Distinguished Flying Crosses and seven other medals. He was credited with shooting down seven Japanese planes. He was called "Jake" in the Navy in place of James. He liked the nickname and kept it when he returned to baseball in 1946.

1838. Jones, James Tilford (1887–1902 OF) "Sheriff." Jones served three terms as Laurel County Kentucky Court Clerk.

1839. Jones, Jessie Frank (1923 P) "Broadway." "Broadway" refers to Jones' flashy dress and love of night life.

1840. Jones, John Joseph (1924 SS) "Binky." "Binky" referred to Jones' size, 5'9" and 154 pounds.

1841. Jones, John William (1923-32 OF) "Johnny on the Spot." In 1932 Jones was batting .351 for Albany in the Eastern League, when the league folded over night. While waiting for an offer from another club, he attended a Philadelphia A's game. When Rodger Cramer of the A's broke his collarbone during the game, Connie Mack had Jones paged and immediately sent him into play. He was really a "Johnny on the spot." Jones was also called "Skins."

1842. Jones, Kenneth Frederick (1924-30 P) "Broadway." According to Lee Allen, Jones actually once lived on Broadway.

1843. Jones, Mack (1961-71 OF) "Mack the Knife." Jones was nicknamed after the character in the hit song "Mack the Knife" made popular by Louis Armstrong in 1957; Bobby Darin, 1959; and Ella Fitzgerald, 1960. The music, written by Kurt Weill, comes from the musical "The Three Penny Opera."

1844. Jones, Nicholas J. (1944-49 AL Umpire) "Red." The nickname refers to hair color.

1845. Jones, Oscar Winfield (1903-05 P) "Flip Flop." Tom Shea reports that Jones was an accomplished gymnast.

1846. Jones, Robert Walter (1917-25 3B) "Ducky." Origin unknown.

1847. Jones, Ryerson L. (1883-84 SS) "Angel Sleeves." Ryerson once wore a jacket on the field, and when the wind blew, his sleeves looked like the sleeves artists paint as those of angels.

1848. Jones, Samuel (1951-54 P) "Toothpick." Jones played with a toothpick in his mouth when he was batting. Another nickname was "Sad Sam" after Samuel Pond "Sad Sam" Jones. It was given to him when he played at Wilkes Barre by sportswriter Bill Phillip. On May 12, 1950, pitching for the Chicago Cubs against Pittsburgh, Jones went into the ninth inning with a no-hit game on the line. He loaded the bases with walks and then struck out the side to complete the no-hitter.

1849. Jones, Samuel Pond (1914-35 P) "Sad Sam." Jones pitched for 22 years in the major leagues and won 229 games. He also pitched in four World Series, but lost both his decisions. He always seemed nervous during the games he pitched which contributed to his nickname. It was assigned to him by writer Bill McGeehan of the *New York Herald Tribune*. He called him "Sad Sam the Sorrowful from Woodsfeld, Ohio." He thought Jones always looked sad and downcast when he pitched.

1850. Jones, Sheldon Leslie (1946-53 P) "Available." This nickname was acquired early in Jones' career when he was pitching for Oklahoma in the Texas League. He would announce to everyone that he was available to pitch when anyone needed help. He once appeared in 19 consecutive games in the minor leagues. Frank Graham suggests that the nickname may have come from the "Available Jones" character in Al Capps "Lil' Abner" comic strip which first appeared in 1934.

1851. Jones, Sherman Jarvis (1960-62 P) "Roadblock." In 1960 while pitching for Tacoma in the Pacific Coast League, Jones won both ends of a doubleheader in relief. A local sportswriter wrote that every time he came in to pitch, the road to home was blocked.

1852. Jones, Stuart (1933–38 P, Negro League) "Slim." Jones was 6'6" and weighed 185 pounds. His blazing fastball once gave him a 32-4 season with the Philadelphia Stars.

1853. Jones, Vernal Leroy (1946–57 1B) "Nippy." Jones was nicknamed after his father. He told me, "My Dad's nickname was 'Nip.' When I was born, they called me Little Nippy."

1854. Jones, William Dennis (1911–12 OF) "Midget." Jones stood 5'6½" tall and weighed 157 pounds.

1855. Jones, William Roderick (1911 1B) "Tex." Jones was not from the state of Texas. "Tex" referred to his large size.

1856. Jones, Willie Edward (1947–61 3B) "Puddin' Head." Jones received his nickname as a boy. It comes from the song "Wooden Head, Puddin' Head Jones." It dates from 1933 with words and music by Alfred Bryan and Lou Handman.

1857. Jonnard, Clarence James (1920–35 C) "Bubber." This is an example of a childhood nickname. Jonnard, as a young boy, was unable to pronounce "brother" properly. It came out "Bubber" and became his nickname.

1858. Jordan, Adolph William (1903–04 2B) "Dutch." "Dutch" refers to Jordan's German background.

1859. Jordan, Baxter Byerly (1927–38 1B) "Buck." Jordan wrote me: "I was 18 years old playing the Piedmont League with the Salisbury Colonials. I played shortstop and had a strong arm and was kind of a showoff. A sportswriter, Shorty Daniels picked up the Buck chant from the fans. He also called me 'Cat Eye' because of my ability to follow the ball at the plate."

1860. Jordan, Clarence Veasy (1901–02 OF) "Slats." Jordan was tall and thin as a teenager. He came to bat seven times in the major leagues without getting a hit.

1861. Jordan, James William (1933–36 2B) "Lord." Origin unknown.

1862. Jordan, Raymond Willis (1912–19 P) "Lanky." "Lanky" refers to Jordan's tall and slim build. He was also called "Rip" which refers to his pitching. He ripped it when he threw the ball.

1863. Jorgensen, Carl (1937 OF) "Pinky." Jorgensen told me that as a child other kids started calling him "Pinky" because he had a brother whose nickname was "Red."

1864. Jorgensen, John Donald (1947–51 3B) "Spider." Jorgensen told me, "At Folson High School in California in the middle 1930s, the basketball coach, William B. Thrasher, said I resembled a black widow spider on the basketball court. I had on a pair of black trunks trimmed in orange and an orange stripe down the side of the trunks."

1865. Joss, Adrian (1902–10 P) "Addie." Joss won 160 games in nine years including four straight 20 wins or more seasons. "Addie" is a takeoff on Adrian.

1866. Joy, Aloysius C. (1884 1B) "Pop." Origin unknown.

1867. Joyce, William Michael (1890–98 3B) "Scrappy." Joyce was an aggressive player who would do anything to win. It was said he was a large edition of John McGraw.

1868. Judd, Thomas William Oscar (1941–48 P) "Ossie." Judd was known by the name of Oscar. "Ossie" is a takeoff on Oscar.

1869. Judy, Lyle Leroy (1935 2B) "Punch." "Punch" is a response to the last name of Judy. The reference is to the famous puppets, Punch and Judy.

1870. Juelich, John Samuel (1939 2B) "Red." The nickname refers to hair color.

1871. Jungels, Kenneth (1937–42 P) "Curly." Origin unknown.

1872. Jurak, Edward James (1982–85 SS) "Lizard." Jurak's sister told me her brother was nicknamed "Lizard" by neighborhood kids, because as a boy he liked to play with lizards in California.

1873. Justis, Walter Newton (1905 P) "Smoke." "Smoke" refers to the speed of Justis' fastball.

1874. Jutze, Alfred Henry (1972–77 C) "Skip." Jutze told me his father nicknamed him "Skip" at an early age. But he does not think there was any particular reason for it.

K

1875. Kaat, James Lee (1959–83 P) "Kitty." The nickname is a response to the last name. Kaat won 283 games in 25 seasons. He also won 16 consecutive gold gloves, so he moved like a cat on the mound.

1876. Kafora, Frank Jacob (1912–14 C) "Tomatoes." Kafora loved to eat tomatoes with every meal.

1877. Kahler, George Rannels (1910–14 P) "Krum." Origin unknown.

1878. Kahn, Owen Earle (1930 PR) "Jack." Kahn appeared in one game in the major leagues as a pinch runner and scored a run. The origin of "Jack," however, is unknown.

1879. Kaiser, Alfred Edward (1911–14 OF) "Deerfoot." Kaiser had speed in the outfield and also on the base paths.

1880. Kaiser, Clyde Donald (1955–57 P) "Tiger." Kaiser told me, "Clyde McCullough, Chicago Cub catcher gave me the nickname because I was always so quiet on the bench and never said anything." Thus "Tiger" is an example of a nickname opposite.

1881. Kaiser, Kenneth J. (1977–88 AL Umpire) "The Hatchet." "The Hatchet" was Kaiser's nickname when he was a professional wrestler.

1882. Kalfass, William Philip (1937 P) "Lefty." Kalfass pitched left handed, but batted right handed.

1883. Kalin, Frank Bruno (1940–43 OF) "Fats." At 6'0" and a little over 200 pounds Kalin appeared on the heavy side.

1884. Kamp, Alphonse Francis (1924–25 P) "Ike." Origin unknown.

1885. Kane, Francis Thomas (1915–19 OF) "Sugar." Sugar is a response to the last name of Kane.

1886. Kane, Harry (1902–06 P) "Klondike." Origin unknown.

1887. Kane, James Joseph (1908 1B) "Shamus." Origin unknown.

1888. Kane, Thomas Joseph (1938 2B) "Sugar." Sugar is a response to the last name of Kane.

1889. Kanehl, Roderick Edwin (1962–64 2B) "Hot Rod." Kanehl had great speed when he first reached the major leagues. In addition, the nickname fit with his first name.

1890. Kappel, Henry (1887–89 SS) "Heinie." "Heinie" denotes Kappel's German background.

1891. Kardow, Paul Otto (1936 P) "Tex." This is a place nickname. Kardow was from Humble, Texas.

1892. Karger, Edwin (1906–11 P) "Loose." Origin unknown.

1893. Karlon, William John (1930 OF) "Hank." Origin unknown.

1894. Karr, Benjamin Joyce (1920–27 P) "Baldy." Karr was 27 before he reached the major leagues and had lost most of his hair.

1895. **Karst, John Gottlieb** (1915 3B) "King." Origin unknown.

1896. **Kavanagh, Charles Hugh** (1914 PH) "Silk." Origin unknown.

1897. **Kay, Walter B.** (1907 OF) "King Bill." Origin unknown.

1898. **Kearns, Thomas J.** (1880–84 2B) "Dasher." Origin unknown.

1899. **Kearse, Edward Paul** (1942 C) "Truck." "Truck" refers to Kearse's build 6'1" and 195 pounds.

1900. **Keck, Frank Joseph** (1922–23 P) "Cactus." According to Tom Shea, the nickname "Cactus" stems from the time Keck pitched in the Texas League.

1901. **Keefe, Timothy John** (1880–93 P) "Sir Timothy." Keefe was a mild-mannered pitcher who won 344 games in just 14 years with a career ERA of .262. "Sir" was in honor of his royal achievements. In 1888 Keefe designed and sold his team, the New York Giants, tight fitting all-black uniforms with raised white letters across the chest that spelled New York.

1902. **Keegan, Robert Charles** (1953–58 P) "Smiley." Keegan told me, "I always grind my teeth when I pitch and it looks as if I am smiling. Dizzy Dean always said I was not serious enough when I was pitching."

1903. **Keeler, William Henry** (1892–1910 OF) "Wee Willie." Keeler was one of the great hitters of the deadball era. He collected 2,962 hits and a career average of .345. He made famous the phrase, "Hit 'em where they ain't." Keeler was a small man at 5'4½" and 140 pounds.

1904. **Keeman, James William** (1920–21 P) "Sparkplug." At 5'6" and 155 pounds, Keeman's build reminded people of a sparkplug.

1905. **Keenan, Harry Leon** (1891 P) "Kid." Keenan was only 17 years old when he made his first and only appearance in the major leagues. He pitched eight innings without allowing a run and banged out two hits in four times at bat.

1906. **Keener, Joshua Harry** (1896 P) "Beams." Origin unknown.

1907. **Keeton, Rickey** (1980–81 P) "Buster." Keeton was nicknamed after the famous comedian Joseph "Buster" Keaton.

1908. **Keifer, Sherman C.** (1914 P) "Katie." Origin unknown.

1909. **Keister, William Hoffman** (1896–1903 SS) "Wagon Tongue." Tom Shea reports that "Wagon Tongue" refers to the large bat Keister used.

1910. **Kelb, George Francis** (1898 P) "Lefty." Kelb pitched left handed and batted left handed. He was also called "Pugger."

1911. **Kell, Everett Lee** (1952 2B) "Skeeter." Everett Kell was the younger brother of George Kell. The nickname refers to Kell's diminutive size, 5'9" and 160 pounds.

1912. **Kelleher, Albert Aloysius** (1916 C) "Duke." "Duke" refers to Kelleher's propensity for fashionable dress.

1913. **Keller, Charles Ernest** (1939–52 OF) "King Kong." Keller was perhaps the strongest player of his era. The nickname refers to the gigantic gorilla by that name from the Hollywood movie. Lefty Gomez once commented, "Keller is the first player to be brought back by Frank Buck."

1914. Kelliher, Frank Mortimer (1919 PH) "Yucca." Origin unknown.

1915. Kelly, Albert Michael (1910 OF) "Red." The nickname refers to hair color.

1916. Kelly, George Lange (1915–32 1B) "High Pockets." Kelly, a Hall of Fame first baseman, was 6'4" with long legs. New York sportswriter, Damon Runyon was the first to use the "High Pockets" nickname.

1917. Kelly, John C. (1879 C) "Honest John." Tristran Coffin in his book, *The Old Ball Game: Baseball in Folklore and Fiction,* relates the story of how Kelly, later to become a National League umpire acquired the nickname of "Honest John" Kelly. "Kelly, it seems, was travelling with a friend one winter night near Akron, Ohio. Their horse lost his footing in a snow drift and bolted. Kelly and his pal leaped from the careening carriage to safety, but the horse ran on. After walking three miles to a farmhouse, Kelly knocked at the door, introduced himself, and asked the farmer if he could hire a conveyance to get back to town. The farmer replied, 'I ain't never heard of ye, but ye look honest to me, John Kelly, and I'll give you a lift!' Harnessing the farmer's best mare to a buckboard, Kelly put down a deposit of two dollars and agreed to bring the animal and the rig back the next day. He and his pal reached Akron safely, but the mare died in the stable before morning. The next day, Kelly returned with the farmer's rig hitched on behind his own buggy and explaining, paid the farmer an extra $20 for the dead mare. 'You're honest John Kelly' the farmer said warmly and that's what he was called 'Honest John' Kelly, for the rest of his days."

1918. Kelly, John Francis (1882–84 C) "Father." Origin unknown.

1919. Kelly, Michael Joseph (1878–93 OF) "King." Kelly was the first great ball player to catch the public's imagination. He was truly the "King" of his time and the most widely known ballplayer before the time of Ruth. Kelly played every position and built the reputation of being the smartest and most daring player of his day. He was by far the most brilliant individualist of his era. He forced a change in the substitution rule, which at the time required the player only to announce to the umpire that he was taking another's place. With Kelly on the bench, a player from the opposing team lifted a foul fly just beyond the reach of the catcher. Kelly leaped from the bench and shouted, "Kelly now catching for Boston" and speared the foul fly bare handed. It was legal, and a new rule had to be instituted to prohibit such plays. Playing the days when there was only one umpire on several occasions when the umpire was looking where a ball was hit to the outfield, Kelly scored from second in a direct line to home plate ignoring third. Kelly was also a king in the pubs of the day. It was said he could drink any two men under the table and often did. He was author of a popular book, *Play Ball,* and had a song written about him, "Slide Kelly Slide."

1920. Kelly, R.B. (1909 SS) "Speed." Kelly possessed great speed on the base paths.

1921. Kelly, William Henry (1920–28 1B) "Big Bill." Kelly was 6'0" and weighed 190 pounds.

1922. Keltz, John E. Joseph (1890 OF) "Chief." "Chief" refers to Keltz's American Indian background.

1923. Kemmerer, Russell Paul (1954–63 P) "Dutch." "Dutch" refers to Kemmerer's German background. He was also called "Kimmersak." According to the biography in the 1960 *Baseball Register,* playing a game of fake batting orders and scrambled names, Kemmerer's name came out Kimmersak and it struck a fancy with his teammates.

1924. Kemner, Herman John (1929 P) "Dutch." "Dutch" denotes Kemner's German background.

1925. Kenna, Edward Aloysius (1928 C) "Scrap Iron." Kenna made up for his small size 5'7½" and 150 pounds with strength and toughness.

1926. Kenna, Edward Benninghaus (1902 P) "The Pitching Poet." Kenna was the son of John E. Kenna, a United States senator from Virginia. He pitched briefly for the Philadelphia Athletics in 1902 posting a 1-1 record. His main interest, however, was poetry not baseball. He could be found writing poetry before and after games in the clubhouse. Lee Allen in his book, *Hot Stove League,* presents a sample of his work from *Lyrics of the Hills* which was written while Kenna was pitching in Wheeling, West Virginia.

"Fall time in the country, when the
Sunshine filters down
The tangled maze of cloud land
And through the beeches brown
In the golden rays it scatters
On the dear old dirty sod
I can trace in wondrous letters
The mystic word of God
And the goodness of the master
Who willed that it should be —
Oh, the olden golden autumn
Is the best of times for me."

1927. Kennedy, Michael Joseph (1879–83 C) "Doc." The following is from an unidentified newspaper clipping dated May, 1891. "When he played in Rochester [Kennedy] in 1876 with the Hop Bitters, he received the sobriquet. In a game with the New Bedfords one day a bleacher crank yelled to Kennedy, 'Say Doctor, give them fellows out in the field a little of that favorite remedy of yours.' Kenny did too. He sent one of them chasing after a four bagger. Ever since he has been called 'Doc.'

1928. Kennedy, Montia Calvin (1946–53 P) "Lefty." Kennedy pitched left handed, but batted right handed.

1929. Kennedy, Sherman Montgomery (1902 OF) "Snapper." Origin unknown.

1930. Kennedy, William Aulton (1948–57 P) "Lefty." Kennedy pitched left handed, and batted left handed.

1931. Kennedy, William V. (1892–1903 P) "Brickyard." Kennedy came from Bellaire, Ohio, famous for its bricks. Kennedy was a brickmaker by trade. People in Bellaire called him "Perk." Sportswriters called him "Wild Bill" and "Roaring Bill" because of his off-the-field antics. Some felt Ring Lardner could have used Kennedy as a model for some of his characters.

1932. Kenworthy, William Jennings (1912–17 2B) "Duke." Kenworthy was known for his fashionable dress.

1933. Keriazakos, Constantine Nicholas (1950–55 P) "Gus." Origin unknown.

1934. Kerlin, Orie Milton (1915 C) "Cy." Origin unknown.

1935. Kern, James Lester (1974–86 P) "Emu." The emu is a tall skinny Australian bird. Mike Shlain quotes Kern, "I got that name from Pat Dobson and Fritz Peterson. I was walking through the clubhouse in 1976. I was six-foot-six at the time and probably weighed 180 pounds. I would squawk occasionally—RUAWWK! They were doing a crossword puzzle and the clue was 'The world's biggest non-flying bird,' and I walked by squawking and it's been 'Emu' ever since." Kern was known as a free spirit. He wore a beard, and a wide-brimmed black Amish hat. He quoted from Confucius to Aquainas. He was generally regarded as a kook and called "Airhead," a nickname he preferred over "Emu." When Kern first arrived in Cleveland in 1974, he was called "The Texas Tornado" because of his good pitching in the Texas League.

1936. Kerr, John Jonas (1914–15 C) "Doc." Many of the players with the nickname of "Doc" had close association with either the medical or dental professions. However, for Kerr the origin of "Doc" is unknown.

1937. Kerr, John Joseph (1943–51 SS) "Buddy." Kerr told me the nickname came from childhood, but he had no idea who was responsible for it.

1938. Kessler, Henry (1876–77 SS) "Lucky." Kessler played for Cincinnati. He had a habit of getting key hits in the seventh inning. Lee Allen reports that at the time O.P. Calor covered baseball for the *Cincinnati Enquirer*. He referred to the seventh inning as the "Lucky Seventh." Because of Kessler's timely hitting in the seventh inning he began to call him "Lucky."

1939. Kibble, John Westly (1912 3B) "Happy." Kibble was known for his pleasant disposition.

1940. Kiefer, Joseph William (1920–26 P) "Smoke." Kiefer had an excellent fastball. He was also called "Harlem Joe" because of his association with New York City.

1941. Kilhullen, Joseph Isadore (1914 C) "Pat." In Kilhullen's case, "Pat" denotes his Irish background.

1942. Killebrew, Harmon Clayton (1954–75 1B) "Killer." Killebrew was one of the great power hitters of all time, belting 573 career homers. A Washington sportswriter gave him the nickname of "Killer" during his rookie year in 1954.

1943. Killefer, Wade (1907–16 OF) "Red." The nickname refers to hair color. Killefer was also called "Lollypop."

1944. Killefer, William Lavier (1909–21 C) "Reindeer Bill." Eddie Gold and Art Ahrens suggest that "Reindeer" refers to Killefer's almost total lack of speed.

1945. Killen, Frank Bissell (1891–1900 P) "Lefty." Killen pitched left handed and batted left handed.

1946. Killian, Edwin Henry (1903–10 P) "Twilight Ed." Killian pitched in an extraordinary number of extra inning games which extended into the twilight hours, when games began at 3:00 P.M.

1947. Kilroy, Matthew Aloysius (1886–98 P) "Matches." "Matches" is a corruption of Matthew. Kilroy struck out 513 batters in 1886 when the pitching rubber was 50 feet. He won 29 games that year but lost a league-leading 34. The next year he won 46 games while dropping 20, but struck out just 217 batters. Another account is that "Matches" comes from Kilroy's rookie year when he burned batters with his 513 strikeouts.

1948. Kimberlin, Harry Lydle (1936–39 P) "Murphy." Kimberlin told me he was nicknamed after relief pitcher John Murphy. He reminded his St. Louis Brown's teammates of him.

1949. Kimbro, Henry Allen (1927–50 OF, Negro League) "Jumbo."

"Jumbo" probably refers to large size, but I cannot document it.

1950. Kimsey, Clyde Lyons (1919–26 SS) "Chad." Origin unknown.

1951. Kindall, Gerald Donald (1956–65 2B) "Slim." At 6'2½" and 175 pounds, Kindall appeared thin.

1952. Kinder, Ellis Raymond (1946–57 P) "Old Folks." Kinder was one of those players who did not acquire a nickname until late in his career. It refers to his age. He was 32 as a rookie and pitched in the majors until he was 43.

1953. King, Charles Frederick (1886–97 P) "Silver." King had prematurely gray hair. He won 206 games in ten years. In 1885 he led the American Association with 45 wins, and an ERA, 1.64. Another account is that King's hair was platinum blond, not gray.

1954. King, Lynn Paul (1935–39 OF) "Dig." Origin unknown.

1955. Kingman, David Arthur (1971–86 OF) "Kong." Kingman was 6'6" and weighed 210 pounds. "Kong" is short for "King Kong" the gigantic ape character in the movie of the same name. Kingman was also called "Sky King" because of his height and also the fact that he worked for United Airline during the off season. A powerful home run hitter, 442 lifetime, Kingman could muster but a .236 lifetime average. He was a liability in the field, where catching a fly ball was always an adventure. One writer suggested he tried to surround ground balls.

1956. Kinsella, Edward William (1905–10 P) "Rube." Kinsella came from the small town of Lexington, Illinois, and was not familiar with big city life. He was nicknamed after "Rube" Waddell.

1957. Kinsella, Robert Francis (1919–20 OF) "Red." The nickname refers to hair color.

1958. Kinzy, Henry Hershel (1934 P) "Slim." Harry, as he was addressed, was 6'4" and weighed 185 pounds.

1959. Kirby, John F. (1884–88 P) "Chickenhearted." A clipping from an unidentified newspaper dated July 6, 1887, characterized Kirby in these words, "He is bull-headed, mulish, ingrate, and apparently without sense of honor or a single manly instinct."

1960. Kirke, Judson Fabian (1910–18 OF) "Jay." Kirke was known by the initial of his first name, "J." In print it came out "Jay."

1961. Kirkland, Willie Charles (1958–66 OF) "Boomer." Kirkland was nicknamed "Boomer" by a fan after he hit four home runs in four days for St. Cloud of the Northern League in 1954.

1962. Kirkpatrick, Edgar Leon (1962–77 OF) "Spanky." While playing for the Kansas City Royals in 1969, a fan started to call him "Spanky" because his uniform was always dirty and his shirt was not tucked in. The reference is to a character in the movie serial "Our Gang," of which an edited version began appearing on television in 1955 under the title "The Little Rascals."

1963. Kirsch, Harry Louis (1910 P) "Casey." Origin unknown.

1964. Kisinger, Charles Samuel (1902–03 P) "Rube." Kisinger came from the small town of Adrian, Michigan, and was not thought to be wise to big city life. He was nicknamed after "Rube" Waddell.

1965. Kison, Bruce Eugene (1971–85 P) "Sweetie." Kison had a small pink face with peach fuzz for whiskers. It made him look no older than 15 when he first came up to Pittsburgh in 1971. Thus his teammates called him "Sweetie." However, this nickname had also been used during his minor league career. He was also called "Stick" in reference to his 6'4", 178-pound build.

1966. Kissinger, William Francis (1895–97 P) "Shaney." Origin unknown.

1967. Klaener, Hugo Emil (1934 P) "Dutch." "Dutch" denotes Klaener's German background.

1968. Klee, Ollie Chester (1925 OF) "Babe." Origin unknown.

1969. Kleinke, Norbert George (1935–37 P) "Nub." "Nub" is a corruption of Norbert. It was first used in childhood.

1970. Kleinow, John Peter (1904–11 OF) "Red." The nickname refers to hair color.

1971. Klem, William J. (1905–40, NL Umpire) "Catfish." Klem had big lips and floppy ears and when making a demonstrative decision, he would let fly a rather fine spray from his mouth. Klem detested the nickname. If he heard a player, manager, or coach use "Catfish" it was certain ejection from the field of play. The same was true if he heard "Cat" or "Catso" come his way. Klem was one of the best known and best loved of all umps. He was often referred to as "The Great Arbitrator." He was credited with the saying, "I never missed one." After retirement Klem related, "What a happy day it was for me when the baseball world tied that egomaniacal sentence to my coattails and never let me forget it. It was worth a million dollars in publicity to me because for all time it singled me out from the other umpires." But he said he was actually misquoted. What he really said was, "I never missed one in my life—HERE," pointing to his head. In 1940 at age 66 he was hit and laid low by a batted ball. When leaving the field a female fan asked, "Were you badly hurt, Pop?" Klem recounted, "I was called everything in my day, all the vile names a scoundrel could lay his tongue to: robber, thief, blind, a wife-beater. But when they called me 'Pop' I knew it was time to quit."

1972. Klepfer, Edward Lloyd (1911–19 P) "Big Ed." Klepfer was 6' and weighed 185 pounds. His career record over six years was 22-17.

1973. Klieman, Edward Frederick (1943–50 P) "Babe." Klieman said there were two Eds in his family and since he was the youngest, he was called "Babe."

1974. Kline, Robert George (1930–34 P) "Junior." Tom Shea indicates "Junior" is a nickname opposite referring to size. Kline was 6'3" and well over 200 pounds. He was also called "King Kong" because of his size.

1975. Kling, John (1900–13 C) "Noisy." This is a nickname opposite. Kling, even as a catcher, rarely said anything to anybody during the course of the game, not even the pitcher.

1976. Klopp, Stanley Harold (1944 P) "Betz." Origin unknown.

1977. Kloza, John Clarence (1931–32 OF) "Nap." Origin unknown.

1978. Klutz, Gene Ellis (1976–83 3B) "Mickey." Origin unknown.

1979. Knabe, Franz Otto (1905–16 2B) "Dutch." "Dutch" denotes Knab's German background.

1980. Knaupp, Henry Antone (1910–11 SS) "Cotton." "Cotton" refers to Knaupp's light blond hair.

1981. Knetzer, Elmer Ellsworth (1909–17 P) "Baron." *The Brooklyn Press* nicknamed him "The Carrick Barron." He was from Carrick, Pennsylvania, of German background, and as handsome as barons are supposed to be.

1982. Knight, Elmer Russell (1922–27 P) "Jack." The nickname comes from childhood. No one wanted to use the name of Elmer.

1983. Knight, John Wesley (1905–13 SS) "Schoolboy." Knight came off the sandlots of Philadelphia to join Connie Mack's A's in 1905. He looked like a schoolboy.

1984. Knight, Jonas William (1884–90 OF) "Quiet Joe." The following description of Jonas Knight appeared in a Cincinnati newspaper on Sept. 6, 1890. "He has less to say than any man ever yet connected with Cincinnati. He is not sullen or moody, but rarely speaks unless spoken to."

1985. Knode, Kenneth Thompson (1920 OF) "Mike." Origin unknown.

1986. Knoll, Charles Elmer (1905– OF) "Punch." Origin unknown.

1987. Knolls, Oscar Edward (1906 P) "Hub." Origin unknown.

1988. Knothe, Wilfred Edgar (1932–33 3B) "Fritz." "Fritz" denotes Knothe's German background.

1989. Knouff, Edward (1885–89 P) "Fred." For no apparent reason "Fred" was used as an alternative to Ed.

1990. Knox, Andrew Jackson (1890 1B) "Dasher." Origin unknown.

1991. Knox, Clifford Hiram (1924 C) "Bud." "Bud" was a childhood family nickname.

1992. Koecher, Richard Finlay (1946–48 P) "Highpockets." Koecher was 6'5" tall with long legs.

1993. Koegel, Peter John (1970–72 C) "Jolly." Koegel was nicknamed when he was playing for Burlington, North Carolina, in 1966 after the Jolly Green Giant in TV commercials. Koegel was 6'6½" and weighed 230 pounds.

1994. Koehler, Horace Levering (1925 OF) "Pip." Origin unknown.

1995. Koestner, Elmer Joseph (1910–14 P) "Bob." Origin unknown.

1996. Kohlman, Joseph James (1937–38 P) "Blackie." The nickname refers to dark hair color.

1997. Kolloway, Donald Martin (1940–53 3B) "Butch." Kolloway explained to me, "When I was six years old I was given the nickname of 'Butch' by my playmates, George Anderson, Ross Stuart and Bill Stoes because I would fight anyone. In baseball I was called 'Ace,' 'Arch' and 'Cab'."

1998. Kolp, Raymond Carl (1921–34 P) "Jockey." Kolp was a polished bench jockey skilled at tormenting the opposition when he was not pitching, with verbal jabs.

1999. Kommers, Fred Raymond (1913–14 OF) "Bugs." Origin unknown.

2000. Konetchy, Edward Joseph (1907–21 1B) "Big Ed." Konetchy was 6'2½" and 195 pounds. In 15 years he amassed 2,148 base hits.

2001. Konikowski, Alexander James (1948–54 P) "Whitey." The nickname refers to very light colored blond hair.

2002. Konstanty, Casimir James (1944–56 P) "Big Jim." Konstanty was one of the few athletes at Syracuse University to letter in four sports which included baseball, basketball, football, and soccer. These accomplishments combined with his 6'1½" and 205-pound frame resulted in the nickname "Big Jim" Konstanty was the first relief pitcher to receive special recognition when he was awarded the National League's Most Valuable Player award in 1950. With the Philadelphia Phillies "Whiz Kids" that year he posted a 16-7 mark and his 74 appearances all in relief included 22 saves. Konstanty was a surprise starter in the first game of the 1950 World Series, and pitched brilliantly in the 1–0 loss to New York Yankee pitcher Vic Raschi.

2003. Kopacz, George Felix (1966–70 1B) "Sonny." Kopacz was a Junior and therefore had the same name as his father. His parents used "Sonny" to differentiate between the two.

2004. Kopf, William Lorenz (1913–23 SS) "Larry." "Larry" was used as an alternative to Lorenz by ballplayers. I could find no explanation as to why Bill or William were not used.

2005. Korcheck, Stephen Joseph (1954–59 C) "Hoss." Korcheck was nicknamed "Hoss" by the publicity director at George Washington University because of his rugged play on the football field. He was also called "Rock" for the same reason.

2006. Kores, Arthur John (1915 3B) "Dutch." "Dutch" refers to Kores' German background.

2007. Korince, George Eugene (1966–67 P) "Moose." Canadian born Korince, received the nickname of "Moose" from a friend because of his size. He was 6'3" and weighed 210 pounds.

2008. Koshorek, Clement John (1952–53 SS) "Scooter." In 1946 with Jamestown in the Pony League, fans thought Koshorek scooted after the ball at shortstop much like Phil Rizzuto. And at 5'6" and 165 pounds he also resembled Rizzuto in size.

2009. Koski, William John (1951 P) "T-Bone." Koski told me that as a 19-year-old rookie he was 6'6" and 190 pounds and had a voracious appetite. One night with roommate Vern Law he ordered a second T-Bone steak dinner. A sportswriter, Les Biederman, saw him do this and told him if he could eat a third, he would pick up the check. Koski did, and Biederman paid. When the story got around, people began calling him "T-Bone."

2010. Koslo, George Bernard (1941–55 P) "Dave." According to the biography in the 1954 *Baseball Register* Koslo adopted the nickname of "Dave" in 1939 as a rookie with Hopkinsville in the Kitty League.

2011. Kosner, Frederick Charles (1931 OF) "Fritz." "Fritz" denotes Kosner's German background.

2012. Koy, Ernest Anyz (1938–42 OF) "Chief." Koy was not of Indian blood, but came from a French-German background. As a schoolboy, however, playmates thought his facial features resembled those of an Indian.

2013. Kracher, Joseph Peter (1939 C) "Jug." Origin unknown.

2014. Kraft, Clarence Otto (1914 1B) "Big Boy." Kraft stood 6' and weighed 190 pounds. But he attained his adult size at an early age which resulted in the nickname.

2015. Krapp, Eugene Hamlet (1911–15 P) "Rubber." Origin unknown.

2016. Kraus, John William (1943–46 P) "Texas Jack." This is a place nickname. Kraus was from San Antonio, Texas.

2017. Krause, Harry William (1908–12 P) "Hal." "Hal" is simply an alternative to Harry.

2018. Kravitz, Daniel (1956–60 C) "Beak." Kravitz possessed a large nose. He was also called "Dusty" as an alternative to Daniel.

2019. Kreiger, Kurt Ferdinand (1949–51 P) "Dutch." "Dutch" refers to Kreiger's German background.

2020. Kreitz, Ralph Wesley (1911 C) "Red." The nickname refers to hair color.

2021. Kremer, Remy Peter (1924–33 P) "Wiz." "Wiz" is short for "Wizzer" which refers to Kremer's fastball. The nickname stems from his minor league playing days.

2022. Kress, Ralph (1927–46 SS) "Red." The nickname refers to hair color.

2023. Krietner, Albert Joseph (1943–44 C) "Mickey." Origin unknown.

2024. Krist, Howard Wilbur (1937–46 P) "Spud." According to Lee Allen, Krist was particularly fond of potatoes.

2025. Kroh, Floyd Myron (1906–12 P) "Rube." Kroh was from the small town of Friendship, New York, and not wise to big city life. He was nicknamed after "Rube" Waddell.

2026. Krueger, Arthur William (1899–1905 SS) "Oom Paul." Krueger was nicknamed after Transvall South African Boer political leader of the time, Paul Krueger, whose nickname was "Oom Paul."

2027. Krug, Everett Ben (1965–69 C) "Chris." Krug was born on Christmas day 1939.

2028. Kuhn, Walter Charles (1912–14 C) "Red." The nickname refers to hair color.

2029. Kunkel, William G. (1968–84 AL Umpire) "Jam." Kunkel may have received this nickname as a pitcher. It may have meant that his pitches jammed batters. However, I have been unable to document this nor can I find "Jam" used for Kunkel when he was playing.

2030. Kuntz, Russell Jay (1979–85 OF) "Rusty." "Rusty" does not refer to hair color. It is used as an alternative to Russell.

2031. Kunz, Earl Dewey (1923 P) "Pinch." Origin unknown.

2032. Kurowski, George John (1941–49 3B) "Whitey." "Whitey" refers to light blond hair color.

2033. Kuzava, Robert LeRoy (1946–57 P) "Sarg." Kuzava told me, "I was a sergeant in the Army during World War II. Ben Epstein, a New York sportswriter, gave me the nickname. In talking to me after I had saved a game, he said I looked like a tough Army Sergeant."

L

2034. Laboy, Jose Alberto (1969–73 3B) "Coco." Laboy was fond of chocolate bars as a youth.

2035. LaChance, George Joseph (1893–1905 1B) "Candy." LaChance had a fondness for all types of sweets. He did not like the nickname.

2036. LaCock, Ralph Pierre, II (1972–80 1B) "Pete." "Pete" in part is derived from the middle name of Pierre, and in part from his father's name. His father, Peter Marshall, was the well known TV-radio personality and master of ceremonies on the NBC "Hollywood Squares" program.

2037. LaCoss, Michael James (1978– P) "Goofy." The nickname of "Goofy" was bestowed by New York Giant third base coach in 1986 because LaCoss did so many crazy things. He is often called "Buffy" by his teammates.

2038. Ladd, Peter Linwood (1979–86 P) "Big Foot." Ladd told me that he has been wearing a size 15 shoe since he was 15 years old. He cannot remember exactly when people started calling him "Big Foot," but it was before the start of his pro career.

2039. Lade, Doyle Marion (1946–50 P) "Porky." Lade told me he got the nickname either from Red Barber or from the author of an article which appeared in *Baseball Magazine*. It refers to the fact that "I am a bit on the chunky side."

2040. Lafferty, Frank Bernard (1876–77 P) "Flip." The nickname refers to his pitching. Lafferty was a flipper.

2041. Lafitte, Edward Francis (1909–15 P) "Doc." Lafitte studied dentistry in 1912 when he was playing for Detroit. He did not, however, become a practicing dentist.

2042. LaForest, Byron Joseph (1945 3B) "Ty." As a kid "Ty" was used as a substitute for Byron.

2043. LaGrow, Lerrin Harris (1970–80 P) "Lurch." LaGrow was 6'5" and 230 pounds. He reminded people, according to Joseph McBride, of the oversized butler on the TV show "The Addams Family."

2044. Lahoud, Joseph Michael (1968–78 OF) "Duck." Lahoud told me he got the nickname because he ran like a duck with a waddle and feet going outward.

2045. Lajoie, Napoleon (1896–1916 2B) "Larry." According to J.M. Murphy, teammate at Philadelphia, pitcher Jack Taylor was responsible for bestowing the nickname in 1896. He had difficulty in pronouncing Lajoie. It has also been reported, by Lee Allen for instance, that "Bollicky Bill" Taylor was the first to use the nickname, but Murphy believes this is incorrect. "Sandy" was the nickname used by hometown friends even though Lajoie's hair was black. Other nicknames used were "Poli" and "Poncy."

2046. Lake, Edward Erving (1939–50 SS) "Inky." The nickname refers to dark complexion.

2047. Lakeman, Albert Wesley (1942–54 C) "Moose." Lakeman was

6'2" and weighed 200 pounds. The nickname was given to him by teammate Jocko Munch when the two were playing for Erie in the Mid-Atlantic League in 1939.

2048. Lally, Daniel J. (1891–97 OF) "Bud." "Bud" was a childhood nickname.

2049. Lamanna, Frank (1940–42 P) "Hank." Origin unknown.

2050. Lamanske, Frank James (1935 P) "Lefty." Lamanske pitched left handed, and batted left handed.

2051. Lamar, William Harmony (1917–27 OF) "Good Time Bill." According to Fred Lieb, playing around and having a good time were more important to Lamar than concentrating on his inherent talent for baseball. In spite of that, Lamar compiled a .310 career average for nine seasons.

2052. Lamline, Frederick Arthur (1912–15 P) "Dutch." The nickname refers to Lamline's German background.

2053. Land, William Gilbert (1929 OF) "Doc." Many of the players with the nickname of "Doc" had a close association with either the medical or dental professions. However, for Land, the origin of "Doc" is unknown.

2054. Landenberger, Kenneth Henry (1952 1B) "Red." The nickname refers to hair color.

2055. Landis, Samuel H. (1882 P) "Doc." Many players with the nickname of "Doc" had a close association with either the medical or dental professions. However, for Landis, the origin of "Doc" is unknown.

2056. Landrum, Terry Lee (1980– OF) "Tito." "Tito" means small in Italian.

2057. Lane, Frank (1948–65 Executive) "Trader Frank." Lane was general manager of six clubs during his career, including the Chicago White Sox, St. Louis Cardinals, and Cleveland Indians. David Voigt writes, "Lane made 24 trades in seven years with the White Sox, dealing so compulsively that his men feared to send out their laundry lest they be gone before pick up time!" Harold Parrott remarks, "The Trader swapped ballplayers like bubble gum cards and he had a thousand stories, a few of which were true. The ballplayers and reporters called him "Motormouth'...." Before his career ended, "Frantic Frank," as some called Lane, had concocted over 500 trades.

2058. Lane, George M. (1882–84 1B) "Chappy." Origin unknown.

2059. Lane, James Hunter (1924 3B) "Dodo." Origin unknown.

2060. Lanford, Lewis Grover (1907 P) "Sam." Origin unknown.

2061. Lang, Martin John (1930 P) "Lefty." Lang pitched left handed but batted right handed.

2062. Lang, Robert David (1975–76 P) "Chip." Lang wrote me, "Before I could walk, I used to wait at the door for my dad to come home from work. I would make sounds like a chipmunk. Since my dad's name was the same as mine, my parents starting calling me Chip."

2063. Lange, Frank Herman (1910–13 P) "Bill." Lange was called "Bill" by the *Chicago Press* after outfielder William "Little Eva" Lange. Lange was also called "Seagan."

2064. Lange, William Alexander (1893–99 OF) "Little Eva." Lange was 6'1" and weighed 180 pounds and was a good hitter with a .350 average for seven years. The "Little Eva" is an opposite nickname and refers to the way Lange walked. It was said he had the strut of a little girl.

2065. Langford, Elton L. (1926–28 OF) "Sam." Langford wrote me, "In 1918 while in the navy I was called Sam after the Negro heavyweight champion Sam Langford. My commander in the navy gave it to me when I was 18 years old. At that time in history, I was not to proud of the nickname."

2066. Lanier, Lorenzo (1971 PH) "Rimp." "Rimp" refers to Lorenzo's small build, 5'8" and 155 pounds.

2067. Lanning, John Young (1936–47 P) "Tobacco Chewin' Johnny." Lanning was rarely seen without a large wad of tobacco in his mouth.

2068. Lanning, Lester Alfred (1916 P) "Red." The nickname refers to hair color.

2069. Lansford, Joseph Dale (1982–83 1B) "Jody." Lansford wrote me that he was called Jody after a cousin by that name.

2070. Lansing, Eugene Edmore (1922 P) "Jigger." Origin unknown.

2071. LaPalme, Paul Edmore (1951–57 P) "Lefty." LaPalme pitched left handed and batted left handed.

2072. Lapihuska, Andrew (1942–43 P) "Apples." Origin unknown.

2073. LaPorte, Frank Breyfogle (1905–15 2B) "Pot." "Pot" is a contraction of the last name, but it may have been reinforced by body build. LaPorte was 5'8" and weighed 175 pounds.

2074. Larkin, Henry E. (1884–93 1B) "Ted." Origin unknown.

2075. Larmore, Robert McCahn (1918 SS) "Red." The nickname refers to hair color.

2076. Larsen, Donald James (1953–67 P) "Night Rider." Larsen was given the nickname of "Night Rider" by Casey Stengel because of his love of night life. He paid little attention to curfews. His day usually started around noon and lasted until the wee hours of the morning. On October 8, 1956, Larsen threw 97 pitches, hurling a perfect game, the first in World Series history. Was he in bed early for once the night before? Nathan Salant quotes Larsen, "Truth of the matter is that one time I did go to bed early, I had the worst game of my career. That was against the Dodgers in game two of the '56 Series. We were ahead 6–0, but I couldn't get anybody out. When Casey Stengel came out to get me I was furious, and I told him that's the last time I'll ever go to bed early." His next start, of course, ended in the perfect game.

2077. Larsen, Erling Adeli (1936 2B) "Swede." Larsen was of Swedish background.

2078. Lary, Frank Strong (1954–56 P) "Mule." When he was in the army, Lary turned over beds in the morning when soldiers overslept with the kick of a mule. Lary was called "Taters" by his teammates because he once wrote that on an order form in a railroad dining car.

2079. Lary, Lynford (1929–40 SS) "Broadway." When Lary first joined the Yankees in 1929, Ruth asked him where he was staying. He replied, "Down on Broadway." Ruth began calling him "Broadway." The nickname was later reinforced by his snappy dress and his love of night life.

2080. Lasher, Frederick Walter (1963–71 P) "Whip." "Whip" referred to Lasher's side arm pitching style.

2081. Lasorda, Thomas Charles (1954–56 P) "El Sorda." As a major league pitcher Lasorda's career was short and not so sweet. He was 0-4 with and ERA of 6.48 in 26 games over three seasons. He really had no public nickname. However, he mentions that when he was playing winter ball in Cuba, fans called him "El Sorda" which he says translates as "The Deaf Woman"!

2082. Lathan, George Warren (1877–84 1B) "Jumbo." Lathan weighed 240 pounds. There is no information on his height. He was also called "Juice" because he always seemed to have tobacco juice dribbling from his chin.

2083. Lathan, Walter Arlington (1880–1909 3B) "The Freshest Man on Earth." Lathan had the reputation of being the most talkative player in the game and an impish clown. He became the first paid coach. Lathan is given credit for originating bench jockeying and ribbing opponents from the coaching box. James Kahn relates the following incident when Lathan was playing third base with Cincinnati in the 1890s and disagreed with a call made by umpire Tom Hurst. "In fury he grabbed his cap off his head and flung it to the ground. As he reached to pick it up, Hurst kicked it up the line. Lathan grabbed it again and slammed it again and Hurst kicked it again. For the next few minutes this pantomime went on until Hurst and Lathan were out at the left field line. The stands howled with glee, the players were doubled over with mirth."

2084. Latimer, Clifford Wesley (1898–1902 C) "Tacks." Origin unknown.

2085. Latman, Arnold Barry (1957–67 P) "Shoulders." Latman at 6'3" and 210 pounds had well-developed shoulders.

2086. Lavagetto, Harry Arthur (1934–47 OF) "Cookie." Lavagetto, an Oakland native, signed to play for Oakland in the Pacific Coast League. The team was owned by Cookie DeVincenzi. At first he was known as "Cookie's Boy." It was then shortened to "Cookie."

2087. Lavan, John Leonard (1913–24 SS) "Doc." Lavan was a practicing physician.

2088. Law, Vernon Sanders (1956–67 P) "Deacon." The nickname of "Deacon" refers to Law's sedate personality.

2089. Lawing, Garland Fred (1946 OF) "Knobby." Lawing told me that he reminded players of his minor league manager, Joe Palluska whose nickname was "Knobby."

2090. Lawrence, Ulysses Brooks (1954–60 P) "Bull." Lawrence was called "Bull" by St. Louis Cardinal manager Eddie Stanky because of his capacity to work at all times.

2091. Lawry, Otis Carroll (1916–17 2B) "Rabbit." At 5'8" and 133 pounds Lawry possessed great speed.

2092. Lawson, Alfred Voyle (1930–40 P) "Roxie." Origin unknown.

2093. Layne, Ivoria Hillis (1941–46 3B) "Tony." Layne explained to me that in 1939 when he was playing for the Chattanooga Lookouts he mispronounced Tony Lazzeri's name. After that his teammates started calling him "Tony."

2094. Lazzeri, Anthony Michael (1926–39 2B) "Poosh 'Em Up." New

York fans of Italian extraction used to Chant to Lazzeri to "Poosh 'Em Up" meaning hit the ball in the stands. The nickname dates to Lazzeri's first year in organized ball at Salt Lake City. When he was struggling, a kind restaurant owner, Tony Roffetti, fed him spaghetti dinners for three straight nights and urged him to "poosh 'em up," meaning to hit.

2095. Leach, Thomas William (1898–1918 OF) "The Wee." Leach was a diminutive outfielder at 5'6½" and 150 pounds. Yet he managed 2,144 hits over 19 campaigns.

2096. Lear, Charles Bernard (1914–15 P) "King." The nickname of "King" is a response to the last name of Lear. It refers to the Shakespearean play "King Lear."

2097. Leard, William Wallace (1917 2B) "Wild Bill." "Wild" refers to Leard's style of play rather than his personality.

2098. Leathers, Harold Langford (1920 SS) "Chuck." Origin unknown.

2099. Lebourveau, DeWitt Wiley (1919–29 OF) "Bevo." Lebourveau was listed in box scores as Lebo, and "Bevo" is a takeoff on that name. Tom Shea, however, points out that Bevo was a malt beverage put on the market during early prohibition days and suggests this accounted for Lebourveau's nickname.

2100. Ledbetter, Ralph Overton (1915 P) "Razor." "Razor" refers to Ledbetter's 6'4" and 190 pounds build. He was also called "Slats."

2101. Lee, Harold Burnham (1930–36 OF) "Sheriff." Lee was never a sheriff. Indeed, before, during or after his baseball career he was not associated with the criminal justice system. Origin unknown.

2102. Lee, Robert Dean (1964–68 P) "Moose." Lee was 6'3" and weighed 225 pounds. He was also called "Truck" because of his size.

2103. Lee, Thorton Starr (1933–48 P) "Lefty." Lee pitched left handed and batted left handed.

2104. Lee, William Crutcher (1934–47 P) "Big Bill." Lee stood 6'3" and weighed 195 pounds. In 1938 he pitched big for the champion Chicago Cubs leading the National League with a 22-9 mark and an ERA of 2.66. But he dropped two games in the World Series to the Yankees.

2105. Lee, William Francis (1969–82 P) "Spaceman." Lee was one of baseball's ultimate flakes of the 1970s decade. He was notorious for making offbeat comments about the game, to players, managers, owners, and sportswriters. He once walked out on the Montreal Expos in protest of what he felt was the unfair treatment and eventual release of second base teammate Rodney Scott. His antics and his point of view are presented in his book with Dick Lally, *The Wrong Stuff.*

2106. Lee, Wyatt Arnold (1901–04 OF) "Watty." "Watty" is a contraction of the first name of Wyatt.

2107. Leever, Samuel (1898–1910 P) "The Goshen Schoolmaster." This is a place nickname. Leever was from Goshen, Ohio. He was a school teacher in the off season in that town.

2108. Lefebure, James Kenneth (1965–72 2B) "Frenchy." Lefebure was of French background.

2109. LeFebure, Wilfrid Henry (1938–44 P) "Lefty." LeFebure pitched left handed and batted left handed.

2110. LeFlore, Ronald (1974–82 OF) "Twinkle Toes Bosco." LeFlore received this nickname from his teammates on the prison baseball team in Jackson, Michigan, in 1971. "Twinkle Toes" referred to his speed and "Bosco" was after the bear in the chocolate milk commercials. LeFlore liked chocolate milk. In 1980 he performed an amazing, but almost forgotten feat. He stole 97 bases for Montreal in only 139 games.

2111. Legett, Louis Alfred (1929–35 C) "Doc." Legett was a practicing dentist.

2112. Lehner, Paul Eugene (1946–52 OF) "Gulliver." In 1951 Lehner was well traveled. He played for the Athletics, White Sox, Browns, and Indians. In 1952 he added the Red Sox. The reference is to the famous child's classic *Gulliver's Travels*.

2113. Lehr, Clarence Emanuel (1911 OF) "King." Lehr is pronounced "Lear," the same as the name of the King in the Shakespearean play.

2114. Leiber, Henry Edward (1933–42 OF) "Goldilocks." The nickname refers to blond hair color. The reference is to one of Grimm's Fairy Tales, "Goldilocks and the Three Bears."

2115. Leibold, Harry Loran (1913–25 OF) "Nemo." Leibold was 5'6½" and weighed 155 pounds. Leibold was nicknamed after the comic strip character Little Nemo in the strip "Little Nemo in Slumberland" created by Winsor McKay which first appeared in the *New York Herald* in 1905.

2116. Leifield, Albert Peter (1905–20 P) "Lefty." Leifield pitched left handed and batted left handed.

2117. Leith, William (1899 P) "Shady Bill." Leith pitched in only one game in the major leagues. In two innings he allowed four hits, walked two and gave up two runs. The origin of Shady Bill, however, is unknown.

2118. Leitner, George Aloysius (1887 P) "Doc." Leitner was a practicing physician and surgeon. He was graduated from Bellview Medical School in New York City.

2119. Leitner, George Michael (1901–02 P) "Dummy." According to SABR researcher Richard Top, Leitner was deaf and dumb.

2120. Lenhardt, Donald Eugene (1950–54 OF) "Footsie." Broadcaster Buddy Blattner of the St. Louis Browns gave Lenhardt the nickname "Footsie." Lenhardt told me it was because he wore a 12 AA shoe and it was difficult to find baseball shoes that would fit.

2121. Lennon, Robert Albert (1954–57 OF) "Arch." Lennon explained to me that teammate Rance Pless at Jacksonville in 1949 gave him the nickname of "Arch." "I was from Brooklyn and sounded like the waiter on Duffy's Tavern radio show."

2122. Lennox, James Edgar (1906–15 3B) "Eggie." "Eggie" is a contraction of Edgar. Lennox was usually addressed as Ed.

2123. Leonard, Elmer Ellsworth (1911 P) "Tiny." This is a nickname opposite. Leonard was a big man, 6'3½" and weighed 210 pounds.

2124. Leonard, Emil John (1933–53 P) "Dutch." He was nicknamed after Hubert "Dutch" Leonard the Red Sox and Tiger pitcher of the preceding decade. Emil, as he was addressed, won 191 major league games, but is the only pitcher to lead both leagues in losses. He dropped 19 with Washington in 1940, and 17 with the Philadelphia Phils in 1948.

2125. Leonard, Hubert Benjamin (1913–15 P) "Dutch." Leonard was of German background. He was the original "Dutch" Leonard. He won a game for the Boston Red Sox in both the 1915 and 1916 World Series.

2126. Leonard, Jeffrey N. (1977– OF) "Hac Man." At Phoenix in the Pacific Coast League, Leonard became alienated and told everyone he would swing at the first pitch no matter where it was for the entire season, and he did. Leonard's moon-faced frown and baleful stare also earned him the nickname of "Penitentiary Face" and "Correctional Institute Face."

2127. Leonard, Walter Fenner (1933–50 1B, Negro League) "Buck." Leonard was nicknamed by a brother who could not pronounce the family nickname for Leonard which was "Buddy." Batting in the fourth slot behind Josh Gibson for the Homestead Grays, Leonard's high batting average and home run production won him the sobriquet of "The Black Lou Gehrig." He was a smooth, sure-handed, left-handed first baseman who had a strong and accurate arm. During the 1940s he was probably the third highest paid player in the Negro leagues behind Page and Gibson.

2128. Lepine, Louis Joseph (1902 OF) "Pete." Origin unknown.

2129. Leppert, Don Eugene (1955–64 C) "Tiger." Leppert told me that his name is sometimes mistaken for Leopard. From that came Tiger. "It happened in 1949. Vern Horscheit, manager of the McAlister Rocket team of the Sooner State League, and my roommate Whitey Herzog started it."

2130. Lerchen, Bertram Roe (1910 SS) "Dutch." Lerchen was of German background.

2131. Lerian, Walter Irwin (1928–29 C) "Peck." Origin unknown.

2132. Lesley, Bradley Jay (1982– P) "The Animal." Lesley stood 6'6" and weighed 200 pounds, and acted like an animal on the field. On the NBC "Game of the Week" broadcast June 18, 1988, he was featured as one of the "Characters of the Game" between innings.

2133. Leverenz, Walter F. (1913–15 P) "Tiny." This is a nickname opposite. Leverenz was 5'10" and weighed 175 pounds.

2134. Leverett, Gorham Vance (1922–29 P) "Dixie." The nickname recognizes Leverett's southern heritage. He was born in Georgetown, Texas.

2135. Leverette, Horace Wilbur (1920 P) "Hod." "Hod" is a takeoff on Horace.

2136. Levsen, Emil Henry (1923–28 P) "Dutch." Levsen was of German background.

2137. Lewis, Edward Morgan (1896–1901 P) "Parson." Lewis had a master's degree from Williams College and was an ordained minister.

2138. Lewis, George Edward (1910–21 OF) "Duffy." The nickname "Duffy" stems from his mother's maiden name.

2139. Lewis, John Kelly (1935–49 3B) "Buddy." Lewis was underage when he signed with Chattanooga in 1934. Manager "Mule" Shirily started calling him "Buddy."

2140. Lewis, William Henry (1933–36 C) "Buddy." "Buddy" was a childhood nickname first used by Lewis' family.

2141. Liber, Charles Edwin (1935–36 P) "Dutch." Liber was of German background.

2142. Libke, Albert Walter (1945–46 OF) "Big Al." Libke was 6'4" and weighed 215 pounds.

2143. Liebhardt, Glenn Ignatius (1930–38 P) "Sandy." The nickname refers to hair color.

2144. Lillie, James J. (1883–86 OF) "Grasshopper." "Grasshopper" refers to Lillie's small stature of which there is some mention in the literature although no firm statistics. There is also mention of his fielding ability which may be related to "Grasshopper" in the sense he was adept at fielding ground balls.

2145. Lillis, Robert Perry (1958–67 SS) "Flea." Lillis was tagged "Flea" by Los Angeles teammate Frank Howard because of his small size. Given that Lillis was 5'11" and 160 pounds, perhaps he was only small from the view of 6'7" and 255-pound Frank Howard.

2146. Lindemann, John Frederick Mann (1901 OF) "Bob." Origin unknown.

2147. Lindsay, Christian Haller (1905–06 1B) "Pinky." The nickname refers to skin complexion. Lindsay's disposition also earned him the nickname of "Cris Crab."

2148. Lindstrom, Fred Charles (1924–36 3B) "Lindy." "Lindy" is a takeoff on the last name of Lindstrom. However, it was reinforced when Charles Lindburg made the first solo plane flight across the Atlantic in 1927. He was called "Lucky Lindy."

2149. Link, Frederick Theodore (1910 P) "Laddie." Origin unknown.

2150. Linton, Claud Clarence (1929 C) "Hustle." Bob, as he was addressed, was known for his aggressive style of play.

2151. Linz, Philip Francis (1962–68 SS) "Super Sub." Linz was the prime example of a role player who could fill in at various positions and do a more than an adequate job. His career consisted of 190 games at shortstop, 102 at second base, 82 at third base, and 22 in the outfield.

2152. Lipon, John Joseph (1942–54 SS) "Skids." Lipon wrote me, "I was never called that [Skids] except in 1941 when I was playing for Muskegon of the Michigan State League. My friends from Detroit used to hitch hike or jump a freight train to come see me play. They would arrive so dirty and grimy that the manager Jack Tighe said they looked as if they came from Skid Row, a run down area of Detroit."

2153. Lipscomb, Gerard (1937 2B) "Nig." Lipscomb had a dark complexion.

2154. Lister, Morris Elmer (1907 1B) "Pete." Origin unknown.

2155. Lively, Everett Adrian (1947–49 P) "Red." The nickname refers to hair color.

2156. Livingston, Thompson Orville (1938–51 C) "Mickey." Livingston received his nickname "Mickey" while playing American Legion ball. Teammates called him that after catcher Gordon "Mickey" Cochrane.

2157. Llenas, Winston Enriquillo (1968–75 2B) "Chilote." Llenas was named Winston after Winston Churchill the English prime minister during World War II. "Chilote" appears to be a childhood nickname that was not used during Llenas' baseball career, however, the origin is unknown.

2158. Loan, William Joseph (1912 C) "Mike." Origin unknown.

2159. Lobert, John Bernard (1903–17 3B) "Honus." Fred Lieb comments that Lobert had many of the same characteristics of Honus Wagner and was also of Teutonic extraction. Lee Allen remarks about Lobert's physical resemblance to Wagner and also the fact that he ran like him.

2160. Locke, Lawrence Donald (1959–68 P) "Bobby." Origin unknown.

2161. Lockwood, Claude Edward (1965–80 P) "Skip." Lockwood told me his pediatrician gave him the nickname of "Skip" at age five because he thought he looked like the skipper of a ship.

2162. Logan, John (1951–63 SS) "Yatcha." "Yatcha" is Ukrainian for John. Logan became noted for what were called Loganisms. For example, after receiving a reward he said, "I will perish this award forever." Speaking at a dinner for Stan Musial he observed, "One of the all-time greats, the immoral Stan Musial." Logan once ordered dessert by saying, "I'll have a pie à la mode with ice cream."

2163. Logan, Robert Dean (1955–65 P) "Lefty." Logan pitched left handed but batted right handed.

2164. Lohrke, Jack Wayne (1947–53 3B) "Lucky." In 1944 as a member of the 35th Infantry Division during World War II, Lohrke was at the Normandy Invasion and the Battle of the Bulge. On four occasions, GI's on both sides of him were killed and he did not even receive a scratch. In 1945 he was scheduled to fly from Fort Dix, New Jersey, to Los Angeles to be discharged but was bumped from the flight. The plane crashed and everyone aboard was killed. In 1946, Lohrke was on a bus trip with the Spokane Indians of the Western International League. When the bus stopped at Ellensburg, Washington, he got word he was to report immediately to the San Diego Padres of the Pacific Coast League. Shortly after, the bus fell off a cliff in the Cascade Mountains and nine players were killed. From then on Lohrke was known as "Lucky."

2165. Lombardi, Ernest Natali (1931–47 C) "Schnozz." "Schnozz" is Yiddish for "nose" of which Lombardi had a whopper. At his eloquent best, albeit tongue in cheek, Lee Allen wrote, "If you did not know that Rostland had written Cyrano de Bergerac long before Ernie Lombardi visited this planet, you would have sworn that the hero was patterned after the big Italian from Oakland, California ... he brought to baseball a nose so lavish in its geography that the more famous schnozzola of Jimmy Durante's seems picayunish by comparison." Lombardi was also called "Bocci" which referred to his fielding lapses.

2166. Lonborg, James Reynold (1965–79 P) "Gentleman Jim." Lonborg was highly regarded as a person. He was thought to be one of the outstanding gentlemen to ever play the game.

2167. Long, Herman C. (1889–1904 SS) "Germany." "Germany" refers to Long's German background. He was also called "The Flying Dutchman" because of his speed on the bases before

Honus Wagner was accorded that nickname.

2168. Long, Nelson (1902 SS) "Red." The nickname refers to hair color.

2169. Lopat, Edmund Walter (1944–55 P) "Steady Eddie." Mel Allen, Yankee broadcaster was responsible for the nickname. From 1948–54 Lopat's record with the Yanks was 17-11, 15-10, 21-9, 10-5, 16-4, and 12-4. The nickname really did fit with Lopat's nervous personality which nearly destroyed his career before he reached the major leagues. He was prone to temper tantrums. Ben Epstein dubbed him "Junk Man" because hitters claimed he threw nothing but garbage, slow stuff such as sliders, curves, screwballs and knucklers, but rarely a fastball over the plate. Honig in his book, *October Heroes,* lets Lopat comment on his thoughts about the nickname. "No, I never minded being called 'The Junk Man.' Never minded it at all. Actually the whole thing was contrived by a friend of mine named Ben Epstein. He was a newspaperman in Little Rock when I was playing there in the early 1940's. We were good friends and we remained good friends on through the years. When I was traded to the Yankees in 1948, Ben was working for one of the New York papers. He wrote an article about me for a sports magazine that year that he entitled 'He Got Plenty of Nothing.' That was a reference to my style of pitching, which consisted of breaking stuff, changes of speed, control, and a hell of a lot of thinking. The season progressed and I kept winning. One day Ben came up to me and said 'Do you mind if I give you a nickname?' 'What kind of nickname?' I asked. 'One that you'll have for as long as you're in the big league and that will be one of a kind.' 'What is it?' 'The Junk Man,' he said. 'Do you mind?' 'Ben' I said, 'I don't care what they call me as long as I can get those batters out and keep collecting my paycheck'."

2170. Lopez, Aurelio Alejandro Rios (1974– P) "Senor Smoke." Smoke refers to this relief pitcher's fastball, his best pitch.

2171. Lord, Briscoe Robotham (1905–13 OF) "The Human Eyeball." Origin unknown.

2172. Lorenzen, Adolph Andreas (1913 P) "Lefty." Lorenzen pitched left handed and batted left handed.

2173. Lotz, Joseph Peter (1916 P) "Smokey." "Smokey" refers to the speed of Lotz's fastball. It was his best pitch.

2174. Louden, William (1907–16 2B) "Baldy." Louden was prematurely bald.

2175. Love, Edward Haughton (1913–20 P) "Slim." At 6'7" Love was about the tallest pitcher of his era. At 195 pounds he appeared slim.

2176. Lowdermilk, Grover Cleveland (1909–20 P) "Slim." Lowdermilk was a shade over 6'4" and weighed 190 pounds.

2177. Lowe, Robert Lincoln (1890–1907 2B) "Link." "Link" was a takeoff on the middle name of Lincoln.

2178. Lowenstein, John Lee (1970–85 OF) "Captain Midnight." Lowenstein was always wearing sunglasses, even for night games.

2179. Lown, Omar Joseph (1951–62 P) "Turk." According to the biography in the 1953 *Baseball Register,* Lown had a fondness for turkey.

2180. Lowry, Samuel Joseph (1942–43 P) "Mose." Origin unknown.

2181. Loyd, John Henry (1903–31 SS, Negro League) "Cachatter." His large out-thrust chin won him the nickname in Cuba of "Cuchara" (Ladel) which was corrupted to "Cachatter" by his teammates. He was 6'2", 185 pounds with enormous hands. He was a fine hitter and a greyhound on the bases. Loyd was considered to be as able a player as Honus Wagner. Because of his large hands he was sometimes called "Shovel." In the later stages of his career, Loyd was called "Pop."

2182. Luby, Hugh Max (1936–44 3B) "Hal." Origin unknown.

2183. Luby, John Perkins (1890–93 P) "Pat." Origin unknown.

2184. Lucas, Charles Frederick (1935 OF) "Fritz." "Fritz" denotes Lucas' German background.

2185. Lucas, Charles Frederick (1923–38 P) "Red." The nickname refers to hair color. Lucas also was referred to as "The Nashville Narcissus." This is a place nickname. Lucas came from Nashville, Tennessee. Some thought he was vain. Lucas was the best control pitcher since 1920, giving up but 455 bases on balls in 2,542 innings pitched. Only once in 16 seasons did he give up more than 50 walks. Lucas was a good hitting pitcher with a career average of .281. He was the first player to collect 100 pinch hits. His career total of 114 is the sixth best mark of all time.

2186. Lucas, John Charles (1931–32 OF) "Buster." Origin unknown.

2187. Lucey, Joseph Earl (1920–25 P) "Scootch." Donald Bagg quotes Lucey, "I don't know where they got that name 'Scootch!' Somebody just threw it at me and it stuck."

2188. Luciano, Ronald M. (1968–80 AL Umpire) "Loosh." Luciano wrote, "The closest I ever came to a nickname was 'Loosh' as in 'that guy must have a screw loosh to play like that'." Luciano thought that a great nickname brought to mind a colorful image.

2189. Ludolph, William Francis (1924 P) "Wee Willie." This is a nickname opposite. Ludolph stood 6'1½" tall.

2190. Luhrsen, William Ferdinand (1913 P) "Wild Bill." Luhrsen, had a strikeout fastball, but his career was hampered by his inability to get the ball over the plate.

2191. Lukon, Edward Paul (1941–47 OF) "Mongoose." Lukon explained to me that "Mongoose" came from a newspaper article which said he was lying in wait. The next day Cincinnati teammates, Joe Beggs and Bucky Walters, began calling him that for a few days. After that said Lukon "it was never used again."

2192. Lumenti, Ralph Anthony (1957–59 P) "Commuter." Lumenti wrote me, "I signed with Washington on Labor Day 1957 and had to return to college at U. Mass. I flew into Washington on weekends to play ball. The publicity director gave me the nickname 'Commuter.' My real nickname is 'Lefty' which was assigned to me by kids in the third grade when we made them up for each other. Mine stuck. I am not sure my mother knows my real name."

2193. Luna, Guillermo Romero (1954 P) "Memo." "Memo" is a corruption of the first and middle names.

2194. Lundy, Richard (1916–48 SS, Negro League) "King Richard." As a shortstop, Lundy had a wide range and a strong arm and was the best at his position during the 1920s. His smooth, graceful and polished play in the field earned him the nickname of "King Richard."

2195. Luque, Adolfo (1914–35 P) "The Pride of Havana." This is a place nickname. Luque was from Havana, Cuba. He gave Cubans a right to be proud of him. He won 193 major league games. In 1922–23 he made an amazing turnabout. In 1922 he led the National League in losses with a 13-23 mark. In 1923 he led the league in wins with a 27-8 mark. Luque was known for his hot temper especially when remarks were made about his dark color.

2196. Lutenberg, Charles William (1894 1B) "Luke." "Luke" is a corruption of the last name instead of Lut.

2197. Lutzke, Walter John (1923–27 3B) "Rube." According to Milton Shapiro, Lutzke was a rough and tumble clown on the diamond, a real rube.

2198. Luzinski, Gregory Michael (1970–78 OF) "The Bull." Luzinski at 6'1" and 240 pounds was a powerful hitter who pounded 307 home runs during his 15-year career. When playing for the Philadelphia Phils a portion of the left field stands where most of his home runs landed was called "The Bull Ring."

2199. Lyle, Albert Walter (1967–82 P) "Sparky." Lyle received the nickname "Sparky" as a child from his father because of his energetic behavior. As a relief pitcher, he had few peers, compiling 238 career saves. He was sometimes called "Count," as in Dracula. He had the ability to draw the life's blood out of an opposing team's rally.

2200. Lynch, Matthew Daniel (1948 OF) "Dummy." According to SABR researcher Richard Topp, Lynch was deaf and dumb.

2201. Lynch, Thomas J. (1888–1902 NL Umpire) "King of the Umpires." The sobriquet was one of deference. Lynch became president of the National League 1910–12.

2202. Lynn, Japhet Monroe (1939–44 P) "Red." The nickname refers to hair color.

2203. Lyons, Edward Hoyte (1947 2B) "Mouse." "Mouse" refers to size. Lyons was 5'9" and 165 pounds.

2204. Lyons, Stephen John (1985–3B) "Psycho." Lyons was nicknamed "Psycho" by other ball players for his unusual behavior on the field. Once when a fan caught a foul ball, Lyons jumped into the stands to congratulate him. On another occasion while on first base, he played tic-tac-toe in the dirt with the first baseman. On July 16, 1990, he slid into first base safely. With dirt in his pants, he forgot where he was and pulled down his pants to his knees and began dusting the dirt from his legs, clad only in shorts and an athletic supporter.

2205. Lyons, Theodore Amar (1923–46 P) "Tex." Lyons, a 260-game winner in the major leagues, was from Louisiana not Texas. The "Tex" nickname came from sportswriter Malcolm MacLean. When he could not find out Lyons' first name at the start of his rookie season, and was late for a deadline, he made up the name of "Tex." Players did not use the nickname, but called Lyons by his middle name, Amar, which he detested.

2206. Lytle, Edward Benson (1890 OF) "Pop." Lytle was 28 years old as a rookie. He was also called "Dad."

M

2207. Maas, Duane Frederick (1955–61 P) "Duke." Maas told me he did not like the name of Duane. As a small boy he asked his father to call him Duke. In one sense, Maas was one of those ball players who nicknamed themselves.

2208. McAllister, Lewis William (1896–1903 OF) "Sport." "Sport" referred to McAllister's flashy dress. He was also called "Cassy."

2209. McArthur, Orland Alexander (1914 P) "Dixie." The nickname denotes McArthur's southern heritage. He was born in Vernon, Alabama.

2210. McAuley, James Earl (1914–25 SS) "Ike." Origin unknown.

2211. McAvoy, James Eugene (1913–19 C) "Wickey." Origin unknown.

2212. McBean, Alvin O'Neal (1961–70 P) "Double O." McBean told me his teammates at Pittsburgh thought he was a dapper dresser. He reminded them of the way Sean Connery dressed in the James Bond movies as secret agent 007 (double 0-7).

2213. McBee, Pryor Edward (1926 P) "Lefty." McBee pitched left handed but batted right handed.

2214. McBride, Arnold Ray (1973–83 OF) "Bake." McBride inherited the nickname of "Bake" from his father, a former pitcher for the Kansas City Monarchs. He did not, however, know its meaning.

2215. McCabe, James Arthur (1909–10 OF) "Swat." McCabe swatted the ball. He was a noted slugger in semi-pro and minor league ball.

2216. McCaffrey, Charles P. (1889 C) "Sparrow." "Sparrow" refers to McCaffrey's small stature.

2217. McCall, Brian Allan (1962–63 OF) "Bam." McCall wrote me that his mother always called him "Bam," the combination of his initials, and that is what he has always been called by others except on formal occasions.

2218. McCall, John William (1948–57 P) "Windy." As a rookie in 1948 he kept asking Ted Williams about his bats. Williams nicknamed him "Windy."

2219. McCall, Robert Leonard (1948 P) "Dutch." McCall told me, "My older brother gave me the nickname when I was very young. I was always getting in trouble, getting in 'Dutch'."

2220. McCarthy, Joseph Vincent (1926–50 Manager) "Marse Joe." Joe McCarthy did not play major league baseball, but he was a superb manager, maybe the best of all time. In 24 years as a manager, 1926–46, 1948–50, his teams never finished out of the first division. He won one pennant with the Chicago Cubs in the National League and eight pennants and seven World Series at the helm of the New York Yankees. His winning percentage of .614 is highest in major league history, as is his World Series winning percentage of .698. In the mid–1920s while managing the Chicago Cubs, he was nicknamed "Marse Joe" by a Chicago sportswriter. "Marse" is a variation of "Massa," a term once used by black slaves meaning "master." In 1926, his rookie year as manager of the Chicago Cubs, he needed nerve, verve and just plain guts to fire Graver Cleveland Alexander for breaking curfew regulations once too often. He also displayed tact and discipline in controlling Hack Wilson's night time activities. With the Cubs and later with the New York Yankees and Boston Red Sox, McCarthy was always a master at extolling the best out of the many star performers under his direction.

2221. McCarthy, Thomas Francis Michael (1884–96 OF) "Little Mac." McCarthy was a 5'7" outfielder. When teamed in the outfield with Hugh Duffy for the Boston Red Sox in the 1890s, the duo was known as the "Heavenly Twins," because of their sparkling play. McCarthy was also called "Foghorn" for his loud voice on the field. Umpire Bill Klem claimed that McCarthy was directly responsible for a rule change concerning a runner taking a base after a sacrifice fly. The old rule said that the runner could not leave the base until the ball had been caught. McCarthy would keep a caught ball bouncing from one hand to the other without holding it until he got near the infield and thus kept the runner stuck on base.

2222. McChesney, Harry Vincent (1904 OF) "Pud." Origin unknown.

2223. McClellan, Harvey McDowell (1919–24 SS) "Little Mac." McClellan was 5'10½" but weighed just 149 pounds.

2224. McClusky, Harry Robert (1915 P) "Lefty." McClusky pitched left handed and batted left handed.

2225. McColl, Alexander Boyd (1933–34 P) "Red." The nickname refers to hair color.

2226. McCormick, Frank Andrew (1934–48 1B) "Buck." McCormick was called "Buck" and "Moose" because of his size, 6'4" and 205 pounds.

2227. McCormick, Harry Elwood (1904–13 OF) "Moose." According to Fred Lieb, "Moose" referred to McCormick's "always charging style of play."

2228. McCormick, Myron Winthrop (1940–51 OF) "Mike." "Mike" was first used in place of Myron by schoolmates in Stockton, California.

2229. McCormick, William J. (1914–15 FL Umpire) "Barry." Origin unknown.

2230. McCovey, Willie Lee (1959–80 1B) "Stretch." Although McCovey was known primarily as a slugger who amassed 521 career home runs and 1,550 RBI's, at 6'4" with long arms he possessed an enormous stretch taking throws at first base.

2231. McCrabb, Lester William (1939–50 P) "Buster." McCrabb wrote me that coach Al Simmons of the Philadelphia A's started calling him "Buster" in 1941 for no reason at all. Teammates then picked up on it. One wonders if perhaps the famous swimmer and popular actor of the period, Larry "Buster" Crabb, might have had something to do with the nickname.

2232. McCreedie, Walter Henry (1905 OF) "Judge." Origin unknown.

2233. McDermott, Frank A. (1912 OF) "Red." The nickname refers to hair color.

2234. McDermott, Maurice Joseph (1948–61 P) "Mickey." "Mickey" was simply a preferred baseball alternative to Maurice. McDermott a good hitting pitcher had a career batting average of .252 and batted over .300 in four seasons.

2235. McDonald, Arch (1934–56 Announcer) "Old Pine Tree." McDonald was the voice of the Washington Senators for 22 years with a brief stint with the New York Yankees in 1939. He was famous for his epigrams, the best known of which resulted in his nickname. When the Senators did something spectacular (which was seldom in the 1930s and 1940s) McDonald would quote from the hillbilly ballad, "They did it. They Cut Down the Old Pine Tree."

2236. McDonald, Charles C. (1912–15 OF) "Tex." McDonald was born and raised in Farmerville, Texas.

2237. McDonald, Jimmie Leroy (1950–58 P) "Hot Rod." McDonald had the reputation of being a showoff and "hot dog." He was hard to discipline and was often in his manager's doghouse.

2238. McDonald, Larry Benard (1988– P) "Big Ben." McDonald is 6'7" tall.

2239. McDonald, Malcolm Joseph (1910– 3B) "Tex." McDonald was born and raised in Galveston, Texas.

2240. McDougal, John Auchanbolt (1895–1905 P) "Sandy." The nickname refers to light blonde hair color.

2241. McDowell, Samuel Edward (1961–75 P) "Sudden Sam." McDowell was a fastball pitcher who many thought did not make the most of his talent. Some even went so far as to call him "Sad Sam." Nevertheless, he led the American League in strike outs five times, twice striking out more than 300 batters. Umpire Bill Kinnon explains why he was called "Sudden Sam." "He had a real herky-jerky motion and could throw the ball like a bullet. And his ball moved. You always had to be especially alert for him; he was so quick that there were times you weren't quite ready to call the pitch." Sparky Lyle mentions another nickname which the players had for McDowell. "We used to call him Teen Angel because he always slicked his hair back. Sam was notorious for getting in the sauce, getting real rowdy, picking a fight, and getting beat up. This one day we were on a plane heading for a road trip, and Sam's hair was blow-dried and he had it combed and styled. Everyone was buzzing 'Teen Angel got his hair done'."

2242. McDuffie, Terous (1932–45 P, Negro League) "The Great." The nickname referred to his fine pitching. McDuffie compiled a winning percentage of .644 for 11 seasons. In 1938 McDuffie led the league in wins, and complete games.

2243. McElveen, Prior Mynatt (1909–11 2B) "Humpy." With names like Prior and Mynatt, McElveen needed a nickname, but the origin of "Humpy" is unknown.

2244. McFarland, Charles A. (1902–06 P) "Chappie." Origin unknown.

2245. MacFayden, Daniel Knowles (1926–43 P) "Deacon Danny." MacFayden received his nickname from Boston Red Sox teammates in the late 1920s, because of his quiet, gentlemanly manner, and his devotion to religion. He often spoke to men's bible classes.

2246. McGaffigan, Mark Andrew (1917–18 2B) "Patsy." Patsy denotes McGaffigan's Irish background.

2247. McGann, Dennis Lawrence (1895–1908 1B) "Cap." Origin unknown.

2248. McGarr, James P. (1984–96 3B) "Chippy." Origin unknown.

2249. McGarr, James Vincent (1912 2B) "Reds." The nickname refers to hair color.

2250. McGee, Francis D. (1925 1B) "Tubby." McGee was overweight early in his playing career.

2251. McGee, William Henry (1935–42 P) "Fiddler Bill." McGee received the "Fiddler" tag because he played the violin. He played in Pepper Martin's "Missouri Mudcats," the hillbilly band which the St. Louis Cardinal's "Gas House Gang" popularized.

2252. McGhee, William Mac (1944–45 1B) "Fibber." McGhee was nicknamed after the main character in the radio serial, "Fibber McGhee and Molly" which aired 1935–52 with actor Jim Jordan as the voice of Fibber.

2253. McGill, William John (1907 P) "Parson." Origin unknown.

2254. McGill, William Vaness (1890–96 P) "Kid." McGill was called "Kid" as a 5'6½", 17-year-old rookie.

2255. McGilvray, William Alexander (1908 PH) "Big Bill." McGilvray's career consisted of two times at bat as a pinch hitter without getting on base. He stood 6'0" and weighed 160 pounds.

2256. McGinnis, Albert (1893 P) "Gus." "Gus," in this case, is a takeoff on the last syllable of the last name.

2257. McGinnity, Joseph Jerome (1899–1908 P) "Iron Man." The nickname has two meanings. The first was a relic of his minor league days at Kansas City. A reporter asked him what he did in the off season. He replied, "I'm an iron man, I work in a foundry." The second meaning refers to his feats on the mound. In 1901 he split ends of doubleheader twice while pitching for Baltimore. The previous year he had won five games in six days pitching for the Brooklyn Superbas. In 1903 he won three doubleheaders in the month of August for the New York Giants. He pitched 434 innings that year and 408 in 1904 in compiling a 35-8 won-loss record.

2258. McGlothin, Eraz Mac (1949–50 P) "Pat." McGlothin told me, "In the Southern League in 1942, a sportswriter thought Eraz was too formal and began calling me Pat because I was Irish. I always kidded them and said they called me Pat because I was Jewish.

2259. McGlothin, James Milton (1965–73 P) "Red." The nickname refers to hair color.

2260. McGlynn, Ulysses Simpson Grant (1906–08 P) "Stoney." Origin unknown.

2261. McGowan, Frank Bernard (1922–37 OF) "Beauty." Origin unknown.

2262. McGowan, Tullis Earl (1948 P) "Mickey." "Mickey" refers to McGowan's Irish background and is a more acceptable baseball name than Tullis.

2263. McGowan, William A. (1925–54, AL Umpire) "Little Joe Chest." McGowan was usually rated the number one umpire in the American League by fans, players, and other umpires. Jimmy Powers wrote, "The fans voted on the best umpires in the league and McGowan was elected number one. The players then sat down to inscribe an epic poem and finally came up with a two-line masterpiece that they set to music. All they had to do to drive

McGowan wild was to chant their poem, 'The American League fans voted me the best; But all the players call me Little Joe Chest'."

2264. McGraner, Howard (1912 P) "Muck." Origin unknown.

2265. McGraw, Frank Edwin (1965–84 P) "Tug." According to Joseph McBride, as a baby McGraw tugged so strenuously at his mother's breast while being nursed, that his parents nicknamed him "Tugger." Another account has it that he tugged at everything as a baby. In either event, it was later shortened to just "Tug."

2266. McGraw, Harry T. (1930–31 1933–34 NL Umpire) "Ted." "Ted" may have been McGraw's middle name and therefore not a nickname. I have not, however, been able to document this.

2267. McGraw, John Joseph (1891–1906 3B) "Little Napoleon." John McGraw stood but 5'7" tall and weighed only 155 pounds. What he lacked in size he more than made up for in his determination and aggressive play. There have been other players and managers whose will to win were as great as McGraw's, but certainly no one who ever played the game showed greater desire. He employed every available tactic and strategy legal or illegal with which he could get away. As a third baseman from 1891–1906, he became famous for attempting to keep runners from scoring by nudging them as they rounded third or hanging on to their belts. In 16 years he batted .334. Adjectives used to describe his play were scrappy, rowdy, pugnacious and ill tempered. His managing career began in 1899 and did not end until 1932. During that period of time his team won nine National League flags and three World Series. In spite of a lifetime winning percentage of .589, his 1915 New York Giants finished dead last. "Little Napoleon" as a nickname referred to McGraw's height and his authoritarian and military style of managing. Douglas Wallop, catches the spirit of "Little Napoleon" in the following description, "...The nickname is well founded in terms of both his autocratic methods and the impression he gave as he directed his team from the third base coach's box—a short, stumpy figure assuming an attitude that seemed always to be the same as the years passed, even when the potbelly became more pronounced and the hair turned gray and then white, the face became grizzled and the small eyes seemed to grow even smaller as they became hemmed in with wrinkles."

As a teenage rookie with the Baltimore Orioles in 1891, McGraw was dubbed "Batboy" by his teammates. However, his rough and rowdy play allowed him to outgrow this nickname in a short period of time. It was replaced with "Muggsy" a nickname which McGraw detested and was only whispered in his presence. It referred to a corrupt Baltimore politician to whom McGraw was thought to resemble physically. In 1891 McGraw was a member of a team touring Cuba after the season. The Cubans appreciated his hard play and nicknamed him "El Mono Amarillo," the yellow monkey, because of his size and the yellow uniforms the team wore.

2268. McGrew, Walter Howard (1922–24 P) "Slim." McGrew was 6'7½" tall and weighed 235 pounds.

2269. McGuire, James Thomas (1884–1912 C) "Deacon." McGuire caught for 26 years in the major leagues. Joe Overfield mentions that he had a quiet demeanor and impeccable personal habits. He did not question umpires decisions. The nickname of "Deacon" comes from the fact that he did not curse or get drunk. Robert

Smith points out that McGuire caught barehanded. "He had extremely large hands, which during the course of his career, had been split, broken and twisted so many times by foul tips they resembled 'a pair of tangled old tree stumps'." David Nemec suggests that perhaps one of McGuire's most impressive accomplishments was catching 220 games after the age of 40.

2270. McGuire, Thomas Patrick (1914–19 P) "Elmer." Origin unknown.

2271. McGunnigle, William Henry (1879–82 OF) "Gunner." The nickname refers to the speed of his throws, but undoubtedly reinforced by the last name.

2272. McIlveen, Henry Cooke (1906–09 OF) "Irish." McIlveen was born in Belfast, Ireland, and was of Irish background.

2273. McIlwain, Stover William (1957–59 P) "Smokey." "Smokey" refers to the speed of his fastball.

2274. McInnis, John Phalen (1909–27 1B) "Stuffy." McInnis was built like a toy bulldog and in 18 seasons had a career batting average of .308. He played in five World Series for three different teams. As a youngster, fans shouted encouragement to him saying, "That's the stuff kid." It became a nickname.

2275. McIntyre, John Reid (1905–13 P) "Handsome Harry." McIntyre was called "Handsome Harry" because of his good looks. He was also referred to as "Daddy of the Spitball." In a nine-year career he managed to win but 71 games against 117 losses. After his baseball career, he became a successful professional gambler, but details on this portion of his life are scanty.

2276. McJames, James McCutcher (1895–1901 P) "Doc." McJames was a practicing physician who worked his way through medical school by pitching major league baseball. In 1898 he won 27 games for Baltimore.

2277. Mack, Cornelius (1886–96 C) "The Tall Tactician." Mack was born Cornelius MacGillicuddy, but changed his name so that it would fit more easily into a box score. He began his 11-year playing career in 1886. Although his lifetime batting average was only .245, he was known as an excellent defensive catcher. Mack was not above using illegal tactics such as tipping the batter's bat or smacking his tongue to lead an umpire into believing the ball had nicked the bat. During his playing days he had no public nickname and was addressed and referred to as Connie. Mack managed from 1894–1950, 53 years. His teams won eight pennants and five World Series yet his winning percentage was below .500, at .484. This was because his teams finished last 17 times. From 1915–21, Mack's Philadelphia Athletics were last in the American League seven straight years. During that period his teams won 323 games and lost 710, a percentage of .312. The 1916 team won only 36 games while losing 117. This may have been the worst team of all time. Through the good years and poor years Connie Mack was a master of baseball strategy. It earned him the nickname of "The Tall Tactician." It was Mack who said, "Pitching is 70% of baseball." Connie was 6'1" and weighed about 170 pounds. He always wore a suit, tie and hat when managing—never a uniform. Mack was soft spoken. Once, when a player accused him of never using profanity, his reply was, "Darn it, I do too." For over half a century he was a familiar, but unusual sight to generations of baseball fans directing his players from the dugout by waving his score card. During the last 20 or so years of his career, sportswriters frequently used "GOM" in print rather than his name. It meant "Grand Old Man." The practice was derived from English newspapers which used those letters in reference to the 19th century British statesman, William Gladstone.

2278. Mack, Frank George (1922–25 P) "Stubby." This is a nickname opposite. Mack stood 6'1½" tall and weighed 180 pounds.

2279. Mack, Joseph (1883–90 2B) "Reddy." The nickname refers to hair color.

2280. McKain, Archie Richard (1937–43 P) "Happy." His uncle called him "Happy" as a boy because he was always whistling and seemed to have a happy-go-lucky attitude.

2281. McKechnie, William Boyd (1907–20 3B) "Deacon." William McKechnie was a major league infielder for 11 years from 1907–20 two of which were spent in the Federal League, 1914–15. His lifetime batting average was .251. McKechnie managed one year in the Federal League, 1915, and 24 years in the National League, 1916–40. During his tenure in the National League, he directed three different teams to pennants, Pittsburgh, St. Louis and Cincinnati. He is the only manager to achieve this feat. In all, teams under his leadership won four pennants and two World Series. Even as a player, McKechnie was highly regarded for his astute knowledge. This ability combined with his soft spoken manner, and the fact that he was a real deacon in the Methodist Church, account for his nickname.

2282. McKee, Raymond Ellis (1913–16 C) "Red." The nickname refers to hair color.

2283. McKeithan, Emmett James (1932–34 P) "Tim." "Tim" denotes McKeithan's Irish background and was a more acceptable baseball name than Emmett.

2284. McKenna, James William (1898–99 P) "Kit." Origin unknown.

2285. McKenry, Frank Gordon (1915–16 P) "Big Pete." Origin unknown. McKenry was also called "Limb," but the origin of that nickname is also unknown.

2286. Mackey, Raleigh (1918–47 C, Negro League) "Biz." Mackey was known as a good hitter, a fierce competitor, with a powerful arm who could throw harder to second base from a squatting position than most catchers could standing up. Many that saw him play felt he was the finest catcher that Negro baseball produced. Although much has been written about Mackey, for instance John Holway devotes 17 pages to his career in his book, *Blackball Stars*, there is not a hint of what the nickname "Biz" meant or how Mackey came by it.

2287. McLarry, Howard Zell (1912–15 1B) "Polly." Origin unknown.

2288. McLaughlin, Michael Duane (1976–82 P) "Bo." McLaughlin wrote me, "A retired man who babysat me at age one had a friend just died whose nickname was Bo. He called me his little Bo. When I was 7 and started playing ball there were 7 kids on the team whose name was Michael. The coach asked if anyone had a nickname. I said mine was Bo and I have been Bo ever since."

2289. McLaughlin, James Anson (1914 OF) "Sunshine." Origin unknown.

2290. McLaughlin, Justin Theodore (1931–33 P) "Jud." "Jud" was a more acceptable baseball name than Justin, thus the takeoff.

2291. McLean, John Bannerman (1901–15 C) "Slasher." McLean caught in the major leagues for 13 seasons, batting .262. In the 1913 World Series he hit .500, 6-12 for the New York Giants. According to Tom Shea his batting style was to slash at the ball.

2292. McLean, William B. (NA Umpire 1871–75; NL Umpire 1876–80, 82–84) "King of the Umpires." McLean was the first umpire to receive this nickname because of the excellent job he did. It dates from 1878. Al Spaulding called McLean "McLean the Quondam Prize Fighter," because he was a professional prize fighter in the off season and an authoritative umpire who was not above enforcing his decisions with his fists if need be.

2293. McLeland, Wayne Gaffney (1951–52 P) "Nubbin." Origin unknown.

2294. McLendon, Gordon (1941–47 Announcer) "The Old Scotchman." In 1949, McLendon began the Liberty Broadcasting System's "Game of the Week" which would be immediately heard on 431 stations. McLendon nicknamed himself "The Old Scotchman" after his Scotch background. His broadcasting career was brief, his other business interests taking up much of his time.

2295. McLish, Calvin Coolidge Julius Caesar Tuskahoma (1944–64 P) "Buster." McLish wrote me, "I was nicknamed by my father because I weighed 12 pounds at birth. I guess it was common in those days to call big babies 'Buster.' I always wondered why I had to have a nickname with all the other names I had been given by my father. One was for an American President, another for a Roman Emperor and a third for an Indian Chief."

2296. McMahon, Henry John (1908 P) "Doc." Many of the players with the nickname of "Doc" had a close association with either the medical or dental professions. However, in the case of McMahon the origin of "Doc" is unknown.

2297. McMahon, John Joseph (1889–97 P) "Sadie." Origin unknown.

2298. McMakin, John Weaver (1902 P) "Spartanburg John." This is a place nickname. McMakin was born and raised in Spartanburg, South Carolina.

2299. McMillan, George A. (1890 OF) "Reddy." The nickname refers to hair color.

2300. McMillan, Norman Alexis (1922–29 3B) "Bub." Origin unknown.

2301. McMillan, Thomas Law (1908–12 SS) "Rebel." While McMillan was born in Pittston, Pennsylvania, he spent his growing up years south of the Mason-Dixon line.

2302. McNabb, Carl Mac (1945 PH) "Skinny." McNabb had a slight build at 5'9" and 150 pounds.

2303. McNair, Donald Eric (1929–42 SS) "Boob." McNair was nicknamed after the Rube Goldberg comic strip character the likeable, innocent, irrational thinking "Boob McNutt." The strip became national in 1918 and appeared through 1934.

2304. McNamara, John Raymond (1927–28 OF) "Dinny." "Dinny" denotes McNamara's Irish background.

2305. McNaughton, Gordon Joseph (1932 P) "Big Train." McNaughton was a 6'1" and 190-pound fastball pitcher who reminded some of Walter "Big Train" Johnson.

2306. McNealy, Robert Lee (1983 DH) "Rusty." Origin unknown.

2307. McPhee, John Alexander (1882–99 2B) "Bid." "Bid" was short for "Biddy" meaning small. McPhee was 5'8" and weighed 150 pounds. He began playing adult baseball at age 16. In 1896, he set the fielding record for second base men with a percentage of .978 which stood for 23 years.

2308. MacPhee, Walter Scott (1922 3B) "Waddy." "Waddy" is a corruption of Walter.

2309. McQuery, William Thomas (1884–1891 1B) "Mox." "Mox" is simply adding McQuery's first initial to "ox." McQuery was 6'4". His exact weight is unknown, but it was over 200 pounds.

2310. McQuillan, Hugh A. (1918–27 P) "Handsome Hugh." McQuillan was regarded as very good looking, especially by women. He also had a place nickname. He was from Astoria, Long Island, New York, and was called "The Astoria Eagle."

2311. McSorley, John Bernard (1884–86 1B) "Trick." According to Furman Bisher, McSorley enjoyed picking up women and provided prostitutes a "trick."

2312. Macullar, James F. (1879–86 SS) "Little Mac." While the exact height and weight of Macullar is unknown, there is indication in reports of his performance that he was small of stature.

2313. McWeeny, Douglas Lawrence (1921–30 P) "Buzz." "Buzz" refers to his pitching. His fastball was said to "Buzz."

2314. Madden, Frank A. (1914 C) "Red." The nickname refers to hair color.

2315. Madden, Leonard Joseph (1912 P) "Lefty." Madden pitched left handed and batted left handed.

2316. Madden, Michael Joseph (1887–91 P) "Kid." In Madden's case "Kid" referred to size. He was 5'7½" and weighed 130 pounds.

2317. Madden, Thomas Joseph (1906–10 OF) "Bunny." Origin unknown.

2318. Madigan, William J. (1886 P) "Tony." Origin unknown.

2319. Madlock, William, Jr. (1973–87 3B) "Mad Dog." While some reports indicate that this four-time NL batting champion was not the easiest person with which to get along, the nickname of "Mad Dog" recalls a specific incident in 1980. Madlock, in an argument, hit umpire Jerry Crawford in the face with his glove. His unruly behavior cost Madlock a $5,000 fine, the largest amount accessed for an on-the-field incident up until that time, and a 15-day suspension, the second longest in major league history up until that time.

2320. Magee, Sherwood R. (1928 NL Umpire) "Sherry." "Sherry" was a takeoff on Sherwood.

2321. Magerkurth, George L. (1929–47 NL Umpire) "Meathead." James Kahn writes about Magerkurth saying his face had an open cherubic quality bearing a remarkable likeness to Herbert Hoover, but, "In anger, however, it seemed to double in size as his jowls reddened and quivered and his neck swelled up over his collar. They called him 'Meathead' but not without penalty. 'Meathead' to Magerkurth was as "Catfish" to Klem. It meant automatic banishment from the game." Magerkurth had been a professional boxer and on several occasions engaged in fisticuffs with players, managers, and fans.

2322. Maglie, Salvatore Anthony (1945–58 P) "The Barber." Maglie was noted for pitching inside to batters and brushing them back. In other words, he gave them a close shave. The nickname may have been reinforced by the fact that Maglie had a dark beard and it often looked as if he needed a shave when he pitched.

2323. Magner, Edmund Burke (1911 SS) "Stubby." The nickname refers to size. Magner stood 5'3" and weighed 135 pounds.

2324. Magoon, George Henry (1898–1903 SS) "Topsy." The origin of "Topsy" is unknown. Magoon was also called "Maggie" which is a takeoff on his last name and has no feminine connotations.

2325. Mahaffey, Lee Roy (1926–36 P) "Popeye." According to Tom Shea, Mahaffey had large prominent eyes.

2326. Mahon, Alfred Gwinn (1930 P) "Lefty." Mahon pitched left handed and batted left handed.

2327. Mahoney, James Thomas (1959–65 SS) "Moe." "Moe" was used as short for Mahoney.

2328. Mails, John Walter (1915–26 P) "The Great." Mails, who won 32 games in a seven-year career, nicknamed himself. He was also called "Duster" after he beaned a batter in the Pacific Coast League in 1915.

2329. Main, Forrest Harry (1948–53 P) "Woody." "Woody" is a response to the first name of Forrest.

2330. Mains, Willard Eben (1888–96 P) "Grasshopper." Tom Shea maintains this is a nickname opposite since Mains was 6'2" and weighed 190 pounds. There is, however, indication that "Grasshopper" referred to Mains underhand style of pitching.

2331. Maisel, Frederick Charles (1913–19 3B) "Flash." Maisel was very fast especially on the base paths. In 1914 he stole 74 bases to lead the American League despite a .239 batting average. He was also called "Fritz" pointing to his German background.

2332. Majeski, Henry (1939–55 3B) "Heeney." Hank, as he was usually addressed, received the nickname of "Heeney" by schoolmates. It is a takeoff on Henry. It was not used much as a baseball nickname.

2333. Malarcher, David J. (1916–34 3B, Negro League) "Gentleman Dave." Malarcher was a smooth fielding third baseman who usually hit in the .300 range. He was one of the few black players with a college education (New Orleans University). This earned him the tag of "Gentleman Dave."

2334. Malbury, Harry William (1955 2B) "Swede." "Swede" calls attention to Malbury's Swedish background.

2335. Malby, Paul Augustus (1913 P) "Biff." Origin unknown.

2336. Maldonado, Candido (1981– OF) "Candy." Unlike some other players with the nickname of "Candy" for example, William "Candy" Cummings, the nickname has no special connotation for Maldonado. It is simply derived from his first name.

2337. Maliho, Emil Pierre (1936 OF) "Lefty." Maliho batted left handed and threw left handed.

2338. Mallonnee, Howard Bennett (1921 OF) "Lefty." Mallonnee batted left handed and threw left handed.

2339. Mallory, James Baugh (1940–45 OF) "Sunny Jim." Mallory wrote me, "During my first year at the University of North Carolina my roommate, Mike Babbit, wingback on the football team, and Bob Smith center on the team gave me the nickname because I was so jovial, smiled a lot and enjoyed a good time."

2340. Malloy, Archibald Alexander (1910 P) "Lick." With a first name of Archibald, Malloy needed a baseball nickname. However, the origin of "Lick" is unknown.

2341. Malone, Pierce Leigh (1928–37 P) "Pat." As a teenager Malone nicknamed himself. In 1929 he led the National League in wins with 22 and strikeouts, 166. He joined the army before World War I and was a member of the calvary at Douglas Arizona in 1916 when General John "Black Jack" Pershing was pursuing Francisco "Pancho" Villa, the Mexican bandit. Because of this experience he was sometimes referred to as "The Black Knight of the Border."

2342. Mancuso, August Rodney (1928–45 C) "Blackie." Before integration in 1947 players with dark complexion sometimes received race-tinged nicknames. This was the case of Gus, as he was usually addressed. Teammate Jim Bottonly gave him the nickname "Blackie" when he was a rookie with the St. Louis Cardinals in 1928.

2343. Mangual, Jose Manuel (1972–77 OF) "Pepe." Origin unknown.

2344. Mangum, Leo Allen (1924–35 P) "Blackie." "Blackie" referred to Mangum's dark hair and complexion.

2345. Manion, Clyde Jennings (1920–34 C) "Pete." Origin unknown.

2346. Mann, Ben Garth (1944 PR) "Red." The nickname refers to hair color.

2347. Manning, Ernest Devon (1914 P) "Ed." "Ed" was used as a short name for Ernest.

2348. Manning, Walter S. (1907–12 P) "Rube." Manning was from the small town of Chambersburg, Pennsylvania. "Rube," after George "Rube" Waddell was a common nickname given to players of rural origin who were less than familiar with big city life.

2349. Mantilla, Felix Lamela (1956–66 2B) "The Cat." Although some fans felt Mantilla had cat-like moves at second base, the nickname is a response to his first name. It is in reference to the comic strip character "Felix the Cat."

2350. Mantle, Mickey Charles (1951–68 OF) "The Commerce Comet." Mantle's father admired catcher Gordon "Mickey" Cochrane so much he gave his son Cochrane's nickname as a first name. As such, it served the purpose of a nickname for Mantle. "The Commerce Comet" is a place nickname. Mantle was from Commerce, Oklahoma. Although Mantle, among other attributes, was known for his speed, this is not what "Comet" refers to. During the 1950 season Mantle hit some long home runs for Joplin of the Western Association. They were called "comets" by fans and sportswriters because of the speed by which they left the park. Manager Casey Stengel sometimes called Mantle "Ignstz" the meaning of which was known only to Stengel. Mantle ended his career with 526 home runs. He was one of the most popular and well known players of all time.

2351. Manuel, Mark Garfield (1905–08 P) "Moxie." "Moxie" referred to Manuel's aggressiveness and get up and go. He had Moxie. This was a slang term popular shortly after the turn of the century.

2352. Manush, Henry Emmett (1923–39 OF) "Heinie." "Heinie" calls attention to Manush's German background.

2353. Mapel, Rolla Hamilton (1919 P) "Lefty." Mapel pitched left handed and batted left handed.

2354. Mapes, Cliff Franklin (1948–52 OF) "Tiger." "Tiger" refers in part to Mapes aggressive style of play plus his build, 6'3" and 205 pounds. He was a real tiger.

2355. Maranville, Walter James Vincent (1912–35 SS) "Rabbit." There are several versions of the "Rabbit" nickname. Maranville did wiggle his ears like a rabbit, but Fred Lieb contends that he looked so much like a rabbit in the face that even his wife called him that. George Sullivan believes that the nickname stems from the handsprings and flips that Maranville did in the base paths plus his antics while waiting for play to resume. One of these was to pretend he was leaning on a wall and then take a tumble as if the wall had collapsed. Finally Harold Kaese reports a quite different account. A small girl saw Maranville in New Bedford, Connecticut, early in his career bouncing around in a pepper game. She said, "You jump just like a rabbit." Until then Maranville had been called "Stumpy." He was 5'5" and weighed 155 pounds.

2356. Marberry, Frederick (1923–36 P; AL Umpire 1935) "Firpo." Marberry reminded people of the Argentine heavyweight boxer Luis Firpo who was knocked out by Jack Dempsey in a famous championship match in September of 1923 when Marberry was a rookie. Starting in 1924 Marberry was the first outstanding pitcher to be used in relief. In that year he started 15 times and relieved 35 times saving 15 games and helping Washington win the A.L. flag. In 1925 he had 55 relief appearances without a start, saving 15 games. He finished his 14-year career with 101 saves. Marberry was an A.L. umpire in 1935. Jocko Conlen thought Marberry was the best looking and best dressed umpire he ever saw. But behind the plate, all he could call were balls. Even though he had been a pitcher, he did not seem to know the strike zone. Marberry was dropped after just one year on the job.

2357. Marcelle (also Marcel, Marcell), Oliver H. (1913–30 3B, Negro League) "Ghost." Marcelle was a 5'9", 160-pound New Orleans Creole with an unmanageable temper. He once hit Oscar Charleston over the head with a bat. He became, however, one of the best defensive third basemen in the Negro leagues. Marcelle was also an effective clutch hitter with a career average of .333 in Negro League competition. I have not been able to find any explanation of the "Ghost" nickname.

2358. Marcum, John Alfred (1933–39 P) "Footsie." According to Tom Shea, Marcum had unusually large feet.

2359. Marichal, Juan Antonio Sanchez (1960–73 P) "The Dominican Dandy." This is a place nickname. Marichal, who won 243 major league games, was one of the first outstanding players to come from the Dominican Republic. He was also often referred to as "Manito."

2360. Marion, John Wyeth (1935–43 OF) "Red." The nickname refers to hair color.

2361. Marion, Martin Whitford (1940–53 SS) "Slats." Bert Shotton gave Marion the nickname of "Slats" because he was tall and thin, 6'2" and 170 pounds. Marion was the best fielding shortstop of his time. In 1944 he was voted the most valuable player in the National League even though he hit only .267 with six home runs. He was very graceful in the field. His ability to get to balls others could not, led to the nickname of "The Octopus." He seemed to have eight tentacles.

2362. Markell, Harry Duquesne (1951 P) "Duke." Markell was born in Paris, France. "Duke" is a play on his French middle name.

2363. Marolewski, Fred Daniel (1953 1B) "Fritz." "Fritz" is an alternative to Fred, but does not imply German background. Marolewski told me a friend of his father's introduced the nickname when he was a child.

2364. Marquard, Richard William (1908–25 P) "Rube." Marquard was nicknamed after George "Rube" Wadell. On opening day 1908 in the American Association, Marquard of Indianapolis bested "Smoky" Joe Wood of Kansas City. An article in the *Indianapolis Star* reporting the game stated, "The right-hander with Kansas City looks like he's going to develop into a great pitcher. They call him Smoky Joe Wood. But we have a left-hander with Indianapolis who's going places too. He resembles one of the great left-handers of all time, Rube Wadell."

2365. Marquart, Albert Ludwig (1931 2B) "Ollie." "Ollie" was used as an alternative to Albert but had no special ethnic identification.

2366. Marquez, Luis Angel (1951–54 OF) "Canena." Marquez was especially fond of bread.

2367. Marquis, Rodger Julian (1955 OF) "Noonie." Marquis told me "Noonie" was a nonsense nickname made up by kids when he was a child.

2368. Marr, Charles W. (1886–91 OF) "Lefty." Marr batted left handed and threw left handed.

2369. Marrow, Charles Kennon (1932–38 P) "Buck." "Buck" is a generic nickname of which the circumstances of origin are almost never documented. It refers to a well developed, virile, aggressive, high spirited young man. The nickname was usually bestowed on the individual during his teenage years.

2370. Marshall, Clarence Westly (1946–50 P) "Cuddles." Marshall was considered to be handsome. Newspaper pictorials compared him to the actor Tyrone Power. Marshall related this story to me, "In 1946 Joe Page gave me the nickname when we were coming home from spring training with the Yankees. I had pitched a good game in Dallas. As we boarded the plane, newspaper men stopped me and asked what they could call me besides Clarence—a nickname. Joe Page told them how all the teenage girls mobbed me and fell over me in the hotel lobby. He said, 'They think he is cuddly.' So, they decided to nickname me Cuddles."

2371. Marshall, Edward Herbert (1929–32 SS) "Doc." I don't know how "Doc" got in the second book. I was always called Eddie except when I had a poor day. I have researched old newspaper clippings for any reference to Doc and found none. The first time Doc was used was well after I retired was by a barber. He greeted me once with "Hi, Doc." He said he picked it up from the record book. I don't know how it got there.

2372. Marshall, Joseph Hanley (1903–06 OF) "Home Run Joe." Marshall hit some long home runs in the minor leagues. However, in 118 times at bat in the major leagues he failed to get any home runs, batting just .178.

2373. Marshall, Michael Allen (1981– OF) "Moose." Marshall was nicknamed "Moose" by Los Angeles fans because of his size, 6'5" and 220 pounds, and his home run power.

2374. Marshall, Roy DeVerne (1912–15 P) "Rube." Marshall was nicknamed after George "Rube" Wadell. But he also had the nickname of "Cy" after Denton "Cy" Young. Both nicknames referred to his small town background and his unfamiliarity with big city life. Combined, his namesakes Wadell and Young won 702 major league games. Unfortunately, Marshall could manage but nine wins during his four-year career.

2375. Marshall, William Riddle (1904–09 C) "Doc." Marshall had an MD degree and was a practicing physician.

2376. Martel, Leon Alphouse (1909–10 C) "Doc." Martel held an MD degree and was a practicing surgeon.

2377. Martin, Alfred Manuel (1950–61 2B) "Billy." In his book with Peter Golenbock, *Number 1,* Martin stated, "I didn't know my real name was Alfred until junior high school. When I was a baby, my grandmother, who spoke Italian, called me Bellitz, which means beautiful. The other kids heard her call me Bellitz and they thought she was saying Billy, and that's what everyone called me." Whether as player or manager, as a fighter, brawler, or umpire-baiter, Martin had few peers in postwar baseball. His relationships with almost everyone he came in contact with on and off the field, friend, or stranger, player or owner became strained at one time or another. His behavior earned him the nickname of "Billy the Brat." His drinking and barroom antics became legendary. He is the only individual in the history of the game hired and fired five times as manager of the same team, to the New York Yankees. In spite of this, many felt his managerial skills to be brilliant. In fact they were called "Billy Ball." Some fans felt, yours truly included, that he might be asked to manage the Yankees once again in the 1990s. But it was not to be. Martin died in a one-vehicle crash outside his upstate New York home on December 25, 1989.

2378. Martin, Alphonse Case (1872–73 P) "Old Slow Ball Phonie." Martin pitched for the Brooklyn Eckfords. He developed a slow pitch which broke down as it crossed the plate. The reverse English on it and the spin was just strong enough so that it hesitated when it came near to the plate and then because of the motion it dropped. It was the first cousin to what shortly later would be called a curve.

2379. Martin, Boris Michael (1944–53 OF) "Babe." Martin told me that "the nickname 'Babe' was given to me by my mother before I went to school because I was the youngest of five children."

2380. Martin, Elwood Good (1917–22 P) "Speed." Martin had a high velocity fastball, but had difficulty in controlling it.

2381. Martin, Harold Wintrop (1906–11 P) "Doc." Martin was a practicing dentist.

2382. Martin, Johnny Leonard Roosevelt (1928–44 OF) "Pepper." Martin was a member and leader of the St. Louis Cardinals' famous "Gas

House Gang" of the middle and late 1930s. Blake Harper, president of the Cardinals' Fort Smith, Arkansas, fan club, called Martin "Pepper" in 1925 because of his aggressiveness gung–Ho play. Martin did not like the nickname and most players called him John or Johnny. But Branch Rickey, Cardinal general manager, in an attempt to make the Cardinals look colorful informed the press that Martin ought to be called "Pepper." It was Rickey who continually told scout Charlie Barrett's tale of driving in Oklahoma at 60 miles per hour and looking up to spy a jackrabbit run by the car with Martin in fast pursuit. "Anyone who can run that fast can play baseball." On February 20, 1934, an article in the *St. Louis Star-Times* called Martin the "Pepper Box Kid." Both Rickey and the press liked to refer to Martin as "The Wild Horse of the Osage." This led to the rumor that Martin was of Indian blood. It was not true. The nickname comes from Martin's involvement with professional football. In 1924 he played for the Homing Indians and Oklahoma pro team. It was sponsored by the Osage Indians. As a hard running halfback, he was noted for his galloping gait. Sportswriters said he ran like a stallion on the prairie. With a little imagination this description led to "The Wild Horse of the Osage" moniker. It must be pointed out, however, that Harold Seymore in his book, *The People's Game,* lists Martin as an Indian player. I have found no other source that verifies this.

2383. Martin, Joseph Clifton (1959–72 C) "J.C.." Family members began calling Martin by the initials of his first and middle name.

2384. Martin, Joseph Samuel (1903 OF) "Silent Joe." Martin did not speak often to other players on or off the field.

2385. Martin, William Joseph (1936–38 3B) "Smoky Joe." Tom Shea reports that Martin was nicknamed after a famous Manhattan fire fighter of the same name.

2386. Martina, John Joseph (1924 P) "Oyster Joe." Martina was from New Orleans, Louisiana, a city where oysters are popular. According to Jack Connelly, Martina was once traded for two barrels of oysters.

2387. Martinez, Carmelo Salgado (1983– OF) "Bitu." Martinez told me, "'Bitu' is short for Bitumu which in Spanish means 'tar.' At about age three I was living in a small town in Puerto Rico. Tar was being put on dusty streets. I asked my mother, 'What is that?' She said, 'Bitumul.' I repeated the word after her. Neighbors thought that was funny and when ever they saw me they would say, 'Bitumul,' and I would repeat it. It became my nickname. When I started playing pro ball, I was called 'Bitu' for short."

2388. Martinez, Felix Anthony (1974–86 P) "Tippy." The nickname of "Tippy" was given to him by an aunt when he was a youngster. It has no special meaning.

2389. Martinez, John Albert (1969–86 C) "Buck." In Martinez's case "Buck" has a specific origin. He told me, "My father being an avid hunter called me 'Buckshot' at birth. My mother wanted to call me 'Buckey.' The compromise was 'Buck'."

2390. Martinez, Rogelio Velos (1950 P) "Limonar." This is a place nickname. Martinez grew up in the town of Limonar in the province of Matanzas, Cuba.

2391. Martini, Guido Joe (1935 P) "Wedo." "Wedo" is a takeoff on the first name of Guido. Martini was also called "Southern" He was born and raised in Birmingham, Alabama.

2392. Massa, Gordon Edward (1957–58 C) "Moose." Massa was 6'3" and 210 pounds.

2393. Massey, Roy Hardee (1918 OF) "Red." The nickname refers to hair color.

2394. Massey, William Henry (1894 1B) "Big Bill." At 5'11" and 168 pounds Massey was probably not big enough to warrant the "Big" nickname, nor small enough for it to be a nickname opposite. The origin is unknown.

2395. Masterson, Paul Nickalas (1940–42 P) "Lefty." Masterson pitched left handed and batted left handed.

2396. Masterson, Walter Edward (1939–56 P) "Bullfrog." Masterson wore tinted glasses because the white gravel around the edge of Comiskey Park in Chicago bothered him when he pitched there. The glare made it difficult for him to see. When he wore the glasses, players called him "Frog" and "Bullfrog."

2397. Mathewson, Christopher (1900–16 P) "Big Six." The brilliant turn of the century pitcher for the New York Giants was so admired and respected that he became a folk hero in his time. He won 374 games in just 17 years. In 1905 he posted a 31-8 won-lost record and an incredible ERA of 1.27. He also won three World Series games that year, all shutouts. The "Big Six" nickname has three possible origins. The first had to do with Mathewson's height. He was 6'1½" and that was considered tall in 1900. Frank Graham reports that when he first came up as a rookie with the New York Giants, a player said, "There is a good looking kid, how tall is he?" Another replied, "Six feet." The first commented, "The biggest six I ever saw." Sportswriter Sam Crane claimed Mathewson was nicknamed after the largest fire engine in New York City. A third account, which Fred Lieb seems to favor, was that he was nicknamed after an important typographical union in New York which was called "Big Six." Regardless of origin, "Big Six" was a newspaper nickname. His wife, friends, and fans called him "Matty," a term of endearment. Some, including Boyman Bulger, referred to Mathewson as "Old Gum Boots" because of his rambling gait.

2398. Mathias, Carl Lynwood (1980–81 P) "Stubby." Mathias wrote me that he got the nickname "Stubby" his first year in pro ball. "I was 5'10" and stocky."

2399. Mathis, Verdell (1940–49 P, Negro League) "Lefty." Mathis pitched left handed and batted left handed.

2400. Matias, John Roy (1970 OF) "Pineapple." Matias was born in Honolulu, Hawaii.

2401. Matthews, Gary Nathanial (1972–87 OF) "Sarg." Eddie Gold and Art Ahrens indicate that "Sarg" points to Matthews take-charge attitude on the playing field.

2402. Matthews, John Joseph (1922 P) "Lefty." Matthews pitched left handed but was a switch hitter.

2403. Mattick, Walter Joseph (1912–18 OF) "Chick." Origin unknown.

2404. Mattox, Cloy Mitchell (1929 C) "Monk." Origin unknown.

2405. Mauch, Gene William (1944–57 2B) "Skip." Mauch told me, "My dad called me Skipper since I was a small boy. Other people just followed up on it." Ironically the nickname fit perfectly since Mauch managed in the major leagues for over a quarter-century after retiring as a player. Baseball managers are often called skippers.

2406. Maul, Albert Joseph (1884–1901 P) "Smiling Al." Origin unknown.

2407. Mauldin, Marshall Reese (1934 3B) "Mark." Mauldin told me he received the nickname of "Mark" from his mother in childhood but does not remember if it has any special meaning.

2408. Mauriello, Ralph (1958 P) "Tami." He was nicknamed after Tami Mauriello a heavyweight boxer who lost a championship fight to Joe Louis in 1946.

2409. May, Frank Spruiell (1917–32 P) "Jakie." A clip in the August 1927 *Baseball Magazine* states, "His proud parents christened him Frank, hence the name Jake which was wished on him early in life, no one seems to know why or when."

2410. May, Merrill Glend (1939–43 3B) "Pinky." Bill James reports, "Merrill May was called Pinkie, according to his son, because 'he had the red ass'." Other accounts, however, state that May was hot tempered and was accorded the nickname of "Pinky" because he was always angry. Merrill entered military service in mid-career in 1943 and never returned to the game.

2411. May, Rudolph (1965–83 P) "Dude." The nickname referred to May's sometimes less-than-stylish dress. Dick Lally reports, "He was particularly fond of a nasty emerald hued suit which when draped on his long, lean form, tended to remind his teammates [Yankees, 1975] of a giant green grasshopper."

2412. May, William Herbert (1924 P) "Buckshot." May was a wild throwing left hander who pitched only two innings in the major leagues.

2413. Mayberry, John Claiborn (1968–82 1B) "Big John." Mayberry was 6'3" and weighed 220 pounds. As John Garritz put it, "The fans dubbed him 'Big John' and no one had to ask why."

2414. Mayes, Adair Bushyhead (1911 OF) "Paddy." Origin unknown.

2415. Maynard, James Walter (1940–46 OF) "Buster." Maynard was a home run hitter in his pre-major league days. They said he "busted the ball."

2416. Mays, Carl William (1915–29 P) "Sub." Mays was an underhand submarine pitcher, and a successful one. In 1921 he led the American League in wins with 27 while losing only nine, for a league leading percentage of .750. In 15 years he won 208 games. Mays is best remembered for his involvement in baseball's only beanball fatality. On August 16, 1920, at the Polo Grounds in the first half of the fifth inning Mays, pitching for New York, hit Cleveland's Ray Chapman in the head with his third pitch. Joseph Overfield describes the event. "There was an ominous crack that was heard all over the Polo Grounds. Mays, thinking his pitch had hit Chapman's bat, fielded the ball and started to throw to Wally Pip at first base, but then he saw Chapman slumped in the arms of catcher Muddy Ruel and he knew the batter had been hit. A doctor was summoned from the stands and Chapman was temporarily revived. Assisted by two of his teammates, he began the long walk to the clubhouse in centerfield, but he soon collapsed and was carried the rest of the way. When a preliminary examination in the clubhouse showed the injury was extremely serious, he was taken to nearby St. Lawrence Hospital, where an operation was performed. He was still under ether when he died at five A.M. the following day, August 17." Although Mays received strong criticism for his admittedly "tight" pitch he was cleared of any criminal charges and continued to pitch in the major leagues for the remainder of the decade. However, as Overfield points out, "In the *New York Times* of August 19, there was an impassioned plea for the development and use of batting helmets, but it was to be more than thirty years before this advice would be heeded."

2417. Mays, Willie Howard (1951–73 OF) "Say Hey." When Mays joined the New York Giants in 1951 he was overwhelmed and bewildered by media attention, new experiences and new faces. Mays developed the habit of saying, almost as a defensive mechanism, "Say Who," "Say What," and "Say Hey." New York sportswriter, Barney Kremenko, began calling Mays "The Say Hey Kid." Giants' sportscaster, Russ Hodges, promoted the nickname of his broadcasts. In 1954, The Treniers recorded a song with Willie Mays, "Say Hey (The Willie Mays Song)" which for a baseball tune gained a large measure of popularity. Johnny Long, Ricky Segall, and the Wanderers also recorded "Say Hey" songs in the same year—sans Mays. "Junior" was Mays' family nickname, and friends often called him "Buck." Mays ended his career with 660 home runs plus a career batting average of .302. He was one of the best known players of all time.

2418. Maxwell, Charles Richard (1950–64 OF) "Smokey." "Smokey" refers to Maxwell's dark complexion.

2419. Mazerowski, William Stanley (1956–72 2B) "Tree Stump." Jim Kaplan argues in his book, *Playing the Field,* that Mazerowski was probably the best fielding second baseman of all time. His nickname is related to his fielding ability. Kaplan writes, "Teammates referred to Mazerowski as 'Tree Stump' because he often kept his vulnerable left foot stationary on double plays. When a runner slid into him, they had to bring out a stretcher—for the runner." Despite his fielding prowess, "Mazz," as he was addressed, may be best remembered for his series winning home run in the ninth inning of the seventh game of the 1960 World Series as Pittsburgh defeated New York 4 games to 3.

2420. Mazzera, Melvin Leonard (1935–40 OF) "Mike." Mazzera told me that "Mike" was a newspaper and radio nickname. He does not know who was responsible for it or what it might have meant. He says he certainly never used it. He calls himself Mel.

2421. Meadows, Henry Lee (1915–29 P) "Specs." Meadows was the first pitcher to wear glasses. As such, in 1915 he was treated, as one writer put it, "as the act between the fat lady and the sword swallower." Nevertheless, he won 188 games in his 15-year career and played in two World Series.

2422. Meadows, Michael Ray (1986 OF) "Louie." Origin unknown.

2423. Medich, George Francis (1972–82 P) "Doc." Medich received the nickname when he played for the Yankee farm team in the New York–Penn League in Oneonta, New York. He was working his way through medical school.

2424. Medwick, Joseph Michael (1932–48 OF) "Ducky." Medwick claimed that when he played for Houston in the Texas League a girl noticed him swimming and remarked, "He swims just like a duck." Branch Rickey spread the story that a girl in the stands at Houston said he walked like a duck. Fred Lieb provides a third account. "The nickname had its beginning in one of Joe's sensational seasons as a Cardinal farm hand in Houston. A girl clapped her hands at a great Medwick play and squealed enthusiastically, 'Isn't he a ducky, wucky of a player?' It got up to the press box, and the boys started calling him 'Ducky Medwick.' The nickname followed him to St. Louis and throughout the big leagues." Medwick detested the nickname and preferred "Mickey." Players often called him "Muscles" because of his great strength.

2425. Mee, Thomas William (1910 SS) "Judge." In the off season he worked as a county clerk, bailiff and finally a county judge in Cook County, Chicago, Illinois.

2426. Meegan, Peter J. (1884–85 P) "Steady Pete." Origin unknown.

2427. Meek, Frank J. (1889–90 C) "Dad." Origin unknown.

2428. Meeker, Charles Roy (1923–26 P) "Lefty." Meeker pitched left handed and batted left handed.

2429. Meers, Russell Harlan (1941–47 P) "Babe." Meers wrote me that he was called "Babe" at birth. His mother was 40 when he was born and already had five children. "I was her baby." He stated that his family and childhood friends use this nickname. In baseball he always went by Russ.

2430. Meier, Arthur Ernst (1906 OF) "Dutch." Meier was of German background.

2431. Meine, Henry William (1922–34 P) "The Count of Luxemburg." Meine had a German background and was addressed as "Heinie." He made his home in Luxemburg, Missouri. "Count" referred to his royal pitching. In 1931 he led National League pitchers in victories with 19.

2432. Meister, Karl Daniel (1913 OF) "Dutch." The nickname denotes Meister's German background.

2433. Meixell, Merton Merrill (1972 PH) "Moxie." Origin unknown.

2434. Mele, Albert Ernest (1957 OF) "Dutch." The nickname denotes Mele's Dutch background.

2435. Mele, Sabath Anthony (1947–56 OF) "Sam." The nickname comes from the first letter of each of Mele's three names and is reinforced by the first name of Sabeth.

2436. Melillo, Oscar Donald (1926–37 2B) "Spinach." In 1927 Melillo contracted Bright's kidney disease. He was placed on a strict diet consisting primarily of spinach for several months. He was also called "Ski" because he admired a Polish football player in Chicago.

2437. Melton, Clifford George (1937–44 P) "Mountain Music." In 1937, pitching for the New York Giants, Melton was the first rookie to win 20 games. He grew up in the Black Mountains of North Carolina, played the guitar and sang country ballads. Melton had a pair of floppy, jug-handled ears. This led to the nicknames of "Rabbit Ears" and "Mickey Mouse." He was 6'5½" and sometimes referred to as "The Towering Cliff of Black Mountain."

2438. Mendez, José de la Caridad Menchez (1908–26 P, Negro League) "El Diamante Negro." Cuban born Mendez was known as "The Black Diamond." At about 5'5", 155 pounds, Mendez possessed a hopping fastball that looked like a pea coming up to the plate, and a curveball that looked as if it was falling off a pool table. In playing against white teams, Menchez gained the reputation of the "Mathewson in Black."

2439. Mendoza, Christobal Rigoberto Carre (1970 2B) "Minnie." Mendoza was Cuban. He was nicknamed after another Cuban ballplayer of the 1950s and '60s whose name resembled his—Orestes "Minnie" Minoso.

2440. Menefee, John (1892–1903 P) "Jock." "Jock" was used as an alternative to John much as Jack is. Menefee was one of the first pitchers to rely on a curveball.

2441. Menoski, Michael William (1914–23 OF) "Leaping Mike." Menoski was noted for his leaping catches in the outfield. He played his first two years in the Federal League and then made a career in the American League.

2442. Mensor, Edward (1912–14 OF) "Midget." Canadian born Mensor, was 5'6" and weighed 150 pounds.

2443. Mercer, George Barclay (1894–1902 P) "Win." Mercer, a short 5'7", but very handsome man, was a versatile performer who played every position except catcher, batting .285 while winning 131 games as a pitcher in nine seasons. There is no indication in the literature that the nickname of "Win" came from his playing career. Joe Oberfield mentions that "he had a weakness for fast women and slow horses, a deadly combination that apparently was to do him in." Heavy in debt with gambling losses, Mercer committed suicide by asphyxiation in the Oriental Hotel, San Francisco, January 12, 1903. While the origin of "Win" is unknown, it may have had something to do with his gambling.

2444. Merena, John Joseph (1934 P) "Spike." Origin unknown.

2445. Merrill, Carl (1990– Manager) "Stump." Merrill never was in the major leagues before he became manager of the New York Yankees. The nickname stems from the coach of the University of Maine, Jack Butterfield, when Merrill was in college. In Merrill's words, "One day I was walking away and I was between two pitchers, both about 6'5". Jack was trying to get my attention. He hollered at me two or three times and I didn't hear him and then he said, 'Hey, you stumpy little devil, turn around'." After that Merrill was known as "Stump."

2446. Merriman, Lloyd Archer (1949–55 OF) "Citation." Merriman was nicknamed "Citation" by sportswriter Bill Bingham of Mobile, Alabama, for the way his hits sped off his bat. The reference is to the race horse, Citation, who was ridden to the triple crown (Kentucky Derby, Preakness, Belmont Stakes) by Eddie Arcaro in 1948.

2447. Merrit, John Howard (1913 OF) "Lefty." Merrit threw left handed but batted right handed. He is one of the few players, with the exception of pitchers to be called "Lefty" when he batted right handed.

2448. Mertes, Samuel Blair (1896–1906 OF) "Sandow." Mertes was very muscular and noted for his strength. He was nicknamed after a famous circus strongman named Sandow who was managed by Flo Ziegfeld.

2449. Messenger, Charles Walter (1909–14 OF) "Bobby." Origin unknown.

2450. Messenger, John Alexander (1924 P) "Bud." For Messenger, "Bud" was a childhood family nickname.

2451. Metha, Frank Joseph (1940 2B) "Scat." "Scat" refers to speed. In 1939 Metha stole 66 bases for Fort Worth in the Texas League.

2452. Metheny, Arthur Beauregard (1943–46 OF) "Bud." Metheny wrote me, "My nickname is very uninteresting. When I was a kid my friends called me their buddy. When I started to play American Legion ball, it was shortened to Bud." Metheny was a college football star before he played major league baseball.

2453. Metkovitch, George Michael (1943–54 OF) "Catfish." According to William Mead, in 1940 Metkovitch caught a three-foot catfish off a bridge. While trying to remove the hook with his foot on the fish's back a sharp fin cut through the crepe sole of his shoe and into his foot. The fin had to be removed by surgery.

2454. Metzger, Clarence Edward (1974–78 P) "Butch." Metzger wrote me, "When I was an infant my older sister Elizabeth, 5 years old, could not pronounce Clarence. She started calling me 'Butch' after the TV character in 'The Little Rascals' show. She thought I was a tough guy. Metzger began his career with 12 straight wins in relief, which is the all-time record. But, this turned out to be two-thirds of his career wins. Cut short by arm trouble he won only 18 games in his career while dropping 9, all in relief.

2455. Meusel, Emil Frederick (1914–27 OF) "Irish." For whatever reason a sportswriter thought Meusel was Irish and nicknamed him that. Emil was the older brother of Bob Meusel. His career average of 11 seasons was .310, Bob's career average for 11 seasons was .309.

2456. Meusel, Robert William (1920–30 OF) "Long Bob." Meusel was 6'3½" and weighed 190 pounds. He was also called "Languid Bob" because he was uncommunicative and tended to play the way he felt that day. Meusel was a member of six Yankee teams which won the A.L. flag, but manager Miller Huggins complained that his attitude was one of just plain indifference. Meusel liked to pal around with "Babe" Ruth, and it was said he did anything the "Babe" wanted him to do.

2457. Meyer, Bernard (1913–25 OF) "Earache." Opponents said that Meyer gave everyone an earache by his constant shouting while a coach with the Phils and Tigers.

2458. Meyer, Lambert Dalton (1937–46 2B) "Dutch." Meyer wrote me, "I was nicknamed after my uncle, the original Dutch Meyers, who was at Texas Christian University as player, coach, and athletic director for 43 years. In June, 1937, when I left T.C.U. several of the Chicago Cub players knew my uncle and started calling me 'Little Dutch.' Later it was shortened to just 'Dutch'." His uncle Leo Robert Meyer was of German background and is a member of the HAF and WFF College Football Hall of Fames.

2459. Meyer, Russell Charles (1946–59 P) "The Mad Monk." When Meyer played football in high school he was nicknamed "Monk" after a great army football player called Monk Meyer who was playing in college at about the same time. Although a likeable fellow off the field, when playing baseball Meyer had a legendary temper which led to the "Mad" moniker. On one occasion when he was removed from a game, he flung the resin bag high in the air, took a few steps and it descended on his head. Another time he injured his foot when he kicked the pitching rubber in anger. He once broke his toe kicking a steel locker in the clubhouse. He was also suspended for ten days for grabbing and holding umpire Frank Dascoli so hard while protesting a safe call on a Jackie Robinson steal of home plate that the buttons popped off of the umpire's jacket.

2460. Meyerle, Levi Samuel (1876–84 3B) "Long Levi." Meyerle was a shade over 6'0" tall which made him one of the taller players of his era.

2461. Meyers, John Tortes (1909–17 C) "Chief." Meyers caught for nine years in the major leagues and batted .291, and played in four World Series, batting .290. Similar to almost all players of American Indian background he was nicknamed "Chief."

2462. Michael, Gene Richard (1966–75 SS) "Stick." Michael was 6'2" and stood very straight. "Stick" comes from his basketball playing days at Kent State University when he weighed less than the 180 pounds he carried while playing baseball.

2463. Middleton, James Blaine (1917–21 P) "Rifle Jim." The nickname refers to the strength of Middleton's pitching arm.

2464. Middleton, John Wayne (1922 P) "Lefty." Middleton pitched left handed and batted left handed.

2465. Midkiff, Ezra Millington (1909–13 3B) "Salt Rock." This is a place nickname. Midkiff was born in Salt Rock, West Virginia.

2466. Mierkowicz, Edward Frank (1945–50 OF) "Autch." Mierkowicz wrote me that as a child he was at a barbeque and he got cold and started sneezing and someone called him A-choo. Later in print in became "Autch" but pronounced like A-choo. However, somewhere along the line researchers must have thought "Autch" was a misprint. For example, in the Macmillan *Baseball Encyclopedia* the A is replaced with a B creating the nickname "Butch."

2467. Miggins, Lawrence Edward (1948–52 OF) "Irish." Miggins was of Irish background. Both his parents were born in Ireland.

2468. Miklos, John Joseph (1944 P) "Hank." Miklos told me, "Johann is German for John. At the age of 14 or 15 my brother started calling me Hans for short. Some people thought my real name was Henry and started using Hank which is short for Henry."

2469. Milan, Jessie Clyde (1907–22 OF) "Deerfoot." Clyde, as he was addressed, was fast on the base paths. In 1912 he led the American League with 88 stolen bases. His career total for stolen bases was 495. Yet Joseph McBride reports, "Chief Bender sarcastically nicknamed Milan 'Deerfoot' because of his lack of speed on the bases."

2470. Miles, Wilson Daniel (1935–43 OF) "Dee." Miles was called Daniel and this was shortened to his initial "D." However, in print it came out "Dee."

2471. Miljus, John Kenneth (1915–29 P) "Big Serb." Miljus, who had a great, but hard-to-control fastball, was 6'1" and one of the few major leagues of Serbian background.

2472. Millan, Felix Bernardo (1966–77 2B) "The Cat." "The Cat" is a response to the name of Felix. The nickname comes from the cartoon character "Felix the Cat."

2473. Miller, Charles Bradley (1889–99 OF) "Dusty." Miller had the habit of raising as much dust as possible when sliding into a base. He hoped the umpire's vision would be impaired and thus the decision would be in his favor.

2474. Miller, Edmund John (1921–36 OF) "Bing." Miller was given the nickname of "Bing" by his brother as a child. It comes from the comic strip character in "Uncle George Washington Bing, the Village Story Teller" that appeared in the Vinton, Iowa, newspaper, *Eagle*.

2475. Miller, Edward Robert (1936–50 SS) "Eppie." Miller was one of the best fielding shortstops of his time despite a .238 batting average for 14 seasons. "Eppie," as a nickname, simply substitutes p's for d's in the short name for Eddie.

2476. Miller, Frank A. (1892–97 2B) "Kohly." Origin unknown.

2477. Miller, Frank Lee (1913–23 P) "Bullet." Miller was a fastball pitcher.

2478. Miller, Frederick Holman (1910 P) "Speedy." "Speedy" refers to the speed of Miller's pitches.

2479. Miller, George Frederick (1884–96 C) "Foghorn." Miller had a loud voice and liked to tell stories. He was also called "Calliope" and was addressed as "Doogie."

2480. Miller, Hugh Stanley (1911–15 1B) "Cotton." The nickname refers to light blond hair color.

2481. Miller, James Eldridge (1944–45 C) "Hack." Miller was strong and well built, 5'11½" and 215 pounds. He was nicknamed after Lawrence "Hack" Miller an outfielder who played 1916–25 and was considered to be one of the strongest men ever to play the game.

2482. Miller, James McCurdy (1901 2B) "Rabbit." "Rabbit" refers to Miller's speed.

2483. Miller, John Anthony (1943–47 P) "Ox." Miller wrote me, "In 1939 I was playing for the team in Lincoln, Nebraska. I pitched two doubleheaders and won all four games. A sportswriter in the morning newspaper said I was strong as an ox. A writer on the evening paper said I was dumb as an ox for pitching so much."

2484. Miller, John Barney (1909–21 1B) "Dots." According to Bill Deane, Cooperstown Baseball Hall of Fame researcher, as a rookie for Pittsburgh in 1909, Miller was working out before a game in Honus Wagner's place at shortstop while Wagner watched from the dugout. A scribe asked Wagner, "Who's that at shortstop?" Wagner, with his German accent replied "Das Miller." When it came out in print in the newspaper "Das" (that is) had been interpreted as "Dots."

2485. Miller, Joseph H. (1884–86 P) "Cyclone." "Cyclone" refers to the speed of Miller's pitches.

2486. Miller, Kenneth Albert (1944 P) "Whitey." The nickname refers to hair color.

2487. Miller, Lawrence H. (1916–25 OF) "Hack." According to Eddie Gold and Art Ahrens, Miller was possibly the strongest player in major league history. He carried 195 pounds on a 5'9" frame. He was nicknamed after the legendary Wrestler Hackenschmidt. Miller's father had been a circus strongman and he must have inherited some of his father's strength. At age 18 he was an apprentice steamfitter. He could lift and carry 250-pound radiators on his back for two blocks and then bring them up several flights of stairs to be installed. During spring training with the Chicago Cubs, he entertained by uprooting trees on Catalina Island. He could bend iron bars with his hands and lift automobiles up by their bumpers. He once pounded a spike through an auto gate at Wrigley Field with his fist, protected only by a rolled up baseball cap. Gold and Ahrens report that this fact has been photographically preserved.

2488. Miller, Leo Alphonso (1923 P) "Red." The nickname refers to hair color.

2489. Miller, Lowell Otto (1910–22 C) "Moonie." According to Frank Graham, when Miller joined the Brooklyn Dodgers in 1910 "the other players took one look at his round face, round blue eyes and promptly dubbed him 'Moonie'."

2490. Miller, Ralph Henry (1921 P) "Lefty." Miller pitched left handed but batted right handed.

2491. Miller, Roscoe Clyde (1901–04 P) "Rubberlegs." Tom Shea attributes the nickname of "Rubberlegs" to the fact that Miller was bounded around between Detroit, New York, and Pittsburgh in a short period of time. Miller was usually addressed as "Roxy," a takeoff on his first name.

2492. Miller, Roy Oscar (1910–14 OF) "Doc." Miller was a practicing physician.

2493. Miller, Ward Taylor (1909–17 OF) "Windy." Miller had the reputation of being outspoken in his behavior.

2494. Miller, Warren Lemual (1909–11 OF) "Gitz." Origin unknown.

2495. Miller, William Paul (1952–55 P) "Hooks." Miller's best pitch was his curveball, which is sometimes called a hook.

2496. Milligan, John (1884–93 C) "Jocko." The evidence is slim, but it would seem for Milligan, the nickname of "Jocko" is no more than an alternative or takeoff on the first name of John having no special meaning.

2497. Milliken, Robert Fogle (1953–54 P) "Bobo." In Milliken's case, "Bobo" is an extension of his short name Bob.

2498. Mills, Abbott Page (1911 3B) "Jack." Origin unknown.

2499. Mills, Abraham G. (1882–85 NL President) "Bismarck of Baseball." As National League president in 1883, he negotiated the first National Agreement, a peace pact with the American Association, then a major league, and the Northwestern League, a powerful minor league. It established an 11-player reserve list, guaranteed territorial rights, set minimum salaries at $1,000 and created a post-season series between the National League and American Association champions. "Bismarck" refers to the great German statesman of the period Otto von Bismarck, whose diplomatic efforts helped keep Europe at peace in the 1880s.

2500. Mills, Howard Robinson (1934–40 P) "Lefty." Mills pitched left handed and batted left handed.

2501. Mills, William Grant (1901 P) "Wee Willie." Mills was 5'7" and weighed 150 pounds.

2502. Milnar, Albert Joseph (1936–46 P) "Happy." Milnar told me that "it was common in my day for players to be nicknamed for comic strip characters. While I was playing sandlot ball other players called me 'Happy' because I loved the game and was always smiling and laughing. It was from the comic 'Happy Hooligan'."

2503. Milne, William James (1948–50 OF) "Pete." "Pete" as a nickname came from childhood playmates but it had no particular meaning.

2504. Milner, Edward James (1980–88 OF) "Greyhound." "Greyhound" refers to Milner's speed in the outfield and on the base paths.

2505. Milner, John David (1971–82 1B) "Hammer." Milner was nicknamed after his boyhood idol "Hammerin'" Hank Aaron.

2506. Milosevich, Michael (1944–45 SS) "Mollie." Milosevich was nicknamed by Benny Bengough when he played for Washington, Pennyslvania in the Penn State League. The nickname carries no feminine connotations. It is a takeoff on the last name.

2507. Milstead, George Earl (1924–26 P) "Cowboy." Milstead's home was in Texas cattle country.

2508. Minarcin, Rudy Anthony (1955–57 P) "Potato Head." Minarcin wrote me that "Buster" (used in the Macmillan *Baseball Encyclopedia* was not his nickname. "My real nickname was 'Potato Head.' When I was about 9 years old, my father gave me a haircut. When I went to the playground, the kids thought I looked like a potato head. An older boy, Steve Kardos gave me the name."

2509. Miner, Ramon Theodore (1921 P) "Lefty." Miner pitched left handed but batted right handed.

2510. Minhan, Edmund Joseph (1907 P) "Cotton." The nickname denotes light blond hair color.

2511. Minner, Paul Edison (1946–56 P) "Lefty." Minner pitched left handed and batted left handed.

2512. Minoso, Saturino Orestes Arrieta Armas (1949–80 OF) "Minnie." "Minnie" is simply a takeoff on the last name of Minoso and was used almost exclusively to refer to this player. Minoso was a very popular player during the years he played with the Chicago White Sox. He retired after the 1964 season. But he returned to play in three games in 1976, and then again in two games in 1980. This means that Minoso is the only player to perform in five decades. It was rumored in 1989, that Minoso might be given the opportunity to appear in a game in the 1990s so that he could become a six-decade player. If so, he would be at least 67 years old when he came to bat.

2513. Minton, Gregory Brian (1975– P) "Moonman." In Minton's own words, "It happened one day during the eight long, long years I spent as a starting pitcher in the San Francisco Giants minor league system. I'd spent the day tubing down a river just outside Phoenix, Arizona. Tubing means you lay on your stomach on an old inflatable inner tube and drift peacefully down the river. Well, it so happened that I forgot one thing—my clothes. And certain parts of my body got very badly sunburned. The burn was so bad, in fact, that I got ugly water blisters on that part of my body that goes over the bullpen fence last. Big blisters, craters. So that night when I walked into the clubhouse and started putting on my uniform, manager Rocky Bridges took one look at me and said my body had more craters than the moon. I became 'Moonman' or 'Moonie'."

2514. Miranda, Guillermo Perez (1951–59 SS) "Willie." Guillermo is synonymous with William. Miranda's older brother started calling him Willie when he was a child.

2515. Mitterling, Ralph (1916 OF) "Sarg." Mitterling held the rank of Sergeant when he was in the army.

2516. Mize, John Robert (1936–53 1B) "The Big Cat." Mize was a slugger who led the National League in home runs three times, slugging average three times and batting average once. He was often called "Big Jawn." It is sometimes forgotten that he was a quick and nimble fielder at first base. Although he did not have exceptional range, he was almost flawless with balls hits to him. This reputation earned him the nickname of "The Big Cat."

2517. Mizell, Wilmer David (1952–62 P) "Vinegar Bend." This is a place nickname. Mizell was raised in the small hamlet of Vinegar Bend, Alabama. After his baseball career, Mizell served as a congressman from the state of Alabama.

2518. Mizeur, Wilbur Francis (1923–24 PH) "Bad Bill." Origin unknown.

2519. Moeller, Joseph Douglas (1962–71 P) "Skeeter." In Moeller's case "Skeeter" does not refer to small body size, since he was 6'5" and weighed 195 pounds. The nickname was given to him by Roy Smalley when his eye swelled shut as a result of a mosquito bite and infection.

2520. Moeller, Ronald Ralph (1956–63 P) "The Kid." Moeller joined the Baltimore Orioles before his 18th birthday.

2521. Mohler, Ernest Follette (1894 2B) "Kid." "Kid" refers to Mohler's size. He was 5'4½" and 145 pounds.

2522. Mohorcic, Dale Robert (1986– P) "Horse." As a 30-year-old rookie in 1986 for the Texas Rangers, he appeared in 12 consecutive games in relief.

2523. Mole, Fenton LeRoy (1949 1B) "Muscles." Mole was 6'1" and weighed 200 pounds. He told me that a sportswriter gave him the nickname because of his home run power while he was playing for the Portland Beavers in the Pacific Coast League.

2524. Molinaro, Robert Joseph (1975–83 OF) "Molly." "Molly" carries no feminine connotations. It is a takeoff on the last name.

2525. Mollwitz, Frederick August (1913–19 1B) "Fritz." The nickname denotes Mollwitz's German background. Fans called him "Zip" but the origin is unknown.

2526. Monahan, Edward Francis (1953 P) "Rinty." Monahan explained to me that he was nicknamed after "Rinty" Monahan a flyweight boxing champion in Ireland in the 1940s who once won 25 bouts in a row. After each win he would serenade the crowd from the center of the ring. Monahan received the nickname from his manager Dave Garcia when he played for Oshkosh in 1949.

2527. Monez, Donald Wayne (1968–83 3B) "Brooks." During his minor league career, teammates said he played third base like Brooks Robinson.

2528. Monge, Isidro Pedroza (1975–84 P) "Sid." Origin unknown.

2529. Monroe, Edward Oliver (1917–18 P) "Peck." Origin unknown.

2530. Montanez, Guillermo Naranjo (1966–82 1B) "Willie." Guillermo is synonymous with William. Thus "Willie" is short for William. In 1970 Montanez was the player the St. Louis Cardinals turned over to Philadelphia when they traded Curt Flood and he failed to report and challenged the reserve clause.

2531. Montefusco, John Joseph (1974–86 P) "The Count." He received his nickname while playing for Amarillo in the Texas League. His last name reminds one of the character in the novel by Alexander Dumas, *The Count of Monte Cristo*. An El Paso, Texas, sportswriter called him "Count Monte."

2532. Montjay, William R. (1883–85 P) "Medicine Bill." Origin unknown.

2533. Moolic, George Henry (1886 C) "Prunes." Origin unknown.

2534. Moore, Alvin Earl (1976–80 3B) "Junior." Origin unknown.

2535. Moore, D.C. (1936–46 C) "Dee." Moore had no other names, just initials. "D" came out "Dee" in print.

2536. Moore, Earl Alonzo (1901–14 P) "Crossfire." Moore had a classic side-arm crossfire delivery. In 1910 he won 20 games for the Philadelphia Phils. In 1912 his arm was broken by a batted ball. His pitching was never quite as effective when he recovered.

2537. Moore, Euel Walton (1934–36 P) "Chief." Moore was of American Indian background. Most players of this ancestry through the 1950s received the nickname of "Chief."

2538. Moore, Eugene, Jr. (1931–45 OF) "Rowdy." This is a nickname opposite. Moore was a strong silent type. An unauthored article in the *Brooklyn Eagle*, July 8, 1939, stated, "The tradition is that Moore says 'hello' when he reports for spring training, 'goodbye' when he leaves for home in October, and nothing much in between."

2539. Moore, Eugene, Sr. (1909–13 P) "Blue Goose." Origin unknown.

2540. Moore, Joe Gregg (1930–41 OF) "The Gause Ghost." This is a place nickname. "Jo Jo," as he was addressed, was from Gause, Texas. The origin of the "Ghost" reference is, however, unknown.

2541. Moore, Lloyd Albert (1936–42 P) "Whitey." The nickname refers to hair color.

2542. Moore, Raymond LeRoy (1952–63 P) "Farmer." Moore was nicknamed "Farmer" by teammates at Fort Worth in the Texas League because he was born and raised on a Maryland tobacco farm.

2543. Moore, Walter (1921–26 SS, Negro League) "The Black Cat." Moore was usually called "Dobie." If this is a nickname, I have not been able to discover its origin. Moore seems to have been called "The Black Cat" by white players in a tribute to his quickness at shortstop. Similar to many of the players in the Negro leagues, Moore was illiterate. A strong hitter, he compiled a career average in the Negro leagues of .360, with a high of .470 in 1924.

2544. Moore, William Allen (1917 3B) "Scrappy." In the minor leagues Moore gained the reputation of being a tough and hustling ballplayer.

2545. Moore, William Austin (1929–34 P) "Cy." Moore was one of many players of this era who came from small towns and were not wise to city life and were given the nickname of "Cy" after Denton "Cy" Young. The nickname was reinforced during his minor league career when he once pitched 60 straight scoreless innings, shades of Cy Young.

2546. Moore, William Wiley (1927–33 P) "Cy." Moore was born in the small town of Bonita, Texas, and received the nickname of "Cy" early in his professional career. He reminded people of Denton "Cy" Young. In his first year with the New York Yankees' championship team of 1927, he became one of the first real relief pitchers. He won 13 games in relief and saved 13 others.

2547. Mootz, J.T. (1936–44 P) "Jake." According to Lee Allen, since Mootz had no first name, somewhere along the line players started to call him "Jake."

2548. Moran, Albert Thomas (1938–39 P) "Hiker." Moran told me that a friend gave him the nickname of "Hiker" when he was a teenage because he liked to take long walks in the Duran Eastman Park in his hometown of Rochester, New York.

2549. Moran, Carl William (1974 P) "Bugs." According to Richard Lindberg, Moran was nicknamed after the famous Chicago gangster "Bugs" Moran. The nickname meant that he was a little strange. Before his first major league game, Carl Moran asked if they played the national anthem or taps!

2550. Moran, Charles Barthell (1903–06 C; NL umpire 1917–39). "Uncle Charlie." Moran had a brief major league career of 25 games in which he batted just .221. However, he became a National League umpire, serving from 1917–39. He was popular and well liked by the players who used "Uncle Charlie" as a term of affection. Moran was also a famous football coach for small Centre College. In 1920 his "Praying Colonels" upset Harvard. In 1951 the Associated Press voted this game the biggest football upset of the first half of the twentieth century. Previously, Harvard had been undefeated in 25 games over two and a half seasons including a Rose Bowl win and a National Championship.

2551. Moran, Roy Ellis (1912 OF) "Deedle." Origin unknown.

2552. Moreland, Bobby Keith (1978– OF) "Zonk." "Zonk" is the sound of the ball when Moreland hits it.

2553. Morgan, Chester Collins (1935–38 OF) "Chick." Morgan told me he picked up the nickname in grade school. Kids called him "Chick" because he was small for his size.

2554. Morgan, Harry Richard (1903–12 P) "Cy." Morgan was from the small town of Pomeroy, Ohio, and not very wise to big city ways. Similar to several other players of the same circumstances, he was nicknamed after Denton "Cy" Young.

2555. Morgan, James Edward (1906 3B) "Red." The nickname refers to hair color.

2556. Morgan, Joe Leonard (1963–84 2B) "Little Joe." The nickname was one of affection and admiration for the 5'7" and 150 pounds Hall of Fame second baseman. Not only did he field his position well, he hit 288 career home runs; attracted 1,865 bases on balls, third on the all time list; and stole 689 bases, seventh on the all time list as of 1990.

2557. Morgan, Tom Stephens (1951–63 P) "Plowboy." Morgan was nicknamed by long time New York Yankee radio and TV announcer, Mel Allen. He called him "Plowboy" because he took so long walking to the mound.

2558. Morrill, John Francis (1876–90 1B) "Honest John." An article in the *New York Clipper* of August 13, 1881, praised Morrill as honest, honorable, affable, and courteous. Richardson points out in his article on Morrill in *19th Century Stars* that when he was given credit as manager in 1883 for a 33-11 winning spree which brought Boston to a first place finish, he said, "Good pitching and catching and lucky hitting won for us. When the season started, I thought we would finish fourth or fifth."

2559. Morris, Edward (1884–90 P) "Cannonball." "Cannonball" referred to the speed of Morris' fastball. Cannonball was a term used for trains which were considered the fastest moving things of the time.

2560. Morrison, John Dewey (1920–30 P) "Jughandle Johnny." Morrison had command of a fine curveball. In a sticky situation in 1922, teammate "Cotton" Tierney yelled to him, "Throw him the jughandle."

2561. Morrissey, John Albert (1902–03 2B) "King." Origin unknown.

2562. Morrissey, Joseph Anselm (1932–36 2B) "Jo Jo." "Jo Jo" was a childhood nickname coming from Morrissey's first name of Joseph.

2563. Morrissey, Michael Joseph (1901–02 P) "Deacon." "Deacon" was a nickname given to players who did not drink, smoke, or curse.

2564. Morse, Newell Obediah (1929 2B) "Bud." "Bud" was a childhood family nickname.

2565. Morse, Peter Raymond (1911 SS) "Hap." "Hap" is short for "Happy" and refers to Morse's disposition.

2566. Morton, Guy, Jr. (1954 PH) "Moose." Morton, who batted only once in the major leagues, was 6'2" and weighed 200 pounds.

2567. Morton, Guy, Sr. (1914–24 P) "Alabama Blossom." This is a place nickname. Morton was born and raised in Vernon, Alabama. The origin of blossom, however, is unknown.

2568. Morton, William P. (1884 P) "Sparrow." "Sparrow" refers to Morton's small stature. His exact height and weight, however, are unknown.

2569. Morton, Wycliff Nathaniel (1961–69 OF) "Bubba." Morton told me he was nicknamed "Bubba" by his parent's after a grandfather who had that nickname.

2570. Moryn, Walter Joseph (1954–61 OF) "Moose." Moryn was 6'2", weighed 200 pounds and was barrel-chested. As one Chicago Cub teammate said, "A real Moose."

2571. Moseby, Lloyd Anthony (1980– OF) "Shaker." According to Tony Kubec, Moseby was a star defensive basketball player in high school. His teammates called him "Shaker" because he was hard to shake.

2572. Moses, Wallace (1935–51 OF) "Peepsight." Moses was nicknamed "Peepsight" by teammates because he always squinted his eyes when he got ready to swing at the ball.

2573. Moskiman, William Bankhead (1910 1B) "Doc." Moskiman attended Cooper Medical School, but dropped out. He never was a practicing physician.

2574. Moss, Howard Glenn (1942–46 OF) "Howitzer." Moss was a power hitter in the minor leagues. In 1947 he hit 53 home runs for Baltimore in the International League.

2575. Mossi, Donald Louis (1954–65 P) "The Sphinx." Mossi possessed protruding ears and facial features which reminded people of the Sphinx Pyramid in Egypt.

2576. Mott, Elisha Matthew (1945 SS) "Bitsy." The nickname refers to Mott's light build and diminutive size, 5'8" and 155 pounds.

2577. Moulton, Albert Theodore (1911 2B) "Ollie." Origin unknown.

2578. Mowrey, Harry Harlan (1905–17 3B) "Mike." Origin unknown.

2579. Mueller, Clarence Francis (1920–35 OF) "Heinie." The nickname refers to Mueller's German background.

2580. Mueller, Donald Frederick (1948–59 OF) "Mandrake the Magician." The nickname was given to Mueller by his teammates because of his deft bat control. "He hits singles like radar." He struck out just 146 times in 4,364 official times at bat in 12 seasons. The reference is to the comic strip, "Mandrake the Magician" which first appeared in 1934; movie serial, 1939; radio program, 1940; TV program, 1954.

2581. Mueller, Emmett Jerome (1938–41 2B) "Heinie." The nickname refers to Mueller's German background.

2582. Mueller, Ray Coleman (1935–51 C) "Iron Man." In 1944 Mueller caught in 155 games for the Cincinnati Reds in a 154-game schedule.

2583. Mueller, William Lawrence (1942–45 OF) "Hawk." Mueller was a converted pitcher. He was learning his trade playing centerfield for Jonesboro in the Class D Northeast Arkansas League. He asked manager John Mostil if he could yell "Hawk, Hawk" instead of "I've got it" to warn off another player that he was going to catch the ball. It was agreed he would do this.

Mueller later moved up to Waterloo in the Three-I-League. Their nickname was "Hawks." In a crucial game with several thousand fans watching, Mueller took after a ball in the gap between left and center field screaming "Hawk, Hawk." He made a diving catch and the crowd rose and cheered in unison "Hawk, Hawk." A nickname was born.

2584. Muff, John Robert (1956–57 P) "Red." The nickname refers to hair color.

2585. Mulcahy, Hugh Noyes (1935–47 P) "Losing Pitcher." Mulcahy was a better pitcher than his 45 won, 89 lost career record would indicate, but he pitched primarily for a weak Philadelphia Phils club. He acquired his nickname because his name so often appeared in box scores as the losing pitcher. Frank Bowles says the nickname was more sympathetic than derogatory.

2586. Mullane, Anthony John (1881–94 P) "Count." Mullane was born in Cork, Ireland, and although Irish, he did not drink or smoke. He was handsome, carried himself with dignity, sported a classic handle-bar mustache, and wore elegant attire. He reminded players and fans alike of an Italian count. Women were attracted to him and he was also called "The Apollo of the Box." When he pitched, more women appeared at games. In the late 1880s this led Aaron Stern, owner of the Cincinnati Reds, to pitch Mullane at home on Mondays and admit women with escorts free of charge. Although this was not the first attempt at a ladies day at the ballpark, Mullane's popularity did much to institutionalize this type of game promotion. In fact Mullane was one of the most popular players, not only of his time, but perhaps in the history of the game up until the Ruth era. In addition to his good looks and baseball skills, Mullane was an expert ice skater, roller skater, boxer and all-around musician. At his Zenith he made up to $6,000 a year, a tidy sum in the 1880s. He was the first ambidextrous pitcher in the major leagues and was a switch hitter. He pitched the first no-hitter in the old American Association. Mullane won 285 games in his 13-year career which included winning 30 games or more for five straight years, 1882–87. In addition to pitching he played 228 games in the infield and outfield. His career batting average was .243. I have always found it strange that such a talented, versatile and popular performer as "The Apollo of the Box," has not found a place in the Hall of Fame.

2587. Mulleavy, Gregory Thomas (1930–33 SS) "Moe." "Moe" is a takeoff on the last name of Mulleavy.

2588. Mullen, Ford Parker (1944 2B) "Moon." Mullen was nicknamed after the comic strip character, "Moon Mullins."

2589. Mullin, George Joseph (1902–15 P) "Wabash George." This is a place nickname. Mullin was raised in the small town of Wabash, Indiana.

2590. Munger, George David (1943–56 P) "Red." The nickname refers to hair color.

2591. Munns, Leslie Ernest (1934–36 P) "Little Nemo." Even though Munns was 6'5" and 210 pounds, he was called "Little Nemo" after the comic strip character who had delusions of grandeur.

2592. Munson, Clarence Hanford (1905 C) "Red." The nickname refers to hair color.

2593. Murphy, Con (1884–90 P) "Razzle Dazzle." Origin unknown.

2594. Murphy, Daniel Joseph (1892 C) "Handsome Dan." Murphy was considered to be very good looking, especially by women.

2595. Murphy, David Francis (1905 SS) "Dirty Dan." Origin unknown.

2596. Murphy, Herbert Courtland (1914 SS) "Dummy." According to researcher, Richard Topp, Murphy was deaf and dumb.

2597. Murphy, John Edward (1912–26 OF) "Honest Eddie." Eddie, as he was addressed, was one of the Chicago White Sox of 1919 who was not involved in throwing the World Series despite the fact that he failed to get a hit in two times at bat as a pinch hitter.

2598. Murphy, John Joseph (1932–47 P) "Fireman." Murphy was one of the first great relief pitchers. He posted a career mark of 73 relief wins and 107 saves in 13 years. He pitched in six World Series getting two wins in relief and four saves. He was also called "Fordham Johnny" because he had attended Fordham University. His friend Pat Malone gave him the nickname of "Grandma" because he did so much complaining especially about meals and service.

2599. Murphy, John P. (1902 3B) "Soldier Boy." Origin unknown.

2600. Murphy, Leo Joseph (1915 P) "Red." The nickname refers to hair color. From 1945–49 Murphy managed the Racine Belles of the All American Girls Baseball League.

2601. Murphy, Robert R. (1918–19 OF) "Buzz." Origin unknown.

2602. Murphy, William Henry (1894–97 SS) "Tot." Murphy was just

5'3" and weighed 125 pounds and called "Midget" as well as "Tot." He was also called "Yale" because he attended Yale University.

2603. Murphy, William N. (1884 OF) "Gentle Willie." Murphy was a very mild mannered individual even when he had been drinking, which was often.

2604. Murray, George King (1922–27 P) "Smiles." Murray had a most likeable disposition and usually had a smile on his face, even in dire circumstances.

2605. Murray, James Francis (1922 P) "Big Jim." Murray was 6'2" and weighed 200 pounds.

2606. Murray, John Joseph (1906–17 OF) "Red." The nickname refers to hair color.

2607. Murray, Raymond Lee (1948–54 C) "Deacon." Murray wrote me, "In 1940, I was in the Eastern League and we rode buses everywhere and raised hell a lot. One night the team sang a hymn and I got up and mocked an old preacher inviting everyone to church. Carl Furillo, Bud Caton, and Mike Madagliat started calling me 'Deacon'."

2608. Murray, William Allenrod (1917 2B) "Dasher." "Dasher" refers to Murray's speed on the bases.

2609. Musial, Stanley Frank (1941–63 OF) "Stan the Man." The nickname of the six-time National League batting champion who recorded 3,630 hits, 1,949 RBI's and 475 home runs is one of the most famous in all of baseball. There is only one—"The Man." Musial received the nickname from an incident occurring in Brooklyn at Ebbets Field where he always hit very well. In a series in 1946, he got so many hits against the Dodgers, that when he came to bat one time, fans exclaimed, "Here comes that man again!" Sportswriters picked it up and started writing about "Stan the Man." The nickname not only stuck, but it also fit. Musial was one of the premier hitters of the late 1940s and early 1950s. Musial told me that as far as he can remember it was 1946 when people started to refer to him as "Stan the Man." It is sometimes forgotten, however, that Musial had a perfectly acceptable baseball nickname before "The Man" moniker. He was called "The Donora Greyhound." This was a place nickname. Musial was born and raised in Donora, Pennsylvania. Greyhound denoted his lean, lissome torso which appeared built for speed, which he possessed. Friends and players often addressed Musial as "Stash."

2610. Myatt, George Edward (1938–47 2B) "Mercury." "Mercury" refers to Myatt's speed on the base paths. He was also called "Foghorn" for his loud voice, especially while playing second base. With a reputation as a womanizer, he was sometimes called "Stud." At one time, Myatt had been a clubhouse aide to Snead Jolly who was called "Big Stud."

2611. Myer, Charles Solomon (1925–41 2B) "Buddy." Myer contended that he had always been called "Buddy" on and off the field for as long as he could remember. It came from childhood. Few remember today that Myer led the American League with a .349 batting average in 1935 or that his career average for 17 seasons was over .300, .303 to be exact.

2612. Myers, Henry Harrison (1909–25 OF) "Hy." "Hy" was just a short take off on the first name of Henry.

2613. Myers, James Albert (1884–91 2B) "Cod." Origin unknown.

2614. Myers, Ralph Edward (1910–15 1B) "Hap." "Hap" is short for "Happy" and refers to Myer's pleasant disposition.

2615. Nagelson, Russell Charles (1968–70 OF) "Rusty." The nickname does not refer to hair color. It is a takeoff on Russell, given to him by his parents at an early age.

2616. Nagle, Walter Harold (1911 P) "Lucky." Origin unknown.

2617. Nahem, Samuel Ralph (1938–48 P) "Subway." Nahem told me "Subway" referred to his underhand delivery. He was dubbed by writer Dan Parlser of the *New York Daily Mirror*.

2618. Naleway, Frank (1924 SS) "Chick." "Chick" refers to Naleway's 5'9", 160-pound build.

2619. Nance, William G. (1897–1904 OF) "Doc." Many of the players with the nickname of "Doc" had a close association with either the medical or dental professions. However, in the case of Nance, the origin of "Doc" is unknown. Nance was also called "Kid" because of his small stature.

2620. Napier, Skelton LeRoy (1912–21 P) "Buddy." "Buddy" was a childhood nickname.

2621. Naranjo, Lazro Ramon Gongalo (1956 P) "Cholly." Origin unknown.

2622. Narleski, William Edward (1929–30 SS) "Cap." Narleski was sent to the minor leagues to learn how to play shortstop. When he returned to the Boston Red Sox, he was asked if he had learned to play short. His reply was, "No, but I know how to wear a high hat."

2623. Narum, Leslie Ferdinand (1963–67 P) "Buster." His first time at bat in the major leagues, playing for

Baltimore he hit a home run off Don Mossi into the upper deck at Tiger Stadium. This earned him the nickname of "Buster." However, as it turned out, Narum was not much of a hitter, even for a pitcher. For his career, he could do no better than seven hits in 118 times at bat for a .059 average.

2624. Nash, Charles Francis (1967–70 1B) "Cotton." Nash wrote me, "'Cotton' was a reflection of my white hair when I was a youth. An uncle originated the name when I was 8 years old in Little League baseball. Several sportswriters made it stick: Truman Stacey of Charles, Louisiana; Larry Boeck of Louisville, Kentucky; Ed Ashford, and Billy Thompson of Lexington, Kentucky." In addition to baseball, Nash played professional basketball.

2625. Nash, James Edwin (1966–72 P) "Jumbo Jim." Nash was 6'5" and weighed 215 pounds.

2626. Nava, Vincent P. (1882–86 C) "Sandy." The nickname refers to hair color.

2627. Navarro, Julio Ventura (1962–70 P) "Whiplash." Navarro told me, "It was my way of throwing and pushing toward third base in a kind of coiling motion. I threw side arm and three-quarters and was kind of slim. 'Whiplash' came from a writer in Tacoma, Washington, where I was in the minor leagues."

2628. Navin, Frank (1905–31 Executive General Manager) "Lucky Frank." Navin bought a small share of the Detroit Tigers with money won in a card game. He was the man responsible for building the championship teams of 1907–09 and the decision to retain Ty Cobb despite his disposition and anti-social behavior. Navin was also called "Jap" due to his "inscrutable features."

2629. Neal, Theophilus Fountain (1905 3B) "Offa." "Offa" is a play on the pronunciation of the middle letters of the first name of Theophilus.

2630. Neale, Alfred Earle (1916–24 OF) "Greasey." In addition to playing baseball, Neale was a great football player and longtime coach of the Philadelphia Eagles. Tom Shea says the nickname of "Greasey" stems form Neale's football playing days at West Virginia Western. He was a ball carrier who slipped through the line like grease. Joseph McBride, on the other hand, reports the nickname comes from childhood. As a boy of Parkersburg, West Virginia, he called one of his friends "Dirty Face" and "Dirty Neck." The boy retaliated by calling him "Greasey" because he worked for a time as a grease boy in a rolling mill.

2631. Necciai, Ronald Andrew (1952 P) "Rocket Ron." Necciai ended the 1952 season pitching in 12 games for the Pittsburgh Pirates. He began the year with Bristol of the Appalachian League where in the first 31 innings he fanned 77 batters. He broke the minor league record for consecutive strikeouts with 12 and pitched a no-hitter.

2632. Needham, Thomas J. (1904–14 C) "Deerfoot." Tom Shea points out that "Deerfoot" is a nickname opposite. As a catcher, Needham was painfully slow on the base paths. "Deerfoot" is a nickname usually reserved for players with great speed.

2633. Neighbors, Cecil E. (1908 OF) "Cy." In Neighbors' case "Cy" is an alternative to Cecil.

2634. Nekola, Francis Joseph (1929–33 P) "Bots." Origin unknown.

2635. Nelson, Albert Francis (1910–13 P) "Red." The nickname refers to hair color.

2636. Nelson, George Emmett (1935–36 P) "Ramrod." "Ramrod" refers to Nelson's build. At 6'3" and 180 pounds, Nelson looked like "Ramrod" on the mound.

2637. Nelson, Glenn Richard (1949–61 1B) "Rocky." Nelson was nicknamed by his St. Louis teammates, but the exact reason is unknown.

2638. Nelson, John W. (1878–90 SS) "Candy." Origin unknown.

2639. Nelson, Lynn Bernard (1930–40 P) "Line Drive." Although Nelson was a good hitting pitcher with a career average of .281, the nickname "Line Drive" does not refer to his hitting, but to the extraordinary number hit off his pitches.

2640. Nelson, Robert Sidney (1955–57 OF) "Tex." This is a place nickname. Nelson was born and raised in Dallas, Texas. At one time in his career he was called "Babe."

2641. Nelson, Rodger Eugene (1967–76 P) "Spider." Nelson's ability to steal bases as a high school ball player led teammates to call him "Spider."

2642. Newhouser, Harold (1939–55 P) "Prince Hal." Newhouser had speed and grace as a pitcher. Detroit newspapers began to refer to him as "Prince Hal" during the war years when he became the best pitcher in baseball. He won 29 games in 1944, 25 in 1945, and 26 in 1946 while dropping just 9 each year for a three-year princely total of 80-27, .747.

2643. Newkirk, Floyd Elmo (1934 P) "Three Finger." Newkirk lost two fingers on his pitching hand in a childhood accident.

2644. Newkirk, Joel Ivey (1919–20 P) "Sailor." Newkirk was in the navy during World War I.

2645. Newlin, Maurice Milton (1940–41 P) "Mickey." "Mickey" was simply an alternative to Maurace.

2646. Newsom, Norman Louis (1929–53 P) "Bobo." Newsom was one of the great characters of the game, pitching for 20 years and winning 211 games, but dropping 222 for a percentage of .487. "Bobo" was like an express train that makes local stops. During his career he went from Brooklyn NL, to Chicago NL, to St. Louis AL, to Washington AL, to Boston AL, to St. Louis AL, to Detroit AL, to Washington AL, to Brooklyn NL, to St. Louis AL, to Washington AL, to Philadelphia AL, to Washington AL, to Philadelphia AL. Newsom could not pronounce "Buck." It came out "Bo." Later he added an extra "Bo" and began calling himself "Bobo" which is the Spanish term for "fool." To reinforce the foolishness, Newsom called everyone else "Bobo." This led to the story that he was called "Bobo" because he used the term for everyone else.

2647. Newsome, Larmar Ashby (1935–47 SS) "Skeeter." Newsome was nicknamed by his uncle because of his small size. During his playing days he weighed 155 pounds on a 5'9" frame.

2648. Newton, Eustace James (1900–09 P) "Doc." Newton was a practicing physician. On August 4, 1905, he was caught by Mike Powers who was also a physician. This might have been the only all-physician battery in baseball history.

2649. Nicholas, Charles Augustus (1890–1906 P) "Kid." Nicholas was 17 years old in 1887 when he won 21 games for Kansas City in the Western League. He was 21 years old and weighed 145 pounds when he broke into the major leagues in 1890 winning 27 games for the Boston National League Club. His youth and slender build led to the "Kid" nickname which stuck with him through his 15-year career which produced an amazing 360 wins. He won 30 games or more in seven seasons.

2650. Nicholas, Frederick C. (1876–82 P) "Tricky." Nicholas is credited with having developed a drop-pitch as early as 1875. It is roughly what would now be called a sinker.

2651. Nicholson, Thomas C. (1888–95 2B) "Beacon." Nicholson was addressed as "Parson" because he would not play on Sunday. "Beacon" denotes his body build. At 6'6" he was a real beacon at second base.

2652. Nicholson, William Beck (1936–53 OF) "Swish." Nicholson had a powerful swing which stirred up a lot of air at the plate when he missed, which was often. Quoting Eddie Gold, "Some say Nicholson squeezed the bat so hard that sawdust would ooze out. And that swing! Brooklyn fans would yell 'Swish' everytime Nicholson would take a tremendous swipe with the bat."

2653. Niebergall, Charles Arthur (1921–24 C) "Nig." The nickname does not denote dark complexion, but is a contraction of the last name.

2654. Nieman, Elmer LeRoy (1943–45 OF) "Butch." Nieman told me, "My father had a butcher shop when I was a little boy. People who traded at the shop called me 'Butch'."

2655. Nieman, Robert Charles (1951–56 OF) "Burly." According to close observers of St. Louis baseball, Nieman was big, strong and just plain slow.

2656. Niekro, Philip Henry (1964–87 P) "Knucksie." Nieko was a knuckleball pitcher all his 24-year career and the pitch carried him to 318 victories, albeit 274 losses.

2657. Niland, Thomas James (1896 OF) "Honest Tom." Origin unknown.

2658. Nill, George Charles (1904–08) "Rabbit." "Rabbit" denotes Nill's speed on the base paths and also his diminutive size, 5'7" and 160 pounds.

2659. Noboa, Milcades Arturo (1984 2B) "Junior." Origin unknown.

2660. Nolan, Edward Sylvester (1878–85 P) "The Only Nolan." In 1875 as a teenager Nolan played for the Paterson, New Jersey Olympics, a crack amateur team. The team drew large crowds which the local paper said came to watch the pitcher known as "the only boy on a team of men." At the age 19 in 1878 Nolan was paid $2,500 to pitch for Indianapolis. In what may have been the first spring training trip a baseball team ever made, moving north from New Orleans, Indianapolis won 11 straight games, six by shutout and Nolan was their only pitcher. From that time on he was known as "The Only Nolan."

2661. Nonnenkamp, Leo William (1933–40 OF) "Red." The nickname refers to hair color.

2662. Northrop, George Howard (1918–19 P) "Jerky Jake." According to Tom Shea, Northrop was always twitching and turning on the mound.

2663. Northy, Ronald James (1942–57 OF) "The Round Man." Worthy had a roly poly build which made him look a great deal heavier than his 200 pounds on 5'10" frame. In his last years in the major leagues he became an excellent pinch hitter, with a life time pinch hit average of .275. He hit three pinch hit grand-slam homeruns.

2664. Novetney, Ralph Joseph (1949 C) "Rube." Origin unknown.

2665. Novikoff, Louis Alexander (1941–46 OF) "The Mad Russian." Novikoff was of Russian background. He was well known for his strange behavior. The 1943 *Baseball Register* credits sportswriter, Eddie West, of the *Santa Anna* (California) *Register,* as the originator of the "Mad Russian tag" when Novikoff was playing for Los Angeles in the Pacific Coast League. Eddie Gold and Art Ahrens give credit to Charlie Grimm when Novikoff first came to the majors with the Chicago Cubs. Richard Goldstein points out that Novikoff had led the Three-I League, the Texas League, the American Association, and Pacific Coast League in batting average before failing in four tries with the Cubs. There were however, explanations. Novikoff said, "I can't play in Wrigley Field because the left-field foul line isn't straight like in other parks, it's crooked." Goldstein goes on to say, "Novikoff had a fear of approaching the ivy-covered walls in Wrigley Field, leading Charlie Grimm to suspect he viewed them as a source of hay fever or perhaps poison ivy. One day Grimm ripped out some vines, rubbed them on his face and hands in the outfielder's presence, and even chewed a few to show they were harmless. But it didn't seem to make an impression." Finally, shortstop teammate Len Merullo gives his impression of "The Mad Russian." "He had a nice family, a wife and a couple of daughters, and he was not a hard drinker, but he loved to have as much beer as he could get in him, and he really enjoyed being around a crowd. He had that big moon face and a big smile, just a very likeable type of guy. He'd tell you stories. He'd lie like hell. You knew he was lying, but he was entertaining."

2666. Nutter, Everett Clarence (1919 OF) "Dizzy." "Dizzy" is a response to the last name of Nutter.

O

2667. Oakes, Ennis Telflair (1909–15 OF) "Rebel." The nickname reflects Oakes' southern heritage. Oakes was born in Homer, Louisiana.

2668. Oana, Henry Kauhane (1934–45 P) "Prince." When Oana first joined the San Francisco Seals, stories were published that he was a Hawaiian Prince. The more he denied them, the more people believed them. When he reported to Detroit in 1943, everyone called him "Prince." He kept telling them "I am just Henry Oana. Call me Hank." However, pitcher teammate Virgil Trucks told a different story. "I really truly believed Hank was a prince. I talked with Hank. I got to know him real well, and he said he definitely was a prince. But you know, not like being next to a queen or king or something like that. He wasn't that type of prince. He was just, you'd say, probably a minor league prince."

2669. Oberlander, Hartman Louis (1888 P) "Doc." Many of the players with the nickname of "Doc" had a close association with either the medical or dental professions. However, in the case of Oberlander, the origin of "Doc" is unknown.

2670. Oberlin, Frank Rufus (1906–10 P) "Flossie." Origin unknown.

2671. O'Brien, Frank Aloysius (1923 C) "Mickey." "Mickey" was a common nickname given to players of Irish background.

2672. O'Brien, John F. (1888–91 P) "Darby." O'Brien was nicknamed after William Darby O'Brien who began his major league career in the American Association one year before John F. O'Brien did.

2673. O'Brien, John J. (1891–99 2B) "Chewing Gum." O'Brien chewed gum in an era in which most other players chewed tobacco.

2674. O'Brien, Thomas Edward (1943–50 OF) "Obie." "Obie" is simply a contraction of O'Brien.

2675. O'Brien, Thomas Joseph (1911–13 P) "Buck." "Buck" is a generic nickname. The circumstances of origin are almost never documented. It refers to a virile, well developed, aggressive, high spirited young man. It is usually bestowed during his teenage years.

2676. Ock, Harold David (1935 C) "Whitey." "Whitey" refers to hair color.

2677. Ockey, Walter Andrew (1944 P) "Footsie." Origin unknown.

2678. O'Conner, John Joseph (1887–1910 C) "Peach Pie." During his amateur career O'Conner played for a team in the St. Louis area called the "Peach Pies." Lee Allen explains the rationale for the nickname. "By reference to him always as 'Peach Pie' Jack O'Conner, newspaper men and fans avoided confusing him with another Jack O'Conner prominent in the game." Jack, as he was addressed, was also called "Rowdy Jack" because of his constant arguing with the umpires."

2679. O'Dea, Paul (1944–45 OF) "Lefty." O'Dea batted left handed and threw left handed.

2680. O'Dell, William Olivar (1954–67 P) "Digger." O'Dell was nicknamed "Digger" by Baltimore teammate, Chuck Deering, after the character in the "Life of Riley" radio and TV show, "Digger O'Dell," the deep voiced friendly undertaker.

2681. Odenwald, Theodore Joseph (1921–22 P) "Lefty." Odenwald pitched left handed but batted right handed.

2682. Odom, David Everett (1943 P) "Porky." Origin unknown.

2683. Odom, Herman Boyd (1925 3B) "Heinie." The nickname reflects Odom's German background.

2684. Odom, Johnny Lee (1964–76 P) "Blue Moon." "Moon" was Odom's childhood nickname because of his moon shaped face. Teammates added the "Blue" because he was often in a depressed mood.

2685. O'Doul, Francis Joseph (1919–34 OF) "Lefty." O'Doul acquired the nickname of "Lefty" at the start of his career when he was primarily a pitcher. He threw left handed, and batted left handed. With a career batting average of .349 in 11 campaigns, the highlight being leading the National League in 1929 with a .399 average, O'Doul became a hero in his hometown of San Francisco. A famous restaurant in that city still bears his name.

2686. Odwell, Frederick William (1904–07 OF) "Fritz." "Fritz" denotes Odwell's German background.

2687. Oertel, Charles Frank (1958 OF) "Ducky." "Ducky" refers to Oertel's size 5'8" and 165 pounds.

2688. Oeschger, Joseph Carl (1914–25 P) "Iron Man." On May 1, 1920, he started and finished a 26 inning 1–1 tie with Brooklyn while pitching for the Boston Braves. The Brooklyn pitcher Leon Cadore also went all the way.

2689. Ogden, Warren Harvey (1922–26 P) "Curly." The nickname denotes the texture of Ogden's hair.

2690. Ogrodowski, Ambrose Francis (1936–37 C) "Brusie." "Brusie" is short for Bruiser. It refers to Ogrodowski's sturdy build and strength.

2691. O'Hara, James Francis (1904 OF) "Kid." "Kid" referred to O'Hara's youthful appearance and size, 5'7" and 150 pounds.

2692. Okrie, Frank Anthony (1920 P) "Lefty." Okrie pitched left handed and batted left handed.

2693. Oldham, John Cyrus (1914–26 P) "Red." The nickname refers to hair color.

2694. O'Leary, Daniel (1879–84 OF) "Hustling Dan." The hustling refers to O'Leary's off the field behavior. He was always on the move entertaining, and trying to wheel and deal.

2695. Oliva, Pedro Lopez (1962–76 OF) "Tony." Oliva used his older brother's (Tony) birth certificate to get a passport into the United States from Cuba. Then he decided to use the name for his baseball career.

2696. Oliver, Albert (1968–84 OF) "Mr. Scoop." Oliver had an uncanny ability of scooping up ground balls and low flying balls in the outfield. The nickname came from fans when he was playing for Gastonia, North Carolina, in the South Atlantic League in 1965.

2697. Oliver, Nathaniel (1963–69 2B) "Pee Wee." According to Joseph McBride, although Oliver was 5'10" and 160 pounds, he looked small in comparison to other Los Angeles Dodger players of the 1960s.

2698. Oliver, Thomas Noble (1930–33 OF) "Rebel." "Rebel" points to Oliver's southern heritage and his southern drawl. He was born in Montgomery, Alabama.

2699. Olivo, Diomedes Antonio Maldonado (1960–63 P) "Guayubin." This is a place nickname. Olivo's home was in Guayubin, Dominican Republic.

2700. Olivo, Frederico Emilio Maldonado (1961–66 P) "Chi Chi." Origin unknown.

2701. Olomo, Luis Francisco Rodriguez (1943–51 OF) "Jibaro." Olomo was the first Puerto Rican to make it to the majors. "Jibaro" refers to his campesino (peasant-farmer) background.

2702. O'Loughlin, Frank H. (1902–18 AL Umpire) "Silk." O'Loughlin once wore a silk hat to a wedding and after that was called "Silk." O'Loughlin was one of the most colorful of all umpires. He was famous for his intonation of "St-r-r-ike Tuh." The quotation "I never missed one in my life" was really O'Loughlin's, although it is usually attributed to Bill Klem. O'Loughlin truly believed he never missed a call.

2703. Olson, Marvin Clement (1931–33 2B) "Sparky." The talkative Olson was a spark plug on the teams he played for.

2704. O'Malley, Walter Francis (1950–79 Owner) "The Big Oom." O'Malley was the owner of the Brooklyn Dodgers and the driving force which brought the team to Los Angeles in 1958. He was regarded as an ultra-shrewd businessman, a tightwad, and a wheeler-dealer type. The monikers "The Big Oom" and "Oom the Omnipotent" refer to these characteristics. The nicknames were given to him by fellow businessmen of Brooklyn who used to meet during the late 1940s and early 50s in room 45 at Brooklyn's Bosert Hotel to wine, dine, and deal.

2705. O'Neal, Oran Herbert (1925–27 P) "Skinny." O'Neal was very thin when he first started in organized baseball. By the time he reached the major leagues he was up to 160 pounds on a 5'11" frame.

2706. O'Neil, James Edward (1880–92 OF) "Tip." Canadian born O'Neil was called "Tip" because of his ability to foul off pitches until he found the one he wanted to hit. In 1887 he batted .435 and scored 167 runs.

2707. O'Neill, Philip Bernard (1904 C) "Peaches." Origin unknown.

2708. Onis, Manuel Dominguez (1935 C) "Curly." Onis wrote me, "I was called curly by my friends at about 15 or 16 when I first started to play sandlot ball. My hair was blond and curly. In 1932 in New York City the Tampa Cuban All Stars played an exhibition game in Harlem against a black team. Fans wanted to know why I had blond hair, blue eyes and reddish complexion. I looked like an Irishman, but was representing Cuba and spoke Spanish. My parents were Spanish not Cuban and I was born in Tampa, Florida."

2709. Ormsby, Emmett T. (1923–41 AL Umpire) "Red." The nickname refers to hair color.

2710. O'Rourke, James Francis (1912–31 3B) "Blackie." During the season O'Rourke developed an exceedingly deep tan.

2711. O'Rourke, James Henry (1876–1904 OF) "Orator Jim."

O'Rourke began his career in the first year of the formation of the National League. After retiring in 1893, he came back to play in one game in 1904. O'Rourke talked like an orator with a full command of the English language which people found outstanding. He was the first club house lawyer. David Phillips says he was a "fountain of rodomontade." Lee Allen in *Hot Stove League* recalls examples. "When he discovered that Louis Sockalexis, a Penobscot Indian signed a contract that forbade drinking, he turned to a friend and said, "I see that Sockalexis must forego frescoing his tonsils with Cardinal brush; it is so nominated in the contract of the aborigine." In 1881 while managing Buffalo, shortstop John Peters asked for a $10 advance. O'Rourke's reply is preserved by Lee Allen. "I am sorry, but the exigencies of the occasion and the condition of our exchequer will not permit anything of that sort at this period of our existence. Subsequent developments in the field of finance may remove the present gloom and we may emerge into a condition where we may see fit to reply in the affirmative to your exceedingly modest request."

2712. O'Rourke, Joseph Leo (1908 SS) "Patsy." "Patsy" denotes O'Rourke's Irish background. It does not refer to feminine characteristics.

2713. O'Rourke, Timothy Patrick (1890–94 3B) "Voiceless Tim." O'Rourke was left with a weak voice after he was hit by a ball in the throat.

2714. Orsatti, Ernest Ralph (1927–35 OF) "Showboat." Orsatti was a flashy dresser. He also was a movie stunt man in the off season and was also called "Hollywood."

2715. Orsino, John Joseph (1961–67 C) "Horse." "Horse," in Orsino's case, refers to size. This catcher was 6'3" and weighed 220 pounds.

2716. Ortega, Filomento Coronado (1960–69 P) "Kemo." Ortega was a Pima Indian born in Arizona. "Kemo" comes from "Kemo Sabe" the name used by the Indian character from the Lone Ranger in the radio, TV and movie shows of the same name. Note this is an example where an American Indian does not have the nickname of "Chief," but at the same time it denotes Indian background.

2717. Orth, Albert Lewis (1895–1909 P) "The Curveless Wonder." Orth managed to win 202 major league games, and even led the American League in wins with 27 in 1906, without the hint of a curveball. Orth was a good hitting pitcher compiling a .273 batting average for 15 seasons, and on occasions played other positions.

2718. Ortiz, Adalberto Colon (1982– P) "Junior." "Junior" refers to Ortiz's seemingly slight build, 5'11" and 174 pounds, and was given to him by players during his minor league career.

2719. Ortiz, Oliviero Nunez (1944 P) "Baby." Oliviero was the younger brother of Robert Ortiz who played for Washington at the same time.

2720. Osborn, Wilfred Pearl (1907–09 OF) "Ossie Green." Origin unknown.

2721. Osborne, Ernest Preston (1922–25 P) "Tiny." This is an example of a nickname opposite. At 6'4" and 215 pounds Osborne was anything but "Tiny."

2722. Osborne, Lawrence Sidney (1937–43 1B) "Bobo." Osborne wrote me, "I signed with Detroit as a 17-year-old teenager out of high school in 1953. Charlie Metro, manager of the Montgomery Grays, spent a lot of time working with me. Several of the older players of this Class A South Atlantic

League team started calling me Charlie's Little Bobo."

2723. Ostergard, Roy Lund (1921 PH) "Red." The nickname refers to hair color.

2724. Ostermueller, Frederick Raymond (1934–48 P) "Fritz." "Fritz" calls attention to Ostermueller's German background. Ostermueller is one of the few pitchers in major league history to win as many as 114 games and still have a career losing record. He dropped 115 decisions.

2725. Ostrowski, Joseph Paul (1948–52 P) "Professor." Ostrowski was a school teacher in the off season.

2726. Otez, William Tilford (1907–11 P) "Steamboat Bill." Otez was nicknamed "Steamboat Bill" by teammate pitcher "Long" Tom Hughes, but he never was able to discover why.

2727. Otis, Harry George (1909 P) "Cannonball." Otis was noted for his fastball, but he also had difficulty in getting it over the plate. He walked 18 batters in his 26.1 innings in the major leagues.

2728. Otis, Paul Franklyn (1912 OF) "Bill." Otis was born Dec. 24, 1889. As of Jan. 1, 1990, at 100 years of age, he was the oldest living ball player. His brother's name was Bill, and he claims that people confused him with his brother. Otis played in four games for the New York Al team in 1912 and made only one hit in 20 times at bat. *But* that hit was off the pitching of Walter Johnson.

2729. Ott, Mary (1940s–60s Fan) "Horse Lady of St. Louis." Ott was a rabid fan, who according to baseball historian, David Nemec, for 25 years had been the scourge of umpires and visiting players to Sportsman's Park.

2730. Ott, Melvin Thomas (1926–47 OF) "Master Melvin." Ott signed with New York Giants at age 16. The "Master" refers to his age. He never played in the minor leagues and had only one season of semi-pro ball competition before joining the Giants. At 5'9" sportswriter Will Wedge of the *New York Sun* called him the "Shetland Pony Outfielder." Ott had a peculiar batting stance in which he took a high-stepped stride just before he swung the bat. It should have taken all his power away and made him a "sucker" for inside fastballs. Most players and coaches in the Giant organization wanted to alter his style, including Casey Stengel, but manager John McGraw would have none of it. He took charge of Ott personally and let him hit the way he wanted to. The Giants, of course, over the next 22 years were rewarded with 311 home runs. The personal treatment Ott received from McGraw led to the sobriquet of "Mr. McGraw's Boy." Ott was soft spoken, well mannered and highly respected. Nathan Salant provides an example of the respect. "As heated and vicious as the old Brooklyn–New York rivalry was, and as nasty as the Dodger fans could get in their home ball park, they always greeted 'Master Melvin' with polite applause, and responded to his home runs with uncharacteristic silence and occasionally, wonder of wonders, a smattering of applause!"

2731. Otto, David Alan (1987– P) "Ave." "Ave" is simply a play on the first name of David.

2732. Outon, William Austin (1933 C) "Chick." Harold Johnson attempts to explain how Outon received the nickname of "Chick." "The nickname 'Chick' was derived from 'Chink'; a title hung on Outon in a peculiar way. North Carolina State was playing Clemson College and the cadets started shouting, 'Plunging Chink' when they could not stop his off tackle plunges. 'I suppose,' he says, 'they thought. I was a Chinaman. I prefer Chick'."

2733. Ovrell, Forrest Gordon (1943–45 P) "Joe." Ovrell told me, "My first manager called me Bullet Joe because of my fastball. Later it became just Joe."

2734. Overall, Orval (1905–13 P) "Big Groundhog." Overall was 6'2" and weighed 215 pounds. He was an agriculture student in California when he received the nickname.

2735. Overmine, Frank (1943–52 P) "Stubby." Overmine was not only short 5'7", but at 175 pounds appeared squatty or "Stubby."

2736. Owen, Arnold Malcolm (1937–54 C) "Mickey." When Owen was playing for Columbus of the American Association, Manager Bert Shotten took one look at his protruding ears and they reminded him of those of Detroit catcher "Mickey" Cochrane. So from then on Arnold Owen, became "Mickey" Owen.

2737. Owen, Frank Malcolm (1901–09 P) "Yip." "Yip" is a place nickname. Owen was born and raised in Ypslanti, Michigan.

2738. Owen, Marvin James (1931–40 3B) "Freck." According to Tom Shea "Freck" is short for "Freckles." Owen's face was covered with them.

2739. Owens, Clarence B. (1916–37 AL Umpire) "Brick." Joseph McBride writes, "Owens was on the receiving end of a brick while umpiring a game in Pittsburg, Kansas. It didn't shake his credo, 'call 'em fast and walk away tough'." On the other hand, Frank Graham and Dick Hyman report in their *Wit & Wisdom: Folklore of a National Pastime* that Owens was called "Brick" "because he was built as solidly as a brick smokehouse and had a spirit as rugged as his body." Mac Davis reports of an incident when catcher Mickey Owen protested one of Owen's calls. Owen told him, "Mickey, if you would only pin back those big ears of yours, I could probably see the ball better."

2740. Owens, Frank Walter (1905–14 C) "Yip." Owens was nicknamed after Frank "Yip" Owen (1901–09).

2741. Owens, James Philip (1955–67 P) "Bear." Teammate Chet Di Emidio of Miami in the KOM League gave him the nickname in 1952. He said Owens always bears down when he is on the mound.

2742. Ozmer, Horace Robert (1923 P) "Doc." Many of the players with the nickname of "Doc" had a close association with either the medical or dental professions. But for Ozmer, the origin of "Doc" is unknown.

P

2743. Paciorek, Thomas Marian (1970–87 OF) "Wimpy." Paciorek received his nickname when he first came up with the Los Angeles Dodgers in 1968 and ate dinner with some of the players. He told me, "All the players who got big bonuses—Valentine, Garvey, Billy Buck—ordered steaks. I didn't particularly like the taste of steak, so I ordered two double cheeseburgers. Tommy [Lasorda] immediately named me 'Wimpy' after the hamburger-loving character from 'Popeye'."

2744. Padden, Richard Joseph (1896–1905 2B) "Brains." Tom Shea states that Padden was an extra astute student of the game.

2745. Padgett, Don Wilson (1937–48 C) "Red." The nickname refers to hair color.

2746. Padgett, Ernest Kitchen (1923–27 3B) "Red." The nickname refers to hair color.

2747. Pafko, Andrew (1943–59 OF) "Pruschka." Chicago Cub manager, Charlie Grimm, nicknamed Pafko in 1944 during his first full year in the major leagues. In Grimm's words, "Andy Pafko was 'Pruschka' to me. My thought was that if he had a carpet bag in his hand he'd look like he'd just got off the boat from one of those old countries." When Pafko first came up to the majors, a book by John R. Tunis, The *Kid from Tomkinsville*, was popular. It was about a young outfielder from small town America. Pafko fit the image and was nicknamed after the small town in Wisconsin where he was from, "The Kid from Boyceville." Later the Chicago Press, and radio announcer Bert Wilson called him "Handy Andy" because he came through in the clutch so many times. Finally Charlie Grimm had another nickname for Pafko. Pafko had a high forehead, so Grimm called him "The Brow" after the character in the Dick Tracy comic strip.

2748. Page, Joseph Francis (1944–54 P) "Fireman." "Fireman" refers to Page's success as a relief pitcher for the New York Yankees. In 1947 he won 14 games in relief and saved 17 more. In 1949 he won 13 games in relief and saved 27 others. Page was a free spirit, a fun loving guy who stayed out late at night, but it never seemed to affect his pitching. It led to the nickname "The Gay Reliever." Page's best pitch was a fastball, and he was often referred to as "Smokey Joe."

2749. Paige, George Lynn (1911 P) "Pat." Origin unknown.

2750. Paige, Leroy Robert (1948–65 P) "Satchel." In 1948 at age 42 Paige became the oldest rookie in major league history and the first black pitcher in the American League. From his start with the semi-pro Mobile Tigers until his stay with the Indianapolis Clowns in 1967, Paige pitched in an estimated 2,500 games and before an estimated 10 million fans. From 1929–58, he played both summer and winter ball in the United States, Canada, Cuba, the Dominican Republic, and Mexico. If he was not the best pitcher in the Negro Leagues, he was by far the most famous and well known. When Paige was seven years old, he began working at the train depot in Mobile, Alabama. It was at this site he earned his nickname. In his own words, "I got me a pole and some ropes. That let me sling two, three, four satchels together and carry them one at a time. The other kids laughed at me and one of them said, 'You look like a walking satchel tree.' They all started yelling it. Soon everybody was calling me that, you know how it is with kids and nicknames. That's when Leroy Paige became no more and Satchel Paige took over. Nobody called me LeRoy, nobody excepting Mom and the government."

2751. Paine, Phillips Steere (1951–58 P) "Flip." Paine told me "Flip" dates from high school when teammates asked if he was going to "Flip [pitch] the game that day." In six major league seasons Paine posted a 10-1 won-lost record, all in relief.

2752. Palmer, Edwin Henry (1917 3B) "Baldy." Palmer was prematurely bald.

2753. Palmer, James Alvin (1965–84 P) "Jockstrap Jim." Palmer who won 268 games for the Baltimore Orioles and four World Series games really did not have a public nickname. However, during the latter stages of his career he made TV commercials for jockey shorts. His near nude form in the shorts on TV led to the locker room nickname. For the same reason he was also called "Cakes."

2754. Pappas, Milton Stephen (1957–73 P) "Gimpy." Pappas wrote me, "I had knee surgery when I was in high school. After that in a game I hit a ball 450 feet and only got a single. My high school teammates started to call me 'Gimpy'." While Pappas did not hit any 450-foot drives as a major leaguer, he did hit 20 home runs while winning 209 major league games.

2755. Parker, Clarence McRay (1937–38 SS) "Ace." Parker played only two years in the major leagues. In 207 times at bat his average was just .179. He was, however, a great football player, elected to both the college football and professional football hall of fames. Parker wrote me, "'Ace' means an expert player, the highest card in the deck. It was given to me by W.N. Cox, sports editor of the *Norfolk, Virginia Pilot* in 1934, my sophomore year at Duke University. After I had an outstanding game, he said Clarence would not fit in the press and he tacked 'Ace' on me and it stuck."

2756. Parker, Clarence Perkins (1915 OF) "Pat." "Pat" recalls Parker's Irish background and replaces Clarence which was not thought to be a suitable baseball name.

2757. Parker, David Gene (1973– OF) "The Cobra." The snake analogy refers to Parker's coiled batting stance and quick striking swing.

2758. Parker, Douglas Woolley (1923 C) "Dixie." The nickname devotes Parker's southern heritage. He was born in Forest Home, Alabama.

2759. Parker, Francis James (1936 SS) "Salty." Parker told me, "When I was 10 years old, I was working in a grocery store in East St. Louis, Illinois. I was always eating salted peanuts. One of the owners of the store, Maurice Holtzman, gave me the nickname."

2760. Parker, Harley Park (1893–1901 P) "Doc." Parker was a medical school student while he was playing baseball. He received his degree from Rush Medical School in Chicago, Illinois.

2761. Parks, Vernon Henry (1921 P) "Slicker." Origin unknown.

2762. Parmelee, Leroy Earl (1929–39 P) "Tarzan." "Bud" as Parmelee was addressed, was nicknamed "Tarzan" by a New York sportswriter while he was pitching for the New York Giants. "His work on the mound usually leaves him out on a limb." The reference is to the hero of the Edgar Rice Burroughs 1914 novel, *Tarzan of the Apes*, which later was made into a series of movies.

2763. Parnell, Melvin Lloyd (1947–56 P) "Dusty." With the Boston Red Sox in 1949, Parnell led the American League in wins with 25, and an ERA of 2.77. But this curveballing pitcher had a habit of throwing the ball into the dirt around home plate and making the dust fly.

2764. Parnell, Roy (1927–43 OF, Negro League) "Red." The nickname refers to light colored hair and skin.

2765. Parnham, James Arthur (1915–17 P) "Rube." Parnham was a small town boy from Heidelberg, Pennsylvania, and not wise to big city ways. He was nicknamed after "Rube" Waddell. In 1923 Parnham won 33 games while losing 7 for the Baltimore Orioles of the International League, ending the season with 20 straight wins.

2766. Parrott, Thomas William (1893–96 P) "Tacky Tom." Parrott was an eccentric, what we would now call a flake. He took great pleasure in playing his cornet in the middle of the night and disturbing people in his boarding house. He loved to ride his bicycle to the ball park. Lee Allen related that in one game he pitched for Cincinnati, "King" Kelly went 4-4 against him. After the game he asked the "King" what he had eaten for breakfast that morning. Kelly said "ham and eggs." That night Parrott stopped at a delicatessen and picked up a supply of eggs and a whole ham.

2767. Parrott, Walter Edward (1892–95 3B) "Jiggs." Origin unknown.

2768. Parsons, Edward Dixon (1939–43 C) "Dixie." Parsons wrote me, "My middle name is Dixon. This plus the fact that I was born in Talladega, Alabama, led Tiny Scurlock, a reporter in Beaumont, Texas, to give me that nickname during spring training of my rookie year."

2769. Parsons, Thomas Anthony (1963–65 P) "Long Tom." Parsons was 6'7" and weighed 210 pounds. In three seasons he posed a 2-13 won-lost record with a career ERA of 4.72.

2770. Partenheimer, Harold Philip (1913 3B) "Steve." Origin unknown.

2771. Pascual, Camilo Alberto (1954–71 P) "Little Potato." His brother Carlos had the nickname of "Potato" meaning shorty. When Washington scout Joe Cambria signed him he began calling him "Little Potato." The nickname referred to birth order, not height. Carlos was 5'6½" tall and Camilo 5'11".

2772. Pascual, Carlos Luis (1950 P) "Potato." Scout Joe Cambria called Pascual "Potato" meaning shorty when he signed him. Pascual was 5'6½".

2773. Paskert, George Henry (1907–21 OF) "Dode." Paskert was addressed as "Dode," the origin of which is unknown. Fred Lieb, however, points out that his nickname was "The Gazelle" because of his speed in the outfield.

2774. Pasquariello, Michael John (1919 C) "Tony." Pasquariello preferred "Tony" to Michael and asked to be called that.

2775. Passarella, Arthur M. (1941–42, 1945–55 AL Umpire) "Pal." Passarella received the nickname "Pal" from his popularity as a semi-pro player.

2776. Passeau, Clyde William (1935–47 P) "Deacon." Passeau was given the nickname of "Deacon" by Manager Charlie Grimm of the Chicago Cubs because of his beetle-eyed stern mouthed visage.

2777. Patek, Freddie Joe (1968–81 SS) "The Flea." Patek, was only 5'5" and weighed less than 150 pounds, yet some observers said he played twice that size during his 14-year career in the major leagues. The smallest player of his time, he was also called "Moochie."

2778. Patterson, Roy Lewis (1901–07 P) "St. Croix Boy Wonder." Patterson was a school boy phenom from St. Croix Falls, Wisconsin. He was the first pitcher to win a game for the Chicago White Sox, opening day, April 24, 1901.

2779. Pattin, Martin William (1968–80 P) "Bulldog." Pattin was called "Bulldog" because he was a battler. He was also called "Duck" by teammates because of his imitation of the Disney character's voice.

2780. Pawelek, Theodore John (1946 C) "Porky." At 5'10" and 210 pounds, Pawelek was on the heavy side.

2781. Payne, Harley Fenwick (1896–89 P) "Lady." Origin unknown.

2782. Pearce, William C. (1908–09 C) "Ducky." Origin unknown.

2783. Pearson, Albert Gregory (1958–66 OF) "The Mighty Mite." Pearson stood 5'5" and weighed 140 pounds. He was nicknamed after the mouse cartoon character of that name.

2784. Pearson, Leonard Curtis (1938–49 OF, Negro League) "Horse." Origin unknown.

2785. Pearson, Montgomery Marcellus (1932–41 P) "Hoot." Pearson was a journeyman pitcher who won exactly 100 games in the major leagues. He pitched one game in each of the 1936, '37, '38 and '39 World Series winning all four for the New York Yankees. He had a fondness for Western songs and movies. One of his favorite stars was "Hoot" Gibson after whom he was nicknamed.

2786. Pecota, William Joseph (1986– SS) "I29." In three years Pecota has made eight trips up and down highway I29 between Kansas City and Omaha, back and forth between the major league team and its AAA team.

2787. Peery, George A. (1927–28 P) "Red." The nickname refers to hair color.

2788. Peete, Charles (1956 OF) "Mule." Peete was a hard worker, but slow of foot. He died in November of 1956 just after his first season in the major leagues.

2789. Peitz, Henry Clement (1894–1913 C) "Heinie." "Heinie" refers to Peitz's German background. Although Peitz was primarily a catcher, he played games at every position including pitcher.

2790. Pena, Alejancho Vasquey (1981– P) "Slow." "Slow" does not refer to Pena's pitches, but to his demeanor. According to broadcaster Vince Scully, Pena marches to his own tune. He does not hurry for anybody or anything.

2791. Pena, Antonio Francesco (1980– C) "El Gato." In the Dominican Republic Pena earned the nickname of "El Gato" because of his cat-like quickness in foiling would-be base stealers. He is especially adept at throwing to first base from a crouch.

2792. Pennington, George Lewis (1917 P) "Kewpie." Origin unknown.

2793. Pennock, Herbert Jefferies (1912–34 P) "The Knight of Kennett Square." This is a place nickname. Pennock was born in Kennett Square, Pennsylvania. Knight refers to his royal pitching. He claimed 240 major league victories and won five World Series games without losing any.

2794. Peploski, Henry Stephen (1929 3B) "Pop." "Pop" did not refer to age, but was simply an alternative to the last name.

2795. Peplowski, Joseph Anthony (1913 3B) "Pepper." "Pepper" did not refer to enthusiastic play, but was just a take off on the last name.

2796. Perdue, Herbert Rodney (1911–15 P) "The Gallatin Squash." This is a place nickname. Perdue grew up in Gallatin, Tennessee. "Squash" refers to Perdue's build, 5'10" and 195 pounds.

2797. Perez, Antansio Rigal (1964–86 1B) "Tony." Latin American player expert, Elmy Martinez points out that Perez's nickname in Cuba was "Tany" which came from his first name. In the United States "Tany" became "Tony." Perez was also called "Big Doggie" for his ability to drive in runs, over 1,650 in his career.

2798. Perkins, Charles Sullivan (1930–34 P) "Lefty." Perkins pitched left handed but batted right handed.

2799. Perkins, Ralph Foster (1915–34 C) "Cy." Perkins was nicknamed by columnist Westbrook Pegler. The reference was to the character "Cy Perkins" in the play "The Old Homestead" which was popular while Perkins was catching for the Philadelphia A's.

2800. Perkins, William George (1928–47 C, Negro League) "Cz." Origin unknown.

2801. Perrin, William Joseph (1934 P) "Lefty."Perrin pitched left handed but batted right handed.

2802. Perrine, John Grover (1907 2B) "Nig." The nickname refers to Perrine's dark complexion.

2803. Perritt, William Dayton (1912–21 P) "Pol." "Pol" is short for Polly, and is a response to the last name of Perritt.

2804. Perry, Melvin Gray (1963–64 OF) "Bob." Perry wrote me, "Leon Wagner gave me the nickname of 'Bullet Bob' because I was so fast. It then became just 'Bob'."

2805. Perry, William Henry (1912 OF) "Socks." "Socks" is short for socker or hitter, of which Perry had little chance to do in the major leagues. He came to bat only 39 times collecting six hits and three walks.

2806. Perryman, Emmett Roy (1915 P) "Parson." According to Tom Shea, the tall, serious appearance of Perryman reminded people of a Parson.

2807. Peters, John William (1915–22 C) "Shotgun." Peters, as a catcher, was noted for his strong throwing arm.

2808. Peters, Oscar C. (1912–14 P) "Rube." Peters was from the small town of Grand Fork, Illinois, and not attuned to big city ways. He was nicknamed after "Rube" Waddell.

2809. Peters, Russell Dixon (1936–47 2B) "Rusty." Rusty does not refer to hair color, but is a take off on the name of Russell.

2810. Peterson, Carl Francis (1955–57 SS) "Buddy." Peterson told me, "I was named Buddy by my father in early childhood, but I don't know why."

2811. Peterson, Charles Andrew (1962–65 OF) "Cap." Peterson wrote me, "'Cap' is no more than using the initials of the three names."

2812. Peterson, Fred Ingels (1966–75 P) "Fritz." Peterson told me the given name of Fred was the same as his father's and grandfather's. "Fritz" was used as an alternative to avoid confusion.

2813. Pettibone, Harry Joe (1983 P) "Jeff." Origin unknown.

2814. Pettit, George William Paul (1951–53 P) "Lefty." Pettit pitched left handed and batted left handed.

2815. Pettit, Leon Arthur (1935–37 P) "Lefty." Pettit pitched left handed and batted left handed.

2816. Petty, Jessie Lee (1921–30 P) "The Silver Fox." Petty was a crafty pitcher who sported a shock of silver grey hair.

2817. Petway, Bruce (1906–25 C, Negro League) "Buddy." "Buddy" was a childhood nickname. Petway was renowned for his crouching snap throws to the bases while catching. He reputedly taught the technique to famed Chicago Cub catcher, Johnny Kline. Petway was a leading home run hero before Josh Gibson came along. He is sometimes referred to as "The Black Babe Ruth."

2818. Pezold, Lorenz Johannes (1914– 3B) "Larry." "Larry" was an alternative to Lorenzo, and more acceptable as a baseball name.

2819. Pezzullo, John (1935–36 P) "Pretzels." Pezzullo had a unique herky, jerky windup which at one point reminded fans of the design of a pretzel.

2820. Pfeffer, Edward Joseph (1911–24 P) "Jeff." Pfeffer was nicknamed by Brooklyn manager Wilbert Robinson and Brooklyn teammates. His bear-like build, 6'3" and 210 pounds reminded them of heavyweight champion boxer, James J. Jeffries.

2821. Pfeffer, Francis Xavier (1905–11 P) "Big Jeff." Information concerning Pfeffer's height and weight is not available. The origin of "Jeff" also is unknown.

2822. Pfeffer, Nathaniel Frederick (1882–97 2B) "Dandelion." Pfeffer had an uncanny ability to cleanly field balls which hugged the ground. They were called "dandelion cutters." He was probably the best second baseman of his time, and he did not use a glove. The German background population of Chicago called him "Unser Fritz" (Our Fritz).

2823. Pfiester, John Albert (1903–11 P) "Jack the Giant Killer." On June 6, 1906, Pfiester pitched the Chicago Cubs to a 19–0 victory over John McGraw's New York Giants. From then on he was called "Jack the Giant Killer." The nickname was reinforced as Pfiester continued to pitch well against the Giants.

2824. Pfirman, Charles H. (1922–26 NL Umpire) "Cy." Origin unknown.

2825. Pfyl, Meinhard Charles (1907 1B) "Monte." "Monte" was used as an alternative to Meinhard, and was a more acceptable baseball name.

2826. Phelan, Arthur Thomas (1910–15 3B) "Dugan." Origin unknown.

2827. Phelps, Ernest Gordon (1931–42 C) "Blimp." Phelps was a large man at 6'2" and during the latter part of his carrer weighed over 250 pounds. He was addressed as "Babe" which denoted his power hitting in the minor leagues and reminded fans of "Babe" Ruth.

2828. Phillippe, Charles Lewis (1899–1911 P) "Deacon." Phillippe had a sedate personality. As Fred Lieb put it, he went about winning 186 games in the major leagues "unostentatiously." He was the best control pitcher of his era. He walked just 363 batters in 2,607 innings. In 1910 he walked only nine batters in 123 innings. In an iron-man performance, he pitched 50 innings in the 1903 World Series and walked only five batters.

2829. Phillips, Albert Abernathy (1930 P) "Buzz." "Buzz" denotes the sound of Phillips' fastball which he was able to throw in only 14 games in the major leagues. However, in 13 times at bat Phillips made 6 hits for a .462 career average including a home run.

2830. Phillips, Clarence Lemual (1934–36 P) "Red." The nickname refers to hair color.

2831. Phillips, Damon Roswell (1942–46 3B) "Dee." Phillips wrote me, "In 1938 my brother Joe and I were playing on the same team. The box score read D. Phillips and J. Phillips. In writing a story, sportswriter Richard Oliver of Ft. Henderson, Texas, added two 'e's' to the 'D' in the box score."

2832. Phillips, Jack Dorn (1947–57 1B) "Stretch." Phillips received his nickname while playing at Norfolk in 1943, because at 6'4" he had a long stretch at first base.

2833. Phillips, John Melvin (1955–64 OF) "Bubba." "Bubba" was a childhood nickname. His brother mispronounced "brother."

2834. Phillips, William Corcoran (1890–1903 P) "Whoa Bill." "Whoa" is the term called when you want a horse to stop. When Phillips was on the mound, he stopped the other team. Because of his grey-white hair, he was also known as "Silver Bill."

2835. Piatt, Wiley Harold (1898–1903 P) "Iron Man." Piatt completed 139 of the 170 games he started as a pitcher. In 1898 as a rookie he won 24 games and lost 14, while pitching 306 innings.

2836. Pickering, Urbane Henry (1931–32 3B) "Dick." Origin unknown.

2837. Pickup, Clarence William (1918 OF) "Ty." Origin unknown.

2838. Picone, Mario Peter (1947–54 P) "Babe." Origin unknown.

2839. Pierce, Raymond Lester (1924–26 P) "Lefty." Pierce pitched left handed and batted left handed.

2840. Piercy, William Benton (1917–26 P) "Wild Bill." Piercy lacked control as a pitcher. In his six-year career, he walked 266 batters while striking out 165.

2841. Pieretti, Marino Paul (1945–50 P) "Chick." Pieretti was called "Chick" and "Pee Wee" because of his size, 5'7" and 150 pounds.

2842. Pierro, William Leonard (1950 P) "Wild Bill." Pierro told me there were two reasons for his nickname. First, he had difficulty finding the plate. Second, "I also had quite a temper and would start a fight at the drop of a hat."

2843. Pierson, William Morris (1918–24 P) "Wild Bill." Pierson lacked control on the mound. In 32 innings pitched in the major leagues, he walked 31 batters while striking out 10.

2844. Piet, Anthony Francis (1931–38 2B) "Tony the Silent." The nickname was given to him by third base teammate "Pie" Traynor, because Piet whooped it up in a boisterous way during the course of games, but seldom spoke off the playing field.

2845. Pieth, Edwin John (1913–15 P) "Cy." Pieth reminded fans of Denton "Cy" Young.

2846. Piey, Charles William (1914 OF) "Sandy." The nickname refers to light hair color.

2847. Pillette, Duane Xavier (1949–56 P) "Dee." Pillette told me, "I grew up in an era when players called their teammates by their initials. Mine are DX. That didn't work so they called me big 'D' and in the newspapers it came out 'Dee.'"

2848. Pillette, Herman Polycarp (1917–24 P) "Old Folks." Joseph McBride suggests that "Old Folks" refers to Pillette's longevity.

2849. Pillion, Cecil Randolph (1915 P) "Squiz." Origin unknown.

2850. Pinelli, Ralph Arthur (1918–27 3B; NL Umpire 1935–56) "Babe." At 10 years old in San Francisco, Pinelli would try to play ball with his older brother Orlando and his friends. When told to go home, "I'd start to bawl and wail at the top of my lungs. I must have had good lungs. 'Ah,' someone would say in disgust, 'let the cry-baby come along.' That's how I got the nickname 'Babe.'" Eight years after his retirement as an active player, Pinelli returned to the major leagues as a National League umpire in 1935 and became one of the most respected "men in blue" through 1956.

2851. Piniella, Louis Victor (1964–84 OF) "Sweet." The nickname referred to Piniella's swing not his personality. His childhood nickname, which he inherited from his father, was "Scrappy, Jr."

2852. Pipgrass, George William (1923–35 P) "Danish Viking." Pipgrass was of Danish background.

2853. Pippen, Henry Harold (1936–40 P) "Cotton." "Cotton" refers to light blond hair color.

2854. Pitko, Alexander (1938 OF) "Spunk." Pitko told me the nickname came from his brother who thought he was a feisty kid.

2855. Pitlock, Lee Patrick Thomas (1970–75 P) "Skip." Pitlock told me he gave himself the nickname just before he enrolled at Southern Illinois University. "I decided I wanted a more athletic name."

2856. Pittenger, Clarke Alonzo (1921–29 SS) "Pinky." Origin unknown.

2857. Pittinger, Charles Reno (1900–07 P) "Togie." According to Fred Lieb, his real nickname was "Horse Face." It was the product of baseball writer and later president of the Philadelphia Phils, Horace Fogal. When a lady wrote into the newspaper asking Fogal not to use the nickname, he wrote back, "Lady, can I help it if he looks like a horse?"

2858. Plant, Edward Stewart (1901–17 P) "Gettysburg Eddie." If ever a player deserved a place nickname it was this Hall of Fame pitcher who won

327 major league games during his 17-year career. Plank was born and raised and died in Gettysburg, Pennsylvania. He attended Gettysburg College and in the off season was a guide at the Gettysburg Civil War battlefield.

2859. Platt, Mizell George (1942–49 OF) "Whitey." The nickname refers to hair color.

2860. Podbielan, Clarence Anthony (1949–59 P) "Bud." "Bud" was a childhood nickname given to Podbielan by his parents.

2861. Podgajny, John Sigmund (1940–46 P) "Specs." Podgajny wore glasses while on the diamond.

2862. Poffenberger, Cletus Elwood (1937–39 P) "Boots." In the three seasons he was in the major leagues, Poffenberger never learned to field his position.

2863. Poindexter, Chester Jennings (1936–39 P) "Jinx." Poindexter was addressed as Jennings. "Jinx" is an interesting combination of letters from his names, probably prompted by the "x" in Poindexter.

2864. Pointer, Aaron Elton (1963–67 OF) "Hawk." Pointer wrote me, "I was called 'Hawk' because of my aggressive play in the outfield for the Houston Astros. I believe it was Jo Morgan who used it first."

2865. Polhemus, Mark L. (1887 P) "Humpty Dumpty." Origin unknown.

2866. Polivka, Kenneth Lyle (1947 P) "Soup." Polivka told me his name means soup in Bohemian.

2867. Polli, Louis Americo (1932–44 P) "Crip." Polli wrote me, "I got hurt playing football in prep school and was on crutches for two weeks. Other players began calling me 'cripple.' Finally, it was shortened to 'Crip.' It has been that way ever since. Most people think it is my first name."

2868. Pool, Harlin Weltz (1934–35 OF) "Sampson." "Sampson" refers to Pool's unusual strength.

2869. Poole, James Ralph (1925–27 1B) "Easy." "Easy" refers to Poole's agreeable personality.

2870. Porter, Andrew (1932–50 P, Negro League) "Pullman." "Pullman" was a response to the last name of Porter. At the time Porter played, many blacks held jobs as porters on railroad Pullman or sleeping cars.

2871. Porter, J.W. (1952–59 C) "Jay." Porter only had initials for his given names. The "J" came out "Jay" in newspaper stories.

2872. Porter, Odie Oscar (1902 P) "Jim." "Jim" was used as a more suitable baseball name than Odie.

2873. Porter, Richard Twilley (1929–34 OF) "Twitchy." Especially in the outfield, Porter could not remain still. He was always moving. Therefore, players and fans alike called him "Twitchy" and "Wiggles."

2874. Porterfield, Erwin Collidge (1948–59 P) "Bob." Porterfield was nicknamed "Bob" by his father when he was six years old and has been known as "Bob" throughout his life.

2875. Porto, Alfred (1948 P) "Lefty." Porto pitched left handed and batted left handed.

2876. Posalla, Leopoldo Jesus (1960–62 OF) "Popy." "Popy" is simply a play on the first and last names and is an alternative to Leopoldo.

2877. Posedel, William John (1938–46 P) "Sailor." Posedel spent time in the navy before he entered organized baseball. He was also called "Barnacle Bill" for the same reason, the reference being to the song written by Hoagy Carmichael, "Barnacles Bill the Sailor." During WWII, Posedel spent another four years in the navy. Two other nicknames indicating his experience in the navy were "Porthole" and "Chief." After his playing career, Posedel became a pitching coach for seven major league teams until his retirement in 1974.

2878. Pott, Nelson Adolph (1922 P) "Lefty." Pott pitched left handed and batted left handed. He pitched two innings in the major leagues and allowed seven hits and seven runs.

2879. Powell, John Wesley (1961–77 1B) "Boog." The nickname was the product of a childhood word for one that gets into mischief. While Powell had an outstanding major league career highlighted by 339 home runs and participation in five American League Championship Series and four World Series, he is probably best known today for his appearances in Miller beer TV commercials.

2880. Powell, Raymond Reath (1913–24 OF) "Rabbit." "Rabbit" refers to Powell's speed on the base paths as well as in the outfield.

2881. Powers, Ellis Foree (1932–33 P) "Mike." For no particular reason, except it was a better baseball name than Ellis, Powers was addressed by the nickname of "Mike."

2882. Powers, John Lloyd (1927–28 P) "Ike." Origin unknown.

2883. Powers, Michael Rily (1898–1909 C) "Doc." Powers was a physician who died a tragic death. He started his eleventh season in the majors catching for Connie Mack's Philadelphia A's, but played in only one game. Fred Lieb describes Powers untimely and painful demise. "On April 26, 1909, whether it resulted from crouching behind the plate, Mike's intestines became locked, so that nutrition could not reach his vital organs. Physicians at Philadelphia's Northwestern Hospital said the popular catcher starved to death." On August 5, 1905, Powers caught for New York Yankee pitcher, Eustace "Doc" Newton. It may have been the only all-physician battery in major league history.

2884. Powers, Philip J. (1878–85 C) "Grandmother." Origin unknown.

2885. Powis, Carl Edgar (1957 OF) "Jug." Origin unknown.

2886. Pratt, Francis Bruce (1921 PH) "Truckhorse." Origin unknown.

2887. Preibisch, Melvin Adolphus (1940–41 OF) "Primo." "Primo" is just a play on the last name and a more acceptable baseball name than Melvin.

2888. Prendergast, Michael Thomas (1914–19 P) "Iron Mike." Origin unknown.

2889. Prentiss, George Pepper (1901–02 P) "Kitten." Origin unknown.

2890. Prescott, George Bertrand (1961 OF) "Bobby." Origin unknown.

2891. Presko, Joseph Edward (1951–58 P) "Little Joe." Presko was 5'9½" and weighed 165 pounds.

2892. Pressnell, Forest Charles (1938–42 P) "Tot." Pressnell wrote me, "My mother gave me that name when I was born because I was so small. I was also the youngest of eight children and my mother called me her little tot."

2893. Price, Joseph Preston (1928 OF) "Lumber." "Lumber" refers to Price's bat. In 1921 for Johnson City, Tennessee, in the Appalachian League, Price led the circuit in batting average .363; total bases, 185; and home runs, 18. Although he had the reputation as a slugger, Price carried the "Lumber" to the plate only once in the major leagues and struck out.

2894. Prichard, Harold William (1957 1B) "Buddy." Prichard told me, "My uncle was named 'Bud.' So he became 'Big Bud' and I was 'Little Bud.' It was when I was about six years old."

2895. Prim, Raymond Lee (1933–46 P) "Pop." Prim pitched for Washington and the Philadelphia Phils in 1933–35 winning three games and dropping seven. He did not reappear for ten years, when at the age of 38 he was recalled by the war-time Chicago Cubs. He was called "Pop" and "Pappy" as his 13-8 record helped the Cubs to the National League flag.

2896. Prince, Robert (1948–75 Broadcaster) "Gunner." Prince was the longtime well-liked voice of the Pittsburgh Pirates. He was nicknamed "Gunner" early in his career when the husband of a woman he was talking to in a bar pulled a gun on him.

2897. Proctor, Noah Richard (1923 P) "Red." Refers to hair color.

2898. Proeser, George (1888–90 OF) "Yats." Origin unknown.

2899. Prothro, James Thompson (1920–26 3B) "Doc." Prothro was a practicing dentist.

2900. Prough, Herschell Clinton (1912 P) "Bill." Prough pitched only three innings in the major leagues allowing seven hits and two runs. The origin of "Bill" is unknown.

2901. Prudhomme, John Olgus (1929 P) "Augie." "Augie" is a play on the name of Olgus.

2902. Pruess, Earl Henry (1920 OF) "Gibby." Origin unknown.

2903. Pruett, Hubert Shelby (1922–32 P) "Shucks." "Shucks" was the strongest expression Pruett ever used in public. In 1922 as a rookie, he faced Babe Ruth 21 times and struck him out 13 times, 10 times in the first 13 times at bat.

2904. Pruiett, Charles LeRoy (1907–08 P) "Tex." Pruiett was not from the state of Texas, but picked up his nickname by pitching in the Texas League before he came to the major leagues.

2905. Pruitt, Ronald Ralph (1975–83 C) "Do It." Pruitt was generally regarded as a flake. Name it and he would do it. While playing for Cleveland he once stood for the national anthem with a two-foot cone-head mask on his head.

2906. Puccinelli, George Lawrence (1930–36 OF) "Count." There is no mention in the literature of "Count" being used as a nickname for Puccinelli. He was, however, called "Pooch," which is a takeoff on the last name.

2907. Purcell, William Aloysius (1879–90 OF) "Blondie." The nickname refers to hair color.

2908. Purdy, Everrett Virgil (1926–29 OF) "Pid." According to Lee Allen, "Pid" referred to Purdy's diminutive size, 5'6" and 150 pounds.

2909. Purnell, Jessie Rhodes (1904 3B) "Scrappy." Purnell had the reputation of a tough, hard-as-nails ball player.

2910. Purtell, William Patrick (1908–14 3B) "The Child Athlete." According to Tom Shea, when Purtell first arrived on the major league scene he had an extremely youthful appearance.

2911. Pyle, Harlan Albert (1928 P) "Firpo." Pyle reminded people of heavyweight boxer Luis Firpo.

2912. Pyle, Harry Thomas (1884–87 P) "Shadow." At 5'8" and 136 pounds, Pyle looked like a shadow as he pitched.

2913. Pyle, Herbert Ewald (1939–45 P) "Lefty." Pyle pitched left handed and batted left handed.

Q

2914. Qualters, Thomas Francis (1953–58 P) "Money Bags." Qualters was one of the bonus babies of the 1950s that never made good. He never won a major league game and he never lost one in 34 appearances over three years. "Money Bags" was a newspaper nickname referring to his bonus status. He told me his real nickname was "Country" given to him by Satchel Paige when he was with Miami. "Country" denoted what Paige called his "two borough stride" when he pitched.

2915. Quarles, William H. (1891–93 P) "The Virginia Grapevine." Bill was born and raised in Petersburg, Virginia. According to an article in *The Boston Globe*, 06/12/1891, the nickname comes from his pitching style in which he raised his left leg up when he was ready to pitch.

2916. Queen, Billy Eddleman (1954 OF) "Doc." Queen wrote me, "I was named after our family doctor whose name was Eddleman, the same as my middle name. So they started calling me 'Doc'."

2917. Quilici, Frank Ralph (1965–70 2B) "Guido." *The Baseball Register* of 1970 reports that Billie Martin, manager of the Minnesota Twins in 1969, gave Frank the nickname because of his Italian background. He also called him "Dago." However, Quilici's own account is quite different. He wrote me, "'Guido' is the Italian pronunciation of 'guy.' It was my Dad's nickname. Ted Uhlaender gave it to me at my first winter league team in St. Petersburg, Florida, in 1961. The players knew I was from Chicago. They thought it fit."

2918. Quinlan, Thomas Aloysius (1913–15 OF) "Finners." Origin unknown.

2919. Quinn, John Edward (1911 C) "Pitt." Origin unknown.

2920. Quinn, Wellington Hunt (1941 P) "Wimpy." Allen reports that Quinn was nicknamed after the cartoon character "J. Wellington Wimpy."

2921. Radatz, Richard Raymond (1962–69 P) "The Monster." Radatz was a 6'6", 230-pound fireballing relief pitcher for the Boston Red Sox when he received the nickname of "The Monster" from opposing batters. In 1963, he won 15 games in relief and saved 25. The next year, he increased his totals to 16 wins and 29 saves.

2922. Radbourn, Charles Gardner (1880–91 P) "Old Hoss." Radbourn was called "Old Hoss" because, like a faithful horse, he was always ready to pitch when the manager gave the word. In 1884, between August 7 and September 6, the Providence Grays won 20 straight games and "Old Hoss" pitched 18 of them. He completed the 1884 season with a 60-12 won-lost record with an Earned Run Average of 1.38.

2923. Radbourne, George B. (1883 P) "Dordy." Origin unknown.

2924. Radcliff, Raymond Allen (1934–43 OF) "Rip." Radcliff had a career batting average of .311 in the major leagues. "Rip" was short for "Ripper" and referred to his hitting ability.

2925. Radcliffe, Theodore (1928–50 C, Negro League) "Double Duty." Although Radcliffe was primarily a catcher, he also pitched. He was called "Double Duty" after a double-header played in Yankee Stadium in 1932 when he caught Satchel Paige's shutout in the first game, and then pitched a shutout himself in the second game. According to Radcliffe, it was writer Damon Runyon who was first responsible for the nickname.

2926. Rader, Douglas Lee (1976–77 3B) "The Red Rooster." For a man of 6'2", 210 pounds, Radar was very quick and agile. He wore his hair long. A shock of his brownish red mane protruded from the back of his cap. Teammates on the Houston Astros thought he looked like the cartoon character "Foghorn Leghorn." The "Red Rooster" tag was reinforced by Rader's fiery temperament and head-first style of play. He was also addressed as "Rojo."

2927. Rader, Drew Leon (1921 P) "Lefty." Raderbaugh pitched left handed but he batted right handed.

2928. Raether, Harold Herman (1954–57 P) "Bud." Raether said his mother gave him the nickname of "Bud" at a very early age, because he was a buddy to his brother.

2929. Ragan, Arthur Edgar (1903 P) "Rip." Origin unknown.

2930. Rakow, Edward Charles (1960–67 P) "Rock." According to his listing in the 1960 *Baseball Register*, "Rock" is just a takeoff on the last name of Rakow.

2931. Ralson, Samuel Beryl (1916 OF) "Doc." Many of the players with the nickname of "Doc" had a close association with either the medical or dental professions. However, in the case of Ralson, the origin of "Doc" is unknown.

2932. Rambert, Elmer Donald (1939–40 P) "Pep." In Rambert's case, "Pep" refers to his enthusiastic play.

2933. Rambo, Warren Dawson (1926 P) "Pete." Rambo wrote me that his father gave him the nickname of "Pete" as a young boy. He went on to add that it was quite common for boys to be nicknamed "Pete" in his hometown of Thoroughfare, New Jersey.

2934. Ramos, Jesus Manuel Garcia (1944 OF) "Chucko." Origin unknown.

2935. Ramos, Pedro Guerra (1955–70 P) "Pete." In Ramos' case, "Pete" is a baseball alternative to Pedro.

2936. Ramsdell, James Willard (1947–52 P) "Willie the Knuck." Ramsdell relied heavily on a knuckleball to carry him through five major league seasons with a 24-39 won-loss record.

2937. Ramsey, Thomas A. (1885–90 P) "Toad." There is no mention in the limited literature on Ramsey that he had any physical characteristics or behavioral characteristics which would remind one of a toad. Although the exact origin of "Toad" is unknown, my guess is that it was no more than a take off on Thomas, that is, "Toad" rather than Tom.

2938. Ramsey, William Thrace (1945 OF) "Square Jaw." Teammates perceived Ramsey to have the physical characteristic of a jaw more square-looking than normal.

2939. Randman, Robert Joyce (1966–67 OF) "Shorty." The nickname refers to height. Randman was 5'9½".

2940. Raney, Frank Robert Donald (1885–90 P) "Ribs." Raney wrote me, "When I was 14 years old, I was 6'4" and weighed 150 pounds. We always played ball with our shirts off and all the kids could see my ribs."

2941. Rapp, Joseph Aloysius (1921–23 3B) "Goldie." The nickname refers to light blond hair color.

2942. Rariden, William Angel (1909–20 C) "Bedford Bill." This is a place nickname. Rariden was born and raised in Bedford, Indiana.

2943. Raschi, Victor John Angelo (1946–55 P) "The Springfield Rifle." Raschi was born in West Springfield, Massachusetts. Thus this is an example of a place nickname. Raschi was a fastball pitcher which in part accounts for the "Rifle" portion of the nickname. This is reinforced by the fact that Springfield, Massachusetts, was the site where the famous Springfield Rifle was developed and manufactured. As a New York Yankee, Raschi pitched in five World Series, started eight games, and won five while dropping three.

2944. Rasmussen, Henry Florian (1915 PH) "Hans." The nickname refers to Rasmussen's German background.

2945. Rautzhan, Clarence George (1977–79 P) "Lance." Rautzhan told me he was named Clarence after his grandfather. The day after he was born his mother thought Clarence was too long and nicknamed him "Lance," and he has been called that ever since.

2946. Ray, Irving Burton (1888–91 SS) "Stubby." Ray was 5'6". There is no data available on his weight.

2947. Ray, James Francis (1965–74 P) "Sting." "Sting" in Ray's case does not refer to his pitching, but simply fits with his last name.

2948. Rayford, Floyd Kinnard (1980–87 3B) "Sugar Bear." His stocky build reminded teammates of the "Sugar Bear" character.

2949. Raymond, Arthur Lawrence (1904–11 P) "Bugs." Raymond was an alcoholic. While under the influence he was know to engage in many strange behaviors. It was said he would drink any type of alcoholic beverage as long as it came in a bottle. "Bugs" refers to his strange behavior while drinking. There is, however, a specific story related to how the nickname may have originated. After a brief stint with Detroit in 1904, Raymond was back in the minor leagues. In 1906, Raymond was dropped by the Atlanta Crackers of the Southern Association for drinking. He attempted to get a contract from the Savannah club of the South Atlantic League who was having a poor season. When the club was reluctant to sign him, he was reported to have said, "I shall pitch Savannah to the pennant." He was signed, won 18 games, and Savannah did, in fact, win the pennant. It was Raymond's crazy boast which led to the nickname of "Bugs."

2950. Raymond, Joseph Claude Marc (1959–71 P) "Frenchy." The nickname refers to Raymond's French Canadian background. He was born in St. Jean, Quebec, Canada. "Frenchy" was what fellow players began to call him at West Palm Beach, Florida, in 1955.

2951. Reardon, Jeffrey James (1979– P) "The Terminator." Reardon as a relief pitcher specializes in saving games in the late innings. He terminates the opposition and the game.

2952. Reardon, John E. (1926–49 NL Umpire) "Beans." Larry Gerlach reports the "Beans" tag came from an incident when Reardon was still in his teens. During a noon-hour game at the Southern Pacific Railroad shops, Lee Allen, a fancy Pullman car painter, yelled, "Come on Baked Beans, old boy, hit one now!" The crowd picked it up and from then on Reardon was "Beans." As an umpire, Reardon made a practice of fraternizing with fans in the stands. His slogan was, "Never too busy to say hello."

2953. Reberger, Frank Beall (1968–72 P) "Crane." With a long neck, and at 6'5", weighing 200 pounds, Reberger reminded fans of a crane when he pitched.

2954. Rector, Connie (1920–41 P, Negro League) "Broadway." Usually "Broadway" refers to fancy dress, but in Rector's case, I cannot document this.

2955. Redding, Richard (1911–38 P, Negro League) "Cannonball." Redding was noted for the overpowering speed of his fastball. He developed a hesitation pitch long before Satchel Paige did, and it was different from Paige's. Balancing on his right foot, Redding, a right handed hurler, would show his back to the batter for a couple of seconds before uncovering one of his blazing fastballs. The maneuver was a sure crowd pleaser. In 1912 with the touring Lincoln Giants, he pitched a perfect game with 17 strike-outs against the Jersey City Skeeters. In that same year, he struck out 24 batters in a game against a team of minor leaguers called "All Leaguers."

2956. Redfern, George Howard (1928–29 2B) "Buck." "Buck" is a generic nickname of which the circumstances of origin are almost never documented. It refers to a well developed, virile, aggressive, high spirited young man. The nickname is usually bestowed on the individual during his teenage years.

2957. Redmond, John McKittrick, Jr. (1935 C) "Red." The nickname refers to hair color.

2958. Redus, Wilson (1934–40 OF, Negro League) "Frog." Redus was just

5'5" and weighed only 155 pounds. His looks reminded people of a frog. His life time average was .323 and in 1926 he hit a career high of .393 for the St. Louis Stars.

2959. Reed, Howard Dean (1958–71 P) "Diz." Reed was an All American pitcher at the University of Texas. The hard throwing right hander reminded people of "Dizzy" Dean.

2960. Reed, John Burwell (1961–63 OF) "Mickey Mantle's Caddy." Reed was a reserve outfielder for the New York Yankees who finished the last inning or two for Mickey Mantle in the outfield when the Yanks had the lead.

2961. Reeder, James Edward (1884 OF) "Icicle." Origin unknown.

2962. Reese, Harold Henry (1940–58 SS) "Pee Wee." In his youth, Reese was a champion marble shooter. A type of marble is called a "Pee Wee." Reese was also called "The Little Colonel" even though he was 5'10". Colonel is of the Kentucky type. Reese was born in Elkon, Kentucky, and in 1939, he led the Louisville Colonels to the American Association pennant. Reese, a Hall of Fame shortstop, played in seven World Series for the Brooklyn Dodgers.

2963. Reeves, Robert Edwin (1926–31 3B) "Gunner." According to Tom Shea, Reeves had a "bazooka for an arm" throwing from third base.

2964. Regan, Philip Raymond (1960–72 P) "The Vulture." Regan was nicknamed by Sandy Koufax after Regan relieved Koufax in the eleventh inning of a 1–1 game and came away with an easy victory. Another account has it that about the same situation existed in a game that Don Drysdale was pitching. In the 1960s, pitchers began calling a save, a "Vultch." A relief pitcher who comes in late in a game and relieves a save or gets a victory is picking over the carcass of the starting pitcher.

2965. Reiber, Frank Bernard (1933–36 C) "Tubby." Although he is listed at 5'8½" and 169 pounds in baseball encyclopedias, Reiber played at a much expanded weight.

2966. Reilley, Alexander Aloysius (1909 OF) "Midget." Reilley was 5'4½" and weighed 148 pounds. He was also called "Duke" because of his snappy dress.

2967. Reilly, Charles Thomas (1889–97 3B) "Princeton Charlie." Reilly was born in New Brunswick, New Jersey, and attended Princeton University. According to Lee Allen, on April 29, 1892, Reilly was sent in to bat for Philadelphia teammate, Kid Carsey in the ninth inning of a game against Chicago, and became the first major league pinch hitter.

2968. Reilly, John Good (1880–91 1B) "Long John." Reilly was a first baseman with long arms and reach. He was 6'3" and weighed 178 pounds.

2969. Reiser, Harold Patrick (1940–52 OF) "Pistol Pete." Reiser was considered one of the great natural talents of baseball. He could run, throw, hit and field with the best of his era. When he first came up to the Brooklyn Dodgers in 1940, he played in two games in which he went seven for seven and was on base 11 straight times. Newspaper reports called him "Pistol Pete." The reference was to a movie serial called "Two Gun Pete." In 1941, his first full year in the majors, Reiser led the National League in hitting with a .343 average. His potential was diminished greatly in future years by his propensity to injure himself by running into outfield walls attempting to catch fly balls.

2970. Reisigl, Jacob (1911 P) "Bugs." According to his relatives, Reisigl was called "Jack." There is no mention in the literature of "Bugs."

2971. Reising, Charles (1884 OF) "Pop." Reising played but two games in the major leagues. Little is known about him or his career, not even his birthdate or how he batted or threw. The origin of the nickname is also unknown.

2972. Reisling, Frank Carl (1904–10 P) "Doc." Reisling was a practicing dentist.

2973. Reitz, Henry P. (1893–99 2B) "Heinie." The nickname refers to Reitz's German background.

2974. Reitz, Kenneth John (1972–82 3B) "The Zamboni Machine." The Zamboni is a machine that cleans the ice at hockey arenas and sucks water from artificial turf at baseball parks. Reitz earned his nickname by fielding everything hit at him at third base.

2975. Rementer, Willis J.H. (1904 C) "Butch." Rementer caught only one game in the major leagues. "Butch" was a childhood nickname.

2976. Remmerswall, Wilhelmus Abraham (1979–80 P) "Win." Remmerswall was born in the Hague Netherlands. He told me he was nicknamed after the English statesman, Winston Churchill, but the Winston was shortened to "Win."

2977. Reniff, Harold Eugene (1961–67 P) "Porky." "Porky" refers to Reniff's build. He was 6'0" weighing 215 pounds.

2978. Renna, William Beneditto (1953–59 OF) "Big Bill." Renna was 6'3" and weighed 218 pounds.

2979. Rennert, Laurence H. (1973–88 NL Umpire) "Dutch." Rennert wrote me, "Dutch was a good old German nickname in Wisconsin. Kids in Oshkosh, Wisconsin, heard the name 'Dutch' used for the Cubs pitcher Leonard. To them it sounded like Rennert. So they started calling me that when I was about 8 or 9 years old."

2980. Rensa, Tony George (1930–39 C) "Pug." Origin unknown.

2981. Repulski, Eldon John (1953–61 OF) "Rip." Repulski had quick hands and wrists. When he hit, he ripped at the ball.

2982. Rescigno, Xavier Frederick (1943–45 P) "Mr. X." "Mr. X" is just a takeoff on the first name of Xavier.

2983. Restelli, Dino Paul (1949–51 OF) "Dingo." Restelli wrote me, "In 1946, when I was playing with the San Francisco Seals, a lady who had a few too many beers was sitting right back of the dugout. When I came to bat in the 6th inning, she was a little tongue-tied, and said, 'come on Dingo, get a hit!' The team heard it, thought it was funny and started using it. Some of my close family still use it today."

2984. Rettig, Adolph John (1922 P) "Otto." The nickname denotes Rettig's German background.

2985. Reulback, Edward Marvin (1905–17 P) "Big Ed." Reulback was 6'1" and weighed 190 pounds. The nickname was reinforced by his sound pitching. In his 13-year career, Reulback had a 181-105 won-lost record with an ERA of 2.28. He pitched in four World Series for the Chicago National League team, winning two games without a loss. On September 26, 1908, Reulback pitched the morning game of a doubleheader and shutout Brooklyn 5-0. In the afternoon game, he again pitched a shutout winning 3–0. It is the only time in major league history a pitcher tossed a shutout doubleheader.

2986. Reuschel, Rickey Eugene (1972 P) "Big Daddy." In the latter stages of his career in the late 1980s, San Francisco Giant teammates began to refer to Reuschel as "Big Daddy." The reference is to his age, experience, good pitching and size. Reuschel is 6'3" and weighs about 240 pounds.

2987. Reynolds, Alle Pierce (1942–54 P) "Superchief." Reynolds was of American Indian background, which accounts for the "Chief" portion of the nickname. "Super" refers to his pitching. Reynolds posted a 182-107 won-lost record in 13 seasons. In addition, he pitched in six World Series for the New York Yankees, winning seven games and saving four others.

2988. Reynolds, Bob (1958–? Broadcaster) "Horse." Reynolds earned his nickname playing 60-minute tackle for Stanford in three straight Rose Bowls, 1934–36. But the nickname fit perfectly when he teamed with Gene Autry, whose nickname was "Cowboy," in broadcasting Dodger baseball games over Los Angeles station KMPC.

2989. Reynolds, Daniel Vance (1945 SS) "Squirrel." Reynolds reported to me that he was nicknamed by sportswriter Tommy Clark, of Martinsville, Virginia, when he first broke into professional baseball. Clark thought he was very fast.

2990. Reynolds, Robert Allen (1969–75 P) "Bullet Bob." Reynolds' best pitch was a blazing fastball.

2991. Reynolds, Robert James (1983 P) "R.J." "R.J." is a nickname made up of the initials of Reynolds' name.

2992. Rhawn, Robert John (1947–49 3B) "Rocky." Origin unknown.

2993. Rheam, Kenneth Johnson (1914–15 1B) "Cy." Origin unknown.

2994. Rhem, Charles Flint (1924–36 P) "Shad." Rhem was from the moonshine county of Rhems, South Carolina. He told the story about the shad fish coming up the river so many times, that town folk started calling him "Shad." Flint, as he was addressed, was a hard drinker. One time before a game, he was supposed to pitch, he brought a pick out to the mound and started slashing at the hard dirt. He had to be removed from the mound and led to the showers before the game ever started and he had thrown a pitch.

2995. Rhodes, James Lamar (1952–59 OF) "Dusty." The use of the nickname of "Dusty" for people with the last name of Rhodes goes back at least 300 years in England, when roads were indeed dusty. This Rhodes was nicknamed by scout Bruce Hays, when he signed his first professional contract. Rhodes is probably best remembered for hitting two home runs and driving in seven runs in three games of the 1954 World Series for the New York Giants.

2996. Rhodes, John Gordon (1929–36 P) "Dusty." "Dusty" is a common nickname for anyone with the last name of Rhodes.

2997. Rhodes, Robert Barton (1902–09 P) "Dusty." "Dusty" is a common nickname for anyone with the last name of Rhodes.

2998. Rhodes, William Clarence (1893 P) "Dusty." "Dusty" is a common nickname for anyone with the last name of Rhodes.

2999. Rice, Edgar Charles (1915–24 OF) "Sam." Rice was one of the premier hitters of his day, compiling a .322 batting average over 20 seasons and .302 in three World Series. Lowell Reidenbaugh provides the classic account of how Rice received the nickname of "Sam." One afternoon in 1915, Clark Griffith announced to the Washington press that the Senators had acquired a player by the name of Rice from the Petersburg Club of the Virginia League, which had just folded. "What's Rice's first name?" a journalist wondered. Without hesitation and hiding the fact he had no idea of the correct answer, the president-manager of the Nats blurted, "Sam." In such a fashion was born a nickname Edgar Charles Rice carried for the remainder of his days. Morris Bealle points out that when Rice stole 33 bases in 1917, newspapers referred to him as "Man of War" after the great race horse.

3000. Rice, Harold Housten (1948–54 OF) "Hoot." Rice's brother is responsible for the nickname "Hoot," which is a takeoff on the middle name of Housten.

3001. Rice, John L. (1955–73 AL Umpire) "Mayor Daily." Tom Gorman writes, "We used to call Rice 'Mayor Daily.' His resemblance to the late Chicago mayor was remarkable. He could have been his twin brother."

3002. Richard, James Rodney (1971–80 P) "J.R." Richard's nickname was no more than his initials. He was also called "Bee" referring to the speed of his fastball. In 1977 and 1978, he led the National League in strike outs, with 303 and 313, respectively. Tragically, his career was ended by illness in 1980.

3003. Richard, Lee Edward (1971–76 SS) "Bee Bee." Richard was a pitcher in high school. It was said he threw so fast the ball looked like a BB coming up to the plate.

3004. Richards, Fred Charles (1951 1B) "Fuzzy." Richards told me his parents nicknamed him "Fuzzy" at an early age because he had white fuzz all over his body.

3005. Richardson, Abram Harding (1897–92 2B) "Old True Blue." While playing for Buffalo 1879–85, the team first wore blue uniforms on the road, and later blue pants at home. The nickname, however, refers to Richardson's all-around team play and his ability to come through in the clutch.

3006. Richmond, Raymond Sinclair (1920–21 P) "Bud." "Bud" was a childhood nickname.

3007. Rickert, Joseph Francis (1898–1901 OF) "Diamond Joe." In his hey day, Rickert was a fan idol and was often the recipient of gifts. One such gift was a diamond stickpin, which resulted in his moniker, "Diamond Joe."

3008. Rickert, Marvin August (1942–50 OF) "Twitch." Origin unknown.

3009. Rickey, Wesley Branch (1905–14 C) "The Mahatma." Branch as he was commonly called, had an undistinguished career as a major league ball player playing a total of 119 games in the years of 1905–07, and 1914. As a catcher he once allowed 13 stolen bases in a single game. Between 1913 and 1925, he managed both the St. Louis Browns and St. Louis Cardinals for a total of ten years with no better than two third place finishes and an overall winning percentage of .473. Rickey's major contributions to baseball were made as an executive with the St. Louis Cardinals and Brooklyn Dodgers. He was an astute business man called the "smartest man in baseball" and the "best salesman." It was he who developed the farm systems of minor league teams, Ladies Day at the ball park and Knot-Hole Gangs for youngsters. By signing Jackie Robinson to a contract in the Brooklyn organization in 1946, Rickey opened the door for black baseball players in organized baseball. Rickey was a thinker and fine speaker who always thought he had something important to say. He liked to lecture players individually and collectively using catchy phrases and parables which often were over their heads. In fact, he appeared most happy when he was pontificating. During the early 1940s, Rickey reminded sportswriters of India's orator-statesman-pacifist, Mahatma Gandhi, and they began to refer to him in print as "The Mahatma."

3010. Rico, Alfredo Curz (1969 OF) "Fred the Barber." Rico began to cut teammates hair for them, and later became a hair stylist.

3011. Riddle, John Ludy (1930–48 C) "Mutt." Origin unknown.

3012. Riebe, Harvey Donald (1942–49 C) "Hank." Riebe wrote me, "In 1940, during my second year in pro-ball in Muskegon, Michigan, a sportswriter named Henderson didn't like using Harvey in his columns and decided to use Hank instead. It was Hank from then on."

3013. Rigler, Charles (1905–22, 1924–35 NL Umpire) "Cy." The origin of "Cy" is unknown. Rigler is usually credited with being the first umpire to raise his right hand to indicate a strike.

3014. Rigney, Emory Elmo (1922–27 SS) "Topper." Origin unknown.

3015. Rigney, William Joseph (1946–51 2B) "Specs." Rigney wore eyeglasses while playing in an era when it was still unusual to do so. He was also called "The Cricket" for the manner in which he hopped around playing second base.

3016. Rile, Ed (1920–30 P, Negro League) "Huck." Origin unknown.

3017. Riley, William James (1879 OF) "Pigtail Billy." Riley wore his hair with a pigtail in back.

3018. Risberg, Charles August (1917–20 SS) "Swede." The nickname refers to Risberg's Swedish background. Risberg was deeply involved in the plot to throw the 1919 World Series when he was playing for the Chicago White Sox. He was one of the eight players Judge Landis banned for life.

3019. Rising, Percival Sumner (1905 OF) "Pop." Origin unknown.

3020. Ritchey, Claude Cassius (1897–1909 2B) "Little All Right." Ritchey was 5'6½" and weighed 165 pounds. He was a good hitter collecting 1,629 hits in 13 seasons, and played an excellent defensive game at second base. Fans said he was a "Little All Right."

3021. Ritter, Louis Elmer (1902–08 C) "Old Dog." Ritter was 26 years old before he reached the major leagues, old for a rookie of the day. However, the exact origin of "Old Dog" is unknown.

3022. Ritter, William Herbert (1912–16 P) "Hank." "Hank" was an alternative to Ritter's middle name of Herbert.

3023. Rivera, Jesus Torres (1975–82 OF) "Bombo." According to SABR Latin American player expert, Peter Bjarkman, "Bombo" refers to macho image.

3024. Rivera, Manuel Joseph (1952–61 OF) "Jungle Jim." Rivera came out of the New York ghetto which some called a jungle. He was a hustler as a kid, and spent ten years in an orphanage. In the army, he served time for sexual assault. As a 30-year-old rookie for the Chicago White Sox, some viewed his behavior as uncivilized. On one occasion he hit a home run, and then slid head long into home plate asking photographers, "Did you get that shot?" After hitting a home run in Kansas City in 1955, he went over to the stands to apologize to Bess Truman that his hit might beat the home club. He ended the visit by saying, "But it was a helluva wallop, eh Bess?"

3025. Rivers, John Milton (1970–84 OF) "Mickey." "Mickey" comes from "Mick the Quick." Rivers had great speed which distracted infielders when he was at bat, and pitchers when he was on base. He was called "Gozzlehead" for his lack of hustle and enthusiasm, and just plain stupidity. Teammates sometimes called him "Mickey Mouth" because when he spoke you knew what he meant, even though it was not what he said.

3026. Riviere, Arthur Bernard (1921–25 P) "Tink." Origin unknown.

3027. Rixey, Eppa (1912–33 P) "Eppa Jephtha." Rixey is a Hall of Fame pitcher who won 251 games over a 21-year career for the Philadelphia Phils and Cincinnati Reds. Lowell Reidenbaugh reports that the use of the middle name "Jephtha" was the creation of Bill Phelon, a Cincinnati writer who took pleasure in creating bizarre nomenclature. Rixey did not seem to object. He said "Eppa Jephtha" sounds like a cross between a Greek letter fraternity and a college yell. Joseph McBride says that Charlie Dryden compared the unusual first name of Eppa with the biblical character Jephtha and tried to convince people that was Rixey's middle name. Rixey denied it. Finally, Lee Allen points out that at 6'6", Rixey was called "The Eiffel Tower of Culpepper," Culpepper, Virginia, being his hometown.

3028. Rizzuto, Philip Francis (1941–56 SS) "Scooter." Rizzuto, was the Yankee shortstop for 13 years, and played in nine World Series. He received his nickname while still an amateur playing in the Queens New York Alliance League. "Scooter" refers to how he took off after ground balls at shortstop.

3029. Roach, Wilbur Charles (1910–15 SS) "Roxy." The nickname is a strange combination of the first two letters of the last name, plus the "x" and "y" letters from the name of the town where he broke into organized baseball Punxsutawney, Pennsylvania.

3030. Robb, Douglas W. (1948–52 NL Umpire, 1952–55 AL Umpire) "Scotty." Robb was of Scottish background.

3031. Robello, Thomas Vardasco (1933–34 2B) "Tony." Robello told me his mother used to pronounce Tommy as Tomme. When he first started to play pro ball, other players heard her and thought she said "Tony." That is what he was called after that.

3032. Roberge, Joseph Albert Armand (1941–46 3B) "Skippy." Roberge was nicknamed after the comic strip character named "Skippy."

3033. Roberts, Charles Emory (1943 SS) "Red." The nickname refers to hair color.

3034. Roberts, Clarence Ashley (1913–14 C) "Skipper." Origin unknown.

3035. Roberts, Dale (1967 P) "Mountain Man." The nickname refers to Roberts' size. He stood a shade over 6'4".

3036. Roberts, James Newsom (1924–25 P) "Big Jim." Roberts was 6'3" and weighed 203 pounds.

3037. Roberts, Leon Joseph (1986 2B) "Bip." Origin unknown.

3038. Roberts, Morganna (1970– Fan) "The Kissing Bandit." Morganna is an exotic dancer with a 60-inch bosom who crashes baseball games as well as other sporting events and interrupts action on the playing field to plant a well-calculated kiss on the unsuspecting cheek of a ballplayer. Inevitably she is escorted from the field by security personnel. Jay Johnstone, a prankster in his own right, wrote, "It was the late Si Burick of Dayton, Ohio, one of the most beloved sportswriters of our time, who wrote about the removal of exotic dancer, Morganna, from a baseball field by four security men, 'And so they escorted her off the field, two a breast'." Pete Rose was the first recipient of Morganna's smooches in 1970. Since that time, she has managed to kiss 22 other players which resulted in 16 arrests. Among those bussed include: George Brett, Mike Schmidt, Nolan Ryan, Dickie Thorn, John Candalaria, and Fred Lynn. Brett was the only player to retaliate. One night with several of his Kansas City Royal teammates, he went to the night club where Morganna was performing. During her act he jumped on stage and kissed her! In an entirely different context, I interviewed Morganna in 1968 when she supposedly was only 15 years old and just starting her career as an exotic dancer. At that time she was called Morganna "The Wild One" and fronted a bosom of a mere 40 inches.

3039. Robertson, Charles Cubertson (1919–28 P) "Racehorse." The nickname "Racehorse" came from Robertson's days in the Texas League and referred to his flat nose not the speed of his fastball.

3040. Robiataille, Joseph Anthony (1904–05 P) "Chick." "Chick" refers to Robiatialle's small 5'8", 150-pound stature.

3041. Robinson, Brooks Calbert (1955–77 3B) "Vacuum Cleaner." Robinson was the Baltimore third baseman for over a score of years and was rated one of the best ever at fielding the position. His uncanny ability to dispose of balls coming his way led to the nickname of "Vacuum Cleaner." He was also called "The Head" by his teammates because of his receding hairline.

3042. Robinson, Frank (1956–76 OF) "The Judge." According to Joseph McBride, when Robinson was playing for the Orioles, after games that had been won, he would preside over a "Kangaroo Court" in the locker room. He would pass out fines to teammates for fielding or mental errors on the field, and inappropriate locker room behavior. In his book, *Extra Innings*, Robinson states that when he was with the Cincinnati Reds in 1956, "My legs were so skinny, that my nickname was 'Pencils'."

3043. Robinson, Jack Roosevelt (1947–56 2B) "Rabbit." As a blocking fullback for Kenny Washington at UCLA, Robinson's speed was denoted by the nickname "Rabbit." This nickname did not stick with Robinson during his baseball career. He was almost universally called "Jackie." In 1947 Robinson broke the color barrier in the major leagues.

3044. Robinson, John Henry (1911–18 P) "Rube." Robinson was a country boy from Floyd, Arkansas, and not used to big city life. He was nicknamed with "Rube" Waddell in mind.

3045. Robinson, Wilbert (1886–1902 C) "Uncle Robbie." For 17 years, 1886–1902, Wilbert Robinson was a superb catcher in the major leagues compiling a life time batting average of .273. During his playing days with the Philadelphia Athletics and Baltimore Orioles, he was called "Yank," "Billy" and "Billy Fish." As a youth, Robinson worked for a butcher and fish dealer. One of his jobs was to drive a wagon and hawl fish from it around town. One day a disgruntled housewife shouted at him: "Come back here Billy Fish and take away your fish. They smell!" A nickname was born. Robinson managed for 18 years in the major leagues with an even .500 record. In 1902, he took the helm of the Baltimore club in mid-season when they were in seventh place, and under his direction they fell to last place. From 1914–31, he managed the Brooklyn Dodgers, winning pennants in 1916 and 1920. Robinson's Falstaffian characteristics fit in perfectly with the zany antics of his Dodger players who earned the collective nickname of "Daffiness Boys." As a manager, Robinson was a lax disciplinarian. This, combined with a benign fatherly attitude toward his players, not only won him respect and admiration, but also the nickname "Uncle Robbie."

3046. Robinson, William Clyde (1903–10 2B) "Rabbit." "Rabbit" refers to Robinson's size 5'5" weighing 145 pounds. He was also called "Tug."

3047. Robinson, William H. (1882–92 2B) "Yank." According to Joseph McBride, Robinson was nicknamed after Yankee Robinson a ninteenth century circus and tent performer who aided the Ringling Brothers in getting their start.

3048. Roche, John Joseph (1914–17 C) "Red." The nickname refers to hair color.

3049. Rodgers, Lee Otis (1938 P) "Buck." In this case "Buck" is brought to mind by the last name. The reference is to the fictional futuristic character of comic strip and movie fame. Rodgers was also called "Lefty." He pitched left handed but batted right handed.

3050. Rodgers, Robert Leroy (1961–69 C) "Buck." "Buck" in this case is brought to mind by the last name. The reference is to the fictional futuristic character of comic strip and movie fame.

3051. Rodgers, Wilbur Kincaid (1915–16 2B) "Raw Meat Bill." Rodgers was an avid hunter of wild game of every description from fowl to wolves.

3052. Roe, Elwin Charles (1938–54 P) "Preacher." Before becoming a professional ball player, Roe seriously considered becoming a clergyman.

3053. Roe, John (1982–88 AL Umpire) "Rocky." Roe wrote me that his favorite player as a kid was Rocky Colovito. At about age nine his father started to call him "Rocky" and it was picked up by everyone else except his mother who always called him Jack. "In fact," he said, "One day when one of the kids came calling for Rocky, my mother told him no Rocky lived there."

3054. Rogan, Wilbur (1917–46 P, Negro League) "Bullet." Rogan got the nickname "Bullet" from the speed of his fastball, but the 5'5", 155-pound pitcher also threw change-ups, curves and spitters. In addition, Rogan was a fine hitter who hit fourth for the Kansas City Monarchs when he was pitching. He also was known as the finest fielding pitcher in Negro baseball history.

3055. Rogers, Orlin Woodrow (1935 P) "Buck." "Buck" is brought to mind by the last name. The reference is to the fictional futuristic character of comic strip and movie fame. Rogers was also called "Lefty." He pitched left handed but batted right handed.

3056. Rogers, Stanley Frank (1938 SS) "Packy." Rogers wrote me, "My nickname came from the prize fighter Packy McFarland. It was given to me by my friends and buddies at an early age."

3057. Rogers, Thomas Andrew (1917–21 P) "Shotgun." Rodgers was a wild, hard-throwing right hander. He walked many more batters than he struck out. In 1916 one of his pitches hit and killed former major league infielder John Lewis Dodge during a Southern Association game in Mobile, Alabama.

3058. Rohe, George Anthony (1901–07 3B) "Whitey." The nickname refers to light blond hair color.

3059. Rojas, Minervino Alejandro Landin (1966–68 P) "Minnie." Rojas wrote me, "In 1962 when I was in the minor leagues, the American announcers had trouble pronouncing my name. So, they just shortened it to Minnie."

3060. Rojas, Octario Victor Rivas (1962–77 2B) "Cookie." In Spanish Rojas' nickname was "Cuqui." In English it became easier to say "Cookie."

3061. Rolfe, Robert Abial (1931–42 3B) "Red." The nickname refers to hair color.

3062. Rollings, William Russell (1927–30 3B) "Red." The nickname refers to hair color.

3063. Rollins, Richard John (1961–70 3B) "Red." The nickname refers to hair color.

3064. Romano, John Anthony (1958–67 C) "Honey." Romano told me, as a baby, family members would look at him and say "Isn't he a honey." Finally, "Honey" became his nickname.

3065. Romberger, Allen Isaiah (1954 P) "Dutch." The nickname refers to Romberger's German background.

3066. Romo, Vicente (1968–82 P) "Heuvo." Romo was nicknamed while he was playing amateur ball in Mexico by his manager who said his face looked like an egg.

3067. Root, Charles Henry (1923–41 P) "Chinski." Root was a 201-game winner over 17 seasons. He was nicknamed by his Chicago Cub teammates because of his protruding chin. Root is the answer to the trivia question "Off whom did 'Babe' Ruth hit his 'called shot' in the 1932 World Series?" According to Eddie Gold and Art Ahrens, Root's version of the "called shot" goes like this, "He didn't point. If he had, I'd have knocked him on his fanny. I'd have loosened him up. I took my pitching too seriously to have anybody facing me do that ... Babe did lift one finger toward our dug out after the first strike and two after the second. The count was 2 and 2 when I threw him a curve on the outside and he hit it over my head and into the bleachers. But he did not point."

3068. Rosado, Luis Robles (1977–80 1B) "Papo." Origin unknown.

3069. Rosar, Warren Vincent (1939–51 C) "Buddy." "Buddy" was a childhood nickname given to Rosar by his uncle. In 1946 Rosar fielded 1.000 in 117 games as catcher.

3070. Rose, Peter Edward (1963–86 OF, 3B, 2B, 1B, Manager) "Charlie Hustle." Tony Kubek, NBC broadcaster and former Yankee shortstop relates the story of how Rose got the nickname of "Charlie Hustle" in the following fashion. "Okay, this is the story on how Pete Rose got his nickname. In spring training of '63, Mickey Mantle, Whitey Ford and I were standing around on the sidelines. Up comes 21-year-old Pete, and the Reds's third-base coach, Reggie Otero, whispers to us, 'Wait'll you get a load of this kid. He goes down to first base in four seconds.' Whitey says, 'Big Deal. Mickey here can get down in 3.5.' Otero says, 'Oh, Yeah? This kid does it on a base on balls.' So Whitey, a great bench jockey starts riding this enthusiastic kid. He starts making fun of him, screaming out, 'Charlie Hustle' this, 'Charlie Hustle' that. The name stuck." Rose became the all time leader in games played, 3,562; times at bat, 14,053; and hits, 4,256. In 1989 Rose was banned from baseball for life for alleged gambling on sports.

3071. Roseman, James John (1882–90 OF) "Chief." Roseman was of American Indian background.

3072. Rosen, Albert Leonard (1947–56 3B) "Flip." In junior high school Rosen was the pitcher, flipper, for a softball team. The kids called him "Flip" and it became his nickname.

3073. Rosen, Emerson Corey (1944–46 P) "Steve." Rosen wrote me about the origin of his nickname. "It was given to me by Hank Hodge, the baseball coach at Clarkson College, Potsdam, New York, in the spring of 1937. He told Paul Kitchell, the Yankee Scout, that he was changing my name so that they would sign me. He also said that no player in the league had the name of Emerson, but he was wrong. There was a player by the name of Emerson Dickman with the Boston Red Sox."

3074. Rosen, Goodwin George (1937–46 OF) "Goody." "Goody" is a fairly obvious play on Rosen's first name.

3075. Roser, John William Joseph (1922 OF) "Bunny." Origin unknown.

3076. Ross, Chester Franklyn (1924–26 P) "Buster." Origin unknown.

3077. Ross, Ernest Bertram (1902 P) "Curly." "Curly" refers to the texture of Ross' hair.

3078. Ross, Lee Ravon (1936–45 P) "Buck." "Buck" is a generic nickname of which the circumstances of origin are almost never documented. It refers to a well developed, virile, aggressive, high spirited young man. The nickname is usually bestowed on the individual during his teenage years.

3079. Rotblatt, Marvin (1948–51 P) "Rotty." "Rotty" is a play on the last name of Rotblatt.

3080. Roth, Robert Frank (1914–21 OF) "Braggo." Roth did a lot of talking, complaining and especially bragging about his playing. In 1917 he stole home six times.

3081. Rounsaville, Virle Gene (1970 P) "The Pearl." The nickname is a response to the first name of Virle.

3082. Routhermel, Edward Hill (1899 2B) "Bobbie." Origin unknown.

3083. Rowe, David (1877–84 OF) "Eli." Origin unknown.

3084. Rowe, Harland Stimson (1916 3B) "Hypie." Origin unknown.

3085. Rowe, Lynwood Thomas (1933–49 P) "Schoolboy." As a youngster he was called "Newsboy" because he delivered newspapers. In 1927 at age 15 he was pitching for the Methodist Church baseball team against the Baptists in El Dorado, Arkansas. The Baptists were batting in the ninth inning with their slugger at the plate. A Baptist fan shouted, "Don't let that schoolboy strike you out." A nickname, which was to stick a lifetime, was born.

3086. Rowell, Carvel William (1939–48 2B) "Bama." "Bama" is a place nickname, short for Alabama. Rowell was born and raised in Citronell, Alabama.

3087. Rowland, Clarence H. (1923–27 AL Umpire) "Pants." Rowland acquired the nickname "Pants" during his minor league playing days when he showed up one day wearing a pair of his brother's oversized knickers which he could hardly keep up. In later years Rowland over-compensated for his nickname by becoming a fashion plate and was regarded as a "Duke" or "Dandy." Rowland managed the Chicago White Sox 1915–18 and guided them to a world championship in 1917.

3088. Roy, Norman Brookes (1950 P) "Jumbo." Roy was 6' and 200 pounds.

3089. Ruberto, John Edward (1969–72 C) "Sonny." Ruberto broke into pro ball at age 18 and was called "Sonny."

3090. Ruble, William Arthur (1927–34 OF) "Speedy." The nickname refers to Ruble's speed in the outfield and on the base paths.

3091. Rucker, George Napoleon (1907–16 P) "Nap." "Nap" is a contraction of Rucker's middle name, but it does not account for his nickname. As a boy in Alpharetta, Georgia, Rucker was fond of confections called "Napoleons" and when his playmates saw the ice-cream peddler coming they would call out, "There's your Napoleon, Rucker." During his playing days Brooklyn fans cut "Napoleon" to just "Nap."

3092. Rucker, John Joel (1940–46 OF) "The Crabapple Comet." Rucker was known for his speed and he was born and raised in Crabapple, Georgia.

3093. Rudolph, John Herman (1903–04 OF) "Dutch." The nickname refers to Rudolph's German background.

3094. Rudolph, Richard (1910–27 P) "Baldy." Rudolph, who won 27 games for the Boston Braves in 1927, had lost most of his hair by the time he reached the major leagues.

3095. Ruel, Harold Dominic (1915–34 C) "Muddy." As a child Ruel fell in a mud puddle and was covered from head to toe with mud. His father said, "Look at Muddy over there." Ruel caught for 19 years in the major leagues and collected over 1,200 hits.

3096. Ruether, Walter Henry (1917–27 P) "Dutch." The nickname refers to Ruether's German background.

3097. Ruffing, Charles Herbert (1924–47 P) "Red." The nickname refers to hair color. Ruffing won 273 games in the major leagues and pitched in seven World Series, winning seven games while dropping two for the New York Yankees. Ruffing was one of the best hitting pitchers of all time with a batting average of .269 with 521 hits, including 36 home runs.

3098. Ruiz, Hiraldo Sablon (1964–71 2B) "Chico." In Ruiz's case, "Chico" means kid. In 1968 he got batting tips from Harry "The Hat" Walker and teammates started to call him "Harry."

3099. Ruiz, Manuel Cruz (1978–80 3B) "Chico." In Ruiz's case, "Chico" means kid.

3100. Runnels, Thomas William (1951–64 1B) "Pete." Runnells told me both his father and older brother had the nickname of "Pete" and it also became his at an early age. He said it often led to confusion, especially when the phone rang and someone wanted to talk to "Pete."

3101. Ruppert, Jacob (1914–39 Owner) "Colonel." In 1914 along with Till Huston, Ruppert, a wealthy New York realtor and brewer, took over the New York American League franchise. Ruppert bought out co-owner Huston in 1923. He received his honorary military title at age 22 while serving on the staff of the governor of the state of New York. Ruppert, as much as anyone else, was responsible for the style and winning tradition of the New York Yankees. He brought Ruth to New York from Boston and built Yankee Stadium. His management of the franchise earned him the nicknames of "Master Builder in Baseball," and "Father of the Yankees."

3102. Rusie, Amos Wilson (1889–1901 P) "The Hoosier Thunderbolt." This is a place nickname. Rusie was from Mooresville, Indiana. He threw so hard that fans wondered why his arm didn't come flying off after the ball. He led the National League in strikeouts five straight years, 1890–94.

3103. Russell, Clarence Dixon (1910–12 P) "Lefty." Russell pitched left handed and batted left handed.

3104. Russell, Ewell Albert (1913–23 P) "Reb." "Reb" denotes Russell's southern background. He was born in Jackson, Mississippi.

3105. Russell, Glen David (1939–47 1B) "Rip." "Rip" is short for "Ripper" and refers to hitting ability. In 1938 Russell collected 216 hits for Los Angeles in the Pacific Coast League.

3106. Russell, John Henry (1922–33 2B, Negro League) "Pistol." Origin unknown.

3107. Russo, Marius Ugo (1939–46 P) "Lefty." Russo pitched left handed but batted right handed.

3108. Russuell, Lloyd Opal (1938) "Tex." "Tex" is a place nickname. Russuell was born in Atoka, Oklahoma, but was raised in West Texas. He played in only two major league games without coming to bat. I have no information on what position he played.

3109. Ruth, George Herman (1914–35 OF) "Babe." George Herman Ruth's nickname, "Babe," is the most famous and well known, of all baseball player nicknames. It is arguable that it may be the most recognizable nickname ever assigned an American. Therefore, its origins deserve attention. There are numerous accounts about how Ruth obtained the nickname of "Babe." Tom Shea, in *Baseball Nicknames 1870–1946*, reports that Ruth received the nickname while he was attending St. Mary's Industrial School in Baltimore. The older and bigger boys refused to let him play in their games because he was "just a babe." One version offered by noted baseball writer, Fred Lieb is quite similar. He states that Ruth received the nickname early in life shortly after coming to St. Mary's. He was teased by the older boys and blubbered, so they called him "Babe." Lieb, however, points out that this incident was denied by a man who attended St. Mary's at the same time Ruth did. Lieb also provides a second account. When Jack Dunn, Baltimore Oriole owner, signed Ruth to a contract in 1914, he was still a minor. Dunn was forced to obtain a court order to relocate him outside of St. Mary's. This led to rumors that Dunn had legally adopted Ruth. It was about this time that Baltimore sportswriters began using the "Babe" nickname in print. None of these accounts is exactly the way Ruth recalls it in his book, *Babe Ruth's Own Book of Baseball*, published in 1928.

It's a funny thing, incidently, how many times a year I get letters asking me how I got my nickname. Some of the newspaper boys made a pretty good yarn out of it one time. They said when I was a little kid I always wanted to play ball with bigger boys, and when they wouldn't let me play I'd cry and howl until I had the whole neighborhood disturbed. The big boys according to this story nicknamed me "Baby" because I cried so much, then shortened it to Babe, as kids will. It's a shame to spoil a good yarn like that, but as a matter of fact the story is all wrong. A man named Steinam, who was coach of the Baltimore Orioles when I joined the club in 1914, gave me the nickname. The first day I reported at the clubhouse he said, "Well here's Jack's newest Babe now."

Interestingly, the circumstances surrounding the nickname are recalled differently by Ruth in *The Babe Ruth Story* (as told to Bob Considine) which was published over two decades later in 1948. It allegedly happened the first time Ruth took the field for spring training in 1914 at Fayetteville, Arkansas.

On that day, Dunn practically led me by the hand from the dressing room to the pitcher's box. I was as proud of my Orioles uniform as I had been of my long pants. Maybe I showed that pride in my face and the way I walked. "Look at Dunnie and his new babe," one of the older players yelled. That started it I guess.

But the clincher came a few days later. Ruth became fascinated with the elevator at the team's hotel. The first he had ever been in. After bribing the operator to let him run it, he nearly decapitated himself by closing the doors with his head striking out.

Dunnie bawled me out until the stuffings ran out of me, and what he didn't say to me the others said for him. But finally one of them took pity on me, shook his head and said "You're just a babe in the woods." After that they called me Babe.

Perhaps it will never be known which, if any, of these accounts is the "true" version of how Ruth's "Babe" nickname originated. Usually, researchers place greater weight on first-person accounts than secondary sources. However, this becomes complicated in Ruth's case. Ruth had two versions of how he got his nickname or did he? Lieb reports that Bill Slocum of the *New York Morning American* was the ghost writer for *Babe Ruth's Own Book of Baseball*, and Bob Considine did the writing for *The Babe Ruth Story*. Were the accounts Ruth's or theirs? Ruth had a notoriously poor memory, especially for names. Lieb comments that "Ruth probably had a low I.Q. Certainly he couldn't remember names, so with everyone it was 'Hello Kid' no matter what the person's age." It is quite possible that Ruth did not remember how he got the nickname "Babe," and just agreed to versions suggested to him. The origin of his nickname was probably of little consequence to Ruth. Be that as it may, Ruth was subject to a number of other nicknames, some of which were far from complimentary. Opposing players called him "The Big Baboon," "The Big Monk," "Monkey," "Nigger" and "Nigger Lips." The baboon and monkey references have their origin in Ruth's first years with the Boston Red Sox. According to Anthony Conner, in *Baseball for the*

Love of It, when Ruth reported to the Red Sox in 1914, he was 19 years old, 6'2" tall and weighed 198 pounds. He had a slim waist, huge biceps and absolutely no manners or social graces. In *The Glory of Their Times*, Lawrence Ritter lets Red Sox teammate Harry Hooper explain what Ruth was like.

> Lord he ate too much. He'd stop along the road when we were traveling and order half dozen hot dogs and as many bottles of soda pop, stuff them in, one after the other, give a few big belches, and then roar "OK boys lets go!" That would hold Babe for a couple of hours, then he'd be at it again. A nineteen-year-old youngster, mind you. He was such a rube that he got more than his share of teasing, some of it not too pleasant. "The Big Baboon" some of them used to call him behind his back....

The derogatory "Nigger" and "Nigger Lips" are thought to come from Ruth's off-season play for various barnstorming teams that often faced Negro teams, or Negro all-star teams, in this country and in Latin America. Don Rogosin in *Invisible Men* points out that Ruth played with such enthusiasm in these exhibitions that "...less capable more prejudiced players referred to him derisively as "Nigger Lips" and falsely questioned his patrimony." However, Ken Sobol in *Babe Ruth & the American Dream* claims "Nipper Lips" was Ruth's nickname at St. Mary's. Leo Durocher who showed little respect for Ruth even when they were teammates, constantly used the "Monkey" and "Nigger" taunts. Ruth retaliated by referring to Durocher as "The All American Out." To say that Ruth did not care for Durocher, is an understatement. If players really wanted to get Ruth's goat, they would call him "Leo," and run like heck. Ruth's teammates and close associates usually called him "Jidge" not "Babe."

"Jidge" is a New England takeoff on George. There is some confusion however, as to how the nickname was spelled. While most sportswriters, Fred Lieb included, used "Jidge" in print, Ford Frick wrote it "Jedgie." In Ruth's *Own Book of Baseball* it is spelled "Jedge": "To the members of the Yankee ball club I'm 'Jedge.' That's a name Benny Bengough [Yankee catcher] tacked on me two or three years ago." Yankee owner Jake Ruppert did not use any nickname choosing to call his star performer Ruth, but because of his strong German accent it came out "Root." As Jimmy Powers points out in *Baseball Personalities*, sportswriters dreamed up a variety of newspaper nicknames for Ruth.

He was the Bambustin' Babe; Manlin "Mandarin"; The Great Gate God; High Priest of Swat; King of Klout; Battering Bambino; King of Diamonds; Caliph of Clout; Potentate of the Pill; Big Boy Blooie; The Sultan of Swat; Behemoth of Bust; Mightiest of the Maulers.

It should not be forgotten that not only was Ruth the subject of a host of nicknames, he was also the creator of them. Because he had such a poor memory for names, he often called people "Kid" or "Pop" with little regard for age. In fact, his universal name for his numerous female liaisons was just "Kid." Because he had difficulty remembering their names he called fellow Yankee teammates infielder Julian Wera "Flop Ears" and pitcher Myles Thomas "Duck Eye." In fact, Ruth called Lou Gehrig "Buster." Finally, although Ruth may have had difficulty with the names of people, he did not seem to suffer the same malady with his bats. Powers explains, "Black Betsy was his helpmate in setting his record of 59 homers. When Betsy was broken, it took two to take her place. Big Bertha and Beautiful Bella helped him hit his famous 60 in 1927." And so, as a collector of nicknames and a bestower of them, Ruth soared above his peers much as he did on the diamond and in many aspects of his private life. Perhaps Lieb sums it up best, "When Babe Ruth was in his prime, they used to say, 'There couldn't be another Babe Ruth.' Baseball just couldn't stand more than one Babe Ruth at one time." Decades later, John Thorn and Mark Rucker wrote in the 1989 *National Pastime:*

> Like no one before him or since, the Babe placed his personal stamp on the game and changed it forever more. His fabulous exploits have often been sung, but remain implausibly epic; our children already think he never truly existed, no more than Paul Bunyon or Superman.

3110. Rutherford, John William (1952 P) "Doc." Rutherford had no formal association with the health field. But this Canadian born player's father was a practicing physician. He received the nickname from teammates on the Dodgers in 1952.

3111. Ryan, Daniel P. (1887–91 P) "Cyclone." "Cyclone" refers to the speed and force of Ryan's fastball.

3112. Ryan, Jack (1908–11 P) "Gulfport." "Gulfport" is a place nickname. Ryan was raised in Gulfport, Mississippi. He spent most of his career in the Texas League as a spitball pitcher. He would chew up slippery ellumand then add coffee grounds to it. This technique earned him the nickname of "Coffee Jack Ryan."

3113. Ryan, James Edward (1885–1903 OF) "Pony." Ryan toiled for 18 years as a major league outfielder mostly for the Chicago National League Club. Although he compiled a career batting average of .309, collected 2,529 hits and in 1888 led the league in home runs, 16. His exploits have all been forgotten today. At 5'9", 160 pounds he was known as the "Pony" outfielder.

3114. Ryan, John Collins (1930–38 SS) "Blondy." The nickname refers to blond hair.

3115. Ryan, Michael James (1964–74 C) "Irish." The nickname refers to Ryan's Irish background. On May 2, 1970, Ryan replaced Phils catcher Tim McCarver who had a broken right hand in a game against the Giants. Five minutes later Ryan broke his left hand.

3116. Ryan, Nolan Lynn (1966– P) "The Ryan Express." The reference is to the 1965 movie "Von Ryan's Express." It is a media nickname applied to Ryan during the latter stages of his career as he continued to set strikeout records and flirt with no-hitters. In 1989 Ryan became the first pitcher to strike out over 5,000 batters. At the end of the 1990 season his total was 5,308. The "Express" rolls on as Ryan pitched his seventh no-hitter early in the 1991 season. However, the ride has not always been smooth as one might expect. Despite the no-hitters and leading the league in strikeouts eleven times, after the 1990 season, Ryan had won just 30 more games than he lost, 302-272, for a winning percentage of .526. This record can be explained in part by the number of free passes on "The Ryan Express." Ryan led the league in bases on balls eight times. Besides being the all-time strikeout leader, he is also the all-time walk king. His total of 2,614 is 781 more than Steve Carlton's second place total of 1,833.

3117. Ryan, Wilfred Patrick Dolan (1919–33 P) "Rosy." Ryan received his nickname from college teammates at Holy Cross College, but claimed he never knew why. Ryan won a game in the 1922, '23, and '24 World Series, all in relief.

3118. Ryba, Dominic Joseph (1935–46 P) "Mike." Lee Allen explains that Ryba "...was a utility player who first reported to the Cardinals when Bill McKechnie managed the team. All though spring training McKechnie called him Mike and Rybe. Frankly puzzled, he asked why. 'My names's not Mike,' he insisted. 'I'm a Pole, not an Irishman' ... 'From now on your name is Mike,' McKechnie told him. 'I don't go for that Dominic'."

3119. Rye, Eugene Rudolph (1931 OF) "Half Pint." The nickname is as much a response to the last name as Rye's size, 5'6", 165 pounds.

S

3120. Sabo, Alexander (1936–37 C) "Giz." Sabo explained to me that as a child he could not pronounce the word whiz. It came out "Giz." Older kids picked this up and started calling him "Giz" as a nickname.

3121. Sabo, Christopher Andrew (1988 3B) "Spuds." Spuds MacKenzie was the name of a dog in beer commercials in the late 1980s. Manager Pete Rose of the Cincinnati Reds thought Sabo bore a resemblance to the dog, because of his flat top hair cut and goggles.

3122. Sadowski, Robert Frank (1963–66 3B) "Sid." Teammates Bill Carpenter and Bill Morton of Winnipeg in the Northern League gave Sadowski the nickname of "Sid" by changing the "a" of the first three letters of his name to "i."

3123. Sage, Harry (1890 C) "Doc." Many players with the nickname of "Doc" have had some experience or association with the medical or dental professions. However, for Sage the origin of "Doc" is unknown.

3124. St. Claire, Edward Joseph (1951–54 C) "Ebba." "Ebba" stems from a child's mispronunciation of Edward.

3125. Salazar, Argenis Antonio Juana (1983 C) "Angel." Origin unknown.

3126. Salle, Harry Franklin (1908–21 P) "Slim." Salle was 6'3" and weighed 180 pounds. He was tall and rangy and called "String Bean" as well as "Slim."

3127. Salmon, Rutherford Eduardo (1964–72 2B) "Chico." "Chico" is a Hispanic nickname meaning kid or small. Salmon, who claimed he was constantly afraid of evil spirits and ghosts, was called "Super Sub" by his Cleveland teammates because he could fill in at so many different positions.

3128. Saltzgaver, Otto Hamlin (1932–45 3B) "Jack." Origin unknown.

3129. Salvo, Manuel (1939–43 P) "Gyp." Salvo was a big, silent type ball player of Sicilian background known for his big wad of chewing tobacco. "Gyp" may be short for Gypsy but I have never seen either used in print for Salvo. Origin unknown.

3130. Samuels, Joseph Jona (1930 P) "Skabotch." Origin unknown.

3131. Samuls, Samuel Earl (1895 3B) "Ike." Origin unknown.

3132. Sanchez, Raul Guadalupe Rodriquez (1952–60 P) "Salivita." "Salivita" means saliva which this Cuban-born pitcher was accused of applying to the ball.

3133. Sand, John Henry (1923–28 SS) "Heinie." The nickname refers to Sand's German background. In 1924, while playing for the Philadelphia Phils, he reported a bribe from New York Giant player Jimmy O'Connell. Later, O'Connell was banned from organized baseball for life.

3134. Sanders, Kenneth George (1964–76 P) "Daffy." According to Sanders, "Daffy" was not really his main nickname. "My nickname was 'Bulldog' because of my tenacity on the mound. It was given to me by Bob Uecker when I was with the Brewers in 1970."

3135. Sanders, Roy Garvin (1917–18 P) "Butch." "Butch" was a childhood nickname. Sanders was also called "Pep" which called attention to the energy he expended on the field.

3136. Sanders, Warren William (1903–04 P) "War." "War" is really a short name using the first three letters of Sanders' first name.

3137. Sanicki, Edward Robert (1949–51 OF) "Butch." Sanicki told me that about age five, "My parents were living in a Polish neighborhood and gave me a skinhead hair cut during the summer which was later called a 'Butch.' It stuck with me as a nickname."

3138. Santana, Rafael Francisco de la Cruz (1983 SS) "Renda Linda." According to Tony Kubec, the nickname means "beautiful gold" and denotes Santana's fielding at shortstop.

3139. Santiago, Jose Guillermo (1954–56 P) "Pants." Santiago was nicknamed by a sportswriter after a game in which he had struck out the side with the bases loaded. "He got 'em by the pants."

3140. Santop, Louis Loftin (1909–26 C, Negro League) "Big Bertha." Santop was a light-skinned Texan who was best known for his Texas-size home runs. The 6'5", 245-pound "Big Top" swung his big bat like a toothpick and liked to boast to opposing pitchers how far he would pound their deliveries, and on occasion would even predict his home runs. In 1912 Santop is credited with hitting a ball over a 485-foot fence in Elizabeth, New Jersey. He was nicknamed after the gigantic German siege gun of World War I.

3141. Sargent, Joseph Alexander (1921 2B) "Horse Belly." "Horse Belly" refers to Sargent's protruding stomach or pot belly.

3142. Satriano, Thomas Victor (1961–72 C) "Satch." "Satch" is a takeoff on the last name of Satriano.

3143. Saucier, Kevin Andrew (1978–82 P) "Hot Sauce." The nickname is a response to the last name.

3144. Sauer, Edward (1943–49 OF) "Horn." Sauer was nicknamed by his teammates for his large Jimmy Durante–type nose.

3145. Sauer, Henry John (1941–59 OF) "The Honker." Hank as he was addressed, similar to his brother Ed, had a prominent proboscis.

3146. Saunders, Russell Collier (1927 OF) "Rusty." "Rusty" is a takeoff on the first name Russell. Although he only played four games in the major leagues, Saunders was a star pro basketball player in the early days of the sport. He led the American Basketball League in scoring during the 1925–26 and 1926–27 seasons.

3147. Saverine, Robert Paul (1959–67 2B) "Rabbit." Saverine wrote me that "Rabbit" stems from his childhood. Kids thought he was very fast of foot.

3148. Sawatski, Carl Ernest (1948–63 C) "Swats." "Swats" did not refer to hitting ability, but is simply a play on the last name of Sawatski.

3149. Sawyer, Carl Everett (1915–16 2B) "Huck." Sawyer reminded people of the main character of Samuel Clemens novel, *The Adventures of Huckleberry Finn.*

3150. Sayler, Philip Andrew (1891 P) "Lefty." Sayler pitched left handed. There is no information on how he batted.

3151. Scales, George (1924–46 3B, Negro League) "Tubby." Scales was 5'11" and weighed 200 pounds. Over 25 seasons he batted .313 with a league leading career high of .392 in 1931.

3152. Scalzi, John Anthony (1939 OF) "Skeeter." "Skeeter" describes Scalzi's small size in the outfield, 5'6".

3153. Scanlan, Frank Aloysius (1909 P) "Dreamy." Origin unknown.

3154. Scanlan, William Dennis (1903–11 P) "Doc." Scanlan was a practicing physician. He was graduated from the Long Island College Hospital of Brooklyn in 1907. Although all four of Scanlan's sons also became physicians, none played professional baseball.

3155. Schacht, Alexander (1919–21 P) "The Crown Prince of Baseball." Schacht pitched for just three years in the major leagues compiling a 14-10 won-lost record. He had no public nickname as a player. After retiring, he developed a new career for himself as a trick artist with a baseball. Schacht then hired himself out to major and minor league clubs as a pre-game, between-games and post-game performer. His act became so popular and well known he was accorded the nickname "The Crown Prince of Baseball."

3156. Schaefer, Herman A. (1901–18 2B) "Germany." The nickname refers to Schaefer's German background. Schaefer is credited with causing the specific rule to be written that bases cannot be run backward, because of his antics of stealing first base from second base.

3157. Schaeffer, Harry Edward (1952 P) "Lefty." Schaeffer pitched left handed and batted left handed.

3158. Schafer, Harry C. (1876–78 3B) "Silk Stockings." Schafer was known for the bright silk stocking he always wore.

3159. Schalk, Raymond William (1912–29 C) "Cracker." When queried, Schalk did not know where his nickname came from or what it meant. However, it is clear it came from playing baseball. There are three possible explanations set forth. Upon seeing Schalk for the first time, a veteran player asked, "Who's that little cracker?" Another story has it he threw the ball back to the pitcher so fast that it cracked when it hit the mitt. Finally, it is recorded that when Schalk squatted behind the plate his rear view was square and small like a cracker box.

3160. Schaller, Walter (1911–13 OF) "Biff." Tom Shea reports that in Schaller's case, "Biff" is short for "Biffer" which in the slang of the day meant slugger.

3161. Schardt, Wilburt (1911–12 P) "Big Bill." Schardt was 6'4" and weighed 210 pounds.

3162. Scharein, Arthur Otto (1932–34 3B) "Scoop." Scharein had great ability to "Scoop" up ground balls at third base.

3163. Scharein, George Albert (1937–40 SS) "Tom." Origin unknown.

3164. Schauer, Alexander John (1913–17 P) "Rube." Schauer reminded people of "Rube" Waddell. Schauer may have been the first major league player born in Russia. At birth he was named Dimitri Ivanovich Dimitnikoff.

3165. Scheer, Henry William (1922–23 2B) "Heinie." The nickname refers to Scheer's German background.

3166. Scheerin, Frederick (1914–15 OF) "Dutch." Similar to "Fritz," as Scheerin was addressed, "Dutch" refers to German background.

3167. Scheffing, Robert Boden (1941–51 C) "Grump." According to Joseph McBride, in 1941 during spring training on Catalina Island, Chicago Cub coach, Charlie Root was playing golf with Scheffing. When Root missed a routine putt on the eighteenth green, Scheffing chewed him out and Root started calling Scheffing "Grump."

3168. Schegg, Gilbert Eugene (1912 P) "Lefty." Schegg pitched left handed and batted left handed.

3169. Schelle, Gerard Anthony (1939 P) "Jim." Origin unknown.

3170. Schemanske, Frederick George (1923 P) "Buck." "Buck" is a generic nickname of which the circumstances of origin are almost never documented. It refers to a well developed, virile, aggressive, high spirited young man. The nickname is usually bestowed on the individual during his teenage years.

3171. Schesler, Charles (1931 P) "Dutch." The nickname refers to Schesler's German backgrouns.

3172. Schillings, Elbert Isaiah (1922 P) "Red." The nickname refers to hair color.

3173. Schirick, Harry Ernest (1914 PH) "Dutch." The nickname refers to Schirick's German background. In his only time at bat in the major leagues, he walked and then stole two bases.

3174. Schlei, George Henry (1904–11 C) "Admiral." Schlei was nicknamed after the popular and controversial Admiral W.S. Schley of whom his name resembled.

3175. Schlesinger, William Cordes (1965 PH) "Rudy." Origin unknown.

3176. Schliebner, Frederick Paul (1923 1B) "Dutch." The nickname refers to Schliebner's German background.

3177. Schlitzer, Victor Joseph (1908–14 P) "Biff." Origin unknown.

3178. Schmees, George Edward (1952 OF) "Rocky." Origin unknown.

3179. Schmidt, Charles (1906–11 C) "Boss." Schmidt was very strong and tough and known for his fighting ability. He once beat Ty Cobb in a fight. He was the "Boss." He was also addressed as "Dutch" because of his German background.

3180. Schmidt, Charles John (1909–15 1B) "Butch." "Butch" is short for "Butcher Boy." Schmidt was a butcher during the off season and owned several shops.

3181. Schmidt, Frederick Albert (1944–47 P) "Tacks." "Tacks" is short for "Tacky" meaning that players found Schmidt's behavior a little strange.

3182. Schmidt, Herman (1913 P) "Pete." Origin unknown.

3183. Schmit, Frederic M. (1890–1901 P) "Crazy." Schmit had a poor command of the English language. When fans laughed at his mispronunciations he never understood why and would ask: "Am I Crazy?" He was also called "Tacky" and "Germany." Fred Lieb recalls that Schmit did a number of odd things one of which was to keep a detailed notebook on batter's weaknesses. One game when Cap Anson came to bat, Baltimore teammate John McGraw asked Schmit what it said about Anson in the notebook. Schmit replied, "It says here I should give Anson a base on balls; that's his weakness."

3184. Schmitz, John Albert (1941–56 P) "Bear Tracks." Joseph McBride states "Bear Tracks" comes from Schmitz's peculiar way of walking. Eddie Gold and Art Aherns on the other hand, point out that Schmitz wore size 14 brogans and he left a track like a bear when he went ice fishing in the woods during the winter.

3185. Schoefield, John Richard (1953–71 SS) "Ducky." Schoefield inherited his nickname from his father who got the nickname from a type of duck common to the Philadelphia area. He writes, "When I started with St. Louis in 1953, my dad met some of the Cardinal players. When they found out that 'Ducky' was his nickname, they started calling me that." Schoefield has the dubious distinction of having played in 19 major league seasons spanning three decades and yet collecting only 699 base hits. That's less than 37 per season.

3186. Schoeneck, Lewis V. (1884–89 1B) "Jumbo." Schoeneck weighed 235 pounds, but there is no information available on his height.

3187. Schreiber, David Henry (1911 P) "Barney." Some fastball pitchers of this era were nicknamed after race car driver Barney Oldfield.

3188. Schreiber, Paul Frederick (1922–45 P) "Von." "Von" refers to Schreiber's German background. Schreiber became a batting practice pitcher for the New York Yankees in 1937, 14 years after he had last pitched for Brooklyn in 1923. The players thought so much of his contribution, they voted him a full World Series share in 1937. On September 4, 1945, he made his debut with the Yanks some 22 years after he had last pitched in the majors. He pitched a total of four innings in two games in 1945.

3189. Schrivener, Wayne Allison (1975–77 SS) "Chuck." Schrivener wrote me, "My nickname comes from the Southern word 'Chuck' which is a term used instead of throw. My dad is responsible for giving me my nickname. He started by saying 'Let's go have a muck!' And it became, 'Let's go Chuck!' I have been Chuck ever since I was 2- or 3 years old."

3190. Schriver, William Frederick (1886–1901 C) "Pop." Schriver assumed the nickname of "Pop" late in his career. His experience included catching for Brooklyn, Philadelphia, Chicago, New York, Cincinnati, Pittsburgh, and St. Louis.

3191. Schroll, Albert Bringhurst (1958–61 P) "Bull." Schroll was 6'2" and 210 pounds, big and strong.

3192. Schuble, Henry George (1927–36 SS) "Heinie." The nickname refers to Schuble's German background.

3193. Schulmerich, Edward Wesley (1931–34 OF) "Iron Horse Wes." Schulmerich was a fullback on the Oregon State football team. He plowed through the opposition with the tenacity of a train or iron horse.

3194. Schult, Arthur William (1953–60 1B) "Dutch." The nickname refers to Schult's German background.

3195. Schulte, Frank (1904–18 OF) "Wildfire." Schulte was a friend and admirer of the great actress, Lillian Russell. One spring Schulte's team, the Chicago Cubs, played an exhibition game in Vicksburg, Mississippi, at the same time Russell's touring group was presenting a performance of a play, "Wildfire." Russell gave a party for Schulte and the rest of the Cub players. In gratitude, Schulte, who owned trotting horses, named his best trotter, "Wildfire." These events were followed closely by sportswriters covering the Cubs spring training activities. Before long, they began to call Schulte "Wildfire."

3196. Schulte, Fred William (1927–37 OF) "Fritz." The nickname refers to Schulte's German background.

3197. Schulte, Herman Joseph (1940 2B) "Ham." Schulte wrote me his mother called him Hahman. "Ham" is a common nickname for people of German background whose name is Herman.

3198. Schulte, John Clement (1923–32 C) "Eagle Eye." Schulte had a good eye at the plate and did not strike out often.

3199. Schultz, George Warren (1955–65 P) "Barney." Schultz told me, while as a baby in his crib, his uncle looked at him and jokingly called him "Barney Google" after the comic strip character. The "Barney" he said, "has stuck with me for life."

3200. Schultz, Howard Henry (1943–48 1B) "Stretch." Schultz was 6'6" and although somewhat awkward at first base he had a long stretch. Schultz played several seasons of professional basketball.

3201. Schultz, Joseph Charles (1912–25 OF) "Germany." The nickname refers to Schultz's German background.

3202. Schultz, Joseph Charles, Jr. (1939–48 C) "Dode." "Dode" was a childhood nickname given to him by his parents. However, Schultz said he had no idea what it meant, if anything.

3203. Schultz, Robert Duffy (1951–55 P) "Bill." Origin unknown.

3204. Schulz, Albert Christopher (1912–16 P) "Lefty." Schulz pitched left handed but batted right handed.

3205. Schumacher, Harold Henry (1931–46 P) "Prince Hal." From 1933–38 New York sportswriters considered Schumacher the second best pitcher in the "Big Apple," second only to "King" Carl Hubbell.

3206. Schumann, Carl J. (1905 P) "Hack." Schumann was big, strong and powerful. The nickname refers to the famous wrestler, Hackenschmidt.

3207. Schuster, William Charles (1937–45 SS) "Broadway." "Broadway" refers to Schuster's love of night life. He was well known for his off-the-field antics and was sometimes called "Monkey on a String." Schuster was also called "Sabu" because of his loud yell which reminded people of the motion picture character Sabu's call to elephants.

3208. Schwamb, Ralph Richard (1948 P) "Blackie." The nickname refers to hair color.

3209. Schwartz, William August (1883–84 C) "Pop." Origin unknown.

3210. Schwartz, William Charles (1904 1B) "Blab." Schwartz was always very talkative about everything.

3211. Schweitzer, Albert Casper (1908–11 OF) "Cheese." "Cheese" is a response to the last name of Schweitzer.

3212. Scoffic, Louis (1936 OF) "Weaser." "Weaser" is a childhood nickname which Scoffic received from a neighbor at the age of 7, when he could not pronounce whistle correctly. He wrote me: "It came out 'Weaser'." Scoffic also told me that when he played for Rochester in the International League, future National League President Warren Giles called him "Scrap Iron" because of the tenaciousness.

3213. Scott, Floyd John (1926–28 OF) "Pete." A 1924 press release listed his middle name as Peter. It would appear that "Pete" was a family nickname.

3214. Scott, George Charles, Jr. (1966–79 1B) "Boomer." The nickname meant he had power at bat and denoted his long home runs.

3215. Scott, James (1909–17 P; 1930–31 NL Umpire) "Death Valley Jim." Scott was nicknamed after Death Valley Scotty, a famous character of the California desert.

3216. Scott, Lewis Everett (1914–26 SS) "Deacon." Scott was a complete gentleman and always had a stern appearance about him. He also happened to be the best bridge player in baseball.

3217. Scott, Marshall (1945 P) "Lefty." Scott pitched left handed but batted right handed.

3218. Scott, Milton Parker (1882–86 1B) "Mikado Milt." Origin unknown.

3219. Scott, Ralph Robert (1972–77 P) "Mickey." Scott told me, "My grandfather used to call me McGee after 'Fibber McGee' on the radio. My parents lengthened it to Mickey and it stuck, thank God. It has been that ever since."

3220. Scrivener, Wayne Allison (1975–77 SS) "Chuck." Origin unknown.

3221. Seale, Johnny Ray (1964–65 P) "Durango Kid." This is a place nickname. Seale grew up in and around Durango, Colorado.

3222. Sears, John W. (1933–45 NL Umpire) "Ziggy." Fred Lieb reports on how John Sears came by the nickname of "Ziggy." "Sears really inherited the name of Ziggy. In 1917, the year before Sears joined the Fort Worth club, a recruit reported to manager Atz carrying a three-month-old baby on one arm and a parrot in a cage on the other, 'Who are you?' Jake asked him. 'I'm Ziggy Sears,' he told him. 'Where's your wife?' Jake wanted to know. 'She's home working,' he said. 'If I make good here, she's going to quit her job and join me'." Atz ordered the rookie to take the kid home to its mother, and go to work at something else, and that was he end of the original Ziggy Sears. When John William Sears reported to Fort Worth the following year, he reminded manager Atz of the unusual rookie of the year before and he immediately bestowed the name 'Ziggy' on our hero, so it probably never will be known what the nickname really meant."

3223. Sears, Kenneth Eugene (1943–46 C) "Ziggy." Sears inherited his nickname from his father, John W. "Ziggy" Sears, a minor league player and major league umpire.

3224. Seaver, George Thomas (1967–85 P) "Tom Terrific." Seaver, a

300-game winner, received his nickname from New York sportswriters during the New York Mets miracle season in 1969 when he led the league with 25 wins and only seven losses for a .781 percentage. He won the National League "Cy" Young award that year.

3225. Sechrist, Theodore O'Hara (1899 P) "Doc." Many of the players with the nickname of "Doc" had experience or association with either the medical or dental professions. However, for Sechrist the origin of "Doc" is unknown.

3226. Secory, Frank Edward (1940–46 OF; 1952–70 NL Umpire) "Deacon." The nickname referred to Secory's impeccable dress.

3227. Sedgwick, Henry Kenneth (1921–23 P) "Duke." The nickname refers to Sedgwick's impeccable dress.

3228. See, Charles Henry (1919–21 OF) "Chad." Origin unknown.

3229. Seeds, Robert Ira (1930–40 OF) "Suitcase." Bib Falk gave Seeds his nickname because he moved from team to team so rapidly it appeared he had to live out of a suitcase. In 1937 with Newark of the International League, he hit 7 home runs and had 17 RBIs in two consecutive games.

3230. Selbach, Albert Karl (1894–1906 OF) "Kip." Fred Lieb suggests that "Kip" may have referred to Selbach's size 5'7" and 150 pounds. Thus it would be the equivalent of runt. Rich Eldred, SABR researcher mentions that Selbach was also called "Barron" and much was made of his German background.

3231. Selkirk, George Alexander (1934–42 OF) "Twinkletoes." Ian Hutchinson points out in the *Canadian Baseball Hall of Fame Magazine,* that Ontario-born Selkirk, was nicknamed by a New Jersey sportswriter who watched him stretch a single into a double. He had a peculiar manner of running on the forward part of his feet putting all the weight on the toes. Selkirk will always be remembered as being the player who replaced "Babe" Ruth in the New York Yankees outfield in 1934 and wore his number 3 on his uniform.

3232. Sell, Elwood Lester (1922–23 P) "Epp." Origin unknown.

3233. Sellers, Oliver (1910 OF) "Rube." Sellers was a small town boy slow to adapt to big city life. He was nicknamed after "Rube" Waddell.

3234. Selma, Richard Jay (1965–74 P) "Mortimer Snerd." Selma reminded teammates of the puppet used by Edgar Bergen.

3235. Sembera, Carroll William (1965–70 P) "The Pencil." At 6' and 150 pounds, Sembera was thin as a pencil on the mound.

3236. Semproch, Roman Anthony (1958–61 P) "Baby." In the minor leagues Semproch was brought along slowly or babied. Managers Hub Kittle at Terre Haute, Indiana, and Charles Gassaway at Wilson, North Carolina, and trainer Pete Ceba, have been acknowledged as using the nickname at the early stages of Semproch's career.

3237. Senerchia, Emanual Robert (1952 3B) "Sonny." "Sonny" is a childhood nickname.

3238. Sessi, Walter Anthony (1941–46 OF) "Watsie." Sessie wrote me that

"Watsie" was a childhood nickname given to him by his brother. It has no particular meaning.

3239. Settlemire, Edgar Merle (1928 P) "Lefty." Settlemire pitched left handed and batted left handed.

3240. Sewell, James Luther (1921–42 C) "Luke." Sewell told me he was given the nickname of "Luke" by one of his first grade school teachers, but the reason is unclear. It may have been a takeoff on Luther.

3241. Sewell, Truett Banks (1932–49 P) "Rip." Sewell's older brother was called "Big Rip." The nickname expressed the idea of ripping it up, or going on a tear. He was called "Little Rip." In 1936 sportswriter Francis Dunn shortened the nickname to just "Rip." In 1941, Sewell was involved in a hunting accident which left him with buck-shot in both legs. It forced him to change his pitching style. He developed a blooper pitch whose nickname, "Eephus," became as famous if not more so than his own nickname. Sewell delivered the pitch with a back spin that sent the ball 20–30 feet in the air at a very slow speed before it came across the plate. Pittsburgh outfielder and teammate, Maurice Van Robays, called it an "Eephus" ball saying, "Eephus ain't no word and that ain't no pitch." Sewell used the pitch with great success and no one ever hit a home run off the pitch until the 1946 All Star Game. Although, he was not expected to pitch in the annual affair because of a sore elbow, Ted Williams, Boston Red Sox slugger was curious about whether Sewell would use the "Eephus" ball if he did pitch. With the American League ahead 9–0 and Sewell in the game pitching for the National League, Manager Charlie Grimm asked Sewell to use the blooper pitch to see if he could wake up the crowd. With two men on base and Ted Williams at bat shaking his head in an appeal not to do it and Sewell nodding to signal he was, Sewell threw two bloopers and a fastball to work the count to two balls and one strike. Then, he threw what he called a "Sunday Super Dooper Blooper" and Williams knocked it out of the park.

3242. Seybold, Ralph Orlando (1899–1908 OF) "Socks." "Socks" means hitting the ball. He socked it. In 1902 Seybold hit 16 home runs to lead the American League.

3243. Seymour, James Bentley (1896–1913 OF) "Cy." According to Fred Lieb, Seymour was a country boy nicknamed after Denton "Cy" Young. In 1905, Seymour missed winning the triple crown in batting by one home run.

3244. Shafer, Arthur Joseph (1909–13 3B) "Tillie." In 1909 manager, John McGraw introduced the rookie Shafer to the New York Giants team in the club house. Outfielder Cy Seymour ran over and kissed Shafer on both cheeks and said, "Tillie, how are you?" The nickname stuck, although the reasons for the feminine tag remains a mystery. Shafer despised the nickname but could not get rid of it. Lee Allen reports Shafer finally quit the game to run a haberdashery rather than continue to face the nickname.

3245. Shaffer, George (1887–90 OF) "Orator." Shaffer was known for his ability to speak. In fact, some said he talked a better game than he played.

3246. Shaffer, John W. (1886–87 P) "Cannonball." "Cannonball" refers to the speed of Shaffer's pitches.

3247. Shaner, Walter Dedaker (1923–29 OF) "Skinny." Shaner's last name reminded people of the character "Skinny Shaner" in the comic strip "Us Boys." Shaner was 6'2", 195 pounds.

3248. Shanks, Howard Samuel (1912–25 OF) "Hawk." Ball players called him "Hawk" because of his ability to chase down fly balls in the outfield.

3249. Shanley, Harry Root (1912 SS) "Doc." Many of the players with the nickname of "Doc" were associated with either the medical or dental professions. However, for Shanley the origin of "Doc" is unknown.

3250. Shannon, John Francis (1892–96 SS) "Frank." "Frank" was used by ball players as an alternative for Francis. Shannon was also called "Tod."

3251. Shannon, Maurice Joseph (1915–26 2B) "Red." The nickname refers to hair color.

3252. Shannon, Thomas Michael (1962–70 3B) "Moonman." Mike, as he was addressed, was known as a clubhouse cut-up or "Moonman." After his retirement, he became a sportscaster for the St. Louis Cardinals.

3253. Shannon, William P. (1914–15 FL Umpire) "Spike." Origin unknown.

3254. Shannon, William Porter (1904–08 OF; 1914–15 FL Umpire) "Spike." Shannon was noted for using his spikes when sliding into a base.

3255. Sharman, Ralph Edward (1917 OF) "Bally." Origin unknown.

3256. Sharpe, Bayard Heston (1905–10 1B) "Bud." "Bud" was a childhood nickname.

3257. Shaughnessy, Francis Joseph (1905–08 OF) "Shag." "Shag" is a contraction of Shaugnessy. Although "Shag" played but nine games in the major leagues, he had a distinguished minor league managerial career.

3258. Shaw, Frederick Lander (1883–88 P) "Dupee." Shaw may have been the first pitcher to use a full windup. His delivery seemed to mystify batters. He talked to batters and told them how great he was, and what dupes they were. When he struck a batter out, he would call to him and say, "Ah, I duped you that time." It got so he began calling himself "Dupee."

3259. Shaw, James Aloysius (1913–21 P) "Grunting Jim." Shaw made a loud and distinct grunting sound when he delivered a pitch, in much the same fashion that many modern day tennis players do when they hit the ball.

3260. Shawkey, James Robert (1913–27 P) "Sailor Bob." Shawkey was an underrated pitcher who won 196 major league games including four seasons in which he won 20 or more games for the New York Yankees. He also pitched in five World Series. He spent most of 1918 in the United States Navy. After that, he was called 'Sailor Bob'."

3261. Shay, Arthur Joseph (1916–18 2B) "Marty." Origin unknown.

3262. Shea, Frank Joseph (1947–55 P) "The Naugatuck Nugget." Shea had a speckled and freckled face and was addressed as "Spec." He had an outstanding rookie year with the New York Yankees in 1947, with a won-loss record of 14-5, and was the winning pitcher in the All Star game. Sportswriters began to call him "The Naugatuck Nugget" after his home town of Naugatuck, Connecticut.

3263. Shea, John Edward (1902 C) "Shorty." Shea was just 5'8" tall. He was also called "Red" because of his hair color. Some encyclopedia's erroneously list his nickname as "Nap."

3264. Shea, Patrick Henry (1918–22 P) "Red." The nickname refers to hair color.

3265. Shears, George Penfield (1912 P) "Scissors." The name of Shears suggests the nickname of "Scissors." This was reinforced by Shears' build, 6'3", 180 pounds.

3266. Sheehan, James Thomas (1936 C) "Big Jim." The nickname refers to body build. Sheehan was 6'2", 195 pounds.

3267. Sheehan, Timothy James (1895–96 OF) "Biff." "Biff" is a childhood nickname. But it may have been reinforced by hitting ability. "Biffer" was sometimes used to indicate a good hitter.

3268. Sheehy, Michael Joseph (1926–87 Clubhouse Manager) "Silent Pete." In 1926 a teenager, Michael Sheehy, was asked by Yankee clubhouse manager, Fred Logan, to help move some trunks in exchange for a free pass to the day's game. Logan liked the youngster and asked him to come back the next day. He did and didn't leave for over 50 years, becoming an institution in the Yankee dressing room. Because he was so quiet and minded his business, Logan called him "Silent Pete." Players shortened it in time to just "Pete." Thus throughout his long association with the Yankees, Michael Sheehy was known as "Pete."

3269. Sheely, Earl Homer (1921–31 1B) "Whitey." The nickname refers to light colored hair.

3270. Sheely, Hollis Kimball (1951–53 C) "Bud." "Bud" was a childhood nickname.

3271. Shelton, Andrew Kemper (1915 OF) "Skeeter." "Skeeter" is a nickname usually reserved for players of small stature. Shelton, however, was not that small, 5'11", 175 pounds.

3272. Shemo, Stephen Michael (1944–45 2B) "Stan." Shemo told me just his friends called him "Stan" when he played pro-ball. "It has no special meaning," he said.

3273. Sherdel, William Henry (1918–32 P) "Wee Willy." Sherdel was 5'10", 160 pounds. He was pitching for Hanover in the Class D Blue Ridge League in 1916. A player on the team said, "He'll never make it. He's too small." From then on he was called "Wee Willie" but Sherdel went on to win 165 major league games and pitch in two World Series.

3274. Sheridan, Eugene Anthony (1918–20 SS) "Red." The nickname refers to hair color.

3275. Sheridan, John F. (1901–14 AL Umpire) "Big Jack." Sheridan was a large man, but there are no statistics available on his exact height and weight.

3276. Sheridan, Neill Rawlins (1948 PH) "Wild Horse." Sheridan wrote me that the nickname of "Wild Horse" came from his "reckless abandon" style of play in the minor leagues.

3277. Sherling, Edward Creech (1924 PH) "Shine." "Shine" is a corruption of Sherling.

3278. Sherlock, John Clinton (1930 1B) "Monk." As a boy playing in the streets of Buffalo, kids thought his batting style, still as a statue, plus his long neck, made him look like a monk.

3279. Sherman, Lester Daniel (1914 P) "General." Sherman was addressed as "Babe" indicating his size, 5'6", 145 pounds. "General" was after the Civil War general, William Tecumseh Sherman.

3280. Shields, Benjamin Cowan (1924–31 P) "Lefty." Shields pitched left handed and batted left handed. He was also called "Big Ben," 6'1½", 195 pounds.

3281. Shields, Francis LeRoy (1915 1B) "Pete." Origin unknown.

3282. Shifflet, Garland Jessie (1957–64 P) "Duck." The origin of "Duck" is unknown. In the minor leagues, his teammates often called him "Shifty," but the origin of this nickname is also unknown.

3283. Shinauet, Enoch Erskine (1921–22 C) "Ginger." An undated *Who's Who* of the period press release, commented on Shinault, "He is known as 'Ginger' and his work behind the bat explains the nickname."

3284. Shines, Anthony Raymond (1983– 1B) "Razor." When Shines was in Junior college, he hit the ball so hard someone said he "sliced up the air."

3285. Shinnick, Timothy James (1890–91 2B) "Good Eye." Shinnick had a good eye for pitches. He walked more times than he struck out. He also had a "good eye" for playing on winning teams.

3286. Shipke, William Martin (1906–09 3B) "Muskrat Bill." Origin unknown.

3287. Shipley, Ernest Raeford (1924–25 1B) "Mule." "Mule" designated Shipley as a plodding, hard working player. It came from his play as fullback as a football player at the University of North Carolina.

3288. Shipley, Joseph Clark (1958–63 P) "Moses." Shipley was nicknamed by teammates at Johnstown in the Eastern League for his similarity in appearance to a character named Moses in the movie *The Searchers*.

3289. Shires, Charles Arthur (1928–32 1B) "Art the Great." Shires was a boxer in the off season and chose that nickname for himself. He also called himself "Whattaman." In baseball, he was best known as a brawler with a mean streak in him. Shires was willing to fight anyone, anytime. In 1929, he even challenged heavyweight champion Gene Tunny to a fight.

3290. Shirey, Clair Lee (1920 P) "Duke." Shirey's snappy dress led teammates to call him "Duke."

3291. Shirley, Alvis Newman (1941–46 P) "Tex." Shirley was usually addressed as "Tex" because he came from Arlington, Texas. He was known to have a temper and short fuse.

3292. Shiver, Ivey Merwin (1931–34 OF) "Chick." Origin unknown.

3293. Short, Christopher Joseph (1959–73 P) "Styles." "Styles" is an opposite nickname. Short had the reputation of being the worst dressed player in baseball. He wore sweaters that were too baggy and carried his clothes while on the road in cellophane bags and newspapers. On one occasion he appeared in the Philadelphia Phils clubhouse in an expensive new powder blue suit. Tim McCarver said the only trouble was the coat sleeves were about four inches too short and the trouser cuffs were about four inches way up his legs.

3294. Shotton, Burton Edwin (1909–23 OF) "Barney." The nickname was bestowed on Shotton by his teammates on the St. Louis Browns because of his speed on the bases. They said he was as fast as the race car driver Barney Oldfield.

3295. Shoun, Clyde Mitchell (1935–49 P) "Hardrock." The nickname came from high school days in Mountain City, Tennessee, where he was known as a rugged football and baseball player.

3296. Shovlin, John Joseph (1911–13 2B) "Brode." Origin unknown.

3297. Shriver, Harry Graydon (1922–23 P) "Pop." Origin unknown.

3298. Shuba, George Thomas (1943–55 OF) "Shotgun." It was said that line drives off his bat went all over the field like pellets out of a shotgun.

3299. Shultz, Wallace Luther (1911–12 P) "Toots." Origin unknown.

3300. Siebert, Wiefred Charles (1964–75 P) "Sonny." "Sonny" is a childhood nickname given to Siebert by his parents.

3301. Siemer, Oscar Sylvester (1925–26 C) "Cotton." The nickname refers to Siemer's light blond hair.

3302. Sievers, Roy Edward (1949–65 1B) "Squirrel." Sievers played basketball at Beaumont High School at St. Louis, Missouri. His teammates said he was always hanging around the cage like a squirrel.

3303. Siglin, Wesley Triplett (1914–16 2B) "Paddy." "Paddy" like "Pat" was a common nickname given to players of Irish-English background. Siglin was a star in the Pacific Coast League and was called "Tornado" and "Old Tornado" as affectionate nicknames.

3304. Silch, Edward (1888 OF) "Baldy." Silch had very little hair by the time he reached his early twenties.

3305. Silvera, Charles Anthony (1948–57 C) "Swede." The name Silvera sounds Italian and it has been erroneously reported that Charlie as he was addressed, was of Italian-German background. Silvera reported to me that he was of Portuguese and Irish extraction. He received the nickname "Swede" at age eight when kids reacted to his raw-boned blond hair. He states, "I was called that all through school, but I was never called 'Swede' during the duration of my entire professional baseball career." Silvera caught for ten years in the major leagues, but played in only 227 games and made only 136 hits. He received seven World Series pay checks while playing for the New York Yankees, but played in only one World Series game. His *career* deserves the nickname of "Stretch."

3306. Silvestri, Kenneth Joseph (1939–51 C) "Hawk." Silvestri had a good throwing arm and had the ability to nail runners attempting to steal bases.

3307. Simmons, Aloysius Harry (1924–44 OF) "Bucketfoot." Simmons developed an unorthodox and unique batting stance usually called "stepping in the bucket." As a right handed batter, he would plant his right foot, and as the ball came to the plate his left foot would stride toward third base. Coaches and managers tried, but could not change his style. However, Simmons was highly successful, compiling a batting average of .334 over 20 years. Nathan Salant quotes Simmons, "I utterly despised that nickname because as far as I was concerned, it questioned my courage. It sounded like I was afraid of the ball. After a while, they stopped calling me by that name, because they knew it made me angry, and the angrier I got, the better I hit."

3308. Simmons, George Washington (1910–15 2B) "Hack." Simmons was nicknamed after the famous wrestler Hackenschmidt.

3309. Simmons, Ted Lyle (1968–89 C) "Simba." At the start of his career Simmons wore his hair long like the mane of a lion. He kept the nickname even after his mane was removed when it caught fire while he was burning leaves.

3310. Simons, Melborn Ellis (1931–32 OF) "Butch." "Butch" was a childhood nickname with the connotation of mischievous.

3311. Simpson, Harry Leon (1951–59 OF) "Suitcase." Simpson was a good journeyman outfielder and first baseman. Yet he was always on the move, back and forth among clubs, 17 times in 11 years.

3312. Simpson, Thomas Leo (1953 P) "Duke." Simpson told me that his older brother's nickname was "Duke." "When I started school, I was called 'Little Duke.' When my brother graduated, the 'little' was dropped since I was the biggest kid in my class."

3313. Sims, Clarence (1915 P) "Pete." "Pete" in Sims' case has no particular meaning. It was just a "better" baseball name than Clarence.

3314. Sims, Duane B. (1964–74 C) "Duke." Minor league manager Mark Wylie of North Platte in the Nebraska State League first called Sims "Duke" because he did not think Duane was a good baseball name, since to him, it had a feminine connotation. During his major league career, Sims' nickname was reinforced by his good looks, fancy dress, and delusions of grandeur.

3315. Singer, William Robert (1964–77 P) "The Singer Throwing Machine." The nickname is a takeoff on the phrase "The Singer Sewing Machine." It was given to Singer by writer Bob Hunter of the *Los Angeles Herald Examiner*. It denotes both Singer's fastball and his endurance on the mound.

3316. Singleton, Bert Elmer (1946–59 P) "Smoky." The nickname refers to the speed of Singleton's fastball. He put smoke on it.

3317. Singleton, John Edward (1922 P) "Sheriff." Origin unknown.

3318. Sisler, George Harold (1915–30 1B) "Gorgeous George." The nickname was used by newspaper writers to celebrate his great hitting and great fielding at first base. He had a career batting average of .345 for 15 seasons and made 2,812 hits.

3319. Sisti, Sebastian Daniel (1939–54 2B) "Sibbi." Sisti told me "Sibbi" is really nothing more than short for Sebastian. "I have had that name for as long as I can remember."

3320. Sketchley, Harry Clement (1942 OF) "Bud." The nickname of "Bud" was given to Sketchley in childhood.

3321. Skinner, Elisha Harrison (1922–23 OF) "Camp." Skinner was named and nicknamed by his parents after his mother's father, Elisha Harrison Camp.

3322. Skizas, Louis Peter (1956–59 OF) "The Nervous Greek." Skizas says he was one of the few players of Greek origin. He told me he did not remember exactly when he got the nickname or whom to attribute it to, but it was during his playing days. "It was because of the gyrations, antics, and unique habits, I displayed while coming up to bat." Mickey Mantle on the other hand, characterizes Skizas as a 1950s pre-hippie from the streets and alleys of Chicago, a guy always on the move, especially with women.

3323. Skopec, John S. (1901–03 P) "Buckshot." Origin unknown.

3324. Skowron, William Joseph (1954–67 1B) "Moose." Skowron says he received his nickname in childhood after his grandfather jokingly called him Mussolini. His family shortened it to "Moose." The nickname was reinforced later by his strength. Joe Pepitone reportedly told him, "They don't call you 'Moose' because you're big and strong. It's because you have a head like one."

3325. Slade, Gordon (1930–35 SS) "Oskie." Slade attended the University of Oregon. One of the cheers for the athletic squads was the yell, "Oski Wah-wah."

3326. Slagle, James Franklin (1899–1908 OF) "Rabbit." Slagle was small and very fast. He was also called "Shorty" and "The Human Mosquito," both nicknames also referring to his small stature.

3327. Slaughter, Byron Atkins (1910 P) "Barney." "Barney" seems to have been an alternative to Byron, although during this period, fastball pitchers like Walter Johnson were called Barney after Barney Oldfield, the race car driver.

3328. Slaughter, Enos Bradsher (1938–59 OF) "Country." Manager Bert Shotton gave Slaughter the nickname of "Country" when he was a rookie with Columbus of the American Association. It was because he was a country boy from the tobacco fields of North Carolina. Shotton also taught Slaughter to hustle, a trait for which he was to become famous, but would never receive a nickname to immortalize his efforts.

3329. Slayback, Elbert (1926 2B) "Scottie." Slayback was of Scottish background.

3330. Sloan, Adam Bruce (1944 OF) "Fatso." Sloan was 5'9", and weighed 195 pounds.

3331. Sloan, Dwain Clifford (1948–49 P) "Lefty." Sloan pitched left handed but batted right handed.

3332. Smajstrea, Craig Lee (1988– 2B) "Alphabet." Smajstrea is of Czech descent. The pronunciation of his name had PA announcers befuddled. Manager Hal Lanier nicknamed him "Alphabet," but his Houston Astro teammates simply call him "Smash."

3333. Small, Clyde Henry (1929–34 P) "Lefty." Harry, as he was addressed, pitched left handed but was a switch hitter.

3334. Smith, Alexander Benjamin (1897–1906 C) "Broadway." As a street name, "Broadway" indicated Smith was streetwise, a gambler, and a dapper dresser.

3335. Smith, Alphonse Eugene (1953–64 OF) "Fuzzy." Smith told me as a minor league player at Wilkes Barre, George Davito, called him "Fuzzy" because his beard grew rapidly.

3336. Smith, Armstrong Frederick (1912 OF) "Klondike." "Klondike" is the name of a vast northern territory in Canada, which at one time was rich in gold ore. Smith was born in London, England. It is possible that he might have spent time in the "Klondike," but, I have found no evidence of this.

3337. Smith, Charles (1924–30 OF, Negro League) "Chino." Smith was a scrappy 5'6" left-handed slugger who, in an abbreviated career batted .446 in regular Negro League play, .423 in exhibitions against major leaguers, and .335 in the Cuban winter leagues. The nickname "Chino" came from the slant across his eyes which gave him an Oriental appearance.

3338. Smith, Charles Marvin (1880–91 2B) "Pop." Smith was given the nickname of "Pop" during the latter years of his career. It was used as a term of respect for his knowledge of the players and the game.

3339. Smith, Clarence Ossie (1913–17 P) "Pop Boy Smith." Smith was very popular as a young ball player, but how this may be related to his nickname is unknown.

3340. Smith, Earl Sutton (1919–30 C) "Oil." When writer Westbrook Pegler was covering the New York Giants, he called Smith "Oil" because of the way Bronx fans pronounced Earl.

3341. Smith, Frank Elmer (1904–15 P) "Piano Mover." Smith was pitching for the White Sox in 1908. He was a sensitive individual who walked out on the team when he was accused of drinking and missing practice sessions. After he was reinstated, the press ridiculed him with nicknames "Piano Mover" and "Piano Keys." Both terms referred to his physique in a negative manner. He was also called "Nig," drawing attention to his dark complexion.

3342. Smith, George Allen (1916–23 P) "Columbia George." Smith attended and played baseball at Columbia University. New York sportswriters gave him the nickname.

3343. Smith, George Henry (1897–1903 2B) "Heinie." "Heinie" denotes Smith's German background.

3344. Smith, George J. (1884–98 SS) "Germany." Smith was of German background.

3345. Smith, Harold Wayne (1956–65 C) "Cura." Smith wrote me, "I was playing in the Mexican Winter League when fans in Guadelahara chanted 'Cura Cura Cura' when I took off my cap for the playing of the national anthem. At age 22, I was becoming bald and I reminded them of an order of Monks who shave their hair so it looks almost like a ring around their heads."

3346. Smith, Henry Joseph (1910 OF) "Hap." "Hap" is short for happy. Smith had a cheerful personality.

3347. Smith, James A. (1898 SS) "Stub." Smith was very short, but his exact height is unknown.

3348. Smith, James Carlisle (1911–19 3B) "Red." The nickname refers to hair color.

3349. Smith, James Lawrence (1914–22 SS) "Bluejacket." Smith was discharged from the navy because of bad eyes. When he showed up at the Bartlesville, Oklahoma, team in 1908, according to Lee Allen, the only clothing he had were old navy uniforms. He wore one for the first game he played. A local sportswriter who did not bother to find out his name listed it as "Bluejacket" in the box score. Smith liked it, and made it his nickname throughout his career.

3350. Smith, John Francis (1883–91 P) "Phenomenal Smith." Smith was one of a few ball players who nicknamed themselves. He called himself "Phenomenal" after pitching a no-hitter for Newark in the Eastern League.

3351. Smith, Lawrence Patrick (1920 C) "Paddy." "Paddy" refers to Smith's Irish background and may even be a takeoff on Patrick.

3352. Smith, Lewis Oscar (1904–11 OF) "Bull." Smith was noted for his strength. He was accorded the nickname of "Bull" while playing football for West Virginia University.

3353. Smith, Lonnie (1978– OF) "Skates." Smith's defensive play has always been erratic because of his tendency to slip in the outfield.

3354. Smith, Marvin Harold (1925 SS) "Red." The nickname refers to hair color.

3355. Smith, Osborne Earl (1978 SS) "The Wizard of Os." Smith is rated as one, if not the best fielding shortstops of all time. During the 1980s he had a lock on the golden glove award. He was truly a wizard at shortstop. The nickname is a takeoff on the 1939 movie, *The Wizard of Oz*.

3356. Smith, Richard Paul (1927 C) "Red." The nickname refers to hair color.

3357. Smith, Robert Walkup (1958–59 P) "Riverboat Smith." Smith told me, "While playing in the Pacific Coast League, Bob Stevens of the *San Francisco Chronicle* wrote that I pitched with all the finesse and cunning of a Mississippi riverboat gambler. I was from Missouri, and the boys in the clubhouse took care of the rest."

3358. Smith, Salvatore Giuseppe (1913 C) "Joe." "Joe" was just an arbitrary name to replace Salvatore. It had no special meaning.

3359. Smith, Samuel J. (1888 1B) "Skyrocket." Origin unknown.

3360. Smith, Walter W. (1928–82 Sportswriter) "Red." Smith began writing about sports in 1928 for *The St. Louis Star*. Over the next five decades he wrote several columns a week for *The Philadelphia Record, The New York Herald Tribune* and *The New York Times*. In 1976 he won a Pulitzer Prize for distinguished commentary. It was said he was the best practitioner of his craft since Ring Lardner. His columns on baseball such as, "Connie Mack's Inevitable Day," "Henry Aaron's Finest Hour," "Miracle of Coogan's Bluff," "Ted Williams Spits," "O'Malley's House of Horrors," and "Loathsome Ploy, & the D.H.," are legendary. Smith had red hair and went by the name of "Red"; even the byline of his columns was Red Smith. Few people even knew his first name was Walter.

3361. Smith, Wilbur Floyd (1909 C) "Wib." "Wib" simply shortens Wilbur, using just three letters of the first name.

3362. Smith, Willard Jehu (1917–18 C) "Red." The nickname refers to hair color.

3363. Smith, Willie (1963–71 OF) "Wonderful Willie." Smith got his nickname for his superb performance for Syracuse in the International League in 1963. His batting average was .380 and as a pitcher he had a 14-2 won-lost record.

3364. Smoyer, Henry Neitz (1912 SS) "Hennie." "Hennie" is no more than an affectionate family pet name for Henry.

3365. Snell, Walter Henry (1913 C) "Doc." Snell was neither a physician or dentist. He was called "Doc" because he coached and taught at Brown University.

3366. Snider, Edwin Donald (1947–64 OF) "Duke." Snider said he received his nickname from his father on the first day he went to kindergarten. He came strutting home and his father said, "Here comes his majesty the Duke." Snider always liked the nickname. "It was better than Edwin, anything would be." During his heavy hitting days (1953–57) when he hit 40 or more home runs each year, he was called the "Duke of Flatbush" by Brooklyn fans and writers. Snider became prematurely grey, and was referred to as "The Silver Fox." Nathan Salant points out that Snider's Dodger teammates had even another nickname for him. Quoting Carl Furillo, "Snider was always crying whenever there were left-handers pitching and he cried when he wasn't hitting the ball, when he was in a slump, and he would cry when the manager didn't take him out.... He was an only child growing up, a mama's boy. They used to call him that. He admitted that himself. 'California Fruit,' we used to call him."

3367. Snipes, Wyatt Beal (1901 PH) "Rock." "Roxy's, as Wyatt was addressed, major league career consisted of only one time at bat. "Rock" as a nickname during the early part of the century was the equivalent of "Batty," a person lacking in mentality. It is short for "Rocks in the Head."

3368. Snodgrass, Amzie Beal (1901 OF) "Chappie." Origin unknown.

3369. Snodgrass, Fred Carlisle (1908–16 OF) "Snow." During his playing years with the New York Giants, there were a number of other players with the firstname of Fred. Players created nicknames to differentiate among them. Snodgrass was called "Sno," the first three letters of his last name. However, when it appeared in print, it tuned up "Snow."

3370. Snover, Colonel Lester (1919 C) "Bosco." An unauthored newspaper report of 1919 described Snover, "He is built like a super-dreadnought." The reference is to a large battleship. How this description may be related to the nickname of "Bosco" is unknown.

3371. Snyder, Charles (1890 OF) "Cooney." Origin unknown.

3372. Snyder, Charles N. (1876–91 C) "Pop." "Pop" was an affectionate nickname given to Snyder during the latter part of his career by fellow players. He was one of the first great catchers, a real student of the game. Snyder stressed team play and is credited as the person who started the system of catcher-pitcher signs.

3373. Snyder, Emanuel Sebastian (1876–84 OF) "Redleg." Snyder played for the Cincinnati Redlegs in 1876, the first year of the National League play. Although he never again played for Cincinnati, he carried the team nickname throughout his career.

3374. Snyder, Frank Elton (1912–27 C) "Pancho." Snyder is a good example of a journeyman player who received too little recognition during his playing days and whose career has all but been forgotten. He toiled 16 years behind the plate for the St. Louis Cardinals and New York Yankees with a lifetime batting average of .265 and appeared in four World Series. "Pancho" refers to the Spanish-Mexican heritage of his native San Antonio, Texas.

3375. Sockalexis, Louis Francis (1897–99 OF) "Chief." Sockalexis appeared in only 94 major league games, all for the National League Cleveland Club, then nicknamed "Naps." But much has been written about his brief career and life. He was a full-blooded Penobscot Indian from Old Town, Maine. His potential as a hitter was as highly regarded as any player of his era. About the time he began his major league career, he discovered the beverage alcohol. Almost immediately, drinking whiskey, as it had been with so many American Indians, became a problem for Sockalexis. It destroyed his baseball career almost even before it got started, and his life as well. He died a beggar on the streets at age 42. Sockalexis was adored by Cleveland fans while he played, and the term "Indians" was sometimes used to refer to the full team. Some researchers believe it was the memory of Sockalexis which led the Cleveland team to eventually change their name to Indians.

3376. Solomon, Eddie, Jr. (1973–82 P) "Buddy." "Buddy" is short for the family pet name for Solomon, "Buddy Jay."

3377. Solomon, Moses H. (1923 OF) "The Rabbi of Swat." Solomon's nickname received much more recognition and enduring fame than his brief major league career which consisted of only two games. Manager John McGraw of the New York Giants had long sought a Jewish ball player to boost attendance. He had high hopes for the hard hitting Solomon who the media had dubbed, "The Rabbi of Swat." Solomon as it turned out was not the answer, and McGraw's quest continued.

3378. Solters, Julius Joseph (1934–43 OF) "Moose." As one writer put it, Solters was big, strong and usually charging.

3379. Somerlott, John Wesley (1910–11 1B) "Jock." "Jock" was just a baseball takeoff on the name of John.

3380. Somers, William (1893 OF) "Kid." Information about Somers is slim. It is not even known what his height and weight were, or from which side he threw and batted, let alone how he came by the nickname of "Kid."

3381. Sommers, Joseph Andrews (1887–90 C) "Pete." Origin unknown.

3382. Sorrells, Raymond Edwin (1922 SS) "Red." The nickname refers to hair color.

3383. Sothoron, Allen Sutton (1914–26 P) "Old Hoss." In 1926, Sothoron was in his last year of eleven he pitched in the major leagues, while doubling as a coach for the St. Louis Cardinals. On August 31, he won the second game of a doubleheader 2–1 on a three hitter to elevate the Cardinals over the Pittsburgh Pirates. They then went on in September to win their first National League flag and defeated the New York Yankees in the World Series. Sothoron was nicknamed "Old Hoss." Ed Burkholder explains one derivation of the nickname "Old Hoss." It means an old fire engine horse that was trained to be ready for action when the fire bell rang, but had been retired. When it heard a fire bell, it would still rear back and get ready to race to a fire even though it might now be hitched to a grocery wagon.

3384. Souchock, Stephen (1946–55 OF) "Bud." The nickname of "Bud" was given to him by his brother when he was a child.

3385. Sparks, Thomas Frank (1897–1910 P) "Tully." Origin unknown.

3386. Speake, Robert Charles (1955–59 OF) "Spook." At 6'1", 175 pounds, Speake was long, lean, bony and some thought "spooky" looking.

3387. Speaker, Tristam E. (1907–28 OF) "The Grey Eagle." Speaker was prematurely grey by age 30. His shock of grey hair could be easily observed as he patrolled center field like a roving eagle. Tris, as he was addressed, was one of the premier hitters of the dead-ball era compiling a lifetime batting average of .344 with 3,515 base hits. Yet as his nickname indicates, he was equally famous for his fielding ability. Many observers feel he may have been the best center fielder of all time. The fact that it has been reported that he once caught a foul fly while playing center field contributed to his reputation. Players called him "Spoke." He was the "Spoke" that kept the team together.

3388. Spear, George Nathan (1909 P) "Kid." There is no available information on Speer's height and weight. However, there is every indication that he was small of stature.

3389. Spencer, Daryl Dean (1952–63 SS) "Big Dee." Spencer was 6'2½", tall by shortstop standards. "Dee" is an expansion of the initial "D." It differentiated Spencer from Don Drysdale, who played at the same time and whose nickname was "Big D."

3390. Spencer, Edward Russell (1905–18 C) "Tubby." According to R.C. Lane, the long time writer for *Baseball Magazine,* Spencer was on the heavy side with very large shoulders. There is no information available on exactly what Spencer weighed or his height. Lane goes on to mention that by age 18, Spencer was able to down a quart of whiskey and still play ball. His career can be described as a "ten-year jag."

3391. Speraw, Paul Bachman (1920 3B) "Polly." The last name is pronounced the same as that of the bird, sparrow. "Polly" thus is related to the pronunciation. Speraw was also called "Birdie."

3392. Spies, Henry (1885 1B) "Harry." "Harry" was used as an alternative for Henry.

3393. Spintz, Joseph Conrad (1930–33 C) "Mule." "Mule" refers to Sprintz's hard work behind the plate. He received the nickname from minor league teammates.

3394. Spratt, Henry Lee (1911–12 SS) "Harry." "Harry" was used as an alternative for Henry.

3395. Squires, Michael Lynn (1975–85 1B) "Spanky." Squires was nicknamed after the character in the movies featuring the "Dead End Kids."

3396. Stafford, Henry Alexander (1916 PH) "Heinie." "Heinie" refers to Stafford's German background.

3397. Stafford, James Joseph (1890 OF) "General." Stafford was interested in military affairs and was a supporter of Antonio Maceo, the Cuban patriot who wanted independence for his country from Spain.

3398. Stafford, John Henry (1893 P) "Doc." Many of the players with the nickname of "Doc" had an association with either the medical or dental professions. However, for Stafford the origin of "Doc" is unknown.

3399. Stahl, Garland (1903–13 1B) "Jake." In 1913, at the end of his career, Stahl refused to play first base because of a foot injury. His teammates thought that he was a loafer and chastised with the nickname "Jaker" which was slang for loafer. By 1915, however, the "Jake" tag was used in a more positive manner when Stahl managed the Boston Red Sox to a World Series victory over the

New York Giants. He was called "Jake the Giant Killer."

3400. Stainback, George Tucker (1934–46 OF) "Goldilocks." The nickname refers to hair color.

3401. Stallcup, Thomas Virgil (1947–53 SS) "Red." The nickname refers to hair color.

3402. Staller, George Walborn (1943 OF) "Stopper." Staller told me that as a young boy, kids started calling him "Stopper." It was a takeoff on Staller.

3403. Stallings, George Tweedy (1890–98 C) "The Miracle Man." Stallings major league career consisted of seven games spread over three years. He had no public nickname. "The Miracle Man" nickname stems from the seventh year of his 13 as a major league manager. In 1914, he managed the Boston "Miracle Team" Braves to the National League flag, despite the fact that they were in last place on the Fourth of July. Stallings was a cultured, handsome, well-educated Southern gentleman from Augusta, Georgia. But as a manager, he was a wild man who made extensive use of profanity and vulgar language. He was also overly superstitious even for a baseball man. He believed in, and used charms, voodoos and hexes. During the later years of his managerial career, he was referred to as "The Big Chief."

3404. Stanek, Albert Wilfred (1963 P) "Lefty." Stanek pitched left handed and batted left handed.

3405. Stanhouse, Donald Joseph (1972–82 P) "Stan the Man Unusual." The nickname was a takeoff on Stan "the Man" Musial. Stanhouse had the reputation as a flake. He engaged in queer antics. For example, when his back was bothering him, he would hang upside down in the bullpen. When he pitched for Baltimore as a relief pitcher, Manager Earl Weaver dubbed him "Full Pack," because he always smoked a full pack of cigarettes when Stanhouse was on the mound. The reason was that Stanhouse even walked batters on 3-2 pitches and loaded the bases before pitching out of jams.

3406. Stanky, Edward Raymond (1943–53 2B) "The Brat." Depending on for whom you rooted, Stanky was either an inspirational leader hollering guy type who could spark a comeback with a walk, or bunt or stolen base, or a loud-mouth, cocky, brawling bench jockey, who even tried to line foul balls into opposing team dugouts. His knack of getting things done with limited ability, infuriated opponents. New York sportswriters called him "that brat from Kensington," after the section of Philadelphia where he was raised. After fights with Len Merullo and Goody Rosen, he was tagged "Muggsy" after John McGraw. This nickname was reinforced when he tangled with Jackie Robinson.

3407. Stanley, Frederick Blair (1969–82 SS) "Chicken." Stanley was pale-skinned, skinny, and looked and walked like a chicken.

3408. Stanley, John Leonard (1911 P) "Buck." "Buck" is a generic nickname of which the circumstances of origin are almost never documented. It refers to a well developed, virile, aggressive, high spirited young man. The nickname is usually bestowed on the individual during his teenage years.

3409. Stanley, Mitchell Jack (1954–78 OF) "Mickey." Stanley's parents decided to call him "Mickey" instead of Mitchell. Stanley, normally an outfielder, played all seven games of the 1968 World Series at shortstop for the

Detroit Tigers, even though he had only nine games of major league experience at that position.

3410. Stanley, Robert William (1977–89 P) "Bigfoot." Stanley wrote me that pitcher Louis Tiant nicknamed him "Bigfoot" in 1978. It was not because of his big feet, but because of his body hair and the way he plodded along as he walked. The reference was to the mythical character of the Northland. Tiant also called him "Vulture" because he would come into a game as a relief pitcher, get in a jam, give up the tying run, and then end up as the winning pitcher taking the win away from the starting pitcher. Tiant called this practice "vulturizing." At about the same time, another Red Sox pitching teammate began calling him "Steamer." This was because of his last name. The reference was to the "Stanley Steamer," an early model car.

3411. Stanton, George Washington (1931 OF) "Buck." "Buck" is a generic nickname of which the circumstances of origin are almost never documented. It refers to a well developed, virile, aggressive, high spirited young man. The nickname is usually bestowed on the individual during his teenage years.

3412. Stargell, Wilver Dornel (1962–82 OF) "Pops." Willie, as he was addressed, really did not have a nickname until 1979, when at the age of 38 he began referring to himself as "Pops." That was the year he led the Pittsburgh Pirates, whose team nickname was "Family," borrowed from the hit record by Sister Sledge "We Are Family," to the world championship.

3413. Stark, Albert D. (1928–35, 1937–39, 1942 NL Umpire) "Dolly." I have found no explanation of "Dolly." It may be possible that it was his middle name or the nickname was derived from his middle name. As an umpire, Stark was very swift of movement, emotional, and high strung. He always seemed to be in the right place at the right time. Faultless in calling ball and strikes, in 1935 in a *Sporting News* poll of 200 players, he was chosen the most popular and respected umpire in the National League.

3414. Stark, Monroe Randolph (1909–12 SS) "Dolly." Origin unknown.

3415. Starr, Raymond Francis (1932–45 P) "Iron Man." A Cincinnati Reds press release in 1942 reports that through 1941 Starr had pitched both ends of 50 double-headers without relief in the minor leagues.

3416. Start, Joseph (1876–86 1B) "Old Reliable." David Porter points out that Start began playing baseball in 1860 at age 17. He was well into his thirties before performing in the first season of the newly founded National League in 1876. "Old Reliable" has two connotations. First, Start was regarded as a power hitter who came through in the clutch. Second, he possessed exceptional skill at catching balls in the clutch, in an era in which fielding left much to be desired.

3417. Staton, Joseph (1972–73 1B) "Slim." Staton was 6'3" and weighed 175 pounds.

3418. Statz, Arnold John (1919–42 2B) "Jigger." Joseph McBride suggests that "Jigger" refers to the golf iron of that name. Statz was one of the best golfers in baseball. Eddie Gold and Art Ahrens report that when Statz was playing with the Chicago Cubs in 1922, teammate Bob O'Farrell nicknamed him "Jigger" because he could never sit still and was always "jigging" around. Statz was just 5'7½" and weighed only 150 pounds, but many expert observers believe he may have been the best fielding center fielder of all time. He played from 1919–42, 8 seasons in the major leagues and 18 in the Pacific Coast League. He played in 3,473 games in the majors and Pacific Coast League more than any other player in history. His 4,093 hits are bested only by Rose and Cobb.

3419. Staub, Daniel Joseph (1963–85 OF) "Rusty." Staub was nicknamed at birth by nurses in the hospital where he was born in New Orleans. When he played for Montreal 1969–71 he acquired the French equivalent of "Rusty," "Le Grand Orange." It was while playing for Montreal in 1969 that Staub became the first player to popularize the use of batting gloves.

3420. Stearns, Norman (1921–42 OF, Negro League) "Turkey." The 6'1", 170-pound Stearns, from 1922–36 hit 160 home runs in the Negro leagues, more than anyone else. Even with his right foot in the bucket, this left handed slugger hit some of the longest home runs in baseball history. The "Turkey" nickname came from the fact that Stearns flapped his elbows when he ran.

3421. Steele, William Mitchell (1910–14 P) "Big Bill." Steele was 6'2" and weighed 195 pounds.

3422. Steelman, Morris James (1899–1902 C) "Farmer." Steelman was a farmer in the off season.

3423. Stein, Justin Marion (1938 SS) "Ott." Stein wrote me that he was nicknamed by teammates in the minor leagues after a famous bowler, Otto Stein from his hometown of St. Louis.

3424. Steinbrenner, George Michael, III (1973–90 Owner) "The Big Ego." In 1973 Steinbrenner headed a 15-man syndicate which purchased the New York Yankees. The highly controversial owner was best known for his interference with the everyday running of the club, making 19 managerial changes in 17 years (including the hiring and firing of Billy Martin five times); disputes with players such as those involving stars Reggie Jackson and Dave Winfield; and constant difficulties with commissioners (eight actions taken against him 1973–89). In August of 1990, Commissioner Fay Vincent forced Steinbrenner out of baseball for associations with confessed gambler, Howard Spina. In spite of all this, to keep perspective, it should be remembered that the Yankees did win five A.L. flags and two World Series during the 17-year Steinbrenner era.

3425. Steiner, James Harry (1945 C) "Red." The nickname refers to hair color.

3426. Steinfeldt, Harry M. (1898–1911 3B) "Battleaxe." Tom Shea points out that "Battleaxe" did not refer to Steinfeldt's temperament but was the name of the branch of tobacco he chewed. Steinfeldt is the answer to the trivia question, "Who was the third baseman who played with the Chicago Cubs famous double-play combination of Tinker to Evers to Chance?"

3427. Stemmeyer, William (1885–88 P) "Cannonball." "Cannonball" refers to the speed of Stemmeyer's fastball. In 1886 he struck out 239 batters.

3428. Stengel, Charles Dillion (1912–25 OF) "Casey." Casey Stengel began his career in organized baseball with Kankakee in the Northern Association in 1910, and it extended 55 years until his retirement as manager of the New York Mets at the end of the 1965 season. Given its length, Stengel's career in baseball was as colorful as anyone ever associated with the game. His playing and managerial days both in the major and minor leagues were filled with antics and incidents which now have become part of the legends and lore of the game. He began his 14-year playing career, 1912–25, with Brooklyn and subsequently played for Pittsburgh, Philadelphia, New York, and Boston, all in the National League. It is sometimes forgotten that Charles Stengel was an excellent outfielder who compiled a lifetime batting average of .284, and .393 in two World Series. Stengel was born and raised in Kansas City. The nickname "Casey" was derived from the initials of his home town K.C. There is more than one version of how this came to be. One is, that when he first came to Kankakee in 1910 he had K.C. stenciled on his baggage and he introduced himself to his teammates by saying "I'm from K.C." A second account is that Stengel talked so much about Kansas City that it quickly became a part of his identity. Yet a third story has it that it was common in those days to nickname minor league rookies by the state or city from which they came. Regardless of the origin, the nickname "Casey," the printed version of K.C., became enduring. There is evidence, however, that during his early playing days Stengel was also called "Dutch" referring to his ancestry, and "Jake" after Jake Stenzel an outfielder of some note in the 1890s. Stengel managed in the major leagues for 25 years with a winning percentage of .508. During his first nine years managing Brooklyn and Boston in the National League his teams finished no higher than fifth place, and in his last four years with the National League New York Mets his teams were dead last four straight times. During the middle period of his managerial career, 1949–60, with the New York Yankees, he masterminded his teams to ten American League flags and seven World Series championships. Due to his success with the Yankees, fans, sportswriters, and broadcasters began to call Stengel "The Professor" and "The Swammi." He was also sometimes addressed as "Doctor" which referred to his own inability to remember names and habit of calling others "Doctor."

3429. Stephen, Louis Roberts (1968 P) "Buzz." Stephen told me that about age two his older sister Tanya could not pronounce "brother." It came out "Bruzzer" which evolved into "Buzzy" and then "Buzz." His wife detests the nickname and does not think it is proper for a grown man.

3430. Stephens, Harry (1880–90s Concessions) "Scorecard Man." Stephens developed the idea of score cards and food concessions at ballparks and by 1900 was supplying the services to most major league franchises. He was also called "Hustling Harry."

3431. Stephens, James Walter (1907–12 C) "Little Nemo." Stephens was 5'6½" and weighed 155 pounds. He was nicknamed after the character in the comic strip. "Little Nemo in Slumberland" created by Winser McKay. It first appeared in the Sunday editions of the *New York Herald* in 1905.

3432. Stephens, Paul Eugene (1921–37 SS, Negro League) "Jake." Holway indicates that Stephens was short, a good base runner, and a great storyteller. However, I can find no information on the origin of the nickname of "Jake."

3433. Stephens, Vernon Decatur (1941–55 SS) "Junior." Stephens had the same name as his father. His family called him "Junior" so as not to confuse him with his father. Stephens was a power hitter, especially for a shortstop. Both players and media recognized this with the nickname of "Buster."

3434. Stephenson, Jackson Riggs (1921–34 OF) "Old Hoss." While "Old

Hoss" may suggest faithful old family horses or fire engine horses of a bygone age, in Stephenson's case it is probably derived from his football days at the University of Alabama. He was called "War Horse" and "Rough House."

3435. Stephenson, Reubin Crandol (1892 OF) "Dummy." Stephenson was totally deaf.

3436. Stephenson, Walter McQueen (1935–37 C) "Tarzan." Stephenson was nicknamed "Tarzan" because of his physical strength, agility and prowess. The reference is to the ape-man character in the novel by Edgar Rice Burroughs first published in 1914. However, it is more likely that Stephenson's nickname came from the comic strip version of the story which appeared in 1929, illustrated by Harold Foster.

3437. Sterrett, Charles Hurlbut (1912–13 OF) "Dutch." "Dutch" refers to Sterrett's German background.

3438. Stevens, Edward Lee (1945–50 1B) "Big Ed." Stephens was 6'1" and weighed 190 pounds.

3439. Stevens, James Arthur (1914 P) "Harry." Origin unknown.

3440. Stewart, Asa (1895 2B) "Ace." Stewart was nicknamed after Asa Brainard the legendary pitcher who pitched every game for the 1869 Cincinnati Red Stockings. The Word Ace meaning good performance may have been derived from Asa.

3441. Stewart, Charles Eugene (1913–14 OF) "Tuffy." In the minor leagues Stewart built the reputation of being a rough and tough ball player who always stuck up for his rights.

3442. Stewart, David Keith (1978– P) "Smoke." "Smoke" refers to Stewart's fastball.

3443. Stewart, Edward Perry (1941–54 OF) "Bud." Stewart wrote me that his parents started calling him "Buddy" as a small boy.

3444. Stewart, Glen Weldon (1940–44 SS) "Gabby." Stewart wrote me, "In the early 1930s while I was playing sand lot ball in Memphis 5 or 6 years before I started playing pro ball, a player called me 'Gabby' because I was so quiet. It was picked up by sportswriter Will Carruthers of the evening daily newspaper."

3445. Stewart, John Franklin (1916–29 2B) "Stuffy." During his minor league days fans would use the expression, "that's the stuff" when Stewart's great speed would enable him to turn a routine ground ball to the infield into a hit.

3446. Stewart, Mark (1913 C) "Big Stick." "Big Stick" means "Big Bat," a good hitter.

3447. Stewart, Veston Goff (1952–56 P) "Bunky." Stewart wrote me, "I was a mischievous child. There used to be a comic strip character in the newspaper my grandfather read regularly. He was always in and out of trouble like me. He was a little boy named Bunky. My grandfather nicknamed me 'Bunky.' The reference is to the comic strip started in 1927 titled "Parlor, Bedroom and Sink, Starring Bunky" and continued to appear in newspapers through the early 1950s.

3448. Stewart, Walter Cleveland (1921–35 P) "Lefty." Stewart pitched left handed but batted right handed.

3449. Stewart, William J. (1933–54 NL Umpire) "The Great Anticipator." Stewart was often accused of making poor calls because he anticipated what was going to happen and made calls prematurely.

3450. Sticker, John A. (1982–93 2B) "Cub." Sticker was a "Cub" in size. He was just 5'3" and weighed 130 pounds.

3451. Stimmel, Archibald Roy (1900–02 P) "Lumbago." Archie, as he was addressed, suffered from rheumatic pain in his lower back.

3452. Stinson, Gorrnell Robert (1969–80 C) "Scrap Iron." Bob, as he was addressed, was nicknamed early in his career by Fresco Thompson of the Los Angeles Dodgers' front office because of his uncanny ability to bounce back after just a few days from a broken jaw injury suffered in 1967 when he was playing for Albuquerque in the Pacific Coast League.

3453. Stirnweiss, George Henry (1943–52 2B) "Snuffy." Stirnweiss suffered from an old football injury which affected his breathing. He also had a sinus condition which he treated by using snuff. In 1945 Stirnweiss won the American League batting title by less than a thousandth of a point, hitting .30854 to Tony Cuccinello's .30845. It was the tightest title race in history.

3454. Stivetts, John Elmer (1889–99 P) "Happy Jack." Stivetts was very friendly, good natured and had a happy-go-lucky attitude.

3455. Stone, Stephen Michael (1943 P) "Rocky." "Rocky" is a takeoff on the last name of Stone.

3456. Stone, William A. (1923 OF) "Tige." "Tige" is short for Tiger and refers to how Stone played the game.

3457. Stoner, Ulysses Simpsen Grant (1922–31 P) "Lib." According to baseball writer Frank C. Lane "Lib" is just a play or takeoff on the name of Ulysses.

3458. Stout, Allyn McClelland (1931–43 P) "Fish Hook." On a fishing trip in Florida a plug with nine hooks landed on Stout's forehead. Two of the hooks took hold and bound the plug to his brow. Fortunately, he was not seriously injured.

3459. Stoval, George Thomas (1904–15 OF) "Firebrand." The "Firebrand" nickname was applied to Stoval during the last two years of his career. He was the first player to jump his contract and join the Federal League. He was the person most responsible for encouraging other players to join the league. During this period of history the Firebrand was the symbol of communist insurrection and anarchy. Stoval's combative personality and turbulent character fit the Firebrand mold.

3460. Strang, Samuel Nicklin (1896–1908 3B) "The Dixie Thrush." "Dixie" refers to Stang's southern heritage. He was born and raised in Chattanooga, Tennessee.

3461. Strange, Alan Cochrane (1934–42 SS) "Inky." "Inky" was a childhood nickname but Strange does not recall what it might mean or how he got it. It may have been because he was a printer in the off season.

3462. Stratton, Monty Franklin Pierce (1934–38 P) "Gander." "Gander" refers to Stratton's build. He was 6'5" and 180 pounds. He looked like a Gander when he pitched.

3463. Strauss, Joseph (1884–86 OF) "The Socker." "Socker" referred to hitting ability. Strauss was also called "Dutch" because of his German background.

3464. Street, Charles Evard (1904–31 C) "Gabby." Street was indeed "Gabby," talking all the time. In addition he had a habit of calling railroad porters "Gabby" to get their attention. During WWI he served in the army overseas with the rank of sergeant. During his managerial career he was referred to as "Old Sarg."

3465. Strickland, George Bevan (1950–60 SS) "Bo." Strickland told me that "Bo" is a childhood nickname. "It is short for boo boos, meaning hurts—cuts and bruises. When I was very young a friend of my grandmother gave me that nickname."

3466. Striker, Wilbur Scott (1959–60 P) "Jake." Striker was born in the small town of New Washington, Ohio. In his own words this how he told me he got the nickname of "Jake." "As a youngster, we had a neighbor man that lived nearby and his name was Jake. I would go to visit him often with my parents or brother and sisters and he would visit us. After a while when people asked me my name, I would say 'Jake.' To this day some people in that community would not be able to tell you my real name."

3467. Strincevich, Nicholas Mihailovich (1940–48 P) "Jumbo." Strincevich wrote me that his father was a very large man and was called "Jumbo" by friends. "After I came along, friends started calling me 'Little Jumbo'."

3468. Stripp, Joseph Valentine (1928–38 3B) "Jersey Joe." Stripp was born and raised in Harrison, New Jersey.

3469. Stromme, Floyd Marvin (1939 P) "Rock." "Rock" refers to Stromme's husky Norwegian build—hard as a rock.

3470. Stroud, Edwin Marvin (1966–71 OF) "The Creeper." Stroud had a hunch-shouldered walk which gave the appearance of creeping up on someone. The nickname came from teammates on Indianapolis team in the American Association. Stroud was also known as "The Streak" because of his great speed. In 1963 he led the Midwest League in stolen bases with 74, the Carolina League in 1964 with 72, and the American Association in 1966 with 57.

3471. Stroud, Ralph Vivian (1910–16 P) "Sailer." Origin unknown.

3472. Struss, Clarence Herbert (1934 P) "Steamboat." Origin unknown.

3473. Stryker, Stearling Alpha (1924–26 P) "Dutch." "Dutch" refers to Stryker's German background.

3474. Stuart, John Davis (1922–25 P) "Stud." "Stud" refers to Stuart's "guts, stamina, determination and confidence" at playing football in West Virginia during his high school days. Although he won only 20 major league games, on July 10, 1923, he pitched and won a double-header for the St. Louis Cardinals allowing the Boston Braves just four runs for the day.

3475. Stuart, Richard Lee (1958–69 1B) "Dr. Strangelove." Stuart was notoriously poor in the field. A Boston sportswriter gave him the nickname in 1963. It is a takeoff on the movie *Dr. Strangelove*.

3476. Stuart, William Alexander (1895–99 SS) "Chauncey." Origin unknown.

3477. Sturdivant, Thomas Virgil (1955–64 P) "Snake." Sturdivant had an outstanding curveball.

3478. Stutz, George (1926 SS) "Kid." In Stutz's case "Kid" refers to both small size, 5'3" and 150 pounds, and the early age he began organized baseball. "Kid" was noted for his ludicrous antics on the field. He was such a clown, that he was called "The Nick Altrock of the Minor Leagues."

3479. **Styles, William Graves** (1919–31 C) "Lena." Origin unknown.

3480. **Sudakis, William Paul** (1968–75 3B) "Suds." "Suds" uses the first three letters and the last letter of the last name for a shortened version of Sudakis.

3481. **Suder, Peter** (1941–55 2B) "Pecky." "Pecky" is a childhood nickname given to Suder by his classmates. He wrote me saying he did not know what the nickname meant.

3482. **Sudhoff, John William** (1897–1906 P) "Wee Willie." Sudhoff was 5'7" and 165 pounds.

3483. **Sukeforth, Clyde LeRoy** (1926–45 C) "Sukey." "Sukey" is simply a short name for Sukeforth.

3484. **Sullivan, Daniel** (1882–86 C) "Link." Origin unknown.

3485. **Sullivan, Florence P.** (1884 P) "Fleury." "Fleury" is an Irish pronunciation of Florence.

3486. **Sullivan, John Frank** (1887–80 1B) "Chub." "Chub" is short for "Chubby."

3487. **Sullivan, John Jeremiah** (1919 P) "Lefty." Sullivan pitched left handed and batted left handed.

3488. **Sullivan, Michael Joseph** (1889–99 P) "Big Mike." Sullivan was 6'1" and 210 pounds. In 11 seasons in the major leagues he won only 54 games while dropping 66.

3489. **Sullivan, Paul Thomas** (1939 P) "Lefty." Sullivan pitched left handed and batted left handed.

3490. **Sullivan, Thomas Jefferson** (1881–84 C) "Sleeper." "Sleeper" appears to be a nickname that Sullivan picked up as a minor league manager rather than a player. He used to transport his ball team from town to town on railroad day-coaches and smoking-cars rather than sleepers. Smoking cars on trains became known to players as "Ted Sullivan Sleepers."

3491. **Summer, John Junior, II** (1974–84 OF) "Champ." The day Summers was born his father looked at him and said, "He's so ugly he looks like he's just gone 10 rounds with Joe Louis." Louis was heavyweight champion of the world in 1948, the year "Champ" was born.

3492. **Summer, Carl Ringdahl** (1928 OF) "Lefty." Summer batted left handed and threw left handed.

3493. **Summers, Oran Edgar** (1908–12 P) "Kickapoo." Summers was of Fox Indian background. "Kickapoo" is the name of the dialect of the Fox Indians who once inhabited the midwestern states.

3494. **Summers, William R.** (1933–50 AL Umpire) "Honest Bill." Summers had a reputation of being fair in his calls. When he was umpiring in the Eastern League, during a game someone called to him, "Hey, Jesse James, get a horse." The next day he rode a horse into the ballpark, fully dressed in uniform and shouted, "Jessie James has arrived. Play ball."

3495. **Sunday, William Ashley** (1883–90 OF) "The Evangelist." Sunday played in the major leagues for eight years and his most crowning achievement was the reputation as one of the heaviest drinkers in the game. This was especially true for the first five years of his career when he played for the Chicago National League team.

Eventually, he found himself playing with the Philadelphia team in 1890. While bar carousing with teammates, a marching band of gospel singers passed. Out of the blue sky Sunday jumped to his feet and declared he was finished with this way of life and was going to devote his service to the work of God. And he did. From 1891–95 he worked for the Young Men's Christian Association in Chicago. In 1896 he became an evangelist. The crowds he drew were so large, and the number of converts so many, that he became the world's leading evangelist of the time. In 1903 he was ordained in the Presbyterian ministry. Another interpretation is that Sunday was not a heavy drinker, but went along on drinking bouts with teammates because he enjoyed the camaraderie. Arthur Bartlet writes of Sunday in his book, *Baseball and Mr. Spalding,* "Until religion took a grip on him, he would take a glass of beer or wine with the boys, but he avoided the hard liquor and the all-night parties." Today, Billy Sunday may be best remembered for his association with the city where he allegedly engaged in his hardest drinking, and did his hardest preaching against it. Songwriter Fred Fisher immortalized Sunday in the still familiar tune "Chicago," with its lyric "Chicago, Chicago, the town that Billy Sunday could not shut down." As a baseball nickname, Sunday's is unique. It is the only example of a player being assigned a nickname after he had completed his major league career, had no further formal association with the game, and for achievements that had nothing to do with the game.

3496. Sundra, Stephen Richard (1936–46 P) "Smokey." "Smokey" refers to Sundra's fastball which he developed early in his career. When he was 17, he was averaging 12 strikeouts per game playing for a men's sandlot team in Cleveland.

3497. Sunkel, Thomas Jacob (1937–44 P) "Lefty." Sunkel pitched left handed and batted left handed.

3498. Surkont, Matthew Constantine (1949–57 P) "Max." As a child, playmates started calling Surkont "Max" in place of Matthew.

3499. Susce, George Cyril Methodius (1929–44 C) "Good Kid." Jim Piersall recalls, "They called him 'Good Kid' because that's what he called everybody else. He didn't pay attention to anybody's name, just called everyone 'Good Kid.' It was like Ted Williams calling a lot of people 'Bush' because he couldn't remember their first names."

3500. Sutcliffe, Charles Inigo (1938 C) "Butch." Sutcliffe told me he got the "Butch" tag from a friend in high school. It was because he was the leader of his team in three sports. And he said, "We always came in first."

3501. Suter, Harry Richard (1909 P) "Rube." "Rube" was a common nickname for players from small towns who were backward in big city ways. Suter was from Independence, Missouri.

3502. Sutherland, Harvey Scott (1921 P) "Suds." "Suds" is a play on the last name, Sutherland.

3503. Sutherland, Howard Alvin (1949 P) "Dizzy." "Dizzy" referred to Sutherland's crazy ways both on and off the field while in the minor leagues.

3504. Sutterhoff, John Gerhard (1898–1905 P) "Sunny Jack." The nickname refers to Sutterhoff's pleasant disposition which he apparently had well before his professional baseball career. In a letter to officials at the Cooperstown Hall of Fame, his son writes, "One of the incidents about which Dad seemed real proud was with Louisville. I'm not sure what year, pitching against Indianapolis on a Sunday, won a single game, pitching again on a holiday on Monday A.M. and Monday P.M., winning both games."

3505. Suttles, George (1918–48 1B, Negro League) "Mule." Suttles was 6'6" and weighed 230 pounds, and swung a 50-ounce bat. He was responsible for some of the longest home runs ever recorded. In the Negro leagues he hit 150 home runs second only to "Turkey" Stearns' 160. Perhaps his longest home run was hit at Havana's Tropical Park where a plaque was placed on the spot at the 500-foot mark where it cleared the wall by 60 feet. The ball was thought to carry 600 feet. The "Mule" nickname comes from the kick of Suttles' bat. Fans used to yell to Suttles, "Kick, mule, kick."

3506. Sutton, Donald Howard (1966–87 P) "Black and Decker." Sutton gained the reputation of cutting the baseball and getting away with it while pitching. It increased his stuff on the ball. Black and Decker is the name of a manufacturing firm which makes, among other things, electric saws. Sutton won 324 games during his major league career and struck out 3,574 batters.

3507. Swacina, Harry Joseph (1907–15 1B) "Swats." Tom Shea reports that the "Swats" nickname is a play on the surname rather than a reference to hitting ability.

3508. Swain, John Hillary (1897–98 P) "Cy." Swain was a small town Ohio boy similar to Denton "Cy" Young for whom he was nicknamed.

3509. Swan, Harry Gordon (1914 P) "Ducky." Origin unknown.

3510. Swander, Edward O. (1903–04 OF) "Pinky." "Pinky" in Swander's case, refers to skin complexion.

3511. Swanson, Arthur Leonard (1955–57 OF) "Red." The nickname refers to hair color.

3512. Swartz, Sherwin Merle (1947 P) "Bud." Swartz wrote me that radio announcer "Dizzy" Dean just started calling him "Bud" on the radio for no reason at all during the short time that he played in St. Louis. It was not a childhood nickname, in fact it had never been used before.

3513. Swartz, Vernon Monroe (1920 P) "Dazzy." Origin unknown.

3514. Sweatt, George (1921–27 3B, Negro League) "Never." The nickname is in part a response to the last name of Sweatt. He was calm, quiet and unassuming. He took everything in stride.

3515. Sweeny, Charles Francis (1914 OF) "Buck." In Sweeny's case there is evidence that the "Buck" nickname referred to toughness and meanness.

3516. Sweetland, Lester Leo (1927–31 P) "Sugar." "Sugar" is just a response to the last name of Sweetland.

3517. Swett, William E. (1890 C) "Pop." Origin unknown.

3518. Swoboda, Ronald Alan (1965–73 OF) "Rocky." Swoboda was nicknamed by his New York Met teammates for the mistakes he made on the field. They said he had rocks in his head.

3519. Sykes, Frank (1915–26 P, Negro League) "Doc." Sykes was a practicing dentist in Baltimore.

T

3520. Taber, Edward Timothy (1926–27 P) "Lefty." Taber pitched left handed and batted left handed.

3521. Tabor, James Reubin (1938–47 3B) "Rawhide." Origin unknown.

3522. Taitt, Douglas John (1928–32 OF) "Poco." In 1926, Taitt batted .369 for the Pocatello Idaho team in the Class D Utah-Idaho League. "Poco" is short for Pocatello and is a place nickname.

3523. Talbot, Fred Leland (1963–70 P) "Bubby." "Bubby" is a mispronunciation of "brother." Talbot's sister is responsible for his childhood nickname.

3524. Tate, Edward Christopher (1885–90 C) "Dimples." Tate did in fact have dimples. However, he was usually addressed as "Pop," a term of affection.

3525. Tate, Lee Willie (1958–59 SS) "Skeeter." "Skeeter" refers to Tate's relatively small size and his ability at shortstop.

3526. Tatum, V.T. (1941–47 OF) "Tommy." According to Lee Allen, Tatum had no first name and somewhere along the line people began to use "Tommy."

3527. Taylor, Arlas Walter (1921 P) "Lefty." Taylor pitched left handed but batted right handed.

3528. Taylor, C.L. (1925 OF) "Chink." Origin unknown.

3529. Taylor, Carl Means (1968–73 C) "Senator." Taylor picked up the nickname of "Senator" from teammates at Pittsburgh, after he claimed that the Pirate management was not playing him regularly because of politics.

3530. Taylor, Charles, I (1904–22 3B, Negro League) "C.I." Taylor's nickname was simply his initials C.I. He was better known for his fairness and honesty on the diamond than his sterling play. For example, Robert Peterson writes of Taylor, "He is supposed to have stolen third base one day in a game at West Baden, sliding in under a cloud of dust to the accompaniment of a safe ruling by the umpire. C.I. rose, brushed himself off, and raised his hand to the crowd and cried, 'Ladies and Gentleman, I am an honest man. The umpire's decision is incorrect. I therefore declare myself out'." Taylor went on to be one of the most successful managers in the Negro leagues.

3531. Taylor, Edgar Reuben (1903 P) "Rube." Taylor was a farm boy from Palestine, Texas, and not attune to big city ways. He is one of several players nicknamed after George "Rube" Waddell. The fact his middle name was Reubin reinforced the nickname.

3532. Taylor, Harry Warren (1932 P) "Handsome Harry." Taylor was considered to be good looking, especially to women.

3533. Taylor, James B. (1879 OF) "Sandy." The nickname refers to hair color.

3534. Taylor, James Wren (1920–35 C) "Zack." Taylor was nicknamed after President Zachary Taylor. "Zack" at one time in his career claimed to be a relative of the tenth president of the United States.

3535. Taylor, John B. (1891–99 P) "Brewery Jack." The nickname refers to Taylor's drinking habits. His career was cut short after nine years. He died of Bright's disease.

3536. Taylor, John W. (1898–1907 P) "Breakman Jack." John W. Taylor's career overlapped with that of fellow right handed pitcher John B. Taylor, whose nickname was "Brewery Jack." This led newspaper writers to call him "Breakman Jack" after his off season occupation. John W. Taylor finished 278 of 286 career starts—97 percent. From June 20, 1901, through August 9, 1906, he finished 187 straight games started and managed to sandwich in 15 relief appearances.

3537. Taylor, Joseph Cephus (1954–58 OF) "Cash." Origin unknown.

3538. Taylor, Leo Thomas (1923) "Chink." Taylor played in only two games, did not come to bat. There is no information on what position he played.

3539. Taylor, Luther Hagen (1900–08 P) "Dummy." Taylor was both deaf and dumb, yet he overcame his handicap and won 115 games in the major leagues.

3540. Taylor, Robert Dale (1957–70 C) "Hawk." Taylor wrote me that at age six or seven, he was given the nickname of "Hawk" by a cousin. It was after the hero of a movie serial popular in the mid–1940s called "Hawk of the Wilderness."

3541. Taylor, Vernon Charles (1952 P) "Pete." Taylor's father nicknamed him "Pete" after the nickname of Hall of Fame pitcher Grover Cleveland Alexander, who he admired.

3542. Taylor, William Henry (1881–87 P) "Bollicky." Origin unknown.

3543. Taylor, William Michael (1954–59 OF) "Moose." The nickname "Moose" refers to Taylor's build. He was 6'3", 215 pounds.

3544. Teachout, Arthur John (1930–32 P) "Bud." "Bud" was a childhood family nickname.

3545. Tebbetts, George Robert (1936–52 C) "Birdie." Tebbetts had a high squeaky voice which reminded people of a bird tweeting. As "Dizzy" Dean was reported to say, "Most of all ballplayers got nicknames, and 'Birdie' Tebbett's is 'Birdie' because he's always ahollerin' like a little ole kinairy bird."

3546. Tebeau, Charles Alson (1895 OF) "Pussy." Origin unknown. I suspect that the nickname "Pussy" is somehow related to the fact that Oliver Tebeau, whose career began before, but overlapped with Charles, was nicknamed "Patsy." However, I have no evidence to support this hypothesis.

3547. Tebeau, George E. (1887–95 OF) "White Wings." "White Wings" was a term used to refer to street cleaners of the era. It was also used to denote garbage workers. Some writers called Tebeau "Fresh Duck" which may be related to "White Wings." To complicate matters further, Tebeau had another nickname, "Hard Call." The meaning of these nicknames and how they related to Tebeau is not clear.

3548. Tebeau, Oliver Wendell (1887–1900 1B) "Patsy." Tebeau was named after Oliver Wendell Holmes, the famous writer poet and physician. One account has it that Oliver was not an acceptable baseball name in the rough and ready section of St. Louis where Tebeau grew up, and that "Pat" replaced it. Bill James provides evidence that it came early in life from his neighbors. It was "Pat" because of his fondness for shoveling sand and carrying a dinner pail. In neither case is the why of "Pat" explained, let alone how "Pat" evolved (if it did) in to "Patsy."

3549. Tekulve, Kenton Charles (1974–89 P) "Bones." Tekulve, an underhanded relief pitcher, was 6'4" and just 175 pounds. When he threw the ball, he looked all bones. Tekulve pitched in 1,050 games, second highest in major league history.

3550. Templeton, Garry Lewis (1976– SS) "Jump Steady." A cousin nicknamed Templeton "Jump Steady" because when he danced to an Aretha Franklin recording of "Rock Steady," he was doing more jumping than rocking.

3551. Terlecki, Robert Joseph (1972 P) "Terk." "Terk" is really a short name for Terlecki using just four letters.

3552. Terry, William H. (1884–97 P) "Adonis." Terry was nicknamed after the youth of Greek mythology, who was so beautiful that he was beloved by both Aphrodite and Persephone. Terry was indeed a handsome youth, worthy of the "Adonis" tag, as a 20-year-old rookie with Brooklyn in 1884. His pitching skills enhanced the nickname.

3553. Terry, William Harold (1923–36 1B) "Memphis Bill." Terry's home town was Memphis, Tennessee.

3554. Tesch, Albert John, Jr. (1915 2B) "Tiny." The nickname refers to Tesch's build, 5'10", 155 pounds.

3555. Tesreau, Charles Monroe (1912–18 P) "Jeff." Tesreau was big and strong at 6'2½", 220 pounds. He was nicknamed "Jeff" after the famous heavyweight prize fighter, Jeff Terseau. Similar to many individuals with nicknames, the nickname becomes so ingrained, that the real name is all but forgotten. As Hy Turkin and S.C. Thompson recall, "A minor victor of this custom was Jeff Tesreau. While he was coaching the Dartmouth baseball team, townsfolk persuaded him to run for public office. He lost the race ... only because local rules specified that a man's legal name must be written on the ballot in order for it to be valid. To the baseball public, which means most of America, the former Giant pitching hero was always 'Jeff'."

3556. Tettelback, Richard Morley (1955–57 OF) "Tut." "Tut" is a takeoff on Tettelback. It recalls the king of Ancient Egypt, Tutankhamen.

3557. Textor, George Bernhardt (1914–15 C) "Tex." "Tex" in this case is an obvious derivation of the last name. It is included simply to illustrate that this "Tex" had nothing to do with the state of Texas.

3558. Thacker, Morris Benton (1958–63 C) "Moe." "Moe" is a takeoff on the name of Morris.

3559. Theobald, Ronald Merrill (1971–72 2B) "Little General." The 5'8" Theobald was an aggressive, take-charge player.

3560. Theodore, Albert Frank (1916–17 P) "Pudgy." At 5'6" and 160 pounds Theodore was thought to be a bit on the heavy side.

3561. Theodore, Charles Harvey (1876–77 1B) "Bushell Basket." SABR researcher, Kevin Grace, indicates that Theodore was an excellent fielding first baseman for his time, with sure hands, like a bushel basket. He was one of the first to leave the base while fielding first base.

3562. Theodore, George Basil (1973–74 OF) "The Stork." Theodore was called "The Stork" by fans because of his 6'4", 190-pound build. He looked very gangly and stork-like in the outfield.

3563. Thesenga, Arnold Joseph (1944 P) "Jug." Thesenga told me, "I got the nickname in high school from friends and sportswriters because I had a jug handle curveball. They liked to use 'Jug' because they could not pronounce my last name. Whenever I joined a new team, people questioned me as to whether I had a drinking problem. They thought the 'Jug' meant I liked liquor."

3564. Thielman, John Peter (1905–08 P) "Jake." "Jake" was simply an alternative for John, which was not uncommon before the turn of the century.

3565. Thies, Vernon Arthur (1954–55 P) "Jake." Thies recalls that a cousin started calling him "Jake" while he was very young, but has no idea why.

3566. Thomas, Chester David (1912–21 C) "Pinch." Thomas had a life time batting average of .237, but in a four year stretch 1915–18, as a pinch hitter, he batted .478, 11 hits in 23 at bats.

3567. Thomas, Clarence Franklin (1925–26 P) "Lefty." Thomas pitched left handed but batted right handed.

3568. Thomas, Claude Alfred (1913 P) "Lefty." Thomas pitched left handed and batted left handed.

3569. Thomas, Clinton (1921–38 OF, Negro League) "Hawk." Thomas was a left-handed power hitting outfielder who was also an exceptional base stealer. The nickname "Hawk," however, refers to his excellent defensive ability in the outfield. He had exceptional range in chasing down balls like a hawk. Thomas was also called "Buckeye" because he first played for the Columbus, Ohio, Buckeyes. His career average for 17 seasons was .300.

3569a. Thomas, David (1930–46 1B, Negro League) "Showboat." "Showboat" refers to Thomas' tendency to show off on the playing field.

3570. Thomas, Fay Wesley (1927–35 P) "Scow." Thomas told me as far as he could remember "Scow" was a "putdown" term for athletes which a fraternity brother called him when he was a pledge in his college days at the University of Southern California. Los Angeles sportswriters picked it up, even though he was usually called "Babe" when playing football.

3571. Thomas, Forrest (1905 P) "Frosty." Origin unknown.

3572. Thomas, James Leroy (1961–68 OF) "Mad Dog." Thomas had a temper. Once while playing golf with a sportswriter in 1961, he became so angered at a poor shot that he hurled his driver so hard that it went through a chain link fence.

3573. Thomas, John Tillman (1951 SS) "Bud." Thomas stated that his parents gave him the nickname of "Bud" so that he would not be confused with his father whose first name was also John.

3574. Thomas, Keith Marshall (1952–53 OF) "Kite." "Kite" is simply a takeoff on the name of Keith.

3575. Thomas, Luther Baxter (1932–41 P) "Bud." Thomas claims that his real nickname was "Lou." He told me he had no idea how "Bud" got started.

3576. Thomas, Myles Lewis (1926–30 P) "Duck Eye." Thomas' eyes were slightly flattened at the top lids, while the bottom was generously curved. Duck's eyes are constructed this way, only more so. Babe Ruth gave Thomas his nickname, because he could not remember his name. Ruth had great difficulty with names.

3577. Thomas, Robert William (1921 OF) "Red." The nickname refers to hair color.

3578. Thomas, Thomas R. (1899–1900 P) "Savage Tom." The nickname refers to the way in which Thomas played the game, and to his size 6'4", 195 pounds.

3579. Thomason, Arthur Wilson (1910 OF) "Silly." Origin unknown.

3580. Thompson, Charles Lemoine (1954–58 C) "Tim." Thompson told me the "Tim" tag came from his father who was called "Tommy" and decided to call him "Tim." Thompson was also called "Burr Head" because of his short hair cut. The first to use that nickname was his 1949 minor league roommate, Tom Lasorda.

3581. Thompson, Eugene Earl (1939–47 P) "Junior." He was called "Junior" because his father, who was a great minor league ball player, had the nickname of "Junior."

3582. Thompson, James Alfred (1914–16 OF) "Shag." "Shag" referred to Thompson's ability to track down fly balls in the outfield.

3583. Thompson, John Dudley (1921 P) "Lefty." Thompson pitched left handed and batted left handed.

3584. Thompson, John P.F. (1882–84 OF) "Tug." Origin unknown.

3585. Thompson, John Samuel (1948–51 P) "Jocko." Thompson wrote me that his wife was responsible for his nickname. He met her for the first time at the start of his minor league career. When they were just introduced, she misunderstood John as "Jocko" and began calling him that.

3586. Thompson, Samuel L. (1885–1906 OF) "Big Sam." Thompson was big in size, 6'2", 210 pounds, and in performance. He was the first National League player to hit 20 home runs in a season, 1889; the first to record 200 hits in a season, 1887; and the first to obtain 300 total bases in a season, 1887. His career total of 128 home runs was more than any other player recorded during the 19th century.

3587. Thomson, Robert Brown (1946–60 OF) "The Staten Island Scott." Bobby, as he was addressed, was born in Glasgow, Scotland, but grew up in Staten Island, New York. In the last game of the 1951 National League season, Thomson hit a three-run home run off Brooklyn Dodger pitcher Ralph Branca in the ninth inning to win the pennant for the New York Giants. So famous was his home run, that it has a nickname of its own, "The Shot Heard 'Round the World."

3588. Thoney, John (1902–11 OF) "Bullet Jack." Origin unknown.

3589. Thormahlen, Herbert Ehler (1917–25 P) "Lefty." Thormahlen pitched left handed and batted left handed.

3590. Thrasher, Frank Edward (1916–17 OF) "Buck." "Buck" is a generic nickname of which the consequences are almost never documented. It refers to a well developed, virile, aggressive, high spirited young man, and

3591. Throneberry, Marvin Eugene (1955–63 1B) "Marvelous Marv." Although Throneberry had been in and out of the major leagues since 1955, he did not receive his nickname until 1962, his last full season in the majors. On May 16, 1962, he was traded from the Baltimore Orioles to the New York Mets for Hobie Landrith and cash. He came to the Mets during their inaugural season in which they were to win 40 games and lose 120. One account has it that in mockingly accessing the trade, a New York sportswriter said that Throneberry's bat might just be what the Mets needed to get moving and dubbed him "Marvelous Marv." Another account has it that his overall bumbling play so endeared him to fans and sportswriters alike, that he was just naturally "Marvelous." For example, on June 17, 1962, he had been with the club just a month when he made a fielding error at first base which cost the Mets four runs. Later on in the game, he hit what should have been a two-run triple. But when he arrived safe at third base, he was called out for not having touched first base. When manager Casey Stengel tried to protest, the first base coach told him, "Forget it Casey, he didn't touch second base either." Roger Creamer reports that sportswriter Jeff Lang came to Throneberry's defense with the tongue-in-cheek statement, "How could he be expected to remember where the bases are? He gets on so infrequently." Writer Jack Bogaczyk presents Marv's version of how the "marvelous" tag originated in these words, "Every writer in New York tries to claim that they hung that [Marvelous] on me, but it was Joan Payson, the lady that owned the Mets," Throneberry said. "She was a real avid fan and she sat right behind the dugout at the Polo Grounds. I hit a home run one day in the ninth inning and won the game, and as I went to the dugout, she said, 'Wasn't that marvelous!'" It is indeed marvelous how much publicity Throneberry managed to get out of the 116 games he played for the Mets in 1962 with .244 batting average.

3592. Thurman, Robert Burns (1955–59 OF) "Owl." Thurman's teammates nicknamed Thurman "Owl" because his eyes gave an owl appearance.

3593. Thurston, Hollis John (1923–33 P) "Sloppy." Thurston may have inherited the nickname "Sloppy" from his father who ran a restaurant in Tombstone, Arizona. It was called "Sloppy's Place," because he used to feed soup to tramps at the back door. Another story reports, however, that "Sloppy" is really a childhood nickname. Thurston made a habit of spilling milk on his clothes. Yet a third account reports that Thurston was always so immaculate that "Sloppy" is an opposite nickname.

3594. Tidrow, Richard William (1972–78 P) "Dirt." Sparky Lyle explains the derivation of "Dirt." "We call him 'Dirt,' a nickname that stuck from when he first came over to the Yankees from Cleveland. When he joined us, before the games, we would play a game called flip. It's usually played behind home plate near the screen, while the other team is taking batting practice.... You bat the ball with your glove over to one of the other guys. Tidrow would be diving after balls getting his uniform filthy. We called him 'Mr. Dirt' after the guy in the Mobil commercials and it stuck with him."

3595. Tierman, Michael Joseph (1887–99 OF) "Silent Mike." Tierman maintained silence and reserve on the field of play even when he disagreed with the umpire. He also disliked publicity and maintained a low profile.

3596. Tierney, James Arthur (1920–25 2B) "Cotton." "Cotton" referred to his thatch of light blond hair.

3597. Tietje, Leslie William (1933–38 P) "Toots." Origin unknown.

3598. Tillman, Kerry Jerome (1982 OF) "Rusty." "Rusty" refers to hair color.

3599. Tinning, Lyle Forrest (1932–35 P) "Bud." "Bud" was a childhood nickname, but the exact origin is unknown.

3600. Tipple, Daniel Slaughter (1915 P) "Rusty." The nickname refers to hair color. Tipple was also called "Big Dan." He was 6', 175 pounds.

3601. Tipton, Eric Gordon (1939–45 OF) "Dukie." Tipton attended and was a great athlete at Duke University. He was also called "Blue Devil" which is the nickname of the athletic teams at Duke University.

3602. Titcomb, Ledell (1886–90 P) "Cannonball." It was said Titcomb had a pitch so fast it would split wood planks.

3603. Titus, John Franklin (1903–13 OF) "Silent John." Titus had the reputation of being so silent that nobody knew when he was around. Even when he spoke, it was softly. "Kid" Gleason once remarked that Titus didn't even make a noise when he spit. He was also called "Toothpick John." He played with a toothpick in his mouth.

3604. Tobin, James Anthony (1937–45 P) "Abba Dabba." Tobin did an imitation of a vaudeville magician's act. In the middle of a trick he would shout, "Abba Dabba, are you ready?" Boston sportswriters often referred to him as "Old Ironsides" calling attention to his rugged appearance and gallant will to win under any circumstances.

3605. Tobin, John Martin (1932 PH) "Tip." Origin unknown.

3606. Tobin, Marion Brooks (1941 H) "Pat." Origin unknown. I have no information on what position Tobin played. He came to bat just one time in the majors.

3607. Tolson, Charles Julius (1925–30 1B) "Slug." "Slug," in Tolson's case, was short for Slugger.

3608. Tomanck, Richard Carl (1955–59 P) "Bones." Tomanck reports that even as a child he was lean and thin. A friend of his father gave him the nickname of "Bones."

3609. Tompkins, Ronald Everett (1965–71 P) "Stretch." The nickname denotes Tompkins' build, 6'4", 200 pounds.

3610. Toney, Fred Alexander (1911–23 P) "Man Mountain." Toney was a mammoth of a man compared to other ball players of his time. He stood a shade over 6'6", and weighed in the neighborhood of 260 pounds. On May 2, 1917, Toney pitched a no-hit game for nine innings, but allowed a hit in the tenth inning to lose the game to James "Hippo" Vaughn, who pitched a no-hitter for ten innings. Vaughn was 6'4" and weighed about 250 pounds at the time. Five hundred pounds of no-hit flesh at once, is a record that may never be broken.

3611. Toporcer, George (1921–28 SS) "Specs." Lawrence Ritter in his book, *Glory of Their Times*, quotes Toporcer. "I had worn glasses practically ever since I'd started school because I was nearsighted. I couldn't see the blackboard without them. In those days, however, nobody played ball with eyeglasses on." Toporcer was the first infielder to wear glasses.

3612. Torborg, Jeffrey Allen (1964–73 C) "Style Master." Torborg does not seem to have had a nickname during his playing days. But according to "Sparky" Lyle, he acquired one while managing Cleveland 1977–79, for being a showoff. "When he walks off the field, he takes tiny little steps so he doesn't step on the foul line. He probably saw that in an old William Bendix movie. It's a pain in the ass watching him walk on the mound. He doesn't say anything to the pitchers anyhow. Today, Nettles hollered at him, 'Hey, Style Master, you have a hair out of place!'"

3613. Torgeson, Clifford Earl (1947–61 1B) "The Earl of Snohomish." "Torgy," as he was often addressed was born and raised in the small town of Snohomish, Washington.

3614. Torkelson, Chester Leroy (1917 P) "Red." The nickname refers to hair color.

3615. Torphy, Walter Anthony (1920 1B) "Red." The nickname refers to hair color.

3616. Torres, Rosendo, Jr. (1971–80 OF) "Rusty." Origin unknown.

3617. Torrienti, Christobel (1914–32 OF, Negro League) "The Cuban Strongboy." The Cuban born Torrienti, at 5'10", 190 pounds was heavily muscled and known for his power hitting which accounts for his nickname. His career average was .352. A confirmed bad ball hitter, he once hit a line drive in Indianapolis so hard that it hit the top of the fence and came back to the right fielder so fast that Torrienti was thrown out at first base. He was referred to as the "Babe Ruth of Cuba."

3618. Tovar, Cesar Leonardo (1965–76 OF) "Pepito." Peter Bjarkman, SABR researcher on Latin American ballplayers, reports that "Pepito" means little Paul. Tovar was 5'9", 155 pounds.

3619. Towne, Jay King (1906 C) "Babe." In Towne's case, "Babe" refers to rural roots. He came from Coon Rapids, Iowa, and was considered a "babe in the woods."

3620. Townsend, Ira Dance (1920–21 P) "Pat." Origin unknown.

3621. Townsend, John (1901–06 P) "Happy." "Happy" refers to Townsend's disposition and personality. When he pitched well, he was called the "Delaware Peach." When he did not pitch well, he was called the "Delaware Lemon." Townsend came from Townsend, Delaware. His name and his hometown name were the same.

3622. Townsend, Leo Alphonse (1920–21 P) "Lefty." Townsend pitched left handed and batted left handed.

3623. Tramback, Stephen Joseph (1940 OF) "Red." The nickname refers to hair color.

3624. Traynor, Harold Joseph (1920–37 3B) "Pie." "Pie" is a childhood nickname, but there are four equally plausible accounts of its origin. An acquaintance says a priest who supervised sandlot games in which Traynor played, used to treat the boys to dessert after the games. All the boys wanted ice cream except Harold, who demanded pie. Another acquaintance states that Traynor was always given a piece of pie as a reward for chasing down and returning foul balls for a local men's team in Somerville, Massachusetts. His mother reported that whenever she sent Harold to the grocery store, he would add pie to her shopping list. Finally, his father thought it had nothing to do with a dessert. "I was a painter and Harold used to come home from those sandlot games all dirty. The word for messed up type is *Pl* and that's where the name really came from."

3625. Treadway, Edgar Raymond (1930 3B) "Red." The nickname refers to hair color.

3626. Tremel, William Leonard (1954–56 P) "Mumbles." Tremel says he is very soft spoken. Joe Garagiola was responsible for nicknaming him "Mumbles."

3627. Trent, Theodore (1927–39 P, Negro League) "Big Florida." This is a place nickname. Trent was from Jacksonville, Florida. He was 6'3" tall.

3628. Trevino, Carlos Castro (1968 OF) "Bobby." Trevino wrote me that his father was a boxer and his nickname was "Bobby." All his father's friends started calling him "Bobby." Later on Trevino says, "People thought that was my real name and sometimes called me Robert instead of Carlos."

3629. Trillo, Jesus Manuel (1975–89 2B) "Indio." "Indio" denotes Trillo's Indian ancestry.

3630. Troaky, Harold Arthur, Jr. (1958 P) "Hoot." Origin unknown.

3631. Trosky, Harold Arthur, Jr. (1958 P) "Hoot." Trosky told me he was raised on a farm and always rose at between 4:00 and 5:00 A.M. When he left the farm, he still got up very early and people started calling him "Hoot Owl." Later it was shortened to just "Hoot."

3632. Troup, Steven Russell (1978 P) "Rainbow." Trout received his nickname while playing high school basketball. A teammate, Doug Rose, said everyone of his shots was a "rainbow," that is, a long arching shot.

3633. Trout, Paul Howard (1939–57 P) "Dizzy." Trout was given the nickname of "Dizzy" by his teammates at Terre Haute in the Triple I League because of his loquacious and fun loving behavior. In spring training 1937, he told everyone to call him "Dizzy" because he talked as much as "Dizzy" Dean. During the latter part of his major league career, he became famous for pulling a large red bandana from his back pocket and wiping his face while on the mound.

3634. Troy, John Joseph (1881–85 2B) "Dasher." Troy was known as an exceptionally good infielder in an era when this was unusual. It was said that he literally dashed down balls at second base.

3635. Troy, Robert (1911 P) "Bun." Origin unknown.

3636. Truby, Harry Garvin (1895–96 2B) "Bird Eye." Origin unknown.

3637. Trucks, Virgil Oliver (1941–58 P) "Fire." "Fire" refers to the speed of Truck's fastball. Jack House, a sportswriter in Truck's hometown of Birmingham, Alabama, gave him the nickname.

3638. Tucker, Thomas Joseph (1887–99 1B) "Foghorn." Tucker had a loud voice on the field. He was also called "Noisy Tom." He continued his noisy ways as a coach. Tucker led the American Association in hitting with a .372 mark in 1889.

3639. Tucker, Thurman Lowell (1942–51 OF) "Joe E." Teammates on the Chicago White Sox thought he bore a striking resemblance to the actor and

...*Officials, Writers, Broadcasters*

comedian Joe E. Brown, who played the title role of the movie version of Ring Lardner's classic baseball story, *Alibi Ike* in 1935.

3640. Turchin, Edward Lawrence (1943 SS) "Smiley." Origin unknown.

3641. Turk, Lucas Newton (1922 P) "Chief." Turk was of American Indian background. "Chief" was a nickname given to almost all ball players with Indian blood.

3642. Turley, Robert Lee (1951–63 P) "Bullet Bob." "Bullet" denotes Turley's fastball which helped him win 21 games for the New York Yankees in 1958 while dropping only seven. He also won two games in the World Series that year while losing one.

3643. Turner, George A. (1893–98 OF) "Tuck." Origin unknown.

3644. Turner, James Riley (1937–45 P) "Milkman Jim." Turner told me, "My uncle owned a milk company and I worked for it during the off season 1935–45. A sportswriter, 'Uncle' Jim O'Leary gave me the nickname during the time I pitched for the Boston Braves, 1937–39."

3645. Turner, Terrence Lamont (1901–19 SS) "Cotton." "Cotton" denotes Turner's blond hair color.

3646. Turner, Thomas Levatt (1915 P) "Tink." The origin of "Tink" is unknown. However, Turner is better known as "Trader" after his brief one game major league career. At Portland, in the Pacific Coast League, he became famous for developing players and trading and selling them. Some of the players he sent to the major leagues include: Mickey Cochrane, Rube Waldberg, Bob Johnson, Doc Cramer and Ferris Fain.

3647. Tutwiler, Guy Isbell (1911–13 1B) "King Tut." "King Tut" is a play on the last name and recalls the Egyptian King, Tutankhamen.

3648. Twinham, Arthur W. (1893–94 C) "Old Hoss." "Old Hoss" was a nickname used for players who were regular work horses. The exact origin for, however, is unknown.

3649. Twinning, Howard Earle (1916 P) "Doc." "Twink," as he was addressed, attended both Swarthmore and Hahnemann medical schools. He was a homeopathic physician.

3650. Twombly, Clarence Edward (1920–21 OF) "Babe." As a school boy, Twombly was a left handed power slugger from Jamaica, Massachusetts. He reminded people of Babe Ruth. The "Babe" tag was reinforced by the fact that Twombly was a cousin of Jack Dunn who discovered and signed Babe Ruth. In 1921, in 87 games with the Chicago Cubs, Twombly hit a lusty .377 including 15 hits in 38 times at bat as a pinch hitter. Strangely, at age 26 he never played in another major league game.

3651. Twombly, Edwin Parker (1921 P) "Cy." Twombly was one of several players who came from small towns and who were nicknamed after Denton "Cy" Young. Twombly was from Graveland, Massachusetts.

3652. Twombly, George Frederick (1914–19 OF) "Silent George." "Silent George" was anything but silent. This is an opposite nickname. Twombly was an inventor, writer, editor, publisher and distributor of a paper products company. He authored a book, *How to Succeed (If Necessary) Without a Ph.D.*

3653. Tyler, George Albert (1910–21 P) "Lefty." Tyler pitched left handed and batted left handed. Teammate on the Chicago Cubs, catcher Bob O'Farrell, recalls that "Birdshot" should have been Tyler's nickname. Tyler was able to fire birdshot from between his teeth by somehow curling his tongue and shooting a toothpick through it. He used to pepper opposing players, umpires and even player's wives that way. The wives especially, never could figure out where all the birdshot was coming from.

3654. Tyler, John Anthony (1934–35 OF) "TyTy." "TyTy" is a takeoff on the nickname of the outfielder Hayden "KiKi" Cuyler who was playing at the same time as Tyler.

3655. Tyson, Cecil Washington (1944 PH) "Turkey." Tyson reports he received his nickname from a sportswriter when he was playing for the Utica, New York, team in the Eastern League. He wrote that: "I did a turkey trot getting down to first base." He also said, "I gobbled like a turkey when I played."

3656. Uhalt, Bernard Bartholomew (1934 OF) "Frenchy." The nickname refers to his French background.

3657. Uhle, George Ernest (1919–36 P) "The Bull." George was exceptionally strong. In 17 major league seasons, he won 200 games while dropping 166. "The Bull" was one of the best hitting pitchers of all time, compiling a career average of .288 with 187 RBIs.

3658. Uhle, Robert Ellwood (1933–40 P) "Lefty." Uhle pitched left handed, but was a switch hitter. In 1923 he started 44 games for Cleveland, the most for any pitcher 1920–41.

3659. Ulisney, Michael Edward (1945 C) "Slugs." Origin unknown.

3660. Ulrich, Frank W. (1925–27 P) "Dutch." The nickname refers to Ulrich's German background.

3661. Upp, George Henry (1909 P) "Jerry." According to Joseph McBride, "Jerryup" used to be an alternative to "giddyup" as an expression to get horses moving. The "Jerry" was inspired by George's last name.

3662. Upright, Roy T. (1953 PH) "Dixie." Roy was a southern boy, having been born and raised in Kannapolis, North Carolina.

3663. Upton, Thomas Hobert (1950–52 SS) "Muscles." In Upton's case, "Muscles" has the opposite meaning. At 6'0", 150 pounds, it did not appear he had any muscles at all.

3664. Ussat, William (1925–27 3B) "Dutch." The nickname refers to Ussat's German background.

V

3665. Vache, Ernest Lewis (1925 OF) "Tex." Vache played in the Texas League before he was called up to the Boston Red Sox.

3666. Vail, Robert Garfield (1908 P) "Doc." Most players with the nickname of "Doc" either had at least some training and experience in either the professions of medicine or dentistry. But the origin of "Doc" for Vail is unknown.

3667. Valdes, Rene Gutierrey (1957 P) "Latigo." "Latigo" or "Whip" refers to Valdes' pitching motion.

3668. Valentine, Fred Lee (1959–68 OF) "Squeaky." Valentine was nicknamed by his aunt while he was a child, but he has no idea what "Squeaky" means. He told me it was not ever used during his playing career.

3669. Valentine, Harold Lewis (1954–55 P) "Corky." His father nicknamed him "Corky" because the comic strip character "Corky" was born at the same time.

3670. Valenzuela, Benjamin (1958 3B) "Papelero." When he was ten years old, Benny was the bat boy for the Los Mochis Sihalo (the Sugar Cain Cutters) team. The players gave him the nickname of "Papelero" because he delivered newspapers.

3671. Valespino, Hilario Borroto (1965–71 OF) "Sandy." Midland, Texas, manager Johnny Welaj gave him the nickname because he thought he looked like Brooklyn outfielder "Sandy Amaros."

3672. Van Alstyne, Clay (1927–28 P) "Spike." Origin unknown.

3673. Van Atta, Russell (1933–39 P) "Sheriff." Russell was involved in law enforcement during the off season. During the 1940s, he was the Sussex County, New Jersey, sheriff.

3674. Van Brabant, Camille Oscar (1954–55 P) "Ossie." "Ossie" is really derived from Oscar, but Van Brabant considers it more of a nickname than a short name. In 1942, while in high school it was suggested to him that "Ossie" would be a more appropriate tag for a baseball player than Camille.

3675. Van Buren, Edward Eugene (1904 OF) "Deacon." Ed refrained from drinking, smoking and swearing.

3676. Vance, Clarence Arthur (1915–35 P) "Dazzy." Lee Allen's account of how Vance received his nickname is a dazzy itself. "Actually, Vance was known as Dazzy by the time he was eleven. As a child in Nebraska, he knew a cowboy who used to look down at his pistol, pat it, and say affectionately 'Ain't it a dazzy?' Vance picked it up and later when he began pitching, he started to refer not to his fastball, but to his change of pace as a 'dazzy' because it was a thing of tantalizing beauty."

3677. Vance, Gene Covington (1970–71 P) "Sandy." "Sandy" told me he was given his nickname the day he was born by his grandfather because of the color of his hair. He went on to say: "Tom Lasorda, my manager in Triple-A ball, nicknamed me 'Dazzy' after the great Brooklyn pitcher. But when I got to the Dodgers, everyone thought 'Sandy' Vance was best. 'Sandy' after the best Dodger pitcher of modern times, and Vance after the greatest old-time Dodger pitcher."

3678. Vance, Joseph Albert (1935–38 P) "Sandy." The nickname refers to hair color.

3679. Vandenberg, Harold Harris (1935–45 P) "Hy." "Hy" says his nickname has been with him since he was four years old. "My brother could not pronounce my name Harold. He called me Hiwald and finally just Hi. It was the baby talk my brother used, and I've carried it to this day." "Hy" has always been amused that so many strangers know his name. He says, "I go to a store and people say 'Hi, how are you?' I go into a restaurant and someone says, 'Hi, can I seat you?'"

3680. Vander Meer, John Samuel (1937–51 P) "The Dutch Master." The Dutch refers to John's ethnic background. Master refers to his unique feat of pitching back-to-back no hitters for Cincinnati in 1938.

3681. Van Robays, Maurice Rene (1939–46 OF) "Bomber." Maurice received his nickname while playing in the lower minor leagues where he built the reputation as a slugger. In 105 games for Ogdenburg in the Canadian American League in 1937 he hit .368 with 43 home runs and 150 RBI's.

3682. Van Wieren, Peter (1976– Announcer) "The Professor." Van Wieren began announcing Atlanta Braves games in 1976, but in that year he also doubled as the club's traveling secretary. He received his nickname because of his reserved and studious nature and the fact he always had a wealth of information on hand, "so you won't run out of things to say."

3683. Van Zant, Richard (1888 3B) "Foghorn." Dick was one of many players whose loud voice on the field of play led to the nickname of "Foghorn." For luck, he carried a pig's ear in his pocket.

3684. Vaughan, Cecil Porter (1940–46 P) "Lefty." Vaughan pitched left handed but batted right handed.

3685. Vaughan, Glenn Edward (1963 SS) "Sparky." Glenn wrote me that Mike White the son of former major leaguer Joyner "Jo Jo" White gave him the nickname during his first year of pro ball at Durham in the Carolina league. He thought Glenn was the spark plug of the team. He also mentions that the nickname may have something to do with the fact that Joseph "Arky" Vaughan was his uncle.

3686. Vaughan, Joseph Floyd (1932–48 SS) "Arky." "Arky" is a place nickname, short for Arkansas. Joe was born in Clifty, Arkansas. Johnson reports that Vaughan received the nickname at age four, but does not describe the circumstances. If so, Vaughan would have received his place nickname at a much earlier age than any of the other 130-odd players with place nicknames.

3687. Vaughn, Frederick Thomas (1944–45 2B) "Muscles." Vaughn had great power and was built on a stocky 5'10", 195-pound frame.

3688. Vaughn, Harry Francis (1886–99 C) "Farmer." Harry was born in Rural Dale, Ohio, and was a farm boy.

3689. Vaughn, James Leslie (1908–21 P) "Hippo." Vaughn was an exceptionally large man for the period in which he played. At 6'4" he began his major league career at about 220 pounds. As time passed, he became larger and larger, some estimate close to 300 pounds by the end of his career. His size plus his lumbering gait on the base paths reminded folks of a hippopotamus. Despite his size or perhaps because of it, Hippo won 20 games or more in 5 of his 13 seasons in the major leagues.

3690. Varner, Glen Gann (1952 OF) "Buck." "Buck" is a generic nickname of which the circumstances of origin are almost never documented. It refers to a well developed, virile, aggressive, high spirited young person. It is usually bestowed upon the individual during his teenage years.

3691. Varney, Lawrence Delano (1902 P) "Spike." Origin unknown.

3692. Varney, Richard Fred (1973–76 C) "Pete." Varney was nicknamed "Pete" by his parents. They thought he looked like his father who was called Pete.

3693. Veach, William Walter (1884–90 1B) "Peek-a-Boo." Veach's normal position was first base. However, in pitching a game for Kansas City in the Union League in 1884 he became bothered with men on base. Manager Ted Sullivan told him not to worry. "Keep an eye on the bench and when I put my hands up fire the ball to first." To do so, Veach had to peek over his shoulder. After he had picked two men off first, the opposing team got wise to him peeking at the bench and stole the signs. Manager Sullivan than had the signal given by a person in the stands, which meant an even more difficult peek for Veach. The opposing team easily discovered these signs also, but from then on Bill was tagged as "Peek-a-Boo" Veach even when he was not pitching.

3694. Veal, Orville Inman (1958–63 SS) "Coot." Veal recalls that he received the nickname while in high school. It is short for "Cooter," but he does not know what it means.

3695. Veil, Frederick Williams (1903–04 P) "Bucky." Veil was signed off the Bucknell College campus and immediately received the nickname of "Bucky." He owns the distinction of being the first relief pitcher in World Series history. He relieved Sam Leever in the second game of the 1903 series for Pittsburgh against the Boston Red Sox. Veil pitched seven innings and allowed just one earned run, but Boston won the game 3–0.

3696. Venable, William McKinley, Jr. (1979–80 OF) "Max." During his high school days, kids started using his middle name and it evolved into "Max."

3697. Venzen, Anthony (1957–71 NL Umpire) "Pope." Origin unknown.

3698. Verban, Emil Matthew (1944–50 2B) "Dutch." Verban was often addressed as "Dutch" in reference to his German background. He was called "The Antelope" because of the graceful way he played second base. To say that Emil was not a power hitter is a gross understatement. From 1941–43 at Asheville, Houston and Columbus in the minor leagues he went 1,661 times at bat without a home run. From 1944–48 he added another 2,423 trips to the plate before finally hitting a homer. He ended his major league career with just that one "dinger" in 2,911 official times at bat.

3699. Verble, Gene Kermit (1951–53 SS) "Satchel." While in grade school Gene used to carry his books to school in a satchel. The kids began to call him that and it became his nickname. He did not like the nickname and retaliated by making up nicknames for the other kids.

3700. Verdal, Albert Alfred (1944 P) "Stumpy." Al was very short when he first started to play baseball and the other kids started to call him "Stumpy." The nickname stuck with him even though he grew to a shade under six feet.

3701. Vernon, James Barton (1939–60 1B) "Mickey." Vernon was addressed by almost everyone as "Mickey." His aunt gave him the nickname when he was just three or four years old, because he liked to listen to the record "Mickey" on the victrola so much.

3702. Versalles, Zoilo Casanova (1959–71 SS) "Zorro." Versalles from the very start of his career in organized baseball had the reputation of being a great fielding shortstop. At his first minor league training camp in Orlando, Florida, a group of players were watching "The Adventures of Zorro" on TV in the clubhouse. As Zoilo walked in one of the players said, "Here comes Zorro now." Another remarked, "The way you play shortstop you are a bandit, just like Zorro, stealing base hits from everybody." Another account attributes the "Zorro" tag to a Washington clubhouse attendant, who in the late 1950s compared the Cuban shortstop in speed, grace and name to the fictional Mexican vigilante popularized on the Walt Disney television series, from 1957–59 starring Guy Williams.

3703. Vick, Henry Arthur (1922–26 C) "Ernie." Origin unknown.

3704. Vickers, Harry Porter (1902–09 P) "Rube." Vickers reminded people of "Rube" Waddell, whose career overlapped with his. Harry was a small town boy from Pittsford, Michigan, and not overly worldly in his ways. He was about the same build as Waddell 6'2", 225 pounds and also threw right handed.

3705. Vico, George Steve (1948–49 1B) "Sam." Vico wrote me that he received the nickname of "Sam" from a teammate, Sid Cohen, while playing for Portland in the Pacific Coast League in the 1940s. He says it was because he wore his pants long!

3706. Vidal, Jose Nicolas (1966–69 OF) "Papito." Origin unknown.

3707. Viola, Frank John, Jr. (1982– P) "Sweet Music." The nickname is a combination of a response to the last name and great pitching. Viola won the American League Cy Young Award in 1988 with a 24-7 won-lost record.

3708. Voiselle, William Symmes (1942–50 P) "Big Bill." Bill was 6'4" and weighed over 200 pounds. "Ninety-Six" was his more popular nickname. He came from the small town of Ninety Six, South Carolina. Note that the town has no hyphen, but the nickname does! Voiselle was the first player to wear the name of his hometown on the back of his uniform — 96.

3709. Von Der Ahe, Christian Frederick Wilhelm (1882–98 Owner) "Der Boss President." The nickname was a comic takeoff on Von Der Ahe's German background and heavy accent, plus his bombastic, compulsive and tyrannical methods of running a ball club. He was a forerunner of both Bill Veeck and George Steinbrenner. He understood little about baseball and was more concerned with selling beer and providing entertainment. The parade of managers he used would have made George Steinbrenner envious. He used five in 1895 alone. He turned Sportsman's Park into what was called "The Coney Island of the West." Bill Veeck's promotions of a half century later could hardly match Von der Ahe's escapades. In addition to a beer garden, Fred Lieb explains, "Chris put a chute-the-chutes in center field, night horse racing, boating, an all-girl cornet band, a wild west showing and boxing.... The Silver Cornet Band was made up of two dozen glamor girls of the nineties. They were the grandmas of the girl orchestras of today, wearing long striped skirts, wide white sailor hats and leg-of-mutton sleeves."

3710. Von Kolnitz, Alfred Holmes (1914–16 3B) "Fritz." The nickname is in reference to Von Kolnitz's German background.

3711. Vorhees, Henry Bert (1902 P) "Cy." Henry came from a small town in Ohio and was the same build as Denton "Cy" Young whose career overlapped with his.

3712. Vowinkel, John Henry (1905 P) "Rip." Vowinkel was a fastball pitcher who "ripped" the ball to the plate.

3713. Waddell, George Edward (1897–1910 P) "Rube." Even by the 1890s, approximately three-quarters of the American population still lived on farms or small towns. When these rural folk came to large metropolitan areas where major league baseball was played, they were often called "Rubes" by city inhabitants. "Rube" was short for Rubin, which was synonymous with farmer. George Waddell fit the stereotype of the classic country yokel, and became one of baseball's most uninhabited eccentrics. The many stories about his escapades have become so legendary that it is difficult to separate fact from fiction. Howard Liss, in his book *Baseball's Zaniest Stars*, presents the following account of how the "Rube" tag was first applied to Waddell. "Back in 1897, Louisville was one of the teams in the National League. One day the tall, gawky young man walked into the team's office. He was wearing a dinky little cap, country-cut clothes and carried a cheap straw suitcase. A Louisville fan noticed him on the street and saw right away that he was no city boy. 'Hey, look at the Rube,' he shouted. Hearing that, Waddell turned, grinned and bowed from the waist. He didn't take offense. In fact, he thought it was funny. And the name stuck." Robert Smith points out, however, that later on Waddell was not as pleased when the "Rube" nickname was used. "Waddell liked to be called Eddie and it was many years before he would answer to Rube. Even then he allowed its use only to his friends, when they greeted him with 'Hey Rube'.... Indeed a man who once clapped him on the shoulder outside a theater and said 'Hello, Rube,' caught a short left on the chin and landed on the seat of his pants at the bottom of a flight of stairs." Waddell's off the diamond antics reinforced the "Rube" nickname throughout his brilliant pitching career

which led to his election to the Hall of Fame. Of the dozens of stories that could be related, the following are representative. Waddell was famous for chasing fire engines. One day while pitching for Connie Mack's "A's," during the game he heard a fire engine pass the stadium and vaulted the centerfield fence to chase it. When he once failed to show up for a game he was scheduled to pitch, club officials finally discovered him wearing a white apron and tending bar in a local pub. On another occasion he was lost to the team for three days, only to reappear dressed up as a drum major leading a parade up Main Street in Philadelphia. On still another occasion when he was missing, he was finally found posing as an automaton in a store window. During, and for some time after, Waddell's career, it became fashionable in baseball to nickname country boys "Rube" even though they may not have been as backward and zany as George.

3714. Wade, Abraham Lincoln (1907 OF) "Ham." "Ham" is simply using the last three letters of Wade's first name to serve as a nickname.

3715. Wade, Jacob Fields (1936–46 P) "Whistlin' Jake." Wade was a fastball pitcher. "Whistlin'" refers to the sound the ball made as he threw to the plate.

3716. Wade, Richard Frank (1923 OF) "Rip." "Rip" refers to how he hit the ball—he ripped it. Six of his 16 major league hits were for extra bases.

3717. Wagenhurst, Elwood Otto (1888 3B) "Woodie." "Woodie" is a takeoff on Wagenhurst's first name.

3718. Wagner, Albert (1898 3B) "Butts." Al was the brother of Honus Wagner, but the origin of his nickname is unknown.

3719. Wagner, Charles F. (1902–18 SS) "Heinie." The nickname refers to his German background.

3720. Wagner, Charles Thomas (1938–46 P) "Broadway." Charlie, as he was usually called, was a sharp dresser who set a fashion pace for his teammates in Boston, in the years before WWII. "Broadway," although a place nickname, in this case, refers to dress not geographical location.

3721. Wagner, John Peter (1887–1917 SS) "The Flying Dutchman." Wagner's German background accounts for his nicknames. He was usually addressed as "Hans" or "Honus" which are the German words for the equivalent of John. Some writers suggest that "Honus" has the connotation of affection and means "Big Olf." Flying refers to Wagner's speed. He stole 722 bases during his career. Dutchman refers to his German background. "The Flying Dutchman" was the title of an opera written by the German composer Richard Wagner. "Honus" was also referred to as "The Peerless Dutchman" and was generally considered as the first great player in the National League.

3722. Wagner, Leon Lamar (1958–69 OF) "Daddy Wags." Leon owned a clothing store in Los Angeles which had the slogan, "Get Your Rags from Daddy Wags."

3723. Wagner, William George (1913–14 P) "Bull." Wagner was 6'1½", 255 pounds and strong.

3724. Walburg, George Elvin (1923–37 P) "Rube." When Walburg entered professional baseball, he reminded many of "Rube" Wadell. He too, was from a small town, Pine City, Minnesota, and had a tall and gangling build. In addition, his first name was also George. The nickname of "Rube" was first used by teammates.

3725. Walczak, Edwin Joseph (1943 2B) "Husky." Ed states, "I was nicknamed 'Husky' by a kid in the fifth grade who thought I was kind of rugged. My whole family calls me this."

3726. Waldbauer, Albert Charles (1917 P) "Doc." Most players with the nickname of "Doc" had some association and or experience in medicine or dentistry. However, for Waldbauer, the exact origin of "Doc" is unknown.

3727. Walker, Albert Bluford (1948–58 C) "Rube." The nickname was given to him by an old time ball player in his hometown of Lenoir, North Carolina. It was used as a term of affection, but it is not clear what the actual connotation was.

3728. Walker, Clarence William (1911–23 OF) "Tilly." According to Richard Topp, SABR researcher, "Tilly" was a name used to refer to "gays" during the time Walker played. The rumor was that Walker had a different sexual persuasion.

3729. Walker, Cleotha (1980–88 2B) "Chico." Origin unknown.

3730. Walker, Erwart Gladstone (1909–12 P) "Dixie." Erwart grew up in the South although he was born in Brownsville, Pennsylvania. As an 18-year-old playing in Zanesville, Ohio, in 1909, the local newspaper headlined one day "Dixie" Walker pitching today. A nickname was born.

3731. Walker, Fred (1931–49 OF) "Dixie." Walker was nicknamed after his father, major league pitcher, Erwart "Dixie" Walker. The "Dixie" refers to Southern origins. Fred was born in Villa Rica, Georgia. In July of 1939, Walker was sold by the Detroit Tigers to the Brooklyn Dodgers for the waiver price. His lusty hitting during the 1940s earned him the title of "The People's Cherce" by Brooklyn fans.

3732. Walker, Frederick Mitchell (1910–15 P) "Mysterious." Mysterious as it may be, little is known about how Walker obtained his nickname. Lee Allen hints that it probably had to do with his temperament.

3733. Walker, Gerald Holmes (1931–45 OF) "Gee." "Gee" is simply an extension of the first letter of Walker's first name. It is really no more than short for Gerald.

3734. Walker, Harry William (1940–55 OF) "The Hat." Harry, the brother of Fred "Dixie" Walker, and son of Erwart "Dixie" Walker, was always playing and toying with his cap when he was batting. Joseph McBride reports that cap manufacturer Tim McAuliffe contended that Walker was the roughest player on caps. He wore out 20 caps per year compared to three for the average player.

3735. Walker, Harvey Willos (1931–45 OF) "Hub." "Hub" was used by newspaper writers in Detroit as a replacement for Harvey in much the same way that "Gee" was used for his brother Harold. Both were rookies for Detroit in 1931.

3736. Walker, James Roy (1912–22 P) "Dixie." Walker was born in Lawrenceburg, Tennessee, and raised in the south.

3737. Walker, Martin Van Buren (1926 P) "Buddy." "Buddy" is a childhood nickname, but the exact origin is unknown. Given that Walker was named after the eighth president of the United States, Martin Van Buren, it is surprising that someone did not give him the short version of Van Buren's nickname, "O.K." (Old Kinderhook).

3738. Wall, Joseph Francis (1901–02 C) "Gummy." Wall had a deformity which forced his gums into prominence. Wall was born in Brooklyn, New York, and when he first became a kid star in baseball, he was called "The Pride of the Sixth Ward." While he only caught in seven games in the major leagues, he owns the distinction of being one of the very few left handed catchers.

3739. Wall, Murray Wesley (1950–59 P) "Tex." Wall was born and raised in the state of Texas.

3740. Wallace, Frederick Renshaw (1919 SS) "Doc." Most of the players with the nickname of "Doc" have had experience in either medicine or dentistry. However, for Wallace the origin of "Doc" is unknown.

3741. Wallace, Harry Clinton (1912 P) "Huck." Wallace reminded people of the character "Huck Finn" created by Samuel Clemens in the novel *The Adventures of Huckleberry Finn*. Wallace was also called "Lefty" because he pitched left handed and batted left handed.

3742. Wallace, James Harold (1942–46 P) "Lefty." Wallace pitched left handed and batted left handed.

3743. Wallace, Roderick John (1894–1902 P) "Rhody." Wallace was usually addressed as Bobby. "Rhody" was a newspaper nickname which was a takeoff on Roderick.

3744. Waller, John Francis (1909 P) "Red." The nickname refers to the color of Waller's hair.

3745. Wallis, Harold Joseph (1975–79 OF) "Tarzan." Joe received his nickname from teammates because of his proclivity for jumping out of motel windows and diving into swimming pools.

3746. Walls, Roy Lee (1952–64 OF) "Captain Midnight." Joe Garagiola and George Metkovich gave Walls the nickname of "Captain Midnight" because of the dark glasses he used. The reference was to the radio and TV character of the same name.

3747. Walsh, Edward Augustine (1904–17 P) "Big Ed." Walsh stood 6'1" and weighed 195 pounds. However, after 1908 when Ed won 40 games for the Chicago White Sox with an ERA of 1.42, "Big" denoted his pitching as much as his size. Walsh's career ERA of 1.82 ranks first among all pitchers to date.

3748. Walsh, James Gerald (1946–51 P) "Junior." Origin unknown.

3749. Walsh, Joseph Patrick (1938 SS) "Tweet." Herb Brett, the Danville, Virginia, manager in 1933, nicknamed Walsh "Tweet" after an old minor league player by that name of whom he was reminded.

3750. Walsh, Michael Timothy (1910–15 3B) "Runt." "Runt" referred to Walsh's size which was not all that small 5'9", 170 pounds.

3751. Walsh, Thomas Leo (1913–15 SS) "Dee." Origin unknown.

3752. Walters, Alfred John (1915–25 C) "Roxy." Walters lasted 11 years in the major leagues but appeared in only 498 games or an average of just 45 per year. The origin of "Roxy" is unknown.

3753. Walters, James Fred (1945 C) "Whale." Fred played major league ball only in the war year of 1945. He was noted for his size. He looked like a whale behind the plate.

3754. Walters, William Henry (1931–50 P) "Bucky." Walters inherited the nickname of "Bucky" from his father. It was given to him by his parents at an early age. However, he wrote me that it evolved into a baseball nickname and was not used much by the members of his family. "Bucky" won 198 games in the major leagues, and it is sometimes forgotten that from 1931–34, he was a third baseman for the Boston Braves and Philadelphia Phils.

3755. Walton, Daniel James (1968–80 OF) "Mickey." Danny was called "Mickey" by his minor league teammates who thought he took after Mickey Mantle.

3756. Waner, Lloyd James (1927–45 OF) "Little Poison." Lloyd was the younger of the two Waner brothers who played outfield together for the Pittsburgh Pirates, 1927–40. The "Little" refers to his relative lack of power compared to his brother Paul. He did not get as many extra base hits, or drive in as many runs. He was, however, almost exactly the same build, 5'9", 150 pounds, in comparison to Paul, 5'8½", 152 pounds. The nickname is a corruption of the word "person." As Lee Allen recounts, it "... came into being when a baseball writer overheard an Ebbets Field fan continually say in Brooklynese, as the Waners came to bat, 'Here comes that big poison,' or 'Here comes that little poison'." With a lifetime batting average of .316 and with 2,459 major league hits, Lloyd was poison to the opposition. As presented by Donald Honig in his book,

October Heroes, Lloyd's version of the origin of the nicknames is slightly different than the account given by Allen. "They used to call us 'Big Poison' and 'Little Poison'. A lot of people have thought we had those nicknames because we were 'poison to the opposing pitchers,' but that isn't the way it came about. It started in 1927, in New York. We were playing the Giants in the Polo Grounds. There used to be this Italian fellow who always sat in the centerfield bleachers. He had a voice on him you could hear all over the ball park. When he hollered out, you heard him no matter where you were.

"Well, Paul and I were hitting well against the Giants. This one day we came out of the club house between games of a doubleheader and this fellow started hollering at us. What it sounded like, was 'Big and Little Poison,' but what he was really saying was 'Big and Little Person.' ... The newspaperman picked it up except they thought he was saying 'Poison' instead of 'Person.' It became a newspaper nickname, because no ball players ever called us that."

3757. **Waner, Paul Glee** (1926–45 OF) "Big Poison." Paul was the oldest of the two Waner brothers who played outfield together for the Pittsburgh Pirates 1927–40. "Big" refers to his greater power, not his size as compared to his brother Lloyd. Paul got more extra base hits and drove in more runs. With a lifetime batting average of .333 with 3,152 hits and 1,309 RBIs, Paul was poison to opponents. For the derivation of the nickname see reference 3756 above, Waner, Lloyd James.

3758. **Wanninger, Paul Louis** (1925–27 SS) "Pee Wee." "Pee Wee" refers to Wanninger's build. Similar to so many shortstops, he was small in stature, 5'7", 150 pounds.

3759. **Ward, Frank Gray** (1883–94 OF) "Piggy." The nickname refers to Ward's build of 5'9", 200 pounds.

3760. **Ward, John Andrew** (1902 OF) "Rube." "Rube" was a nickname given to players who came from small towns and were less than worldly in their knowledge of big city life. John grew up in the small Ohio town of New Lexington.

3761. **Ward, Joseph Nicholas** (1912 OF) "Hap." "Hap" is short for "Happy" and refers to Joe's disposition, even though he failed to reach base in his two times at bat in the major leagues.

3762. **Ward, Richard** (1934–35 P) "Ole." Origin unknown.

3763. **Warden, Jonathan Edgar** (1968 P) "Warbler." Jon explains his nickname in these terms, "When I came up to the Detroit Tigers in 1968, I was always whistling. Sliding instructor, Bernie Deviverious could not pronounce my name and labeled me 'Warbler.' I didn't like it and thank God it has not followed me after baseball."

3764. **Wares, Clyde Ellsworth** (1913–14 SS) "Buzzy." Clyde was given the nickname of "Buzzy" by teammate Jack Leary because he was always talking baseball.

3765. **Warhop, John Milton** (1908–15 P) "Crab." Jack, as he was addressed, had a "complaining disposition." He was also called "chief" a nickname usually reserved for players of American Indian blood. The pronunciation of his name Warhop sounded to some like "Warhoop." Warhop is the answer to the trivia question, "Off what pitcher did Babe Ruth hit his first home run in 1915?"

3766. Warmoth, Wallace Walter (1916–23 P) "Cy." Warmoth was from the small farm town of Bone Gap, Illinois. He was nicknamed after the great Denton "Cy" Young who also was a small town boy when he first entered organized baseball.

3767. Warneke, Lonnie (1930–46 P; NL Umpire 1949–55) "The Arkansas Humming Bird." Warneke was born in Mt. Ida, Arkansas. David Porter reports that a St. Louis sportswriter was impressed with his lively fastball and darting form of delivery. It reminded him of a humming bird. Joseph McBride attributes the nickname to Lon's singing and playing guitar in Pepper Martin's "Mudcat Band" when he was with the St. Louis Cardinals. After his playing days, Warneke had a short career as a major league umpire from 1949–55.

3768. Warner, Hoke Hayden (1916–21 3B) "Hooks." "Hooks" is usually a nickname given to pitchers with good curveballs. For Waner, it is simply a corruption of his first name Hoke.

3769. Warstler, Harold Burton (1930–40 SS) "Rabbit." The nickname was applied to Warstler's speed and size of 5'7½", 150 pounds, at playing shortstop. He was a "good field, no hit" shortstop.

3770. Washer, William (1905 P) "Buck." "Buck" is a generic nickname. The circumstances of origin are almost never documented. It refers to a virile, well developed, aggressive, high spirited young man, usually bestowed during teenage years.

3771. Waters, Fred Warren (1955–56 P) "Innocent Fred." The nickname comes from the bland and innocent expression he carried on his face even when circumstances might indicate otherwise.

3772. Wathan, John David (1976–85 C) "Duke." John was nicknamed after the actor, John "Duke" Wayne whom he was thought to resemble. Manager "Whitey" Herzog of Kansas City called him "Cornfield" because he came from Iowa.

3773. Watson, Charles John (1913–15 P) "Doc." Charles was nicknamed after the famous character "Dr. Watson" in the Sherlock Holmes tales by Sir Arthur Conan Doyle.

3774. Watson, John Reeves (1918–24 P) "Mule." John Watson had the same workman-like qualities as Milton Watson who preceded him in the major leagues by two years. Fred Lieb attributes the nickname "from the mules that pulled the plows in the cotton fields of his birth place, Homer, Louisiana." Watson is the only pitcher since 1901 to pitch three complete game doubleheaders, twice in 1918, and once in 1921.

3775. Watson, Milton Wilson (1916–19 P) "Mule." "Mule" denotes the workman-like qualities of Milt's pitching. He was always ready.

3776. Watson, Robert Jose (1966–84 1B) "Bull." Watson was 6'1½", and over 200 pounds. He was nicknamed "The Bull" by his high school coach because of his size and strength.

3777. Watson, Walter L. (1887 P) "Mother." Watson was known as a perfect gentleman. "Mother" was a term used in this era for such an individual who did not smoke, drink, swear, or brawl.

3778. Watt, Frank Marion (1931 P) "Kilo." "Kilo" is short for kilowatt. The nickname is a play on the name of Watt.

3779. Watwood, John Clifford (1929–39 OF) "Lefty." He batted left handed and threw left handed.

3780. Weatherly, Cyril Roy (1936–50 OF) "Stormy." "Stormy" is a takeoff on Roy's last name. It was given to him by a fan while he was playing for New Orleans in 1935.

3781. Weaver, Arthur Coggshall (1902–08 C) "Six O'clock." Weaver was tall and very thin, especially for a catcher. Behind the plate, fans said he looked like the hands of a clock at dinner time.

3782. Weaver, George Daniel (1912–20 SS) "Buck." "Buck" is a generic nickname. Weaver was one of the eight men on the 1919 White Sox ("Black Sox") team that were accused of throwing the World Series. "Buck" was banned for life after the 1920 season, which turned out to be his best in terms of batting average of .333, runs scored 104, and RBI's 75. Known as a good fielding third baseman, Weaver was charged with 71 errors at shortstop in 1912. Although I find no evidence of it, Fred Lieb suggests that Weaver was nicknamed after William "Farmer" Weaver who was addressed as "Buck."

3783. Weaver, James Brian (1967–68 P) "Fluss." Origin unknown.

3784. Weaver, James Dement (1928–39 P) "Big Jim." Jim was 6'6" and weighed 230 pounds.

3785. Weaver, Montgomery Morton (1931–39 P) "Prof." Monte, as he was addressed, had been awarded two college degrees and had a job teaching analytical geometry before he reached the major leagues.

3786. Weaver, William B. (1888–94 OF) "Farmer." Weaver was a farm boy from Parkersburg, West Virginia. Fred Lieb states he was usually called "Buck," and that he was original "Buck" Weaver. Other "Buck" Weavers, such as George "Buck" Weaver were nicknamed after him.

3787. Webb, Cleon Earl (1910 P) "Lefty." He pitched left handed and batted left handed.

3788. Webb, James Laverne (1932–45 SS) "Skeeter." Fred Lieb hits the nickname on the head when he comments that Webb was "small but pestiferous." "Skeeter" was not much of a hitter with a lifetime average of .219, but he was an excellent shortstop.

3789. Webb, Samuel Henry (1948–49 P) "Red." The nickname refers to hair color.

3790. Weeghman, Charles A. (1914–21 Owner) "Lucky." Weeghman founded the Chicago entry in the Federal League 1914–15. Their nickname was "Whales." He built what is now called Wrigley Field. He owned the Chicago Cubs 1916–21 before selling out to P.K. Wrigley. The nickname "Lucky" refers to Weeghman's meteoritic rise in the diner business in Chicago, from pennies to millions in a short period of time.

3791. Weidman, George E. (1880–88 P) "Stump." Baseball encyclopedias do not provide information on Weidman's height and weight. From newspaper pictures he looks short and squatty. This probably accounts for his nickname. During the five-year period 1882–86 "Stump" won 75 games, but dropped a whopping 125. In other words, he averaged 15 wins and 25 losses for five straight seasons.

3792. Weigel, Ralph Richard (1946–49 C) "Wig." The nickname "Wig" simply uses three letters of Ralph's last name.

3793. Weik, Richard Henry (1948–53 P) "Legs." Weik had long legs. As a pitcher at 6'3½" and 180 pounds, he appeared as all legs when he threw the ball.

3794. Weike, John Garabaldi (1883–84 OF) "Podgie." Origin unknown.

3795. Weiland, Robert George (1928–40 P) "Lefty." He pitched left handed and batted left handed. His younger brother Ed Weiland, who also spent two years in the major leagues and pitched and batted left handed, had no public nickname at all.

3796. Weilman, Carl Woolworth (1912–20 P) "Zeke." "Zeke" has been used as a nickname as short for physique. Carl was 6'5½" and 180 pounds. The exact origin of "Zeke" is unknown.

3797. Weimer, Jacob (1903–09 P) "Tornado Jake." "Tornado" refers to Weimer's blazing fastball.

3798. Weinert, Philip Walter (1919–31 P) "Lefty." Weinert pitched left handed and batted left handed.

3799. Weingartner, Elmer William (1945 SS) "Dutch." The nickname refers to Weingartner's German background.

3800. Weis, Arthur John (1922–25 OF) "Butch." "Butch" was a childhood nickname, but the exact origin is unknown.

3801. Weiser, Harry Budson (1915–16 OF) "Bud." Strictly speaking "Bud" qualifies as a short name not a nickname since it is derived from Budson. I document it, because some modern day writers suggest it is a play on Harry's last name. He was not nicknamed after Budweiser beer.

3802. Welch, Frank Tiguer (1919–27 OF) "Bugger." Origin unknown.

3803. Welch, Herbert M. (1925 SS) "Dutch." The nickname refers to Welch's German background.

3804. Welch, Michael Francis (1880–92 P) "Smiling Mickey." Mickey comes from Michael and Welch's Irish background. According to Robert Tiemann, SABR 19th century baseball expert, whenever Welch was pitching in a tight spot characteristically, he would have a grin of determination on his face. The nickname was given to him by cartoonist E.V. Munktrick. On September 10, 1889, Welch became the first pinch hitter in major league history and he struck out.

3805. Welday, Lyndon Earl (1907–09 OF) "Mike." Origin unknown.

3806. Welde, Wilbur (1930–31 P) "Biggs." Origin unknown.

3807. Wells, Gregory De Wayne (1981–82 1B) "Boomer." Wells played briefly for Toronto for two years and then went to Japan. At 6'6" and 250 pounds, he earned the nickname of "Boomer" when in 1984, he became the first Gaijin (foreign-born player) to win a triple crown when he led the Hankyu Braves to the Japan Pacific League championship.

3808. Wells, Willie (1925–49 SS, Negro League) "El Diablo." The 5'7", 160-pound Wells was the premier Negro league shortstop from the late 1920s until the middle 1940s. He compiled a career batting average of .332 in the Negro leagues, and .392 against major leagues in exhibition games. He led the Negro National League with .400 in 1929, and .409 in 1930. When he played in Mexico he was called "El Diablo" "The Devil."

3809. Welsh, James J. (1890–95 C) "Tub." "Tub" is short for "Tubby." Welsh was 5'11", and weighed in the neighborhood of 230 pounds.

3810. Wensloff, Charles William (1943–48 P) "Butch." Wensloff related that Aaron Robinson gave him the nickname of "Butch" during his rookie year with the Yankees in 1943. It was because he was always "cutting up" in the club house.

3811. Wenz, Frederick Charles (1968–70 P) "Fireball." Wentz was noted for his fastball. He struck out 38 batters in 42 innings of a brief major league career in which he compiled a 3-0 won-lost record.

3812. Wera, Julian Valentine (1927–29 3B) "Flop Ears." Wera was a reserve third baseman with the 1927 Yankees. Babe Ruth could not remember his name and called him "Flop Ears" because of his protruding ears.

3813. Werden, Percival Wherritt (1884–97 1B) "Moose." Perry was called "Moose" because of his size of 6'2" and 220 pounds. Werden was one of the few players to have devoted his talents to three teams in three major leagues in three years of service, although not consecutively—1884 St. Louis, Union League; 1888 Washington, National; 1890 Toledo, American Association.

3814. Werhas, John Charles (1964–67 3B) "Peaches." John says his nickname stems from his college days while playing for the University of Southern California. He was spiked during a fight in a game against a Marine team at Camp Pendleton. It required several stitches in his knee. The next day at the game Marines in the stands began to tease and ride him by shouting, "Are you all right, Peaches?" His college coach Rod Dedeaux picked it up. When he signed with the Dodgers in 1960 the club house man, Jim Muke kept it going.

3815. Werle, William George (1949–54 P) "Bugs." During his college days, Werle was interested in the study of insects. Fellow students began to call him "Bugs."

3816. West, Jim (1930–47 1B, Negro League) "Shifty." "Shifty" may refer to West's tendency to be always on the move, never standing still while playing first base. However, I cannot document this.

3817. West, Joseph (1976–78 NL Umpire) "Cowboy Joe." West made several records with a country western band, Texas Cookin.

3818. West, Milton Douglas (1884–90 OF) "Buck." "Buck" is a generic nickname. The circumstances of origin are almost never documented. It refers to a virile, well developed, aggressive, high spirited young man, usually bestowed during teenage years.

3819. West, Weldon Edison (1944–45 P) "Lefty." West pitched left handed but batted right handed.

3820. Wetzel, Franklin Burton (1920–21 OF) "Buzz." Wetzel played with great enthusiasm and lots of energy. It was said he was always buzzing on the diamond.

3821. Wetzel, George William (1885 P) "Shorty." There is no available data on Wetzel's height. Origin unknown.

3822. Weyhing, August (1888–1901 P) "Rubber-Winged Gus." Gus got his nickname from his practice of always soaking his arms in hot water and never letting a trainer touch it. He said it kept his wing loose. This habit enabled him to pitch for 14 years with great success without ever suffering a sore arm. During that period, he pitched over 4,324 innings, winning 264 games and losing 234.

3823. Wheat, Zachary Davis (1909–27 OF) "Buck." "Buck" for Wheat in not of the generic variety. It is a takeoff on his last name. It brings to mind the popular type of breakfast food "buckwheat cakes," a type of pancakes. It was mostly a newspaper nickname since Wheat was usually addressed as "Zack." Playing for Brooklyn in an era when Babe Ruth was a hero for the Yankees and John McGraw's Giants were winning pennants like they were going out of style, Wheat was voted the most popular player in New York. "Zack" was noted for his ability to hit curveballs and was one, if not the best curveball hitter of his era.

3824. Wheeler, Donald Wesley (1949 C) "Scotty." The nickname refers to Wheeler's Scottish background.

3825. Wheeler, George Harrison (1910 PH) "Heavy." "Heavy" may have indicated Wheeler's playing weight, but he is listed at 5'9½" and 180 pounds. Exact origin unknown.

3826. Whitaker, Louis Rodman (1977– 2B) "Sweet Lou." Lou was nicknamed by his teammates for the sweet way he swings the bat.

3827. Whitaker, Walter Elton (1916 P) "Doc." Whitaker was a practicing dentist.

3828. White, Albert Eugene (1940–47 OF) "Fuzzy." Origin unknown.

3829. White, George Frederick (1895 P) "Deke." "Deke" is a shortened and corrupted nickname for Frederick.

3830. White, Guy Harris (1901–13 P) "Doc." White was one of the first major league players to graduate from college and go directly into the major leagues. He was a member of Georgetown University's first graduating class in the School of Dentistry in 1901. In addition to winning 190 major league games and practicing dentistry in the off season, "Doc" composed popular songs and was a vaudeville performer. The well known baseball writer, Ring Lardner, wrote the lyrics to White's most famous song, "Little Puff of Smoke, Goodnight," 1910.

3831. White, James Laurie (1896–90 3B) "Deacon." White was first introduced to the game of baseball in his teens by a disabled Civil War veteran in his hometown of Caton, New York. He became one of the first great ball players starting his major league career at age 29. He was called "Deacon" because he did not smoke, drink, or gamble. Lee Allen, however, points out that White was also a Sunday school superintendent. According to Allen, White may have been one of the last persons to believe that the earth was flat. He spent many off-the-field hours trying to convince fellow players that they were living on a flat plane and not a globe.

3832. White, Joyner Clifford (1932–44 OF) "JoJo." When White arrived to join the Detroit Tigers in 1932, players asked him where he was from. In a deep southern accent, he said "Georgia." But to the players, it sounded like "Jo-Jo."

3833. White, Oliver Kirby (1909–11 P) "Redbuck." Red refers to hair color. White was also called just "Buck." It was short for "Buckeye." White was born and raised in Hillsboro, Ohio.

3834. White, William Henry (1877–86 P) "Whoop-La." White, a three-time 40-game winner, used to scream something like "Whoop-La" when he retired opposing batters. He often did this literally, by hitting them. The fact that he was the first major league pitcher to wear glasses, did not improve batter's morale when facing White. It was

White's intimidating pitches which led to a rule change. In 1884, the American Association adopted a rule that a player struck by a pitch, automatically was awarded first base.

3835. Whitehead, John Henderson (1935–42 P) "Silent John." Whitehead was a man of few words. He rarely spoke until spoken to.

3836. Whitehouse, Charles Evis (1914–19 P) "Lefty." Whitehouse pitched left handed but was a switch hitter.

3837. Whitman, Myron Claude (1944–45 C) "Red." The nickname refers to hair color.

3838. Whitman, Walter Franklin (1946–48 SS) "Hooker." Frank, as Whitman was usually addressed, was nicknamed "Hooker" by his high school basketball coach. He was a hook-shot artist.

3839. Whitney, Arthur Carter (1928–39 3B) "Pinky." Whitney was nicknamed at an early age by his brother who thought he resembled the cartoon character, "Pinky Thompson," who wore a baseball cap and carried a bat on his shoulder.

3840. Whitney, Frank Thomas (1876 OF) "Jumbo." In this case, "Jumbo" is an opposite nickname. At 5'7", 150 pounds, Whitney was small, not large.

3841. Whitney, James E. (1881–90 P) "Grasshopper." One account states that Whitney had a head about the size of a wart, and a forehead which slanted at an angle of 45 degrees. A second version attributes the "Grasshopper" nickname to the peculiar manner in which Whitney ran the bases.

3842. Whitted, George Bostic (1912–22 OF) "Possum." Whitted loved to hunt and raise hunting dogs. Fried Lieb says he was raised in Carolina possum-hunting country. Whitted was also called "Poffin Belly," which called attention to his pot belly.

3843. Widner, William Waterfield (1887–91 P) "Wild Bill." Widner at times had difficulty in locating the plate. He walked more batters than he struck out.

3844. Wietelmann, William Frederick (1939–47 SS) "Whitey." "Whitey" is derived from the last name of this player, not the color of his hair.

3845. Wiggs, James Alvin (1903–06 P) "Big Jim." Wiggs stood 6'4" and weighed over 200 pounds.

3846. Wihtol, Alexander Ames (1979–82 P) "Sandy." "Sandy" refers to Wihtol's hair color.

3847. Wilber, Delbert Quentin (1946–54 C) "Babe." Wilber reports that he was the youngest in his family and called "Baby" and "Babe." After his first year he said, it was not used as a baseball nickname.

3848. Wilhelm, Charles Ernest (1953 SS) "Spider." Wilhelm writes, "I didn't ever know what my nickname was until opening day 1947, when I was with Federalsburg, Maryland, in Class D ball. The public address announcer said 'Leading off and playing shortstop, "Spider" Wilhelm.' My manager, Pep Rambert, thought I was so small and so fast at shortstop that I looked just like a lot of little spider legs in the field."

3849. Wilhelm, Irwin Key (1903–21 P) "Kaiser." Wilhelm had as much difficulty in his career as the German kaiser for whom he was nicknamed. In a nine-year career, he managed to lose 108 games while winning just 58.

3850. Wilkie, Aldon Jay (1941–46 P) "Lefty." Wilkie pitched left handed and batted left handed.

3851. Wilks, Teddy (1944–53 P) "Cork." As a relief pitcher, Wilks had an assortment of pitches and deliveries from overhand to submarine. During the years 1946–48, he made 77 consecutive appearances in relief without being charged with a defeat. This performance led one of his catchers, Joe Garagiola to nickname him "Cork." He put the cork on the bottle of the opposing team.

3852. Will, Robert Lee (1957–63 OF) "Butch." Will was nicknamed as a child by his father and brother Elmer. He says, "They thought I was a 'chunk'."

3853. Williams, Alva Mitchel (1911–18 C) "Buff." Origin unknown.

3854. Williams, August Joseph (1911–15 OF) "Gloomy Gus." "Gus," as he was addressed, was a confirmed recluse, keeping to himself whenever possible. In addition, he always seemed to have a sad look on his face.

3855. Williams, Charles (1915–34 P, Negro League) "Lefty." Claude, as Williams was sometimes addressed, won 29 games and lost only one for the Homestead Grange in 1930. His only loss was to Dick "Cannon Ball" Redding. He pitched left handed, but I have not been able to discover if he also batted left handed.

3856. Williams, Claude Preston (1913–20 P) "Lefty." Williams pitched left handed but batted right handed.

3857. Williams, David Carter (1913–14 P) "Mutt." At 6'3½", 195 pounds, Williams resembled the tall character in the comic strip "Mutt and Jeff."

3858. Williams, Dewey Edgar (1944–48 C) "Dee." "Dee" is just an extension of the first two letters of Williams' first name.

3859. Williams, Donald Reid (1963 P) "Dino." "Dino" is short for dinosaurs, after the cartoon character. Williams was 6'5" and weighed about 225 pounds.

3860. Williams, Fred (1912–30 OF) "Cy." Williams led the National League in home runs four times, and was the first senior circuit star to hit over 200 home runs. "Cy" refers to his country background. He came to the major leagues from the rural area of Wadena, Indiana, without any minor league experience.

3861. Williams, Fred (1945 1B) "Pap." The circumstances of Williams' nickname may be unique. In his own words, "In grammar school a close friend of mine and I were talking about ball player's nicknames. We decided we should have nicknames. I chose 'Daddy Skeeter' for him and he gave me 'Pap Skeets.' It was later shortened to 'Pap'."

3862. Williams, James Thomas (1899–1909 2B) "Buttons." "Buttons" refers to Williams' small size. He was also called "Home Run" when he belted nine in his rookie year before the turn of the century.

3863. Williams, Joe (1897–1932 P, Negro League) "Smokey Joe." Williams was 6'5", or some say 6'6", and half Indian. He threw an overhand fastball said to be faster than any other Negro League pitcher. He was first called "Cyclone." It was not until the mid-1920s that the "Smokey Joe" tag was applied, indicating he was still throwing hard well into his fourth decade. A strike-out artist, it was not unusual for him to fan 20 or more batters in a game. In a 12-inning night game, he struck out 27 Kansas City Monarchs while pitching for the Homestead Grays. Williams was 54 years old at the time. Quite a feat, even though poor lighting aided his cause.

3864. Williams, John Brodie (1914 P) "Honolulu Johnny." Williams was born in Honolulu, Hawaii, 60 years before the islands became the 50th American state in 1959.

3865. Williams, Marshall McDiarmid (1916 P) "Cap." Origin unknown.

3866. Williams, Rees Gephart (1914–16 P) "Steamboat." Origin unknown.

3867. Williams, Robert Fulton (1940–46 P) "Ace." "Ace" is a nickname usually applied to players of extraordinary ability. However, for Williams, the exact origin of "Ace" is unknown.

3868. Williams, Theodore Samuel (1939–60 OF) "The Splendid Splinter." When Williams was a rookie with the Red Sox he was tall, skinny, and gangly-boned. This combined with his explosive hitting accounts for the nickname. Williams was also called "The Thumper," referring to his hitting. American League players often called him "Big Guy" acknowledging his number one status as a hitter. "The Kid" was yet another nickname for Williams in his early years and has been attributed to Johnny Orlando, Red Sox equipment manager. Finally, Williams sometimes called himself "Teddy Ball Game." From time-to-time, sportswriters would use this nickname in print. Williams, the last player to hit .400 or better in a season (.406 in 1941) is generally considered to be one of the greatest "pure" hitters of all time. He won 6 batting titles with a career average of .344 and 521 home runs.

3869. Williams, Walter (1964–75 OF) "No-Neck." Williams was just 5'6" tall with a very short neck. When he was in the outfield, from the grandstand, it appeared he had no neck at all.

3870. Williams, Walter Merrill (1898–1903 P) "Pop." Origin unknown.

3871. Willis, Charles William (1925–27 P) "Lefty." Willis pitched left handed and batted left handed.

3872. Willis, Joseph Denk (1911–13 P) "Big Joe." The nickname refers to Willis' size and body build at an early age, 6'1", 185 pounds.

3873. Willis, Lester Evans (1947 P) "Lefty." Willis pitched left handed and batted left handed. He was also called "Wimpy."

3874. Willoughby, Claude William (1925–31 P) "Weeping Willie." Origin unknown.

3875. Wills, Elliott Taylor (1977–82 2B) "Bump." Former major leaguer, Maury Wills, the father of Elliott "Bump" Wills, admired Chalmers "Bump" Elliott, a great University of Michigan football player and later coach of the University of Illinois football team. He named and nicknamed his son after him.

3876. Wilshere, Vernon Sprague (1934–36 P) "Whitey." The nickname refers to hair color.

3877. Wilson, Arthur Earl (1908–21 C) "Dutch." The nickname refers to Wilson's German background.

3878. Wilson, Charles Woodrow (1931–35 SS) "Swamp Baby." Wilson grew up in the swamp country of South Carolina. But the exact origin of the nickname is unknown.

3879. Wilson, Francis Edward (1924–28 OF) "Squash." Origin unknown.

3880. Wilson, Frank Hoxie (1918–27 OF) "Kid." Usually "Kid" is a nickname for either a very young and or small player. Neither was true for Wilson. In his case "Kid" may be an opposite although the origin is unknown.

3881. Wilson, George Archer (1884 OF) "Hickie." The nickname refers to skin blemishes.

3882. Wilson, George Frank (1911–14 C) "Squanto." "Squanto" may be of American Indian derivation, but the origin is unknown.

3883. Wilson, George Peacock (1934 PH) "Icehouse." "Icehouse" was the nickname given to Wilson during his college days, playing halfback for the football team at St. Mary's University in California. He was cool in tough situations.

3884. Wilson, George Washington (1952–56 OF) "Teddy." Wilson had a trial with the Red Sox and was sent back to the minor leagues. In all confidence, he said he would be back and "hit better than Ted Williams." After this, he was called "Teddy."

3885. Wilson, Gomer Russell (1924 P) "Tex." Wilson was born and raised in Trenton, Texas.

3886. Wilson, Howard Paul (1899–1904 P) "Highball." Origin unknown.

3887. Wilson, Howard William (1906 P) "Chink." Some people believed Wilson's facial features resembled those of individuals of Chinese background, but the exact origin of the nickname is unknown.

3888. Wilson, James (1923–40 C) "Ace." "Ace" denotes Wilson's superior play behind the plate, but the nickname does not seem to have been used very often. Almost universally, Wilson was known as Jimmy.

3889. Wilson, John Francis (1934–42 P) "Black Jack." Wilson recounts, "I had a very heavy beard. On the day I pitched I wouldn't shave. With my cap pulled down low on my face, it looked black. Sportswriters in Boston picked this up and gave me the nickname of 'Black Jack'."

3890. Wilson, John Nicodemus (1913 P) "Lefty." Wilson pitched left handed but batted right handed.

3891. Wilson, John Owen (1908–16 OF) "Chief." "Chief" indicates Wilson's American Indian background. Most Indian ball players received the nickname of "Chief."

3892. Wilson, Judson (1924–45 3B, Negro League) "Boojum." Wilson was only an average fielding third baseman, but was an exceptional hitter with a career average of .375. John Holway says that many old-timers rate Wilson the best of Negro League hitters. He was called "Boojum" from the sound of his drives as they bounced off outfield walls. When he played in Cuba he was known as "Jorocon," the bull.

3893. Wilson, Lester Wilbur (1911 OF) "Tug." Origin unknown.

3894. Wilson, Lewis Robert (1923–34 OF) "Hack." At 5'6", 190 pounds, Wilson was built close to the ground and his compact frame allowed him to generate strength and power at the plate. In 1930, he hit 56 home runs for the Chicago Cubs, a National League record, and drove in 190 runs, a major league record. The nickname "Hack" indicates his strength and power. It is short for Hackenschmidt, the name of the strong man heavyweight wrestling champion of the early years of the 20th century. While "Hack's" bouts with the bottle are legendary, his frequent over indulgence in alcoholic beverages does not account for the following incident. In the fourth game of the 1929 World Series, the Chicago Cubs were leading Connie Mack's Philadelphia A's 8-0 in the seventh inning. "Mule" Hass, A's outfielder hit a long high fly ball to center field, which Wilson lost in the sun and it dropped for a three run homer. The A's scored 10 runs in the inning and went on to beat the Cubs 10-8. From then on, Wilson was called "Sunny Boy" by Chicago fans.

3895. **Wilson, Michael** (1983-87 OF) "Tack." Origin unknown.

3896. **Wilson, Robert James** (1951-60 C) "Red." The nickname refers to hair color.

3897. **Wilson, Roy Edward** (1928 P) "Lefty." Wilson pitched left handed and batted left handed.

3898. **Wilson, Samuel Marshall** (1921 C) "Mike." Origin unknown.

3899. **Wilson, Thomas G.** (1914 C) "Slats." "Slats" denotes Wilson's build, 6'1½", 160 pounds. The nickname was reinforced by the fact his position was catcher. Most catchers have had a more stocky physique.

3900. **Wilson, William Clarence** (1920 P) "Mutt." At 6'3", 165 pounds, Wilson resembled the tall character in the comic strip "Mutt and Jeff."

3901. **Wilson, William Hayward** (1980 OF) "Mookie." "Mookie" is a childhood mispronunciation of the word milk. Wilson's family was responsible for the nickname.

3902. **Wiltse, George LeRoy** (1904-15 P) "Hooks." Wiltse was known for his outstanding curveball, which helped him win 23 games in 1908, and 20 in 1909.

3903. **Wiltse, Harold James** (1926-31 P) "Whitey." The nickname refers to hair color.

3904. **Wiltse, Lewis DeWitt** (1901-03 P) "Snake." Similar to his brother, George, Wiltse's best pitch was his curveball.

3905. **Wineapple, Edward** (1929 P) "Lefty." Wineapple pitched left handed and batted left handed.

3906. **Wineford, James Head** (1932-38 P) "Cowboy." Origin unknown.

3907. **Wingo, Absalom Holbrook** (1919-28 OF) "Red." The nickname refers to hair color.

3908. **Winham, Lafayette Sylvester** (1902-03 P) "Lave." "Lave" is a corruption of Lafayette, shorter and easier to say.

3909. **Winn, George Benjamin** (1919-23 P) "Breezy." Winn was of a talkative nature. He was also called "Lefty." He pitched left handed and batted left handed.

3910. **Winsett, John Thomas** (1930-38 OF) "Long Tom." The nickname denotes Winsett's height 6'2".

3911. **Winter, George Lovington** (1901-08 P) "Sassafras." Origin unknown.

3912. **Winters, Jessie Franklin** (1919-23 P, Negro League) "T-Bone." Origin unknown of this nickname. Winters was also known as "Nip." He was the left-handed ace of the Hilldale Club in the Eastern League. He was the most effective pitcher in that league. In 1924 he won three games in the World Series against the powerful Kansas City Monarchs. The origin of "Nip" is unknown.

3913. Wirtz, Elwood Vernon (1921–24 C) "Kettle." Origin unknown.

3914. Wise, Kendall Cole (1957–60 2B) "Casey." Wise wrote me, "I used the initials of my name KC to be called by. During my days in the minors, players and sportswriters began to put the two together and call me 'Casey.' I was often compared to Casey Stengel coming out on the losing side of the comparison money-wise (no pun intended)."

3915. Wistert, Frances Michael (1934 P) "Whitey." The nickname refers to hair color.

3916. Wisterzil, George John (1914–15 3B) "Tex." Wisterzil was born in Detroit, Michigan, but he spent so much time in the state of Texas, he received the nickname of "Tex."

3917. Witek, Nicholas Joseph (1940–49) "Mickey." "Mickey" is derived from "Nickey." People thought it was easier to say than "Nickey."

3918. Withrow, Frank Blain (1920–22 C) "Kid." "Kid" is a nickname opposite. Withrow was a 29-year-old rookie when he arrived in 1920 to play for the Philadelphia Phils.

3919. Withrow, Raymond Wallace (1963 OF) "Corky." Withrow wrote me, "When I was 3–4 years old, I had a cow-lick in the crown of my hair. There was a comic strip with a little boy with a cow-lick in his hair and my dad started calling me by that boy's name, Corky."

3920. Witt, George Adrian (1957–62 P) "Red." The nickname refers to hair color.

3921. Witt, Lawton Walter (1916–26 OF) "Whitey." The nickname refers to hair color.

3922. Wittig, John Carl (1938–49 P) "Hans." "Hans" denotes Wittig's German background.

3923. Wolf, Walter Francis (1921 P) "Lefty." Wolf pitched left handed but batted right handed.

3924. Wolf, William Van Winkle (1882–92 OF) "Chicken Wolf." According to SABR researcher Philip Von Vorries, Wolf was nicknamed by teammate Pete "the Gladiator" Browning when they were both playing for Louisville of the American Association. Before a game, Wolf disobeyed manager John Dyler's orders and gorged himself on stewed chicken. During the game, he was charged with several errors.

3925. Wolfe, Roy Chamberlain (1912–14 OF) "Polly." Origin unknown.

3926. Wolfe, Wilbert Otto (1903–06 P) "Barney." Origin unknown.

3927. Womack, Horace Guy (1966–70 P) "Dooley." Womack told me, "My parents had a friend named Dool. They added an 'ey' and named me after him. With a name like Horace, wouldn't you go by Dooley?"

3928. Womak, Sidney Kirk (1926 C) "Tex." Womak was born in Greensburg, Louisiana, but spent so much time in the state of Texas, he earned the nickname of "Tex."

3929. Wood, Charles Aster (1930–31 P) "Spades." There are several versions of how the "Spades" nickname came into being, but they differ only slightly from the one given to me by Wood's wife. "He was attending a Methodist's institution, Wofford College, in Spartanburg, South Carolina.

At that time in 1928, strict blue laws were observed. Playing cards was frowned on. On Sunday evening, March 18, 1928, Charles and three other boys skipped evening vespers to play bridge. On one of the deals Charles received 13 spades. He made 283 points without doubling. One of the player's father worked on the local newspaper, he wrote a story on the remarkable incident. When the college authorities read about it, they were shocked. The outcome was that Charles was expelled from school at 19, in his sophomore year. From then on, he was known as 'Spades'." He was a remarkable baseball player and well known in local circles. He was quickly signed by the Pittsburgh Pirate club. Less than two years later, he was playing in the major leagues. A serious injury to his pitching arm ended his career after just two years.

3930. Wood, Charles Spencer (1923 SS) "Doc." Most players with the nickname of "Doc" have been associated with either the medical or dental professions. However, for Wood the origin of "Doc" is unknown.

3931. Wood, George A. (1880–92 OF) "Dandy." It was said that "George Wood cut a fine figure." He was considered very handsome by women and was famous for his large moustache.

3932. Wood, Joe (1908–20 P) "Smoky Joe." Even at 5'11", 180 pounds, Joe Wood appeared frail. It surprised everyone that he had a blazing fastball, some said the equal of that of the great Walter Johnson. In 1912, he posted a 34-5 won-lost record with an ERA of 1.91. The nickname of "Smoky Joe" was given to him before he had pitched in a major league game. Wood was born Howard Ellsworth Wood. His parents nicknamed him "Joey." After he had achieved some fame, he had his name changed to Joe Wood.

3933. Woodhead, James (1879 3B) "Red." The nickname refers to hair color.

3934. Woodman, Daniel Courtenay (1914–15 P) "Cocoa." Origin unknown.

3935. Woodruff, Orville (1904–10 3B) "Sam." Origin unknown.

3936. Woods, Jim (1953–75 Announcer) "The Possum." Woods worked with Mel Allen 1953–56 on the Yankee broadcasts, but was fired to make way for ex–Yankee shortstop Phil Rizzuto. He was nicknamed by Enos Slaughter who saw his burr haircut and said, "I've seen better heads on a possum." Wood also did New York Giant games until they left for the West Coast. Then he joined Bob Prince in Pittsburgh from 1958 to 1975.

3937. Wooten, Earl Hazwell (1947–48 OF) "Junior." Wooten was nicknamed "Junior" by teammate John Wilson when both were with the Chattanooga team in the Southern League. Wilson called Wooten "Junior" because he was much younger than Wilson.

3938. Workman, Harry Hall (1924 P) "Hoge." "Hoge" is a takeoff on Harry.

3939. Works, Ralph Talmadge (1909–13 P) "Judge." Origin unknown.

3940. Worthington, Allan Fulton (1953–69 P) "Red." The nickname refers to hair color.

3941. Worthington, Robert Lee (1931–34 OF) "Red." The nickname refers to hair color. According to Tom Shea, Worthington was also called "Colonel Rhubarb." The "Colonel" was an honorary title Kentucky-style, and "Rhubarb" recognized his red hair.

3942. Wright, Burnis (1932–45 OF, Negro League) "Wild Bill." Origin unknown.

3943. Wright, Edward Yatman (1918 SS) "Ceylon." Wright grew up in the small town of Ceylon, Minnesota.

3944. Wright, Forrest Glenn (1924–35 SS) "Buckshot." Glenn as he was usually addressed, was given the nickname of "Buckshot" when he was playing for Kansas City in the American Association in 1922. It refers to his fast throwing arm, which rarely missed its target. It was, interestingly, an almost underhanded throw.

3945. Wright, Wayne Bromley (1917–23 P) "Rasty." Wayne Wright was nicknamed "Rasty" after William "Rasty" Wright who played in 1890.

3946. Wright, William Robert (1946–58 P) "Lefty." Wright pitched left handed and batted left handed.

3947. Wright, William Simmons (1909 P) "Lucky." Origin unknown.

3948. Wright, William Smith (1890 OF) "Rasty." Origin unknown.

3949. Wrigley, George Watson (1896–99 SS) "Zeke." Origin unknown.

3950. Wuestling, George (1929–30 SS) "Yats." Origin unknown.

3951. Wynn, Early (1939–63 P) "Gus." Three hundred–game winner Early Wynn was nicknamed by teammate Ellis Clary in 1937, when they were both playing for Stanford in the Florida State League. Clary said he just looked like a "Gus." Joseph McBride suggests that Clary might have been reminded of a wrestler, Guss Sonnenburg.

3952. Wynn, James Sherman (1963–77 OF) "Toy Cannon." Although of relatively small size, 5'10", 160 pounds, Wynn demonstrated explosive power at the plate. Balls came off his bat as if shot out of a cannon. The "Toy Cannon" tag was given to him by Houston Astro fans.

3953. Wynnegar, Harold Delano (1975–78 C) "Butch." Wynnegar was chubby as a child, and an aunt gave him his nickname, because she thought he looked like a "Butch."

3954. Wyse, Henry Washington (1942–51 P) "Hooks." Wyse was known for his curveball. Manager Charlie Grimm called him "Hankus Pankus" for no particular reason.

3955. Yale, William M. (1905 1B) "AD." Origin unknown.

3956. Yarnell, Waldo William (1926 P) "Rusty." The nickname refers to hair color.

3957. Yarrison, Byron Wadsworth (1922–24 P) "Rube." "Rube" refers to Yarrison's rural background and country ways.

3958. Yaryan, Clarence Everret (1921–22 C) "Yam." "Yam" refers to Yaryan's big feet. It was said he wore shoes as large as violin cases.

3959. Yates, Albert Arthur (1971 OF) "Bunny." Origin unknown.

3960. Yatkeman, Morris (1924–82 Clubhouse Manager) "Butch." Yatkeman began work for the St. Louis Cardinals in 1924 as visiting team batboy and later became one of the most famous of clubhouse managers. "Butch," as he was universally known for 48 years, referred to his diminutive size.

3961. Yeabsley, Robert Watkins (1919 PH) "Bert." Origin unknown.

3962. Yeager, George J. (1896–1902 C) "Doc." Many of the players with the nickname of "Doc" had close associations with either the medical or dental professions. For Yeager, however, the origin of "Doc" is unknown.

3963. Yeager, George Y. (1898–1908 3B) "Little Joe." "Little Joe" was used by fellow players as a term of affection.

3964. Yeargin, James Almond (1922–24 P) "Grapefruit." Origin unknown.

X-Y-Z

3965. Yellowhorse, Moses J. (1921–22 P) "Chief." "Chief" was a nickname given to almost every player of Indian blood through the 1950s. He was named after a famous yellow pony who was of great ability in aiding Indians in hunting buffalo.

3966. Yerkes, Charles Carroll (1927–33 P) "Lefty." Yerkes pitched left handed but batted right handed. Although Carroll, as he was addressed, pitched in five major league seasons his won-lost record was only 1-1.

3967. Yewric, Thomas J. (1957 C) "Kibby." Yewric told me as a child his brother called him "Kibby." It meant he was nosy.

3968. Yingling, Earl Hershey (1911–18 P) "Chink." The nickname stemmed from his last name which sounded Chinese. Neither his facial features nor body size looked Chinese.

3969. York, James Edward (1919–21 P) "Lefty." He pitched left handed and batted left handed.

3970. York, Rudolph Preston (1934–48 1B) "The Big Indian." York claimed he was a "whole lot [Cherokee] Indian." Rudy, as he was addressed, was a powerful hitter with 277 home runs to his credit in 13 seasons. In 1934 as a rookie for Detroit, he hit 35 home runs, 18 in the month of August. He was such a poor fielder, however, of the Dave Kingman type, that sportswriters used to say, "He must be part Indian and part first baseman."

3971. Yost, Edward Frederick (1944–62 3B) "The Walking Man." Yost, usually a lead-off man, earned his nickname by an uncanny ability to attract walks. Just an average hitter with a career batting average of .254 and with only modest power, 139 home runs in 18 campaigns, Eddie accounted for 1,614 bases on balls. He ranks seventh on the all-time list behind six great hitters: Joe Morgan, Ruth, Williams, Yastremski, Mantle and Ott. Yost led the American League in walks six times. His highest total achieved was 151 in 1956. Only Ruth and Williams drew more bases on balls in a season than "The Walking Man."

3972. Young, Charles (1915 P) "Cy." One of several players by the name, of Young who were nicknamed after the greatest player with that name, Denton "Cy" Young. He was however, usually addressed as Charlie.

3973. Young, Denton True (1890–1911 P) "Cy." Although there are slight variations in accounts by different writers, all seem to agree on the essential facts of the event that led to Denton being assigned the nickname of "Cy." Daley's classic report goes like this, "When this gangling farm boy strode off an Ohio ridge for a baseball tryout in 1890, he had no nickname. But he got the nickname and the job in the same afternoon. George Moreland, the Canton manager, tested him by the simple expedience of having him pitch to his star hitter. The big farmer—6'2" and 210 pounds—had no uniform, no catcher. But the batter couldn't nick him for a loud foul. 'How's that kid pitcher?' asked the owner afterwards. 'Just look at the grandstand' was the reply! The owner looked up and almost swooned. Board after board of the backstop had been splintered. "Pears as though a cyclone struck it,' he remarked." The "Cyclone" designation soon was shortened to "Cy." Without attempting to dispute this account, it should be pointed out that in 1890, there was already a fast-balling right handed major league pitcher with the nickname of "Cyclone" who won 32 games for Cincinnati in 1889. See entry for Duryea, James Whitney.

3974. Young, Harlan Edward (1908 P) "Cy the Third." Both Denton "Cy" Young, and Irving "Cy" Young were pitching in the major leagues, when Harley, as he was addressed, broke in as a rookie in 1908. "The Third" was used to distinguish among them. Undoubtedly the "Cy" was after Denton Young. The distinction was hardly necessary, since Harlan lasted but one year in the majors.

3975. Young, Irving Melrose (1905–11 P) "Young Cy." When Irv, as he was addressed, broke in with the Boston National League teams in 1905, Denton "Cy" Young, after whom he was nicknamed, was pitching for the Boston American League team. "Young Cy" or "Cy the Second" were used to distinguish between them. This distinction was needed especially in 1905 when Denton started 33 games and finished 32, and Irv started 42 games and finished 41. It seemed every other day a "Cy" was pitching in Boston!

3976. Young, Lemuel Floyd (1933–45 2B) "Pep." Lem was nicknamed after Ralph "Pep" Young a second baseman who preceded him and whom he was thought to resemble in enthusiastic style of play.

3977. Young, Norman Robert (1936–48 P) "Babe." Origin unknown.

3978. Young, Ralph Stuart (1913–22 2B) "Pep." "Pep" refers to Young's enthusiasm and chatter at second base.

3979. Youngblood, Arthur Clyde (1922 P) "Chief." Similar to other players nicknamed "Chief," Youngblood was of American Indian descent. His career consisted of but 4⅓ innings pitched in the major leagues.

3980. Youngs, Ross Middlebrook (1917–26 OF) "Pep." Ross was known for playing the game with a "peppy" boyish enthusiasm.

3981. Yount, Herbert Macon (1914 P) "Hub." "Hub," as he was addressed, was short for Herbert. Yount was also called "Ducky." While the origin of this nickname is unknown, it was not because of his height — 6'5".

3982. Yowell, Carl Columbus (1924–25 P) "Sundown." It was said Yowell did his best pitching during twilight hours.

3983. Zabel, George Washington (1913–15 P) "Zip." His nickname refers to the way he pitched. He put zip (speed) on the ball. June 17, 1915, Zabel zipped through a major league record of 18⅓ innings of relief as the Cubs beat the Dodgers 4–3 in 19 innings.

3984. Zachary, William Chris (1944 P) "Chink." His facial features, but not his build, were thought to look Chinese.

3985. Zacher, Elmer Henry (1910 OF) "Silver." "Silver" referred to Zacher's grey hair, and was preferable to the name of Elmer.

3986. Zardon, Jose Antonio Sanchez (1943 OF) "Guieno." "Guieno" means Guinea hen. It refers to Zardon's speed in the outfield and base paths.

3987. Zarilla, Allen Lee (1943–53 OF) "Zeke." Shortstop teammate, Vern "Junior" Stephens, on the St. Louis Browns gave Zarilla the nickname "Zeke" because it rhymed with sneak. He thought he was sneaky fast, and called him "Sneak Zeke."

3988. Zdeb, Joseph Edmund (1977–79 OF) "Mad Dog." Zdeb was nicknamed by Royal's manager Whitey Herzog during spring training camp in 1977. It refers to his all out hustle. It looked as if he was playing mad.

3989. Zeider, Rollie Hubert (1910–18 2B) "Bunions." Zeiders suffered from bunions. In 1913, when star first baseman Hal Chase was traded from the New York Yankees to the Chicago White Sox for Zeider and for William "Babe" Borton, a New York sportswriter remarked in disgust that the Yanks had traded a star for a bunion and an onion. Onion referred to Borton's inability to get along with other players. Zeider was also called "Hook" and "Polly" because of his long nose. When Ty Cobb nearly amputated his bunions with his spikes sliding into second base, newspaper accounts called Zeider the "Bunion King."

3990. Zernial, Gus Edward (1949–59 OF) "Ozark Ike." Although he was born in Beaumont, Texas, broadcaster Fred Haney of the Hollywood Stars in the Pacific Coast League nicknamed Gus "Ozark Ike" after the rustic cartoon character. Playing the outfield Zernial often looked both rustic and rusty.

3991. Zettlein, George (1876 P) "The Charmer." Zettlein always had a grin or smile on his face with which to charm both fans and opposing players.

3992. Zimmer, Charles Louis (1884–1903 C; NL Umpire 1889, 1904–05) "Chief." Zimmer was one of the great catchers of the 18th century. He is best remembered for using beefsteak as padding in his light mitt behind the plate, catching one of Cy Young's no hitters and hitting perhaps the longest home run of all time. So the story goes, at the old Boston National League park, he hit a home run over the fence which landed on a car of the Boston-Albany Railroad and was not recovered until it reached Fall River. "Chief" was not an Indian. In 1886 he was playing for Poughkeepsie. The team's nickname was Indians. Zimmer was the head man of the team and everyone addressed him as "Chief."

3993. Zimmer, Donald William (1954–65 3B) "Popeye." Zim was nicknamed after the famous cartoon character because of his tobacco-filled bulging jowls.

3994. Zimmerman, Henry (1907–19 3B) "Heinie." The nickname stems from Henry's German background. While playing third base for the New York Giants, "Heinie" became the goat of the 1917 World Series when in the sixth and final game of the series, he chased Eddie Collins of the White Sox across the plate with what turned out to be the winning run.

3995. Zipfel, Marion Sylvester (1961–62 1B) "Bud." According to Zipfel's own account, "My twin sister and I had three older brothers. They called us 'Buddy' and 'Sissie.' Later, I became just 'Bud.' In baseball I was really called 'Zip' more than 'Bud,' not only because of my name, but because of my speed." By the 1980s, few baseball fans remembered the name of Zipfel until it became part of the title of a book written by Rich Marazzi and Len Fiorito about the present circumstances of former major league players of the 1960s—*Aaron to Zipfel.*

3996. Zoldak, Samuel Walter (1944–52 P) "Sad Sam." Zoldak often had a sad look on his face.

3997. Zuber, William Henry (1936–47 P) "Goober." The nickname is no more than a play on Bill's last name. "Goober" rhymes with Zuber.

3998. Zupo, Frank Joseph (1957–61 C) "Noodles." "Noodles" refers to Zupo's Italian background and love of pasta.

3999. Zwilling, Edward Harrison (1910–16 OF) "Dutch." "Dutch" refers to Zwilling's German background. Since 1910, Zwilling has remained the last name in alphabetical order on the all time major league roster list. "Dutch" replaced Frank Zinn, who had held the dubious honor since 1888, replacing "Chief" Zimmer who in 1884 had ousted George Zettlin, who had held the distinction since 1876. And, as one great baseball writer once wrote, "You can look it up."

II. All American Girls Baseball League Players

All American Girls Baseball League Player Nicknames

Compiled by Brenda S. Wilson

The All American Girls Baseball League was a dream come true for some 558 women who played the game of baseball in the United States from 1943 to 1954. The All American Girls Baseball League was the only full-scale professional major league baseball accessible to women. Women played ball in Wrigley Field, Comiskey Park, and Yankee Stadium. It was women professional ball players who played the first night baseball game on Wrigley Field. On July 18, 1944, portable lights were installed for a night-time doubleheader featuring four of the League's teams. Although the occasion was a war-related event to pay tribute to Red Cross blood donors and other supporters of the Red Cross, some 20,000 spectators appeared to witness this unique event.

Philip K. Wrigley, entrepreneur and owner of the Chicago Cubs, created a National Girls Softball League in 1943. Due to the World War II manpower shortage, Wrigley started women's softball in the event that major league baseball was cancelled. Wrigley saw women ball players serving as inspiration examples to other women who had entered the labor force. The players were to symbolize America's home front heroes. Due to his emphasis on building home front morale, Wrigley established the League as a non-profit professional organization. During the first year, the players signed a league contract, rather than a team contract. Thus, the League did not start out with a reserve clause.

Although the League began as the National Girls Softball League, after 1948 it became a baseball league and the name changed to the All American Girls Baseball League. The League played by major league baseball rules. Not only did the League follow major league rules, they may have been instrumental in the adoption of the designated hitter rule, which allowed a batter for each team to bat without taking a field position. This rule was adopted by the All American Girl Baseball League in 1950, and later adopted by the American Baseball League.

The transition from softball to baseball occurred with the conversion of underhand pitching, to sidearm pitching in 1946, to overhand pitching in 1948. By 1954, the only difference between major league baseball and the women's professional baseball was a five foot difference in the base path distance. The variations in size and distance were designed to fit the perceived strength disparities of the average woman ballplayer and to allow an entry adjustment from softball. The changes in women's baseball mirrored the evolution of men's baseball.

During the League's 11 year history, 14 midwestern cities, including Chicago, served as host to the league teams. Women from all over the United States and Canada played a 125 game season from mid–May to early September. Each season ended with championship playoffs and All Star games. By 1948, the league had over one million fans. Players were paid salaries roughly equivalent to those of male minor league players in AA classification. Former minor and major league players, such as Hall of Famers Jimmy Foxx, Max Carey, and Dave Bancroft, served as team managers. In all, 19 former major league ballplayers served as managers for the League.

To make women's participation in baseball acceptable, spring training also included training at Helena Rubenstein's Charm School. Wrigley's marketing strategy was to have the women project ultra-feminine characteristics along with their ability to play ball. To create a feminine look, the players wore short-skirted uniforms with satin shorts designed by Wrigley's wife. Each team had a female chaperon who was responsible for the conduct, care and appearance of the team's ball players. A chaperon often served as a counselor, surrogate parent, disciplinarian, friend, and trainer to the team's players.

By 1954, the League folded and its memory faded just about as quickly as it had been conceived. The war was over and woman's place, once again, was back in the home. Although the public was quick to forget, the women baseball players never did. This memorable experience was recaptured during the 1980s with annual old-timer exhibition games. By 1986, a player's association was formed in hopes to gain national recognition as professional baseball players. After some 30 years, the other major league in America sport's history was recognized. In 1988, the League's history and the names of the women who played in the League were acknowledged with a permanent display in the Cooperstown Baseball Hall of Fame.

The list that follows is the only known compilation on the subject. All known positions are given rather than just the primary position. In some cases no position has been specified because the information is not available.

4000. Adams, Evelyn Edell (1946 3B/SS) "Tommie." The name stems from her childhood days of being called a "Tomboy." Sportswriter Hank Wolf changed "Tomboy" to "Tommie" during her early softball career. The name was used when she played basketball in 1937, and was carried over into her professional baseball career.

4001. Applegren, Amy Irene (1944–53 1B/P) "Lefty." The name is the result of Applegren being left handed. Since a left handed first baseman or pitcher was considered advantageous for her team, she was taught to play these positions at the early age of 11 when she first joined organized ball. The name "Lefty" was adopted as she continued to pitch and play first base.

4002. Appugliese, Lucille Marie (1944–45 C) "Lulu." The name stems not from her first name, but from a reference to her ball playing. Sportswriter Jack Canberry of the *Denver Post* wrote after watching her play, "She sure is a Lulu of a ball player."

4003. Armstrong, Charlotte (1944–45 P) "Skip." "Skip" is a shortened version of the name "Skipper." A hometown sportswriter is credited with first using the name "Skipper" when he referred to Armstrong as the "Skipper of her ship," denoting her strong pitching ability that led her team to many victories during the season. She earned the name while playing fast-pitch ball before she joined the AAGBL. The name remained with her during her professional career and later life.

4004. Arnold, Lenna (1948–49 P) "Sis." A childhood family nickname.

4005. Baker, Mary (1943–53 C/IF) "Bonnie." Origin unknown. Baker was selected as the All Star catcher in 1943 and 1946. She served as player-mana

ger of the Kalamazoo Lassies in 1950. She was considered one of the most attractive players in the league. Baker was also a former fashion model before she joined the league in 1943.

4006. Barker, Lois Anna (1950 3B/RF) "Tommie." Her family expected her to be a boy when she was born. The name Thomas Henry was reserved for Barker with anticipations of her being a baby boy. Although she was never given the name Thomas Henry, she was called "Tommie." Very few people know her given name.

4007. Barney, Edith (1948–49 C) "Little Red." "Red" was a reference to Barney's red hair. Instead of "Rex Barney" the major league baseball player, she became "Red Barney" taking the "Red" from "Red" Barber, a radio sports announcer. She acquired the name "Red" from her friends and teammates during her teens playing ball. Later when she played pro ball, "Little" was attached to "Red," because there was another player named "Red." Barney became known as "Little Red" because she was much shorter than Fran Janssen the Grand Rapid's pitcher who was also called "Red."

4008. Barr, Doris (1944–46 P) "Dodie." Origin unknown.

4009. Batikis, Annastasia (1945 CF) "Stash." "Stash" comes from having Annastasia as a first name and playing ball on a boy's team. She was given the name by some of the boys she played ball with in elementary school. She was first called "Stashia" which was changed to "Stacy" which was changed to "Stash." Before the name "Stash" stuck, she was called "Shorty," "Lefty," "Speedy," and "Pork Chop."

4010. Baumgartner, Mary Louise (1949–54 C) "Wimpy." The name comes from the cartoon character "Wimpy" who always ate hamburgers. Her oldest sister started calling her "Wimpy" when she was around the age of four, because she always wanted hamburgers for every meal. "Wimpy" was often shortened to "Wimp."

4011. Bell, Virginia Louise (1948 Util) "Ginger." Though the name is often a substitute for Virginia, this was not the case for Bell. "Ginger" was a reference to her personality. She was described as a spicy and snappy baby because at a very early age she began to walk without ever crawling. It was her father who is credited with first calling her "Ginger" after he proclaimed her to be "full of ginger."

4012. Berger, Marguerite Eloise (1944 2B) "Sonny." The name stems from a error in the *Miami Herald* sport's report. After pitching a winning game, the newspaper reported, "M. Berger, pitcher, was supported by *his* teammate, Tommy Moore." The newspaper assumed that Tommy referred to a male ball player. Thus, M. Berger must also be male. The next day at practice the team teased Berger by calling her "Son." The idea caught on and "Son" became "Sonny."

4013. Bergmann, Erma M. (1946–51 P/OF) "Bergie." "Bergie" was derived from her last name Bergmann. It was her teammates who first called her "Bergie," and the fans popularized it.

4014. Berthiaume, Elizabeth Anne (1945–46) "Bo Bo." Berthiaume was called "Bo Bo" by her fans while playing pro-ball before she was married. This name had no significant meaning. Later when she married while still playing in the league, she was called "Wiggles" because of her movement at the plate when she was batting. "Wiggles" also went well with her married name Wicken.

4015. Blumutta, Catherine Elizabeth (1944–54) "Swish." Her basketball coach called her "Swish" because of her style of shooting baskets. Blumutta aimed her hook and long shots at the basket rim and never used the backboard. Even though the name had nothing to do with baseball, it followed her throughout her baseball career.

4016. Briggs, Wilma Hannah (1948–54 OF) "Briggsie." "Briggsie" is an extension of the name Briggs. Players of the AAGBL were the first to start calling her "Briggsie." Briggs liked the idea because she had never been referred to by her last name before.

4017. Brown, Patricia Irene (1950–51 P) "Specs." The name is a reference to her wearing eyeglasses. "Specs" is short for spectacles meaning eyeglasses. A sportswriter attached this name to her because not too many girls wore glasses and played baseball. Once when she pitched a three-hitter, the headlines read: "Specs Brown Pitches 3-Hitter." The name was never used by her fellow teammates who usually referred to her as "Pat" or "Brownie."

4018. Brumfield, Dolores B. (1947–53 2B/OF) "Dolly." Brumfield acquired the name "Dolly" because she was so young when she joined the league. She was one of the league's youngest players. She was 14 when she reported to Havana, Cuba, for spring training. Daisy Junor is credited with first calling her "Dolly" after spring training in Cuba. Being older and married, Junor took on the role of Brumfield's "unofficial" chaperon while they were in Cuba. Before baseball, she was known as "Puddin" by her family. Later, when she was teaching she was called "Dee." Brumfield's mother often said she knew what group of friends were calling by what name they used on the telephone. Brumfield led the Kenosha Comets in hitting in 1951, and finished second in league hitting in 1953.

4019. Burkovich, Shirley (1949–51 IF/OF) "Hustle." Burkovich earned her nickname from her teammates because of her on the field hustle during a game.

4020. Callaghan, Margaret Ethel (1944–49 2B/3B) "Calhoun." There was no known meaning attached to the name "Calhoun." It seems that a Fort Wayne fan referred to Callaghan as "Calhoun" and the team picked it up and started calling her "Calhoun." Callaghan was a reliable infielder. She was the leading fielder at third base in 1944 and 1945. In 1946, she had the most putouts in the league at third base.

4021. Castillo, Ysora (1949–51) "Chico." "Chico," meaning kid, refers to Castillo's Spanish roots. She was from Havana, Cuba.

4022. Cione, Jean (1945–54 P/1B/OF) "Cy." "Cy" is a derivative of the last name of Cione.

4023. Clark, Corrine M. (1947) "Corky." "Corky" was the result of her teammates trying to come up with a nickname that would go with Corinne. When she first started playing softball, her mother felt no one could replace Corinne with a nickname. Finding a nickname became a challenge for the team.

4024. Cook, Donna (1946–54 P/OF) "Little Cookie." The term "Cookie" is a derivation of Donna Cook's last name. The "little" was added to "Cookie" when her younger sister started to play in the AAGBL in 1949. The name was used to distinguish the two sisters apart. Ironically, the name was not a reference to Cook's size or age.

4025. Cook, Doris (1949–53 P/OF) "Big Cookie." Doris Cook received the name "Big Cookie" when she joined the AAGBL. The name was used to distinguish her from her older sister Donna who was already playing for the league. There was no special meaning attached to the term "Big," because she was neither larger in size nor older in age.

4026. Cordes, Gloria (1950–54 P) "Cordie." "Cordie" is a derivation of the name Cordes. AAGBL teammates were the first to call her "Cordie" because it was much easier to use and remember in field chatter than her last name Cordes. As the team pitcher, her name was called quite often during the game. Cordes was selected for 1952 All Star team, after pitching 24 consecutive complete games that season.

4027. Cornett, Betty Jane (1950–51) "Curly." The name is a reference to her hair, even though Cornett's hair is not curly. Teammates, "Smokey" Mandella and "Hustle" Burkovich, are credited with first using "Curly." Cornett acquired the name in the fall of 1949 on her way to Rookie Camp in Indianapolis, Indiana. Wanting to look her best for such a grand occasion, Cornett had curled her hair. Since her hair was naturally straight, the curl was only temporary. At the train station and throughout the trip, Cornett met many of her future teammates. As the trip progressed, Cornett was confronted with a long layover and rainy weather. As the rain came tumbling down, so did Cornett's curls. The other players soon realized that the curls were not for real and started calling her "Curly."

4028. Crawley, Pauline (1946–51 CF) "Hedy." The name "Hedy" was the result of Crawley comparing herself to the glamorous Hedy Lamarre. As a joke, her high school classmates started calling her "Hedy." The name stuck and following her throughout her professional career and later life.

4029. Daetweiler, Louella Mildred (1944 C) "Daets." "Daets" is a derivation of the last name Daetweiler. Daetweiler received the name while in grammar school and it followed her through her ball career and in later life.

4030. Dancer, Faye Katherine (1944–50 OF/IF/P) "Tiger." Dancer's father began calling her "Tiger" when she was very young because of her zestful attitude toward playing baseball. On the weekends, her father would take her and her brother to the playground to play ball. Because she was more interested in playing ball than her brother, her father started calling her "Tiger." Her zestful attitude not only earned her the name "Tiger," but a reputation of being a player who believed her job was to stir up the fans and make the game interesting. She was known to pull such capers as turning cartwheels as she left center field, and stopping the game from the outfield so that she could get a drink. She was truly a "Tiger" of an entertainer for both her fans and teammates. Dancer stopped using the name of "Tiger" after her father, who inspired her love for baseball, died.

4031. Dapkus, Eleanor Virginia (1943–50 OF/P) "Slugger." Dapkus earned the name "Slugger" her first year playing pro ball when she hit ten home runs. She set an all time league record, which remained unbroken until 1952. She was also called "Ace" when she was pitcher for the Racine Belles. "Ace" was a reference to her excellent pitching ability that came as a surprise to the fans and players because she usually played outfield. Dapkus was the first to earn the Player of Year award twice, once in 1947 and again in 1949.

4032. Davis, Gladys (1943–47 SS) "Terrie." Origin unknown.

4033. Decambra, Alice (1946–50 2B/P) "Big Al." Origin unknown.

4034. Deegan, Mildred Eleanor (1943–52 C/P) "Deegie." "Deegie" is an extraction from her last name Deegan. Since her team manager only referred to the players by their last names, Deegan asked him if she could be called "Deegie" instead of Deegan because she did not like being called Deegan. The name was never used after her ball career.

4035. Descombes, Jeneane (1954 P) "Lefty." "Lefty" referred to Descombes being a left handed pitcher. She acquired the name while she was the bat girl for her hometown men's baseball team. An old-timer from the men's baseball team first called her "Lefty." He taught Descombes how to pitch left handed and encouraged her to become a left handed pitcher. The name stuck and so did the lessons. Descombes became a left handed pitcher for the Grand Rapids Chicks.

4036. Dokish, Juanita (1954) "Lee." The nickname "Lee" was the name Dokish received early in life. It seems that her younger sister could not pronounce the name Juanita, and started calling her "Leela." "Leela" was later shorten to "Lee" and the nickname has remained with Dokish ever since.

4037. Doyle, Cartha Lynn (1946) "Duckie." The name is a shortened version of "Ducksoup" meaning the player is an easy out at the plate. While Doyle was playing softball, a cousin started calling her "Ducksoup." Her teammates picked up on the "Ducksoup" and shortened it to "Duck." After she joined the league, she was called "Duckie." Even though the name's origin has a negative note concerning her ball playing, Doyle preferred to be called "Duckie" because most people had difficulty pronouncing her first name.

4038. Drinkwater, Maxine (1954 1B/2B/3B) "Mac." "Mac" is a derivation of her first name Maxine. Her brothers and friends first started calling her "Mac" when she was very young. The name stuck and followed her through her ball career.

4039. Earp, Mildred (1946–50 P) "Mid." "Mid" is simply a short name taken from the name Mildred.

4040. Eisen, Thelma (1944–52 OF) "Tiby." "Tiby" is a childhood name given to Eisen by her family. The name served as a substitute middle name. Eisen was from a Jewish family that did not give middle names at birth. When she started to school this became an important issue to her. Eisen's family gave her the nickname "Tiby" as a replacement for not having a middle name. The nickname stuck and followed her throughout her life. Few know her by her given name, Thelma. Eisen was one of the few players who also served as a team manager for the league. In 1946, she played on the All Star team, tied the league record in triples, and was second in stolen bases.

4041. Eisenberger, Joan Marie (1942–54 2B) "Bergie." "Bergie" is a derivation of the name Eisenberger. The opposing team players first started calling her "Bergie" when she played in the league. Often her own teammates would refer to her as "Bugger" instead of "Bergie" as a tease.

4042. Emerson, June (1948–49) "Venus." The term "Venus" was a reference to the armless Greek statue, Venus de Milo. Emerson received the nickname during a particular game, when she lost sight of the ball and it hit her on the head, bounced off, and was caught by the second baseman who turned it into a double play. Since Emerson's contribution to the play was by her head and not her arms, her teammates called her "Venus" to denote her ability to play baseball without using her arms or hands.

4043. Fenton, Peggy Lou (1945) "Lefty." Fenton was called "Lefty" throughout her ball career because she was a left handed athlete.

4044. Filarski, Helen Margaret (1944–50 3B) "Fil." "Fil" was derived from her last name Filarski. The name was first used in a game when the players yelled "Fil" to direct her attention to a short bunt. It was a questionable play as to who should get the ball, her or the pitcher. Although she married during her career and her last name changed to Steffes, the nickname "Fil" remained.

4045. Fischer, Alva Jo (1945–48 P) "Tex." Origin unknown.

4046. Fisher, Lorraine Rose (1947–49 P) "Fish." The name is a shortened version of her last name Fisher. She received the name "Fish" during childhood, and it followed her through her ball career and later in life.

4047. Flaherty, Mary J. (1948) "Irish." Flaherty was given the name "Irish" by her friends in Connecticut because she looked Irish and was.

4048. Florreich, Kathleen Lois (1943–50 P) "Flash." During her baseball career she earned the name "Flash" because of her speed and strong pitching arm. She was well known for stealing bases and pitching a pretty mean fastball.

4049. Gascon, Eileen Virginia (1949–51 Util) "Ginger." Gascon's mother started calling her "Ginger" because of her perky personality when she was around five years old. The name followed her through her ball career and later life.

4050. Geissinger, Jean Louise (1950–54 2B) "Squeaky." Due to the high pitch of Geissinger's voice, which could always be heard during infield chatter, she became known as "Squeaky." The name made her very self-conscious of her voice so she resorted to whistling instead of chattering during the games. The name stuck throughout her professional career.

4051. Gianfrancisco, Philomena Theresa (1945–49 RF) "Frisco." "Frisco" is an abstraction from her last name Gianfrancisco. Player Alma Ziegler tagged her with "Frisco" during a game in an attempt to get a rally going when she was up to bat. It probably seemed easier to say "Come on Frisco" than "Come on Gianfrancisco." She was sometimes called "Philharmonica," if the players were into teasing her.

4052. Goldsmith, Bethany Joan (1949–51 P) "Torchy." Being a redhead and pitching a mean fastball earned Goldsmith the name "Torchy." It was her teammates on the Kenosha Comets team who first called Goldsmith "Torchy."

4053. Habben, Caroline Elizabeth (1953–54 OF/C) "Hab." "Hab" is a shortened version of her last name Habben. It seems that Caroline was just too long to use on the ball field. The name was never used after her ball career.

4054. Harnett, Ann (1943–47 3B) "Tootie." Origin unknown. Harnett was the first ball player that was signed by Philip K. Wrigley to play in the AAGBL. In 1943, she played on the All Star team and led the league in extra base hits (26) and RBIs (69).

4055. Harney, Elise Juanita (1943–48 P) "Lee." Harney was given the name "Lee" because the name Elise was unusual and the players had difficulty pronouncing it correctly. Her teammates in the Chicago Softball league started calling her "Lee," and she has been known as "Lee" ever since.

4056. Harrell, Dorothy Harriet (1944–50–52 SS) "Snookie." Harrell's grandmother started calling her "Snookie" soon after she was born. She had a boy cousin called "Snooky" who was older. Her parents spelled her name with an "ie" instead of "y" because she was a girl. The name was used when she first started playing ball at the age of 13 and was continued throughout her career.

4057. Havlish, Jean Ann (1953–54 SS) "Grasshopper." Developing her own unique playing style earned Havlish the name "Grasshopper." When she played shortstop for the Fort Wayne Daisies, she would get low to the ground in a ready stance. From the first baseman's position, Havlish's stance looked like a grasshopper. The team's first baseman, Betty Weaver Foss, is credited with first using the name "Grasshopper."

4058. Haylett, Alice Marie (1946–49 P) "Al." "Al" is a shortened version of the name Alice. Although "Al" can be derived from Alice, this is not commonly practiced. It probably was used because of it's masculine connotation and Haylett being a female playing a traditionally all-male sport. The name was given to her when she first started playing ball, and it followed her through her professional career. Haylett set the all time league ERA (0.77) and winning percentage (.833) in 1948. She had a lifetime ERA of 1.92. Her favorite pitches included a curveball, slider, and an overhand fastball with a rise.

4059. Heafner, Ruby E. (1946–51 C) "Rebel." She was called "Rebel" because of her North Carolina roots and her outspoken demeanor. Her friend, Vivian Kellogg, gave her the name while on tour in the South in 1947. Heafner never missed an opportunity to play up to the crowds and her teammates grew to depend on her constant chatter and occasional "rebel yell." She was often accused of claiming that all umpires were Yankees.

4060. Heim, Kay Ann (1943–44 C) "Heimie." "Heimie" is a derivation of Heim. She acquired the name from her baseball fans when she played in the Edmonton, Alberta, Canada, city league, which was popularized by the sportswriters. When she came to the United States to play pro ball, the name followed her.

4061. Hickson, Irene Mae (1943–51 C) "Choo Choo." The name comes from the song "Chattanooga Choo Choo." Hickson was from Chattanooga, Tennessee. The name was the result of a sports cartoon that pictured Hickson riding on top of a train. The cartoon caption read, "The 'Choo Choo' gets around the bases ... she has scored another Belles Run." Hickson was also called "Hick" by the opposing team fans which referred to her southern heritage. Hickson considered the name "Hick" as a personal insult. Hickson was a member of the 1943 All Star team and the leading hitter (.417) in the 1943 AAGBL championship playoff. She was also the league's oldest regular player.

4062. Hill, Joyce Elaine (1945–51 1B) "Farmer." "Farmer" refers to Hill being born and raised on a farm. Player Jo Hasham started calling her "Fahma" which was her pronunciation of the word farmer.

4063. Hohlmayer, Alice Marie (1946–50 1B/P) "Lefty." "Lefty" was given to Hohlmayer because she was a left handed ball player. She acquired the name when she first started playing at the early age of nine. The name following her throughout her career. While pitcher for the Kenosha Comets in 1948, she pitched 42 scoreless innings.

4064. Horstman, Catherine (1950–54 3B) "Horsey." "Horsey" is a derivation of the last name Horstman. Her Fort Wayne Daisy teammates were the first to call her "Horsey." Horstman played on the 1946 All Star team.

4065. Hutchinson, Anna May (1944–50 P/C) "Hutch." "Hutch" is a shortened version of Hutchinson. Players of her high school softball team were the first to call her "Hutch." The name stuck and followed her through her ball career and later in life. She was selected to the 1946 and 1947 All Star teams. She pitched the most games (51) of the season in 1946. In 1947, she also won more games (27) and pitched more innings (360) than any other pitcher in the league.

4066. Jackson, Lillian Nimmo (1943–45 OF) "Birddog." In admiration, teammate Faye Dancer began to call Jackson "Birddog." Jackson's speed and accuracy in playing the outfield appeared to Dancer as a good birddog after birds. During the time the team was traveling on the road, Dancer brought a picture of a birddog from the restaurant where she had dinner to Jackson. Dancer had convinced the owner to give her the picture for her friend "Birddog."

4067. Jacobs, Janet Elizabeth (1945) "Peanut." "Peanut" was an appelation acquired at an early age by virtue of playing baseball with an older brother and his friends. Jacobs' brother bestowed the name on Jacobs because she was his younger sister.

4068. Janssen, Frances Louise (1948–52 P) "Big Red." "Red" is a reference to Janssen's red hair. She was first called "Red" when she played basketball and softball in Fort Wayne. It was not until she played professional baseball that the name "Big Red" was used. "Big Red" was adopted in 1948 because there were two redheads on the Grand Rapids team. Since Janssen was much taller (5'11"), she became "Big Red." Although her hair is no longer red she is still known as "Big Red."

4069. Jenkins, Marilyn M. (1952–54 C) "Jinx." There is no significant meaning attached to the name "Jinx." It probably was chosen because it went well with Jenkins. Player Alma Zeigler is credited with first using "Jinx."

4070. Johnson, Arleene Cecelia (1945–48 3B/SS) "Johnnie." The name was derived from her last name. Although the name has masculine connotations, it was not a reference to her personal or physical characteristics. Her team roommates started calling her "Johnnie" and the name was popularized by the team during her ball career. After she married and her last name changed to Noga, she was still known as "Johnnie." Johnson set the league's fielding record at third base in 1946 (.928) and 1947 (.942).

4071. Jurgensmeier, Margaret Ann (1951) "Jurgy." "Jurgy" is a shortened version of her last name. "Jurgy" was given to her when she first started playing ball before she joined the AAGBL. The name stuck and was popularized by the fans during her ball career. "Jurgy" appeared to be the family nickname. Her father, John Jurgensmeier, who played all sports, was called "Jurgy," and her two brothers were also called "Jurgy."

4072. Kamenshek, Dorothy M. (1943, 51–53 1B) "Kammie." "Kammie" is a derivation of the name Kamenshek. When she joined the Rockford Peaches team there were four Dorothy's on the team. They all were given a nickname. The name stuck through her ball career and later in life. Kamenshek led the league in batting in 1946 and 1947 with averages of .316 and .306 respectively.

4073. Keagle, Merle (1946–47 IF/OF) "Pat." Origin unknown.

4074. Kellogg, Vivian Caroline (1944–54 1B) "Kelly." The name evolved because of her last name. Teammates started calling her "Kelly" the first year she joined the league. Kellogg later became a team manager in the league.

4075. Kelly, Jacqueline (1947–53 Util) "Scrounger" and "Babe." Origin unknown.

4076. Kerrar, Adeline (1944 C) "Short Stuff." "Short Stuff" refers to Kerrar's height. Her height of 5'1" became quite noticeable to the fans when she was the catcher for a pitcher who was 6'3". It was the fans who first started calling her "Short Stuff." Although she caught for other pitchers who were not tall, she was always known as "Short Stuff" throughout her ball career.

4077. Kerrigan, Marguerite Thresea (1950–52) "Kerry." "Kerry" is an extraction from her last name. Kerrigan received the name because her father would not allow anyone to shorten Marguerite. Thus, her high school friends started calling her "Kerry." The name stuck through high school and followed her through her ball career and later in life. After baseball when she worked in telephone sales, her name "Kerry" often drew inquiries from customers as to whether she was Irish or a redhead. Ironically, she is both. It can be speculated that the name's origin could have been due to just such characteristics as her red hair and Irish roots.

4078. Kerwin, Helen Irene (1949–50 C/1B/OF) "Pepper." Having a nickname was a very important for members of Kerwin's seventh grade softball team. One of the players thought everyone should have a nickname and named Kerwin "Pepper" after first trying "Dizzy" and "Speedy." On another team, a member also carried the issue of nicknames to the extreme. Here the team member turned in a line-up card to the public address announcer with a nickname for each player even if the players did not have nicknames. After the game, the team manager banded all nicknames except for Kerwin's nickname, because she already had her nickname "Pepper" before she played for the team. "Pepper" was also shortened to "Pep."

4079. Kissel, Audrey Susan (1944 2B) "Pigtails." "Pigtails" is a reference to Kissel's hairstyle. She always wore her hair in pigtails during the game to keep it out of her face. Her teammates picked up on this and started calling her "Pigtails."

4080. Kline, Maxine Louise (1948–54 P/OF) "Max." "Max" is a shortened version of the name Maxine. Although the name is a male name, it had no masculine connotations. She received the name from her parents when she was very young. The name followed her through her ball career and later in life.

4081. Klosowski, Dolores (1943–44 1B) "Lefty." Playing first base left handed earned Klosowski the nickname, "Lefty. She received the name before she joined the league while playing softball. The name was used throughout her career.

4082. Kobuszewski, Theresa Agnes (1946–47 P) "Terry." "Terry" was a replacement for the name "Tracy." Her mother first started calling her "Tracy" when she was a small child, because she was always outside and loved playing ball. "Tracy" was said to fit better than Theresa. However, when she joined the league "Tracy" was changed to "Terry" by her teammates.

4083. Koehn, Phyllis Carol (1943–49 LF/P) "Sugar." Harold Isabell, one of the top ten radio announcers of the 1940s, started calling her "Sugar Koehn" because her last name is pronounced "cane."

4084. Kotil, Arlene (1949–51 IF) "Riley." The name comes from the television program, "The Life of Riley." It was a reference to Kotil having an easy life. Kotil's grandmother often relieved Kotil of her chores so she could have more time to play ball. Kotil's parents started calling her "Riley" to prevent her ball friends calling her "Lefty," because she played ball left handed. The name stuck, and Kotil was known throughout her career as "Riley" and not "Lefty."

4085. Kotowicz, Irene Katherine (1945–50 P/OF) "Ike." "Ike" was given to her in grammar school to replace the name Irene. The name continued to be used during her ball career.

4086. Kunkel, Anna Marie (1950 OF) "Kunk." "Kunk" was a shortened version of her last name Kunkel. Team players were the first to start calling her "Kunk." The name stuck even after she married and her last name changed to Huff.

4087. Leduc, Neola G. (1951–54 P/OF) "Pinky." Although the meaning of the name is unknown, it was Rita Briggs, a fellow teammate and friend, who first called Leduc "Pinky." It seems that Leduc and Briggs were walking down the street one day when Rita took it upon herself to call Leduc "Pinky," and the name stuck.

4088. Lee, Dolores (1952–54 P/IF) "Pickles." Origin unknown.

4089. Leonard, Rhoda Ann (1946 2B/RF) "Nicky." "Nicky" comes from "Nike" which was a mispronunciation of the nickname "Mike." It seems that Leonard's older brother wanted a little brother when Leonard was born and began calling her "Mike." When her younger brother was born he could not pronounce "M" so he called her "Nike." Eventually everyone began calling her "Nicky." "Nicky" followed her through her ball career and later in life.

4090. Lessing, Ruth Elizabeth (1944–49 C) "Tex." "Tex" alludes to Lessing's hometown roots. Being from San Antonio and the only Texan in the AAGBL in 1944 earned her this distinguished name. She played on the 1946, 1947 and 1948 All Star teams. She holds the league catching record for most games played in a season (125 in 1948).

4091. Lonetto, Sarah Magdalen (1947–48 P) "Tomato." There is no significant meaning attached to the name. It probably stems from sounding like her last name Lonetto. Catcher Dottie Chapman and her husband first started calling her "Tomato" when Lonetto played for the Muskegon Lassies. Lonetto was the team's pitcher and Chapman was her catcher.

4092. Lovell, Jean L. (1948–54 C) "Grumpy." Taking her ball career as serious business earned Lovell the name "Grumpy" from the other players on her team. Beginning her career toward the end of the league years, many players were beginning to realize that their future in pro ball was limited. By the early 1950s many of the teams were starting to fold. Lovell was determined that the team she played for would not fold, if the players were serious about playing ball. This attitude did little to prevent what Lovell feared. In 1950 and again in 1951, the teams Lovell played on folded at the end of the season.

4093. Machado, Helene Patricia (1946–47 OF) "Chow." Earning the reputation of eating tough meat landed Machado the name "Chow." During spring training in Cuba, the steak that was served to the players was always tough and many players refused to eat it. Hating to see the steak go to waste, Machado would collect the uneaten steak and feed it to the dogs in the street. Having the reputation of a hearty eater, Machado's teammates thought she wanted it for herself and started calling her "Chow."

4094. MacLean, Lucella Catherine (1943–52 C/RF/1B) "Frenchy." "Frenchy" was given to MacLean by her team manager when she played for the Edmonton Orange Crust Fast Ball Team. It referred to her using her hands a lot when she was talking.

Although MacLean acquired the name during her ball career, it did not follow her throughout her league years. After joining the league, some negative remarks were made to her concerning the name "Frenchy." She immediately dropped the name "Frenchy" and insisted on being called either Lu or Lucella.

4095. Maguire, Dorothy Mayme (1944–47 C/OF) "Mickey." The name "Mickey" has long been associated with the game of baseball, and "Mickey" became associated with Maguire because the name seemed to fit well with her last name. It stands to reason that the two names could have gotten together because both are of Irish descent. Maguire was called "Mickey" when she first joined the league and the name stuck throughout her career.

4096. Mahoney, Emily Marie (1947–48 OF) "Red." Mahoney acquired the name "Red" while attending Girl Scout Camp. The name was a reference to Mahoney's red hair. The name stuck, and at the age of 23 when she joined the league she became known as "Red Mahoney" to her fans. To Mahoney, "Red" seemed much more appropriate for playing ball than Marie.

4097. Mandella, Lenora Dolores (1949–52 P) "Smokey." "Smokey" was originally an adaptation from the cartoon character "Smokey Stover" who was a fireman. Mandella's neighbor, Mr. Johnston, is credited with first calling her "Smokey." When Mandella was about two years old, she was known to pick up cigarette butts off the street and separate the tobacco from the paper. During her ball career, the name was associated with her strong pitching ability.

4098. Mansfield, Marie Margaret (1950–54 IF) "Boston." Mansfield acquired the name "Boston" because it alluded to her hometown of Boston, Massachusetts.

4099. Meier, Naomie Lavern (1946–51 OF) "Sally." Meier's mother began calling her "Sally" while she was a very young child. The name stuck and followed her through her baseball career and in later life.

4100. Metrolis, M. Norma (1946–50 C) "Trolley." "Trolley" evolved from "Trol" which was extracted from her last name Metrolis. "Trolley" was given to her when she first started playing ball. The name followed her through her ball career and was shortened to "Trol" later in life.

4101. Meyer, Rita Ann (1946–50 SS/P) "Slats." Meyer was named after Marty "Slats" Marion who played shortstop for the St. Louis Cardinals. Her teammates started calling her "Slats" because she played like Marion. At shortstop, she was quite an impressive sight with her strong arm and deep range. Meyer ranked in the top third of the league batters during her career.

4102. Moczynski, Betty Jane (1943 OF/C) "Moe." The name is derived from her last name Moczynski. A ball player from her hometown team started calling her "Moe" because she could not pronounce Moczynski. The name stuck throughout her ball career and later in life.

4103. Moore, Dolores Jean (1952–54 1B) "Babe." Her brother named her "Babe" after the great female athlete "Babe" Didrikson Zaharias when she was 12 years old. Moore acknowledged that it was a great feeling to be named after such a great athlete. The name was popularized during her ball career. She is still known as "Babe" to her family.

4104. Mudge, Nancy (1950–54 2B) "Smudgie." "Smudgie" is a derivation of her last name, Mudge. She was given the name when she was a sophomore in college by her friends. The name was later used during her ball career. She was the second baseman for the 1954 All Star team.

4105. Mueller, Dolores M. (1949 P/3B) "Champ." Mueller's playground teacher started calling her "Champ" when she was seven years old. She acquired the name because she always wore her father's baseball medals when she came to the playground. Being determined to live up to her father's reputation, her teacher proclaimed Mueller as the champion ball player of the playground. The name was used throughout her career.

4106. Mueller, Dorothy (1947–53 P/1B) "Sporty." Origin unknown.

4107. Nelson, Helen (1943) "Little One." Being small in stature earned Nelson the name "Little One."

4108. Nesbitt, Mary Lillian (1943–50 P/1B/OF) "Lefty." Being a left handed ball player earned Nesbitt the name "Lefty" from the coaches and players early on in her ball career. She was known as "Lefty" until she was married. After marriage, her last name was changed to Wisham, and her nickname changed to "Wish." Her husband's nickname was also "Wish" and as a couple they were known as "Wish and Wish." The changing of her nickname was probably a reflection of the rarity of a player getting married and continuing to still play ball. Nesbitt played on the 1943 All Star team and was the top batter for the Peoria Redwings in 1948 (.292).

4109. Nicol, Helen M. (1943–54 P) "Nickie." The name originated from the pronunciation of Nicol which sounds like "nickel." She was called "Nickie" when she first started grammar school, and it has followed her through her ball career and later in life. "Nickie" is often shortened to "Nick."

4110. O'Brien, Eileen (1946) "Obe." "Obe" was derived from her last name O'Brien. She acquired the name while playing ball in Chicago in 1936, and it followed her throughout her career and later in life.

4111. O'Hara, Janice W. (1943–50 1B) "Jerry." During World War I, the name "Jerry" referred to a person who was of German descent. Being the only Irish person in a German Lutheran grade school earned O'Hara the name "Jerry." O'Hara was given the name "Jerry" as an acknowledgment of acceptance by her German school classmates. The name probably stuck because she often had problems getting people to pronounce her first name as "Ja-neice" rather than "Jan-us." The name was continued after grade school, throughout her ball career, and later in life.

4112. Olinger, Marilyn (1948–53 IF) "Corky." Although the meaning is unknown, the nickname "Corky" resulted from a joke during her childhood days. Her sister and neighborhood friends are credited with tagging her with the name.

4113. Paire, Lavone (1944–53 C) "Pepper." "Pepper" referred to Paire having red hair. She led all catchers in the AAGBL in fielding in 1950 (.979).

4114. Peppas, June Anne (1948–54 P/1B/OF) "Wiggles." "Wiggles" was a reference to Peppas' preparation in the batting box. A sportswriter is credited with first calling her "Wiggles." She had a habit of wiggling to adjust her belt once she was up to bat. All her wiggling paid off during the final game of the final season of the AAGBL in 1954, when Peppas drove in four runs. It was her hit that helped the Kalamazoo Lassies to win the season's championship upsetting the Fort Wayne Daisies. Peppas played on the 1953 and 1954 All Star teams.

4115. Perlick, Edthe Lillian (1943–49 OF) "Speedy Edie." Usually addressed as "Edie," Perlick was also called "Speedy Edie," because of her fast speed on the bases and outfield. Player Jo Winters is credited with first using "Speedy" when Perlick played for the Racine Belles.

4116. Peters, Marjorie Lillian (1943–44) "Pete." "Pete" is a derivation of the name Peters. Player Helen Nelson is credited with first calling her "Pete" when Peters played for the Rockford Peaches.

4117. Petras, Ernestine Ceciela (1944–52) "Teeny Pigtails." Usually addressed as "Teeny," which is a derivation of her first name Ernestine, she was also called "Teeny Pigtails." She was known for wearing her hair in pigtails during the games. Petras later became the team manager for the Kenosha Comets in 1951.

4118. Pieper, Marjorie L. (1946–47 SS) "Peeps." Pieper received the name "Peeps" because of the sound of her last name. Player Rita Briggs is credited with first calling her "Peeps."

4119. Pollit, Alice (1947–53 SS/Util/IF) "Al." "Al" is derived from the first name of Alice.

4120. Pratt, Mary (1943–47 P) "Prattie." The name was derived from her last name Pratt. She acquired the name while in college, and it was used during her ball career.

4121. Pryer, Charlene Barbara (1946–52 2B/OF) "Shorty." The name "Shorty" was her father's nickname. Both Pryer and her father played baseball in their hometown at the same time. Because Pryer and her father were both short, sportswriters referred to her father as "Shorty" and Pryer as "Shorty, Jr." After her father quit playing, the "Jr." was dropped and Peyer was called "Shorty." Pryer was a member of the 1951 All Star team.

4122. Redman, Magdalen Marie (1948–54 C/2B/3B/OF) "Minnie." Redman earned the name "Minnie" because she was a great fan of Orestes "Minnie" Minoso of the Chicago White Sox. It was her AAGBL teammates who first started calling her "Minnie."

4123. Reynolds, Mary Francis (1946–49 3B) "Windy." The name alludes to Reynolds' ability to carry on chatter during the ball game. A sports announcer first called Reynolds "Windy" while she was playing ball in Miami Beach, Florida. In 1950, Reynolds became the team manager for the Peoria Redwings.

4124. Richards, Ruth (1947–54 C/OF) "Richie." "Richie" is a derivation of the last name, Richards. Players on the Grand Rapids Chicks' team started calling her "Richie," the first year she played pro ball. Richards played on the 1950 and 1952 All Star teams.

4125. Ricketts, Joyce Elaine (1953–54 OF) "Rick the Hick." The name comes from her last name Ricketts and refers to her small town roots. Alma Ziegler is credited with first using the name. Ziegler was notorious for coming up with a nickname for her teammates. Ricketts was told by her chaperon that getting a nickname from Ziegler meant you were an accepted member of the team.

4126. Risinger, Helen Earlene (1948–54 P) "Beans." Risinger's father gave her the name when she was very young, because she once cried to eat pork and beans for breakfast. During her baseball career, she was often called "Bean Pole" because she stood 6'1" and weighed only 138 pounds.

4127. Romatowski, Jenny Anne (1946–54 C/3B/OF) "Romey." Although the name is often thought to be taken from her last name, it alludes to the long distances she roamed to play ball. Her friend, Lorraine Fisher, is credited with calling Romatowski "Romey." Romatowski was a member of the 1954 All Star team and the 1954 Kalamazoo Lassies Championship team.

4128. Roth, Eilaine May (1948–51 3B/OF) "I." Roth was called "I" because her first name sounded like it started with an "I" and her twin sister's first name sounded like it started with an "E." Roth's brother used the names to distinguish between their first names. The name followed her throughout her ball career and later in life.

4129. Roth, Elaine Marjorie (1948–51 OF) "E." Roth's brother Harold started calling her "E" as a way to get her attention when she was very young. Roth's twin sister is named Eilaine, whom he named "I." "E" and "I" were much more easier to say than their given names. The name was continued through her ball career because Roth and her sister both played professional ball.

4130. Rukavina, Theresa May (1950–53) "Rookie." Every team had one or two rookies to start off a new season. When Rukavina joined the league, she automatically was "Rook-a-vina." The name was shortened to "Rookie." Later, when she received a contract from the Kalamazoo Lassies, her name appeared on the contract as "Terry" which led to her teammates on the new team to start calling her "Terry."

4131. Ruknke, Irene R. (1942–47 SS) "Runk." "Runk" was derived from the nickname "Little Runk." When Ruknke and her sister played for the same team in Chicago, the players started calling Ruknke "Little Runk" and her sister "Big Runk." Her sister was 5'6" and she was 5'4". The "Little" was dropped after Ruknke went on to play pro ball, and her sister did not.

4132. Rumsey, Janet J. (1951–54 P) "J.R.." "J.R." is Rumsey's initials. She acquired the name during her ball career.

4133. Russo, Margaret Ann (1950–54 SS) "Rookie." Russo earned the name "Rookie" because it was her first year in the league, and she was also the youngest player on her team. With those odds, it did not take veteran player Nancy Warren long to tag Russo with the name "Rookie."

4134. Sams, Doris Jane (1946–53 P/OF) "Sammye." "Sammye" is a derivation of the name Sams. Although the name is a male name, it has no masculine connotation. She acquired the name from a friend about a year before she started playing professional ball. She liked the name more than Doris and encouraged the players to call her "Sammye." The name caught on and followed her through her career and later in life. In 1952, Sams hit 12 home runs setting a new league record.

4135. Sands, Sarah Jane (1943–54 OF/C) "Salty." Sands was named after a man in Bloomsbury, Pennsylvania, who was called "Old Salty Hazard." Her father started calling her "Salty" when she was about five years old because she, like "Old Salty Hazard," had a habit of wearing summer clothes in the winter and winter clothes in the summer. In her second season of play, she made the second All Star team.

4136. Satterfield, Doris (1948–53 Util/OF) "Sadie." Origin unknown.

4137. Schroeder, Dorothy Agusta (1943–54 SS) "Little Miss Pigtails." A Fort Wayne sportswriter named Schroeder "Little Miss Pigtails" because she wore her hair in two long braids during the game. "Little Miss" probably evolved because Schroeder was only 15 years old when she joined the league. The name was never used by her teammates who preferred to call her "Dottie." Schroeder was a member of the 1952, 1953, and 1954 All Star teams. She was the only player to play all 12 seasons of the AAGBL.

4138. Sero, Dora (1942–50 OF) "Baser." "Baser" was a term Sero used to describe her playing position. On Sero's first day on the field as a pro, veteran player Sophie Kury asked her what position she played. Sero replied, "I'm a Baser." Kury screamed, "Baser" and from that day she was called "Baser."

4139. Sherriff, Vivian M. (1944 3B) "Andy." The name was derived from her married name Anderson. Sherriff's teammates started calling her "Andy" when she started to play professional ball. The name probably came about as a way of bringing attention to how unusual it was for a player to be married and continue to play ball.

4140. Shively, Twila Irene (1945–46 LF/1B) "Twi." Shively's brother started calling her "Ki Ki" when he was a baby. Her father extended "Ki Ki" into "Ki Ki Cuyler" after the old-time baseball player, Hazen Cuyler, because Shively loved playing baseball. Later "Ki Ki Cuyler" was changed to "Twi Twi Cuyler" and then shortened to "Twi" during her years with the AAGBL. In 1946, Shively scored the most runs (76) for the Grand Rapids Chicks.

4141. Smith, Helen L. (1947–48 OF) "Gig." "Gig" is an abbreviation that stands for "Government Issued Grip." This was an army expression meaning a black mark given to a person during inspection. Smith was given the name "Gig" when she was in army because she innocently asked its meaning. Although she rarely received a "Gig," she was stuck with the name. It was carried over into her ball career and later in life.

4142. Steck, Etna Mae (1948–49 OF) "El." Although "El" is derived from Steck's first name, "El" is not usually considered a short name for Elma. Steck acquired the name while playing amateur ball and it stuck throughout her ball career.

4143. Steele, Joyce Maureen (1953) "Lucky." Making the tryouts for the AAGBL earned Steele the name "Lucky." Her hometown high school is credited with first calling her "Lucky." Although Steele made the tryouts, she was sent back home to finish high school before she was allowed to play. When she arrived home, her high school had made a banner which bore the words "Welcome Home, Lucky." The name stuck and followed her throughout her ball career.

4144. Stevenson, Rosemary (1954) "Stevie." Although the name is derived from her last name, "Stevie," it probably alluded to Stevenson's participation on an all-male softball team. She was given the name by her male teammates when she first played organized ball at the age of 11 for a men's softball team. The name was continued during her playing years with the league.

4145. Stoll, Nancy Jane (1946–54 OF) "Jeep." The name referred to her stature of being short and built low to the ground. While traveling with the AAGBL, her three roommates started calling her "Jeep" because she was only 5' tall and they were considerably taller.

4146. Studnicka, Mary Lou (1951–53 P) "M.L." "M.L." are the initials for the name Mary Lou. Alma Ziegler is credited with first calling her "M.L." when she played for the Grand Rapids Chicks. She became known as "M.L." because she refused to answer to the name "Mare," which was short for Mary.

4147. Stuhr, Beverly Joyce (1949–50) "Shorty." Being 5'1" earned Stuhr the name "Shorty" by her teammates during her ball career.

4148. Taylor, Eunice Marion (1950–51 C) "Dustie." "Dustie" comes from Taylor getting quite dirty and dusty as catcher for the team. One of Taylor's teammates, who did not like her first name Eunice, started to call her "Dustie" instead.

4149. Tetzlaff, Doris Ella (1944–49 3B) "Tetz." "Tetz" is a shortened version of the name, Tetzlaff. Her Milwaukee Chicks' teammates were credited with first calling her "Tetz." The name was only used during her ball career.

4150. Thomas, Marva Lee (1951) "Tommy." "Tommy" was derived from the player's last name, Thomas.

4151. Thompson, Viola (1944–47 P) "Tommie." "Tommie" is a derivation of the last name, Thompson.

4152. Trezza, Elizabeth (1944–50) "Moe." "Moe" was given to Trezza by her teammates because she had a habit of calling everyone "Moe." When Trezza first joined the league she called all the players "Moe." Trezza had trouble remembering the players names. Consequently, the name "Moe" was pinned on her as a joke. It remained with her through her career. Interestingly, the nickname "Moe" was also given to Trezza's brother by his army buddies during World War II. It is not known if Trezza's brother got the name for the same reason.

4153. Tronnier, Ellen Jane (1943 OF) "Hornet." The name refers to Tronnier's collection of hornets' nests. When Tronnier was young she liked to collect hornets' nests and put them under her bed. Tronnier's mother happened to tell some of the players how there were hornets always flying around the house because of the nest under her bed. From then on, she was known as "Hornet."

4154. Voyce, Inez Ferne (1946–53 1B) "Hook." Alma Ziegler who played second base on Voyce's team started calling her "Hook" because she was left handed. Voyce was also called "Lefty."

4155. Vukovich, Francis (1950 P) "Bebop." Vukovich's love for jazz music earned her the name "Bebop." She was known for playing the radio and listening to jazz music.

4156. Waddell, Helen Jessie (1950–51) "Chippie." Although no meaning is attributed to the name "Chippie," it probably is a reference to her lighthearted personality. She was also called "Chipper." Waddell acquired the name from friends while playing softball, and the name followed her throughout her ball career.

4157. Wagoner, Elizabeth Ann (1948–54 OF/P) "Waggie." The name is a derivation of her last name Wagoner. Her teammates referred to her as "Waggie" when she played for the AAGBL. Wagoner was also called "Rabbit" by her team chaperon, because she was such a fast runner.

4158. Walulik, Helen (1948–50 P) "Hensky." "Hensky" was derived from the name "Henny," which was a childhood nickname used by her younger siblings. It seems that her younger brothers and sisters were unable to pronounce Helen. A neighborhood boy changed the name to "Hensky" because of her Polish origin. The name "Hensky" followed her through elementary school, high school, and her ball career.

4159. Wanless, Betty (1953–54 Util/OF) "Duke." Origin unknown.

4160. Warren, Nancy (1946–54 P/SS) "Hank." "Hank" originated during Warren's childhood days. When Warren was young, she went on a family fishing trip and became very homesick. To overcome her homesickness, she became obsessed with eating during the trip. Because of her interest in eating, her family started calling her "Hungry Hank." After she started to play softball, the name was shortened to "Hank," and was used as a reference to the baseball player Hank Greenberg.

4161. Weaver, Betty Colleen (1950–54 1B/3B) "Metropolis Mauler." The name means "Super Woman." Teammates started calling her "Metropolis Mauler" after the name appeared in a sports article. Metropolis, Illinois, was Weaver's hometown, which was also the hometown of the comic book hero character, "Superman." "Mauler" was probably attached to "Metropolis" because of her performance at bat. She won the league's batting championship in 1950 and 1951 with averages of .346 and .368 respectively. In 1953, Weaver led the league in most runs (99), most hits (144), and the most stolen bases (80).

4162. Weeks, Rossey Louise (1947) "Flash." "Flash" alludes to Weeks' fast speed running the bases. Her coach and manager, M.E. Welborn, is credited with first calling her "Flash" when she played for the Seaboard Meteors Softball Club in 1944. Not only did Weeks earn the name of "Flash" while playing for the Seaboard Club, she was voted the Most Valuable Player of the year by her teammates. Weeks went on to play for the AAGBL in 1947 and her nickname and reputation followed. Unfortunately, her career was shortened by an injury to her hand during her first year of play.

4163. Wegman, Marie Elizabeth (1947–50 1B/2B/3B/SS) "Blackie." "Blackie" refers to the color of Wegman's hair. Her father started calling her "Blackie" when she was a small child because Wegman had dark colored hair, and her younger sister had blonde hair. Wegman's younger sister's nickname was "Whitey." The name was carried over into her ball career because Wegman and her sister both played on the same hometown team. The name followed her throughout her ball career, even though her sister did not continue to play. A sportswriter once claimed that the name came from her teammate "Gabby" Ziegler, but this was not the case.

4164. Westerman, Helen (1944 C) "Pee Wee." "Pee Wee" is a reference to Westerman's small size. She was popularized by the media as the "petite blue-eyed blonde weighing only around 95 pounds, fragilely built." There was also mention of her very small hands.

4165. Wigiser, Margaret (1944–45 OF) "Wiggie." "Wiggie" is a derivation of the last name, Wigiser.

4166. Wiley, Janet Nancy (1950–51 1B) "Pee Wee." Wiley was named after her brother whose nickname was "Pee Wee." The name seemed to fit because she was the smallest and youngest girl who played sandlot ball in her neighborhood. When she joined the league, she brought the nickname with her.

4167. Wirth, Senaida (1946–50 SS) "Shoo Shoo." Origin unknown.

4168. Wisniewski, Constance Rose (1944–52 P/OF) "Ironwoman." Wisniewski earned the name "Ironwoman" when she pitched a doubleheader and won both games. Her manager, wanting to boost attendance, scheduled two games in one day and publicized that "Ironwoman Wisniewski" would be pitching both games. After the game, the name was popularized by the press and followed her for a couple of years. Wisniewski was chosen the player of the year in 1945 because of her outstanding underhand pitching. In 1945, she faced more batters, pitched more innings, and worked more games than any other pitcher in the league. When the league made the transition from underhand to overhand pitching, Wisniewski became less known by the name "Ironwoman." The name was never picked up by her teammates who preferred to call her "Connie." Wisniewski was the league's first Most Valuable Player in 1945. She also was the pitcher for the 1946 All Star team. She played as an outfielder on the 1948, 1949, 1951, and 1952 All Star teams.

4169. Wuethrich, Lorraine Ruby (1943–44 SS/3B) "Lolly." Wuethrich's elementary school friends are credited with first calling Wuethrich "Lolly." Although there is no specific meaning attached to the nickname, a teacher once told Wuethrich that the name referred to a person who was lazy.

4170. Youngberg, Renae Audrey (1951–54 SS) "Ray." "Ray" comes from Youngberg's initials, R.A.Y. Her Grand Rapid teammates were the first to call her "Ray."

4171. Ziegler, Alma Kathryn (1944–54 P/2B) "Gabby." "Gabby" alludes to Ziegler's chattering during a game. She was well known for her vociferous style while on the field. It is not known who first used the name, but all who knew her during her career would agree it was a most fitting name. Ziegler was also called "Ziggy" or "Zig," which were derivations of her last name. Ziegler served as the Grand Rapid Chicks team captain from 1944 to 1954, and was very active in nicknaming other team players. She was Player of the Year in 1950, and played on the 1950 and 1953 All Star teams.

4172. Zeigler, Marie Ellen (1953) "Little Zig." Zeigler was named "Little Zig" after the player, Alma Ziegler, who was sometimes called "Zig."

Appendix A: Negro League Players

Robert Peterson in his book, *Only the Ball Was White*, identified 2,495 players who played in the upper echelons of the Negro leagues from 1884–1950. He was able to provide both first and last names of 1,912. Of this number, he lists the nicknames of 382. Starting with Peterson and using the fine research efforts of other Negro League scholars such as Jack Clark and especially John Holway, I was able to identify 83 players with nicknames who at least one of these experts would rate of "star" quality. There are probably other "stars" who had public nicknames which as yet I have not been able to identify. In this respect the list is quite incomplete. Nevertheless, it does represent the first attempt to compile a list of the nicknames of important players in the Negro leagues who never played in the major leagues. The data for each entry may be found in Part I. Players, Umpires, Managers, Officials, Sportswriters, Broadcasters, Owners, Fans.

Newton Henry Allen "Colt"
David Barnhill "Impo"
Lloyd Bassett "Rocking Chair Catcher"
James Thomas Bell "Cool Papa"
Willard Brown "Home Run"
Thomas Butts "Pee Wee"
Walter Cannady "Rev"
George Carr "Tank"
Oscar McKinley Charleston "The Black Ruth"
Francisco Coimbre "Pancho"
Andy Cooper "Lefty"
Willie Cornelius "Sug"
John Wilbain Crutchfield "The Black Lloyd Waner"
Raymond Dandridge "Hooks"
John Davis "Cherokee"
Lorenzo Davis "Piper"
Elwood De Mose "Bingo"
Martin Dihigo "El Maestro"

William Dismukes "Dizzy"
Herbert Albert Dixon "Rap"
Charles Dougherty "Pat"
William Drake "Plunk"
Luther Favrell "Red"
Andrew Foster "Rube"
John W. Fowler "Bud"
Joshua Gibson "Boxer"
Charles Grant "Chief Tokahoma"
Frank Grant "Black Dunlap"
Claude Grier "Red"
Arthur Henderson "Rats"
J. Preston Hill "Pete"
Crush Holloway "Crush"
Jessie Hubbard "Mountain"
Robert Hudspeth "High Pockets"
Clarence Jenkins "Fats"
George Johnson "Chappie"
Grant Johnson "Home Run"
Oscar Johnson "Heavy"
William J. Johnson "Judy"

Stuart Jones "Slim"
Henry Allen Kimbro "Jumbo"
Walter Fenner Leonard "Buck"
John Henry Loyd "Cachatter"
Richard Lundy "King Richard"
Raleigh Mackey "Biz"
David J. Malarcher "Gentlemen Dave"
Oliver H. Marcelle (also Marcel, Marcell) "Ghost"
Verdell Mathis "Lefty"
Terous McDuffie "The Great"
José de la Caridad Menchez Mendez "El Diamante Negro"
Walter Moore "The Black Cat"
Roy Parnell "Red"
Leonard Curtis Pearson "Horse"
William George Perkins "Cz"
Bruce Petway "Buddy"
Andrew Porter "Pullman"
Theodore Radcliffe "Double Duty"
Connie Rector "Broadway"
Richard Redding "Cannonball"
Wilson Redus "Frog"
Ed Rile "Huck"
Wilbur Rogan "Bullet"
John Henry Russell "Pistol"
Louis Loftin Santop "Big Bertha"
George Scales "Tubby"
Charles Smith "Chino"
Norman Stearns "Turkey"
Paul Eugene Stephens "Jake"
George Suttles "Mule"
George Sweatt "Never"
Frank Sykes "Doc"
Charles Taylor I "C.I."
Clinton Thomas "Hawk"
David Thomas "Showboat"
Christobel Torrienti "The Cuban Strongboy"
Theodore Trent "Big Florida"
Willie Wells "El Diablo"
Jim West "Shifty"
Charles Williams "Lefty"
Joe Williams "Smokey Joe"
Judson Wilson "Boojum"
Jessie Winters "Nip"
Burnis Wright "Wild Bill"

Appendix B: Umpires

The nicknames of umpires, let alone the origins of their sobriquets, are much more difficult to research than those of ballplayers. Umpires truly become invisible men. They come, do their job, retire, and then seem to fade out of memory. Their lives are submerged in history. Only recently have umpires become legitimate subjects for systematic research. As yet, the literature is scant. Therefore by definition the list of umpire nicknames provided below is incomplete. But it is, to my knowledge, the first attempt to compile one. I suspect, however, because of their attempt to keep a low public profile, umpires as a group attracted a much lower percentage of public nicknames than did ballplayers. Thus the list may not be as incomplete as it first seems. For example, by far the most popular nickname among ballplayers is "Lefty." I did not find any "Lefty" umpires! The data for each entry may be found in Part I. Players, Umpires, Nonplayer Managers, Officials, Sportswriters, Broadcasters, Owners, Fans.

Emmett L. Ashford "Pata Ditas"
E. Lee Ballanfant "Joe Doaks"
Albert J. Barlick "Prodigy"
Tyton R. Boggess "Dusty"
William E. Bransfield "Kitty"
George W. Burnham "Watch"
William J. Byron "The Singing Umpire"
John B. Conlan "Jocks"
Thomas H. Connolly "Mr."
Henry C. Crawford "Shag"
David L. Davidson "Satch"
John J. Doyle "Dirty Jack"
John F. Dwyer "Blinky"
Robert D. Emslie "Blind Bob"
Robert V. Ferguson "Death to Flying Things"
John F. Flaherty "Red"
Arthur F. Frantz "Bud"
John H. Gaffney "King of the Umpires"

Thomas D. Gorman "Easy"
William J. Guthrie "Bull-Necked Bill"
William E. Haller "Fox"
Douglas H. Harvey "God"
Eugene Henry "Ted"
Howard E. Holmes "Ducky"
Harry Howell "Handsome"
R. Cal Hubbard "Big Cal"
Edwin H. Hurley "Butch"
Nicholas J. Jones "Red"
Harry S. Johnson "Steamboat"
Kenneth J. Kaiser "The Hatchet"
William J. Klem "Catfish"
William G. Kunkel "Jam"
Ronald M. Luciano "Loosh"
Frank H. O'Loughlin "Silk"
Thomas J. Lynch "King of the Umpires"
William J. McCormick "Barry"
William A. McGowan "Little Jo Chest"

Harry T. McGraw "Ted"
William B. McLean "King of the Umpires"
Sherwood R. Magee "Sherry"
George L. Magerkurth "Meathead"
Frederick Marberry "Firpo"
Charles B. Moran "Uncle Charlie"
Emmett T. Ormsby "Red"
Clarence B. Owens "Brick"
Arthur M. Passarella "Pal"
Charles H. Pfirman "Cy"
Ralph A. Pinelli "Babe"
John E. Reardon "Beans"
Laurence H. Rennert "Dutch"
John L. Rice "Mayor Daily"
Charles Rigler "Cy"
Douglas W. Robb "Scotty"
John Roe "Rocky"
Clarence H. Rowland
James Scott "Death Valley Jim"
John W. Sears "Ziggy"
William P. Shannon "Spike"
John F. Sheridan "Big Jack"
Albert D. Stark "Dolly"
William J. Stewart "The Great Anticipator"
William R. Summers "Honest Bill"
Anthony Venzen "Pope"
Lonnie Warneke "The Arkansas Humming Bird"
Joseph West "Cowboy Joe"
Charles L. Zimmer "Chief"

Appendix C: Influential Nonplaying Baseball Personalities

In addition to umpires, there are a number of other individuals who never played any major league baseball but had important roles in its development. Many of them had nicknames. They include: nonplaying managers, league officials, sportswriters and broadcasters, owners, general managers, club house attendants, and last but not least fans. They deserve recognition. The list below is not comprehensive. It includes only those individuals that I have run across in the course of the research on major league player nicknames. The data for each entry may be found in Part I. Players, Umpires, Nonplayer Managers, Officials, Sportswriters, Broadcasters, Owners, Fans.

Marion Danne Adair "Bill"
Mel Allen "The Voice"
Gene Autry "Singing Cowboy"
Walter Lanier Barber "The Ol' Redhead"
Edward G. Barrow "Cousin Ed"
Joseph Borden "Josephus the Phenomenal"
Sam Breadon "Lucky Sam"
Jack Brickhouse "Hey Hey"
Walter Owen Briggs "Spike"
Walter Owen Briggs, II "Spike"
James David Bristol "0010"
John T. Brush "Tooth"
August Adolphus Busch, Jr. "Big Eagle"
Joseph D. Cantillon "Pongo Joe"
Harry Caray, Jr. "Skip"
Henry Chadwick "Father of Baseball"
Albert Benjamin Chandler "Happy"
Hilda Chester "Howling Hilda"
Howard Cosell "Howard the Humble"
James Creighton "Unbeatable Jimmy"
Harry Tillis Crosby "Bing"
Arthur Dixwell "Hi Hi Dixwell"
William D. Eckert "The Unknown Soldier"
Bob Elson "The Old Commander"
Charles O. Finley "Charlie O."
Curt Gowdy "The Cowboy"
William Augustus Greenlee "Big Red"
Al Helfer "The Ghost of Hartsdale"
Lolly Hopkins "Megaphone Lolly"
Frank Lane "Trader Frank"
Joseph Vincent McCarthy "Marse Joe"
Arch McDonald "Old Pine Tree"
Gordon McLendon "The Old Scotchman"
Carl Merrill "Stump"
Abraham G. Mills "Bismark of Baseball"
Frank Navin "Lucky Frank"
Walter Francis O'Malley "The Big Oom"

Mary Ott "Horse Lady of St. Louis"
Robert Prince "Gunner"
Bob Reynolds "Horse"
Morganna Roberts "The Kissing Bandit"
Jacob Ruppert "Colonel"
Michael Joseph Sheehy "Silent Pete"
Walter W. Smith "Red"

George Michael Steinbrenner, III "The Big Ego"
Harry Stephens "Scorecard Man"
Peter Van Wieren "The Professor"
Christian Frederick Wilhelm Von Der Ahe "Der Boss President"
Charles A. Weeghman "Lucky"
Jim Woods "The Possum"
Morris Yatkeman "Butch"

Bibliography

Abramovich, Joe, comp. *Baseball Register*. St. Louis: The Sporting News, 1964.
_____, comp., with Paul Rickart. *Baseball Register*. St. Louis: *The Sporting News*, 1966.
Abrens, Arthur. "The Daily Dahlen in 1894." *The Baseball Research Journal*, 4 (1975): pp. 57–60.
Addie, Bob. "The Big Brown Squirrel." *Baseball Digest*, 16 (1957), Dec.: pp. 69–73.
Alexander, Charles. *John McGraw*. New York: Viking, 1988.
_____. *Ty Cobb*. New York: Oxford University Press, 1984.
Alexander, Grover Cleveland. "How I Lost the World Series," in Sidney Offit, ed., *The Best of Baseball*. New York: Putnam, 1936, pp. 22–29.
Allen, Lee. *The American League Story*. New York: Hill & Wang, 1962.
_____. *The Cincinnati Reds*. New York: Putnam, 1948.
_____. *Cooperstown Corner: Columns from the Sporting News, 1962–1969*. Cleveland: Society for American Baseball Research, 1990.
_____. *The Hot Stove League*. New York: Barnes, 1955.
_____. *The National League Story*. New York: Hill and Wang, 1961.
_____. *100 Years of Baseball*. New York: Bartholomew House, 1950.
_____. "The Player Who Helped Nab Al Capone." *The Sporting News*, May 17, 1969, p. 10.
_____. "Red, Lefty and a Few Animals," in Charles Einstein, ed., *The Fireside Book of Baseball*. New York: Simon and Schuster, 1956, pp. 6–10.
_____. *The World Series: The Story of Baseball's Annual Championship*. New York: Putnam, 1969.
Allen, Maury. *Bo: Pitching and Wooing*. New York: Dial Press, 1973.
_____. *The Incredible Mets*. New York: Paperback, 1969.
Alston, Walter, with Jack Tobin. *A Year at a Time*. Waco, Texas: Word, 1976.
Amman, Larry. "Newhouser and Trout in 1944," *Baseball Research Journal*, 12 (1983): pp. 18–22.
Anderson, Wayne. *Harmon Killebrew: Baseball's Superstar*. Salt Lake City: Deseret, 1971.
Anson, Adrian. *A Ball Player's Career: Personal Experiences and Reminiscences*. Chicago: Era, 1900.
Barber, Red, and Robert Creamer. *Rhubarb in the Catbird Seat*. New York: Doubleday, 1968.
Bartlett, Arthur. *Baseball and Mr. Spalding: The History and Romance of Baseball*. New York: Farrar, Straus & Young, 1951.
Barrow, Edward, with James Kahn. *My Fifty Years in Baseball*. New York: Coward-McCann, 1951.
Baseball Alumni News. Falls Church, Va.: Major League Baseball Players Association, Sept. 1986.
Baylor, Don, with Claire Smith. *Don Baylor*. New York: St. Martin's, 1989.

Bealle, Morris. *The Washington Senators.* Washington, D.C.: Columbia, 1947.
Beaton, Rod. "Galarraga Solved." *USA Today,* April 26, 1989.
Benchley, Robert. "The Silent Art of Joe Jackson." *Everybody's Magazine,* 44 (1921), Feb.: pp. 30-31.
Berke, Art. *Unsung Heroes of the Major Leagues.* New York: Random House, 1976.
Berkow, Ira. "An Evening with the Kid." *New York Times,* Nov. 12, 1988.
"Big Daddy Has Big Day." *Greensboro News & Record,* Aug. 24, 1989.
Bilovsky, Frank, and Rich Westcott. *The Phillies Encyclopedia.* New York: Leisure, 1984.
Bisher, Furman. "A Short History of Baseball Nicknames." *Sky,* July, 1980: pp. 61-62.
Block, Cy. *So You Want to Be a Major Leaguer.* New York: Metropolitan Life, 1965.
Bloodgood, Clifford. "A Down Home Rival of Schoolboy Rowe." *Baseball Magazine,* 50 (1935), Aug., p. 407.
———. "The Lesser Known Buddy of the Washington Club." *Baseball Magazine,* 52 (1937), Jan., pp. 345.
Bodley, Hal. "Madlock Looks Past Baseball's Oversights." *USA Today,* June 13, 1983.
Boggess, Dusty (as told to Ernie Helm). *Kill the Ump.* Dallas: Lone Star Brewing, 1966.
Bonner, M.G. *Baseball Rookies Who Made Good.* New York: Knopf, 1954.
Boren, Steve. "The Bizarre Career of Rube Benton." *The Baseball Research Journal.* 12 (1983): pp. 180-83.
Borst, Bill. *The Pride of St. Louis: A Cooperstown Gallery.* St. Louis: Krank, 1984.
Boswell, Thomas. *The Heart of the Order.* New York: Doubleday, 1989.
Bouton, Jim. *Ball Four.* New York: Dell, 1970.
———. *I'm Glad You Didn't Take It Personally.* New York: Dell, 1971.
Bowles, Frank. "Statistics of Fair Play." *The National Pastime.* Manhattan, Kansas: Ag, 1984, pp. 74-81.
Brown, Warren. *The Chicago Cubs.* New York: Putnam, 1946.
Bruce, Janet. *The Kansas City Monarchs: Champions of Black Baseball.* Lawrence, Kansas: University of Kansas Press, 1985.
Brundidge, Harry. "Buzz Arlett—The Game's Big Mystery." *The Sporting News,* Dec. 17, 1931, p. 15.
Buck, Ray. *Dave Parker, the Cobra Swirl.* Chicago: Children's Press, 1981.
Bulkley, George. "See You Later Lou," in Sidney Offit, ed., *The Best of Baseball.* New York: Putnam, 1956, pp. 124-31.
———. "Why Did Mickey Smile?" *The Baseball Research Journal,* 11 (1982): pp. 127-29.
Burkholder, Ed. *Baseball Immortals.* Boston: Christopher, 1955.
Burns, Ed. "Truck Hannah, Angel Pilot, Holds Work Record as Catcher—185 Games in Year." *Chicago Tribune,* June 1, 1939.
Busch, Thomas. "Story of Charles Victor (Y) Faust." *Baseball Research Journal,* 12 (1983): pp. 82-86.
Carmichael, John. "The Chicago White Sox," in Ed Fitzgerald, ed., *The Book of Major League Baseball Clubs: The American League.* New York: A.S. Barnes, 1952.
———. *My Greatest Day in Baseball.* New York: Grosset & Dunlap, 1963.
———, ed. *Who's Who in the Major Leagues,* 15th ed. Chicago: Inland Lithograph, 1947.
Chass, Murry. "Baseball's Bonus Beauties: 187." *The Sporting News,* Nov. 16, 1987, pp. 48-49.

Church, Seymour. *The History, Statistics & Romance of the American National Game from Its Inception to the Present Time. Vol. I, 1845-1871.* Princeton: Pyne, 1902 (reprint, 1974).
Clark, Ellery. *Boston Red Sox: 75th Anniversary History 1901-1975.* Hicksville, N.Y.: Exposition, 1975.
Coffin, Tristram. *The Old Ball Game: Baseball in Folklore and Fiction.* New York: Herder & Herder, 1971.
Cohane, Tim. "Frank Lane: Baseball's Noisiest Dynamo." *Look,* 20 (1956), June 12: pp. 123ff.
Condon, David. *The GoGo Chicago White Sox.* New York: Coward-McCann Sports Library, 1960.
Conlon, Jocko, and Robert Creamer. *Jocko.* New York: J.B. Lippincott, 1967.
Considine, Tim. *The Language of Sport.* New York: World Almanac, 1982.
Cooney, Byron. "Montana Men Who Play Big League Baseball." *Dillon (Montana) Examiner,* Oct. 13, 1922.
Cope, Myron. "Customer's Man with a Fastball." *Saturday Evening Post,* Aug. 4, 1956, pp. 30ff.
Cosell, Howard, with Peter Bonventure. *I Never Played the Game.* New York: Avon, 1985.
Couzens, Gerald. *A Baseball Album.* New York: Lippincott & Crowell, 1980.
Creamer, Robert. *Babe: The Legend Comes to Life.* New York: Simon & Schuster, 1974.
Curran, William. *Big Sticks: The Batting Revolution of the Twenties.* New York: Morrow, 1990.
———. *Mitts.* New York: Morrow, 1985.
Daley, Arthur. *Times at Bat: A Half Century of Baseball.* New York: Random House, 1950.
Dark, Alvin, and John Underwood. *When in Doubt, Fire the Umpire.* New York: Dutton, 1980.
Davids, L. Robert. "Bud Fowler: Black Baseball Star," in Richard Puff and Mark Rucker, eds., *The Empire State of Baseball.* Garrett Park, MD: Society for American Baseball Research, 1989, pp. 5-6.
Davis, Mac. *Great American Sports Humor.* Garden City, N.J.: Blue Ribbon, 1950.
———. *Lore and Legends of Baseball.* New York: Lantern, 1953.
———. *Sports Shorts: Astonishing But True.* New York: Bantam, 1959.
De Gregorio, George. *Joe DiMaggio: An Informal Biography.* New York: Stein & Day, 1973.
Deutsch, Jordan, Richard M. Cohen, Roland Johnson, and David Neft. *The Scrapbook History of Baseball.* Indianapolis: Bobbs-Merril, 1975.
Dreisewerd, Edna. *The Catcher Was a Lady: The Clem Dreisewerd Story.* Hicksville, N.Y.: Exposition, 1978.
Durant, John. *The Story of Baseball in Words and Pictures.* New York: Hastings House, 1973.
Durocher, Leo. *The Dodgers and Me: The Inside Story.* New York: Ziff-Davis, 1948.
———, with Ed Linn. *Nice Guys Finish Last.* New York: Pocket, 1975.
Durso, Joseph. *Casey: The Life and Legend of Charles Dillon Stengel.* Englewood Cliffs, N.J.: Prentice Hall, 1967.
Duxbury, John, ed. *Baseball Register.* St. Louis: *The Sporting News,* 1969.
———, comp., with Clifford Kachline. *Baseball Register.* St. Louis: *The Sporting News,* 1967.

Evers, Johnnie, and Hugh Fullerton. *Baseball in the Big Leagues.* Chicago: Reilly & Britton, 1910.

Farrington, Dick. "Rip Radcliff Who Hits Best with Two Strikes on Him, Rapping at Door of Bat Title After Worst Major Slump," *The Sporting News,* Aug. 29, 1940, p. 15.

Fay, Bill. "Belles of the Ball Game." *Colliers,* Aug. 13, 1949, p. 44.

Feller, Bob. *Strikeout Story.* New York: Bantam, 1947.

Ferguson, John. "A 'Reluctant Rookie' Turns Tiger with Tulsa." *The Sporting News,* Sept. 9, 1972, p. 45.

Fidler, Merrie A. *The Development and Decline of the All-American Girls Baseball League.* Unpublished M.S. Thesis, department of physical education, University of Massachusetts: Amherst, Mass., 1976.

Finch, Robert, L.H. Addington, and Ben Morgan, eds. *The Story of Minor League Baseball.* Columbus, Ohio: Stoneman, 1953.

Fitzgerald, Ed. "Ewell Blackwell: The Whip of the Reds." *Sport,* 11 (July, 1951): pp. 48–54.

Flood, Curt, with Richard Carter. *The Way It Is.* New York: Pocket, 1971.

Foltz, Wendy. "'Bugs' Grover Pitched for the Tigers 50 Years Ago." *Battle Creek Michigan Enquirer News,* June 20, 1963.

Ford, Whitey, Mickey Mantle and Joseph Durso. *Whitey & Mickey.* New York: Signet, 1977.

_____, with Phil Pope. *Slick: My Life In & Around Baseball.* New York: Dell, 1987.

Forsyth, Frederick. "Money with Menaces" in *No Comebacks: Collected Stories.* New York: Bantam, 1983, pp. 126–49.

Freehan, Bill, Steve Gelman and Dick Schapp, eds. *Behind the Mask.* New York: World, 1970.

Frick, Ford. *Games, Asterisks and People: Memoirs of a Lucky Fan.* New York: Crown, 1973.

Frommer, Harvey. *Baseball's Greatest Rivalry: The New York Yankees and Boston Red Sox.* New York: Atheneum, 1982.

Fullerton, Hugh. "The Lure of the Bleachers." *American Magazine,* 77 (May, 1914): pp. 29–33.

Gage, Tom. "Call Him What You Will, But He's Guillermo Now." *The Sporting News,* May 9, 1988, p. 14.

Gallager, Mark. *The Yankee Encyclopedia.* New York: Leisure, 1982.

Garagiola, Joe. *It's Anybody's Ballgame.* Chicago: Contemporary, 1988.

Garritz, John. *The George Brett Story.* New York: Coward, McCann & Geoghegan, 1981.

Gerlach, Larry. *The Men in Blue: Conversations with Umpires.* New York: Viking, 1980.

Gershman, Michall. "Smokey Joe's Shining Season." *Sports Heritage,* Sept./Oct., 1987, pp. 42–48.

Geuliotti, Joe. "The 'Can' Brings Charisma to Beantown." *The Sporting News,* June 24, 1985, p. 17.

Gittlitz, Hy. *Don't Kill the Umpire.* New York: Grosby, 1957.

Gold, Eddie. "Mighty Swish Beats Blackwell." *Vine Line* (the official newspaper of the Chicago Cubs) 1 (March, 1986): p. 22.

_____, and Art Ahrens. *The Golden Era Cubs: 1876–1940.* Chicago: Bonus, 1985.

_____, and Art Ahrens. *The New Era Cubs: 1941–1985.* Chicago: Bonus, 1985.

Gold, Victor. "Nine for Baseball." *The American Spectator,* Sept., 1937, p. 27.

Golenbock, Peter. *Bums: An Oral History of the Brooklyn Dodgers.* New York: Putnam, 1984.
Gorman, Tom. *Three and Two.* New York: Scribner's, 1979.
Graffis, Herb. "Queens of Swat." *Click,* Sept. 1944, pp. 48–50.
Graham, Frank. *The Brooklyn Dodgers: An Informal History.* New York: Putnam, 1945.
———. *The New York Giants: An Informal History.* New York: Putnam, 1952.
———. "The Singles Hitter of the Giants." *Sport,* 15 (Aug. 1955): pp. 40ff.
———, and Dick Hyman. *Wit and Wisdom: Folklore of a National Pastime.* New York: David McKay, 1962.
Granger, David. "Doc-umenting the History of a Nickname." *New York Times,* Nov. 11, 1984, Sec. 5, p. 2.
Grayson, Harry. *They Played the Game.* New York: Barnes, 1944.
Green, Paul. "Baseball of Happy Chandler." *Sports Collectors Digest,* 10 (Nov. 1983): pp. 28ff.
Grimm, Charlie, with Ed Prell. *Jolly Cholly's Story: Baseball, I Love You!* Chicago: Henry Regvery, 1968.
Grosshandler, Stan. "Relief Pitchers: Specialists in Crisis." *Baseball Digest,* 31 (May 1972): pp. 22–27.
———. "Where Have Those Grand Old Nicknames Gone?" *Baseball Research Journal,* 7 (1978): pp. 61–63.
Haag, Ken. "Nicknames: The Lure & Lore of Baseball." *Sports Collectors Digest,* July 14, 1989, p. 52.
Haber, Bill. "In Pursuit of Bull Durham." *Baseball Research Journal,* 12 (1983): pp. 106–08.
Ham, Bus. "Senators Expect Narum to Win 15." *Washington Post,* Feb. 3, 1965.
Hano, Arnold. *Roberto Clemente: Batting King.* New York: Putnam, 1968.
Harris, Sheldon. *Blues Who's Who: A Biographical Dictionary of Blues Singers.* New York: Da Capo, 1979.
Harris, Stanley. *Playing the Game: From Mine Boy to Manager.* New York: Frederick A. Stokes, 1925.
Harwell, Ernie. "Billy O'Dell," in Ray Robinson, ed., *Baseball Stars of 1959.* New York: Pyramid, 1959, pp. 97–102.
———. "The Game for All America," in Charles Einstein, ed., *The Fireside Book of Baseball.* New York: Simon & Schuster, 1956, p. 183.
Henkey, Ben. "Prize Winning Rookies." *The Sporting News,* Nov. 8, 1969, p. 34.
Herkowitz, Mickey, and Steve Perkins. *Everything You Always Wanted to Know About Sports and Didn't Know Where to Ask.* New York: Signet, 1977.
Hernandey, Keith, and Mike Bryan. *If on First.* New York: Penguin, 1986.
Herzog, Whitey, and Kevin Horrigan. *White Rat: A Life in Baseball.* New York: Harper & Row, 1987.
Hirshberg, Al. *The Braves: The Pick & the Shovel.* Boston: Waverly, 1948.
———. "The Pinky in the Red Sox Boot." *Sports Illustrated,* 3 (July 25, 1955): pp. 48–51.
Hoffman, John. "Chicago's Nuts About Chico." *Complete Baseball,* 2 (Fall 1950): pp. 56–59.
Holahan, David. "Nicknames and the Refrigerator." *Christian Science Monitor,* Dec. 19, 1985, p. 15.
Hollander, Zander, ed. *Baseball Lingo.* New York: Norton, 1967.
Holmes, Tommy. "The Strange Case of Thomas Baker." *Baseball Digest,* 14 (March 1955): pp. 19–21.

Holway, John. *Black Stars: Negro League Pioneers.* Westport, Conn.: Meckler, 1988.
———. *Voices from the Great Black Baseball Leagues.* New York: Dodd, Mead, 1975.
Honig, Donald. *Baseball America: The Heroes of the Game and the Times of Their Glory.* New York: Macmillan, 1985.
———. *The October Heroes.* New York: Simon & Schuster, 1979.
Hutchinson, Ian. *Salutes Cooperstown on Its 50th Anniversary.* Toronto: The Canadian Baseball Hall of Fame and Museum, 1989.
Isaminger, James. "Mack's Robert Taylorish Southpaw." *Philadelphia Inquirer*, May 9, 1940.
Ivor-Cambell, Frederick. "Henry Chadwick," in David Porter, ed., *Biographical Dictionary of American Sports: Baseball.* New York: Greenwood, 1987, pp. 82–83.
Jackson, Donald. "He Welted the Sphere a Prodigious Biff." *Smithsonian*, April, 1989, p. 184.
Jackson, Reggie, with Mike Lupica. *Reggie.* New York: Ballantine, 1984.
"Jakie May of the Cincinnati Reds." *Baseball Magazine*, 42 (August, 1927): p. 398.
James, Bill. *Historical Baseball Abstract.* New York: Villard, 1986.
Johnson, Harold. *Who's Who in Major League Baseball.* Chicago: Buston, 1933.
Johnstone, Jay, with Rick Talley. *Over the Edge.* Chicago: Contemporary, 1987.
———, with ———. *Temporary Insanity.* New York: Bantam, 1985.
Jordan, Pat. *The Suitors of Spring.* New York: Warner, 1973.
Jordan, David. *A Tiger in His Time: Hal Newhouser and the Burden to Wartime Ball.* South Bend, IN: Diamond Communications, 1990.
Josselyn, Talbert. "Better Than the Best." *Colliers*, 115 (July 7, 1945): pp. 69ff.
Joynik, Tom. "Hurricane Hazel in 1957." *The Baseball Research Journal*, 12 (1983): pp. 83–86.
Kaese, Harold. *The Boston Braves.* New York: Putnam, 1948.
———. "The Boston Braves," in Ed Fitzgerald, ed., *The Book of Major League Baseball Clubs: The National League.* New York: Barnes, 1952, pp. 68–100.
Kahn, James. *The Umpire Story.* New York: Putnam, 1953.
Kahn, Rodger. "Markell, N.Y. Policeman, Eyes Beat with Phillies." *New York Herald Tribune*, Dec. 28, 1953.
Kahn, Roger, and Al Helfer, eds. *The Mutual Baseball Almanac.* New York: Doubleday, 1954.
Kaplan, Jim. *Playing the Field.* Chapel Hill, N.C.: Algonquin, 1987.
Kavanaugh, Jack. "No Touch at Second." *Sports History*, May, 1988, pp. 16–24.
Kiersh, Edward. *Where Have You Gone Vince Dimaggio?* New York: Bantam, 1983.
Kiner, Ralph, with Joe Gergen. *Kiner's Korners.* New York: Arbor House, 1987.
Kinnaird, Clark, Walter Johns and Ralph Hollenbeck, eds. *Big League Baseball.* New York: Avon, 1951.
Kinsella, W.P. *Shoeless Joe.* New York: Ballantine Books, 1982.
Kofender, Bill. "Gals Play Ball Too." *Sports Graphics*, June, 1947, pp. 8–9.
Kofoed, J.C. "The Silent Infielder." *Baseball Magazine*, 13 (Oct. 1914): pp. 77–82.
Kuehnert, Marty. "Horner Is 'Mr. Hom-Ah' in Japan." *The Sporting News*, June 29, 1987, p. 12.
Kuenster, John. *From Cobb to Catfish: 128 Illustrated Stories from Baseball Digest.* Chicago: Rand McNally, 1975.
Lally, Dick. *Pinstriped Summers.* New York: Arbor House, 1985.
Lane, F.C. "The Firebrand of the Federal League." *Baseball Magazine*, 13 (July 1914): pp. 25–32.

———. "Smoky Joe Wood," in Sidney Offit, ed. *The Best of Baseball*. New York: Putnam, 1956, pp. 61–67.
Lane, Frank. "He Earned the Nickname 'Bing'." *Baseball Magazine*, 44 (Dec. 1929): pp. 293–94ff.
———. "His Name Was So Long They Called Him 'Lil'." *Baseball Magazine*, 38 (Feb. 1927): pp. 399–400.
———. "The Most Remarkable Comeback on Record." *Baseball Magazine*, 21 (July 1918): pp. 263–67.
Langford, Jim. *The Game Is Never Over: An Appreciative History of the Chicago Cubs, 1948–1980*. South Bend, Ind.: Icarus, 1980.
Langford, Walter. "Pinky Whitney: Philly Star from Another Era." *Baseball Digest*, June 1988, pp. 69–71.
Lardner, John. "Spitball Is a Horrid Word." *Sport*, Feb. 1955: pp. 21ff.
———. "That Was Baseball: The Crime of Shufflin' Phil Douglas." *New Yorker*, 33 (May 12, 1956): pp. 136ff.
Lasorda, Tommy, and David Fisher. *The Artful Dodger*. New York: Arbor House, 1985.
Lawler, Joe. "High Octane for the Gas House Gang." *Sports History*, (March, 1988): pp. 18–25.
LeFlore, Ronald, with Jim Hawkins. *One in a Million*. New York: Warner, 1978.
Leggett, William. "The Mouse Who Builds the Mountains," in Ellen Pearson, ed. *Great Stories from Sports Illustrated*. Middleton, Conn.: American Education Publications, 1972.
Lewis, Franklin. *The Cleveland Indians*. New York: Putnam, 1949.
Libby, Bill. *Charlie O. and the Angry A's*. Garden City, N.Y.: Doubleday, 1975.
Lieb, Fred. *Baseball as I Have Known It*. New York: Tempo, 1979.
———. "Baseball—The Un That Belongs to Us," in Sidney Offit, ed. *The Best in Baseball*. New York: Putnam, 1956, pp. 213–18.
———. *The St. Louis Cardinals*. New York: Putnam, 1944.
Lieb, Frederick. *The Baltimore Orioles: The History of a Colorful Team in Baltimore and St. Louis*. New York: Putnam, 1955.
———. *Connie Mack: Grand Old Man of Baseball*. New York: Putnam, 1945.
———. *The Detroit Tigers*. New York: Putnam, 1946.
———. "Nicknames." *The Sporting News*, Nov. 18, 1943, p. 7.
———. "Noah's Ark Spawned Big-Time's Nicknames." *The Sporting News*, Dec. 21, 1963, pp. 38–40.
———. *The Pittsburg Pirates*. New York: Putnam, 1948.
Lindberg, Richard. *Who's on Third? The Chicago White Sox Story*. South Bend, Ind.: Learus, 1983.
Linn, Ed. *Steinbrenner's Yankees: An Inside Account*. New York: Holt, Rinehart & Winston, 1982.
Liss, Howard. *Baseball's Zaniest Stars*. New York: Random House, 1971.
Lowry, Philip. *Green Cathedrals*. Cooperstown, N.Y.: Society for American Baseball Research, 1986.
Luciano, Ron, and David Fisher. *The Fall of the Roman Umpire*. New York: Bantam, 1986.
———, and ———. *The Umpire Strikes Back*. New York: Bantam, 1982.
Lukas, J. Anthony. "Trials of a Rookie." *New York Times Magazine*, April 1, 1979, pp. 23ff.
Lyle, Sparky, and Peter Golenbock. *The Bronx Zoo*. New York: Dell, 1979.
McBride, Joseph. *High and Inside*. New York: Warner, 1980.

McConnell, Robert. "Three Shots of Rye." *The Baseball Research Journal*, 9 (1980): pp. 80–82.
McCoy, Bob. "That Fabulous '87 Series." *The Sporting News*, Oct. 5, 1987, p. 10.
McCoy, Hal. "Spuds'll Take the Work." *The Sporting News*, May 9, 1988: p. 22.
MacFarlane, Paul. *Daguerreotypes of Great Stars of Baseball*. St. Louis: The Sporting Views, 1968.
McGarigle, Bob. *Baseball's Great Tragedy: The Story of Carl Mays, Submarine Pitcher*. New York: Exposition, 1972.
McGowen, Roscoe. "Who's a Screwball?" in Sidney Offit, ed. *The Best of Baseball*. New York: Putnam, 1956, pp. 118–23.
McGraw, John. *My Thirty Years in Baseball*. New York: Arno, 1974.
Mack, Connie. *My 66 Years in the Big Leagues*. Philadelphia: John C. Winston, 1950.
Mandel, Mike. *SF Giants: An Oral History*. Santa Cruz, Calif.: Mike Mandel, 1979.
Mann, Arthur. "Droll Fellows," in Sidney Offit, ed. *The Best in Baseball*. New York: Putnam, 1956, pp. 162–67.
Mantle, Mickey, with Herb Gluck. *The Mick*. New York: Doubleday, 1985.
Marazzi, Rick, and Len Fiorito. *Aaron to Zipfel*. New York: Avon, 1985.
———— and ————. *Aaron to Zuverink*. New York: Avon, 1982.
Marcin, Joe. ed. *Baseball Register*. St Louis: The Sporting News, 1970, 1971.
Martin, Billy, and Peter Golenbock. *Number 1*. New York: Delacorte, 1980.
Masin, Herman. *Curve Ball Laughs*. New York: Pyramid, 1955.
May, Frank, ed. *The Amazing Braves*. Atlanta: Philmay, 1982.
Mayer, Ronald. *The 1937 Newark Bears: A Baseball Legend*. East Hanover, N.J.: Vintage, 1980.
Meany, Thomas. "Lopat—The Junk Man." *Baseball Digest*, 11 (June 1952): pp. 94–97.
Merin, Samuel. "A Newcomer to the Mound." *Baseball Magazine*, 50 (Sept. 1938): p. 470.
Millard, Tex. *Cuttin' the Corners*. South Brunswick, N.Y.: Barnes, 1966.
Miller, Cary. "Will the Thrill." *Beckett Baseball Card Monthly*, July 1989, pp. 6–7.
Milne, Robert. "The Leading Hitter of the Browns." *Baseball Magazine*, 51 (Dec. 1936): p. 294.
Mitchell, Fred. "Pendleton Twists Ankle, Replaced by Lawlers in Card's Line-Up." *Chicago Tribune*, Oct. 1987, 10.
Molter, Harry. *Famous Athletes of Today*. New York: Page, 1953.
Mosedale, John. *The Greatest of All: The 1927 New York Yankees*. New York: Dial, 1974.
Mote, James. *Everything Baseball*. New York: Prentice Hall, 1989.
Munson, Thurman, with Martin Appel. *Thurman Munson: An Autobiography*. New York: Coward, McCann, & Geoghegan, 1979.
Murdock, Eugene. "Some Called Him Tarzan." *The Baseball Research Journal*, 10 (1981): pp. 106–11.
————. "They Called Him Unser Choe." *Baseball Research Journal*, 6 (1977): p. 37–46.
Murphy, J.M. "Napoleon Lajoie: Modern Baseball's First Superstar." *The National Pastime*, 1988, pp. 1–79 (entire issue).
Musial, Stan, Jack Buck and Bob Broeg. *We Saw Stars*. St. Louis: Bethany, 1976.
Nadel, Eric, and Craig Wright. *The Man Who Stole First Base*. Dallas: Taylor, 1989.
Nagel, Walter. *Five Straight Errors on Ladies' Day*. Caldwell, Id.: Caxton, 1965.
Nash, Bruce, and Allan Zullo. *The Baseball Hall of Shame*. New York: Wallaby, 1985.

Neft, David, Lee Allen, Robert Markel, John Tattersall, Neil Armann and Jordan Deutsch, ed. *Baseball Encyclopedia*. New York: Macmillan, 1969.
Nelson, Kevin. *Greatest Stories Ever Told About Baseball*. New York: Perigee, 1986.
Nemec, David. *Great Baseball Feats, Facts and Firsts*. New York: New American Library, 1987.
Newman, Rose. *The California Angels*. New York: Simon & Schuster, 1982.
Nightingale, Dave. "A Batting Champion Gone to Pot." *The Sporting News*, May 16, 1988, pp. 18–19.
Obojski, Robert. *Bush League: A History of Minor League Baseball*. New York: Macmillan, 1975.
O'Gara, Rodger. "Bump Will Sees Good and Bad in Being Son of Famous Dad." *The Sporting News*, August 23, 1975, p. 25.
Okkonen, Marc. *The Federal League of 1914–1915: Baseball's Third Major League*. Garrett Park, MD: Society for American Baseball Research, 1989.
Oknent, Daniel, and Harris Lewine, eds. *The Ultimate Baseball Book*. Boston: Houghton-Mifflin, 1984.
———, and Steve Wulf. *Baseball Anecdotes*. New York: Harper & Row, 1989.
O'Neal, Bill. *The Texas League 1888–1987: A Century of Baseball*. Austin, Texas: Eakin, 1987.
O'Neill, Frank. "Bingo Binks 'Magnificent Unpredictable' Keeping Senators in Scrap for Pennant." *The Sporting News*, September 20, 1945, p. 9.
Overfield, James. "William Ellsworth Hory, 1862–1961." *National Pastime*, 2 (1982): pp. 70–72.
Overfield, Joe. "Derby Day: Man of Many Hats." *Bison Gram*, 5:3 (May 1989): pp. 30–31.
Overfield, Joseph. *The 100 Seasons of Buffalo Baseball*. Kenmore, N.Y.: Partners', 1985.
———. "Tragedies and Shortened Careers," in John Thorn and Pete Palmer, eds. *Total Baseball*. New York: Warner, 1989.
Palmer, Harry. *Stories of the Baseball Field*. Chicago: Rand McNally, 1890.
Parrott, Harold. *The Lords of Baseball*. New York: Praeger, 1976.
Patten, William, and J. Walker McSpadden. *The Book of Baseball: The National Game from the Earliest Days to the Present Season*. New York: Collier, 1911.
Peary, Danny, ed. *Cult Baseball Players: The Greats, the Flakes, the Weird, and the Wonderful*. New York: Simon & Schuster, 1990.
Perry, Gaylord, with Bob Sudzk. *Me and the Spitter*. New York: Signet, 1974.
Peters, Mason. "Hertford Honors Hunter with Merry Party Today." *Greensboro News & Record*, May 9, 1987, pp. C-1, 2.
Peterson, Robert. *Only the Ball Was White*. New York: McGraw-Hill, 1970.
Petreman, David. "Cultural & Linguistic Unawareness: Nicknaming Latino Major League Ballplayers." Paper presented at the popular culture meetings, Toronto, Canada, 1991.
Phillips, David. *That Old Ball Game*. Chicago: Henry Regnery, 1975.
Pickard, Charles, and Clifford Kachline, comps., with Paul Rickart. *Baseball Register*. St. Louis: The Sporting News, 1965.
Piersall, Jimmy, with Richard Whittingham. *The Truth Hurts*. Chicago: Contemporary.
Pinella, Lou, with Maury Allen. *Sweet Lou*. New York: Putnam, 1986.
Pinelli, Babe (as told to Joe King). *Mr. Ump*. Philadelphia: Westminster, 1953.
Polner, Murray. *Branch Rickey*. New York: New American Library, 1982.
Pope, Edwin. *Baseball's Greatest's Managers*. New York: Doubleday, 1960.

Porter, David, ed. *Biographical Dictionary of American Sports: Baseball.* New York: Greenwood, 1987.
Povich, Shirley. "This Morning." *Washington Post,* August 30, 1944.
Powers, Jimmy. *Baseball Personalities.* New York: Rudolph Field, 1949.
"A Quiet Iceman Cometh to Pirates." *The Sporting News,* Sept. 21, 1987, p. 17.
Quimby, Allen. "An Afternoon with Rod Lucas." *The Baseball Research Journal,* 10 (1981): pp. 28–33.
Rathgeber, Bob. *Cincinnati Reds Scrapbook.* Virginia Beach: J.V.C. Corp. of Virginia, 1982.
Reichler, Joseph, ed. *Baseball Encyclopedia,* 7th ed. New York: Macmillan, 1988.
Reidenbaugh, Lowell. *Baseball's Hall of Fame Cooperstown.* St. Louis: The Sporting News, 1986.
———, and Craig Carter. *Take Me Out to the Ball Park.* St. Louis: The Sporting News, 1987.
Remas, Mike. "Players of Old Had More Colorful Nicknames." *Baseball Digest,* August, 1972, pp. 85–87.
Rebalow, Harold, and Meir Rebalow. *Jewish Baseball Stars.* New York: Hippocrene, 1984.
Rice, Grantland. "A Tip to Teddy," in Sidney Offit, ed. *The Best of Baseball.* New York: Putnam, 1956, pp. 15–16.
Ritter, Lawrence. *The Glory of Their Times* (new enlarged ed.). New York: Vintage, 1985.
———, and Donald Honig. *The Image of Their Greatness: An Illustrated History of Baseball from 1900 to the Present.* New York: Crown, 1979.
Robinson, Ray. *Baseball's Most Colorful Managers.* New York: Putnam, 1970.
Roeder, Bill. "The Amazing Story of Brooks Lawrence." *Sport,* May 1957, pp. 42ff.
Roff, Elwood. *Baseball and Baseball Players.* Chicago: Roff, 1912.
Romig, Ralph. *Cy Young: Baseball's Legendary Giant.* Philadelphia: Dorrance, 1964.
Rose, Pete, and Roger Kahn. *Pete Rose: My Story.* New York: Macmillan, 1989.
Rosenbaum, Art. "Nicknames Still in Vogue in Major Leagues." *Baseball Digest,* August 1981, pp. 88–90.
Rumill, Ed. "He Could Be the Fastest Man in Baseball." *Christian Science Monitor,* May 5, 1971, p. 17.
Saccucci, Fluffy. "The Kissing Bandit." *Sports Collectors Digest,* Jan. 19, 1990, pp. 260–62.
Safire, William. *Safire's Political Dictionary.* New York: Ballantine, 1978.
Salant, Nathan. *Superstars, Stars and Just Plain Heroes.* New York: Stein & Day, 1982.
Salsinger, H.G. "Jake Wade, Who Snapped Allen's Victory String, Keeps Knocking at the Door." *Detroit News,* Jan. 3, 1938.
Schaap, Dick. *Steinbrenner.* New York: Avon, 1982.
Schacht, Al. *My Own Particular Screwball.* Ed Keyes, ed. New York: Doubleday, 1955.
Scheiffele, Fred. "Billy Evans and His Lucky Star." *Baseball Magazine,* 47 (July 1932): p. 358.
Schlain, Bruce. *Oddballs.* New York: Penguin, 1989.
Schlossberg, Dan. *Barons of the Bullpen.* New York: Grosset & Dunlap, 1975.
———. *The Baseball Book of Why.* Middle Village, N.Y.: Jonathan David, 1984.
———. *The Baseball Catalog.* Middle Village, N.Y.: Jonathan David, 1980.
Schoor, Gene. *The Pee Wee Reese Story.* New York: Messner, 1956.
———. *Seaver.* Chicago: Contemporary, 1986.

Scully, Gerald. *The Business of Major League Baseball.* Chicago: University of Chicago Press, 1989.
Seymour, Harold. *Baseball: The Early Years.* New York: Oxford, 1960.
———. *The People's Game.* New York: Oxford, 1990.
Shapiro, Milton. *Heroes Behind the Mask.* New York: Messner, 1968.
———. *Laughs from the Dugout.* New York: Messner, 1966.
Shatzkin, Mike. *The Ballplayers: Baseball's Ultimate Biographical Reference.* New York: Morrow, 1990.
Shea, Thomas. *Baseball Nicknames 1870–1946.* Hingham, Mass.: Gates-Vincent, 1946.
Sifakis, Carl. *The Dictionary of Historic Nicknames.* New York: Facts on File, 1984.
Simons, Herbert. "Life of an Ump," in Sidney Offit, ed. *The Best of Baseball.* New York: Putnam, 1956, pp. 156–61.
Silverman, Al. "The Hawk on the Bench." *Sport,* Jan. 1958, p. 84.
Simpson, Doug. "The Earl of Snohomish." *The Baseball Research Journal,* 11 (1982): pp. 155–60.
Skipper, James K., Jr. "Baseball's 'Babes'—Ruth and Others." *Baseball Research Journal,* 13 (1984): pp. 24–26.
Slocum, Bill. "Hub on Matty?" in Kinnaird, Clark, Walter Johns and Ralph Hollenbeck, eds. *Big League Baseball.* New York: Avon, 1951.
Smith, Curt. *Voices of the Game: The First Full-Scale Overview of Baseball Broadcasting, 1921 to the Present.* South Bend, Ind.: Diamond Communications, 1987.
Smith, H. Allen. "The Nature of Nicknames." *Holiday,* 40 (Oct. 1966): pp. 24–32.
Smith, Ira. *Baseball's Famous First Basemen.* New York: Barnes, 1956.
———. *Baseball's Famous Outfielders.* New York: Barnes, 1954.
———. *Baseball's Famous Pitchers.* New York: Barnes, 1954.
———, and H. Allen Smith. *Low and Inside: A Book of Baseball Oddities and Curiosities.* Garden City, N.J.: Doubleday, 1949.
———, and ———. *Three Men on Third.* Garden City, N.J.: Doubleday, 1951.
Smith, Ken. "He's Called Mandrake Mueller." *Baseball Digest,* 14 (May 1955): pp. 15–24.
Smith, Myron, comp. *Baseball: A Comprehensive Bibliography.* Jefferson, N.C.: McFarland, 1986.
Smith, Robert. *Baseball: A Historical Narrative of the Game, the Men Who Have Played It, and Its Place in American Life.* New York: Simon & Schuster, 1947.
———. *Heroes of Baseball.* Cleveland: World, 1952.
Sobel, Ken. *Babe Ruth and the American Dream.* New York: Ballantine, 1974.
Spink, C.C. Johnson. "We Believe." *The Sporting News,* Jan. 4, 1975, p. 10.
Spink, J.G. "Diamond Slang," in Fred Lieb, Bob Burnes, J.G. Taylor Spink, Les Biederman, *Comedians and Pranksters of Baseball.* St. Louis: Spink, 1966, pp. 46–58.
Spink, J.G. Taylor. "Looping the Loops." *The Sporting News,* Aug. 23, 1945, p. 2.
———, comp., with Paul Rickart. *Baseball Register.* St. Louis: *The Sporting News,* 1941, 1942, 1943, 1945, 1946, 1947, 1948, 1949.
———, comp., with ———, and Joe Abramovich. *Baseball Register.* St. Louis: *The Sporting News,* 1950–61.
Stein, Fred. *Under Coogan's Bluff.* Glenshaw, Penn.: Automated Graphic Systesm, 1978.
Stein, Harry. *Hoopla.* New York: St. Martin's, 1983.
Steinbuck, Jack. "Glamour Girls of Big-League Ball." *Magazine Digest,* July 1946, pp. 68–71.

Stewart, Wayne. "The Man Who Owned Babe Ruth." *Sports Heritage.* May/June 1987, pp. 54–57.
Stockton, Roy J. "How Duster Mails Collects on Color." *Baseball Magazine,* 41 (Feb. 1926): p. 406.
Stump, Al "Requiem for a Mad Russian," in William A. Wise, ed. *Cavalier's Major League Baseball 1961.* Greenwich, Conn.: Fawcett, 1961, pp. 58–60.
Sullivan, George. *Baseball's Wacky Players.* New York: Dodd Mead, 1984.
Sullivan, Timothy. *Humorous Stories of the Ball Field.* Chicago: Massachusetts, Donahue, 1903.
Terzian, James. *The Kid from Cuba: Zoilo Versalles.* Garden City, N.J.: Doubleday, 1967.
Thompson, Stephen. "The American Indian in the Major Leagues." *Baseball Research Journal,* 12 (1983): pp. 1–7.
Thorn, John, and Bob Carroll, eds. *The Whole Baseball Catalogue.* New York: Simon & Schuster, 1990.
_____, and Pete Palmer, eds. *Total Baseball.* New York: Warner, 1989.
Tiemann, Robert, and Mark Rucker, eds. *Nineteenth Century Stars.* Kansas City: Society for American Baseball Research, 1989.
Tingley, Ken. "Will Baseball Nicknames Strike Out?"*Kiwanis Magazine,* May 1990, pp. 26–28.
Tomlinson, Gerald. "A Minor-League Legend: Buzz Arlett, the 'Mightiest' Oak," *Baseball Research Journal,* 17 (1988): pp. 13–16.
Trachenburg, Leo. "Remembrances of Waite Hoyt." *Yankees Magazine.* Sept. 1988, pp. 22–24.
Treat, Roger. *Walter Johnson: King of the Pitchers.* New York: Messner, 1948.
Turkin, Henry, and S.C. Thompson. *The Official Encyclopedia of Baseball,* 10th ed. Cranbury, N.J.: Barnes, 1979.
Tygiel, Jules. *Baseball's Great Experiment: Jackie Robinson and His Legacy.* New York: Vintage, 1983.
Vanderberg, Bob. *Sox: From Lane and Fain to Zisk and Fisk.* Chicago: Chicago Review Press, 1984.
Vecsey, George. "Country Boy Runs Home." *New York Times,* July 26, 1985.
Veeck, Bill, with Ed Linn. *The Hustler's Handbook.* New York: Putnam, 1965.
_____, with _____. *Veeck as in Wreck.* New York: Putnam, 1965.
Verrell, Gordon. "Moose Makes Healthy Start." *The Sporting News,* May 23, 1988, p. 20.
Vogt, D.C. *Baseball History in Limerick Verse and Sketch.* Milwaukee: Greenfield House, 1981.
Voigt, David Q. *American Baseball: From the Gentleman's Sport to the Commissioner's System.* University Park: Pennsylvania State University Press, 1966.
Von Bovier, Philip. "Requiem for a Gladiator." *Baseball Research Journal,* 12 (1983): pp. 147–57.
Wallop, Douglass. *Baseball: An Informal History.* New York: Norton, 1969.
Walton, Ed. *The Rookies.* New York: Stein & Day, 1982.
Ward, John. "Lena Blackburne, a Player of the Old School." *Baseball Magazine,* 44 (Oct. 1929): p. 494.
Ward, John J. "The Unluckiest Man in Baseball." *Baseball Magazine,* 22 (Feb. 1919): pp. 223–24.
Warfield, Don. *The Roaring Redhead: Larry MacPhase, Baseball's Great Innovator.* South Bend, Ind.: Diamond Communications, 1987.
Whiteford, Mike. *How to Talk Baseball.* New York: Dembner, 1983.

White Sox 1966 Year Book. Chicago: Chicago White Sox, 1966.
Wielgus, Chuck, Alexander Wolff, and Steve Rushin. *From A-Train to Yogi: The Fan's Book of Sports Nicknames.* New York: Harper & Row, 1987.
Williams, Joe. "Yankees' Warmup Pitcher Sheds Wraps, Stops Raps." *The Sporting News,* Sept. 13, 1945, p. 5.
Williams, Ted, with John Underwood. *My Turn at Bat: The Story of My Life.* New York: Simon & Schuster, 1969.
Wurman, Richard. *Baseball Access.* Los Angeles: Access, 1984.

Index

Abba Dabba 3604
Abdul Jibber-Jabber 331
Abe 343
Abner 561
Ace 1029, 1032, 1712, 1997, 2755, 3440, 3867, 3888, 4031
Ach 967
AD 3955
Addie 1865
Admiral 244, 3174
Adonis 384
Airhead 1935
Al 259, 713, 4058, 4119
Alabama Blossom 2567
Alamazoo 1781
Alderman 394
All American Out 982
Alphabet 3332
Andy 4139
Angel 3125
Angel Jack 8
Angel Sleeves 1847
Angleworm 3
Animal, The 2132
Antelope, The 3698
Apples 2072
Appollo of the Box, The 2586
Arbie 797
Arch 1997, 2121
Arkansas Humming Bird, The 3767
Arky 3686
Arm, The 1430
Art the Great 3289
Astoria Eagle, The 2310
Augie 1202, 2901
Autch 2466

Available 1850
Ave 2731
Axel 1014
Ayrriba 639

Babe 12, 21, 150, 260, 269, 279, 329, 472, 787, 811, 845, 936, 1036, 1254, 1519, 1579, 1968, 1973, 2379, 2429, 2640, 2838, 2850, 3109, 3279, 3619, 3650, 3659, 3847, 3977, 4075, 4103
Babe Ruth of Cuba 3617
Babe Ruth of the Citrus Circuit, The 260
Babe Ruth of the Rookies 1278
Babe Ruth's Caddy 482
Babe Ruth's Legs 482
Baby 73, 2719, 3236
Baby Bull, The 570
Baby Doll 1761
Baby Face 384
Bad Bill 786, 994, 2518
Bad News 1247, 1436
Bake 2214
Bald Billy 162, 1747
Baldy 1835, 1894, 2174, 2752, 3094, 3304
Ball Hawk 939
Bally 3255
Bam 2217

Bama 3086
Barber, The 2322
Barnacle Bill 2877
Barney 1813, 3187, 3199, 3294, 3327, 3926
Barnyard 1558
Baron 1981
Barrego 52
Barry 2229
Baser 4138
Batboy 2267
Battleaxe 3426
Battleship 1386
Beacon 2651
Beak 2018
Beams 1906
Beanie 1444
Beans 2952, 4126
Beany 1760
Bear 435, 1219, 1310, 2741
Bear Tracks 1775, 3184
Beau 220
Beau, The 189
Beauty 137, 2261
Bebop 4155
Bedford Bill 2942
Bedford Sheriff 1156
Bedrock 204
Bee 3002
Bee Bee 3003
BeeBee 112
Beetle 121
Ben 1221
Bergie 4013, 4041
Bernie 1768
Bert 300, 1245, 1325, 3961
Beto 108
Betz 1976

356 Index

Beverly 193
Bevo 2099
Bid 2307
Biddy 918
Biff 2335, 3160, 3177, 3267
Big 1462
Big Al 2142, 4033, 4033
Big Baboon, The 3109
Big Bear, The 1256
Big Ben 516, 2238, 3280
Big Bertha 3140
Big Bill 7, 117, 311, 425, 481, 587, 902, 1770, 1921, 2104, 2255, 2394, 2978, 3161, 3421, 3708
Big Bo 344
Big Boy 2014
Big Cal 1709
Big Cat 1240
Big Cat, The 2516
Big Chief, The 3403
Big Cookie 4025
Big D 961
Big Daddy 1127, 2986
Big Dan 403, 3600
Big Dave 817
Big Dee 3389
Big Doggie 2797
Big Eagle 467
Big Ed 866, 1015, 1561, 1972, 2000, 2985, 3438, 3747
Big Ego, The 3424
Big Florida 3627
Big Foot 2038
Big Groundhog 2734
Big Guy 3868
Big Indian, The 3970
Big Jack 3275
Big Jawn 2516
Big Jeff 2821
Big Jim 180, 646, 1212, 2002, 2605, 3036, 3266, 3784, 3845
Big Joe 3872
Big John 305, 2413
Big Mike 3488

Big Monk, The 3109
Big Oom, The 2704
Big Pete 2285
Big Poison 3757
Big Red 1383, 4068
Big Serb 2471
Big Six 101, 2397
Big Stick 3446
Big Stud 1821
Big Tex 638
Big Tom 1349
Big Train 2305
Big Train, The 1813
Bigfoot 3410
Biggs 3806
Bill 11, 25, 49, 1153, 2063, 2728, 2900, 3203
Billiken 1701
Billy 1499, 2377, 3045
Billy Fish 3045
Billy the Brat 2377
Bing 79, 757, 2474
Bingo 264, 875
Binky 1840
Bip 3037
Bird, The 1125
Bird Dog 1678
Bird Eye 3636
Birddog 4066
Birdie 744, 3391
Bismarck of Baseball 2499
Bitsy 2576
Bitu 2387
Biz 2286
Blab 3210
Black Babe Ruth, The 2817
Black Cat, The 2543
Black Dunlap 1366
Black Jack 445, 3889
Black Knight of the Border, The 2341
Black Lloyd Waner, The 769
Black Lou Gehrig, The 2127
Black Marquard 937
Black Mike 652

Black Ruth, The 591
Blackie 549, 689, 808, 878, 881, 1996, 2342, 2344, 2710, 3208, 4163
Blade, The 1443
Blazer 586
Blazer, The 292
Blimp 1530, 2827
Blind Bob 1045
Blinky 986
Blitzen 235
Blix 929
Blond Guy 1538
Blondie 290
Blondy 3114
Bloody Jake 1072
Blower 417
Blue Devil 3601
Blue Goose 2539
Blue Moon 2684
Blue Sleeve 1481
Bluegill 1716
Bluejacket 3349
Bo 213, 888, 1757, 2288
Bo-Beau 220
Bo Bo 4014
Boardwalk 407
Bob 437, 1019, 1146, 1332, 1995, 2146, 2804, 2874
Bobbie 3082
Bobby 2160, 2449, 2890, 3628
Bobo 1658, 2497, 2646, 2722
Bock 123
Boileryard 636
Bomber 3681
Bombo 3023
Bones 126, 1039, 3608
Bonnie 1655, 4005
Boo 1122
Boob 2303
Boog 2879
Boojum 3892
Boom Boom 199
Boomer 1792, 1961, 3214, 3807
Boon 1514

Index   357

Booster 1376
Booter 1612
Bootnose 1641
Boots 848, 1368, 1654, 2862, 3370
Boss 3179
Boston 4098
Bots 2634
Bow Wow 85
Boxer 1304
Boy Manager, The 335
Boy Wonder 1493, 1548
Boze 239
Bozo 614
Braggo 3080
Brains 2744
Brat, The 3406
Breezy 3909
Brick 2739
Brickyard 1931
Briggsie 4016
Broadway 982, 1150, 1839, 1842, 2079, 2954, 3207, 3334, 3720
Brock 823
Brode 3296
Brooks 2527
Brooks Robinson of the Negro Leagues 799
Brow, The 2747
Brownie 1022, 1174, 4017
Bruce 684
Bruno 253, 297, 431
Brusie 2690
Bruz 1455
Bub 2300
Bubba 611, 1161, 1489, 2569, 2833
Bubber 1857
Bubbles 1474
Buck 196, 201, 379, 443, 449, 480, 550, 765, 804, 1005, 1067, 1078, 1196, 1197, 1198, 1200, 1201, 1216, 1324, 1379, 1593, 1751, 1754, 1859, 2127, 2226, 2369, 2389, 2417, 2675, 2956, 3049, 3050, 3055, 3078, 3170, 3408, 3411, 3690, 3770, 3782, 3786, 3818, 3823
Bucketfoot 3307
Buckeye 1370
Buckshot 423, 2412, 3323, 3944
Bucky 364, 877, 1415, 1493, 1759, 3695, 3754
Bud 62, 186, 257, 275, 278, 299, 619, 774, 1186, 1194, 1204, 1429, 1469, 1485, 1522, 1546, 1725, 1991, 2048, 2450, 2452, 2564, 2762, 2860, 2928, 3006, 3256, 3270, 3320, 3384, 3443, 3801, 3995
Buddy 97, 147, 214, 256, 284, 294, 295, 319, 355, 383, 768, 790, 856, 1307, 1387, 1456, 1491, 1518, 1599, 1729, 1937, 2139, 2140, 2611, 2620, 2810, 2817, 2894, 3069, 3376, 3737
Buff 3853
Buffalo Bill 1647
Buffy 2037
Bug 1653
Bugger 3802, 4041
Buggs 1006, 2970
Bugs 229, 448, 1404, 1999, 2549, 2949, 3815
Bull 977, 978, 980, 981, 1016, 1575, 1815, 2090, 3352, 3723, 3776
Bull, The 1119, 2198, 3657
Bull Dog 336, 1134, 1592
Bull-Necked Bill 1416
Bulldog 2779, 3134
Bullet 2477, 3054
Bullet Ben 231
Bullet Bob 2990, 3642
Bullet Joe 469
Bullfrog 893, 2396
Bump 1426, 3875
Bumper 1826
Bumpus 1833
Bun 3635
Bunch 1316
Bunion King 3989
Bunions 202, 3989
Bunk 676
Bunky 3447
Bunny 388, 705, 1081, 1534, 2317, 3075, 3959
Bunt 1217
Burly 2655
Burrhead 912, 1085
Bush 185, 326, 334
Buster 15, 87, 370, 409, 462, 562, 596, 1199, 1278, 1673, 1907, 2186, 2231, 2295, 2415, 2623, 3076, 3433
Butch 26, 232, 374, 844, 1012, 1541, 1565, 1626, 1733, 1997, 2454, 2654, 2975, 3135, 3137, 3180, 3310, 3500, 3800, 3810, 3852, 3953, 3960
Butcher Boy 20, 235
Butterball 333
Buttercup 890
Buttermilk Tommy 945
Buttons 389, 3862
Butts 3718
Buzz 86, 353, 513, 952, 1008, 2313, 2601, 2829, 3429, 3820
Buzzy 3764
Bye Bye 128

Index

Cab 1997
Cachatter 2181
Cactus 738, 1796, 1900
Cakes 2753
Calhoun 4020
California Bill 425
California Fruit 3366
Calliope 2479
Camera Eye 272
Camp 3321
Candy 776, 1488, 2035, 2336, 2638
Candy Ben 255
Candy Man, The 508
Canena 2366
Cannonball 736, 2559, 2727, 2955, 3246, 3427, 3602
Cap 73, 623, 630, 767, 1083, 2247, 2622, 2811, 3865
Captain Hook 59
Captain Midnight 2178, 3746
Carney 1162
Carpet Sweeper, The 1672
Casey 666, 1431, 1825, 1963, 3428, 3914
Cassy 2208
Cat, The 373, 2349, 2472
Catfish 1730, 1961, 2453
CB 456
Ceylon 3943
Cha Cha 570
Chad 1950, 3228
Chairman of the Board 1169
Champ 3491, 4105
Chancer 1030
Chappie 590, 1300, 1358, 1797, 2244, 3368
Chappy 2058
Charlie Hustle 3070
Charlie O 1130
Charmer, The 3991
Chauncey 3476
Chauncy 963

Cheese 3211
Cherokee 834, 1141
Chesty 723
Chewing Gum 2673
Chi Chi 2700
Chick 105, 106, 337, 363, 520, 538, 568, 575, 770, 820, 997, 1236, 1246, 1428, 1504, 1661, 2403, 2553, 2618, 2732, 2841, 3040, 3292
Chicken 1526, 3407
Chicken Wolf 3924
Chickenhearted 1959
Chico 515, 532, 533, 1061, 1116, 1117, 1257, 1582, 3098, 3099, 3127, 3729, 4021
Chief 24, 223, 293, 341, 597, 605, 1004, 1467, 1487, 1502, 1648, 1922, 2012, 2461, 2537, 2877, 3071, 3375, 3641, 3891, 3965, 3979, 3992
Chief Tokahoma 1364
Chief Whitehorn 800
Child Athlete, The 2910
Childe Harold 1773
Chile 1337
Chili 824
Chilote 2157
Chink 1543, 3887, 3968, 3984
Chino 3337
Chinski 3067
Chip 227, 2062
Chipper 4156
Chippie 4156
Chippy 1270, 2248
Choke 'em Charlie 1593
Cholly 1047, 2621
Choo Choo 657, 4061
Choppy 10
Chow 4093
Chris 2027

Chub 669, 3486
Chubby 852
Chuck 610, 1042, 2098, 3189, 3220
Chucko 2934
Chummy 1371
Circus Solly 1640
Citation 2446
Cito 1269
Clancy 782
Cleary Daddy 759
Climax 296
Clinkers 1082
Coalyard Mike 1457
Coaster Joe 688
Cobra, The 2757
Cobra Joe 1195
Coca 1417
Cocky 661, 1085
Coco 2034
Cocoa 3934
Cod 2613
Coffee Jack Ryan 3112
Colby Jack 701
Coldwater Jim 1720
Colonel 206, 1124, 3101
Colonel Rhubarb 3941
Colt 39
Columbia George 3342
Columbia Lou 1278
Comet 80
Commerce Comet, The 2350
Commuter 2192
Connie 1791, 4168
Cookie 771, 2086, 3060
Cool Papa 219
Cooney 3371
Coonie 289
Coot 3694
Cordie 4026
Cork 3851
Corky 3669, 3919, 4023, 4112
Cornfield 3772
Cornhusker Express, The 93
Corns 358

Correctional Institute
  Face 2126
Cot 850
Cotton 371, 1836,
  1980, 2480, 2510,
  2624, 2853, 3301,
  3645
Count 503, 916, 2199,
  2586, 2906
Count, The 2531
Count of Luxemburg,
  The 2431
Country 837, 854,
  1550, 2914, 3328
Cousin Ed 171
Cousin Egbert 171
Cowboy 1484, 1823,
  2507, 3906
Cowboy Joe 3817
Cozy 917, 919
Crab 3765
Crab, The 452, 1075
Crabapple Comet, The
  3092
Cracker 1450, 3159
Crane 2953
Crash 838
Crazy 3183
Crazy Horse 772
Creeper, The 3470
Creepi 750
Cricket, The 3015
Crip 2867
Crooning Joe 554
Crossfire 2536
Crow, The 3015
Crown Prince of Baseball, The 3155
Crungy 756
Crush 1659
Crybaby 639
Cub 3450
Cuban Strongboy, The
  3617
Cuckoo 607
Cuddles 2370
Cuke 172
Cully 1528
Cuno 164
Cupid 600
Cura 3345

Curley 410, 441, 933,
  1871, 2689
Curly 2708, 3077,
  4027
Curry 1166
Curveless Wonder, The
  2717
Cut Rate 1745
Cy 27, 146, 291, 298,
  338, 616, 1090, 1123,
  1213, 1670, 1934,
  2374, 2545, 2546,
  2554, 2633, 2799,
  2824, 2845, 2993,
  3013, 3243, 3651,
  3711, 3766, 3860,
  3972, 3973, 4022
Cy the Third 3974
Cyclone 2485, 3111,
  3863, 3973
Cyclone Jim 984
Cz 2800

Dad 635, 1438, 2206,
  2427
Dad Gum 100
Daddy 609
Daddy of the Spitball
  2275
Daddy Wags 3722
Daets 4029
Daff 1249
Daffy 855, 3134
Dago 1393, 2917
Daisy 835
Dandelion 2822
Dandy 3931
Danish Viking 2852
Danny 216, 1377
Dapper Dan 1703
Darby 2672
Darkie 642
Darling, The 322
Dasher 1898, 1990,
  2608, 3634
Dashing Dan 715
Dauntless Dan 1258
Dauntless Dave 801
Dave 1619, 2010

Dazzy 3676, 3677
Deacon 406, 924,
  1824, 1834, 2088,
  2269, 2281, 2563,
  2607, 2776, 2828,
  3216, 3226, 3675,
  3831
Deacon Danny 2245
Dear Old Rodger 685
Dearfoot 191
Death to Flying Things
  585, 1114
Death Valley Jim 3215
Dee 721, 2470, 2535,
  2831, 2847, 3751,
  3858, 4018
Deeby 1175
Deedle 2551, 4034
Deek 807, 879
Deerfoot 145, 1879,
  2469, 2632
Deke 3829
Del 1691, 1693, 1694
Delaware Lemon 3621
Delaware Peach 3621
Denny 957
Der Boss President
  3709
Derby 442
Derby Day 649
Desperate 194
Dewey 1071
Diamond Jim 360,
  1283,
Diamond Joe 3007
Dibby 1163
Dick 464, 726, 1353,
  1478, 1525, 2836
Dig 1954
Digger 2680
Dim Dom 792
Dimples 1743
Ding Dong 221
Dingle 764
Dingo 2983
Dining Car Addict
  437
Dinny 2304
Dino 3859
Dinty 141, 1273
Dirty 254

Dirty Al 1241
Dirty Dan 2595
Dirty Jack 949
Dirty Man, The 1241
Disco Danny 1168
Divvy 819
Dixie 537, 826, 1698, 2134, 2209, 2758, 2768, 3662, 3730, 3731, 3736
Dixie Thrush, The 3460
Diz 2959
Dizzy 854, 903, 2666, 3633
Do It 2905
Dobie 2543
Doc 21, 55, 109, 181, 340, 471, 529, 555, 698, 734, 735, 778, 813, 1011, 1017, 1073, 1098, 1271, 1295, 1314, 1441, 1449, 1531, 1740, 1817, 1927, 1936, 2041, 2053, 2055, 2087, 2111, 2276, 2296, 2371, 2375, 2376, 2381, 2423, 2492, 2573, 2619, 2648, 2669, 2742, 2760, 2883, 2899, 2916, 2931, 2972, 3110, 3123, 3154, 3225, 3249, 3365, 3398, 3649, 3666, 3726, 3740, 3773, 3820, 3827, 3930, 3962
Doc Twink 3649
Doctor 3428
Dr. K 1342
Dr. Strangelove 3475
Dode 32, 268, 393, 613, 2773, 3202
Dodie 4008
Dodo 88, 265, 2059
Dolly 1374, 1375, 3413, 3414, 4018
Dominican Dandy, The 2359

Don Jose Blocke el Dirigente de Aquadilla Teborines 298
Donora Greyhound, The 2609
Donie 470
Donk 1516
Doogie 2479
Dooley 3927
Dordy 2923
Dory 853, 1037
Dot 1225
Dots 2484
Double Duty 2925
Double Joe 987
Double O 2212
0010 (Double O Ten) 396
Double X 1191
Doughnut Bill 534
Downtown 420
Dracula 323
Dreamy 3153
Droopy 1066
Duck 2044, 2779, 3282
Duckie 4037
Ducky 886, 1437, 1554, 1662, 1663, 1667, 1846, 2424, 2687, 2782, 3185, 3981
Dude 287, 582, 1065, 2411
Duffy 988, 2138
Dugan 2826
Duke 382, 526, 880, 1062, 1097, 1687, 1912, 1932, 2207, 2362, 2966, 3227, 3290, 3312, 3314, 3366, 3772, 4159
Duke of Flatbush 3366
Duke of Tralee, The 380
Dukie 3601
Dummy 861, 969, 1704, 2119, 2200, 2596, 3435
Dumplings 1607
Dupee 3258

Durango Kid 3221
Duster 2328
Dustie 4148
Dusty 125, 306, 699, 2473, 2763, 2995, 2996, 2997, 2998
Dut 576
Dutch 136, 198, 240, 310, 313, 378, 399, 876, 894, 904, 935, 956, 1109, 1158, 1280, 1505, 1570, 1573, 1587, 1615, 1634, 1652, 1858, 1923, 1924, 1967, 1979, 2006, 2019, 2052, 2124, 2125, 2130, 2136, 2141, 2219, 2430, 2432, 2434, 2458, 2979, 3065, 3096, 3166, 3171, 3173, 3176, 3179, 3194, 3437, 3463, 3473, 3660, 3664, 3698, 3799, 3803, 3877, 3999
Dutch Master, The 3680
Dutchman 1218, 1220
Dynamo 603

E 4129
Eagle Eye 1555, 3198
Earache 2457
Earl of Snohomish, The 3613
Easy 1349, 2869
Ebba 3124
Ed 659, 2347
Ee-Yah 1782
Eggie 2122
Egyptian 1533
Eiffel Tower of Culpepper, The 3027
El 4142
El Diablo 3808
El Diamante Negro 2438
El Divino Loco 1338

El Gato 2791
El Grande Burro 418
El Maestro 896
El mono amarillo 2267
El Sambo Maravelloso 799
El Sorda 2081
Eli 1630, 3083
Elmer 304, 675, 727, 2270
Elmer the Great 199
Emu 1935
Epp 3232
Eppa 1805
Eppa Jephtha 3027
Eppie 153, 2475
Ernie 3703
Evangelist, The 3495
Eyechart 1419
Ez 589

Faceless Functionary, The 1009
Farmer 217, 458, 2542, 3422, 3688, 3786, 4062
Fat Freddie 1147
Fat Jack 1138
Father 1918
Father of Baseball 573
Father of the Yankees 3101
Fats 238, 640, 806, 1779, 1883
Fatso 3330
Fatty 394, 1182
Feather 608
Fibber 2252
Fiddler 179, 711
Fiddler Bigg 2251
Fidgety Phil 668
Fido 132
Fifth Avenue 982
Fil 4044
Filipino 47
Filthy McNasty 1241
Finn 174
Finners 2918
Fire 637, 3637

Fireball 3811
Firebrand 3459
Fireman 208, 2598, 2748
Firpo 2356, 2911, 4046
Fish Hook 3458
Fitz 1207
Flaco 82
Flakey 365
Flame 869
Flame, The 976
Flame Thrower, The 1094
Flash 80, 1048, 1092, 1152, 1311, 1345, 2331, 4048, 4162
Flea 643, 2145
Flea, The 2777
Fleury 3485
Flip 2040, 2751, 3072
Flip Flop 1845
Flop Ears 3812
Floppy 1509
Flossie 2670
Fluss 3783
Flying Dutchman, The 2167, 3721
Foggy 854
Foghorn 356, 2221, 2479, 2610, 3638, 3683
Footer 1809
Foots 751
Footsie 212, 283, 2120, 2358, 2677
Fordham Flash, The 1218
Four Sack 985
Fox 1446
Foxy Grandpa 139
Foxy Ned 1461
Frank 3250
Frantic Frank 2057
Freck 2738
Fred 1989
Fred the Barber 3010
Frenchey 324
Frenchy 1184, 1282, 2108, 2950, 3656, 4094
Freshest Man on Earth,

The 1083
Frisco 4051
Fritz 369, 439, 719, 932, 1135, 1568, 1988, 2011, 2184, 2331, 2363, 2525, 2686, 2724, 2812, 3196, 3710
Frog 2958
Frosty Bill 966
Full Pack 3405
Fungo 1595
Fuzzy 3004, 3335, 3828

Gabber 1333
Gabby 1506, 1822, 3444, 3464, 4171
Gabe 1276
Gallatin Squash, The 2796
Gander 3462
Gates 427
Gato 1115
Gause Ghost, The 2540
Gay Castillian, The 1339
Gay Reliever, The 2748
Gazelle, The 2773
Gee 72, 3733
Gee Gee 1296, 1330
General 766, 3279, 3397
Gentle Jeems 1248
Gentle Willie 2603
Gentleman Dave 2333
Gentleman Jake 812
Gentleman Jim 2166
Gentleman Joe 277
Gentleman John 1050
Gentlemanly Bobbie 618
Georgia Peach, The 650
Germany 2167, 3156, 3183, 3201, 3344
Gettysburg Eddie 2858
Ghost 2357

362 Index

Ghost of Hartsdale,
  The 1550a
Giant Killer, The 597,
  722
Gibby 2902
Gid 1259
Gig 4141
Gil 1244
Gilly 260, 1711
Gimpy 418, 2754
Ginger 195, 622, 3283,
  4011, 4049
Gink 1560
Gitz 2494
Giz 3120
Gladiator, The 430
Glass Arm Eddie 411
Glider 51
Glider, The 589
Gloomy Gus 3854
Goat 58, 651
God 1511
Goldbrick 639
Golden Boy 422
Golden Greek, The 22
Goldie 2941
Goldilocks 2114, 3400
Gomer 1629
Goo Goo 1239
Goober 3997
Goobers 368
Good Eye 3285
Good Kid 3499
Good Time Bill 2051
Goody 3074
Goofball 1261
Goofy 1339, 2037
Goose 1002, 1351, 1352
Gorgeous George 3318
Gorilla 1318
Goshen Schoolmaster,
  The 2107
Governor 1027
Gozzlehead 3025
Grand Old Man 2277
Grandmother 2884
Grapefruit 3964
Grasshopper 2144,
  2330, 3841, 4057
Gray Flamingo,
  The 377

Greasey 2630
Great, The 2242, 2328
Great Anticipator, The
  3449
Great Arbitrator, The
  1971
Great Gabbo, The
  1232
Great Lakes Dread
  Naught 437
Greek George 1284
Grey Eagle, The 3387
Greyhound 2504
Grin 357
Groove 192
Grump 1744, 3167
Grumpy 4092
Grunting Jim 3259
Guayubin 2699
Guido 2917
Guieno 3986
Guinea 1821
Gulfport 3112
Gulliver 2112
Gumby 1253
Gummy 3738
Gunboat 1412
Gunner 512, 2271,
  2896, 2963
Gus 215, 1933, 2256,
  3951
Gussie 1251
Gyp 3129

Hab 4053
Hac Man 2126
Hack 1046, 1049, 2481,
  2487, 3308, 3894
Haddie 1312
Hairbreadth Harry 1451
Hal 2017, 2182
Half Pint 3119
Ham 1739, 3197, 3714
Hammer 2505
Hammerin' Hank 1381
Hammerin' Henry 1
Hammond Hummer 3
Handsome 1697
Handsome Dan 2594

Handsome Harry 1697
Handsome Hugh 2310
Handsome Jack 528
Handsome Ransom
  1753
Handy Andy 1603,
  2747
Hank 1267, 1350,
  1392, 1748, 1893,
  2049, 2468, 3012,
  3022, 4160
Hankus Pankus 3954
Hans 4, 177, 1406,
  2944, 3721, 3922
Hap 660, 1722, 2565,
  2614, 3346, 3761
Happy 440, 580, 1112,
  1172, 1507, 1643,
  1650, 1671, 1743,
  1939, 2280, 2502,
  3621
Happy Jack 499, 598,
  3454
Hard Rock 1811
Hardrock 40, 3295
Harlem Joe 1940
Harry 2275, 3098,
  3392, 3394, 3439
Harry the Horse 805,
  1544
Hartford Jack 1099
Harvard Eddie 1365
Hat, The 3734
Hatchet, The 1881
Hawk 361, 536, 846,
  1486, 2583, 2864,
  3248, 3306
Head, The 3041
Heathcliff 1792
Heavy 286, 1807,
  3825
Hedy 4028
Heeney 2332
Heimie 4060
Heinie 183, 200, 236,
  1024, 1400, 1549,
  1552, 1772, 1890,
  2352, 2431, 2579,
  2581, 2683, 2789,
  2973, 3133, 3165,
  3192, 3343, 3396,

Index 363

3719, 3994, 3364, 4158,
Herky 1621
Herky Jerky 1684
Herschel 639
Heuvo 3066
Hey Hey 385
Hi 218, 1774
Hi Hi Dixwell 907
Hick 486, 530, 4061
Hickey 1639
Hickie 3881
Hickory 892, 1750, 1795
Hickory Bob 1479
Higbe 1494
High Pockets 1384, 1714, 1916
Highball 3886
Highpockets 1727, 1992
Hiker 2548
Hillbilly 261
Hinkey 1434
Hippity 1676
Hippo 3689
Hit Man 999
Ho Jo 1800
Hob 1616
Hobby 1421
Hobie 1121
Hod 1026, 1170, 2135
Hodge 247
Hog 1780
Hoge 3938
Hoke 898
Hollywood 2714
Home Run 124, 426, 964, 1790, 1798, 3862
Home Run Harry 831
Home Run Joe 2372
Hondo 1583, 1657, 1692
Hondo Hurrican, The 1509
Honest Bill 3494
Honest Eddie 2597
Honest Jack 352
Honest John 61, 1069, 1917, 2558

Honest Tom 2657
Honey 155, 1668, 3064
Honker, The 3145
Honolulu Johnny 3864
Honus 2159, 3721
Hook 982, 1357, 1571, 3989, 4154
Hooker 3838
Hooks 437, 716, 799, 815, 1742, 1804, 2495, 3768, 3902, 3954
Hoosier Schoolmaster 30
Hoosier Thunderbolt, The 3102
Hoot 1076, 1306, 2785, 3000, 3630, 3631
Hopalong 1702
Horn 3144
Hornet 4153
Horse 2522, 2715, 2784, 2988
Horse Belly 3141
Horse Face 2857
Horse Lady of St. Louis 2729
Horsey 4064
Hoss 342, 2005
Hot Potato 1453
Hot Rod 1889, 2237
Hot Sauce 3143
Houston 1785, 1786
Howard the Humble 714
Howitzer 2574
Howling Dan 1703
Howling Hilda 599
Hub 68, 1498, 1987, 3735, 3981
Huck 252, 1274, 3016, 3149, 3741
Hug 1715
Human Eyeball, The 2171
Human Flea, The 317
Human Mosquito, The 3326
Human Rain Delay, The 1473

Hummer 857, 960
Humphrey 262
Humpty Dumpty 2865
Humpy 2243
Hunkey 1620
Hurricane 1532
Husk 579
Husky 3725
Hustle 2150, 4019
Hustling Dan 2694
Hustling Harry 3430
Hutch 506, 4065
Hy 2612, 3679
Hypie 3084

I 4128
Icebox 577
Icehouse 3883
Iceman 974
Icicle 2961
Ignstz 2350
Ike 321, 400, 567, 709, 871, 1884, 2210, 2882, 3131, 4085
Immortal Azue, The 110
Imp 209
Impo 161
Inch 1331
Incredible Hulk, The 947
Indian Bob 1810
Indians' Bambino 437
Indians Bologna 437
Indio 3629
Ink 3461
Inky 2046
Innocent Fred 3771
Irish 697, 706, 1187, 1497, 1602, 2272, 2455, 2467, 3115, 4047
Iron 827
Iron Duke 1442
Iron Hands 1614
Iron Horse 1278
Iron Horse Wes 3193

364 Index

Iron Man 504, 827, 2257, 2582, 2688, 2835, 3415
Iron Mike 2888
Iron Pony 42
Ironwoman 4168
I29 2786
Itzy 1110
Izzy 1637

J.C. 2383
J.R. 3002, 4132
Jack 35, 793, 809, 1091, 1096, 1480, 1763, 1878, 1982, 2498, 2970, 3128
Jack the Giant Killer 2823
Jackrabbit 1309
Jacques 1183
Jake 563, 742, 1160, 1203, 1302, 1837, 2547, 3399, 3432, 3466
Jake the Giant Killer 3399
Jakie 2409
Jam 2029
Jap 143, 2628
Jasper 831
Jay 44, 1222, 1669, 1960, 2871
Jeep 1459, 1540, 1717, 4145, 4145
Jeff 2813, 2820
Jelly 1778
Jerky Jake 2662
Jerry 3661, 4111
Jersey 122, 197
Jersey Joe 3468
Jess 911
Jessie 1765, 1766
Jet 1784
Jibaro 2701
Jidge 3209
Jigger 276, 2070, 3418
Jiggs 922, 923, 2767
Jim 190, 438, 2872, 3169

Jing 1812
Jingles 729
Jinx 2863, 4069
Jittery Joe 245
Jo Jo 2540, 2562
Jock 2440, 3379
Jockey 1088, 1998
Jocko 679, 681, 1128, 1164, 1447, 2496
Jockstrap Jim 2753
Jodie 207
Jody 2069
Joe 312, 788, 847, 1321, 2733, 3358
Joe Doaks 134
Joe E 3639
Johnnie 4070
Johnny on the Spot 1841
Jojo 3832
Jolly 1993
Jolly Cholly 1395
Jolly Green Giant, The 822
Joltin' Joe 901
Jorocon 3892
Josephus the Phenomenal 325
Josh 263
Jot 1334
Jud 560, 2290
Judge 732, 1405, 2232, 2425, 3939
Judge, The 3042
Judy 1814
Jug 1287, 2013, 2885
Jughandle Johnny 2560
Jumbo 167, 173, 424, 551, 833, 1034, 1471, 1949, 2082, 3088, 3186, 3467, 3840
Jumbo Jim 2625
Jumpin' Joe 965
Jumping Jack 1829
Jungle Jim 3024
Junie 67
Junior 350, 785, 1209, 1317, 1974, 2534, 2659, 2718, 3433, 3748, 3937

Junk Man 2169
Jurgy 4071

Kaiser 3849
Kammie 4072
Kangaroo 1830
Kansas Cyclone, The 1813
Katie 1908
Kelly 1664, 4074
Kemo 2716
Kentucky Colonel, The 671
Kerry 4077
Kettle 3913
Kewpie 168, 2792
Kibby 3967
Kickapoo 3493
Kid 130, 187, 476, 478, 502, 542, 652, 873, 975, 1000, 1048, 1083, 1179, 1329, 1576, 1905, 2254, 2316, 2521, 2619, 2649, 2691, 3380, 3388, 3478, 3880, 3918
Kid, The 548, 2520, 3868
Kid from Boyceville, The 2747
Kiddo 829
Kiki 783
Kiko 1255
Killer 1942
Kilo 3778
Kimmersak 1923
King 114, 120, 398, 656, 1895, 1919, 2096, 2113, 2561
King Bill 1897
King Carl 1710
King Kong 1913, 1974
King of the Umpires 1235, 2201, 2292
King Richard 2194
King Tut 3647
Kip 3230

Kissing Bandit, The 3038
Kit 544, 2284
Kitten 2889
Kitten, The 1425
Kitty 366, 367, 1875
Klondike 942, 1886, 3336
Knee High 1603
Knight of Kennett Square, The 2793
Knobby 2089
Knuckles 615
Knucksie 2656
Kohly 2476
Kong 1955
Krum 1877
Kunk 4086

Laddie 2149
Lady 129, 2781
Lance 2945
Languid Bob 2456
Lanky 1862
Larrupin Lou 1278
Larry 2004, 2045, 2818
Latigo 3667
Laughing Larry 951
Lave 3908
Laz 1264
Leaky 1104
Lean 280
Leaping Mike 2441
Lee 133, 4036, 4055
Lefty 5, 48, 64, 65, 81, 98, 113, 154, 156, 157, 193, 248, 267, 273, 307, 314, 330, 410, 437, 450, 474, 492, 525, 527, 546, 559, 578, 595, 629, 703, 733, 749, 752, 810, 821, 898, 909, 910, 914, 1033, 1095, 1103, 1118, 1126, 1132, 1145, 1242, 1285, 1290, 1293, 1294, 1320, 1339, 1340, 1341, 1347, 1382, 1399, 1403, 1411, 1529, 1545, 1547, 1579, 1589, 1591, 1604, 1605, 1627, 1631, 1677, 1690, 1713, 1719, 1749, 1764, 1769, 1787, 1794, 1832, 1882, 1910, 1928, 1930, 1945, 2050, 2061, 2071, 2103, 2109, 2116, 2163, 2172, 2192, 2213, 2224, 2315, 2326, 2337, 2338, 2353, 2368, 2395, 2399, 2402, 2428, 2447, 2464, 2490, 2500, 2509, 2511, 2679, 2681, 2685, 2692, 2798, 2801, 2814, 2815, 2839, 2875, 2878, 2913, 2927, 3049, 3055, 3103, 3107, 3150, 3157, 3168, 3204, 3217, 3239, 3280, 3331, 3333, 3404, 3448, 3487, 3489, 3492, 3497, 3622, 3653, 3658, 3684, 3741, 3742, 3779, 3787, 3795, 3798, 3819, 3836, 3850, 3855, 3856, 3871, 3873, 3890, 3897, 3905, 3909, 3923, 3946, 3966, 3969, 4001, 4009, 4035, 4043, 4063, 4081, 4108, 4154
Legs 3793
Lem 761
Lena 280, 3479
Levy 1140
Li'l Abner 1056
Lib 3457
Lick 2340
Lief 1057
Lightning 1746
Limb 2285

Limonar 2390
Lindy 2148
Line Drive 2639
Link 2177, 3484
Lip, The 982
Lippy 982
Little All Right 3020
Little Bing 78
Little Colonel, The 2962
Little Cookie 4024
Little Eva 2064
Little Globe Trotter, The 996
Little Italian, The 1322
Little Joe 2556, 2891, 3963
Little Joe Chest 2263
Little Kong 243
Little Louie 74
Little Mac 2221, 2223, 2312
Little Miss Pigtails 4137
Little Napoleon 2267
Little Nel 1190
Little Nemo 2591, 3431
Little One 4107
Little Phil 1281
Little Pid 1028
Little Poison 3756
Little Potato 2771
Little Professor, The 900
Little Red 4007
Little Steam Engine, The 1248
Little Zig 4172
Liz 1229
Lizard 1872
Loco 1584
Lofty 433
Lolly 4169
Long Bob 1077, 2456
Long Charlie 1827
Long Herm 249
Long Jim 1646
Long John 66, 2968
Long Levi 2460
Long Pants 1710

366 Index

Long Tom 1718, 2769, 3910
Lonnie 1335
Loose 1892
Loosh 2188
Lord 1861
Losing Pitcher 2585
Lou 395
Louis 2422
Louisiana Lightning 1409
Low 606
Lucky 1696, 1938, 2164, 2616, 3790, 3947, 4143
Lucky Frank 2628
Lucky Sam 372
Luke 1068, 2196, 3240
Lulu 4002
Lumbago 3451
Lumber 2893
Lurch 2043
Luscious Luke 77

M.L. 4146
Mac 4038
Mack 1618
Mack the Knife 1843
McLean the Quondam Prize Fighter 2292
Mad 1521
Mad Dog 2319, 3988
Mad Hungarian, The 1707
Mad Monk, The 2459
Mad Russian, The 2665
Maggie 2324
Magician, The 6
Magnet, The 19
Mahatma, The 3009
Mail Carrier 671
Major 1422, 1689
Man Behind the Yankees 171
Man Mountain 3610
Mandrake the Magician 2580
Mandy 401

Manito 2359
Mark 2407
Marse Joe 2220
Marshalltown Infant, The 73
Marty 3261
Mary 495
Mary Ann 916
Master Builder in Baseball 3101
Master Melvin 2730
Mastodon Moundsman, The 437
Matches 1947
Matty 2397
Max 3498, 3696, 4080
Mayor Daily 3001
Meathead 2321
Mechanical Man 1279
Medicine Bill 2532
Megaphone Lolly 1675
Memo 2193
Mento 9
Meow 1319
Mercury 2610
Metropolis Mauler 4161
Mex 1581
Mickey 652, 760, 887, 1131, 1369, 1427, 1535, 1978, 2023, 2156, 2234, 2262, 2424, 2645, 2671, 2736, 3025, 3219, 3409, 3701, 3755, 3917, 4095
Mickey Mantle's Caddy 2960
Mickey Mouse 2437, 3025
Mid 4039
Midget 1120, 1854, 2442, 2602, 2966
Mighty Mite, The 1715, 2783
Mikado Milt 3218
Mike 339, 683, 927, 1985, 2158, 2228, 2420, 2578, 2881, 3118, 3805, 3898
Milkman Jim 3644
Miner 419

Minnie 2439, 2512, 3059, 4122
Miracle Man, The 3403
Mr. 690
Mr. Automatic 515
Mr. Chips 604
Mr. Cub 138
Mr. Ho-Mah 1681
Mr. McGraw's Boy 2730
Mr. October 1754
Mr. Scoop 2696
Mr. X 2982
Mississippi Mudcat, The 468
Moe 465, 1154, 1193, 2327, 2587, 4102, 4152
Mollie 2506
Molly 731, 2524
Money Bags 2914
Mongoose 2191
Monk 644, 962, 2404, 3278
Monkey 1173, 1686, 3109
Monkey on a String 3207
Monte 2825
Monty 178
Monster, The 2921
Moochie 2777
Mookie 3901
Moon 1303, 1445, 1492, 2588
Moon Man 1818
Moonie 2489, 2513
Moonlight 1361
Moonlight Ace 1231
Moonman 2513, 3252
Moose 31, 414, 617, 959, 998, 1100, 1396, 1420, 1515, 2007, 2047, 2102, 2226, 2227, 2373, 2392, 2566, 2570, 3324, 3378, 3813
Mortimer Snerd 3234
Mose 2180
Moses 3288

Index 367

Mother 3777
Motormouth 285, 2057
Mountain 1708
Mountain Man 3035
Mountain Music 2437
Mouse 2203
Mouth, The 714
Move Up Joe 1289
Mox 1143, 2309
Moxie 1563, 2351, 2433
Muck 2264
Mudcat 1367
Muddy 3095
Muggsy 40, 2267, 3406
Mul 1651
Mule 895, 1093, 1516, 2078, 2788, 3287, 3393, 3774, 3775
Mumbles 3626
Murphy 1948
Muscles 1243, 2424, 2523, 3663, 3687
Muskrat Bill 3286
Mutt 3011, 3857, 3900
Mysterious 3732

Nails 991
Nap 1977, 3091
Nardi 695
Nashville Narcissus, The 2185
Naugatuck Nugget, The 3262
Ned 755
Needle 628
Nemo 1237, 2115
Nervous Greek, The 3322
Newt 1728
Nick 34, 547, 1458
Nick Altrock of the Minor Leagues, The 3478
Nickie 4109
Nicky 4089
Nig 246, 631, 642, 777, 1226, 1356, 2153, 2653, 2802, 3341
Nigger 3109
Nigger Dark 642
Nigger Lips 3109
Night Rider 2076
Nin 33
Ninety-Six 3708
Nino 308, 1063
Nip 3912
Nippy 1853
Nitro 775
Nixey 496
Noisy 633, 1975
Noisy Tom 3638
No-Neck 3869
Noodles 1433, 3998
Noonie 2367
No Votes 639
Nub 1969
Nubbin 2293
Nubs 1828

Oats 872
Obbie 1007
Obe 4110
Obie 2674
Octopus, The 2361
Offa 2629
Oil 3340
Oil Can 347
Oisk 1059
Ol' Redhead, The 144
Old Ironsides 3604
Old Aches and Pains 77
Old Anse 73
Old Commander, The 1038
Old Coonskin 825
Old Dog 3021
Old Folkes 90
Old Folks 1952, 2848
Old Fox, The 1393
Old Gum Boots 2397
Old Hick 530
Old Hig 1600
Old Home Remedy, The 146
Old Hoss 84, 2922, 3383, 3434, 3648
Old Ironsides 3604
Old Pard 135
Old Pete 430
Old Pine Tree 2235
Old Reliable 1569, 3416
Old Roman, The 673
Old Sarg 3464
Old Scotchman, The 2294
Old Slow Ball Phonie 2378
Old Sport 376
Old Stubblebeard 1394
Old Tornado 3303
Old True Blue 3005
Old Wax Figger 1553
Ole 3762
Ollie 211, 1224, 1466, 2365, 2577
Ona 915
One Arm Daily 789
Onkel Frantz 1218
Only Nolan, The 2660
Oom Paul 880, 2026
Oom the Omnipotent 2704
Orange-Outang 107
Orator 3245
Orator Jim 2711
Oskie 1868, 3325, 3674
Ossie Green 2720
Ott 3423
Otto 2984
Ox 404, 1010, 1344, 2483
Oyster 460
Oyster Joe 2386
Ozark Ike 3990

Pa 1476
Packy 3056
Paddy 188, 958, 1189, 2414, 3303, 3351
Pal 2775

Index

Pancho 655, 672, 1585, 3374
Pants 3087, 3139
Pap 3861
Papelero 3670
Papito 3706
Papo 3068
Pappy 432, 2895
Parakeet 1223
Pard 1051
Parisian Bob 552
Parson 2137, 2253, 2651, 2806
Partridge 16
Pat 71, 309, 498, 670, 739, 858, 865, 937, 1206, 1468, 1734, 1941, 2183, 2258, 2341, 2749, 2756, 3606, 3620, 4017, 4073
Pata Ditas 94
Patcheye 1313
Patsy 488, 2246, 2712
Pea Ridge Day 849
Pea Soup 968
Peaceful Valley 882
Peach 1133
Peach Pie 2678
Peaches 841, 1362, 2707, 3814, 4067
Pearl, The 3081
Pebbly Jack 1326
Peck 2131, 2529
Pecks 794
Pecky 3481
Peco 1301
Pee Wee 392, 479, 1523, 2697, 2841, 2962, 3758, 4164, 4166
Peek-a-Boo 3693
Peekskill Pete 747
Peeps 4118
Peepsight 2572
Peerless Dutchman, The 3721
Peerless Leader, The 579
Pencil, The 3235
Pencils 3042

Penguin 571
Penitentiary Face 2126
Penny 119
People's Cherce, The 3731
Pep 621, 692, 864, 1159, 1343, 2932, 3976, 3978, 3980
Pepe 1210, 2343
Pepito 3618
Pepper 103, 625, 632, 2382, 2795, 4078, 4113
Pepper Pot 176
Perk 1931
Peruchin 570
Pete 32, 41, 210, 569, 584, 593, 674, 791, 1148, 1188, 1567, 1608, 1611, 1736, 1788, 2036, 2128, 2154, 2345, 2503, 2933, 3100, 3182, 3213, 3268, 3281, 3313, 3381, 3692, 4116
Phantom, The 1776
Phenomenal Smith 3350
Philabuck 565
Philharmonica 4051
Piano Keys 3341
Piano Legs 1346, 1598
Piano Mover 3341
Piccolo Pete 1023
Pickles 897, 4088
Pid 2908
Pidge 429
Pie 3624
Pig Pen 1241
Piggy 3759
Pigtail Billy 3017
Pigtails 4079
Pimba 51
Pinch 2031
Pineapple 2400
Ping 303
Pink 1527
Pinky 1475, 1601, 1863, 2147, 2410, 2856, 3839, 4087

Pip 1994
Piper 839
Pistol 3106
Pistol Pete 2969
Pitching Pachyderm 437
Pitching Poet, The 1926
Pitt 2919
Platanito 1814
Plowboy 2557
Plunk 954
Podgie 3794
Poet, The 589
Poffin Belly 3842
Poison 69
Poker Bill 534
Pol 2803
Polly 2287, 3391, 3925, 3989
Polo 70
Ponca City Lou 647
Ponderosa 437
Pongo Joe 511
Pony 3113
Pooch 160, 2906
Poodles 1737
Poosh 'Em Up 2094
Pop 73, 572, 707, 899, 979, 1106, 1177, 1385, 1435, 1793, 1819, 1866, 2206, 2794, 2895, 2971, 3019, 3190, 3209, 3297, 3338, 3372, 3870, 4078
Pop Boy Smith 3339
Pope 3697
Popeye 1055, 2325, 3993
Pops 3412
Popy 2876
Pork Chop 1638, 4009
Porky 270, 1700, 2039, 2682, 2780, 2977
Porthole 2877
Portland Bill 1770
Poss 1070
Possum 463, 3842
Possum, The 3936
Pot 2073

Potato 2772
Potato Head 2508
Pound Cake 1495
Prattie 4120
Preacher 934, 1102, 1537, 3052
Pretzels 1298, 2819
Prexy 96
Pride of Havana, The 2195
Pride of the Sixth Ward, The 3738
Pride of the Yankees 1278
Primo 2887
Prince 2668
Prince Hal 594, 2642, 3205
Princeton Charlie 2967
Prodigy 149
Prof 3785
Professor 402, 2725
Professor, The 3428, 3682
Prunes 2533
Pruschka 2747
Psycho 2204
Pud 2222
Puddin 4018
Puddin' Head 1856
Pudge 1058, 1142, 1272, 1460
Pudgie 867
Pug 37, 230, 566, 1391, 2980
Pugger 1910
Pullman 2870
Pumpsie 1378
Punch 1869, 1986
Put Put 93
Putsy 485

Queen of the Bleachers 599
Quick 1297
Quiet Joe 1984

R.J. 2991
Rabbi of Swat, The 3377
Rabbit 14, 234, 359, 487, 1227, 1265, 1327, 1715, 2091, 2355, 2482, 2658, 2880, 3043, 3046, 3147, 3326, 3769, 4157
Rabbit Ears 2437
Racehorse 3039
Rae 282
Rage 1087
Rainbow 3632
Rainman 224
Rajah 1682
Rambo 889
Ramrod 2636
Rap 905
Rapid Robert 1111
Rasty 3945, 3948
Rats 1557
Rattle Snake 127
Raw Meat Bill 3051
Ray 1208, 1439, 4170
Razor 2100, 3284
Razzle Dazzle 2593
Reb 3104
Rebel 18, 704, 1724, 2301, 2667, 2698, 4059
Red 54, 57, 115, 142, 148, 152, 165, 166, 170, 228, 266, 274, 302, 320, 328, 346, 362, 416, 444, 466, 494, 497, 500, 501, 540, 553, 564, 678, 687, 710, 730, 737, 814, 836, 883, 921, 931, 933, 946, 948, 983, 1003, 1020, 1040, 1074, 1080, 1084, 1107, 1137, 1139, 1149, 1214, 1389, 1413, 1414, 1472, 1510, 1539, 1610, 1622, 1624, 1632, 1665, 1700, 1844, 1870, 1915, 1943, 1957, 1970, 2020, 2022, 2028, 2054, 2068, 2075, 2155, 2168, 2185, 2202, 2225, 2233, 2259, 2282, 2314, 2346, 2360, 2393, 2488, 2555, 2584, 2590, 2592, 2600, 2606, 2635, 2661, 2693, 2709, 2723, 2745, 2746, 2764, 2787, 2830, 2897, 2957, 3033, 3048, 3061, 3062, 3097, 3172, 3251, 3264, 3274, 3348, 3354, 3356, 3360, 3362, 3382, 3401, 3425, 3614, 3615, 3623, 3625, 3744, 3789, 3837, 3896, 3907, 3920, 3933, 3940, 3941, 4096
Red Devil 1681
Red Mahoney 4096
Red Rooster 454
Red Rooster, The 2926
Red Top 1817
Redbuck 3833
Reddy 1181, 1372, 1388, 2299
Redleg 3373
Reds 2249
Redskin 23
Reindeer Bill 1944
Renda Linda 3138
Rev 509
Rhino 1623
Rhody 3743
Ribs 2940
Richie 4124
Rick 1668
Rick the Hick 4125
Rifle Jim 2463
Rig Pete 784
Riley 4084
Rimp 2066
Rinty 2526
Rip 510, 658, 662, 663, 696, 1432, 1862,

Index

2924, 2929, 3105, 3241, 3712, 3716
Riverboat Smith 3357
Road Runner 645, 1263
Roadblock 1851
Roaring Bill 1517, 1931
Rob 1260
Rock 107, 1230, 2005, 2930, 3367, 3469
Rock of Snohomish, The 107
Rocket 638
Rocket Ron 2631
Rocking Chair Catcher 182
Rocky 386, 602, 2637, 2992, 3053, 3178, 3455
Rod 859
Rojo 2926
Rollicking Rollie 1556
Romey 4127
Rookie 4130, 4133
Rope, The 348
Roscoe 717
Rosy 522, 3117
Rotty 3079
Roudy Bill 718
Rough 535
Round Man, The 2663
Roundman 990
Rowdy 1031, 2538
Rowdy Dick 176
Rowdy Jack 2678
Roxie 2092
Roxy 762, 2491, 3029, 3752
Rubber 2015
Rubber-Winged Gus 3822
Rubberhead 1536
Rubberlegs 2491
Rube 13, 28, 233, 381, 863, 885, 1021, 1035, 1176, 1180, 1299, 1956, 1964, 2025, 2197, 2348, 2364, 2374, 2664, 2765, 2808, 3044, 3164, 3233, 3704, 3713,
3724, 3727, 3760, 3957
Rudy 3175
Rugger 83
Runk 4131
Runt 728, 3750
Rusty 1288, 1398, 2030, 2306, 2615, 2809, 3146, 3419, 3600, 3616, 3956
Ryan Express, The 3116

Sabu 3207
Sad Sam 1373, 1849, 2241, 3996
Sadie 1688, 2297, 4136, 4136
Sage 1717
Sailer 3471
Sailor 2644, 2877
Sailor Bob 3260
St. Croix Boy Wonder 2778
Sal 507
Salivita 3132
Sally 4099
Salt Rock 2465
Salty 2759, 4135
Sam 375, 724, 779, 2060, 2065, 2435, 2999, 3705, 3935
Sammy 1644, 4134
Sampson 2868
Sandow 2448
Sandy 56, 694, 1588, 2045, 2143, 2240, 2626, 2846, 3671, 3677, 3678, 3846
Sara 242
Sarg 682, 2033, 2401, 2515
Sarge 116
Sassafras 3911
Satch 818, 3142
Satchel 2750, 3699
Say Hey 2417
Say Hey Kid, The 2417
Scat 556, 840, 2451
Schnozz 2165
Schoolboy 1706, 1983, 3085
Scissors 1185, 3265
Scoop 3162
Scoops 517, 518, 519, 702
Scootch 2187
Scooter 2008, 3028
Scorecard Man 3430
Scottie 3329
Scotty 29, 163, 1741, 3030, 3824
Scrap Iron 205, 720, 1262, 1520, 1925, 3452
Scrappy 539, 1867, 2544, 2909
Scroggy 973
Scrounger 4075
Scuzzy 1397
Sea Lion 1440
Seacap 607
Seattle Bill 1771
Senor Smoke 2170
Sep 1252
Shad 175, 2994
Shadow 541, 2912
Shady Bill 2117
Shag 574, 741, 1001, 3257
Shags 1679
Shaker 2571
Shakes 1731
Shamo 665
Shamus 1887
Shaney 1966
Shanty 1642
Sharpie 982
She 920
Sheriff 288, 387, 693, 1079 1233, 1238, 1268, 1490, 1838, 2101, 3317, 3673
Sherry 2320
Shifty 3282, 3816
Shine 712, 3277
Shoeless Joe 1752
Shoo Shoo 4167
Shook 412
Shooty 111
Short Stuff 4076

Shortwave 176
Shorty 740, 860, 884, 1228, 1695, 2939, 3263, 3326, 3821, 4009, 4121, 4147
Shotgun 592, 1261, 2807, 3057, 3298
Shoulders 8, 2085
Shovel 1628
Show Boat 1136
Showboat 2714
Shucks 2903
Shufflin' Phil 941
Sibbi 3319
Sid 1577, 1597, 2528, 3122
Silent Cal 225
Silent George 1559, 3652
Silent Joe 2384
Silent John 1315, 1723, 3603, 3835
Silent Pete 3268
Silk 1896, 2702
Silk Stockings 3158
Silver 1157, 1401, 1511, 1953, 3985
Silver Bill 2834
Silver Fox, The 2816, 3366
Simba 3309
Simon 171
Singer Throwing Machine, The 3315
Singing Cowboy 104
Singing Umpire, The 484
Sir Richard 700
Sir Timothy 1901
Sir Walter 1813
Sis 1674, 4004
Six O'clock 3781
Skabotch 3130
Skates 3353
Skeeter 159, 258, 1911, 2519, 2647, 3152, 3271, 3788
Skeets 891
Skids 2152
Skinny 413, 1359, 1363, 2302, 2705, 3247

Skins 1841
Skip 514, 763, 943, 1410, 1767, 1874, 2161, 2405, 2855, 4003
Skipper 926, 1211, 3034
Skippy 483, 3032
Skoonj 1230
Sky King 1955
Skyrocket 3359
Slasher 2291
Slats 280, 832, 1860, 2361, 3899, 4104
Sled 36
Sledge Hammer 315
Sleeper 3490
Sleepy Bill 461, 1816
Sleth 1155
Slewfoot 473
Slick 558, 653, 1169, 1503, 1806
Slicker 2671
Sliding Billy 1452
Slim 493, 1041, 1044, 1178, 1470, 1483, 1496, 1852, 1951, 1958, 2175, 2176, 2268, 3126, 3417
Slim Jim 995
Slouth Foot 579
Slow 2790
Slow Joe 950
Slug 459, 1544, 3607
Slugger 4031
Slugs 3659
Smash 3332
Smiles 2604
Smiley 271, 1902, 3640, 3640
Smiling Al 2406
Smiling Mickey 3804
Smiling Stan 1423
Smoke 1590, 1873, 1940, 3442
Smokey 46, 2173, 2273, 2418, 3496, 4097
Smokey Joe 2748, 3863
Smoky 446, 1086, 3316

Smoky Joe 2385, 3932
Smudge 1821
Smudgie 4104
Snags 1542
Snake 851, 913, 1574, 3477, 3904
Snake, The 1195
Snake Man, The 953
Snap 972
Snapper 1266, 1929
Snipe 680, 1465
Snitz 75, 428
Snooker 89
Snookie 4056
Snooks 944
Snooze 1354
Snow 3369
Snuffy 3453
Socker, The 3463
Socks 1645, 2805, 3242
Soldier 543
Soldier Boy 781, 2599
Sonny 906, 1680, 1755, 2003, 3089, 3237, 3300, 4012
Soup 505, 2866
Sour Mash 803
Souther 2391
Southern Gentleman, The 671
Sox 1735
Spaceman 2105
Spades 3929
Spanky 1962, 3395
Sparkplug 1904
Sparky 14, 59, 2199, 2703, 3685
Sparrow 2216, 2568
Spartanburg John 2298
Spec 3262
Special Delivery 1831
Specs 648, 1477, 1609, 2421, 2861, 3015, 3611, 4017
Speed 1275, 1920, 2380
Speedy 2478, 3090, 4009
Speedy Edie 4115
Sphinx, The 2575

Index

Spider 624, 1864, 2641, 3848
Spike 327, 349, 390, 391, 2444, 3253, 3254, 3672, 3691
Spinach 2436
Spitball 60
Spittin' Bill 908
Splendid Splinter 3868
Splinter 1292
Spoke 1043, 3387
Spook 1758, 3386
Spooks 1286
Sport 2208
Sporty 4106
Spot 251, 1089
Springfield Rifle, The 2943
Spud 581, 843, 1803, 2024
Spuds 3121
Spunk 2854
Squack 753
Squanto 3882
Square Jaw 2938
Squash 3879
Squat 799
Squeaky 151, 301, 345, 3668, 4050
Squirrel 2989, 3302
Squiz 2849
Stan 3272
Stan the Man 2609
Stan the Man Unusual 3405
Stash 1336, 2609, 4009
Steady Eddie 2169
Steady Pete 2426
Steamboat 955, 1799, 3472, 3866
Steamboat Bill 2726
Steamer 1151, 3410
Steve 397, 2770, 3073
Stevie 4144
Stick 1965, 2462
Still Bill 1613
Sting 2947
Stinky 830
Stonewall 1756
Stoney 2260

Stooping Jack 1348
Stopper 3402
Storm 828
Stormy 3780
Strawberry Bill 241
Streak, The 3470
Stretch 354, 1407, 2230, 2832, 3200, 3609
String 1250
String Bean 3126
Stub 421, 3347
Stubby 1054, 2278, 2323, 2398, 2735, 2946
Stud 2610, 3474
Stuff 235
Stuffy 475, 2274, 3445
Stump 1013, 2445, 3791
Stumpy 2355, 2700, 3700
Style Master 3612
Styles 3293
Sub 2416
Subway 2617
Sudden Sam 2241
Suds 1165, 3480
Sug 708
Sugar 489, 490, 1885, 4083
Sugar Bear 290, 2948
Sugar Boy 938
Suitcase 3229, 3311
Sukey 3483
Sun 795
Sundown 3982
Sunny Boy 3894
Sunny Jim 332, 989, 1424, 2339
Swammi, The 3428
Sunset Jimmy 451
Sunshine 2289
Super Jew 1053
Super Joe 588
Super Sub 2151, 3127
Superchief 2987
Sure Shot 971
Swamp Baby 3878
Swamper 982
Swampy 925

Swat 2215
Swats 3148
Swede 453, 523, 524, 868, 1464, 1562, 1656, 1801, 2077, 2334, 3018, 3305
Swedish Wonder 1448
Sweet 2851
Sweet Lou 1806, 3826
Sweet Music 3707
Sweetbreads 118
Sweetie 1965
Swish 654, 2652, 4015, 4015
Symphony 612

T-Bone 1323, 2009, 3912
Tabasco Kid, The 1022
Tack 3895
Tacks 2084, 3181, 3183
Tacky Tom 2766
Tall Tactician, The 2277
Tami 2408
Tank 531
Tarzan 2762, 3745
Taters 2078
Teach 491
Ted 131, 1572, 2074, 2266
Teddy 3884
Teddy Ball Game 3868
Teeny Pigtails 4117
Terminator, The 1564, 2951
Terrie 4032
Terry 4082, 4130
Tetz 4149
Tex 102, 521, 545, 641, 725, 746, 1060, 1578, 1635, 1705, 1721, 1777, 1789, 1855, 1891, 2205, 2236, 2239, 2640, 2904, 3108, 3291, 3665, 3739, 3885, 3916, 3928, 4045, 5090
Texas Jack 2016

Texas Ranger, The 1496
Texas Tornado, The 1935
Texas Wonder, The 1636
Three Finger 2643
Three Finger Brown 419
Three Star 1566
Thumper 874
Thumper, The 3868
Tiby 4040
Tido 796
Tige 3456
Tiger 1625, 1880, 2129, 2354, 4030
Tillie 3244
Tilly 272, 1380, 3728
Tim 447, 1390, 2283
Tin Man 415
Tink 3026, 3646
Tiny 316, 583, 1360, 2123, 2133, 2721
Tioga 457
Tip 2706, 3605
Tippy 2388
Tito 1192, 1223, 1586, 2056
Toad 2937
Tobacco Chewin' Johnny 2067
Toby 2, 99, 1482
Tod 436, 842, 3250
Togie 2857
Tom 3163
Tom Terrific 3224
Tomato Face 773
Tomatoe 4091
Tomatoes 1876
Tommie 4000, 4006, 4151
Tommy 4150
Tony 802, 862, 2093, 2318, 2695, 2774, 2797, 3031
Tony C 677
Tony the Silent 2844
Tookie 1308
Tooth 434
Toothpick 1848

Toothpick John 3603
Tootie 4054
Toots 3299
Top Cat 1792
Topper 3014
Topsy 1508, 2324
Torchy 4052
Tornado 3303
Tornado Jake 3797
Tot 2602, 2892
Towering Cliff of Black Mountain, The 2437
Toy Bull Dog 720
Toy Cannon 3952
Toy Trojan 1075
Trader 1680
Trader Frank 2057
Treads 1809
Tree Stump 2419
Trick 2311
Tricky 2650
Trojan 1075
Trolley 4100
Trolly Line 477
Troy Terrier 993
Truck 992, 1463, 1899
Truckhorse 2886
True Gun 1500
Tub 3809
Tubby 2250, 2965, 3151, 3390
Tuck 3643
Tucker 95, 1820
Tuffy 3441
Tug 92, 2265, 3893
Tully 3385
Tun 237
Turk 50, 780, 1101, 2179
Turkey 1402, 3420, 3655
Turkey Mike 928
Turkeyfoot 405
Tweet 3749
Twi 4140
Twilight Ed 1946
Twink 3649
Twinkle Toes Bosco 2110
Twinkles 1685
Twinkletoes 3231

Twitch 3008
Twitchy 2873
Ty 1205, 1551, 2042, 2837
TyTy 3654

Ubbo Ubbo 1683
Ug 557
Uke 620
Unbeatable Jimmy 748
Uncle Bill 53
Uncle Charlie 2550
Uncle Robbie 3045
Uncle Tom 140
Union Man 1649
Unit 1808
Unknown Soldier, The 1009
Unser Choe 1524
Unser Fritz 2822

Vacuum Cleaner 3041
Venus 4042
Victory 1105
Vinegar Bend 2517
Vinegar Bill 1064
Virginia Grapevine, The 2915
Voice, The 38
Voiceless Tim 2713
Volga Batman, The 59
Von 3188
Vulture 3410
Vulture, The 2964

Wabash George 2589
Waddy 2308
Waggie 4157
Wagon Tongue 17, 1909
Wahoo Sam 743
Waiter 671
Walking Man, The 3971
War 3136

374   Index

Warbler 3763
Warrior 1215
Watch 455
Watsie 3238
Wattie 1660
Watty 2106
Weasel 373
Weasel, The 250
Weaser 3212
Webbo 634
Wedo 2391
Wee, The 2095
Wee Willie 627, 798, 1903, 2189, 2501, 3482, 3273
Weeping Willie 3874
Wentz 1171
Whale 3753
Whammy 940
What's the Use 601
Whattaman 3289
Wheels 545
Wheezer 870
Whip 2080
Whip, The 281
Whiplash 2627
Whispering 1717
Whispering Bill 169
Whistler 1418
Whistlin' Jake 3715
Whitey 45, 76, 93, 1025, 1108, 1169, 1305, 1328, 1408, 1594, 1606, 1617, 1732, 2001, 2032, 2486, 2541, 2676, 2859, 3058, 3269, 3844, 3876, 3903, 3915, 3921
Whiz 1277
Whoa Bill 2834
Whoop-La 3834
Whoops 745
Wib 3361
Wickey 2211
Wid 691
Wig 3792
Wiggie 4165
Wiggles 2873, 4014 4114
Wild Bill 686, 930, 1445, 1726, 1738, 1931, 2097, 2190, 2840, 2842, 2843, 3843, 3942
Wild Elk of the Wasatch, The 1596
Wild Horse 3276
Wild Horse of the Osage, The 2382
Wildfire 3195
Wiley 970
Will the Thrill 626
Willie 1580, 2514, 2530
Willie the Knuck 2936
Willy 1234
Wimpy 1467, 2743, 2920, 3873, 4010
Win 184, 2443, 2976
Windy 226, 359, 2218, 2493, 4123
Wish 1018, 4108
Witto 43
Wiz 2021
Wizard 1633
Wizard of Oz, The 3355
Wobby 1454
Wonderful Willie 3363
Woodie 3717
Woody 1048, 1666, 1783, 2329
Workhorse 754

Yam 3958
Yank 408, 3045, 3047
Yankee Clipper 901
Yatcha 2162
Yats 2898, 3950
Yip 2737, 2740
Yo Yo 91, 816, 1052
Yogi 243
Young Cy 3975
Youngy 1802
Yucca 1914

Zack 3823
Zamboni Machine, The 2974
Zaza 1512
Zeke 158, 222, 318, 3796, 3949, 3987
Zig 4171
Ziggy 1513, 3222, 3223, 4171
Zip 664, 1762, 2525, 3983, 3995
Zonk 2552
Zorro 3702

www.ingramcontent.com/pod-product-compliance
Ingram Content Group UK Ltd.
Pitfield, Milton Keynes, MK11 3LW, UK
UKHW041921140426
5217IPUK00014B/258